D0946864

FOUNDATIONS OF REHABILITATION TEACHING
WITH PERSONS WHO ARE BLIND OR VISUALLY IMPAIRED

Paul E. Ponchillia
and
Susan V. Ponchillia

Printed in the United States of America

2003 reprinting

Library of Congress Cataloging-in-Publication Data

Ponchillia, Paul E.
Foundations of rehabilitation teaching with persons who are blind or visually impaired / Paul E. Ponchillia and Susan V. Ponchillia.
p. cm.
Includes bibliographical references (p.) and index
ISBN 0-89128-939-9 (cloth : alk. paper)
1. Blind—Rehabilitation—Study and teaching. 2. Visually handicapped—Rehabilitation—Study and teaching. 3. Rehabilitation—Study and teaching. I. Ponchillia, Susan Kay Vlahas. II. Title.
HV1598.P65 1996 96-28125
371.91'—dc20 CIP

Photo Credits

American Foundation for the Blind, 103, 105; Arkenstone, 193 (right); Center for Independent Living, 234; Janet Charles, American Foundation for the Blind, 281, 290, 291; Greg Dorata, American Foundation for the Blind, 99 (lower left); Yusef El-Amin, Library of Congress, National Service for the Blind and Physically Handicapped, 188 (bottom left); Howe Press, 128; Natalie Knott, 303; New Mexico School for the Visually Handicapped, 197 (bottom); Precision Vision, 104; TeleSensory Corporation, 101, 160, 161 (top left), 192; Ruth Solomon, 98, 99 (upper left, upper right, lower right), 100, 118, 127, 135, 136, 158, 161 (bottom right), 180, 181, 185, 187, 188 (top right), 189, 196, 197 (top), 202, 221, 229, 232, 233, 241, 255, 256, 257, 265, 270, 271, 273, 277, 285, 286, 289; Xerox Imaging Systems, 193 (left).

Dedication

WE DEDICATE this book to Dr. Ruth Kaarlela, our friend and teacher, in recognition of the importance of her role in the development of the discipline of rehabilitation teaching. Although she was not the first university-based educator of rehabilitation teachers, she is certainly the foremost, and her work is a major factor in the continuation of university rehabilitation teaching programs. She, more than anyone before or after her, conveyed the philosophy that persons who are blind deserve the highest quality of instruction during their rehabilitation. We were fortunate enough to have been educated at Western Michigan University during her tenure, where she assisted us in forming our own philosophies of rehabilitation teaching and furnished us with the skills needed to put those philosophies into practice. This book is a direct result of her educational efforts. If Dr. William Moon was the founder of home teaching, Dr. Kaarlela is truly the founder of rehabilitation teaching. Thank you, Ruth.

CONTENTS

FOREWORD

The primary purposes of the American Foundation for the Blind (AFB) at its inception in 1921 were to conduct research, collect and disseminate information, and improve services for blind and visually impaired people. Seventy-five years later, AFB is involved in a wide range of activities and initiatives nationwide, but these purposes still stand. One of AFB's critically important contributions to the field of visual impairment and blindness has been the key role it has played in building the knowledge base of the field. It has supported training and education efforts, advocated for the establishment of programs, conducted research, and helped document the knowledge that professionals who worked with persons who were blind or visually impaired needed in order to perform effectively. With the publication of *Foundations of Rehabilitation Teaching,* this historic tradition continues.

Although the roots of rehabilitation teaching extend back to the earliest efforts to provide assistance to persons who were blind, the body of knowledge and procedures developed to help blind and visually impaired individuals learn adaptive techniques for independent living has not until now been comprehensively recorded in a text. Now, however, individuals studying the discipline of rehabilitation teaching have available to them in one source much of the essential knowledge that they need to pursue their profession. We at AFB are proud to have helped the authors of this textbook disseminate material of such importance to the widest audience possible.

There are many indications of the establishment and growth of a professional endeavor, and the publication of a textbook on the subject is surely one of them. With the appearance of *Foundations of Rehabilitation Teaching,* a vital part of the field has reached a milestone in its development, much to the benefit of the professionals who pursue this discipline and the individuals to whom they provide services.

Carl R. Augusto
President
American Foundation for the Blind

PREFACE

The onset of blindness or visual impairment has an enormous impact on every aspect of an individual's life, both personally and vocationally. In general, it affects the ability to perform the activities of daily life, travel independently, and obtain and utilize information, all of which are crucial skills needed for success both on the job and in one's personal life. Teaching alternative methods of accomplishing these essential tasks is at the core of the rehabilitation teacher's efforts.

Rehabilitation teachers have long known the importance of building a solid foundation of prevocational skills as a basis for individuals' vocational rehabilitation training and successful employment, as well as for enhancement of their self-esteem and self-image. However, until now, rehabilitation teachers have not had the benefit of a comprehensive compilation of the essential information needed to perform their job. At last, thanks to the efforts of Dr. Paul Ponchillia and Dr. Susan Ponchillia, rehabilitation teaching has a codified and organized text that can be used by practitioners and students alike.

Although each person with impaired vision has unique needs and requires an individualized plan of instruction, this volume synthesizes and systematizes the nuts and bolts of rehabilitation teaching. And, in the course of doing so, it also provides a broad overview and philosophical principles of the profession.

The publication of *Foundations of Rehabilitation Teaching* marks the first time that a comprehensive work has been written on rehabilitation teaching. It heralds a new affirmation of the importance of the profession for individuals with impaired vision. The book provides long overdue recognition of rehabilitation teachers themselves and their valuable contribution to human service. May this publication serve as a catalyst for more such publications on one of the most critical aspects of the entire rehabilitation process—rehabilitation teaching!

Thank you, Paul and Sue. All of us in the service of persons with impaired vision are indebted to you for sharing your wisdom and experience.

Patricia Bussen Smith, Ed.D.
Department Chairperson
Coordinator, Rehabilitation Teaching of the Blind Programs
Department of Rehabilitation
University of Arkansas at Little Rock

ACKNOWLEDGMENTS

We sincerely thank all who participated, directly or indirectly, in the production of this text. We are especially grateful to those who served as reviewers and who spent innumerable unsung hours reading the manuscript as it was being written. Without their input, the book would surely be a significantly less accurate document. This talented group of fellow rehabilitation teachers included Donald Blasch, Thomas Ciesielski, Audrey Davis, Don Golembiewski, Ruth Kaarlela, Lynne Luxton, Judy Matsuoka, Maureen Moore-Strainge, Michael Nelapovich, Alice Raftary, Julia Richardson, Ramona Sangalli, Patricia Bussen Smith, Beth Trotta, and others from the United States. A special thanks to our international reviewers: Cheryl Richesin (Brantford, Ontario, Canada), Marta Csattos-Tolnay (Budapest, Hungary), Yoshie Morita (Tokyo, Japan), Simon Leung (Palmerston North, New Zealand), and Nkechinyere (Kate) Edoga (Lagos, Nigeria).

This text would not say what we meant it to without the suggestions, questions, and nagging of editors Natalie Hilzen and Ellen Bilofsky, whom we hold in great regard. They are brilliant, and we are indebted. We also send our love and appreciation to our parents and grandparents for all their support and assistance.

Special thanks also go to our friend Ruth Solomon for her photographic expertise. Also, we express appreciation to Patrick Howell, who designed the original graphics for the abacus section "just for fun," in spite of never having made our acquaintance. We would be remiss without thanking Alice Ransler, our secretary, for keyboarding, spell checking, running hither and yon, and always maintaining a smile. The help of numerous students at Western Michigan University Department of Blind Rehabilitation is also gratefully acknowledged; in particular, Barbara Louton (South Africa) and Mary Wilson, who typed, searched library shelves, and read and proofread innumerable passages on cassette tape; and especially Julie Hapeman and Mary Szekely, who helped pull this all together during their studies at WMU.

The financial support and patience of our departmental chairperson, Dr. William Wiener, were especially appreciated, as was the time he took from a busy schedule to write the Introduction. Thanks also to all the fine staff members and graduate assistants who helped with computer problems, literature searches, photography, and a hundred other details. Finally, thanks to Janet Pisaneschi, Dean of the College of Health and Human Services, and to the administration of Western Michigan University.

INTRODUCTION

Foundations of Rehabilitation Teaching is the first comprehensive book intended to assist in the preparation of rehabilitation teachers for work with people who are blind. It has been a long time in the making and promises to serve as an effective teaching tool as well as a means of further standardizing the practice of rehabilitation teaching. Much credit must be given to Paul and Sue Ponchillia for this massive undertaking. The past eight years of their lives have been devoted to the development of this text. Version after version was written and improved upon as they neared their goal of a book that could serve both students following the university rehabilitation teaching curricula and those practitioners working within the profession.

The need for this book has become obvious over the years from the constant requests for information on rehabilitation teaching received by Western Michigan University's Department of Blind Rehabilitation. In the past, the department had published monographs addressing such issues as independent living skills and independent eating skills, which offered many within the field information about the skills needed to work with clients who are blind or visually impaired. Although these early efforts, along with works by other authors, contributed to practice, they served only as a stopgap measure while the field awaited a more comprehensive offering.

Historical Background

As the field of rehabilitation teaching began to evolve, it struggled to define itself and to find a means to prepare practitioners. It can be argued that rehabilitation teaching began in the 1850s in England at the Home Teaching and Visiting Society of London. In the United States, rehabilitation teaching began in Philadelphia in 1882 when Frank Battles, Superintendent at the school for the blind, met with Dr. William Moon to discuss how to serve blind adults. During the remainder of the 19th century and into the middle of the 20th century, home teaching, as it was then called, continued to develop in the United States. During that time, the skills necessary to teach blind people to become independent were handed down from teacher to teacher through in-service training at agencies and schools and through short-term courses sometimes taught at a university. As one might expect with such diversity in personnel preparation, the roles of the teacher became quite varied, including not only the teaching of such skills as braille, activities of daily living, crafts, use of talking books, and other activities deemed to be helpful, but also incorporating such counseling tasks as case finding, friendly visiting, and elements of social work services.

In light of this great diversity of function, many attempts were made to define rehabilitation teaching and professionalize its services. One of the earlier attempts at self-examination occurred when the Rehabilitation Teaching Division of the American Association of Workers for the Blind (AAWB) conducted meetings to explore professional standards. In 1941 these meetings resulted in a national certification program for the purpose of monitoring the preparation of individuals who would enter rehabilitation teaching. Various studies were conducted over the years to identify the job responsibilities of rehabilitation teachers and to standardize services. Such studies included AAWB self-studies, the Cosgrove Report (Cosgrove, 1961), the report of the Commission on Standards and Accreditation for the Blind (1966), and role and function studies by Leja (1990). Today the roles of the profession are diverse and well documented. Rehabilitation teachers have been described as well-rounded practitioners who provide a variety of adaptive skills that are designed to return the individual to full independence.

Professional preparation of rehabilitation teachers began with the first university degree program in rehabilitation teaching at Western Michigan University in 1963. Further professionalization continued to unfold with the addition of other university rehabilitation teaching programs such as at Boston College, Florida State University, the University of Arkansas at Little Rock, Dominican College, Northern Illinois University, Cleveland State University, San Francisco State University, Hunter College, Pennsylvania College of Optometry, and the University of Massachusetts. A major landmark in personnel preparation was reached in 1988 when the Association for the Education and Rehabilitation of the Blind (AER) joined with the American Foundation for the Blind (AFB) to outline a university approval process to establish adequate curriculum, resources, and personnel for university training programs (Wiener and Luxton, 1994).

Compiling the essence of rehabilitation teaching into this single text, *Foundations of Rehabilitation Teaching,* will have the effect of further defining and developing the profession. The individual preparing to become a rehabilitation teacher will be able see the full scope of the profession. It will no longer be necessary to assemble materials from a variety of sources. Instead, this text can be used as the main source of information and can be supplemented by other resources (suggested throughout the individual chapters and in the appendixes) that provide greater detail in specific content areas.

Knowledge Base

Foundations of Rehabilitation Teaching draws upon the knowledge base accumulated since the beginning of the profession. Early practice was based upon clinical experience gathered by blind and sighted teachers of persons who are blind. As the profession developed, experimental studies using both traditional research design and small-subject design were used to validate existing teaching procedures and develop new insights. The volume at hand has integrated both the experiential and the experimental information in a way that respects the old and adds to it new information that has been tested.

A quick review of the table of contents of this text shows the richness of the material provided within. The book is organized into five parts. Part 1 provides an overview of the profession and other background information, including a history of rehabilitation teaching. Part 2 provides the reader with the foundation needed for evaluation, planning, and delivery of services. Part 3 through Part 5 correspond to the essential function of the rehabilitation teacher: instruction in the areas of adaptive communication, activities of daily living, and management skills. Within the scope of these major sections are chapters that provide the latest information on the essential instructional areas. An individual instructor or a reader working alone may find that another order of presentation is preferable for particular skills, or perhaps that some skills need to be presented before assessment or planning is discussed. Since each chapter is a self-contained unit, and the text contains extensive cross-referencing to related topics, the book is easily adapted to a variety of uses or approaches.

The final chapter of the book gives us a glimpse into the future of the profession. With the rapid pace of technological development, what is speculation today will be reality by the time the book is read, and devices presented as leading-edge technology may soon be outdated. The reader must keep in mind the necessity of keeping abreast of the day-to-day developments in assistive technology. In this regard, the extensive Resources section will be most helpful. The appendixes provide materials that will be useful while the reader is studying the various chapters and also later when the practitioner is taking on a professional role with clients. They provide a rich source of teaching resources and also a wealth of information to assist the teacher with questions that are certain to surface during practice. The Learning Activities will be useful both to the instructor and the student working alone. Appendix A focuses on certification and other professional issues. Appendix B answers many important questions that relate to working with individuals with multiple disabilities and other conditions. The forms that are collected in Appendix C will prove invaluable to students and practitioners alike, and the Glossary will form a lexicon for the field. The Resources section will enable the teacher to identify specific sources of help as well as information.

At the Crossroads

The profession of rehabilitation teaching is at a crossroads. There are not enough professionally prepared rehabilitation teachers to meet the needs of persons with visual impairments. In many locations, agencies attempt to make up for this shortage by providing teachers with short-term training. Often these individuals do not have the breadth of knowledge or a high enough level of skill to bring their students to their full potential. The Rehabilitation Teaching Division of AER recognizes this problem and has committed itself to developing a program to prepare rehabilitation teaching aides who can work under the direction of professionally prepared rehabilitation teachers. It is hoped that *Foundations of Rehabilitation Teaching* will be useful also to this emerging group of assistants as they join with professionals to improve services for people who are blind.

In conclusion, this text will further advance the skills of the rehabilitation teacher and help with the training of assistants. If the profession is to expand and services are to improve, it is necessary to establish a solid theoretical foundation for professionals. This volume will both provide the groundwork on which to build and will serve as a launching platform for further professional growth. We at Western Michigan University are proud of the small part that we have played in the development of this profession and are particularly proud of the contribution of Paul and Sue Ponchillia in adding to the knowledge base of rehabilitation teaching through their research and their untiring work to author this book.

William R. Wiener, Ph.D.
Chairperson and Professor
Department of Blind Rehabilitation
Western Michigan University

PART ONE

The Profession of Rehabilitation Teaching

CHAPTER 1

An Introduction to the Profession

KEY CONCEPTS IN THIS CHAPTER

- **Rehabilitation teaching and its purposes**
- **The rehabilitation system for blind and visually impaired people and its subsystems**
- **The structure of the federal vocational rehabilitation system**
- **The other professionals with whom rehabilitation teachers work**
- **The terminology used to describe the segment of the population with visual impairments**
- **The demographics pertaining to individuals with visual impairments**
- **The effects of common types of visual impairments on visual functioning**

Rehabilitation teaching has evolved from its early days, when blind persons used their personal knowledge and experience as a basis for assisting others who were blind, to its modern status as a field of highly educated professionals (Leja, 1990). A rehabilitation teacher is a professional whose primary goal is the rehabilitation of individuals who are visually impaired—that is, the provision of instruction and guidance to help individuals to acquire the skills and knowledge to manage their daily lives (Asenjo, 1975b) and to achieve self-confidence and self-sufficiency at their highest attainable level (LaGrow, 1992).

The loss of visual functioning that results from a visual impairment causes an individual to lose self-confidence in his or her ability to conduct everyday life and to perform in a job (Carroll, 1961). Before vocational issues can be addressed, the person must first adjust to the losses of self-image and life skills that he or she may have experienced. The rehabilitation services that are provided to people with visual impairments address both personal and vocational needs, helping individuals to develop personal confidence and skills of everyday living through instructional efforts as well as to gain or regain job skills through vocational training and placement. The instructional phase, generally termed *personal adjustment training*, is the area in which a rehabilitation teacher functions.

THE PROFESSION OF REHABILITATION TEACHING

The Rehabilitation Teacher

Rehabilitation teachers may hold such job titles as independent living specialist, living skills instructor, vision rehabilitation specialist, or blind rehabilitation specialist, among others. Whatever the title, a rehabilitation teacher's primary role is to instruct people with visual impairments in utilizing the adaptive skills that allow them to cope with the demands of everyday life. Rehabilitation teachers generally teach the following categories of activities (Ponchillia & Kaarlela, 1986; Wiener & Luxton, 1994):

- *low vision skills:* employment of usable vision and of low vision devices and techniques
- *communication:* instruction in adaptive skills and alternative forms of reading, writing, mathematical calculations, and listening as well as assistive technology
- *personal management:* personal hygiene, grooming, medicinal management, and clothing care
- *orientation and movement* in familiar indoor environments
- *home management:* general home care, kitchen skills, home repairs, and bookkeeping skills
- *leisure-time activities:* handicrafts, adapted games, and active forms of recreation.

Methods of instruction in these skills are covered in Part 3 of this book. Rehabilitation teachers also perform case management and administrative tasks such as assessing clients, planning services, making referrals, keeping records, and managing time and materials, which are covered in Part 2 and Part 4. The remainder of Part 1 will serve as an introduction to the profession of rehabilitation teaching and the rehabilitation system in which its practitioners function, a brief overview of the people served by the profession and the types of visual impairments they experience, and, in Chapter 2, a survey of the history of rehabilitation teaching.

When rehabilitation teachers instruct clients with congenital visual impairments, they function more or less as traditional teachers, since their primary function is to impart knowledge or skills. When working with people who have adventitious or acquired impairments, however, rehabilitation teachers also strive to help clients regain the level of self-confidence they experienced prior to becoming visually impaired. Regaining the ability to function independently and effectively in daily life leads to a sense of control, self-determination, and power, which, in turn, helps the individual's self-image return to its preimpairment level (Carroll, 1961; Tuttle, 1984). Therefore, along with teaching specific skills, enhancing the client's self-confidence and self-image is an important goal of rehabilitation teaching.

The Rehabilitation Team

In general, rehabilitation teachers work either in rehabilitation centers, where clients gather for instruction and may reside temporarily, or from a field office or local agency in a community setting while providing their actual services in clients' own homes. In either case, rehabilitation teachers function as a part of an interdisciplinary team, whose composition varies depending on the work setting.

The team working in a residential center is large, often containing as many as seven distinct professionals. A member of each of the following groups is usually included:

- *Rehabilitation teachers* working in centers typically provide instruction in the areas of communication and daily living.
- *Rehabilitation counselors* or *social workers* usually serve as agency case managers and in some cases provide therapeutic counseling.
- *O&M instructors* teach people with visual impairments to travel.
- *Low vision specialists* assess functional visual ability, prescribe or obtain devices to increase that ability, and train individuals to use visual aids properly.
- *Occupational therapists* are less commonly members of rehabilitation teams, but they serve the valuable function of training or retraining individuals in motor skills.

- *Medical personnel*, such as nurses, are employed in many residential rehabilitation centers to provide traditional medical services to clients with special needs and to deliver instruction in such areas as diabetic self-care and sex education.
- *Psychologists* function as therapeutic counselors and also assess clients' potential through the administration and interpretation of standardized tests of intelligence, personality, adjustment to visual impairment, vocational interest, and the like.

In the United States, a rehabilitation team located at a field office sometimes consists of as few as two members: a rehabilitation teacher and a rehabilitation counselor or social worker (see the next section on the rehabilitation system for an explanation of how these offices are organized). However, field offices commonly provide job placement and O&M services as well. Because states are responsible for providing vocational services, their provision is optional for local private nonprofit agencies.

Field-based rehabilitation teams in Canada are less numerous than in the United States but tend to provide more comprehensive services. At the divisional (provincial) level, they generally consist of a counselor, a rehabilitation teacher, a mobility instructor, a family worker, a vision rehabilitation specialist (low vision specialist), a career development specialist, a library specialist, a worker who provides services to senior citizens, and a technology consultant.

THE REHABILITATION SYSTEM

In North America, rehabilitation teachers practice their profession within a large network consisting of five major subsystems, each of which will be discussed in turn. They are

- the federal-state vocational rehabilitation system in the United States, administered by the Rehabilitation Services Administration (RSA) of the U.S. Department of Education, Office of Special Education and Rehabilitative Services, which serves primarily adults
- the Canadian National Institute for the Blind (CNIB), which serves blind adults in Canada
- the U.S. Department of Veterans Affairs (VA), formerly the Veterans Administration, which serves veterans
- the private nonprofit sector, which serves both children and adults in the United States and Canada
- the Office of Special Education Programs, also part of the U.S. Department of Education, Office of Special Education and Rehabilitative Services, which primarily serves children through its educational services.

The Federal-State Vocational Rehabilitation System

The federal-state rehabilitation system in the United States, administered by RSA of the U.S. Department of Education, is by far the largest of the subsystems that serve people with visual impairments. As such, the vocational rehabilitation system supported by RSA serves as the most widespread model for provision of rehabilitation services to people with visual impairments. Thus, the organization of services described throughout this text is based largely on the principles and practices used in this vocational rehabilitation system.

In the United States, a vocational rehabilitation agency exists in each state and is responsible for training or retraining individuals with disabilities to become employable or to benefit from independent living services. Criteria for eligibility for services vary from state to state. In some states there are two vocational rehabilitation agencies, one serving people who have visual impairments and another serving people with other disabilities. In other states, one umbrella agency is responsible for services to people with all types of disabilities.

This vocational rehabilitation system has its legislative and financial roots in the Federal Civilian Vocational Rehabilitation Act of 1920 and subsequent amendments, which provide the legal base for building rehabilitation facilities, training rehabilitation personnel, and providing rehabilitation services (Bledsoe, 1972). Until 1978, RSA funds were limited largely to services for individuals with disabilities who demonstrated significant potential for return to gainful employment. ("Homemaker" is also considered a vocational goal and is commonly used for older visually impaired clients.) However, the amendments of 1978 expanded the service boundaries to include independent living services for disabled persons who have nonvocational goals. Thus, two major programs have resulted from the vocational rehabilitation legislation: the Vocational Rehabilitation Program, aimed at employment, and the Independent Living (IL) Program for nonvocational clients.

Direct services to clients are funded by federal-state partnership but are provided through a system of individual state agencies. The costs of service delivery are generally shared between federal and state governments on an 80 percent federal to 20 percent state basis. The current trend, however, is toward less federal and more state responsibility for funding.

The state agencies that provide vocational rehabilitation services under RSA range from divisions of large social service umbrella agencies to separate state commissions under the direct supervision of the governor. Regardless of the administrative structure of the agency, the vocational rehabilitation services provided are relatively uniform from state to state. The agencies generally provide the following sequence of services:

- determining eligibility for services
- conducting a program assessment
- writing a program plan
- delivering personal adjustment training
- providing vocational services.

A vocational rehabilitation counselor will first determine whether a client is eligible to receive services. Then the program assessment helps to identify the client's vocational or independent living goals (see Chapter 3), and the planning phase culminates in a written plan for meeting them (see Chapter 4). Rehabilitation teachers may be involved in these initial functions, but they are largely carried out by vocational rehabilitation counselors. The rehabilitation teacher functions primarily in the personal adjustment training phase, along with mobility instructors and counselors, in which clients are taught adaptive living skills. Rehabilitation teachers conduct their own assessment and planning as they begin this work. Finally, vocational services might include assessment of job skills, ranging from standardized testing of vocational interest and aptitude to measurement of performance in simulated job situations; job training, including instruction in the skills needed to perform specific jobs, job-seeking skills, and education at the community college or university level; and, eventually, placement in a work setting. The placement phase is often marked by a variety of challenges, because the number of job possibilities may be affected by the nature of a client's visual impairment and, more important, because potential employers commonly underestimate the abilities of people with visual impairments (Dickey & Vieceli, 1972; Ryder & Kawalec, 1995). Services are terminated when clients obtain their vocational goals, withdraw from services, or are unsuccessful in achieving their goals.

Canadian National Institute for the Blind

The Canadian system of rehabilitation services for people who are visually impaired differs from the U.S. vocational rehabilitation system in that services are provided by CNIB, which is for the most part a private agency. Approximately one-third of its funding comes from the Canadian government, one-third from the United Way, and one-third from private donors. It operates through division offices in each province, and services are provided through 52 rehabilitation services centers. (In the province of Quebec, direct services are delivered through private agencies not affiliated with CNIB, such as Institute Nazareth et Louis Braille.)

The unique geographical difficulties created by Canada's varied population and large land mass have recently prompted a movement toward providing core services to the areas covered by the division offices. Each center is designed to deliver library, personal adjustment, counseling, family counseling, and career development services. In addition, equity of services to clients is ensured by assigning professionals through a formula based on a worker-client ratio.

Although the administrative structure of the Canadian system differs from that of the United States, the services provided are similar. As is the case in each state vocational rehabilitation agency, personal adjustment training is offered in both residential centers and field-based home settings. Rehabilitation teaching services, case management procedures, and vocational services are also similar.

Veterans' Services

The services provided by the Department of Veterans Affairs for blind veterans in the United States are aimed primarily at personal adjustment training, which is delivered through a series of regional VA medical centers across the country. These Blind Rehabilitation Centers, which date back to the 1940s, served as models for the development of most modern-day residential centers (Asenjo, 1975a). The centers, which are located in the eastern, midwestern, southeastern, southwestern, and western regions of the United States, are known for their outstanding facilities and comprehensive services.

Recently, the VA has introduced field services through Visual Impairment Service Teams (VIST) and through Blind Rehabilitation Outpatient Services (BROS). VIST coordinators are responsible for case management, follow-up, vocational placement, and other support services, and BROS workers are responsible for adaptive skills instruction. Rehabilitation teachers function as team members both in the VA residential centers and on the VIST teams.

Private Sector Services

Rehabilitation services are also available through private agencies funded by contracts with state vocational rehabilitation agencies, clients' fees, United Way contributions, various foundation grants, private contributions, and, to some extent, the sale of products manufactured on the premises. Private agencies commonly offer personal adjustment training in residential or community-based programs, house low vision clinics, provide sheltered employment, and work diligently to modify the public perception of blindness.

Rehabilitation teachers working in private agencies function in much the same manner as they do in the federal-state system. However, private agencies are more likely to require professional certification of a rehabilitation teacher (Leja, 1990).

Educational Services

Educational programs for children with disabilities in the United States were established by P.L. 94-142, the Education for All Handicapped Children Act of 1975 and modified by the 1990 Individuals with Disabilities Education Act, known as IDEA (P.L. 101-476). This legislation requires school personnel to make accommodations in programming and in physical facilities so that all disabled children can receive a free and appropriate education in the least restrictive environment possible. Services for children who are visually impaired are usually delivered by a special teacher of visually impaired students and include educational instruction, adaptive communication skills, sometimes daily living skills, and consultation with general education teachers.

Rehabilitation teachers currently teach daily living skills in some residential schools for children with visual impairments and in some mainstream schools. There is likely to be an increased role for school-based rehabilitation teachers in the future because there is a perceived need to increase training for youngsters in daily living skills (Spungin, 1987), and teachers of visually impaired students seldom have enough time to provide all the instruction that would be desirable.

THE CLIENTS OF REHABILITATION TEACHERS

Who are the people receiving services from rehabilitation teachers within this vast system? The individuals who experience visual limitations are as diverse as the members of the general population of which they are a subset. Although they share the commonality of limited vision, they share little else. Even their visual impairments do not make them a homogeneous group, because the causes and circumstances surrounding vision loss are infinitely varied.

The Language of Visual Impairment

Because of the diversity of the visually impaired population, numerous terms are used to describe different segments of the group. Unlike descriptors used in the hard sciences or life sciences, however, the terms used to describe people with visual impairments tend to be overlapping, vaguely defined, and applied interchangeably. For example, terms such as *visually impaired, visually handicapped,* and *blind* are all sometimes used to describe the entire population. In addition, certain descriptors go in and out of vogue as the language of the general population changes. Whereas *partially sighted* once described people with useful but limited vision, the newer expression *low vision* has now taken its place.

As a result of the confusion over terminology and the recognition of the diversity among people with visual impairments, there is a tendency among recent writers to define terms more broadly (Barraga, 1976; Scholl, 1986b) and to use functional definitions that provide more concrete descriptions of individuals' vision in terms of their actual abilities rather than arbitrarily chosen numeric measurements and boundaries. One term is still defined objectively, however, because it is frequently used in the vocational rehabilitation system as one of the criteria by which eligi-

SIDEBAR 1.1

The Definition of Legal Blindness

The definition of legal blindness is based on visual acuity and visual field, with consideration of the type of corrective lenses worn during testing.

- *Visual acuity*—the sharpness or clearness of vision—is measured by the ability to recognize letters or other graphic symbols. It is expressed as two numbers, the first of which is the distance in feet at which the person being tested is able to identify the form being viewed, and the second of which is the distance at which the normal eye can discern the form. Therefore, an acuity expressed as 20/20 indicates that the person being tested has normal vision. A person who has an acuity of 20/180 is able to see at a 20-foot distance an object that a person with normal vision can see from 180 feet away.
- *Visual field*—the area visible to the eye—is measured by the angle of the cone shape formed by the area that can be seen without shifting the gaze when looking at a point straight ahead. As peripheral, or side, vision is lost, the angle decreases, causing a "tunnel vision" effect.

To be considered legally blind, a person must have a visual acuity of 20/200 or less in the better eye after best correction, or the visual field must subtend an angle of 20 degrees in the better eye. The corrective lenses being worn during the examination must be standard, that is, of the type used to correct myopia, hyperopia, or astigmatism (Vaughan, Asbury, & Riordan-Eva, 1995).

bility for service is determined. This term is *legal blindness* (see Sidebar 1.1).

The definition of legal blindness is considered by some to be an arbitrarily chosen parameter that does not relate to functional ability in a concrete way. People who fall within the boundaries of legal blindness range in visual ability from having no usable vision or light perception to being able to read newspaper print. Perhaps more important, some people who experience significant functional limitations are not legally blind according to the definition used and therefore may not qualify for vocational rehabilitation services.

Common terms related to blindness and visual impairment as defined by the authors are listed in Table 1.1, and many more are defined in the Glossary. It should be noted that these terms are generally defined functionally, and that some have broad meanings and others more specific ones. For example, *visually impaired* is used to refer generally to the entire group of people with visual impairments, whereas *blindness* is limited to those with no functional vision.

Table 1.1. Definitions of Common Terms Related to Blindness and Visual Impairment

Term	Definition
Blindness	Lack of functional vision.
Functional	Related to use; useful.
Functional vision	A degree of vision sufficient to be of use in performing a given task.
Legal blindness	A visual acuity of 20/200 or less in the better eye after standard correction, or a visual field of 20 degrees or less in the better eye.
Low vision	A degree of vision that is functional but limited enough to interfere with the ability to perform everyday activities and that cannot be corrected with standard eyeglasses or contact lenses.
Visual acuity	The ability to discern form visually; the sharpness or clearness of vision.
Visual disability	A limitation in functional ability resulting from visual impairment.
Visual field	The area that is visible without shifting the gaze.
Visual handicap	The psychological, social, or economic effects resulting from a visual impairment.
Visual impairment	Any degree of vision loss, including total blindness, that affects an individual's ability to perform the tasks of daily life.

Sources: Ian L. Bailey and Amanda Hall, *Visual Impairment: An Overview* (New York: American Foundation for the Blind, 1990): and Kathleen Mary Huebner, Jeanne Glidden Prickett, Therese Rafalowski Welch, and Elga Joffee, Editors, *Hand in Hand: Essentials of Communication and Mobility for Your Students Who Are Deaf-Blind,* Vol. 2 (New York: AFB Press, 1995), Glossary.

Demographics of Visual Impairment

The people who receive services from rehabilitation teachers in the United States generally fit under the large umbrella created by the definition of legal blindness because blindness agencies that provide vocational rehabilitation programs for visually impaired people usually require a client to be legally blind. In order to plan for services to individuals with visual impairments, it is essential to know how many such individuals there are and how they are distributed within the general population. At first glance, the literature on prevalence of visual impairments in the United States appears to be confusing because there is a great deal of variation among the reported estimates. However, this wide variation is a reflection of differences in definitions, primarily relating to severity of visual impairment.

There are three major sources of estimates commonly used in the United States: (1) figures based on the National Health Interview Survey conducted by the National Center for Health Statistics (National Center for Health Statistics, 1995); (2) figures based on the Survey of Income and Program Participation conducted by the U.S. Bureau of the Census (McNeil, 1993); and (3) a set of figures used to estimate the federal budgetary cost of blindness (Chiang, Bassi, & Javitt, 1990), which are based on the results of the Baltimore Eye Study

(Tielsch et al., 1990) and model reporting area statistics from the former U.S. Department of Health, Education, and Welfare, now the Department of Health and Human Services (*Statistics on Blindness in the Model Reporting Area*, 1973). The first two reports distinguish between nonsevere and severe visual impairment, based on self-reports of functional impairment in reading (whether the respondents had difficulty reading newsprint or were unable to do so, using their normal eyeglasses or contact lenses). The third report made projections using clinical measures of acuity from the Baltimore Eye Study that correspond to an administrative definition of legal blindness.

As would be expected, using a broader definition of visual impairment, such as the "newsprint" definition, yields a larger estimate of the visually impaired population than does using the more narrow definition of legal blindness. Table 1.2 illustrates the range of estimated prevalence of nonsevere and severe visual impairments and legal blindness, based on selected reports.

Table 1.2. Selected Estimates of the Prevalence of Visual Impairment in the United States, Early 1990s

Category	Estimated Number (millions)	Rate per 1,000 Population
Functional limitation in seeing, nonsevere[a]	8.1	41.4
Severe visual impairment[b]	4.3	17.3
Functional limitation in seeing, severe[a]	1.6	8.2
Legal blindness[c]	1.1	4.5

[a]Ages 15 and older, 1991–92 figures. From J. M. McNeil, *Americans with Disabilities: 1991–92: Data from Survey of Income and Program Participation*, Current Population Reports, Household Economic Studies, P70–33 (Washington, DC: Bureau of the Census, U.S. Department of Commerce, December 1993).

[b]All ages. Estimates for 1990, based on 1977 National Health Survey figures corrected for methodological problems. From K. A. Nelson and G. Dimitrova, "Severe Visual Impairment in the United States and in Each State, 1990," *Journal of Visual Impairment & Blindness, 87* (March 1993), pp. 80–85.

[c]All ages, 1990 figures. From Y. Chiang, L. J. Bassi, and J. C. Javitt, "Federal Budgetary Costs of Blindness," *Milbank Quarterly*, 70(2) (1992), pp. 319–340.

Prevalence data demonstrate clearly the effect of aging on the rate of visual impairment (see Table 1.3). Relatively few individuals are blinded when young, whereas approximately two-thirds of those defined as either severely visually impaired (Nelson & Dimitrova, 1993) or as legally blind (Chiang, Bassi & Javitt, 1990) are over the age of 65. Therefore, the typical client of a rehabilitation teacher is usually an older person who is frequently more interested in learning adaptive skills than job skills.

Types of Visual Limitations

Because there is such a wide variety of visual impairments, and each individual's vision is different, a detailed clinical discussion of the types and causes of visual impairments is beyond the scope of this book. This section gives an overview of the most common visual problems and causes of vision loss. (For more detailed information, see Agency for Health Care Policy and Research, 1993; Goldberg, 1986; Vaughan, Asbury, & Riordan-Eva, 1995).

Visual impairments, as reflected in the definition of legal blindness, limit either visual acuity or visual field or both. Limitations of acuity may relate to maladies of the *cornea*, the normally transparent covering of the front of the eyeball, but more commonly result from opacities of the *lens* of the eye, the part of the eye that changes shape to focus light rays on the *retina*. *Cataracts*, which are the most frequent disorder of the lens, cloud the entire visual field. In addition, bright light or light reflected from shiny surfaces (glare) increases the difficulty of seeing. Therefore, the affected person has trouble with reading and other near-vision tasks as well as with distance vision and moving through unfamiliar environments (Jose, 1983a).

Visual field limitations generally take one of three forms—*central* loss, *peripheral* loss, or *irregular* loss—depending on where in the visual field the disruption of vision occurs. The most common central field loss is caused by a condition

Table 1.3. The Effect of Age on Prevalence of Legal Blindness

Age (years)	Number of Legally Blind Individuals	Percentage of Total Cases	Rate per 1,000 Population
Under 20	53,260	4.8	0.7
20–64	337,102	30.5	2.3
65 years and over	713,264	64.6	23.4
Totals	1,103,626	99.9[a]	4.5

Source: Adapted from Y. Chiang, L. J. Bassi, and J. C. Javitt, "Federal Budgetary Costs of Blindness," *Milbank Quarterly,* 70(2) (1992), pp. 319–340.

[a]Percentages do not add to 100 because of rounding.

often found in elderly persons, known as *macular degeneration.* The *macula* is the central portion of the retina that is responsible for acuity. Therefore, a central field loss is essentially a loss of acuity in the center of vision, but peripheral sight is often unaffected. In beginning stages of loss, a diffuse spot appears in the center of vision, which some persons describe as a blue dot. As the person ages, the occlusion generally becomes denser and more obtrusive. The functional result of such a loss is a severe limitation in reading and other near-vision tasks (Jose, 1983a). Individuals with a central field loss learn *eccentric viewing*—that is, turning the eye to look around the blind spot.

The most common causes of peripheral field loss are *retinitis pigmentosa* and *glaucoma.* Retinitis pigmentosa is an inherited disease that results in the progressive destruction of cells within the retina. Glaucoma is a group of conditions in which small retinal blood vessels are damaged as a result of extreme interocular pressure. In both cases, the peripheral field is gradually reduced, resulting in a narrow tunnel of vision, sometimes to the point of total blindness. Although the outer boundaries of vision are lost, central acuity may be unaffected. In such cases, near-vision tasks can often be accomplished, but movement in unfamiliar surroundings is generally difficult. In addition, since the peripheral portion of the retina is responsible for night vision, people with these conditions may be functionally blind after dark (Jose, 1983a).

The loss of visual field in randomly placed, irregular patches is most frequently the result of *diabetes mellitus.* Diabetes causes circulatory problems that damage the tiny blood vessels in the retina. This condition is referred to as *diabetic retinopathy* which not only affects the field of vision, but may also cause extreme acuity problems as a consequence of interocular bleeding. Blood components leak into the eye, blocking the course of light from cornea to retina. Therefore, the practical problems imposed by diabetic retinopathy fluctuate greatly and range from limitations in carrying out tasks that require near vision to difficulties with mobility. Diabetes is a leading cause of blindness.

SUMMARY

Rehabilitation teachers serve in a variety of roles, teaching a variety of tasks to people whose needs, cultures, and abilities are as individual as they are. Despite the diversity of their roles, rehabilitation teachers are clearly defined as service providers whose emphasis is on providing rehabilitation instruction and guidance in daily living skills to people who have visual impairments.

Chapter 2 continues this survey of the field of rehabilitation teaching by providing a history of the profession. By understanding the unique roots of rehabilitation teaching in the work of itinerant home teachers a century ago, one can better comprehend the current development of the field. Parts 2, 3, and 4 of this book will detail the actual process and content of the rehabilitation teacher's work.

CHAPTER 2

The Evolution from Home Teaching to Rehabilitation Teaching

KEY CONCEPTS IN THIS CHAPTER

- **The social evolution of persons who are blind**
- **The early roots of rehabilitation teaching**
- **The founding of home teaching**
- **The expansion of home teaching settings and roles in the first half of the 20th century**
- **The activities in the 1950s that defined present-day rehabilitation teaching**
- **The present status of rehabilitation teaching**

A profession is more than a job or a collection of skills. A profession such as rehabilitation teaching comes into being through a gradual process of development that eventually results in a unified discipline with a specific body of knowledge and standards. Rehabilitation teaching has a long history, and it is still evolving. This chapter presents an overview of the history of rehabilitation teaching as a professional discipline, from its earliest beginnings as an individualistic, charity-based endeavor to its current status as a profession with standardized activities and knowledge.

HISTORICAL ROOTS

Modern-day rehabilitation teaching is the product of a long evolutionary process that began centuries ago, as people who were blind began a tortuous journey toward social equality. Lowenfeld (1973) described that journey as having the following four stages:

- *Separation.* From earliest times, prior to and during the Greek and Roman era, people who were blind were separated from society. The extreme form of this was exemplified by the common Greek and Roman practice of annihilating blind individuals. Although exceptional blind individuals such as the poet Homer were venerated, they were still accorded separate status from the rest of society.
- *Ward status.* Ward status for blind people, in which society protected them and provided food and shelter for their welfare, was common from the early centuries A.D. through the Dark Ages, as is often reflected in the Bible. Early writings describe hospices, hostels, and "support homes" for blind people (Wagg, 1932).
- *Self-emancipation.* The movement toward self-emancipation was becoming evident beginning in the 16th century, as demon-

strated by numerous references to talented individuals with visual impairments, such as the English mathematician Nicholas Saunderson, the road builder John Metcalf, and the Austrian child musician, Maria Theresa von Paradis, who was given a pension by Empress Maria Theresa (Farrell, 1956).

- *Integration.* Integration, the final and still ongoing stage, had its beginning in the 1700s. The most important and first step in the integration process was the inclusion of children who were blind in educational programs, of which blind rehabilitation and rehabilitation teaching were later offshoots. The first such program was initiated by Valentin Haüy in Paris in the early 1780s (Lowenfeld, 1973). Although the initial focus was on academic skills, additional subject areas such as music, leisure skills, and home management were added as educators began to realize the potential of people with visual impairments. Schools similar to Haüy's were quickly developed in Germany, Austria, England, and Russia.

In the early 1830s, three American schools began operations almost simultaneously in Massachusetts, New York, and Pennsylvania. The leader of the day in education for people who were blind was Samuel Gridley Howe of the New England Asylum for the Blind, which would later become the well-known Perkins School for the Blind in Watertown, Massachusetts. Howe was especially noted for his strong belief in social integration, for being the first to educate a deaf-blind person, and for his role in establishing the first state school for the blind in Ohio in 1837 (Lowenfeld, 1973).

Pioneers such as Howe set the stage for rehabilitation teaching through the teaching techniques they developed and the precedents they set. For example, Haüy trained his students in vocations like chair caning and weaving, Johann Wilhelm Klein of Vienna wrote the first instructional materials for blind persons, and Howe described techniques for working with persons who are deaf and blind. Haüy and Howe were also pioneers in what was perhaps the most significant advance for blind people: the development of tactile methods of written communication, which is discussed in detail in Chapter 7. Over the years, a number of systems were proposed and tried, including negative typecasting, Boston line type, Moon type, and New York Point, before, amidst much contention, braille finally became the most widely used system.

REHABILITATION TEACHING: A HISTORY

The methods and techniques that would become the basis of rehabilitation teaching were developed in educational settings. However, the profession itself had its beginnings in the notion of bringing services to blind people in their homes, and the teachers involved were themselves usually blind. From these beginnings, which might be considered the initiation phase, the profession rapidly expanded until attempts at standardization and formal definition formed the profession of rehabilitation teaching as it is known today.

Initiation

Dr. William Moon, who himself became blind as a young man, can be considered the first rehabilitation teacher. He began teaching in England and later initiated the first service delivery program to people who were visually impaired in their homes in the United States (Dickinson, 1956; McKay, 1965). In conjunction with John Rhoads of the Pennsylvania Bible Society, Moon founded the Pennsylvania Home Teaching Society and Free Circulating Library for the Blind in Philadelphia in the 1880s (Dickinson, 1956; McKay, 1965). Their goal was to teach persons who were blind to read the scriptures through a program of home-based instruction. As the idea of home-based instruction spread, the name "home teacher" became the standard for these teachers for nearly a century.

Expansion

In the period following Moon's pioneering work, around the turn of the century, the provision of home teaching services expanded. New programs appeared, and the types of services offered increased. It quickly became apparent that individuals receiving home teaching services needed more than just reading and writing skills and that they were capable of learning what would become known as daily living skills.

Volunteer home teachers, who were turn-of-the-century graduates of what was then known as the Perkins Institution, were among the first to note a need for instruction in handicrafts for income generation and in living skills for survival (McKay, 1965). These teachers, almost exclusively women, were paid as little as $1 a day and traveled with sighted guides, whom they had to pay out of their own pockets (Koestler, 1976). Kimball (1908), a home teacher in Rhode Island, noted that she had been asked to teach reading and writing, but found greater needs in her clients. At the same time, Kelly (1908) reported that her clients in Maryland had learned to read New York Point and Moon type, write New York Point, write with a pencil, travel with a cane, crochet, and knit. In addition, a blind man by the name of Javal (1905), in an early autobiography, wrote of his need and ability to perform daily living chores. Koestler (1976), in her history, also noted that home teachers offered instruction in finger-reading systems, handicrafts, and daily living skills. Foley (1919), the first home teacher in California, expanded the home teacher's duties further when she added educational placement of children with visual handicaps, blindness-prevention instruction, attempts at changing public attitudes, and location of suitable employment sites. Connecticut offered home teaching services as early as 1893 (Dickinson, 1956); by 1926, they were offered in 25 states (Koestler, 1976).

Simultaneously, however, an alternative to home-based teaching was developing. The large number of disabled servicemen who survived World War I prompted the establishment of residential rehabilitation facilities. The first was St. Dunstan's Hostel for Blinded Soldiers and Sailors, founded in England in 1915 (Wagg, 1932), followed closely by its U.S. counterpart, a unit at Evergreen Hospital in Baltimore in 1918. World War II brought further refinement of the concept of residential rehabilitation of blind veterans within the Veterans Administration, and the idea spread to state agencies. By 1950, 30 states operated residential rehabilitation centers (Asenjo, 1975a).

The increase in blind rehabilitation programs led to a need for more trained teachers to work in homes and residential centers for blind rehabilitation. The Canadians were the first to respond to this need, and a teacher training program was initiated by the Canadian National Institute for the Blind in 1919 (Kaarlela, 1966). Others were soon established at Columbia University in 1921, and at the Pennsylvania Institute for the Instruction of the Blind in 1924 (Dickinson, 1956). The latter, which was founded by Dr. Olin E. Buritt at Overbrook in Philadelphia, was the best known.

Definition

The burgeoning roles of home teachers and a national recognition of the need for standardization of practices in the area of human services prompted the American Foundation for the Blind (AFB) and the American Association of Workers for the Blind (AAWB) to organize the first meeting on professional standards for home teachers in 1938 (Cosgrove, 1961; Dickinson, 1956). A seven-member panel put forth a set of recommendations for home-teaching standards, and in 1941, AAWB accepted the first standards for certification of home teachers (Cosgrove, 1961). The two-level system emphasized both training and specific skill achievements. Class 1 certification required at least two years of college, including social work, and applicants had to demonstrate proficiency in grade 2 braille, typing, and handicrafts. In addition to these requirements, Class 2 certification required rehabilitation teachers to be college graduates and to have four semester hours of educational psychology.

In spite of these early efforts at standardization, in the 1950s and 1960s several authors were still noting the need to better define the role of the home teacher (Anderson, 1965; Cosgrove, 1961; Dickinson, 1956; Gissendanner, 1955; McKay, 1965). Home teachers active in AAWB, noting that the discipline had become overly diverse, undertook the task of defining it. A 1955 survey of members of home teaching organizations and the AAWB (Gissendanner, 1955) demonstrated the diversity of roles resulting from the expansion period of rehabilitation teaching. Among the 112 people who responded, all of the following subjects were taught:

- braille
- typing
- crafts
- Moon type
- penmanship
- cane travel
- homemaking
- use of adaptive appliances
- card games
- manual language
- English
- New York Point
- music
- social adjustment.

In addition, they reported working in preschool nurseries, being public speakers, and delivering talking books; and 31 supplemented their incomes with home-based employment. Besides the subjects assumed to be part of the home teacher's job, respondents noted that their duties often included:

- public relations
- social activities
- recreation
- arranging for medical care
- case recording
- assisting in placement
- writing letters for clients
- distributing canes
- supervising women in sheltered workshops
- training volunteers
- investigating potential foster home sites.

Dickinson (1956) continued the investigation by surveying agencies that employed home teachers. Sixty administrators reported even broader perceptions of home teachers' responsibilities, including such additional activities as collecting chairs for caning and selling home crafts. These administrative expectations of home teachers far exceeded the present duties and perceptions of rehabilitation teachers practicing today.

Although the Gissendanner and Dickinson studies were informative, they lacked scientific methodology. As a result, Cosgrove (1961) undertook a major federally sponsored study of the functions, qualifications, and training of the home teacher. It, too, had inherent research weaknesses, particularly in its small sample size, but it is generally considered a landmark work. The author interviewed 50 home teachers functioning under a variety of titles. The findings about the home teachers' roles were similar to those of earlier studies. The lack of standardization in the field was clear. The investigator found no standard assessment practices or curricula among agencies, caseloads varying in size from 20 to 300 people, and a range of 12 to 50 visits to clients made in an average two-week period.

The personal characteristics of the group were also similar to those of home teachers studied earlier. Most were women; most had visual impairments; and educational levels varied from less than high school level to college degrees in psychology, sociology, home economics, and occupational therapy. Nearly half were certified by AAWB.

Fueled by these three studies, debate about the roles of home teachers ensued. Dickinson (1963) expressed a need to limit the services offered by home teachers. He believed home teachers should be teachers first, then counselors, community referral sources, and interpreters of blindness to the community at large. Complex family counseling, counseling of deep-seated emotional problems, child welfare, placement, transportation of books to the library, and social visiting all fell outside the home teacher's realm. In addition, he felt strongly that the teaching role should be focused on rehabilitation goals, rather than on goals like "occupying idle hands," as had been done with handicrafts in the past.

Although most home teachers seemed to agree with Dickinson's philosophy, there was some disagreement on the issue of whether they were teachers or social workers (Anderson, 1965; Cosgrove, 1961; Kaarlela, 1966; Magill, 1959; McKay, 1965). McKay (1965) pointed out the role of the home teacher and the learning of adaptive skills in facilitating adjustment to blindness. However, there were those who felt that adjustment was a consequence of teaching; thus, home teachers should primarily be teachers (Anderson, 1965). Anderson's perception of the purpose of home teaching was threefold: to instruct, to impart information, and to interpret the meaning and effects of blindness to clients, their families, and the community. In some regards, the ongoing disagreement was based on semantics, since, Anderson argued, many who called themselves social workers actually performed teaching functions by their own descriptions.

The AAWB Board of Certification developed a statement of philosophy in 1959 (Cosgrove, 1961), indicating that the home teacher should be involved in casework as well as in instruction. In addition, AAWB's stance was that home teachers should recognize the needs of the individual, interpret those needs to the community, possess leadership skills, adjust quickly to the needs of persons who are blind, and be able to develop and implement a plan of action for meeting their needs (Cosgrove, 1961; Magill, 1959).

Refinement

Perhaps the symbol of rehabilitation teaching's movement out of the struggle to define itself into the phase of refining the profession was the name change that took place in 1965 as a result of the COMSTAC (Commission on Standards and Accreditation of Services for the Blind) Report (1966; Leja, 1990). This document attempted to set forth standards for every area of services to people who are blind. Rehabilitation teacher became the new job title, and AAWB soon accepted this term for certification purposes.

Because academic preparation and specialized training for rehabilitation teaching are still somewhat varied, there remains an admixture of philosophies and beliefs in the field. However, there is a great deal of evidence demonstrating that rehabilitation teaching has truly become a profession. The next section explores the professional status of rehabilitation teaching today.

PROFESSIONAL STATUS

Rehabilitation teaching is a relatively young profession, and it therefore is not as fully developed as some that have been in existence for a longer time. According to Raelin (1985), a profession is defined by the following characteristics, exemplified by its practitioners:

- special expertise normally gained through a prolonged specialized training in a body of abstract knowledge
- autonomy—that is, the perceived right to make choices concerning both the means and the ends of the work
- commitment to the work and the profession
- identity with the profession and other professions
- ethics—a felt need to render service without concern for self
- collegial maintenance of standards, as through certification.

Despite its relative youth, rehabilitation teaching is well along the path to professionalism in each of these areas.

Professional Knowledge

The expertise of rehabilitation teachers lies in the knowledge of adaptations for people with visual impairments in the areas of communication and the tasks of daily living, as presented in Parts 3 and 4 of this book. The body of knowledge used within the discipline of rehabilitation teaching has been developed primarily through practice, although theory in rehabilitation, adult education, and social work has been incorporated into the profession as it is taught today. Over the years, people with visual impairments and rehabilitation teachers have found adaptive techniques that increase the independence of people with visual impairments. The teaching techniques utilized today have been validated for the most part through successful use over time. Development of knowledge through trial and error is highly inefficient, however, and, because it is not based on scientific or systematic investigation, can lead to incorrect conclusions. Therefore, techniques need to be validated through research. Over the past few years there has been an increasing amount of applied research, professional discussion, and collaborative exploration in the field in areas such as attitudes about blindness and attitude change, stereotypic behaviors and their alleviation, measurement and enhancement of tactile sensitivity, diabetic management, outcomes of rehabilitation teaching, use of computers, teaching techniques, visual efficiency, recreational games, and professional relationships. Such efforts indicate that rehabilitation teachers are building the knowledge base of the profession.

Professional Qualifications

The first university-based training program in rehabilitation teaching in the United States was begun at the master's level at Western Michigan University in 1963 (Kaarlela, 1966). This new program was soon followed by similar programs at Boston College and Cleveland State University, which no longer exist, as well as at Northern Illinois University in DeKalb; the University of Arkansas at Little Rock; Hunter College of the City University of New York; Pennsylvania College of Optometry in Philadelphia; and San Francisco State University; and more recently at the University of Massachusetts at Boston; Dominican College in Orangeburg, New York; and Florida State University in Tallahassee. Standardization of university curricula was undertaken through a joint effort of Division 11, Rehabilitation Teaching and Independent Living, of the Association for Education and Rehabilitation of the Blind and Visually Impaired (AER) and AFB and was approved by the AER board of directors in fall 1990 (Wiener & Luxton, 1994).

The best estimate of the influence that more than 30 years of professional training has had on qualifications of rehabilitation teachers comes from a scientific survey of 209 practicing rehabilitation teachers conducted in 1989 by Leja (1990) in which he found that 42 percent of his subjects held degrees in rehabilitation teaching. This means, however, that the majority of rehabilitation teachers are still taught in settings other than university training programs. Since there is little standardization of training methods outside universities, it is doubtful that such training courses are inclusive.

Table 2.1 compares Leja's findings about the personal characteristics and qualifications of rehabilitation teachers today with those of three other studies conducted earlier in the profession's history (Cosgrove, 1961; Dickinson, 1956; Young, Dickerson, & Jacobson, 1980). Educational qualifications have improved since Dickinson's era, when only 59 percent of rehabilitation teachers held college degrees of any sort, with 96 percent of rehabilitation teachers holding degrees in 1989. In addition, the percentage of agencies requiring a degree have increased from 38 percent in 1956 (Dickinson, 1956) to 100 percent in 1982 (Nelipovich, Godley, and Vieceli, 1982). As can be seen, the profession continues to be dominated by women. There is also evidence that the profession is becoming competitive in attracting practitioners from more varied backgrounds, since less than 40 percent of rehabilitation teachers were legally blind in 1989, whereas 86 percent were in 1956, and virtually all home teachers were blind at the profession's beginning. The 44 percent of rehabilitation teachers who achieve certification has changed little since 1963.

Professional Roles

The responsibilities of rehabilitation teachers burgeoned in the early days of home teaching, as mentioned earlier, but tasks such as those described by Dickinson (1956) as being too general or beyond the home teacher's abilities are not included in later studies (Leja, 1990; Nelipovich et al., 1982; Young et al., 1980). Leja utilized a validated Job Tasks Inventory to determine the activities of the 209 rehabilitation teachers he surveyed and found that the tasks fell into the three broad categories of teaching, case management, and professional or administrative activities. The most frequently performed tasks were the teaching activities of plan writing (discussed in Chapter 4) and instruction in various daily living skills and the case management tasks of scheduling, counseling clients in one form or another, and contacting other community agencies. The administrative task of attending staff meetings was also a frequent job activity. (Leja's findings about the roles of rehabilitation teachers are presented in more detail in the discussion of case management in Chapter 17.) The frequency of plan writing as a task of today's rehabilitation teachers seems to be a direct result of the increased formality in the field of blind rehabilitation.

A more recent study of rehabilitation teachers' roles and functions conducted by Beliveau-Tobey and De l'Aune (1991) with the goal of identifying training needs corroborates Leja's findings and provides further evidence of the evolution of rehabilitation teaching from the earlier "jack-of-all-trades" roles of home teachers to today's better-defined teaching, case man-

Table 2.1. Qualifications and Personal Characteristics Reported by Rehabilitation Teachers, 1956 to 1990

	Survey			
Characteristics	Dickinson (1956) (*N*=241)	Cosgrove (1961) (*N*=50)	Young et al. (1980) (*N*=78)	Leja (1990) (*N*=209)
Female	73%	77%	[a]	81%
Legally blind	86%	94%	[a]	38%
High school diploma or less	41%	24%	3%	2%
College degree	59%	68%	97%	96%
Master's degree	[a]	[a]	46%	51%
Rehabilitation teaching degree	[a]	[a]	1%	42%
Rehabilitation teaching certification	[a]	42%	[a]	44%

Sources: R. M. Dickinson, "The Discipline of Home Teaching," *Proceedings of the Thirtieth Convention of the American Association of Workers for the Blind* (New York: American Foundation for the Blind, 1956), pp. 21-28; E. Cosgrove, *Home Teachers of the Adult Blind: What They Do, What They Could Do, What Will Enable Them to Do It* (Washington, DC: American Association of Workers for the Blind, 1961); P. S. Young, L. R. Dickerson, and W. H. Jacobson, "A Study of the Job Responsibilities of the Field of Rehabilitation Teaching," *Journal of Visual Impairment & Blindness,74* (1980), pp. 386-389; and J. A. Leja, "The Job Roles of Rehabilitation Teachers of Blind Persons," *Journal of Visual Impairment & Blindness, 84*(4) (1990), pp. 155-159.

[a] No data available.

agement, and administrative functions. They pointed out that, although other professions such as rehabilitation counseling have been heavily studied, there continues to be a need for updating the studies of the role and functions of present-day rehabilitation teachers.

Professional Certification

As mentioned earlier, certification of home teachers by AAWB was initiated in 1941. The standards were amended significantly in 1963, when training of rehabilitation teachers was moving to the academic setting, and six times since then. The certifying body for rehabilitation teachers remained AAWB until 1984, when that organization underwent a consolidation and subsequent name change. The new organization, AER (see Sidebar 2.1), adopted a system of continually renewable professional certification. The current designations are Professional Rehabilitation Teacher Certification, Types AA and A. Type AA certification was designed specifically for graduates of university-based training programs in rehabilitation teaching, and Type A is for persons with other degrees, such as rehabilitation or education, who received specific on-the-job

SIDEBAR 2.1

The Professional Organization and Literature

The Association for Education and Rehabilitation of the Blind and Visually Impaired (AER) is the international membership organization for professionals who work with people who are visually impaired. The association's beginnings date back to the early 1900s as the American Association of Workers for the Blind (AAWB). Since that time, it has undergone several reorganizations and name changes, the most significant and most recent of which was the 1984 consolidation with the Association for the Education of the Visually Handicapped (AEVH). During the first year of its existence it was known as the AAWB-AEVH Alliance, but later became AER. Biennial international conferences sponsored by AER are held in the summer of even-numbered years, and regional conferences are scheduled throughout the United States and Canada during alternate years. In addition, state and provincial chapters generally meet one or more times per year.

AER is composed of subgroups, called divisions, based on specific areas of interest. Division 11, Rehabilitation Teaching and Independent Living, is one of the largest. As is the case with the general structure of AER, Division 11 is governed by elected officers and a board of directors serving two-year terms to coincide with biennial meetings of AER. The members of the board are elected and each represents one of AER's United States/Canadian geographic regions. Division 11 accomplishes much of its work through committees, including the Certification Committee. Division 11 conducts business meetings and organizes programming at the biennial international conferences, and its members are active at regional and state chapter meetings. One of the goals of Division 11 is to promote high-quality teaching. Therefore, continuing education units are generally made available from conferences and workshops to enhance the knowledge of rehabilitation teachers and to assist them in certification renewal.

AER publishes the quarterly peer-reviewed journal, *RE:view*, which is free to members, and contains a variety of articles. Members of Division 11 also publish a quarterly newsletter, *RT News*. In addition, the *Journal of Visual Impairment & Blindness*, a peer-reviewed journal published bi-monthly by the American Foundation for the Blind, is available at a discounted price to AER members.

training from agencies in skills for working with people who are blind. Although similar to previous standards, the knowledge and skills required for certification today have been updated, and documentation of credentials is more stringent. (See Appendix A for more information on the certification process.)

Professional Ethics

One of the essential characteristics of a profession is standardization of the behaviors of its members. Basic to this premise is the existence of a code of ethics, which describes acceptable practices relating to confidentiality, fairness, equal treatment of clients, remuneration and rewards from clients, quality of service, interprofessional respect and teamwork, commitment to clients, and other such issues. AER Division 11 members voted to accept a code of ethics for rehabilitation teachers at the AER national conference in 1986. A more concise version replaced it in 1990, and it is included in Appendix A.

The Rehabilitation Teacher Code of Ethics is divided into six sections, each of which details the professional's commitment to a significant aspect of the profession. The sections cover the rehabilitation teacher's relationship to

- *clients*—including issues of respect, advocacy, confidentiality, safety, evaluation, empowerment, and professional relationships
- *community*—including the obligation to present factual material about visual impairment to the public and to avoid exploitation of clients during this activity
- *profession*—including the promotion of professional training and the responsibility to add to the body of professional knowledge, to promote quality services, to report unethical practices, and to support other professionals
- *colleagues and other professionals*—including the need to function as a cooperative team member and to make referrals to qualified professionals when the client's needs are beyond the rehabilitation teacher's expertise
- *professional business practices*—including adherence to agency practices and policies, avoidance of private practice that conflicts with agency service, and guidelines for handling gifts from clients
- *private employment practices*—including boundaries for ethical business practices.

PROFESSIONAL PRACTICE

It has been a long and difficult struggle to establish rehabilitation teaching as a profession. The Epilogue discusses some of the challenges rehabilitation teaching faces today and in the future as it continues this ongoing process of development. The brief discussion in this chapter indicates its attainment of professional status. The detailed body of knowledge presented throughout the rest of this book reinforces that professionalism.

This overview of the profession of rehabilitation teaching has made clear that rehabilitation teachers perform a wide variety of tasks in their different roles in the course of their work. Part 2 of this book covers the process of rehabilitation teaching—how the teacher meets and assesses the client, how the two together decide what services and instruction the client will receive, and how the rehabilitation teacher plans the instructional sequence.

PART TWO

The Process of Rehabilitation Teaching

CHAPTER 3

The Assessment Process

KEY CONCEPTS IN THIS CHAPTER

- The purpose and need for assessment
- The levels of assessment in the overall rehabilitation process
- Rehabilitation teaching's three-part assessment of personal adjustment clients
- The process of assessing case files
- The process of conducting an assessment interview
- The process of conducting an observational assessment
- The Case File Summary Form
- The Interview Assessment Form

The initial assessment provides the cornerstone on which rehabilitation teaching services are built. Assessment is the process through which the teacher determines the present needs and skill levels of the client. Thus, an assessment provides the teacher with well-documented information on which to base an instructional plan. The assessment is also valuable in building rapport with the client, since instruction that underestimates or overestimates the learner's knowledge and abilities can result in unnecessary frustration or feelings of being patronized. According to the theory of Piaget, choosing the correct starting point for instruction is imperative, since it is basic to optimal learning (cited in Ginsberg & Opper, 1988). Also, because caseloads tend to be large and people with visual impairments are often on waiting lists for services, the rehabilitation teacher must know precisely where to begin instruction in order to make the most effective use of time.

LEVELS OF ASSESSMENT

In a typical state vocational rehabilitation program in the United States, assessment takes place at several levels, which are shown in Table 3.1:

- Eligibility determination measures whether the individual meets the criteria for service.
- Program assessment, usually conducted by the vocational rehabilitation counselor, but in some states the responsibility of the rehabilitation teacher, determines what major services the individual will receive and results in the Individualized Written Rehabilitation Program or, in Canada, the Individual Program Plan (see Chapter 4).

Table 3.1. Outline of Client Assessment

Level of Assessment	Procedure
Eligibility determination	The vocational rehabilitation counselor coordinates testing for the medical eye examination report and completes intake procedures.
Program assessment	The vocational rehabilitation counselor conducts diagnostic testing, determines the vocational goal with the client, and writes an Individualized Written Rehabilitation Program (IWRP) or Individual Program Plan (IPP) describing the services required to meet the vocational goal.
Personal adjustment assessment	The rehabilitation teacher conducts an assessment of the client through a case file review, an interview, and direct observation; and writes a service plan describing the specific skills to be taught to help the client adjust to vision loss.
	During ongoing assessment, the rehabilitation teacher determines the client's specific needs on a daily basis and writes a lesson plan for how to teach each of the skills listed on the service plan.
Vocational assessment	Following personal adjustment training, the vocational rehabilitation counselor coordinates a specialized assessment to determine the client's needs relating to his or her vocational goal.

- Personal adjustment assessment, conducted by the rehabilitation teacher, determines which skill areas will be taught.
- Vocational assessment determines the person's potential for employment.

This discussion will focus on the personal adjustment assessment, for which the rehabilitation teacher is responsible. How the teacher translates the assessment into a set of goals (the service plan) and the specific steps to reach them (lesson plans) is covered in Chapter 4 on the planning process.

The rehabilitation teacher usually begins his or her part of the assessment when personal adjustment training services are prescribed as a result of the program assessment. If services are to be provided in the person's home, the rehabilitation teacher is responsible for the entire personal adjustment assessment, and all areas of communications and daily living are included. If the person is to be served in a residential center, this level of assessment is generally conducted by a rehabilitation counselor or a team of instructors and counselors. The rehabilitation teacher working in the residential center is usually responsible only for the assessment of the particular subject areas that he or she teaches. Information gathered during the rehabilitation teacher's assessment comes from three major sources: the case file, personal interviews, and direct observation.

ASSESSMENT OF CASE FILE

The case file, which usually reaches the rehabilitation teacher some time prior to the first meeting with the referred client, provides a historical overview. The case file may contain only a few documents establishing the client's eligibility for services, or it may be several inches thick, depending on the extent to which the person has utilized services in the past. In either case, one would expect to find information relating to the following:

- eye condition
- medical history
- educational history
- vocational history
- social history

- rehabilitation history
- psychometric testing history
- personal characteristics.

Case records provide valuable information for planning services. Data gleaned from eye reports are especially helpful. The person's visual acuity is a good predictor of visual ability, and age at the onset of the disability is a good predictor of conceptual knowledge. Medical records describe other disabilities or conditions or medication regimens. It is important to be aware of any medication the client is taking, because the side effects of certain prescription drugs can interfere with learning or affect scheduling. Information on prior educational performance is also useful, because such performance has been shown to relate to an individual's ultimate success in training (Scholl, Bauman, & Chrissey, 1969).

Vocational information found in case files is useful because types of former employment give some indication of the visually impaired person's skills. A specified vocational goal can indicate the importance of teaching certain job-related skills during personal adjustment training.

The social history in a case file is usually a narrative report written by a social worker or counselor. It provides data relating to the client's background in the family or other living situations. The social history narrative may indicate the family's perception of the disability, the degree of support to be expected from family members, the role of the visually impaired member in the family, and the family's degree of support from others.

Reports from rehabilitation teachers who have provided training in the past are particularly valuable. They are good indicators of learning potential, and they describe the individual's levels of various skills. In addition, results of standardized tests serve as indicators of the client's vocational preference, intelligence, dexterity, personality, and degree of adjustment to the impairment.

However, data collected from records have certain inherent weaknesses. Outdated information, biased reports, and results of inappropriate testing can be particularly problematic. Obsolete and consequently inaccurate information is often found in eye reports or medical histories. For example, visual acuity is subject to overnight alterations, and medications are changed frequently. Reporter biases are also commonly reflected in case files. Social histories, for example, may provide false information based on the interviewer's prejudices, and rehabilitation teachers' reports regarding performance may be inaccurate, as a result of bias on the part of the instructor or lack of objective measures of performance. Psychometric information may also be inaccurate because the interviewer was not familiar with special testing conditions or adaptive tests for individuals who are visually impaired. Despite the value of having case files for background information about the person, therefore, one should recognize that a service plan and a service provider's knowledge of his or her client cannot be based on such files alone.

Reading case records takes time and it is helpful to determine beforehand what information is important to gather. Many agencies have developed simple forms to expedite the review. Examples of two completed Case File Summary Forms are presented in Figures 3.1 and 3.2. (A blank copy of this form appears in Appendix C for readers' use.) Following are the case histories on which the two Case File Summary Forms are based to illustrate the kinds of information that is condensed in these two summaries:

> Judy H. is a bright young woman who is eager to find employment in the area of drug abuse counseling. Her initial loss of vision occurred when she was 10 years old as a result of diabetes. At age 23, shortly after she had completed a master's degree program and taken a job in a group home for adults with developmental disabilities, she experienced a significant retinal hemorrhage that left her with considerably decreased functional vision. During two subsequent job interviews, she was upset to find her-

Case File Summary Form

Name Judy H.

Address 235 Fourth Avenue, New City

Date 2/22/96 **Age** 23 **Gender** F

Education Master's degree in social work

Visual impairment history

Cause Diabetic retinopathy, vitrectomy

Age of onset Diabetes, age 10; retinopathy, age 23

Prognosis Progressive, further decrease probable

Acuity Distance OD 20/200 OS 20/400

Near OD 20/100 OS 20/400

Counts fingers 1 foot, left

Field Not available

Comments Vision has been decreasing; a +6.00 microscopic system improves reading to 20/40

Medical history

Disabilities Insulin dependent, abnormal thyroid, can't stand for more than four hours per day

Medications Insulin injections

Comments Not allowed to lift more than 20 pounds

Vocational history

Present Residential services coordinator

Past Pharmacy technician, MSW student

Goal Full-time social work employment

Comments Makes use of CCTV and modified tape recorder at current employment

(continued on next page)

Figure 3.1. Sample Case File Summary Form

Social history

Marital status Married

Living situation Lives with husband

Living situation goal Same

Client support Client is self-supporting ($30,000/year, full medical benefits)

Family/group support Family is supportive

Testing history

Low vision evaluation (10/18/95)

College evaluation 5/6 to 5/10/94

Rehabilitation history

Past year None

Number of weeks of previous training 1 week training, 4/29/94

Setting State residential rehabilitation center

Activities of daily living training Client performed independently and successfully in all areas

Communication Able to use low vision aids (magnification, illumination), recording (modified recorder), and computer to accomplish communication tasks. Had introduction to braille

Other If vision decreases, will need more training in adaptive techniques and advanced braille, with emphasis on more tactile skills

Figure 3.1. Sample Case File Summary Form *(continued)*

self unable to answer questions about how she would keep track of information about her clients. This led to her request for further training at the rehabilitation center where she had previously had one week of training, particularly in the areas of braille and adaptive computers. Her past history with personal adjustment training indicates that she is an outstanding learner and would benefit from such training.

Dr. Richard K. was referred to the agency two weeks after he was accidentally shot in both eyes. An interview at the hospital found him strongly denying his nearly total loss of vision, with such statements as "I just hope I get my sight back in time for the basketball league championships next month." The ophthalmologist's reports indicated the likelihood of a permanent significant loss. Dr. K.'s past history, which included a job as a plant disease researcher for the State Department of Agriculture, and his tenacious spirit would appear to make him an ideal rehabilitation client. He is easy to talk to on the topics of fishing, nature, hiking, camping, and the like. Recent reports from his wife indicate that he is going to work every day but that he is bored with his job, which is now limited to answering questions on the telephone about plant diseases.

Case File Summary Form

Name Richard K.

Address 3715 Briarcliff Road, Parksville

Date 12/16/95 **Age** 31 **Gender** M

Education Ph.D. in Biology

Visual impairment history

Cause Gunshot wounds, both eyes

Age of onset Age 30

Prognosis Unknown. Client expects to regain vision

Acuity Light perception O.U.

Field

Comments

Medical history

Disabilities None

Medications Cortical steroid, antidepressant

Comments

Vocational history

Present Plant pathologist, pending return of sight

Past Plant pathologist, disease research

Goal Greenhouse and landscape business operator

Comments He continues to work answering questions about plant diseases for state residents. His original job was in a plant disease clinic, where he diagnosed diseases and conducted plant disease research. He is interested in the outdoors.

(continued on next page)

Figure 3.2. Sample Case File Summary Form

Social history

Marital status: Married

Living situation: Lives with wife, daughter (age 4), son (age 2)

Living situation goal: Same

Client support: Client is self-supporting ($40,000/year, full medical benefits)

Family/group support: Family is supportive. Neighbor reads him the paper and takes him fishing

Testing history

No previous standardized tests

Rehabilitation history

Past year: No previous training

Number of weeks of previous training: ______

Setting: ______

Activities of daily living training: ______

Communication: ______

Other: ______

Figure 3.2. Sample Case File Summary Form *(continued)*

THE ASSESSMENT INTERVIEW

Perhaps the most crucial part of the assessment process is the initial assessment interview. This meeting is when the instructor begins to obtain his or her own firsthand information about the client, and together instructor and client establish the client's needs. The major purposes of this interview are to verify the information gathered from case records, to establish rapport, to determine the client's personal needs and desires, and to inform the client of the services that the rehabilitation teacher can offer.

A well-structured interview involves the following four sequential steps (Benjamin, 1981):

- preparation
- the opening
- the body
- the closing.

These will be discussed in turn.

Preparation

Preparation is the cornerstone of the interview process, because it lays the essential foundation for effective service delivery. The success of the assessment interview depends in large part on the rehabilitation teacher's ability to maintain a meaningful dialogue with the client. Therefore, the rehabilitation teacher should become aware of some basic principles of interpersonal communication. There are many potential obstacles to communication, and before attempting to conduct an interview, the teacher should consider which ones are likely to surface and how to eliminate them.

As part of this process, the rehabilitation teacher needs to evaluate his or her attitudes toward religious and ethnic groups, people with disabilities, people with different cultural backgrounds, socioeconomic subgroups, and other minorities. Those who are subject to biases easily recognize prejudice; unfortunately, it is often difficult to recognize one's own biases or lack of cultural knowledge, and these factors serve as threats to communication. Because this subject is of such importance, it is covered in more detail in Chapter 5 on the learning and teaching process.

In addition, many factors relating to interpersonal dynamics need to be considered carefully, because they can have a significant impact on client-teacher interaction. Unless the client feels comfortable with the teacher, it may be difficult to establish a working relationship. A fundamental obstacle to communication can be the client's perception of the teacher's attitudes toward him or her. Problems frequently arise, for example, if the teacher's perception of himself or herself as being in the role of "helper" leads to a patronizing or demeaning behavior toward the client. If a teacher has the attitude that he or she holds all the answers to the client's problems, for example, the client may perceive that the teacher is not paying attention to the client's unique situation. In essence, difficulties relating to this issue may be connected to the teacher's reason for entering a helping profession. Many people become rehabilitation teachers because they want to help persons in need. The operative question, however, is *why* they desire to help. Perhaps some people want to help others for purely altruistic reasons, but it appears more likely that helping fulfills a basic human "need to be needed." Therefore, it is important for rehabilitation teachers to understand that the helping relationship is beneficial not only to those receiving a service, but also to those delivering it. This awareness strengthens the relative equality of the participants in the helper-helpee relationship. If this concept is not understood, the teacher's perception of his or her role can become overinflated, leading in turn to behavior that may be overly authoritarian or overly solicitous.

Self-centeredness on the part of the interviewer is another factor that can interfere with communication. Overconcern with oneself is commonly the result of nervousness, especially when someone is inexperienced. For this reason, rehabilitation teachers who are beginning their careers may want to be sensitive to the influence of feelings of awkwardness or uncertainty. However, seasoned professionals as well may find that nervousness on meeting new clients has an initial effect on their behavior. This problem may manifest itself in such ways as overattention to paperwork or participation in meaningless conversation for long periods of time. Nervousness and feelings of inadequacy can affect virtually all novice interviewers from time to time, but coping mechanisms can be used to overcome these feelings. One strategy would be to plan the interview well in advance and even to practice it if necessary. Another would be to engage in a few minutes of informal dialogue on general topics, such as the weather, the person's living quarters, or the surrounding neighborhood.

Overconcern with self can also sometimes be a function of a need to be in control. People who have a tendency to dominate the conversation or interrupt others should monitor themselves by audio- or videotaping themselves as they interact with others before they attempt actual interviews (Benjamin, 1981). If negative behaviors are present, they can be replaced by positive ones, such as encouraging input from the client, allowing him or her to complete responses, or promoting decision making on the client's part.

Many other obstacles to communication are related to the person being interviewed rather than to the interviewer; for example, the client's degree of adjustment to the loss of sight or his or her personality or personal attitudes. Depression or anger, inherent shyness, or prejudicial feelings toward being helped are common hurdles to be overcome. Because this topic is a complex one, it is also presented in more detail in Chapter 5 on the learning and teaching process.

After potential obstacles to communication are considered and plans are made to overcome them, another crucial step in preparing for the opening phase of an interview is to gather information from the case file that will be useful. Facts about the situation that resulted in the client's visual impairment, about the family, or about prior employment are especially useful. They furnish the interviewer with an unlimited supply of material for leading questions that help both the interviewer and client to get beyond any initial nervousness. Leading statements or questions such as "I see you grew up on a farm," "So you have two children," or "The job you did sounds interesting. What was it like?" are good icebreakers.

The Opening

The opening phase of the interview represents the initial contact with the client, during which the rehabilitation teacher

- establishes contact
- begins to develop rapport
- introduces the agency's goals.

This phase begins with the first telephone contact and continues through the initial stages of the first meeting.

The first verbal interaction between client and teacher usually takes place on the telephone. The teacher introduces himself or herself, states his or her agency affiliation, and establishes a time for the initial interview. At the time of the first face-to-face contact, the teacher restates his or her name and agency affiliation and describes the agency's broad goals.

In general, the initial contact is best handled in a relatively formal way. In practical terms, this means that the new client interviewee should be addressed as Mr., Mrs., or Ms. After this introduction and a few minutes of informal conversation based on the case file review, the body of the assessment can begin.

The Body

The assessment itself is carried out during the third phase, or body, of the assessment interview. The rehabilitation teacher's goals at this point are to determine the client's perceived needs, knowledge of the impairment, and abilities and to describe the services to be offered. The Rehabilitation Teacher Interview Assessment Form presented in Figure 3.3 serves as an outline for this process. (A blank copy of the form appears in Appendix C for readers' use.) This example was completed for the following client:

> Mrs. Rachel S. has a central visual loss from macular degeneration but did not think that she was eligible for services for the blind because she has remaining peripheral vision. She experiences difficulty accomplishing tasks related to seeing small print such as reading the newspaper, telephone books, food labels, and stove dials. As a busy mother with two small children, she finds the limitations caused by her vision loss very frustrating. When her husband inquired at the local library about books on tape, the librarian alerted the couple to the services of the State Commission for the Blind as well as the local Library for the Blind and Physically Handicapped.

As an adult who became visually impaired only recently, Mrs. S. represents a typical rehabilitation teaching client. The reader should be aware that in interviewing a client with a congenital disability, although the areas requiring assessment remain the same, wording of the questions used to elicit the information may need to vary to reflect the in-

Rehabilitation Teacher Interview Assessment Form

Name Rachel S. **Date** 9-26-95

Address 324 South Street, Waterford **Interviewer** Robert Z.

Other disabilities Slight hearing impairment in left ear

Living situation Lives with husband, daughter (4), and son (2)

Immediate dangers She is in no danger since her husband meets most of her survival needs. Also, her mother stays with her during the day while her husband is at work.

Accuracy of knowledge of eye condition Knows that her central vision is beyond repair and that her peripheral vision will probably not be affected.

COMMUNICATION

Reading

A. Current reading ability She cannot read newspapers, telephone books, or standard print books, but can read newspaper headlines, some food labels, and her own printing if large.

B. Past reading interests Mystery novels, westerns, and art-related books. Subscribed to Ladies' Home Journal.

C. Use of tape recorder Doesn't have a cassette player.

D. Knowledge of Talking Books Knows little about the program, but has read several books on a disc player her husband brought home two months ago.

Writing

A. Present handwriting skills Minimal handwriting use. Currently writes notes to husband and kids. Expressed difficulty in writing in straight line.

B. Keyboarding (typewriter and/or computer; past and present experience) Has never been exposed to computers. Worked in an office as a clerk-typist. Has made no attempt at typing since her vision loss.

C. Use of tape recorders (past and present experience) Has used a stereo cassette player, but never used a tape recorder.

Mathematics (past and present abilities and responsibilities)

Was responsible for the family bookkeeping before sight loss, but her husband now does the accounting. Stated that she missed being able to write checks. Used a calculator frequently in the past.

(continued on next page)

Figure 3.3. Sample Rehabilitation Teacher Interview Assessment Form

ACTIVITIES OF DAILY LIVING

Home Management (all past and present methods, responsibilities, and experiences)

A. Food preparation *Microwave is operated by heat-sensitive push buttons—can't tell what does what. Self-reported fear of stove. Formerly prepared about 50 - 60% of meals. Took special pride in baking skills.*

B. Cleaning *Did most of the sweeping, laundry, and about 50% of the total housekeeping in past. Does most laundry, makes beds, does dishes now.*

C. Home repairs *Most of repair chores done by workmen, but she had done some minor plumbing and electrical chores. Has tried nothing since vision loss.*

Personal Management (all past and present abilities)

A. Grooming/makeup *No problems reported*

B. Medicinal management *Takes blood pressure medication and an antidepressant. Identified the two types of pills by their color.*

C. Clothing identification and care *Is still able to distinguish clothing by color. Does laundry.*

D. Money identification *After minimal instruction she could identify all bill denominations by the print patterns on backs of bill, even though she could not read the numbers.*

E. Telling time *Has difficulty reading her digital watch face.*

F. Telephone use *Reports that she uses her index finger and counts the individual keys to find the number she wants. Much frustration expressed.*

Leisure Pursuits (past interests and present use)

No interest expressed because of frustration of trying and failing at needlepoint, but once did this extensively.

Indoor Mobility

A. Present difficulties *No difficulty reported.*

B. Knowledge of sighted guide techniques *None.*

C. Visibility in living situation (lighting and contrast) *Kitchen area is dark due to heavy window drapes and poor lighting, but remainder of house is well lighted.*

Figure 3.3. Sample Rehabilitation Teacher Interview Form *(continued)*

dividual's situation. One of the first items on the Interview Assessment Form is designed to verify the information in the case file regarding the client's other disabilities and to determine the client's perception of them. This information can be gathered by asking, "Do you have any other disabilities that you feel interfere with your daily routine?" In the example in Figure 3.3, the client did have a slight hearing impairment, which did not significantly affect her need for instruction or services.

It is important to ascertain the client's living situation early in the assessment. Persons who live alone pose a special consideration. The rehabilitation teacher needs to assess their ability to meet basic survival needs even before assessing their daily living skills. Immediate survival needs include access to food, shelter, and transportation and the ability to administer one's own medications. The following questions should be asked to ascertain whether the client's survival needs are being met:

How are you managing to get meals?

Are you able to pay rent or house payments?

Can you set the thermostat?

Are you able to pay for heating fuel?

How are you getting to doctors' appointments, the grocery store, and other crucial destinations?

Are you taking any medications? If so, how do you know when to take them?

How do you know which pill is which?

If it is obvious that the client has support from others, such as a spouse, and is in no immediate danger, these questions need not be immediately addressed unless another indication emerges of the client's need for help in these areas. Since Mrs. Rachel S. had good family support, these questions did not need to be specifically addressed at this point.

Because misconceptions and misunderstandings concerning eye conditions are common, the next step in the assessment is to evaluate the client's knowledge of his or her impairment. In most cases the information needed can be obtained by asking: "Do you mind describing what happened at the time of your loss of sight?" and following up with related questions. Simple misunderstandings can be addressed immediately. For example, if Judy H., the drug abuse counselor with diabetic retinopathy, says, "If only I hadn't changed insulin brands, I never would have lost more sight," the rehabilitation teacher can say, "You needn't feel guilty. Additional vision losses are common with diabetic retinopathy." However, if gross misconceptions are discovered, the individual should be referred to an ophthalmologist or to an agency counselor. For example, Dr. K.'s belief that his vision will clear enough to allow him to play at next month's basketball championships is probably irrational and should perhaps be discussed with a counselor, but only the ophthalmologist can address the probable outcome of his gunshot injuries.

After these initial steps, the rehabilitation teacher can begin assessing the client's communication and daily living skills. As can be seen on the Interview Assessment Form, the primary skill areas within those categories are reading, writing, mathematics, the ability to move through the indoor environment safely, personal management, home management, and leisure pursuits. In every area, both past and present abilities should be ascertained.

Reading

The reading assessment should cover the client's present visual ability, past reading interest, experience with tape recorders, and knowledge of the Talking Book Program. Specific questions to ask a newly visually impaired client include:

What kinds of things did you read before your sight loss?

Are you able to see well enough to read anything now? If so, what?

Do you use any types of visual reading aids?

Have you used a tape recorder in the past? If so, can you describe how?

Do you know about the Talking Book Program? If so, can you describe how you use it?

Writing

The writing assessment should cover handwriting skills and keyboarding ability on both a typewriter and a computer. Questions might include:

Have you used a typewriter in the past? If so, please describe how.

Have you used a computer? If so, please explain how.

Have you tried writing since you lost your vision?

Do you presently use a typewriter or computer? If so, how do you manage?

Mathematics

The mathematics assessment should investigate the client's need and ability to calculate mathematical problems. Appropriate questions to be asked might be:

Have you had much need in the past to do mathematical calculations? If so, please describe what you did and how.

Are you currently able to do a math problem, such as adding the cost of purchases made at the grocery store?

Have you had any experience with calculators? If so, please describe it.

Indoor Mobility

The mobility assessment should investigate the person's knowledge of sighted guide techniques, the relative degree of visibility within the living environment, and fears and problems related to moving through it. Questions to ask might be:

Are you able to walk with other people? If so, how do you do it?

Are you having any difficulties getting around your house or property? If so, what are they?

If the person has functional vision, the interviewer would also want to know:

Are there any particular places in the house where you have more difficulty seeing?

Personal Management

The personal management assessment should cover hygiene, grooming, management of medicines, clothing care, identification of money, timekeeping, and telephoning skills. With the exception of toothbrushing, skills such as bathing and other hygiene-related tasks need not be investigated specifically, because they do not usually pose a problem for most clients unless the client has another disabling condition. Questions relating to this area include:

Are you able to take care of toothbrushing, shaving, cosmetics, and hair care now? If so, how are you doing it?

What kinds of cosmetics did you use before your vision loss?

Are you able to identify the clothing in your closet? If so, how do you do it?

Were you responsible for washing and ironing your clothing before your vision loss?

Are you able to manage the washing and ironing now? If so, how do you do them?

Are you able to keep track of time in any way? If so, could you explain your method?

Have you continued to use the telephone? If so, what method do you use to dial?

Home Management

The home management assessment should explore the client's past responsibilities in home care and current skills in food preparation, cleaning, and home repair. Suggested questions are:

Were you responsible for any of the housework or meals before your sight loss? If so, please explain how.

How have you taken care of leaky faucets or other maintenance problems in the past?

Are you able to get your cleaning and cooking done now? If so, how are you managing these chores?

Have you attempted any repair chores? If so, how have you done them?

Where do you plan to live following rehabilitation training?

Leisure Pursuits

The leisure pursuits assessment should identify the client's personal interests and abilities. Suggested questions might be:

Did you have any craft hobbies before losing your sight? If so, what were they?

Did you have any other hobbies then, such as card playing?

Did you have any active recreational pursuits in the past, such as jogging? If so, what were they?

Are you able to do any of these things now? If so, would you describe them?

The rehabilitation teacher can also use the interview to assess some skills in a more concrete way. Teaching the simple skills of signature writing, telling time, coin identification, dialing the telephone, and walking with a guide provide opportunities for assessing the client's use of residual vision, fine motor coordination, motor memory, tactile acuity, directional orientation, cognitive ability, and gross motor coordination (Raftary, 1977). These activities also afford the client a chance to experience an initial success, and they demonstrate the benefits to be gained from working with a rehabilitation teacher. For example, giving Dr. K. some tips on how to record information from the telephone might help the rehabilitation teacher gain his confidence and willingness to participate in further teaching sessions.

Individuals who have recently become visually impaired commonly vent feelings of frustration and hopelessness during the initial interview. It is common to encounter statements such as: "I don't think sitting around listening to books all day sounds like much of a life," or, as Mrs. S. said, "Yeah, I used to cook, but now I can't even pour a cup of coffee." The rehabilitation teacher may be tempted to counter with a detailed description of how much better the client's life will be when he or she learns all the adaptive skills the teacher has to offer. Although some encouragement is certainly appropriate, the teacher must be careful not to overdo it. It is unlikely that simply asserting the potential for learning will affect the client's attitudes, and in some cases the client may not, in fact, be capable of performing at the level predicted. Furthermore, exaggerating the possibilities may cause the client to disregard them completely.

In most cases, it is probably best to make a statement that acknowledges the problem and the possibility of addressing it, without making specific promises—for example "I'm pretty sure I can help you with some of the problems you are having in the kitchen. We'll talk about it in detail later." The interviewer can win the client's confidence, however, by responding to statements that indicate a special need or interest. For example, if the client says: "Handwriting has really become a problem. I always write over lines, and sometimes I find myself writing off the right side of the page," the rehabilitation teacher can explain guides or even demonstrate how a signature guide is used (see Chapter 8). Finding one or two specific problems that can be easily solved through adaptation will convince the client of the instructor's worth and will help get a "foot in the door."

The Closing

The final phase of an assessment interview is the closing. Although closing the interview might appear to be simple, it is sometimes complicated by the fact that the client may not want the visit to end. Because full caseloads generally require rehabilitation teachers to visit several households per day, however, it is important to close the interview in a timely manner.

The teacher's intention to close the interview is generally conveyed by a summary statement (Benjamin, 1981), for example, "Well, it appears you're doing pretty well, but we have several areas to work on over the next few weeks. Would you like to start next time with an introduction to the Talking Book Program?" The implication of such statements is not always perceived by the client, so a more direct approach may be required. One may need to say, for example, "I'm terribly sorry, but I must leave to see my next client, so shall we set up our next appointment?" In addition, there will be times when the newly referred person will need psychological support during the rehabilitation teacher's initial visits. Therefore, it is good practice to allow more time than usual and to schedule new clients for the last appointment in the day, if possible.

In the course of closing the interview, the teacher should also set a time for the next appointment and make sure the client knows how to contact the teacher. The teacher's office telephone number should be furnished in an accessible medium.

DIRECT OBSERVATIONAL ASSESSMENT

The third and final part of the rehabilitation teaching assessment process is direct observational assessment of the actual behavioral abilities of the client. For most clients, the assessment interview will have yielded all the information needed to begin writing an instructional plan that will list the areas and specific skills in which the client needs instruction, as explained in the next chapter. Once the teacher and client begin the first lessons, ongoing direct observational assessment of the client's performance and of the living environment continues to yield a great deal of useful information. For example, an initial lesson in Dr. K.'s kitchen would probably be an orientation session in which Dr. K. describes the room. Observation would tell the teacher whether Dr. K. knows kitchen utensils, organizational methods, and the uses of kitchen appliances. Similarly, the teacher can easily observe Dr. K.'s dressing habits, ability to move through an indoor environment, and cleaning abilities. After a few lessons, the teacher will have a good idea of Dr. K.'s fine motor skills, problem-solving ability, degree of useful vision, and motivation.

On rare occasions, however, a client will have a misconception of his or her skills and may not be capable of functioning at the levels he or she reports during the assessment interview. In this case, the rehabilitation teacher needs to identify the client's performance levels more directly through some type of testing. Unfortunately, testing is threatening to many individuals, and it can jeopardize the success of rehabilitation if the client perceives the teacher as questioning his or her honesty. If not handled properly, this situation can disrupt the rapport between teacher and learner and might even damage the client's self-confidence. Therefore, the rehabilitation teacher should place major emphasis on administering testing in a nonthreatening way.

The easiest means to accomplish this is through the observational assessment. If the teacher suspects the client cannot operate the telephone efficiently, for example, he or she need not confront the individual by saying: "You're going to have to show me that you can use the phone," or "Let's test your telephone dialing skills now, so you can prove you're capable." Rather, the assesser can either wait until the need to use the telephone arises naturally or design another lesson in which using the telephone is routinely required. For example, the telephone might be used in conjunction with a patch cord to record information obtained from a retail store about tape recorders or from a local transit company about bus routes.

If the teacher's observation demonstrates that the client cannot perform at the level reported in the assessment interview or is performing unsafe techniques, the teacher's response can create another point of possible conflict. Here again, the teacher need not be confrontational. Rather than responding with: "I'm afraid you're not doing it as well as you think," or "No, that's not the way it's done," one might say: "It's great that you have worked that method out on your own. I have a couple of others that work well, too. Some people with visual impairments use them successfully. I can show you during our next appointment."

In certain situations, objective scores, such as measures of braille accuracy or typing speed, are necessary and appropriate. One notable area is assessing low vision, which is discussed in Chapter 6. There are no commonly used standardized tests for assessing performance in the personal adjustment training subject areas, but methods of establishing objective scores are discussed in Chapter 17.

Along with the case file and interview assessments, observational assessment and testing, if necessary, yield all the information required to create a sound plan through which to serve the client. The process of plan writing is discussed in the next chapter.

CHAPTER 4

The Planning Process

KEY CONCEPTS IN THIS CHAPTER

- **The need for and purpose of written plans**
- **The relationship between assessment and planning**
- **The development of behavioral objectives**
- **The levels of planning in the rehabilitation process**
- **The function and completion of IWRP or IPP forms in the planning process**
- **The development of a service plan**
- **Rehabilitation teaching lesson plans**
- **Task-analyzed lesson plans**

The assessment process discussed in Chapter 3 is the prerequisite to designing individualized teaching plans for a particular client. Once the client's abilities, needs, and desires are ascertained, rehabilitation professionals can formulate written documents detailing the sequential sets of steps through which rehabilitation will be accomplished. Such written plans are helpful to the client, teacher, and administrator. They benefit the client by ensuring a logical sequence of instruction and by informing him or her of the agency's services and expectations. The teacher benefits because plans provide objectives with measurable outcomes, contribute to the efficient use of time, and alleviate the potential stress of being unprepared for a lesson. For administrators, plans provide a means to measure the outcomes of teaching and the overall service program.

The planning process is an organized one. It begins with setting broad goals that are required by federal or agency guidelines and proceeds to more specific plans that set forth the services and areas of instruction to be offered to the client. Three types of written plans are usually required during the rehabilitation process. From most general to most specific, they are the following:

- The Individualized Written Rehabilitation Program (IWRP) in the United States or the Individual Program Plan (IPP) in Canada
- the service plan
- lesson plans.

Each type of plan is based on one of the levels of the assessment process described in Chapter 3.

The IWRP or IPP is written on the basis of the program assessment conducted by a vocational rehabilitation counselor after the client's eligibility for vocational rehabilitation services is established. It is the most general plan, since it describes which of the agency's services—such as personal adjustment training or vocational training—will be offered to the client. In the United States, a transition plan is now required for young people with visual impairments who have been receiving services through the educational system and who need a combination of educational and vocational services to prepare for life after leaving school. The transition plan is generally comparable to the IWRP or IPP.

The service plan is written by the rehabilitation teacher based on the personal adjustment training assessment, which is described in more detail in Chapter 3. The service plan lists the specific skills to be offered within each of the subject areas taught by rehabilitation teachers, such as handwriting, keyboarding, and the like. Lesson plans result from the assessment of the learner's needs within each instructional area and are specific outlines of the individual lessons to be provided.

This chapter will examine each of these types of written plans in detail, including the information to be included and how to formulate goals and objectives with the client. The specific skills referred to in this chapter are detailed in the individual chapters on instructional skills in Parts 3 and 4. First, however, it is necessary to understand the way in which these plans specify what rehabilitation services will try to accomplish and how. This statement, known as the *behavioral objective,* is the basic unit of all written plans, whether broad or specific, used in the rehabilitation process.

BEHAVIORAL OBJECTIVES

A behavioral objective, also known as an instructional or a performance objective, is a concisely written statement of the expected outcomes of instruction (Yeadon, 1974). The behavioral objective provides the framework for a structured lesson in which the lesson's content and successful completion are defined and made measurable. Consider the following example:

> When presented with 25 grade 2 braille sentences, the learner will read them aloud with 90 percent accuracy.

Note that this behavioral objective has three integral parts: the *condition,* the *behavior,* and the *criterion used to measure performance* (Magers, 1962). Examples of conditions, behaviors, and criteria commonly used in behavioral objectives written by rehabilitation teachers are listed in Table 4.1.

The Condition

The condition—in this example, "When presented with 25 grade 2 braille sentences . . . "—is a brief description of the circumstances in which the behavior will be observed. It might refer to the amount of physical space allotted, the materials available, the amount of information given, reference materials allowed, or other descriptions of the situation with which the learner is presented.

The Behavior

The behavior in a behavioral objective is an observable action taken by the learner that he or she wishes to achieve. In the example, the behavior is ". . . will read them aloud . . ." The way a behavior is measured depends in part on whether it stems from the *cognitive, affective,* or *psychomotor* domains (Magers, 1962).

Cognitive behaviors are responses that demonstrate a degree of knowledge or intellectual understanding of a subject, for example, recalling information, describing a technique, or mentally calculating a mathematics problem. The affective domain relates to an individual's interests, attitudes, and preferences. Affective behaviors are, for the most part, measured by psychometric tests or other ways of detecting observable behaviors that themselves may reflect a change in affect. For example, renewal of interest in an old hobby may reflect an attitude change in someone who had formerly demonstrated signs of depression. Psychomotor responses are perhaps the most easily recognized, because they require physical movements. Sweeping, walking, and tracking in a straight line while reading braille would be considered psychomotor behaviors.

Other examples of behaviors that are part of behavioral objectives are listed in Table 4.1.

The Criterion

The third component of a behavioral objective, the performance criterion, is the yardstick by which achievement of the behavior is measured. The criterion in the example is ". . . with 90 percent accuracy." Criteria for other objectives might be the neatness of work, number of consecutive successful completions, number of correct steps, and degree of safety; additional examples are given in Table 4.1.

The choice of which criterion to use is based on the nature of the behavior being observed. If the activity results in numerous products, such as words in typing or braille, it is easily measured in such terms as writing speed or percentage of words brailled accurately. If the activity is a single act requiring several steps, however, such as filling a glass of water or cooking an item properly, the measure would be a more subjective judgment of quality. In the former case, the criterion could be quantified as the number of consecutive trials of filling the glass to the desired level without spilling. In the latter case, the criterion might be the degree of doneness of the food cooked or the amount of assistance that was required from the teacher during the lesson.

The level of performance at which a behavior is considered to have been successfully executed depends on the importance of the behavior. If the behavior is related to safety, for example, measuring insulin, the criterion is likely to be 100 percent

Table 4.1. Examples of Conditions, Behaviors, and Criteria Found in Rehabilitation Teachers' Behavioral Objectives

Subject Area	Condition	Learner's Behavior	Performance Criterion
Communication	When given a modified tape recorder and a cassette...	...the learner will verbally describe the parts of the recorder...	...with 90% accuracy.
	When given a radio, patch cord, cassette recorder, and cassette...	...the learner will attach the patch cord and manipulate the controls on both machines to record directly from the radio	...without assistance.
	When given 10 dictated sentences and a full-page writing guide...	...the learner will scriptwrite all the sentences...	...with 90% of the words legible.
Activities of Daily Living	When presented with a razor and shaving cream...	...the learner will shave his face...	...leaving no visible whiskers.
	When presented with 10 prelabeled garments from her closet...	...the learner will identify...	...9 correctly.
	When presented with five items of canned food and a pocket magnifier...	...the learner will verbally identify the items...	...correctly four out of five times.
	When shown a vacuum cleaner and its replacement belt...	...the learner will remove the worn belt and replace it with the new one...	...correctly two out of three times.
	When given a pot of coffee and a mug...	...the learner will pour the liquid into the mug...	...to the proper level without spilling.

accuracy. If the learner has a vocational goal related to a skill such as typing, the criterion would also need to be relatively high accuracy. By contrast, the criterion need not be stringent for an activity such as setting a home thermostat, since an error becomes quickly apparent and poses no real safety hazard. The specified level of performance should not be so low, however, that the client would fail frequently when attempting the task following rehabilitation, since the resulting frustration would likely discourage the use of that skill. In most cases, such criteria as 80 or 90 percent accuracy, two or three consecutive successes, or the teacher's subjective judgment of "consistently" are probably sufficient.

IWRP AND IPP

Behavioral objectives are used at every level of the planning process. As already indicated, the first written plan to be completed for the client specifies his or her overall vocational goal and the plans to achieve it. In the United States, this plan is known as the IWRP, and is mandated by the 1992 amendments to the Rehabilitation Act (Rubin & Roessler, 1995). The IPP, its equivalent, is utilized throughout Canada. This first step in the planning process is generally the responsibility of a rehabilitation counselor, but its completion is a rehabilitation teaching function in some state vocational rehabilitation systems. In either case, the rehabilitation teacher needs a thorough understanding of the process.

At the first meeting with the client, he or she is informed of possible services to be delivered, of eligibility requirements, and of his or her rights and responsibilities. The client's program of services (personal adjustment training, vocational training, and so forth) is then jointly constructed by the counselor and the client as they complete the IWRP. The IWRP must be reviewed annually and may be amended if the client's needs change.

An IWRP must contain the following information:

- a vocational objective
- the date services begin and the date by which the vocational objective is to be achieved
- the specific services to be offered
- objective criteria, evaluation procedures, and schedules for determining progress
- a description of the Client Assistance Program (Roessler & Rubin, 1992).

Other information commonly found includes the degree of the client's responsibility in the program and the client's view of the objectives and services. Figure 4.1, which appears at the end of this chapter, shows an example of an IWRP. This form was completed for a client named Arthur R., a 46-year-old computer programmer who was totally blinded in an accident in the home. Among the general descriptive information such as the client's name and address and the assigned case number, the case status refers to the client's progress through the rehabilitation process—for example, if he or she is a new client, has been evaluated, is receiving personal adjustment training, and so forth.

The vocational objective section of the IWRP is of primary importance, because it is a statement of the overall desired outcome of the agency's services—that is, the type of job the client will try to obtain. It is best written as a behavioral objective, complete with a condition, a behavior, and a criterion, as it is for Mr. R.'s objective of returning to his job as a computer programmer, but many IWRPs contain only a job title. In either case, the vocational objective must contain a formal job title that is listed in the *Dictionary of Occupational Titles* (U.S. Dept. of Labor, 1991), with the appropriate code number if available. This section of the IWRP must also contain a brief explanation of why the objective is considered realistic. Supporting information should include the client's strengths and weaknesses in the physical, intellectual, and psychosocial areas; his or her vocational interest and history; and the feasibility of obtaining employment in the local job market (Roessler & Rubin, 1992).

The description of planned services is an important part of the IWRP, because each service provides the client with some skill or commodity that will enable him or her to reach the vocational goal. Specifying an overall beginning and a completion date for the planned services forces the plan writer to estimate carefully the amount of time it would take to prepare the client to perform the job listed in the vocational objective. The rest of this section of the IWRP lists the services to be offered, in chronological order. The following information must be provided regarding each service:

- a behavioral objective
- a brief description of each service
- the dates on which services are to be initiated and completed
- the cost of each component of the service and the total cost
- a description of how progress will be evaluated.

Any number of types of services can be offered, but they must be chosen from the following 13 categories:

1. counseling and guidance
2. physical and mental restoration, including corrective surgery and ocular prosthetic devices
3. vocational and other training services, including remedial education
4. monetary maintenance and transportation during other rehabilitation services
5. services to the family deemed necessary to the adjustment of the individual
6. interpretive services for those who are deaf
7. reading and personal adjustment services
8. provision of telecommunications and other technological aids
9. placement in suitable employment
10. postemployment services if the client's job is in jeopardy
11. assistance in obtaining occupational licenses, tools, equipment, and initial stocks for small businesses
12. job coaching services
13. assistance in obtaining other goods and services that might aid the client in obtaining employment (Mund, 1978).

As can be seen from the preceding list, these categories of services are inclusive and varied enough to encompass a wide range of assistance. Some services are aimed at improving the appearance of the client, through such measures as fitting ocular prosthetics, purchasing job-related clothing, and procuring dentures. Some, such as providing hearing aids or eye surgery, are intended to increase the individual's ability to function. Others, such as counseling, family counseling, and personal adjustment training, address the person's psychological and physical adjustment to vision loss. Still others, such as job training, higher education, and monetary maintenance and transportation for clients enrolled in training programs, are focused on providing employment skills. And an additional group of services, which include job placement, obtaining vocational licenses, and purchasing tools and initial stock for small business ventures, are aimed specifically at finding employment.

In the example presented in Figure 4.1, Mr. R. will receive four planned services from a total of six categories: personal adjustment training and counseling from categories 1 and 7; adaptive computer training from category 3, with transportation from category 4; physical restoration in the form of prosthetic eyes from category 2; and provision of adaptive computer equipment from category 8.

The section of the IWRP entitled Client's Responsibility is usually a listing of what is expected of the client. Mr. R.'s IWRP requires him to receive the planned services, furnish his own living expenses during computer training, obtain Medicare reimbursement for the prosthetic devices, and make an attempt to regain his former job. This section may also include space for the client's views regarding the objectives and services, to give the client the opportunity to agree or disagree with the content of the program. In the case of Arthur R., the client objected to the specific brand of adaptive computer equipment being purchased. The inclusion of these elements in the IWRP encourages the involvement of the client in the planning process.

The final section requires the client's signature, indicating his or her understanding of and agreement with the plan, and outlines the client's right to request further review and representation under the Client Assistance Program (CAP). This program is intended to furnish clients with a personal advocate for services. Vocational rehabilitation agencies are required by federal legislation to inform clients about CAP provisions. As indicated in Arthur R.'s IWRP, he was informed about CAP services so that if he is dissatisfied with the services he is being provided, he can contact the CAP worker, who then investigates the complaint and serves as an advocate on his behalf.

Figure 4.2, which appears at the end of this chapter, is an example of the Canadian form, the IPP, completed for a client named Marjorie M., whose objective is to brush up on O&M, typing, and braille skills in order to enter a business college and eventually work as an executive secretary. The form is similar to the IWRP in outlining specific goals, specific services to implement them, and specific dates for services.

THE SERVICE PLAN

If the IWRP or IPP specifies personal adjustment training as one of the planned services, the next plan that will be written is the service plan. Rehabilitation teachers use the information gathered during their three-part assessment process to design a plan for each individual client. Writing new individual behavioral objectives for every client in an agency would require far more planning time than is often practical or feasible. Therefore, agencies usually have lists of objectives or behaviors that serve as goals for service plan forms. The service plan is an outline of all the skills to be taught by the rehabilitation teacher. When completed, the service plan form lists expected outcomes for the client. Although a service plan is not required by law as the IWRP is in the United States, in many ways the service plan serves as the overall blueprint for the rehabilitation teacher to follow throughout the client's personal adjustment training program.

As can be seen in the example presented in Figure 4.3 at the end of this chapter, the service plan is divided into the two overall categories of communication and activities of daily living. Within each is a listing of the major teaching areas, such as braille, computers, handwriting, home management, kitchen skills, and the like. Each area is subdivided into long-term objectives, which are related to the long-term goals to be reached within that major area, and into specific short-term objectives as well. (See the chapters in Parts 3 and 4 for more information on the specific instructional areas and the contents of the long-term and short-term objectives listed for each.) For illustrative purposes, the sample service plan form in Figure 4.3 presents an exhaustive list of long- and short-term goals, but it could easily be shortened for use in a practical teaching setting. To organize the information needed to achieve a long-term goal, it may be useful to think in terms of instructional units, as shown in the sample service plan.

For example, within the area of teaching braille and other tactile communication systems, there are four long-term goals, or units, including reading grade 1 braille, reading grade 2 braille, writing braille, and reading the Fishburne Alphabet. The short-term goals are the instructional steps that would be required to reach the long-term goal. Each of these steps usually represents one lesson that is an average of one hour long. All or only some of the short-term objectives within each of these units might be appropriate for an individual, depending on that person's goals and current skills. Thus, if a client wants to learn grade 1 braille to be able to label personal items, all the short-term objectives under "reading grade 1 braille" and the objectives under "braille writing" relating to slate writing and labeling would be required to meet the goal.

The sample service plan form in Figure 4.3 was completed for a client named Lillian P. In reviewing the following case study description of her situation, it will be helpful for readers to compare the needs she has expressed and those reflected in the rehabilitation teacher's assessment with the lesson objectives selected for Mrs. P. in her service plan.

> Mrs. Lillian P. is a 70-year-old woman who lives alone in a six-room house in a small rural town. Three years ago, glaucoma limited her peripheral vision to 12 degrees in both eyes. Her visual acuity is 20/80 in the left eye and 20/200 in the right. Her visual condition is considered stable as a result of recent corrective surgery.
>
> Mrs. P. has a slight hearing loss in her left ear, but is otherwise healthy. Her IWRP specifies 30 hours of home instructional services. She has received low vision services, at which time she was given a short training session on the use of handheld and headborne near-vision devices, which were dispensed. (See Chapter 6 for a discussion of low vision services and devices.)
>
> Mrs. P. was a homemaker until her husband's death 10 years ago. Since then she has worked as a housekeeper for an elderly gentleman, but her loss of vision forced her to quit. She wishes to continue in her present living situation with support from a local Meals on Wheels program and occasional visits from her 45-year-old daughter, who will help her with bookkeeping matters. She expresses interest in continuing her knitting and sewing hobbies and in returning to a local bridge club. She was an avid reader, but feels her magnifiers cause her eyes to tire too quickly.
>
> Her major form of correspondence with friends was through handwritten letters. Mrs. P. also expressed concern about home cleaning, meal preparation, hair care, and makeup needs. She had no experience with tape recorders or typewriters, but uses the telephone with ease.
>
> A two-week assessment demonstrated that Mrs. P. possesses more than adequate intelligence and dexterity to accomplish most rehabilitation tasks. She poured liquids accurately, but showed apprehension in regard to knives and expressed fear of the stove. She was able to identify food articles in her cupboards visually, could describe articles of clothing given to her randomly, and could read with magnifiers at a rate of 70 to 80 words per minute. Her home is relatively dark, particularly in the kitchen and bathroom, where she has difficulty functioning. She expressed a desire to learn, but feels dependent on her daughter and has surrendered much control to her.

As can be seen in the sample completed service plan, many possible objectives were passed over in the list, which reflects the need to set priorities in order to keep her plan under the 30 hours of instruction specified in her IWRP. Nothing was selected from the Braille and Other Tactile Systems area (see Chapter 7) because Mrs. P. uses low vision devices to meet her spot-reading needs, such as setting the thermostat (see Chapter 6), and she can readily identify her clothing and the food in her cupboard with her functional vision. Also, the Computer Technology area was passed over (see Chapter 9) because no need for it was indicated in her assessment data.

The objectives in the Low Vision section relating to modifying the environment for better visibility were selected because they will give her the knowledge to improve the poor visual conditions noted in the kitchen and bathroom. The two objectives under the unit relating to reading will increase her reading efficiency and may eliminate some of her reading discomfort. Handwriting with bold-line guides was selected because writing letters is a concern for her, and her vision is good enough to see the dark, wide lines on the guide and to read her own enlarged script (see Chapter 8).

The objectives selected under Listening and Recording that relate to the National Library Service for the Blind and Physically Handicapped Talking Book Program were indicated by the fact that although Mrs. P. could read 70 to 80 words per minute with visual aids, she tired easily and could not read for long periods. The Talking Book Program, a service that provides recorded novels on cassettes, will give her a comfortable means by which to continue reading (see Chapter 10). The objectives under the tape recording unit will give her a way to store information such as recipes or instructions for craft projects, and knowing how to clean a tape recorder will increase the efficiency of the recorder and the machines provided by the Talking Book Program. Under the area of Mathematics, she will be taught to use a large display calculator to help her regain some control over her finances.

In the broad area of Daily Living Skills, in the section on Orientation and Movement in the Home Environment, only protective techniques that might prevent minor injuries resulting from collision were selected because Mrs. P. has significant travel vision. Under Kitchen Skills, her fear of stoves and knives are addressed, as are adaptations to kitchen timing, microwave cooking, and cookbooks. The objectives selected under Home Management will give her a way to monitor cleanliness and keep her orientation when sweeping or mopping a large area, and all the Household Safety training objectives were selected because Mrs. P. intends to live alone. The skills to be taught under Personal Management were makeup and hair care, which will help her maintain a good appearance. Under Leisure-Time Activities, needlecrafts and card playing were chosen because Mrs. P. expressed interest in these activities.

Because in general the rehabilitation teacher's time and rehabilitation funds are limited, when formulating service plans it is necessary to choose only those objectives that are absolutely required to enable clients to reach their goals, as was done with Mrs. P. Since each objective takes time to achieve, efficient planning is essential to guarantee efficient use of time.

The process for determining the total number of hours of service to be provided for personal adjustment training varies greatly from agency to agency, but generally all require some preplanning. In most cases, the counselor who writes the IWRP is responsible for this task, but he or she may request assistance from the rehabilitation teacher. In such cases, the service plan becomes the major tool for determining time allotment. Transforming objectives in the service plan into hours of services to be provided requires careful consideration. A good rule of thumb is that each lesson objective listed on the service plan requires one hour of teaching. If 20 objectives are checked off, therefore, the client's program would be expected to take approximately 20 hours. As a rehabilitation teacher becomes familiar with the process of estimating hours, however, it becomes clear that the time involved in reaching certain objectives varies. Some lesson objectives require only 15 or 20 minutes, whereas others can be attained only after two or more hours of teaching. When several objectives are included in a service plan, however, they tend to average out to a requirement of approximately one hour each.

If the rehabilitation teacher does not play a role in setting the number of service hours to be provided, there may be times when the goals of the service plan must be carried out under limits determined by the rehabilitation counselor who wrote the IWRP. If, for example, the counselor allows only 20 hours for personal adjustment training, but the rehabilitation teacher's service plan demonstrates a need for 40 hours of instruction, the teacher's task becomes difficult. In this situation, the teacher can contact the counselor, and then perhaps the supervisor, to request an increase in teaching hours based on the results of the rehabilitation teaching assessment. If negotiations produce no change in the time allotted, the rehabilitation teacher may have to set priorities among the objectives and select the 20 most important ones for the client. Factors to consider in setting such priorities include:

- the client's survival needs, such as the availability of food in a home setting
- the need to alleviate dangerous situations, such as poor visibility of an open staircase in the home
- the skills needed to achieve the client's vocational goal, such as keyboard training for someone aimed at secretarial work

- the skills needed to fulfill the client's personal priorities, such as home cleaning skills for someone to whom cleanliness and order are important
- the client's abilities, such as intellectual capacity or physical dexterity, as demonstrated in the assessment.

In the case of Mrs. P., since the number of service hours was limited to 30, priority was given to reading, personal and household appearance, and safety. The first two were assigned more importance because of her expressed interest in them, and safety was addressed because Mrs. P. lives alone and must know how to take such emergency measures as using the fire extinguisher and shutting off the water supply. Although activities such as crafts would surely be of benefit to Mrs. P., they were given low priority because she did not express great interest in them and because they would not have as significant an effect as the safety concerns.

THE LESSON PLAN

Once the necessary objectives have been selected, planning proceeds to the most specific level: the development of individual lesson plans. The lesson plan, the culmination of the planning process, is a written description of the instructional procedure to be followed in individual lessons. Lesson plans are especially helpful when the instructor is inexperienced, when the instructional unit is complex, or when the rehabilitation teacher's daily planning time is limited. Because there is seldom adequate time for planning, the lesson plans used by rehabilitation teachers are not generally written anew for each individual or for every class. Rather, one plan is written to cover an entire instructional unit, such as slate writing, using adaptive timepieces, or using an adapted tape recorder. These unit lesson plans can be consulted and modified to meet the individual student's needs. Sample lesson plans are found in the instructional chapters in Parts 3 and 4 of this book.

A workable outline for rehabilitation teaching lesson plans is as follows:

I. Objective—the specific behavioral objective to be reached during the lesson
II. Materials—items required to carry out the instruction
III. Assessment—a list of questions or activities designed to measure the adequacy of skills that are prerequisite for the particular lesson
IV. Procedure—specific descriptions of the sequential steps to be followed in teaching the lesson
V. Memoranda—notes relating to common difficulties or reminders to the teacher
VI. Evaluation—the behaviors to be observed and measured at the end of the lesson
VII. Assignments—a list of suggested practice activities to reinforce learning.

Procedure

All parts of the lesson plan are important, but the heart is the procedure section. It can be difficult to write, because it requires the rehabilitation teacher to predict how the lesson will flow. Following these suggestions may simplify the process of preparing the procedure section:

1. Prepare an outline of the major steps in the lesson.
2. Perform the activity yourself and jot down the required steps.
3. Write the plan to a degree of specificity sufficient for a substitute teacher to follow it.
4. Consider the outline to be a generic plan for the average learner.

Although it is tempting to write plans to the degree of specificity dictated by the teacher's own knowledge level, he or she should include enough detail in the event that a substitute teacher must present the lesson to the client. Figure 4.4 presents a sample lesson plan for teaching slate writing. Note the degree of specificity included (for example, paper insertion and hand position), which provides reminders of important steps the teacher should present. (Chapter 7 presents detailed information about writing with a slate and stylus). The outline of the procedure section includes:

A. Uses and general information

B. Orientation to parts

C. Paper insertion

D. Embossing

The first two subheadings work well for most lessons that involve teaching someone to use a device. Reviewing the uses of a device may often seem unnecessary, but it informs the client about why he or she might want to possess the skill involved. Orientation to the parts of the device is generally a prerequisite for using it. The last two subheadings in this example are the steps in the operation of the slate and stylus. The activities required for operating a device are most easily ascertained by actually performing the skill. In this case, one can sit down with the slate, stylus, and paper and note the specific behaviors required to use it.

Task-Analyzed Lesson Plans

The task-analyzed lesson plan is an important variation on the lesson plan that is used when learners have developmental disabilities, closed head injuries, or other conditions that hamper learning. Task analysis is a process in which activities are subdivided into their simplest parts. Thus, the primary difference between task-analyzed plans and the standard lesson plan is the degree of detail written into the procedures section and perhaps in the scope of what might be covered in a one-hour lesson. By analyzing the procedures in this level of detail, the teacher ensures that all the necessary steps are included in the lesson, thus promoting maximum learning and avoiding discouraging outcomes. The following situation illustrates the benefits of developing a task-analyzed lesson plan.

> Jonathan C. was a young man of 22 years with a cognitive disability. He attended a day activity program where some 20 individuals received daily living skills training and were taught skills that could qualify them to work in the agency's workshop. As the only blind client in the agency, Mr. C. posed some special challenges for the agency's daily living skills instructor, who contacted the local rehabilitation center for help. The instructor explained that although all the clients were required to brush their teeth each morning, Mr. C. could not, which meant that the instructor had to take the time to do it for him.
>
> The rehabilitation teacher who was assigned to Mr. C. had no experience with task analysis and proceeded to use her standard toothbrushing lesson plan. It soon became apparent, however, that the standard instruction, "Have the learner brush the front surface of her or his teeth," was not sufficient for Mr. C., because there are in reality four front surfaces to brush (top left, top right, bottom left, and bottom right), and all these surfaces require a different wrist action. Although most clients might be able to adjust to the different movements required without detailed instruction, the subdivided steps had to be addressed individually over several sessions before Mr. C. could successfully accomplish the complete toothbrushing task.
>
> When Mr. C. was initially asked to brush front surfaces of his teeth, the rehabilitation teacher had no adequate way of measuring daily progress because Mr. C. could not accomplish the task in its entirety. However, when the task was broken down into four steps, the teacher was able to document that progress had been made when the top left teeth were brushed successfully. This was reinforcing to both the teacher and the client, and encouraged them to continue until the entire task was learned successfully.

The approach to writing task-analyzed lesson plans is similar to that for the standard lesson plan, in that the teacher works through the activity and jots down the steps, but in this case, every step must be recorded. For example, in the standard lesson plan for slate writing shown in Figure 4.4, step 4 under subhead E, Embossing with the stylus, reads: "Have the learner emboss full cells until all six dots are formed consistently." A task-analyzed procedure for the same activity might require as many as 13 steps simply to cover embossing the first three positions of the first cell. Assuming that all the material up to that point in the lesson had been covered, the task-analyzed procedure would include the following steps:

1. Have the learner locate the slate which has the paper inserted.
2. Place the slate in front of the learner with the hinge at left and paper sticking out of the slate toward him or her.
3. Have the learner locate the stylus.
4. Have the learner pick up the stylus with the dominant hand.
5. Have the learner grasp the wooden knob properly.
6. Have the learner locate the top right cell with index finger of the nondominant hand.
7. Have the learner place the tip of the stylus in that cell.
8. Have the learner push the tip of the stylus into the upper right corner with index finger of the nondominant hand.
9. Have the learner hold the stylus straight up and down and push it into the paper until it makes a "popping" sound.
10. Have the learner move the tip of the stylus down along the right side of the cell until it "catches."
11. Have the learner straighten the stylus and apply pressure until the paper "pops."
12. Have the learner slide the tip of the stylus down along the right side until it stops.
13. Have the learner straighten the stylus and apply pressure until it "pops."

Although working through a task analysis for an activity can be somewhat tedious, it is an excellent tool for a teacher who has little experience in teaching clients with learning limitations, because it offers a simple step-by-step guide. In addition, it provides a practical means by which to measure progress of clients who do not progress as quickly as most. Whereas the rehabilitation teacher using the standard lesson plan in Figure 4.4 could not record progress on part d until the equivalent of completing all 13 steps was accomplished, the teacher using a task-analyzed plan would know that learning had occurred even if two or three beginning steps were mastered.

SUMMARY

The plans designed by rehabilitation teachers help them tailor the services and instruction they provide to the client's needs, teach effectively, make the best use of teaching time, and measure the outcomes of instruction. Once these plans are written and agreed to, the rehabilitation teacher can proceed to instruction in the specific skills that have been selected. In doing so, it will be helpful for the teacher to know some basic principles of teaching and learning and particularly the factors that affect how people with visual impairments learn. These areas are covered in the next chapter.

State Commission for the Blind
Individualized Written Rehabilitation Program

CLIENT DESCRIPTION

1. **Name and Address**

   Arthur R.

   213 Prairie Ave.

   Piqua, MI 19008

2. **Case Number** 210.89

3. **Case Status** 08

4. **Date** 1/15/97

5. **Type** ☒ Original ☐ Amendment ☐ Annual ☐ Closure

SECTION I—VOCATIONAL OBJECTIVE

At the completion of agency services, the client will be employed as a computer programmer at a salary commensurate with that occupation.

DOT Number 0101010101

Plan Justification

Mr. R. had performed as a computer programmer for 12 years prior to his complete loss of sight. His employment record was flawless; he has the physical and mental capacity to perform this job, and he wants to return to his former employment. The employer indicates this to be feasible as well.

Deficits

Mr. R. demonstrates little adjustment to his new blindness; he also has few adaptive living and communication skills; he has no knowledge of adaptive computer technology; and he has unsightly eyes as a result of his accidental blindness.

SECTION II—PLANNED SERVICES

Service Personal adjustment/counseling: Client will undergo personal adjustment training and counseling at the state rehabilitation center.

(continued on next page)

Figure 4.1. Sample Completed Individualized Written Rehabilitation Program (IWRP)

Objective

Upon completion of the personal adjustment training program at the state rehabilitation center, the client will perform the adaptive skills required for daily living and noncomputer job skills and will exhibit behaviors and skills necessary for adjusting to and coping with blindness sufficient to allow him to enter a vocational training program.

Description

The state center provides comprehensive adjustment counseling, and it provides training in communications, daily living, mobility, etc.

Service dates **Begin** 2/15/97 **End** 6/15/97

Cost $600 per week, transportation $75

Total cost $7,275

Funding source VR

Progress evaluation Monthly staff meetings and reports at center.

Service Vocational training: Client will receive adaptive computer training.

Objective

At the completion of an adaptive computer training program, the client will perform the skills at a level required to return to his former employment.

Description

The 3-semester-hour course offered by the local community college trains individuals to use voice output computers.

Service dates **Begin** 9/1/97 **End** 12/15/97

Cost Tuition $450, transportation $200, books $100

Total cost $750

Funding source VR

Progress evaluation Monthly grade review with client

(continued on next page)

Figure 4.1. Sample Completed IWRP *(continued)*

Service Physical restoration: Client will be fitted with two prosthetic eyes.

Objective

After receiving two prosthetic shells, the client will regain physical appearance acceptable for employment.

Description

Dr. Norr produces prosthetic shells that fit over existing globes. The service will require four visits and another follow-up visit two months after fitting.

Service dates **Begin** 6/15/97 **End** 12/15/97

Cost $1,000 per eye, inclusive

Total cost $2,000

Funding source Medicare

Progress evaluation Monthly contact with optician

Service Electronic aids: Purchase adaptive speech output equipment.

Objective

Following the purchase of a speech synthesizer, the client will operate his computer at a level sufficient to allow him to return to work.

Description

A Brand X speech synthesizer will be purchased, and the vendor will install it upon delivery.

Service dates **Begin** 9/1/97 **End** 9/1/97

Cost $1,528.51

Total cost $1,528.51

Funding source Employer

Progress evaluation Postpurchase on-site evaluation

(continued on next page)

Figure 4.1. Sample Completed IWRP *(continued)*

SECTION III—CLIENT'S RESPONSIBILITY

Client will

A. Complete the personal adjustment training program successfully.

B. Complete the adaptive computer training program with a grade of C or above.

C. Submit Medicare/Medicaid forms for payment for prosthetics.

D. Provide maintenance costs during computer training.

E. Make a significant effort to return to work.

Client's view of objectives and services

The client agrees with the plan, but prefers a Brand Z speech synthesizer. However, the state purchasing contract requires Brand X. He has agreed reluctantly to accept Brand X.

SECTION IV—CLIENT'S UNDERSTANDING AND AGREEMENT

I have discussed this plan with my counselor, have a copy of it, and I understand and accept the provisions outlined.

I understand that the planned employment outcome and the financial support provided for it by the rehabilitation agency are dependent upon my meeting the responsibilities outlined in the previous section. I further understand that failure to meet these responsibilities may result in termination of my program.

I understand that I may discuss problems or disagreements with the IWRP with my counselor. If I am dissatisfied, I may request an informal review with my counselor's supervisor for administrative review. I understand that if, after review, I continue to be dissatisfied, I will be assisted with application for a Fair Hearing with the Agency.

I understand that the Client Assistance Program is available to assist and/or represent me in the administrative review and fair hearing. I have been informed that the CAP worker is ____________________ and he can be reached at ____________________.

I understand that all services of this agency are provided on a nondiscriminatory basis without regard to race, color, creed, gender, age, national origin, or disability.

I further understand that services provided under this IWRP are subject to change on the basis of circumstances such as available funds or educational programs, and is not a binding contract.

____________________________________ ______________

Client's Signature **Date**

____________________________________ ______________

Counselor's Signature **Date**

Figure 4.1. Sample Completed IWRP *(continued)*

Individual Program Plan

Client Name: Marjorie M.

Client Short-Term Goal: Review and update O&M and personal communication skills in order to prepare for entry into the George Brown College Office Automation Program

Client Long-Term Goal: Obtain employment in a business office as an executive secretary.

Client's Goals	*Implementation Process*	*Target Date*
1. Client will review grade 2 braille skills and aim for a reading of 65 WPM.	Grade II braille instruction by the rehabilitation teacher to commence 5/9/95.	12/20/95 estimated completion date
2. Client will review personal typing skills and achieve an average of 20 WPM.	Personal typing review by the rehabilitation teacher to commence 10/12/95	1/7/96 estimated completion date
3. Client will update orientation and mobility skills and receive familiarization to new neighborhood.	Orientation and mobility update to commence on 9/9/95.	2/1/96 estimated completion date
4. Client will complete assessment for entry into the George Brown College Office Automation Program (OAP).	OAP staff to provide assessment 3/4/96–4/15/96.	4/15/96 estimated completion date
5. Client will successfully complete the fall 1996 OAP program.	September 1996 program to commence 9/10/96.	January 1997 estimated completion date

Additional Information

____

____

____

____

I have reviewed the above information and agree with the program plan outlined.

Client's Signature	**Case Manager's Signature**	**Date**

Figure 4.2. Sample Completed Individual Program Plan (IPP)

Service Plan

Instructions
Place a check mark on the line in front of each of the objectives that are required to meet the client's program goals. If additional objectives are needed, please write them in the space provided at the end of this form.

Name Lillian P.

Date 7/18/96

Instructor Perelli

COMMUNICATION SKILLS

I. Low Vision

A. At the completion of the unit describing environmental visibility, the learner will modify his or her environment to a level that maximizes his or her visual performance.
- ✓ 1. When asked, the learner will describe the effects of size, contrast, and illumination on environmental visibility to a level that demonstrates an adequate knowledge.
- ✓ 2. When given a location in his or her living quarters, the learner will modify it to achieve maximum visibility.

B. At the completion of the vision training unit, the learner will perform reading and other functions to a level sufficient to meet his or her daily needs.
- ___ 1. When asked, the learner will describe his or her best eye placement for eccentric viewing to a level that demonstrates adequate knowledge.
- ✓ 2. When presented with a hand-held magnifier, the learner will read labels, dial settings, etc., with 90% accuracy.
- ___ 3. When presented with a stand magnifier, the learner will read and describe the material with 90% accuracy.
- ___ 4. When presented with a headborne microscope, the learner will read and describe material with 90% accuracy.
- ✓ 5. When presented with a telemicroscope, the learner will read and describe material with 90% accuracy.
- ___ 6. When presented with a closed-circuit television system, the learner will read and describe material with 90% accuracy.
- ___ 7. When presented with a telescope, the learner will use it to view television and for other indoor purposes at a level sufficient to meet daily needs.

II. Braille and Other Tactile Systems

A. Upon completion of the grade 1 braille training unit, the learner will read grade 1 braille at a level sufficient to meet his or her information-storage, reading, and labeling needs.
- ___ 1. When presented with a braille training manual, the learner will read letters A through E with 90% accuracy.
- ___ 2. When presented with a braille training manual, the learner will read letters F through J with 90% accuracy.

(continued on next page)

Figure 4.3. Sample Completed Service Plan Form

___ 3. When presented with a braille training manual, the learner will read numbers with 90% accuracy.
___ 4. When presented with a braille training manual, the learner will read letters K through O with 90% accuracy.
___ 5. When presented with a braille training manual, the learner will read letters P through T with 90% accuracy.
___ 6. When presented with a braille training manual, the learner will read letters U through Z with 90% accuracy.
___ 7. When presented with a braille training manual, the learner will read necessary braille punctuation signs with 90% accuracy.
___ 8. When presented with a braille training manual, the learner will read necessary composition signs with 90% accuracy.
___ 9. When presented with a braille training manual, the learner will read two pages of uncontracted braille with 90% accuracy.

B. Upon completion of the grade 2 braille training unit, the learner will read grade 2 braille at a level sufficient to meet his or her information-storage and reading needs.
___ 1. When presented with a braille training manual, the learner will read alphabet word signs with 95% accuracy.
___ 2. When presented with a braille training manual, the learner will read short form word signs with 95% accuracy.
___ 3. When presented with a braille training manual, the learner will read the signs for *and, with, for, of,* and *the* with 95% accuracy.
___ 4. When presented with a braille training manual, the learner will read part word signs with 95% accuracy.
___ 5. When presented with a braille training manual, the learner will read lower signs with 95% accuracy.
___ 6. When presented with a braille training manual, the learner will read initial letter signs with 95% accuracy.
___ 7. When presented with a braille training manual, the learner will read final letter signs with 95% accuracy.
___ 8. When presented with a braille training manual, the learner will read cookbook units of measure with 95% accuracy.

C. Upon completion of the braille writing training unit, the learner will emboss braille at a level sufficient to meet his or her information-storage and labeling needs.
___ 1. When presented with a standard slate, paper, and a stylus, the learner will emboss two pages with 95% accuracy.
___ 2. When presented with a braillewriter and paper, the learner will emboss two pages with 95% accuracy.
___ 3. When presented with vinyl labeling tape and other materials, the learner will emboss braille labels with 95% accuracy.
___ 4. When presented with braille writing materials, the learner will write the descriptions and addresses of four sources of braille materials with 95% accuracy.

D. At the completion of the Fishburne Alphabet training unit, the learner will read and write it at a level sufficient to meet his or her needs.
___ 1. When presented with letters A through E, the learner will read them with 90% accuracy.

(continued on next page)

Figure 4.3. Sample Service Plan Form *(continued)*

___ 2. When presented with letters F through M, the learner will read them with 90% accuracy.
___ 3. When presented with letters N through Z, the learner will read them with 90% accuracy.
___ 4. When presented with labels, the learner will read them with 95% accuracy.
___ 5. When presented with the embossing device, the learner will produce the letters of the alphabet with 95% accuracy.

III. Handwriting

A. Upon completion of the handwriting training unit for those who have congenital visual impairments, the learner will write words that are legible to a degree sufficient to meet his or her daily needs.
___ 1. When presented with the letters in his or her name, the learner will identify them with 90% accuracy.
___ 2. When presented with the letters of his or her last name and shown how they are connected, the learner will write them until 90% are legible.
___ 3. When presented with the letters of his or her first name and shown how they are connected, the learner will write them until 90% are legible.
___ 4. When presented with a standard signature guide and pencil, the learner will write his or her signature legibly in 90% of attempts.
___ 5. When presented with the remaining letters in the alphabet and given a full-page writing guide, the learner will write them until 90% of the attempts are legible.
___ 6. When presented with a full-page writing guide, the learner will write a one-page letter with 90% of the words legible.

B. Upon completion of the script-writing training unit for those with adventitious impairments, the learner will use handwriting devices at a level sufficient to meet his or her daily needs.
___ 1. When presented with the more rigid and structured writing guides, the learner will write 90% of his or her words legibly.
___ 2. When presented with the flexible baseline and other less structured guides, the learner will write 90% of his or her words legibly.
_✓_ 3. When presented with bold-line writing guides, the learner will write 90% of his or her words legibly.
_✓_ 4. When presented with the writing guide of choice, the learner will write a two-page document with 90% of the words legible.
___ 5. When asked, the learner will write the names, addresses, and descriptions of two major sources of handwriting aids legibly.

C. Upon completion of the raised-line drawing board training unit, the learner will use a raised-line drawing board to read and produce graphic representations to a level sufficient to meet his or her graphic needs.
___ 1. When presented with tactile drawings, the learner will describe them at a level demonstrating that the graphics are recognized.
___ 2. When presented with a raised-line drawing board, the learner will produce drawings that can be recognized visually in four out of five attempts.

IV. Typewriting/Keyboarding

A. Upon completion of the informal typing training unit, the learner will type documents at a level sufficient for such correspondence.

(continued on next page)

Figure 4.3. Sample Service Plan Form *(continued)*

___ 1. When presented with a typewriter, the learner will identify the parts necessary for paper insertion and keyboard input with 90% accuracy.
___ 2. When presented with a typewriter and paper, the learner will insert the paper and use the letters of the home row with 90% accuracy.
___ 3. When presented with a typewriter and paper, the learner will insert the paper and use the remaining keys utilizing the first fingers with 90% accuracy.
___ 4. When presented with a typewriter and paper, the learner will insert the paper and use the remaining keys utilizing the second fingers with 90% accuracy.
___ 5. When presented with a typewriter and paper, the learner will insert the paper and use the remaining keys utilizing the third fingers with 90% accuracy.
___ 6. When presented with a typewriter and paper, the learner will insert the paper and use the remaining keys utilizing the fourth fingers with 90% accuracy.
___ 7. When presented with a typewriter and paper, the learner will insert the paper and perform the following adaptive skills at a level sufficient for informal correspondence: (a) set margins, (b) set tabs, (c) correct known keystroking errors, (d) maintain a bottom margin, and (e) mark the closing for subsequent signature.
___ 8. When presented with a typewriter, paper, and envelope, the learner will type an informal letter with 90% accuracy.

B. Upon completion of the business typewriting training unit, the learner will type formal documents at a level sufficient for business correspondence.
___ 1. When presented with a typewriter and paper, the learner will type a three-page document with less than three mistakes per page.
___ 2. When presented with a typewriter, paper, and a business envelope, the learner will type a three-page business letter in the proper formats with less than three mistakes per page.

V. Computer Technology

A. Upon completion of the computer literacy training unit, the learner will describe the uses and major parts of computers at a level sufficient to allow him or her to draw conclusions regarding their usefulness to him or her personally.
___ 1. When asked, the learner will, from memory, describe the major uses of computers to a level indicating an overall understanding.
___ 2. When asked, the learner will, from memory, describe the major parts of a computer to a level indicating an overall understanding of their interrelationship and functions.
___ 3. When asked, the learner will, from memory, define computer terminology to a level indicating an overall understanding.

B. Upon completion of the computer utilization training unit, the learner will perform the necessary functions at a level sufficient to meet his or her word-processing and information-storage needs.
___ 1. When presented with a word-processing program and a voice, large-print, or braille output microcomputer that has been configured by the instructor, the learner will type 60 lines with less than five mistakes.
___ 2. When presented with a word-processing program and a voice, large-print, or braille output microcomputer, the learner will save, retrieve, and print a file and review the directory with 90% accuracy.
___ 3. When presented with a word-processing program and a voice, large-print, or braille output microcomputer, the learner will perform the editing functions (delete, insert, block, search, etc.) with 90% accuracy.

(continued on next page)

Figure 4.3. Sample Service Plan Form *(continued)*

___ 4. When presented with a microcomputer, a word-processing program, and a speech synthesizer, the learner will produce and read a two-page document with 95% accuracy.
___ 5. When presented with a microcomputer, a word-processing program, and a braille output system, the learner will produce and read a two-page document with 95% accuracy.
___ 6. When presented with a microcomputer, a word-processing program, and an electronic screen magnification system, the learner will produce and read a two-page document with 95% accuracy.
___ 7. When presented with a computer and an optical character recognition system (scanner), the learner will read documents and store them as text files that contain fewer than 10 mistakes per page.
___ 8. When presented with an adapted microcomputer and the appropriate software, the learner will perform utility functions (copy, format, etc.) with 90% accuracy.
___ 9. When presented with an adapted microcomputer and database software, the learner will store and retrieve information with 90% accuracy.
___ 10. When presented with a braille input–speech output computer, the learner will store and retrieve files with 90% accuracy.
___ 11. When asked, the learner will describe five major sources of computer access devices.

VI. Listening and Recording Devices

A. Upon completion of the tape recorder training unit, the learner will use a tape recorder at a level sufficient to meet information-storage and retrieval needs.

_✓_ 1. When presented with a standard cassette recorder and a blank tape, the learner will record three separate segments on two sides and retrieve them quickly and efficiently.
___ 2. When presented with an adapted cassette recorder and a blank cassette tape, the learner will consistently record information on different tracks at different speeds and retrieve that information quickly and efficiently.
___ 3. When presented with an adapted cassette recorder and a blank tape, the learner will record and locate voice- and tone-indexed segments with 90% accuracy.
_✓_ 4. When presented with a tape recorder, head-cleaning supplies and a demagnetizer, the learner will consistently clean and demagnetize the heads without harming the machine.
___ 5. When presented with a radio or tape player with an output jack, a cassette recorder, a patch cord, and a blank tape, the learner will consistently record information clearly and completely.
___ 6. When presented with damaged cassette tapes and the proper repair materials, the learner will consistently demonstrate the techniques required to restore them to working order.
___ 7. When presented with live lectures, a tape recorder, and a system for condensing and storing notes, the learner will produce outlines of the information presented by the lecturer that contain 95% of the pertinent information.
___ 8. When asked, the learner will describe the Recording for the Blind program to a level that demonstrates a working knowledge of their services.
___ 9. When read a list of recording resources, the learner will record and index those he or she desires and retrieve them quickly and efficiently.

B. Upon completion of the National Library Service for the Blind and Physically Handicapped (NLS) and radio reading service training unit, the learner will utilize the services and products of the programs to a level sufficient to meet his or her pleasure-reading needs.

(continued on next page)

Figure 4.3. Sample Service Plan Form *(continued)*

✓ 1. When presented with the services of the NLS and radio reading services, the learner will apply for those desired.
___ 2. When presented with a Talking-Book Easy Cassette Machine and a recorded cassette, the learner will consistently play a book without restarting it and demonstrate an understanding of the content.
___ 3. When presented with a Talking-Book Machine disc player and a book on disc, the learner will consistently place the needle in the proper position and demonstrate reading comprehension without scratching the record.
✓ 4. When presented with a Talking-Book Cassette Machine and a recorded cassette, the learner will consistently find specific page locations on different tracks and demonstrate an understanding of the book's content.

VII. Mathematics

A. Upon completion of the adaptive calculator training unit, the learner will use a calculator at a level sufficient to meet his or her daily needs.
✓ 1. When presented with a large-display calculator, the learner will perform the four basic mathematical functions (addition, subtraction, multiplication, and division) with 95% accuracy.
___ 2. When presented with a talking calculator, the learner will perform the basic mathematical functions with 95% accuracy.
___ 3. When presented with a scientific calculator, the learner will perform the necessary functions with 98% accuracy.
___ 4. When presented with a list of calculator resources, the learner will record those he or she desires.

B. At the completion of the abacus training unit, the learner will perform the four basic mathematical functions at a level necessary to meet his or her daily needs.
___ 1. When presented with a Cranmer abacus, the learner will add three-digit numbers with 95% accuracy.
___ 2. When presented with a Cranmer abacus, the learner will subtract three-digit numbers with 95% accuracy.
___ 3. When presented with a Cranmer abacus, the learner will multiply three-digit numbers with 95% accuracy.
___ 4. When presented with a Cranmer abacus, the learner will divide three-digit numbers with 95% accuracy.
___ 5. When presented with a list of abacus resources, the learner will record those he or she desires.

DAILY LIVING SKILLS

VIII. Orientation and Movement in the Home Environment

A. Upon completion of the orientation and movement training unit, the learner will move through his or her home environment efficiently.
___ 1. When traveling with a sighted guide, the learner will move through his or her environment safely and efficiently.

(continued on next page)

Figure 4.3. Sample Service Plan Form *(continued)*

___ 2. When moving through familiar environments, the learner will use searching and trailing techniques to move through his or her environment safely and efficiently.

___ 3. When moving through familiar environments, the learner will use orientation techniques to move through his or her environment safely and efficiently.

___ 4. When moving through familiar environments, the learner will use diagonal cane technique to move through his or her environment safely and efficiently.

B. When presented with the self-protection training unit, the learner will function safely in familiar environments.

✓ 1. When presented with a familiar environment, the learner will use protective techniques to a level that ensures minimal risk.

___ 2. When presented with a familiar environment, the learner will describe its safety hazards and suggest ways that it might be modified to minimize risks.

IX. Kitchen Skills

A. Upon completion of the cold foods training unit, the learner will prepare foods that need not be heated to a level sufficient to meet his or her lunch and snack needs.

___ 1. When asked, the learner will consistently describe the kitchen area and its contents to a level indicating a working knowledge.

___ 2. When presented with common kitchen utensils, the learner will describe their functions to a level indicating a working knowledge.

___ 3. When presented with various pouring tasks, the learner will consistently fill containers with hot and cold liquids to a proper level without spilling.

___ 4. When presented with bread and a butter knife, the learner will consistently spread various semisolid foods evenly and with thorough coverage.

___ 5. When presented with various can openers, the learner will consistently open cans safely and efficiently.

___ 6. When presented with various volumetric measuring devices, the learner will consistently measure solids, semisolids, and liquids at a level to meet recipe needs.

✓ 7. When presented with kitchen knives, the learner will consistently slice, dice, and peel various foods safely and efficiently.

___ 8. When presented with soiled dishes and work area, the learner will consistently clean them safely and efficiently.

B. Upon completion of the simple hot foods training unit, the learner will prepare snacks, lunches, and simple dinner meals at a level sufficient to meet his or her daily needs.

✓ 1. When presented with a hot beverage device, the learner will consistently prepare various instant foods safely and efficiently.

___ 2. When presented with a toaster or toaster oven, the learner will consistently prepare prepackaged foods safely and efficiently.

✓ 3. When presented with an electric or gas stove, the learner will consistently perform the following: (a) describe stove dials, (b) describe dial marking methods, (c) detect heat from the burner, (d) center pots and pans on a burner, (e) set stove dial in the correct position, and (f) detect boiling liquid safely and efficiently.

___ 4. When presented with a frying pan and various foods, the learner will consistently fry them safely and to the proper level of doneness.

(continued on next page)

Figure 4.3. Sample Service Plan Form *(continued)*

✓ 5. When presented with an oven, a timer, and various foods, the learner will consistently bake them safely and to the proper level of doneness.
✓ 6. When presented with a microwave oven and various foods, the learner will cook them safely and to the proper level of doneness.
___ 7. When presented with an adapted form of a simple cookbook or list of instructions from food containers, the learner will use it to prepare foods to meet his or her needs.
___ 8. When presented with foods of his or her choice, the learner will prepare a full-course meal efficiently and to the proper level of doneness.

C. Upon completion of the elaborate hot foods training unit, the learner will prepare appetizers, dinners, and desserts, to a level sufficient to meet his or her daily needs.
✓ 1. When presented with a cookbook of his or her choice, the learner will adequately describe how it could be adapted to meet his or her needs.
___ 2. When presented with an electric mixer and various foods, the learner will consistently mix them safely and thoroughly.
___ 3. When presented with a food processor and various foods, the learner will process foods safely and efficiently.
___ 4. When presented with a slow cooker and various foods, the learner will prepare them to a proper level of doneness.
___ 5. When presented with a broiler and various foods, the learner will prepare them to a proper level of doneness.
___ 6. When presented with a wok and various foods, the leaner will prepare them to a proper level of doneness.
___ 7. When presented with soufflé equipment, the learner will prepare a soufflé to a proper level of doneness.
___ 8. When presented with the equipment and foods of his or her choice, the learner will prepare a full-course meal (appetizer, entrée, and dessert) efficiently and to the proper level of doneness.

X. Personal Management

A. Upon completion of the clothing care training unit, the learner will maintain his or her desired appearance.
___ 1. When asked, a learner who had no former concept of clothing styles and colors will consistently describe them to a level that indicates understanding.
___ 2. When presented with various articles of clothing and the appropriate materials, the learner will label and later consistently identify them with 80% accuracy.
___ 3. When presented with various articles of clothing and the appropriate materials, the learner will consistently prepare them for storage on hangers, in closets, and in suitcases, so that they are unwrinkled and neat in appearance.
___ 4. When presented with various articles of clothing and the appropriate materials, the learner will consistently sort, wash, dry, and iron them so that they are clean and unwrinkled.
___ 5. When presented with various types of shoeware, the learner will consistently clean and polish them so that they are unsoiled and neat in appearance.
___ 6. When taken to a laundromat, the learner will consistently use the facilities to wash and dry his or her clothing quickly and efficiently.

B. Upon completion of the personal care training unit, the learner will perform hygiene, grooming, and routine health skills at a level sufficient to meet his or her needs.

(continued on next page)

Figure 4.3. Sample Service Plan Form *(continued)*

___ 1. When presented with standard bathroom facilities, a learner with multiple handicaps will consistently bathe him- or herself to a level that maintains personal cleanliness.
___ 2. When presented with the materials of choice, the learner will consistently care for his or her teeth at a level sufficient to maintain dental hygiene.
___ 3. When presented with the materials of choice, the learner will consistently care for feminine menstrual needs to a level sufficient to maintain personal hygiene.
___ 4. When presented with the materials of choice, the learner will consistently shave to a desired level of personal appearance.
✓ 5. When presented with the materials of choice, the learner will consistently apply cosmetics to a desired level of personal appearance.
✓ 6. When presented with the materials of choice, the learner will consistently care for hair to a desired level of personal appearance.
___ 7. When presented with methods of measuring insulin, the learner will choose the one most appropriate and consistently measure it at a level sufficient to ensure adequate and safe administration.
___ 8. When presented with his or her ocular prosthetic devices, the learner will consistently perform the skills necessary to maintain a desired level of personal appearance.
___ 9. When presented with his or her medications, the learner will mark and later consistently identify them at a level sufficient to ensure safe and adequate administration.

C. At the completion of the telephone training unit, the learner will utilize a telephone at a level sufficient to meet his or her daily needs.
___ 1. When presented with a rotary dial telephone and 10 numbers, the learner will successfully contact 9.
___ 2. When presented with a touch-pad telephone and 10 telephone numbers, the learner will successfully contact 9.
___ 3. When presented with a telephone of the learner's choice, he or she will contact local information banks and retrieve information with 90% accuracy.
___ 4. When asked, the learner will describe all the special services of the local telephone company.

D. At the completion of the time and money training unit, the learner will tell time and identify money at a level sufficient to meet his or her daily needs.
___ 1. When presented with a raised-dot or large-print watch, the learner will consistently read the time and set it to within five minutes of the correct time.
___ 2. When presented with a talking watch or clock, the learner will consistently use all its functions to a level sufficient to meet his or her needs.
___ 3. When presented with coins, the learner will identify them correctly with 99% accuracy.
___ 4. When presented with paper money, the learner will describe an identification method and identify random selections with 99% accuracy.
___ 5. When presented with adaptive checking or banking materials, the learner will write checks correctly, enter balances in the ledger, and use an automated teller machine with 99% accuracy.

XI. Home Management

A. Upon completion of the home management training unit, the learner will perform home care skills to a level sufficient to meet his or her daily needs.

(continued on next page)

Figure 4.3. Sample Service Plan Form *(continued)*

___ 1. When asked, the learner will describe the following to a level at which training can begin: (a) clean and dirty, (b) dust and dusting, (c) wash and rinse, and (d) polish and polishing.
_✓_ 2. When asked, the learner will describe to a degree indicating adequate knowledge adaptive methods for: (a) maintaining spatial orientation in large areas, (b) thoroughly covering a surface to be cleaned, and (c) monitoring cleanliness.
_✓_ 3. When presented with the proper materials, the learner will consistently dust, wash, and polish various flat surfaces so they are clean and shiny.
_✓_ 4. When presented with a broom, a dustpan and two vinyl floors, the learner will clean them until they are free of dirt.
___ 5. When presented with a dust mop and two vinyl floors, the learner will clean them until they are free of dirt.
___ 6. When presented with a wet mop, water bucket, cleaning fluid, and two vinyl floors, the learner will clean them until they are free of dirt.
___ 7. When presented with vacuum cleaner and two carpeted floors, the learner will clean them until they are free of dirt.
___ 8. When presented with bedclothes, the learner will consistently make a bed neatly and evenly.

XII. Home Mechanics

A. Upon completion of the home mechanics training unit, the learner will perform home repair tasks at a level sufficient to meet his or her daily needs.
___ 1. When presented with a saw, a saw guide and a clamp, the learner will consistently cut boards safely and with minimal veer.
___ 2. When presented with a hammer, nails, and a board, the learner will consistently drive nails safely and with minimal bending.
___ 3. When presented with three grades of sandpaper and a board, the learner will consistently distinguish the grade of the sandpaper and sand a board until smooth.
___ 4. When presented with common hand tools, the learner will consistently use them properly.
___ 5. When presented with a standard faucet, the learner will consistently replace the washers without damaging the mechanism and so that it does not leak.
___ 6. When presented with a standard toilet, the learner will consistently describe the function of each part and consistently disassemble and reassemble the mechanism in such a way that it functions properly.
___ 7. When presented with a standard hinged door, the learner will consistently disassemble and reassemble the doorknob so that it functions properly.
___ 8. When presented with common drain-cleaning tools, the learner will consistently describe their use to a level indicating the necessary knowledge to use them.
___ 9. When presented with an electric wall plug and a disattached cord, the learner will consistently reattach it, so that the wires are not crossed and it will conduct electricity.
___ 10. When presented with a fuse box, the learner will consistently describe its parts and replace fuses safely and effectively.

B. At the completion of the household safety training unit, the learner will demonstrate a knowledge of serious safety issues and their solutions to a level necessary to manage a home independently.
_✓_ 1. When presented with a fire extinguisher, the learner will consistently use it in the proper manner for putting out various types of household fires.
_✓_ 2. When presented with a smoke alarm, the learner will consistently replace the batteries and demonstrate an adequate knowledge of how it is used.

(continued on next page)

Figure 4.3. Sample Service Plan Form *(continued)*

✓ 3. When presented with a fuse box, the learner will consistently turn it off when asked to do so.
✓ 4. When presented with the main shutoff valve for the household water supply, the learner will consistently turn it off when asked to do so.

XIII. Leisure-Time Activities

A. Upon completion of the crafts training unit, the learner will prepare craft items to meet his or her daily needs.
___ 1. When presented with prepackaged craft kits, the learner will consistently produce craft items at a level sufficient to meet his or her needs.
___ 2. When presented with the proper materials, the learner will produce woodcraft items at a level sufficient to meet his or her needs.
___ 3. When presented with the proper materials, the learner will produce tying-craft items at a level sufficient to meet his or her needs.
✓ 4. When presented with the proper materials, the learner will produce needlecraft items at a level sufficient to meet his or her needs.
___ 5. When presented with the proper materials, the learner will produce clay, pottery, or dough craft at a level sufficient to meet his or her needs.
___ 6. When presented with the proper materials, the learner will produce paper craft items at a level sufficient to meet his or her needs.
___ 7. When presented with the proper materials, the learner will produce decoupage craft items at a level sufficient to meet his or her needs.
___ 8. When presented with the proper materials, the learner will produce leather craft items at a level sufficient to meet his or her needs.
___ 9. When presented with the proper materials, the learner will produce woven craft items at a level sufficient to meet his or her needs.

B. Upon completion of the sewing training unit, the learner will perform sewing activities at a level sufficient to meet his or her daily needs.
___ 1. When presented with a regular or self-threading needle, thread, and the appropriate needle-threading devices, the learner will thread the needle consistently.
___ 2. When presented with appropriate sewing materials, the learner will consistently reattach buttons.
___ 3. When presented with appropriate sewing materials, the learner will consistently mend seams.

C. Upon completion of the recreation training unit, the learner will perform selected activities at a level sufficient to meet his or her daily needs.
___ 1. When presented with board games, the learner will play them at a level sufficient to meet his or her needs.
✓ 2. When presented with card games, the learner will play them at a level sufficient to meet his or her needs.
___ 3. When asked, the learner will consistently describe methods for adapting mainstream recreational or leisure-time activities.

Figure 4.3. Sample Service Plan Form *(continued)*

An Initial Slate-Writing Lesson

I. Objective: When presented with 8½" x 11" braille paper, vinyl labeling tape, a standard 28-cell slate or E-Z Read slate, and a stylus, the learner will emboss braille characters with 90% accuracy.

II. Materials: Braille paper, standard 28-cell slate or E-Z Read slate, stylus

III. Assessment: Does the learner know braille?

IV. Procedure

- A. Uses (reasons for learning to use the slate)
    1. Portability
    2. Relatively low expense
    3. Uses of specifically designed slates for tasks such as labeling, writing postcards, and doing mathematics
- B. Orientation to parts of the slate and stylus
    1. With slate in a closed position: windows, orientation marks indicating each group of five cells from right to left, hinge, bottom plate
    2. With slate in an open position: cell indentations on bottom plate, paper pegs
    3. Stylus: handle, point
- C. Paper insertion for standard slate
    1. Have the learner lay the slate on the table with the hinge left and windows up.
    2. Ask the learner to open the slate like a book.
    3. Have the learner place a sheet of paper against the bottom of the upper pegs and along the hinge (to prevent excess holes and ensure straight insertion).
    4. Have the learner push the lower pegs through the paper and then close the slate.
- D. Paper insertion for E-Z Read slate
    1. Have the learner place the closed slate in front of him or her, face down with hinge at right.
    2. Have the learner open the slate, noting the pegs.
    3. Have the learner line the paper up on the hinge and bottom of upper pegs.
    4. Have the learner push the lower pegs through the paper.
    5. Have the learner close the slate and turn it over.
- E. Embossing with the stylus
    1. Have the learner hold the stylus on or just above the joint where the index finger meets the hand; the index finger of the right hand should be curled over the top of the handle.
    2. Have the learner place the point of the stylus in the first cell, second row. Explain that the first line is too close to the top when beginning a new page.
    3. Tell the learner to use the index finger of the left hand as the guide finger, which moves from cell to cell and line to line to guide the stylus.
    4. Have the learner emboss full cells until all six dots are formed consistently.
        - a. Stress that the stylus point enters the cell from the first (right) side to emboss dots right to left.
        - b. Stress using the left index finger to locate and press the point into dot positions 1, 2, and 3.
        - c. Stress the importance of a light touch to prevent paper tearing.
        - d. Stress holding the stylus perpendicular to the slate surface to prevent the paper tearing.
        - e. Stress the importance of keeping the guide finger in constant contact with the frame.
    5. Have the learner emboss cell corners until he or she makes them consistently.
    6. Have the learner move the paper by placing thumbs over the lower pegs, removing the paper, and placing the lower set of holes on the top set of pins, feeling for them with the thumbs through the existing holes.

(continued on next page)

Figure 4.4. Sample Lesson Plan for Teaching Slate Writing

7. Have the learner emboss the braille alphabet, or the portion that he or she knows, until he or she is competent.
8. Have the learner emboss words, phrases, and sentences until he or she is accurate 90% of the time.
9. Have the learner identify specific braille characters in cell locations using orientation marks to locate them and the tip of the stylus to identify them.
10. Have the learner remove the paper and correct mistakes accurately.

V. Memoranda
   A. The slate may be accepted more readily if it is taught before the braillewriter.
   B. An enlarged model of a slate window may be needed for initial conceptualization.
   C. Many learners place too much pressure on stylus.
   D. Stress use of the first finger on the nondominant hand for orientation purposes.

VI. Evaluation
   Have the learner emboss 10 lines of dictated material, and check for the quantity and type of errors made.

VII. Assignments
   A. Have the learner compile names, addresses, and telephone numbers of friends and family.
   B. Have the learner label articles such as cassette tapes, compact discs, computer disks, etc.

Figure 4.4. Sample Lesson Plan *(continued)*

CHAPTER 5

Learning and Teaching

KEY CONCEPTS IN THIS CHAPTER

- **The definition of learning**
- **The major learning theories**
- **The major theories of adult development and their effects on learning**
- **The effect of aging on learning**
- **The effect of life events and transition on learning**
- **The effect of life experience and cultural background on learning**
- **The process of adjustment to vision loss and its effect on learning**
- **The effect of visual impairment on learning**
- **Methods for instructing adults with severe visual impairments**

The assessment and planning processes are integral parts of rehabilitation teaching, but the actual instruction that takes place is the key to the success of rehabilitation. Myriad variables interact to determine the learner's ability to assimilate the information offered by the instructor. Paramount among them are the following:

- the instructor's perception of learning
- the learner's stage of adult development
- the learner's proximity to a major life event or a life transition phase, such as vision loss
- the learner's age
- the learner's life experience and cultural background
- the learner's degree of adjustment to blindness
- the effect that early sight loss may have had on the learner.

The beginning sections of this chapter are theoretical, discussing major theories about variables that affect an individual's ability to learn and cope with significant life events. As such, they are somewhat clinical and present research based on groups of people. The purpose is to offer a framework on which education and rehabilitation teaching can be based, not to imply that all clients will act alike or should be taught in the same manner. The remainder of the chapter focuses on the effects on learning of adjusting to vision loss in particular and specific approaches to teaching adults who are visually impaired.

Variables in adult learning are too numerous to allow general conclusions to be drawn about best practice. Although various principles have been proposed by writers in the past, they have been challenged to such a degree that they appear to hold little practical value (Merriam & Caffarella, 1991). The only assumptions that can be made are that adults differ distinctly as learners from children; each is an individual with his or her own experiences, beliefs, level of intelligence, stage of human development, and degree of adjustment to vision loss. As a group, they are accustomed to determining their own destinies, they expect to be treated as individuals, they behave within an accepted set of social norms determined by work and community, and they engage in learning for the purpose of reaching a goal that will help them in some practical way (Merriam & Caffarella, 1991). Consequently, adults would not generally be expected to learn best in a setting based on traditional children's classrooms, where teachers determine what is to be learned, maintain an authoritarian posture, and use standard textbooks and teaching methods for large groups.

Because adults are so individualistic, the only practical way to determine their beliefs, learning abilities and styles, degree of self-esteem, and so on is by interacting with them through the initial assessment and through frequent teaching situations. At the very least, the following questions related to the factors that affect learning that will be discussed in this chapter should be answered during this process:

- A "humanistic" approach—one that considers an individual's emotions and potential for growth—would generally be considered best for most clients, but is it good for this particular learner?
- Does this client expect to be a self-directed learner or will he or she require a more directed approach?
- Does the learner require specific modifications because of a mental or physical disability?
- Is the learner facing a significant life event and transition other than loss of vision?
- Does this learner have strong ethnic or cultural beliefs, and if so, what are they?
- What level of adjustment to loss has the learner achieved?
- If the learner had a visual impairment at an early age, what effect has it had on concepts, motor abilities, and self-esteem?

In most rehabilitation settings instructors work with clients individually or in small groups, and this affords the perfect environment for determining their specific needs. Knowledge of the variables that affect adult learning can provide the instructor with a basis on which informed decisions can be made about individual learners.

FACTORS AFFECTING LEARNING

The Rehabilitation Teacher's Approach to Learning

Since the major function of rehabilitation teachers is to instruct visually impaired individuals in adaptive skills, they are teachers and their clients are learners. Therefore, it is necessary for rehabilitation teachers to understand what learning is and to know the major theories about the process of learning. Learning can be defined in a simplistic way as a behavioral change that results from experience (Merriam & Caffarella, 1991). However, the process of learning has been described in numerous ways, some of which will be briefly summarized here. (For a more thorough review of this subject, readers should consult the work of Merriam & Caffarella, 1991.) The major learning theories can be grouped into four orientations: behaviorism, cognitivism, humanism, and social learning (Merriam & Caffarella, 1991).

Behaviorists, such as Skinner (1974), base their theory on the premise that learning is measured in observable behaviors and that learning results from environmental factors. Therefore, learning is a function of what is presented in the learner's environment, and it is fostered by immediately reinforcing or rewarding the behaviors considered positive, and, conversely, not rewarding those considered negative. Merriam and Caffarella (1991) suggested that educational tools such as behavioral objectives, systematically designed instruction, programmed instruction, and computer-assisted instruction are recent manifestations of behaviorist thinking. These teaching tools are all based on the notion of breaking learning tasks into smaller segments or tasks and then monitoring for a "correct behavioral response as a result of learning," which is then promptly rewarded.

Cognitivists challenge the behaviorists and hold that learning should be measured not by viewing individual events, such as observable behaviors, but by considering patterns of behavior (Hergenhahn, 1988). According to cognitivists, learning is a cognitive, or thinking, process in which humans consider all the ingredients of a problem (information received in a learning situation) and arrive at solutions (reorganize the information based on experience, prior knowledge, maturity, and so on). The essence of the difference between behaviorist thinking and that of cognitivists is in the locus of control. That is, behaviorists propose that the environment controls learning, whereas cognitivists believe that control of learning comes from within the individual. These theorists believe that the learner's role is an active one and that it is self-directed and that new information is manipulated to fit present knowledge (Bruner, 1965).

Humanists, such as Maslow (1970) and Rogers (1983), consider learning from the perspective of the human potential for growth, and this perspective includes the affective or emotional aspects of the individual as well as cognition (Merriam & Caffarella, 1991). Rogers proposed that learning should include five characteristics:

- Learning entails *personal involvement*—the affective (emotional) and cognitive (intelligence) aspects of a person involved in the learning event.
- Learning requires *self-initiation*—a sense of discovery coming from within.
- Learning is *pervasive*, resulting in a change in attitude and behavior of the individual.
- Learning entails *evaluation* to determine whether the experience is meeting a need.
- Learning is *experiential*—a total experience.

Consequently, the instructor must utilize methods that promote self-initiation and make use of instructional methods that consider the learner's emotions.

The fourth and final learning orientation, *social learning theory*, is based on the idea that people learn from observing other people, and, as Merriam and Caffarella (1991) note, "by definition, such observations take place in a social setting" (p. 134). According to this theory, an individual sees a behavior, mentally stores it, visualizes situations in which it might be used in the future, and uses it when the appropriate time presents itself. Proponents of this theory suggest that learning involves both the influence of the environment (as in behaviorism) and the individual's own inner thought processes. As such, the locus of control of the learning is thought to reside in both external and internal sources. Social learning theorists suggest that positive role models are effective teachers and that learning can occur in all aspects of an individual's life, both inside and outside the classroom.

It is not expected that a rehabilitation teacher would base his or her teaching style totally on any one of the theories just described. Still, an individual teacher's set of beliefs might lead him or her to adopt one of these theories as most useful. However, each theory has been strongly supported by research, and each has its strengths in terms of meeting the individual needs of particular learners and clients. For example, those who learn best in small structured increments or who do not seem to be motivated to learn would in all likelihood do well under the principles of behaviorism, while those who are highly self-motivated might perform best as a result of the methods suggested by cognitivists. But because a newly blinded client's adjustment to loss has psychological implications (as discussed later in this chapter), the humanistic approach would also appear to be a highly suitable method, since learning and self-image rebuilding are so closely related. It is therefore essential to consider the needs and characteristics of the individual learner and to apply the theories and methods that appear to be most effective for that person's circumstances.

Combinations of the methods suggested by the theorists may also be useful when working with any particular client. For example, the behavioral objectives discussed in the previous chapter and the systematic approach utilized in the chapters of this text that deal with teaching specific adaptive skills can be combined with the caring, interactive style of the humanists to ensure an objective program that also fosters the rebuilding of the client's self-image and involves his or her own background experiences and motivation.

Stages of Adult Development

Humans pass through a series of developmental milestones throughout life. Psychological theorists and researchers such as Erikson (1950), Gould (1978), Jung (1933), Kohlberg (1990), Levinson (1986), Loevinger (1976), and Perry (1968) have described each phase or stage as characterized by certain beliefs and behaviors. Thus, the teaching methods deemed best for a learner at one stage may not be appropriate for someone at a different stage. In particular, the theories of educating children will not be appropriate to meet the learning needs of adults. Moreover, readers should keep in mind that the stage of development for individuals who have developmental disabilities in addition to their vision loss would not necessarily correspond to the expected stage or phase for persons of their age.

There are two basic schools of thought regarding adult development. One relates "phases" of life to chronological age. The other describes development as taking place in "stages" or levels of attainment not tied to age (Lasker, Moore, & Simpson, 1980). Those holding to the phasic theories believe that people move through a series of eras in their lives akin to seasons of the year (Erikson, 1950; Gould, 1972, 1978; Jung, 1933; Levinson, 1978, 1986). Levinson (1978) described four major phases, including the dependence of childhood (age 3–17 years), the commitments of early adulthood (22–40 years), the responsibilities of middle adulthood (45–60 years), and the wisdom of late adulthood (age 65 and older). He also described short transitional periods between these phases (ages 17–22, 40–45, and 60–65) that are characterized by uncertainty and redefinition (see the discussion of life events and transition in this chapter).

Teaching strategies can be planned according to phasist theories such as Levinson's broad eras of development. Even without his evidence, it would be logical to instruct those in the childhood era in a different manner from those adults in the middle or older phases. Also, the tumultuous transition periods between phases might be expected to disrupt learning in some way.

The theories suggested by the phasic theorists are helpful, but perhaps too broad or general to be of significant practical use. However, the ideas proposed by the stagists, particularly those of Loevinger (1976), appear to have a great deal of relevance for adult learning. Loevinger's major emphasis was on "ego development," which she described as a person's way of making sense of the world, or a mental process for understanding and acting. Her theory holds that people move through a sequence of stages, from being unable to distinguish oneself from others, to being introverted and self-protective, to wanting to conform and be like others ("conformant"), to wanting to be recognized as an individual, to understanding the value of others, and finally to knowing one's inner self. Loevinger developed a standardized test to identify an individual's stage of development, which was administered randomly to adults in the United States. The results indicated that the population is distributed fairly evenly throughout all but the highest stages. In general, about 37 percent were considered to be in the conformant stage, and a similar percentage (36 percent) had developed beyond to a stage of greater self-awareness or autonomy (Lasker & Moore, 1980).

Loevinger (1976) found that an individual's stage of development profoundly affected his or her attitude toward learning. Thus, people in the conformant stage believe that others are the sources of knowledge, that the instructor is an authority or lecturer, and that the learner parrots what he or she has been taught. By contrast, those in the later stages believe that the source of knowledge is their own life experience, that the instructor is a role model or evaluator, and that the learner has a responsibility for his or her own learning.

These attitudes affect how the individual responds in a teaching situation. The conformant learner takes less responsibility in the learning and expects to be told how to accomplish a task, whereas those who have developed beyond that stage would feel more comfortable learning through observation and participating in problem solving. Therefore, identifying a student's learning styles is important for the teacher. (For more details about how different life stages affect learning and development, readers should consult the works of Levinson [1986] and/or Loevinger [1976] and the review presented in Merriam and Caffarella [1991]).

The individual's attitude toward learning becomes apparent through his or her willingness to be an active learner. The following two cases illustrate the kinds of clues that would lead a rehabilitation teacher to an understanding of a student's preference or style regarding learning and teaching.

> When questioned about which kitchen skills and which foods he would prefer to work on, Tony V., a rehabilitation client, responded, "I don't know. You're the boss. Whatever you think is best for me." When asked, "I know you typed a good deal before your vision loss, so would you investigate the computer keyboard and try to identify the keys?" Tony V.'s response was, "Oh, I'm not sure. Would you please show me?" His responses indicate that he may be a conformant learner.

> Jennifer P. responded to questions about her interest in taking a braille class with specific information, saying "I really think I will enjoy braille, and since I'll only be here for about six weeks, I'd like to learn as much of it as possible. I can study it at night in my room." When asked to investigate the computer keyboard, "Yes," she replied, "I think I can. It looks like the keys along the top are number keys just like on the typewriter."

Obviously, Tony V. requires more direction from the instructor than does Jennifer P. It is important for the reader to understand, however, that suggestions about how to approach different types of learners relate only to the teaching style used, not to the structure of the lesson or to performance outcomes. The teacher would need to follow the lesson plan for keyboarding (see Chapter 9) with Jennifer P. just as with Tony V. If Jennifer P. was unable to identify all the parts of the keyboard, the instructor would point out the remaining important parts listed in the lesson plan.

Aging

Since rehabilitation teachers frequently work with elderly clients, it is important to consider whether aging affects the ability to learn. Traditionally, learning ability has been viewed as a function of intelligence. Although there are many variables that determine the ability to learn, intelligence is probably the strongest determinant and has been the most thoroughly studied. Therefore, this discussion of aging and learning is primarily based on the effect of age on intelligence.

Whether or not intelligence declines with age is a topic that has been debated and studied for years. Early researchers concluded that intelligence peaks in the second decade and decreases thereafter (Jones & Conrad, 1933; Thorndike, 1932). However, recent researchers report little change in intelligence before the age of 50 or 60 years (Arenberg, 1974; Kidd, 1973; Schaie & Labouvie-Vief, 1974; Schaie & Stroether, 1968). In addition, there appears to be little change in some individuals' intelligence when studied at a very old age. Field, Schaie, and Leino (1988) found that less than half of their study group of individuals aged 73 to 93 years had significant loss of intelligence, and some were found to have little loss at 92 years of age.

The question of whether aging affects intelligence is in part a matter of how intelligence is defined. The traditional view of intelligence is that it is a single quality possessed by humans and that it can be measured through psychometric tests. In recent years, however, theorists have proposed that intelligence is composed of multiple factors (Merriam & Caffarella, 1991). These authors hold that those who view intelligence as a single entity tend to find that intelligence peaks earlier in life than do those who feel intelligence is a group of factors.

The most recent theories based on multiple factors tend to measure intelligence in terms of how individuals conduct their everyday lives, rather than on a single test score. Gardner (1983, 1990) described seven types of intelligence—linguistic, logical-mathematical, spatial, kinesthetic (muscle/joint memory), musical, intrapersonal (understanding oneself), and interpersonal (understanding others)—which vary greatly within a given individual. Sternberg (1985, 1990) holds a similar view, basing intelligence on the individual's ability to solve problems in everyday situations. Those who believe that intelligence is a measure of practical ability based on multiple factors theorize that aging may cause losses in one or more factors, but that the other factors can easily compensate for the loss (Cattell, 1987). In fact, Baltes, Dittmann-Kohli, and Dixon (1984) showed that certain factors of multiple intelligence could be selectively enhanced in order to compensate for the loss of others.

It is important to remember, however, that the process of aging affects the individual as a whole and its impact is not confined to intelligence. Physical effects such as loss of sensory ability are also accruing. Since people require good sensory and physical functioning to learn optimally, any physical losses would be expected to limit the potential for learning. One of the most significant factors to remember in considering the effects of aging on intelligence and learning is that the potential for disease and multiple disabilities increases with age (Michaels, 1993; Orr, 1992). Schaie and his colleagues believe strongly that people maintain a more than adequate amount of intelligence to meet their needs until disease interferes (Schaie & Willis, 1991). Thus, intellectual losses from Alzheimer's disease, weakness from heart disease, loss of tactile sensitivity from poor circulation, and losses of many other kinds—rather than loss of intelligence—are what may challenge the abilities of older individuals who are in learning situations.

Based on recent research on intelligence and learning, therefore, it does not appear that aging itself interferes with learning significantly. Of particular relevance to rehabilitation teachers is the evidence that some factors of intelligence might be selectively enhanced in order to overcome any losses in others. For example, if a client is having difficulty with certain kinesthetic tasks—those involving muscle and joint movement—perhaps he or she can be taught to use other aspects of intelligence to problem solve.

> Lucy S., an elderly client with a central field loss, had also lost the ability to perform the physical operations necessary to turn food that was cooking on the stovetop, and was therefore unable to prepare it in the way she always had in the past. However, she was able to use a microwave oven and a slow cooker as alternatives.

Because multiple disabilities are common among elderly clients, the rehabilitation teacher must also be familiar with the effects that various physical and mental conditions may have on learning and with methods of adapting one's teaching approach to compensate for them. Although it is not within the scope of this book to cover these in detail, some of the limitations frequently caused by disease or disability are listed in Appendix B. For further information, readers are encouraged to consult the work of Brodwin, Tellez, and Brodwin (1995) and Stolov and Clowers (1981).

The Effect of Life Events

Life events are significant occurrences that act as markers in the human life cycle, causing periods of disorientation and reorientation and representing important turning points in life (Merriam

& Caffarella, 1991). They can be personal, such as birthdays or marriage or the experience of a major transitional phase in life, such as adolescence. They can also be cultural, affecting large groups, such as wars, social movements, or catastrophes. Life events are generally considered as processes, rather than single events in time, that have repercussions well before and after the actual event (Schlossberg, 1987; Schlossberg, Lynch, & Chickering, 1989).

Persons who are in a transitional phase of their life as a result of a major life event frequently exhibit identifiable strengths and weaknesses. The weaknesses, such as immobilization and rapid swings in emotion, are generally understood and expected (Sugarman, 1986). Surprisingly, however, one of the strengths frequently engendered by such experiences is an increased willingness to engage in new educational activities (Brookfield, 1987). In fact, Aslanian and Brickell (1980) believed that most people cope with transition in this way.

Sugarman (1986) identified the following seven stages that accompany a wide range of transitions:

- immobilization
- mood reactions (depending upon the nature of the life event)
- minimization of the event's impact
- letting go or breaking with the past
- testing or exploring the new situation
- searching for meaning in the experience
- integration (feeling at home with the change).

As a life event, a significant vision loss surely can cause the most difficult of transitions. Sugarman's (1986) model of the stages in coping with transition essentially coincides with traditional ideas in the field of blind rehabilitation about adjustment to vision loss (Cholden, 1958; Schulz, 1980; Tuttle, 1984). Sugarman's stages can be helpful in predicting the behavior of personal adjustment clients. They will be discussed as they relate to vision loss in particular later in this chapter.

Success in coping with life events and moving through these various stages appears to depend on many factors, including the degree to which the individual views the transition as positive or negative, the person's inner strengths, the extent of external support available, and strategies for coping (Schlossberg, 1987). Schlossberg also felt that coping was enhanced by helpers and that exploring the transition, developing problem-solving strategies, and learning coping skills were important.

Schlossberg's suggestions, although not specifically developed for the field of rehabilitation, apply to the role the rehabilitation teacher plays in the adjustment process by promoting problem solving and teaching adaptive skills. They also indicate that clients may need to discuss their loss of sight in order to move to the stage Sugarman described as letting go. In addition, theories about life events suggest that rehabilitation clients are probably ready to be in a learning environment and that rehabilitation teachers can foster coping by suggesting coping strategies and by teaching skills that promote coping.

Although the negative characteristics of persons in transition such as immobilization and emotional swings may interfere with instruction (see the discussion of adjustment to vision loss later in this chapter), it is helpful to bear in mind that clients might, as a result of their changing lives, be more open to learning than they would be otherwise (Merriam & Caffarella, 1991). Indeed, in the authors' experience, the vast majority of clients are extremely receptive to learning once the initial stages of adjustment have passed.

Life Experience and Cultural Background

Experiential Background

Because knowledge is gathered and beliefs are established by the individual through prior experiences, experience is an important factor to consider in the rehabilitation process. Prior knowledge is the base on which methods of adult education are anchored (Merriam & Caffarella, 1991), including rehabilitation teaching. Since most instructional areas entail common activities of daily living, nearly all adults will have had some concrete or abstract experience with them. Assessment is designed to pinpoint the client's degree of knowledge of particular skills (see Chapter 3), and instruction is begun at that point. In addition, prior knowledge of the practical uses of particular skills (such as having a method to keep track of addresses and telephone numbers) allows the adult learner to relate new learning (how to tape record the information) to previous practice (writing the addresses), rather than simply memorizing what is being taught. Reliance on prior knowledge also makes the instructional process simpler, because analogies—such as the analogy between storing information on cassette tapes and storing information on computer disks—can be used effectively in instruction.

The formation of attitudes or beliefs through experience is complex and extremely difficult to measure. Attitudes toward learning or instructors may stem from preschool experiences; negative attitudes toward being helped may have originated during the Great Depression years; and fears may have been formed in infancy. Negative attitudes and fears are especially difficult to recognize since they are generally viewed as undesirable traits and are usually kept hidden, as in the following example:

> Walter A., a Vietnam veteran with a service-connected vision loss, extended his negative attitude about his former superiors in the service to the rehabilitation teachers employed by the Veteran's Affairs Blind Rehabilitation Center. He expressed a desire to move ahead with the personal adjustment goals he had agreed on with his instructors. However, staff members were perplexed by what seemed to be personality clashes with all teachers except one, another veteran, whom Walter A. viewed as "an equal." Once staff members initiated discussion about the issue, they were able to help Walter A. to realize that his attitude about previous supervisors was affecting his learning success.

Cultural Background

The influence of cultural factors on beliefs and attitudes is especially important to anyone intending to instruct adults. Because the populations of the United States and Canada are both extremely ethnically varied, an awareness of the cultural effects on the teacher-learner relationship is necessary to achieve optimal learning. It is impossible to know all the do's and don'ts of interacting with people from all the cultures represented in North America, but some principles are generally applicable.

Most cultures can be analyzed by investigating their values, language, actions, and possessions (Brokenleg, 1987). These factors will strongly affect the content of lessons in such areas as kitchen skills and leisure activities. Cultural education is beyond the scope of this book, but because rehabilitation teachers so frequently encounter clients from diverse cultures, it is important for them to know how to examine information in this regard. Brokenleg (1987) suggested that human service professionals who plan to work with a particular ethnic group should use the four categories mentioned as guides when searching for specific information about that culture. Such information might be gathered from clergy, local human service workers, cultural centers, libraries, and, of course, from the client. Whatever the source, the information will be invaluable in building rapport with a given client and in planning the instructional process that will work best for him or her.

Values. Behaviors and reactions arising from cultural values can be unanticipated or misinterpreted by uninformed instructors. For example, dogs are considered unclean by Muslims, which could lead to difficulty for teachers who use dog guides and work with Muslim clients. (Teachers with dogs might ask clients of the Muslim faith if it would be a problem to bring a dog to the lesson.) Also, using tape recorders or computers would not be acceptable in work with people from an Amish community. Traditional male and female roles differ among cultural groups, and these variations, if unknown to or ignored by the rehabilitation teacher, could complicate the relationship between teacher and learner. For example, some people, such as women from the Middle East, might be uncomfortable touching or being touched by a member of the opposite sex during a lesson on sighted guide technique (see Chapter 12).

Even traditional views about personal independence in some cultures may be sufficiently different from dominant North American ideas that they cause misunderstandings that might affect the planning and implementation of the instructional program. An example found in some Native American cultures relates to the "Circle of Life," a recurring theme of life and health. According to this perspective, we are born into a circle of extended family and community that supports us and that we, in turn, support. In such a traditional extended family, it is common to find other family members taking on the roles of those who no longer can perform certain tasks. Thus, a mother who can no longer cook, clean, or grocery shop because of vision loss might express interest in being able to accomplish these tasks independently because she wishes to continue to support her family; but they, in turn, may not encourage her to learn new ways to perform these tasks from a rehabilitation teacher because the family views it as their new responsibility (Ponchillia, 1993b).

Language. The differences in meanings and use of words among ethnic minorities can also interfere with communication. For example, for reasons related to both cultural values and language, members of the native American Sioux tribe have no word for *time*. The result is that the client's concept of keeping appointments might be completely different from that of the rehabilitation teacher. Some cultures believe that saying or pretending a thing can cause it to occur. It is therefore important to be aware of how one phrases things that might be perceived as negative (Locust, 1990). For example, in a discussion of cultural beliefs and native peoples with diabetes and visual impairment, one of the authors pointed out that saying to a Native American client, "Your foot looks infected. You should see a doctor so you don't get gangrene and need to have it amputated," may lead the individual to think the rehabilitation teacher is wishing him or her "bad" (Ponchillia, 1993b, p. 335). A more positive way to phrase concern might be, "Your foot looks infected. People with diabetes have problems like these and need to go to the doctor for treatment when there is an infection." Such examples highlight the need for attending to the learner's understanding of and reaction to language used during lessons.

Actions. Certain actions that would be considered unremarkable by most people in mainstream North American society may not be acceptable to people in other cultural groups. Making eye contact, for instance, has an entirely different connotation for Native Americans or people from Asian countries than it does for many North Americans. It can be perceived as a sign of disrespect, particularly when directed toward elderly people.

Conversely, the omission of certain actions may hamper interaction with clients. For example, in many instances, clients with Asian or other cultural backgrounds may expect visitors to remove their shoes before entering the house, and some may follow a custom of greeting elderly family members first (*Culturgram '92: Taiwan*, 1992) and would expect the instructor to do so even if the elder is not the client. Another Asian custom observed in Taiwan and elsewhere is presenting all new acquaintances with a business card upon being introduced (J. Leja, personal communication, September 1995). This action is considered of great importance, giving the card bearer more credibility, perhaps, and is not viewed as something to do as an afterthought at the end of an appointment with a client "so you can contact me if you have any questions." Even without further study of cultural differences, one can avoid difficulties in such situations by being polite, respectful of elderly family members who happen to be in the home, and by being observant.

Possessions. The items associated with different cultures, such as foods, can also pose potential intercultural problems. Foods and their preparation methods differ significantly among ethnic and other groups, as do methods of measuring ingredients for recipes. Other possessions of people from other cultures, such as the types of clothing that are worn or handicrafts that are made, might also differ. These factors will affect the content of lessons on such topics as kitchen skills and leisure activities.

Given this understanding of potential cultural differences among clients, rehabilitation teachers should be prepared to teach alternate methods or activities based on clients' needs and to ask questions about such factors as traditional crafts or the traditional way that members from a cultural group perform the skills being taught. For example, if it is traditional to use a large knife and quick rocking motions for dicing or slicing vegetables, as it is in Japan, the teacher who commonly teaches the use of a small paring knife for the same task may need to be the party who changes methods, rather than the client. Although it is difficult to prepare sufficiently beforehand to understand all the cultural differences one might encounter, rehabilitation teachers should be alert to clues (shoes lined up at the doorway, reluctance to touch a guide's elbow), and should be sensitive enough to make inquiries about other aspects of a client's cultural background that might affect personal adjustment training. For further information, readers can consult Storti (1994) and Culturgrams, mini-descriptions of customs and courtesies of more than 100 areas of the world, published by the David M. Kennedy Center for International Studies, Brigham Young University, Provo, Utah.

EFFECT OF VISUAL IMPAIRMENT ON LEARNING

To this point, this chapter has focused on members of the general population. The discussion that follows will present the particular effects that severe visual impairments may have on learning. It should be kept in mind, however, that people who are visually impaired differ from others only in regard to that particular characteristic. Therefore, the theories discussed earlier apply to this population as they do to everyone.

Adjustment to Vision Loss

The onset of blindness or visual impairment is a life event that elicits responses similar to those of any other serious life event that causes a significant transition. Therefore, the seven stages that accompany transition suggested by Sugarman (1986) that were presented earlier in this chapter can apply to adjustment to vision loss. Sugarman's stages are in fact similar to those described by blindness professionals (Cholden, 1958; Schulz, 1980; Tuttle, 1984), and since Tuttle (1984) relates his phases specifically to vision loss, his ideas will be presented here.

Although an in-depth discussion of these phases is beyond the scope of this book, further reading of Tuttle's work is advisable for an understanding of the behavior of clients adjusting to vision loss. Tuttle (1984) terms this process "adjusting with vision loss" and does not confine it to those with adventitious impairments. He includes those with congenital impairments in his description of adjustment because he believes that adjustment to even a prenatal loss begins when the child becomes aware that he or she is different from others and that the process of adjustment is identical, regardless of when the onset of vision loss occurs.

Self-Esteem and Acceptance

To best understand the theories of adjustment, it is necessary first to be aware of the relationship between self-esteem and adjustment and to the concept of acceptance of loss. Most theorists, including Carroll (1961), Cholden (1958), Schulz (1980), and Tuttle (1984), have described the process of adjusting to loss of sight as a sequential set of phases through which the newly visually impaired person travels. They believe that the loss of sight is a serious blow to self-esteem—the individual's feelings of self-worth, ability, and significance (Coopersmith, 1967). An individual's level of self-esteem is determined both by internal factors—such as perception of success, defenses, values, and aspirations (Coopersmith, 1967)—and by external factors, particularly the way in which others react to one's behavior (Tuttle, 1984). New sight loss, which makes even the simplest daily tasks seem difficult or impossible, causes devaluation of self, and the pity shown by well-meaning people reinforces the lowered self-esteem.

Adjusting to the loss is considered by those adhering to this theory as learning to accept the reality of the new situation and then finding ways to live with it (Acton, 1976, p. 149). Some believe as Carroll (1961) did, that accepting means that the person must "die" as a sighted person and that self-esteem is completely reorganized (see Sidebar 5.1). Others hold that the self-esteem undergoes a lesser change that involves accepting blindness as one of the individual's attributes (Tuttle, 1984). In either case, these theorists all believe that rehabilitation instruction cannot be successful without the individual's acceptance of the loss.

Dodds and his colleagues have challenged this theory, suggesting a more cognitively based one (Dodds, 1987; Dodds, Bailey, Pearson, & Yates, 1991). They assert that there is no need to require acceptance of the loss as a prerequisite to skills training. Rather, they hold that skills training should begin quickly and that the gains made in doing practical tasks will initiate adjustment. Although maintaining that acceptance of the loss is critical, the authors prefer the latter approach because learning practical adaptive skills promotes acceptance by demonstrating that the loss is not as devastating as it once appeared. Therefore, the

Death and Rebirth: The Origins of Blind Rehabilitation Theory

SIDEBAR 5.1

Carroll (1961) was among the first to express the theory that loss of vision produces a severe blow to self-image, and modern rehabilitation practices are based on the writings of Carroll and his cohorts. In his classic monograph, *Blindness: What It Is, What It Does and How to Live With It*, Carroll (1961) described in detail the losses that resulted from a visual impairment and suggested rehabilitation regimens to overcome them. The modernized versions of Carrol's adaptations are still being used today.

The theory has met with widespread acceptance but has been criticized by some for the analogy Carroll drew between blindness and death. Although the reactions to new blindness are virtually the same as those ascribed to impending death by Kubler-Ross (1970), the analogy may seem extreme, particularly to those who are visually impaired. It has been interpreted, perhaps erroneously, to mean that blindness is so terrible that it is like death itself. Another interpretation is that Carroll meant the analogy to relate blindness and rehabilitation to death and rebirth in a Judeo-Christian sense that movement into a new life must begin with the acknowledgment of the end of a former one. In any case, the model has proved valuable as a practical tool for rehabilitation.

Carroll (1961) stated that the sighted self must die before the blind one could grow, implying to some that a person should not enter rehabilitation until that stage was reached, because he or she would not be ready for it. The concept of "acceptance" seems to have stemmed from this aspect of Carroll's writings. Dying as a sighted person has apparently been equated to accepting one's blindness. The common use of the word "acceptance" carries the connotation that one must think of blindness in a positive way, and this produces some strong reactions from many clients.

authors believe, personal adjustment training should be initiated as quickly as possible following sight loss, even though the client's initial reactions to the loss, including anger and irrational thoughts, may make the rehabilitation teacher's job difficult, as discussed in the next section.

Phases of Adjustment

The phases described by Tuttle (1984) in adjusting to vision loss include

- trauma
- shock and denial
- mourning and withdrawal
- succumbing and depression
- reassessment and reaffirmation
- coping and mobilization
- self-acceptance/self-esteem.

Tuttle believes that individuals move through these phases in a sequential manner. However, the length of time spent in each and the degree to which persons return to former stages is highly individualistic. Some people move through the series of phases quickly, some might revert back to former phases, and others may remain in one or another phase for the remainder of their lives.

The trauma phase is the actual loss itself, or, in the case of a congenital impairment, the point at which a child becomes aware that he or she is different from his or her friends. In the case of adventitious loss, the extent and duration of the trauma varies from the sudden onset that results from accidents or retinal detachment to the slow development of progressive diseases such as chronic glaucoma, diabetes, or retinitis pigmentosa, in which the trauma can recur numerous times.

The shock and denial phase is characterized by immobilization. The harsh reality of the loss of vision is so devastating that the "self" is protected by automatic body responses that serve as psychological defense mechanisms (Cull, 1972; Schulz, 1980). These defense mechanisms are subconscious psychological reactions that protect the ego during periods in which unacceptable realities prevail.

Denial, a defense mechanism characterized by the tendency to ignore the problem subconsciously, serves to buffer the individual from the loss and give him or her time to deal with it. Denial commonly takes two forms: first, denial that the loss happened at all, followed by denial of its permanence. It is extremely important for rehabilitation teachers to be aware of denial of permanence because the great majority of clients think the vision loss is temporary, and, therefore, they often see no need for adaptive skills instruction at this stage of adjustment. As individuals become aware of the reality of the loss, they move into the mourning and withdrawal phase. At this point, they have realized the effects of the loss, and they mourn the loss of the ease with which they conducted their lives in the past. Often, they withdraw. *Withdrawal* is a defense mechanism characterized by a decrease in the need for social interaction, and it takes the form of avoiding people or retreating into thought when in the company of others. Individuals also become extremely egocentric during this phase.

As time passes, the individual moves away from the psychological defenses of the two earlier stages, which are replaced by conscious decisions, and thought becomes more rational. Many individuals become acutely aware of the limitations they face and commonly think or say, "I can't." In essence, they succumb to the loss, and depression results. In the authors' experience, this is a period in which depression comes and goes without warning, sometimes numerous times in a day or even an hour. Sugarman (1986) called this phase the mood reaction stage, which he described as an emotional roller coaster. Deep depression and threats of or even attempts at suicide are also sometimes exhibited during this time.

The reassessment and reaffirmation phase brings a self-evaluation of the individual's personal attributes, and decisions are made about which characteristics to keep, which to eliminate, and which to change (Tuttle, 1984, pp. 193–194). This phase is the equivalent of Sugarman's (1986) "letting go" stage, in which the individual begins to see that it is possible to live with the impairment. Perhaps most important, it is a time during which the individual may decide which of the limitations accompanying the impairment can be overcome.

Coping and mobilization behaviors begin to appear as the individual actually begins to overcome limitations to change the attitude that the disability is devaluating. This period is the time of learning and applying adaptive skills in daily life. The last phase, self-acceptance/self-esteem, is a return to the old self and to the former level of self-confidence. The individual accepts blindness or visual impairment as one of his or her personal characteristics along with all the others.

Because adjustment theories such as Tuttle's hold that the loss of sight is so tied to self-esteem, the role of the rehabilitation teacher and the purpose of adaptive skills instruction go well beyond imparting knowledge to the learner and become a kind of counseling-by-teaching. As in any type of counseling situation, the professional must be keenly aware of the need to build the client's confidence during lessons. It is not enough to teach someone to perform skills well; he or she must also know how the skill will help in the attainment of individual goals. The teaching must also be done with as much understanding and respect as possible to foster the goal of self-acceptance.

The individual's emotional upheaval and the use of denial during early phases of adjustment to vision loss can be disruptive to learning. Denial, basically the opposite of acceptance, may mean that the rehabilitation instruction process cannot go on because the client has not accepted his or her loss of vision. However, the authors' experiences indicate that, in fact, instruction can help someone work through the process of denial.

> George R., a 30-year-old man who was blinded in an automobile accident, was sure he would regain his vision after surgery, which was scheduled three months in the future. He resisted attempts to convince him to go to a residential program, telling his counselor that he would not need adaptive skills because his sight would return. After finally agreeing to try the program and experiencing just one week of successes in personal adjustment training, he had faced the reality that the upcoming operation would, even if successful, not return his vision to normal. As he became aware that blindness was not as debilitating as he had once thought, he moved into the beginning of the reassessment phase.

It should also be noted that, in general, denial cannot be broken down by confrontation, and attempts to do so can cause damage to rapport with a client or even termination of services. Potok (1980), an individual who experienced vision loss and entered a rehabilitation center, described how having professionals directly confronting him about "a need to admit that he was blind" caused him great anger and resulted in his leaving the rehabilitation facility. Denial is most commonly encountered at the time of the rehabilitation teacher's assessment, and reactions such as "I don't need any of this because I'm going to see again" may be heard a great deal. One approach is to respond with such statements as "I really hope you do get your vision back. I know you're having some trouble at present, so let's see if we can make things easier for you now." The individual may in fact regain some vision, but regardless of what happens later, he or she can benefit from services at the present time. The remainder of the assessment should identify needs that will convince the person of the benefits of training and that can be used for the purpose of overcoming denial.

Clients in early stages of adjustment may also exhibit reactions reflecting egocentricity and rapid mood swings. Every word the instructor speaks may be analyzed for its meaning, and angry responses are not unusual. For example, when Miriam S.'s teacher mistakenly asked her to move to her left instead of right, causing Miriam to bump into a table, the client responded angrily, "I thought you were a professional. You don't even know your right from your left. I can't believe it!" Knowing that the extreme display of feeling was in all likelihood due to a lack of adjustment and that it was not intentionally directed at her, the teacher responded simply by apologizing.

Although rare during the instructional process, threats or even attempts at suicide do sometimes occur. These threats may take the form of statements such as, "I think I'll just step out in front of a car during mobility training today and put us all out of our misery," or "Maybe I'll do myself a favor tonight and jump off the bridge down the street." Statements of this nature can be relatively common during early training phases, but they should be taken seriously and reported to the counseling or psychological staff immediately. If threats of suicide are encountered in the client's home, community crisis personnel should be contacted. (See Chapter 17—dealing with case management—for more information on community resources.)

For many clients who reach the succumbing and depression ("I can't") stage, most of the irrational thought exhibited in earlier phases of adjustment has passed. Now the individual may be ready to deal with facts, although they still may cause sadness. It is not easy to overcome the resistance of someone who feels "I can't," so the rehabilitation teacher may need to become a salesperson of sorts. A useful tack to take is to identify one or two lost abilities that are especially important to the person and concentrate on restoring them. A person can frequently be moved from depression and into reassessment in this way.

> Patricia L., a 52-year-old hairdresser with diabetes and a recent severe sight loss, entered a rehabilitation center with a son at one elbow and her husband at the other. Her family literally lifted her through the door because of her fear of moving without sight. This client was afraid of going up the stairs to her bedroom, even with physical support. She cried for hours that evening and was extremely disoriented for two or three days. In her intake interview it was discovered that she viewed her inability to prepare food for her family as the most devastating of her losses. By the end of the first week of personal adjustment training and only four lessons on adaptive kitchen skills, she was using the stairs, had become oriented to the building, and spoke positively about "beating blindness" for the remainder of her time at the center.

Although not all clients respond like this one, perseverance is key for most rehabilitation teachers faced with teaching clients who are in the throes of a difficult adjustment.

Teaching becomes simpler once a client has reached the reassessment and reaffirmation phase. At this time, many individuals may actively be seeking solutions to their challenges and are evaluating their abilities. In that case, they should be encouraged to become an active part of the planning process, be given tasks that require problem solving, and be made aware of the part each lesson plays in the attainment of their goals. This change to a positive outlook is every rehabilitation teacher's goal for clients, and it is the reward all hope for.

Instruction from this point on generally focuses on confidence building and a return to self-esteem. The important point to bear in mind during this stage of instruction is that skills need to be mastered sufficiently so that the client will be independent and successful when services are terminated. A quick once-over lesson on a tape recorder, a complex cooking lesson, or instruction in using a low vision device may result in temporary success at the end of the lesson, but may not be adequate for lasting confidence. If the client returns home and fails at early attempts to undertake tasks on his or her own, the new techniques learned during training may be abandoned.

Early Vision Loss

Congenital visual impairments, as defined here, have their onset during prenatal or early childhood development. Generally, the earlier they occur, the more profound they tend to be (Scholl, 1986b). Because congenital vision losses affect early childhood development, the effects are likely to be more complex than they will for individuals who experience later (adventitious) losses. Early onset affects the cognitive, psychomotor, and affective domains of development in ways that can have consequences for an adult's ability to perform the skills taught during personal adjustment training.

Cognitive Domain

Limitations on learning in the cognitive domain relate primarily to the nature and extent of the individual's body of knowledge, which may be restricted as a result of learning without visual input. When sight is severely limited, learning tends to occur through the less efficient senses of touch and audition (Lowenfeld, 1973; Scholl, 1986a).

The sense of touch is relatively concrete, in that nearly everyone can use their sense of touch to identify objects placed in their hands without training. However, the tactile sense is limited in scope and range. Many items are too far away, too small or large, too hot or cold, or moving too fast to explore tactilely.

Hearing is beneficial for learning because it has a larger physical range than does touch. However, the usefulness of this sense is limited by the individual's inability to direct it and by its relatively abstract nature. That is, the sounds one hears are not always emitted from something tangible and may not easily be related to their sources. If a child never connects the ticking of a clock to the clock itself, for example, the information has no practical meaning. Concepts involving space present particular challenges. The spatial relationship of one's self to objects and of objects to other objects (mental mapping) may be extremely difficult to comprehend without sight (Cratty, 1971; Barraga, 1986). Although the sense of sight has its own limits of scope and range, it is superior in these respects to the senses of audition and touch. Unless parents or teachers intervene, the result of limited access to information is that severely visually impaired children may not have as broad a knowledge base or degree of conceptual development as sighted youngsters.

Rehabilitation teachers will encounter these limitations in concept development frequently in the area of daily living skills. Concepts that are easily understood through vision, such as mixing ingredients or browning fried foods, may be difficult for their clients.

> Molly W., a totally blind 19-year-old in a summer rehabilitation program, was able to define mixing as stirring two substances until they become one. However, she admitted that she really did not understand how that could happen. Consequently, the instructor demonstrated the concept by having her use her hands to feel how water and pancake mix can become a homogeneous mixture.

Another common practical problem may arise when an instructor expects a client to understand the relationship of one piece of furniture to another in the client's living quarters. Often clients may know how to find each object from a landmark such as a doorway, but they may not know how to get from one object to another. One technique that has proved helpful to individuals who read braille is the use of the familiar braille cell dot positions to relate one object to another. For example, "The chair is at dot 1, the end table is at dot 2, the door at dot 3," and so on. This technique is also useful for dividing an area to be scrubbed or swept.

Psychomotor Domain

The development of motor skills in infants and children is measured through the milestones of grasping, sitting independently, crawling, standing, and walking. In general, children with severe visual limitations tend to attain these milestones at later ages than do children with normal vision (Ferrell, 1986). Because the motivation for movement comes primarily from visual stimulation, there may be little reason for preschoolers with severe visual limitations to reach for objects or move toward them if they do not know they are there. Thus, there tends to be limited exploration, limited overall body movement, and limited learning about the environment. As a result of this and because motor skills are to some extent learned through observations (Lowenfeld, 1973), movements tend to be less fluid and deviations in posture and gait more common in youngsters with severe visual impairments (DiFrancesco, 1980).

Thus, rehabilitation teachers who work with adults with severe congenital visual impairments may need to cope with clients' limited dexterity and, in some cases, limited range and degree of movement. Mixing ingredients in a large bowl may be difficult, for example, because the client's stirring motion may be limited to a few inches in the center of the bowl, and the action may not be vigorous enough to accomplish the task. Remediations include modeling the action so the person can follow the hand movements necessary to do the task or providing concrete feedback about how well the mixture is blended by adding something to it that can be perceived tactilely.

Lack of motor involvement during childhood development often manifests itself in repetitive behavior such as rocking, head swinging, and eye poking (Griffin, 1981). These behaviors are known as stereotypic behaviors. Stereotypic behaviors can be likened to the repetitive behaviors many people engage in, such as drumming their fingers on a tabletop, but stereotypic behaviors are notable because of their extraordinary frequency or intensity. Stereotypic behaviors can be distracting to others and perhaps lead them to believe falsely that someone who exhibits them is developmentally delayed, autistic, or emotionally disturbed (Huebner, 1986; Swallow & Huebner, 1987). In general, people who exhibit stereotypic behaviors are not consciously aware of them, which makes the behaviors difficult to control. In many cases, constant feedback given during concentrated periods of observation has yielded significant benefits (Blasch, 1978). More recently, electronic feedback devices that alert the user to the behavior have shown promise (Bringle, 1987; Felps & Devlin, 1988; Osman, 1987). The rehabilitation teacher may occasionally need to help a client eliminate stereotypic behaviors (or the parents of a young congenitally blind child) with developing strategies for controlling his or her repetitive movements (LaGrow & Repp, 1984).

Affective Domain

The affective domain can be viewed as development of behaviors related to people (emotional, social, and personality development) (Piaget, 1981). A visual impairment can sometimes have little direct influence on the affective development of a child. However, indirect influences can often be significant (Scholl, 1986a).

Normal affective development begins when the mother first holds her newborn, initiating bonding. It is the beginning of a long period of affective development that should culminate ultimately in an independent, self-confident adult. The infant learns to love and be loved, eventually learns to interact with family and then friends, and learns about relationships and social behaviors (Joffe & Vaughn, 1982). A severe visual impairment requiring long periods of hospitalization that interferes with the parent's ability or willingness to nurture the infant can have a strong limiting effect on affective development, as can a lack of eye contact between parent and child. Relationships with siblings can be negatively affected if it appears that the child with a visual impairment requires more of the parents' attention (Scholl, 1986a).

According to Warren (1984), social development of students with visual impairments seems to differ from that of nondisabled peers, and Bauman (1973) reported that degree of vision is frequently related to level of social development. In extreme cases, it seems that early visual impairment may influence affective behaviors in young adults and in adults, who may either be overdependent on others or reject assistance because of fear of imposing, may behave inappropriately, or may avoid learning situations in which they feel they might fail (Scholl, 1986a).

Affective development begins from the first moments of life, so clients whose affective behaviors have been influenced by early visual impairment are not likely to alter old behaviors or develop new ones overnight. Rehabilitation teachers can help such clients, however, by making practical suggestions that improve self-esteem and nurture independent living skills. For example, individuals who exhibit either too much willingness to depend on others for assistance or a reluctance to ask for assistance when necessary can be helped by discussing which tasks are reasonable to do independently and which tasks might be facilitated by arranging for assistance from volunteers, family members, or friends. In addition, rehabilitation teachers can teach skills that help clients make optimal use of assistance. The two following examples demonstrate these principles:

Annette G. consistently "burned out" volunteers by asking for assistance with paying her telephone, utility, and installment loan bills. What should have been a brief and simple task was complicated by the fact that Annette G. received her social security check at a post office box located across town, so the volunteer's first task was to drive Annette G. to the post office to pick up her check. Then, because Annette G. did not use a checking account to pay bills, she asked the volunteer to drive her to the bank to cash her check, to the telephone business office to pay that bill, to the utility company office, and finally to the lending company to pay the loan installment. Each office was located in downtown areas with inadequate parking, so the volunteer was additionally stressed by circling to locate nearby parking and then assisting Annette G. to the building.

The rehabilitation teacher helped Annette G. recognize that her demands were excessive, given that alternatives were available. First, she moved her post office box to a location within walking distance. She was helped to open a checking account and arrange for direct deposit of her social security check. The rehabilitation teacher taught her specific skills such as writing checks using a check guide or template (see Chapter 8), and addressing envelopes, so Annette G. only needed the assistance of volunteers to read her mail and run occasional errands. She was later overheard passing on these suggestions to other clients.

Kristy S. was a totally blind full-time college student with a busy schedule, but she was determined to be independent and not ask for assistance in accomplishing daily living tasks such as grocery shopping. Grocery shopping involved an hour-long bus trip each way, using a backpack and folding grocery cart to transport the groceries home. Kristy had mastered orientation within her favorite grocery store and selected most food items by memorizing their locations and using tactile clues. However, her reluctance to ask for assistance while searching along the aisles for grocery items made the task time consuming. Kristy S. admitted that grocery shopping took too much of her time, and she occasionally came home with such unwanted items as green tea instead of regular, mayonnaise instead of salad dressing, and ground turkey instead of hamburger. She also admitted that she wished she could learn about new products the grocery had, but "didn't want to bother anyone" by asking for help.

Although all the possible psychological reasons why Kristy S. felt reluctant to ask for assistance could be speculated about, it was the behaviors that could be changed. During discussions about alternatives to her grocery-shopping method, Kristy S. learned that her knowledge of store layout would assist her in making a grocery list; that most stores have procedures and personnel to assist shoppers with special needs; and that she needed only to call ahead to arrange for a personal shopper to assist her in selecting groceries and examining new products (see Chapter 13). She also learned that the store was willing to select and deliver grocery items for a small charge, which freed considerable time that could be devoted to schoolwork.

Rehabilitation teachers can also help clients who may have developed inappropriate social behaviors or low self-esteem related to visual impairment. For example, since social relationships are often enhanced by one's appearance in public, at least initially, they may give clients feedback about whether mannerisms and behavior are appropriate and offer suggestions for ways a person with visual impairment can stay abreast of latest fashions and hairstyles (see Chapter 14). Finally, since self-esteem is always enhanced by being successful, rehabilitation teachers can assist students by ensuring that lesson goals can be successfully achieved.

TEACHING LEARNERS WITH VISUAL IMPAIRMENTS

In this section, the focus of attention shifts from the learner to the teacher. Since, as noted earlier, adults are considerably different as learners from children, teachers of adults need to use different techniques and approaches than they would in the traditional children's classroom. Although the topic of teaching adults cannot be addressed in detail in this text, there is a significant body of literature on working with adults (see, for example, Merriam & Caffarella, 1991) that readers may wish to consult, and some tips for teachers are presented in Sidebar 5.2.

In addition to being aware of the needs of adult learners, rehabilitation teachers need to take into consideration the special needs of learners who are visually impaired. The effective instruction of adults with visual impairments is a complex task. However, the insights gained from knowing how the impairment may affect the individual and the learning process helps in deriving practical principles for rehabilitation teaching. Three important aspects of instruction will be emphasized here:

- communicating effectively
- monitoring the speed of delivery of the lesson
- reinforcing success in learning.

Enhancing Instructional Communication

Teaching an individual who is blind or visually impaired might at first glance appear to be a difficult task. However, if the instructor is aware of the circumstances inherent in communicating with learners who have limited or no vision and knows the methods used to overcome barriers, the teaching is little different than it is with any learner.

In all instructional communication, there is a verbal and nonverbal component. For example, as an instructor explains the process of tying a square knot to most learners, he or she also demonstrates the movements required to complete the task while the learner visually observes. Similarly, a classroom lecturer will enhance complex explanations with visual aids such as pictures, graphs, or scale models. Lecturers also commonly use gestures such as pointing and accompanying phrases such as "over there" and "that one." If the learner is visually impaired and is not able to see these aids and gestures, much of the information being presented is lost.

Knowing that the learner cannot see nonverbal cues, an inexperienced instructor who is faced with introducing a new method or device to someone with limited or no vision might automatically attempt to describe it verbally in great detail. If the technique or object being described is simple, this method works well. Words alone are inadequate, however, when describing visually complex manipulations or items. For example, imagine trying to describe completely verbally how to tie shoes.

Since the verbal part of instruction is sometimes difficult, a nonverbal component is often required. Therefore, the instructor needs to understand the methods for enhancing verbal instruction as well as for presenting the nonverbal part in a way that can be understood by individuals with severe visual impairments. The communication barriers caused by visual impairment can usually be overcome through the following methods:

- using precise language
- using analogies
- using auditory cues
- giving the learner more descriptive responsibility
- using tactile modeling demonstrations
- presenting tactile or highly visible scale models
- manipulating learner movements.

In general, the three most commonly used techniques are using verbal descriptions for sim-

Tips on Teaching Adult Learners

Determine the learner's needs and interests. This is a basic part of a routine assessment, but it is important for the teacher to keep it in mind when planning lessons. This information will help when trying to follow other tips, such as increasing motivation, finding relevant practical examples, and providing reinforcing lessons.

Explore the factors and circumstances that affect learning. As discussed in the early part of this chapter, the instructor needs to pay attention to the client's background, learning style, age, and other factors that affect how he or she will learn.

Discuss goals with the learner. Goals can be established by mutual agreement, or, if the client seems reluctant to provide input, the teacher can state goals for him or her. Goals help to provide structure and meaningfulness to individual lessons.

Tell the learner how the lesson will be of use. Adults learn better if they know why they "need to know."

Use the learner's prior knowledge and experience. Students feel valued if their personal expertise in an area is recognized. The instructor can use prior knowledge as a starting point for providing new information and as a basis for analogies to make explanations clearer.

Provide practical examples. Most people learn best by doing. Applying information on use of a telephone patch cord by asking a student to call her favorite gourmet coffee shop to record verbal directions from the bus stop to the door is more reinforcing than simply discussing how a patch cord could be used.

Increase motivation. The instructor may have to be creative in finding the best motivators for each individual or type of lesson. For example, learning handwriting for the first time can be tedious for someone without vision, but setting the goal as being able to sign greeting cards "with love, Aunt Lucy," can be more motivational than simply knowing one can write the alphabet.

Provide reinforcing lessons. An example of reinforcement is selecting brownies instead of a casserole to make during an early baking lesson. Family members, neighbors, or staff and students at a rehabilitation center will certainly provide positive reinforcement and attention!

Assign "homework." Homework can be reading a page of braille aloud on cassette, typing a grocery list, or handwriting a letter to a friend. Learners who are self-motivated will likely accept it as part of their responsibility, while more conformant learners will follow the instructor's request; both will benefit from continuity and repetition.

Discuss the teacher's observations about the student's learning characteristics. Observations related to the learner's preferred mode of input and output for information (verbal, tactile, auditory, or written) or the best time of day for certain activities can be helpful in promoting the most effective teaching and learning. For example, if the teacher notes that the student's tactile or visual reading is flawless in the morning but worse in the afternoon, it might be helpful to point it out so that primary reading activities could take place earlier in the day.

Share performance evaluations. Knowing that he or she learned 20 of the 26 letters of the braille alphabet, for example, gives the learner positive reinforcement for his or her mastery of learning, which increases self-esteem and motivation for further efforts.

ple tasks, having the learner describe newly introduced devices, and using modeling for tasks requiring movement. The other techniques have more specific applications, but all should be part of the rehabilitation teacher's repertoire.

Using Precise Language

Terms such as "there," "here," "thing," and "stuff" should be avoided. Specific names of items such as computer components or tape recorders and their parts and precise descriptions of the steps required in the performance of a skill should be used. Therefore, if the teacher refers to the "paper advance button" on a braillewriter, there should be no question in the student's mind about what item is being referred to. If attempting to describe a complex movement, such as tying a shoe, the task should be broken down into its simplest parts and each part taught separately and in sequence.

Using Analogies

Assuming that the learner is not a very young child, analogies can help clarify explanations and descriptions. For example, as noted earlier, while explaining the function of a computer disk, the instructor might draw on an adult's previous experience to compare it with an audio cassette or a compact disk using the following parallels: "You said you were familiar with cassette tape recorders, so we can compare this computer disk to a cassette tape. As you speak into the tape recorder, it places your voice on the tape, which you can listen to later. The computer disk does the same for information typed into it; that is, you can type what you want on the computer and store it electronically on the disk and save what you have typed, then use that information in the computer at a later time."

Using Auditory Cues

It is relatively easy for most people with normal hearing to locate the direction of a sound. Therefore, auditory cues can be used to give orientation during lessons. For example, in telling a person who is blind how to get to a specific location in a room, it is simple for the instructor to go to the desired location and give an auditory cue, such as a tap on a kitchen counter and saying: "right here." Although this method is effective for locating places in a room or perhaps on a tabletop, hearing is not discerning enough for it to be helpful in pointing out specific parts of typewriters, tape recorders, and other objects.

Instructors should be aware of the merits of various sound-emitting devices. Electronic beepers or portable radios are commonly used as sound beacons to mark desired locations, such as outbuildings on a client's property or a counter in a kitchen. In general, they are helpful, but beacons with very high-pitched sounds tend to be difficult to locate; those with lower pitches are best. Also, in large areas, such as gymnasiums or swimming pools, these devices may be confusing because of echoes.

Using Learner Description

Using the learner's description and words for objects solves the problem posed by the learner's inability to easily see the gestures made by the instructor. When teaching someone who can see well, it is common to point to the parts of a device and to name them. The underlying communication problem is only operative in one direction though, from teacher to learner, not from learner to teacher. If the learner points to parts and names them, the problem is avoided because the teacher can monitor the learner's gestures. A good deal of the awkwardness of trying to tell someone who cannot see how to locate a specific machine part can be avoided by having students tactilely or visually investigate devices such as tape recorders or talking calculators. For example, the teacher might say: "I know you told me that you used a tape recorder in the past. Would you take a few minutes to investigate this machine and describe it and its parts for me?" As the parts are encountered, they can be named, establishing a common language that can be used from that point on. For example, during future lessons, the instructor simply says: "find the on/off switch," rather than: "move over to the left side of the machine, then move up about half way, then right an inch or two and you will find the on/off switch." This technique also sometimes eliminates the client's need to learn new terms. For example, if a client describes a switch on a Talking-Book Cassette Machine as a "toggle switch" (see Chapter 10), there is no need for the teacher to introduce the equivalent term "rocker switch."

Using Modeling

If the instructor is teaching a movement that is required to do a particular task, he or she can use modeling in much the same way as when teaching learners with unimpaired vision. The only difference is that the learner with low vision may need to be close enough to see and the tactile learner will need to touch the teacher as the movement is made. For example, if the instructor is demonstrating how to turn a hamburger with a spatula, the blind client would hold the wrist and the spatula blade to monitor it.

Using Scale Models

In the same way that a scale model of a molecule helps the biology teacher, an enlarged model of something too small to feel or see with limited vision can be helpful in rehabilitation teaching. For example, the braille cell window of a slate is too small for many people to explore tactilely, but an enlarged cardboard model can give the student a better understanding of how the braille slate window actually looks. Models can also be used to show the individual steps in a complex task, such as tying a knot (Canadian Council of the Blind, 1993; Hoshiyama, 1989). A series of such steps can be glued to cardboard or tacked to wood to facilitate investigation.

Maps of areas too large to investigate, such as the layout of the rehabilitation center or the position of a bus stop on a city block, can also facilitate understanding. These maps may be made with bold lines or shown on a closed-circuit television for clients with low vision (see Chapter 6) or made with a raised-line drawing board (see Chapter 8). Raised-line drawing boards can also be used to explain a concept that is best represented by a drawing, such as a typical line graph encountered in sociology classes or the layout of a stovetop that is too hot to touch.

Using Manipulation

Occasionally, it is necessary to actually manipulate the learner's movements in order to make an action understood. For some clients, for example, the arm swing in bowling is best demonstrated by having the individual hold the ball and moving his or her arm. This technique is generally considered the least favorable instructional method because it is somewhat intrusive and the learner may feel as though someone else is controlling his or her movements. If manipulation is required, the instructor must be sure to ask permission first.

Monitoring Speed of Delivery

The speed of delivery of information is of particular importance, because if concepts are introduced too quickly, learning does not occur; and if they are offered too slowly, the learner loses interest. The primary tool for monitoring speed of instruction is ongoing evaluation. During lessons, evaluation is accomplished by making sure that the learner understands the major concepts presented before the next is introduced. Although the principle is simple, the techniques for measuring learning may not be. One of the most common mistakes made by new instructors is asking questions that require simple yes-or-no answers, such as "Do you understand?" "Is that clear?" or "Easy, huh?" Generally, learners will respond to such questions affirmatively unless they are especially assertive, and the instructor receives little information about what has actually been learned. Therefore, behavioral measures must be the ultimate determinant of learning.

The speed of instruction within a lesson can be determined by making sure that the client is able to perform the essential tasks before the next concept is introduced. For example, if a lesson in recording is being taught, the client must first know the machine's keyboard. Having the learner successfully demonstrate the use of each of the recorder's play mode keys will indicate his or her readiness to move to recording. The same concept holds true when determining delivery speed from lesson to lesson. The learner needs to reach the performance objectives written in the lesson plan before proceeding to the next lesson. Therefore, ongoing evaluation not only informs the rehabilitation teacher of how much the student understands during the lesson, but also provides the final picture of the student's performance at the end of the lesson, as demonstrated in the following example:

> Carolyn H.'s rehabilitation teacher realized during an introductory tape recording lesson that Carolyn H. was familiar with all of the controls typically found on tape recorders, but could not consistently point out or locate correct keys on the particular modified adapted tape recorder being taught (see Chapter 10), although she had improved by the end of the first lesson. The teacher's evaluation helped him plan the next lesson, which required Carolyn H. to locate various keys a number of times while listening to several address and recipe tapes.

The related topics of how to measure and report learners' performance are covered in Chapter 17 on case management.

Reinforcing Learning

It is generally understood that learners need feedback on how they are performing and that well-timed and appropriate positive reinforcement is a good motivational teaching tool. It is perhaps important to mention that feedback from the teacher, such as "Nice job," "Yup, that's it!" or "Great work! Only five more to go" is necessary when significant learning has occurred. However, too much reinforcement or reinforcement of extremely simple tasks may serve to discourage adult learners. Overly exuberant exclamations of "Wow!" "Wonderful!" or "Unbelievable!" at the identification of each braille character in a reading lesson are examples of going overboard.

As the reader moves on to the chapters in Parts 3 and 4 on the specific adaptive skills that rehabilitation teachers are called on to teach their clients, he or she may consider how the principles of learning and teaching presented in this chapter would apply to the presentation of particular lessons. And, as the new rehabilitation teacher begins to work with clients, he or she will no doubt find it useful to return to the concepts described in this chapter in order to relate them to practical situations.

PART THREE

Communication Skills

CHAPTER 6

Low Vision Skills

KEY CONCEPTS IN THIS CHAPTER

- **The role played by rehabilitation teachers on the low vision rehabilitation team**
- **The methods used by rehabilitation teachers in assessing low vision**
- **The factors affecting the ability to see objects clearly**
- **Nonoptical methods of enhancing low vision**
- **Optical systems used to enhance low vision**
- **Methods used to train individuals with low vision to read with a near-vision optical device**
- **Methods used to train individuals with low vision to use a closed-circuit television system**
- **Methods of assessing individuals with low vision**
- **Methods of training individuals to read with near-vision devices**

Prior to about 1975, the discipline known as blind rehabilitation was based largely on the adaptive techniques used by persons who were totally blind (Rosenthal, 1991). As a result, those who had useful vision were commonly introduced to these techniques as if they, too, were totally blind. Since we now recognize that most individuals who are visually impaired have some functional (useful) vision and have the potential to use it, rehabilitation teachers today provide somewhat different instruction, no longer emphasizing tactile techniques only. In fact, a new subdiscipline of rehabilitation teaching termed *vision rehabilitation* has been developed. Vision rehabilitation is based on the premises that use of limited functional vision can generally be enhanced, and that its enhancements should be a major focus of rehabilitation.

A degree of vision that is functional but limited enough to interfere with the ability to perform everyday activities and that cannot be corrected with standard eyeglasses or contact lenses is known as *low vision.* A commonly used definition of low vision (Resources for Rehabilitation, 1993) refers to visual impairments that leave the individual with some residual vision. Many professionals consider an acuity of 20/70 or less to be low vision. The World Health Organization (WHO) defines moderate low vision as acuity of 20/70 to 20/160 in the better eye with best possible correction; severe low vision is defined as ranging between 20/200 and 20/400 or marked by a visual field of 20 degrees or less (Greenblatt, 1989).

Jose (1983b) proposed a model for providing vision rehabilitation services that consists of three parts: preclinical assessment, clinical services, and training phases and instructional services. The rehabilitation teacher generally conducts the preclinical phase, which includes an informal assessment of the degree of functional vision of the individual and his or her adjustment to the impairment. This functional assessment is usually conducted as part of the observational portion of the initial assessment in the client's home (see Chapter 3) and is a practical testing of his or her ability to utilize remaining vision. In some cases, rehabilitation teachers who specialize in low vision also assist in the clinical phase, in which optometrists or ophthalmologists in the low vision clinic conduct more sophisticated tests to determine the client's visual status, prescribe types of magnifiers or other aids that would be of benefit, and show the client how to use the prescribed aids. Rehabilitation teachers also function in the instruction and training phase, which includes teaching visual and tactile adaptive techniques to the client with low vision and provides a sequential introduction to and reinforcement of the proper use of prescribed low vision aids in a practical setting. Before considering the specific methods of assessing individuals with low vision, it is necessary to review the factors that affect how such individuals see and the adaptations that are available to assist them.

FACTORS AFFECTING VISIBILITY

In order for a rehabilitation teacher to assist an individual with low vision in attaining the best possible visual efficiency, the teacher must understand the factors that affect visibility, or the ease with which objects are seen. The most important variables to consider are

- illumination
- contrast
- size.

Illumination

Illumination, the amount of light reflected from the surface of the viewed object into the eye, is critical to visibility. Generally, as the degree of illumination is increased, so is visibility—at least, up to a point. An individual's pathology and current level of vision will also affect the amount of light needed to see an object. Therefore, one of the first assessments a rehabilitation teacher makes in a client's home is the adequacy of the lighting. Perhaps because normal vision is extremely efficient, lighting in the average home is rarely optimal. As a result, the simple addition of lights in the environment may be all that is required to solve certain problems. Adding a light in the kitchen, for example, may eliminate difficulties with tasks such as pouring liquids or peeling potatoes.

Other factors relating to illumination, such as glare and the learner's degree of sensitivity to light, also determine how well an object is seen. If reflected light strikes the eye at an angle, or is bright enough to cause the eye to close or blink, glare results and interferes with visual tasks. Glare can be controlled by adjusting the angle of the light source or by placing the object to be viewed on a less shiny or more absorptive surface (Carter, 1983a). Thus, if the person with low vision places a potato to be peeled on a towel that covers the shiny surface of the kitchen counter or moves the light source from the front to his or her side, the individual will see the potato more easily.

If the client's eye condition results in photophobia (oversensitivity to light), too much illumination can be detrimental and may even decrease visual efficiency. In such cases, reflected light can be controlled with sunglasses or light filters added to prescription glasses. Ambient light—the light that exists in the surrounding environment—must also be controlled, particularly if it is sunlight. This can be accomplished by suggesting that the client wear a visor or cap with a protruding bill or use sunglasses that have shields mounted on the sides and top. Indoors, shades and blinds or curtains may help control the sunlight entering the room, and dimmer switches can be used to adjust the level of artificial illumination.

Contrast

The degree of color difference between an object and the surface against which it is being viewed is termed *contrast.* Increasing contrast between an object and the background generally improves its visibility. Glare interferes with contrast by making objects appear closer in color.

Creating contrast is an especially helpful technique for people with low vision because it can be done with little effort or expense. Whereas increasing lighting may require expensive fixtures or installation costs, it is a simple matter to increase the contrast of an object by placing something of a significantly different color behind or beneath it. For example, filling a glass with milk is made easier by placing a dark towel or tray under it. This principle can also be used for such tasks as filling insulin syringes or doing handicrafts. In addition, contrast can sometimes be increased by wearing yellow sunlenses. Yellow filters tend to turn blues, grays, and purples to black and thus increase contrast between the object and lighter surroundings. Such modifications also make reading print easier. Placing a yellow acetate sheet over reading material tends to make print, especially faint or colored print, appear blacker, thus increasing contrast (Watson & Berg, 1983). A typoscope, which is a sheet of black paper or plastic with a window cut out to isolate one line of print at a time, can also be used to increase contrast and reduce glare reflected from a white page. The typoscope further assists the reader by blocking out extraneous material, thereby directing the eye to the correct line.

Size

Degree of visibility is also affected by the size of the object to be viewed. Perception of size can be manipulated by increasing the actual size of the object to be viewed, by bringing it closer to the eye, or by creating a larger image of the object through magnification. Increasing physical size is not usually practical, with the exception of providing larger print for reading. As anyone who has experienced limited vision quickly learns, however, it is a simple matter to bring the object closer to the eye, and thus increase the size of the image of the object on the retina. As a result of this phenomenon, known as *relative-distance magnification,* when the distance from eye to object is decreased by one-half, the size of the retinal image doubles. The rehabilitation teacher will often find that low vision clients have discovered this principle long before their first visit for services. However, many elderly people have become accustomed to holding their materials at a comfortable distance in order to focus properly over the years before they lost additional vision, and they may need to have reinforcement and assurance that a new habit of holding materials closer is beneficial rather than harmful to their eyes. The apparent size of objects can also be increased by the use of optical low vision aids, which are discussed in the next section. Low vision aids also assist individuals in adapting to a limited visual field.

LOW VISION DEVICES

Low vision devices are designed to alter the way in which the image of an object reaches the eye. The types in common use include:

- telescopes
- microscopes
- telemicroscopes
- optical magnifiers
- electronic magnifiers
- prisms (Jose, 1983c).

Although rehabilitation teachers are not generally trained to prescribe optical aids, demonstration of low vision devices to the client should be part of the teacher's initial preclinical low vision assessment (Carter, 1983b; Jose, 1983b).

Since many newly referred people with recent vision loss are told by their regular eye care specialist, "I'm sorry, there's nothing else we can prescribe that will help you to see," they may not see the value of traveling to a clinic or other service center for a complete low vision workup. However, such a workup is essential. If an appropriate assessment is made and appropriate low vision devices are demonstrated, based on the initial assessment, the individual may see the value of pursuing further assessment (and prescription) by a specialist in low vision. Therefore, it is important that rehabilitation teachers have knowledge of the variety of devices, their uses, and training techniques.

Telescopes

Telescopes are generally used for viewing objects at a distance of more than 20 feet, but some are used within 2 feet of objects to be viewed. The handheld types are used for viewing traffic lights, bus signs, and the like; those mounted on spectacles or attached to them as loupes are used for activities performed for long periods, such as watching television, reading sheet music, or watching sporting events; and those mounted within other lenses are helpful for spotting a distant object while traveling on foot and help to eliminate fatigue from having to hold the telescope to the eye.

The *bioptic telescope* is used in combination with standard refractive error lenses (hence the name "bi-optic") and is effective for those who need to check distant objects frequently while moving about. Bioptics have a distance or reading telescope fitted into the standard prescription lens so the user can look through either the telescope or the standard lenses, depending on the task. This system allows some users to drive with their refractive lenses, and also monitor signs and landmarks with the distance telescope. However, because telescopes limit the visual field, make objects appear closer, and make moving objects appear to be moving at an increased rate of speed, they are not practical to use continuously while walking or driving.

Microscopes

Microscopes are headborne or spectacle-mounted lenses used to accomplish near-vision tasks. They have a close working distance (2 to 20 cm.) and create enlarged images on the retina, which has the same effect as bringing the object closer to the eye. Microscopes are used for reading as well as for other near activities that require the hands to be free. Among their disadvantages, they restrict the field of view significantly, and the short working distances they require means that people needing high degrees of magnification must hold reading material or other objects close to their faces.

Telemicroscopes

A *telemicroscope* is, as the name implies, a combination of a telescope and a microscope and is gen-

Spectacle-mounted and handheld telescopic low vision devices.

A microscopic low vision device mounted on spectacles.

erally prescribed for tasks to be completed at a distance of 20 to 100 cm. (Kennedy, 1991). Telescopes limit how close to a task the user can focus; the telemicroscope solves this problem by attaching a reading cap to the front lens. Telemicroscopes are either spectacle mounted or handheld and serve as near-vision aids when the microscopic lens is attached. Their strength is versatility, since they allow the user to view both near and far objects without changing low vision aids.

Optical Magnifiers

Magnifiers are also near-vision aids, but differ from microscopes in that they are held near the object to be viewed and are used at any distance from the eye, although holding them closer to the eye increases the field of view. Because the distance from eye to magnifier can be greater than with microscopes, which is initially more comfortable for the user, and because magnifiers are relatively easy to learn to use, they are popular with novice users of low vision devices. Although magnifiers increase the image size of objects viewed, a disadvantage is that they restrict the field of view by enlarging a relatively small portion of it.

A telemicroscopic low vision device.

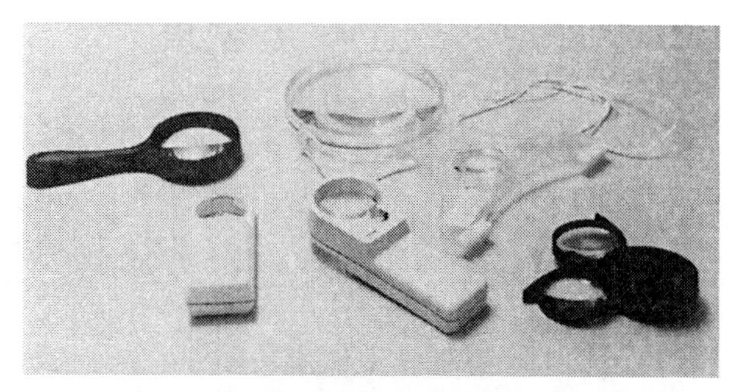

A variety of handheld magnifiers.

Handheld magnifiers are the most commonly owned optical aid (Whitten, 1986), because they are versatile, relatively inexpensive, and readily available to the general public. Handheld magnifiers are primarily used for spot reading, such as for food labels, thermostats, telephone dials, restaurant menus, and the like.

Some magnifiers are mounted on stands that build in the correct focal distance (the distance between the lens and the object being viewed) (see Sidebar 6.1), making them especially useful to individuals with tremors or other motor-control problems (Jose, 1983c), and some are fitted with illuminators for use in dark environments, thus pairing control of size and control of illumination in one device. Stand magnifiers, particularly those with

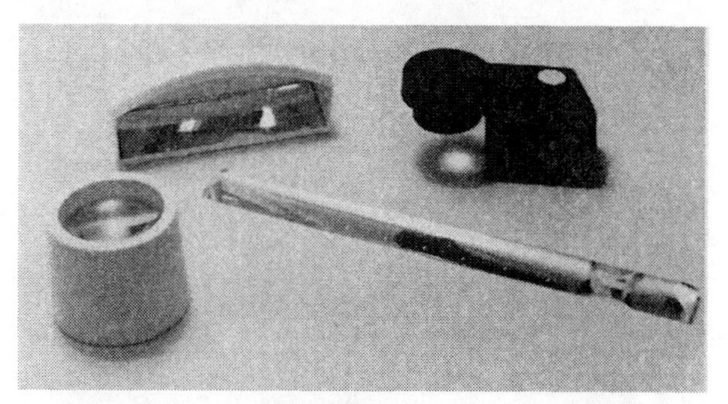

Various types of stand magnifiers, including a prism magnifier (top left) and bar magnifier (bottom right). Some have built-in illumination.

SIDEBAR 6.1

Focal Distance and Working Distance

In considering the performance of low vision devices, two factors that need to be understood are *focal distance* and *working distance.* The focal distance is a property of the lens and is generally the distance at which the lens must be placed from the object in order for the object to be in sharp focus. The working distance is the distance at which an object is held from the eye of the viewer, and it will vary depending on a number of factors, including whether the person is using a handheld or spectacle-mounted lens, his or her viewing habits, the optical device, and the task. The stronger the lens, the shorter the focal distance; but, in general, close working distances are less comfortable to the user than longer ones. If the user is unable to use the device at a comfortable working distance, the rehabilitation teacher may need to explore with a low vision professional other options for modifying the working distance. (For further information on the technical aspects of this topic, the reader can consult, for example, Jose, 1983d and 1983e, and Whitney, 1975.)

attached sources of lighting, are especially effective during the early training phases for people with low vision. However, they restrict the field of view significantly, and many people will not use them following rehabilitation training (Whitten, 1986).

Full-page magnifiers are requested by many people with low vision, because they theoretically allow the user to view an entire page of text at one time. They provide so little magnification, however, that they are useful only to people with significant functional vision.

A full-page magnifier.

Electronic Magnifiers

Electronic magnification provided through a *closed-circuit television (CCTV)* system is another option for people with low vision. The CCTV uses a video camera to focus on the material to be viewed, and the enlarged image is displayed on a television monitor. A CCTV provides clear images at extremely high levels of magnification—up to 80 times, depending on the size of the screen—and does not require users to hold material near their faces (AFB National Technology Center, 1996; Uslan, 1993, 1994a, 1994b; Uslan & Ren Shen, 1996). Using a CCTV is also less fatiguing than using magnifiers with powers greater than 5X (the image is magnified five times). CCTVs allow people with severely limited vision to read, write, and perform many daily living or vocational tasks comfortably.

Most CCTVs are not very portable and are relatively expensive when compared to more common optical aids (Jose, 1983e; Moss, 1992). However, the price of CCTVs is decreasing, and several hand-held models are now available that allow the user to carry the device to stores, libraries, or other

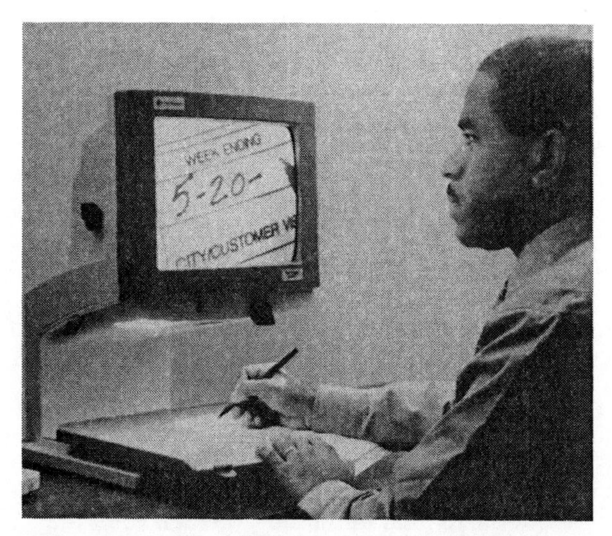

A closed-circuit television (CCTV) system.

locations. Given the rapid development in this area, readers are urged to contact the AFB National Technology Center as well as manufacturers of low vision aids and devices (see Resources section) for information on the most recent products.

A CCTV may be an appropriate aid for an individual when the following factors are present (Silver & Fass, 1977; De Witt, Schreier, & Leventhal, 1988):

- The optical devices currently used do not provide sufficient magnification.
- Increased contrast or reversed image improves performance.
- Long periods of reading or writing are necessary.

Prisms and Mirrors

Prisms and mirrors do not increase the size of the object or image; these optical aids are used when there are limitations in the individual's visual field. Prisms bend light rays to place images on the retina that are not being viewed directly. Mirrors provide similar benefits. Both are especially useful for increasing the viewing area of persons with localized losses of vision in the visual field, particularly those who have limited side or central vision. The prism is mounted on a lens. The user moves his or her gaze to the prism to monitor the blind side. The user can become more aware of peripheral objects by scanning systematically into the prism (Finn, Gadbaw, Kevorkian, & De l'Aune, 1975; Jose, 1983c).

Low Vision Devices in Use

A variety of factors affect the successful use of optical devices (Greig, West, & Overbury, 1986). They include:

- the ease with which the device can be used
- the cost of the device
- the relative comfort with which the device can be used
- the user's previous knowledge of low vision devices
- the individual's appearance while using the device.

As might be expected based on these factors, a study of former rehabilitation clients by Whitten (1986) found that people most commonly utilized the simplest and least expensive devices: handheld magnifiers for near-vision tasks and handheld telescopes for distance. Among those who could read using low vision devices but not with the naked eye, both ownership and use of near-vision devices was high. However, ownership was also high among those whose vision was so limited that they could not read standard print even with the use of a low-vision device. This apparent contradiction gives cause for concern, since it appears that some clients may be attempting to use devices that do not appropriately meet their needs. A possible explanation is that some people with low vision may be reluctant to use nonvisual alternatives to accomplish near-vision tasks and are seeking some way to increase their vision. Consequently, such individuals may, at least during the early stages of adjustment, be particularly anxious for low vision specialists to prescribe devices. Therefore, the rehabilitation teacher should ensure that such individuals receive an especially thorough low vision assessment that takes all factors into account.

FUNCTIONAL VISION ASSESSMENT

Perhaps the most important conclusion that can be drawn from what is known at present about the use of low vision aids is the importance of a sound assessment to accurately determine a client's needs so that the best possible adaptations can be suggested. This process helps to determine whether an individual has enough sight to perform communication, mobility, and daily living tasks visually.

The rehabilitation teacher's assessment of the client's functional vision is generally conducted before the client's first low vision clinic visit as part of the teacher's observational assessment. This assessment will not provide sufficiently scientific data for making prescriptions, but it can give the clinical low vision team functional information on which to base their assessment and can provide the rehabilitation teacher with information on how best to instruct the client.

The assessment process conducted in the client's everyday environment (home, workplace, recreational setting, and the like) consists of both observation and actual measurement. Because the client's abilities may differ greatly in regard to near, intermediate, and distance tasks, all three should be evaluated.

Observational Assessment

Jose (1983c) has suggested that the observational portion of a vision assessment focus on the following areas:

- *Present ownership and use of low vision devices:* The rehabilitation teacher should note the types of optical devices owned and the degree to which they are being used. This information can indicate whether further training or reevaluation of the prescription is needed.
- *Light and dark adaptation:* Light sensitivity and problems in adapting to light or dark are indicated by avoidance of light sources such as windows.
- *Accommodation:* The eye changes refractive power to focus on near objects by a process called accommodation (Vaughan, Asbury, & Riordan-Eva, 1995). Individuals with accommodation problems will not be able to hold items close to their eyes, may complain of headaches when doing near-vision tasks, and may have fluctuating vision when working at close distances.
- *Fixation:* Fixating is the act of holding one's gaze on a particular target. People with fixation problems will be unable to move their gaze from one place to another easily or will lose their place frequently while attempting to read.
- *Tracking:* Tracking is the ability to follow a moving object or target with the eyes, and is also the skill involved in following a line of type across and locating the next line. Rehabilitation teachers should look for awkwardness in following moving objects when assessing tracking skills.
- *Binocularity* and *convergence:* Binocularity is the ability to focus both eyes on one object and fuse the two images into one. Convergence refers to the process of directing the visual axes of the eyes to a near point. Difficulties in both abilities manifest themselves in similar ways: awkwardness in picking up objects, double vision, crossed eyes, inability to bring the eyes together, avoidance of near-vision tasks, and an abnormal amount of head turning are common signs.
- *Scanning:* Scanning is the ability to search for and locate items such as objects in the

environment or words or lines on a page. Problems in scanning are common. They are usually the result of visual field deficiencies and are manifested by unusual head movements, inability to move the gaze from one object to another, bumping into or tripping over objects, and difficulty seeing large items or colors.

- *Visual-motor coordination:* If the client exhibits poor hand-eye coordination, visual-motor coordination may be faulty.
- *Figure-ground perception:* Limited figure-ground skills will be demonstrated by an inability to find one object among many, difficulty finding objects right in front of the individual, and generally overlooking detail.
- *Depth and space perception:* Depth and space problems show up in poor hand-eye coordination and improper sequencing of letters when reading.

Observation of a client's general behavior yields useful information regarding visual abnormalities and gives some indication of his or her visual acuity. In order to pinpoint the client's ability to function visually, however, it is necessary to conduct some actual measurements. These will yield rough numeric estimates of visual acuity for the clinical low vision team, and, just as important, give the rehabilitation teacher specific information on the client's ability to function visually.

Measurement

Distance Vision Assessment

Carter (1983b) suggested several methods that can be used to make informal determinations of acuity. He recommended that these be done under existing lighting conditions, but that subjective data relating to light intensity and direction should be recorded. Everyday objects, such as a notebook or appointment book, can be used to make a rough determination of the acuity of distance vision. The object is moved toward the client, starting from a distance of about 10 feet, and two measurements are reported to the low vision clinician: the greatest dimension of the object (its height or width at its largest point) and the distance from the object to the eye in feet when it is first seen.

Distance acuity can also be determined by using one of the charts designed for that purpose. The most common among them are the familiar Snellen, Feinbloom, and New York Lighthouse charts (see Resources section), but the rehabilitation teacher should consult the low vision clinical team for their recommendation. Regardless of which is used, the examiner should have the client attempt to identify the largest figure on the chart with the worse eye at a distance of 10 feet (Carter, 1983b). If it cannot be identified at that distance, the examiner should move the chart closer to the client until he or she can just identify the largest figure. If the chart cannot conveniently be moved, the client should be instructed to walk toward the chart until he or she can just

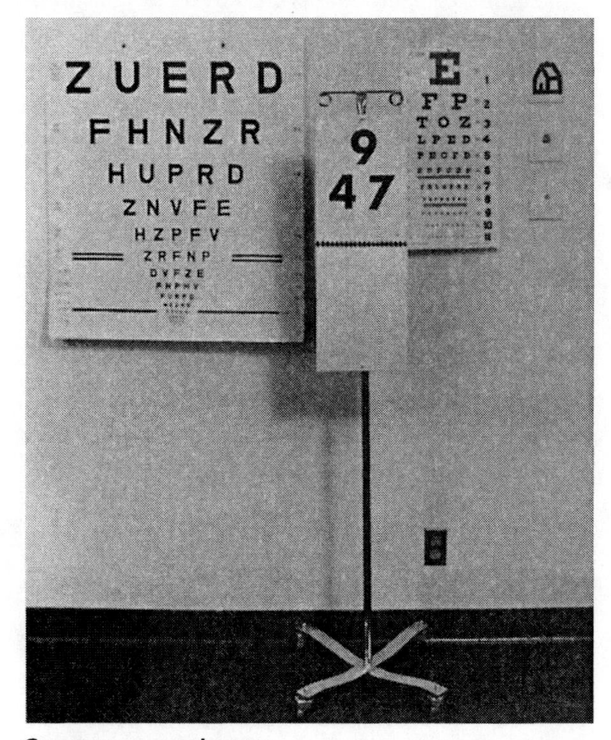

Common eye charts.

identify the largest figure. The distance at which the figure is identified should be recorded as the numerator and the size of the figure as the denominator (for example, a 20/400 letter identified at 3 feet would indicate an acuity of 3/400). The better eye should be examined next, then both eyes together (binocular acuity). Natural lighting should be used, and the head position should be chosen by the client (Carter, 1983b).

Near-Point Vision Assessment

Near-point acuity and functional ability can be determined in a similar manner to assessing distance vision, and this assessment is especially useful for the kinds of skills taught by rehabilitation teachers. Environmental conditions, especially the degree and direction of lighting, should be noted. Also, since reading is the most important near-point task for most people, standard size letters should be used as the target. The person being tested should hold the reading material at whatever working distance he or she is most comfortable.

Figure 6.1 lists some common reading materials and their average print sizes that can be used for this purpose. A functional assessment can also include checking to see which household items, such as bills and canned good labels, the client can read.

Near-point test charts are also available from numerous sources, but clinicians should be consulted before choosing one. In the special circumstance that the person being tested is illiterate, a chart that uses symbols instead of letters should be used.

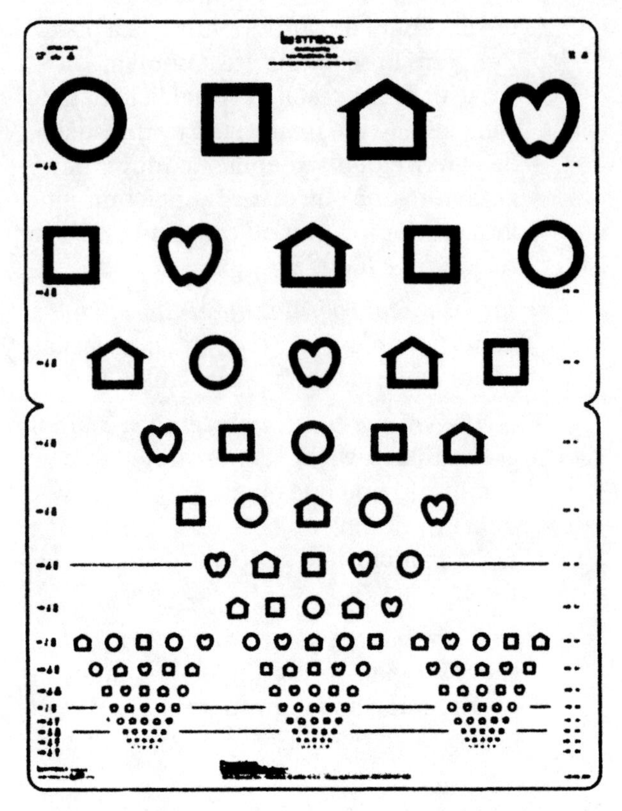

Charts that use symbols, such as these LEA Symbols, can be used with children or adults who do not read letters.

Reading Material	Average Type Size
Want ads	5 point
Bible	6 point
Telephone book	6 point
Newspaper articles	7 point
Adult-level books	10–12 point
Large-print books	18 point

Figure 6.1. Common Reading Materials and Their Average Type Sizes

Visual Field Assessment

The area that can be seen by the eye without shifting the gaze is known as the visual field. Normal visual fields in each eye are approximately 60 degrees to the nasal side, 90 degrees to the temporal side, 50 degrees superior (above), and 70 degrees inferior (below) the center of a fixation point (Carter, 1983b)). There is a small blind spot where the optic nerve leaves the retina to reach the visual cortex of the brain.

Perhaps the most useful information about the size and functioning area of the visual field and the effect on the individual with low vision is gained through observation. Many of the abnormalities described in the section on observational assessment stem from field limitations. Loss of peripheral vision causes individuals to try to maximize their vision by moving their small field of view around to scan the environment. Loss of central vision is often manifested by attempts to see around the affected area. If such behaviors as head tilting, excessive scanning, and fixing the gaze away from the object being observed are present, this indicates a restricted central field that is interfering with the acuity test, and the examiner should note the behaviors along with the acuity measurement. The visual field assessment should then follow the acuity testing.

Confrontation Field Testing. One of the simplest informal measures of visual field for peripheral measurements is termed confrontation field testing. The subject is placed facing the tester at a distance of 20 inches or one-half meter and asked to fix his or her gaze on the tester's nose, occluding (covering) first one eye and then the other. The tester makes sure that the gaze remains fixed, while he or she moves a highly visible object in the size range of 10 to 20 millimeters in a semicircular fashion from behind the subject's head to the tester's face, keeping the target at the same distance from the subject's eye. The subject indicates when he or she first perceives the object. The tester passes the target in and out of the person's field of view several times until the subject's peripheral field is determined. If the visual field is restricted to the circumference of the face at this distance, it is probably an indication that the individual's visual field is about 15 degrees, and he or she would be considered legally blind.

Chalkboard Tangent Screen. The chalkboard tangent screen is a useful tool for measuring central fields (Carter, 1983b). The subject is asked to fix his or her gaze one eye at a time on a dot on a chalkboard 1 meter away. If the subject cannot see the dot on the chalkboard in the center of the visual field, a large *X* can be drawn on the board, and he or she should attempt to fixate on the point at which they intersect. The examiner then passes a target of a highly contrasting color from the outer perimeter of the subject's visual field toward the center at 14 to 16 different locations around the board. As the subject indicates when he or she first sees the object, the examiner marks each spot on the board. The test is most accurate if the target is the smallest that the person being tested can see at that distance. The examiner can reproduce the resulting graphic representation of the subject's central vision on paper. If the chalkboard test is not practical in the client's home, a simple tangent screen can be constructed from a dark cloth and other materials.

Grid Testing. A similar near-point test of central field vision can be done using standard graph paper placed 14 inches from the subject. Again, the subject fixes on a central mark, and reports whether any part of the chart looks wavy, distorted, or missing. In an informal visual assessment, this test can serve as an early warning of central field damage and give a rough indication of where the damage is located. In the clinical setting, this test is known as the Amsler grid (Carter, 1983b) (see Figure 6.2).

Color Discrimination. Color discrimination is such a common problem for those with cataracts and other eye pathologies that an informal test should be conducted. Color discrimination functionally affects many people each day when they attempt to identify clothing. Although it will not serve for clinical purposes, an informal assess-

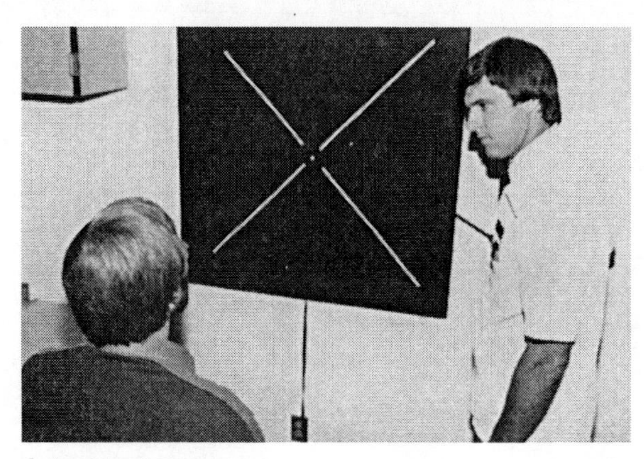

A tangent screen.

ment can be made by asking clients to identify the color details of their own clothing or home decor or of colored sheets of paper under conditions of good illumination.

TRAINING FOR PEOPLE WITH LOW VISION

Once assessment of the client's functional vision is complete and the clinical team has concluded its work, the rehabilitation teacher can begin teaching adaptive techniques and use of any prescribed low vision devices. Many clients receive limited training with their new device in the clinical setting, but rehabilitation teachers can continue the training in the client's everyday environment while the client performs everyday tasks.

People who have some functional vision often have discovered many techniques for enhancing their vision by the time a rehabilitation teacher first sees them. Indeed, as is the case in all areas of rehabilitation teaching, clients often have created new and novel ways of accomplishing tasks that will add to the instructor's repertoire. Many clients, however, will have no knowledge of adaptive skills. For them, daily chores can be monumental obstacles that can discourage experimentation and slow the process of recovering their independence and self-image, and training them to be as efficient as they can possibly be will expedite the rehabilitation process.

As discussed earlier, illumination, contrast, and size are the major variables determining environmental visibility. All three should be considered in the training regimen.

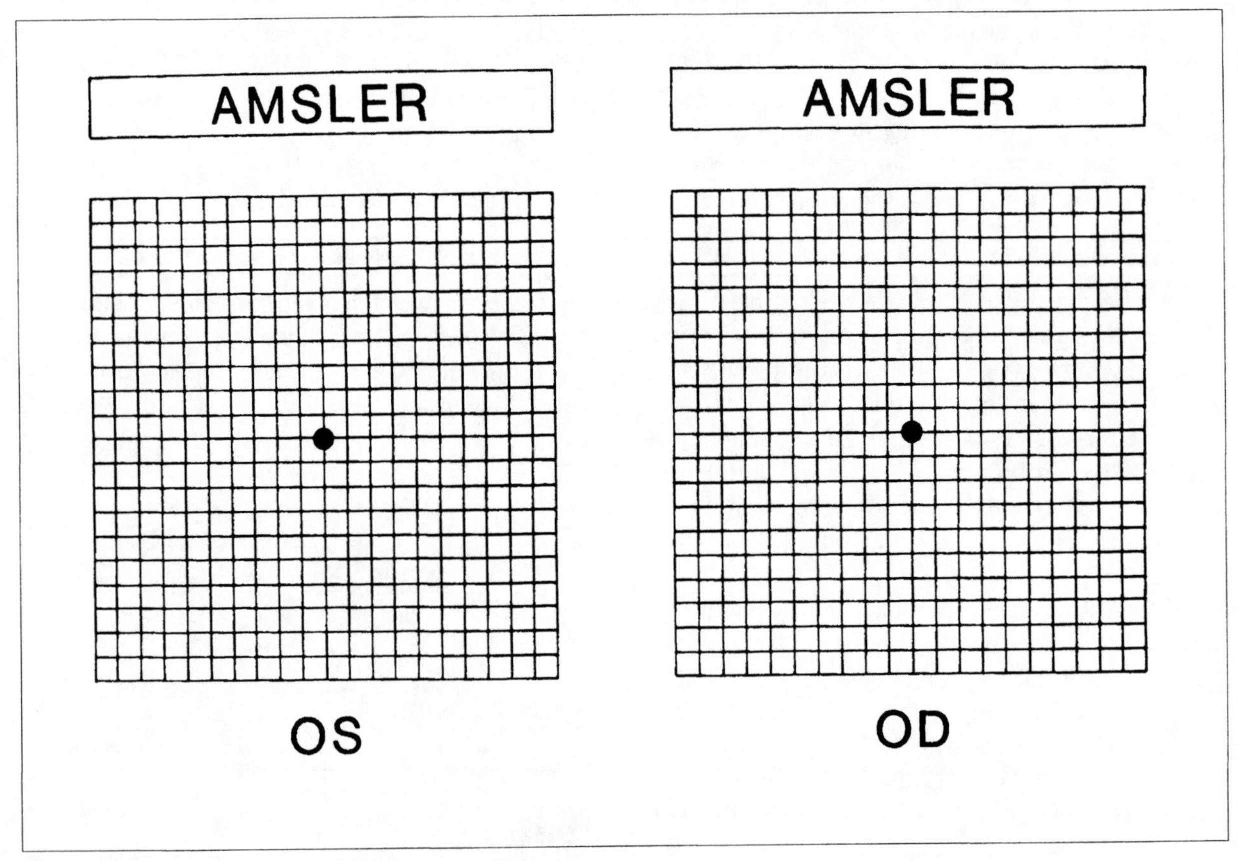

Figure 6.2. An Amsler Grid
The Amsler grid is used to test central field vision.

Illumination

Training related to illumination consists of assisting the learner to determine the best types, intensity, and placement of lights, and teaching him or her to recognize the effects and sources of glare. Reading, writing, performing food preparation, or working on a craft project are good exercises for this purpose. The rehabilitation teacher and client can experiment with different natural and commercial light sources, light intensities, directions of light source, and absorptive backgrounds. In addition, particularly if the client is photophobic, the rehabilitation teacher should try different colors and strengths of sunglasses recommended by the low vision team. When clients fully understand these concepts, they should be encouraged to assess their lighting needs room by room. For more details about such an assessment, Dickman (1983) provides a thorough discussion of environmental modifications.

Contrast

The rehabilitation teacher can make similar use of tasks involving daily living skills and written communication to demonstrate the effects of variation in contrast on visibility. For example, it is easy to show the effects of contrast on ease of mobility within the home by adding contrasting accents such as skid-proof throw rugs, table coverings, and the like (Dickman, 1983).

Size and Optical Devices

Modifying the size of objects to be dealt with in the daily routine is generally more difficult than varying contrast. Some items, such as the printed word, yarn for knitting, or playing cards, are readily available in larger form for easier viewing, and the client can be made aware of the phenomenon of relative-size magnification, but the major way of increasing size is through optics.

Training is especially important in the use of near-point low vision devices, because they are difficult to focus for new users and commonly restrict the field of view, so that users experience the same problems as do people with a peripheral field loss. Consequently, training entails instruction in the proper methods of focusing and in locating, tracking, and fixating on the task to be viewed. Watson and Berg (1983) describe training techniques for developing these skills.

Focusing

To teach focusing of low vision devices, Watson and Berg (1983) suggest that the trainer occlude the individual's worse eye and instruct him or her to use only the center of the device. The effect of the focal length of the optical device on visibility is demonstrated by moving a target in and out of focus. If the client experiences problems in focusing, the instructor can attach a stiff object cut in a length equal to the focal distance of the lens to the front of it to provide a physical reminder of where to hold the lens relative to the object, or the client can temporarily switch to a stand magnifier, which places the lens the correct distance away from reading material.

Locating

Locating a target when using a near-point device can be difficult for many clients because the area that is magnified is small. The difficulties encountered are much akin to those experienced when trying to tactilely locate a raised symbol with a fingertip. The field of view for searching is small and so is the target, which makes finding it through random searching within a larger area extremely tedious and difficult. As with tactile search methods (see Chapter 12), systematic patterns are helpful. For example, to locate the beginning of the first line of print on a page, the individual finds the left edge of the paper or the binding of the book, moves up to the top of the page and then down and to the right to begin reading. Watson and Berg (1983) also suggested placing the target on a stand and having the client find the target with the naked eye, place his or her finger on it, and then locate the target using the aid by following the arm down to it.

People who continue to have problems in locating targets after these interventions are presented should perhaps be trained by using a bioptic system (see the section on telescopes earlier in this chapter) so that they can locate the target through the nonmicroscopic lens and then drop the head a bit to view it through the microscope. Or, the target can be placed in a window with a red border above and a green one below, so that the individual can use the association of color with the upper or lower boundaries of the object to indicate which way to shift his or her gaze to locate the target (Watson & Berg, 1983).

Tracking

Problems in tracking are associated primarily with the task of reading. They are manifested by the inability to move from the end of one line to the beginning of the next. Again, this can be likened to the tactile task required in reading braille, and Watson and Berg (1983) suggest tracking techniques that are virtually the same as those used in braille instruction (see Chapter 7). At the end of the print line, the client visually follows the line just read back to its beginning and drops down to the next line or places a finger at the beginning of the line as a place marker and returns to it when the line is completed. Watson and Berg also suggest using a typoscope or ruler to move down from line to line. In addition, exercises can be utilized to practice tracking. As in braille teaching, the client simply tracks lines without reading them or tracks a series of solid horizontal lines with the low vision device. If the instructor places a number or word at the end of the line for the client to read, it is easy to determine whether each line was tracked successfully.

Fixating

Fixating, which is the act of holding one's gaze on a particular target, is especially difficult for people with central field losses, because they must fix their gaze not on the target but on a spot that allows the target to be viewed by the peripheral retina. The technique of fixating on a spot away from the target that allows the person to see it is termed *eccentric viewing*. In this process, the central blind spot, or scotoma, is in effect moved to the side of the object to be viewed. Again, a technique such as eccentric viewing may have been discovered by client prior to the rehabilitation teacher's intervention. With some experimentation, the most appropriate eccentric viewing point can be determined. Practice with reading, writing, or daily living tasks will reinforce eccentric viewing. Using large targets with good color contrast is suggested during the training phase.

CCTVs

In general, the difficulty of using optical low vision devices increases significantly as the power of the device increases. The difficulties of keeping an object in focus, tolerating close working distances, and dealing with the extremely restricted visual fields of high-powered magnifiers discourage many people from using them. Consequently, when a client requires high degrees of magnification, CCTV systems become a feasible option. Training programs in using CCTVs stress manipulation of the controls and of the materials under the camera. Problems of locating, tracking, and fixation are also inherent with CCTVs, and training regimens should include the appropriate adaptive techniques. (Watson and Berg, 1983, p. 348, present a detailed description of the training sequence, and a sample lesson plan for teaching the CCTV appears in this chapter.)

Training with the CCTV is similar to that for other magnification devices. The control features, such as those governing focus, magnification, contrast, brightness, background and foreground color, and electronic text marking are usually taught first. The more difficult portion of training involves the manipulation of the X-Y table, which is the platform that holds the material to be viewed on some CCTVs. The user must become accustomed to the relationship between the movement of the material on the X-Y table

Teaching the Use of a CCTV

I. Objectives
   A. When presented with textbooks and reference books, the learner will use the CCTV to locate specified sections quickly and efficiently.
   B. When presented with reading materials with various sizes of type, the learner will use the CCTV to read them at a speed of 40 wpm and be able to describe their contents.

II. Materials
   A. CCTV
   B. Reading materials
      1. 24-point handmade print or Feinbloom Reading Card
      2. 18-point print, from large-print *Reader's Digest* or other large-print book
      3. 10–12 point print documents, such as standard books
      4. 8–10 point print, such as paperback books
      5. 7-point print, such as newspapers
      6. 6-point print, such as a telephone directory or want ads
      7. A standard dictionary

III. Assessment
   A. Can the learner read enlarged or magnified print?
   B. Can the learner use other near-point reading aids?
   C. What types of reading materials were read before the vision loss?
   D. What types of reading materials will be read vocationally?

IV. Procedure
   A. Uses: Explain reading, writing, vocational, and personal uses.
   B. Orientation to parts of the CCTV
      1. Have the learner locate the significant parts of the CCTV.
      2. Point out following if missed:
         a. Gross parts: camera, monitor, table
         b. Monitor: on/off switch, contrast, brightness, polarity switch
         c. Camera: focusing, magnification, line markers, height controls, aperture
         d. X–Y table: margin settings
      3. Operation
         a. Determine best magnification.
            (1) Demonstrate the highest magnification.
            (2) Decrease the magnification until the learner cannot read.
            (3) Increase magnification again until the learner can read.
            (4) Repeat procedure under reverse polarity.
            (5) Record working distance and magnification setting.
         b. Familiarize the learner with reading.
            (1) Have the learner read 24-point print while the instructor tracks.
            (2) Familiarize the learner with fixation methods if necessary.
            (3) Familiarize the learner with controls.
               (a) Preset the device at best visibility and have the learner turn the machine on.

(continued on next page)

Teaching the CCTV (continued)

(b) Have the learner experiment with and determine the best contrast.
(c) Have the learner experiment with and determine the best brightness and contrast.
(d) Have the learner experiment with and determine the better polarity.
(e) Have the learner experiment with and determine the best aperture setting.
(f) Have the learner experiment with and determine the best magnification.
(g) Have the learner experiment with and determine the best focus.
(h) Have the learner experiment with and determine the best relationships among controls.

4. Familiarize the learner with the X–Y table.
   a. Choose a nonglossy picture large enough for the learner to see with the unaided eye.
   b. Show it to the learner and have him or her describe it and place it on the X–Y table.
   c. Have the learner touch the table and ask him or her to follow its movements while viewing the screen.
   d. Move the table, showing parts of picture, and have the learner describe the relationship between movement and image.
   e. Have the learner manipulate the table to locate picture parts.
5. Familiarize the learner with location methods.
   a. Place a document with 18-point print on the table.
   b. Have the learner locate the left edge of paper.
   c. Have the learner move to the top of page.
   d. Have the learner move down and to the right to locate the first sentence.
   e. Have the learner repeat until comfortable.
   f. Replace the document with a page containing two to three 1" x 1" symbols.
   g. Demonstrate an "X" searching pattern by moving the table diagonally from top left to bottom right and from bottom left to top right of the page.
   h. Have the learner locate each symbol until comfortable.
6. Familiarize the learner with scanning.
   a. Place a document on the table that contains a series of horizontal 1-inch-thick lines that are preceded by and followed by a different number.
   b. Demonstrate tracking from left to right, retracing that line and dropping to the next.
   c. Have the learner repeat the procedure until comfortable.
   d. Replace document with double-spaced reading material in 18-point print.
   e. Have the learner read and track until comfortable.
7. Familiarize the learner with other print sizes and styles.
8. Familiarize the learner with the functions unique to that particular CCTV.

V. Memoranda

A. If scanning is a problem, use a typoscope or electronic line markers on the CCTV.

(continued on next page)

Teaching the CCTV (continued)

B. Reassess the learner's lowest useful magnification after some practice.
C. The learner may need to cover one eye.
D. Use background lighting, but eliminate screen glare.
E. Point out the cost of this device at the beginning of instruction.

VI. Evaluation
A. Have the learner find five specified sections in a standard textbook or novel.
B. Have the learner locate five specified words in a dictionary.
C. Have the learner read a passage from a standardized reading series and determine the number of words read per minute and the degree of comprehension.

VII. Assignments
A. Have the learner practice locating passages of a pleasure book.
B. Have the learner practice reading a pleasure book for longer periods each day.

and the resulting image on the television or video screen. This takes much practice, since a movement of the table in one direction allows the viewer to see the part of the reading material on the opposite side of the table. For example, moving the table to the right brings the left side of the target into view, and moving it toward the viewer displays the target's upper edge. Training is especially important with these devices because developing familiarity with these movements can be difficult for the untrained user.

Stress

Since there is tedium involved in learning to use one's remaining vision and to manipulate optical devices, the instructor should be aware of the effects of physical and mental stress on both the client's visual ability and skill performance. Increasing muscle tension restricts blood flow and can affect eye physiology and muscle control (Huxley, 1975). Therefore, the instructor should allow for periods of relaxation during a training phase consisting of short sessions. Nonoptical devices such as a gooseneck lamp and a reading stand or combination cushion-bookrest to support the reading material in a comfortable position are helpful in avoiding muscle tension.

TACTILE VS. LOW VISION ADAPTATIONS

At the beginning of this chapter, the retreat from the historical emphasis on teaching all visually impaired people as though they were totally blind was described. As the pendulum swung away from this approach, however, the backlash led many professionals to dismiss out of hand any notion of using tactile adaptations for people with low vision—to reject, for example, the idea of occluding (blindfolding) low vision learners to improve their "blindness skills" (LaGrow & Ponchillia, 1989).

Rather than considering the question of whether to teach tactile *or* visual techniques—a false dichotomy similar to the braille-or-print issue—it is important for rehabilitation teachers to consider each individual's situation. If a person with low vision can use her or his vision to read recipes and package labels but has a visual field defect that causes problems in locating items in the cupboard or on the countertop, then lessons should include both visual and tactile training. The cook can then utilize his or her remaining vision for the reading tasks and exercise tactile search patterns to locate elusive items. In that event, an occluder would be used initially, with the learner's agreement and understanding, to reinforce tactile methods.

In recent years, the issue of whether to encourage persons with low vision to read using braille or print has provoked renewed discussion. Rehabilitation teachers can help the low vision learner decide whether learning extensive braille is desirable, basing their input on knowledge of the learner's present and anticipated visual reading skills and the possible results that could be expected from learning braille. The factors that go into this decision are discussed next in Chapter 7, which also describes the instructional process once the decision is made to teach braille or another form of tactile communication to a client.

CHAPTER 7

Braille and Other Tactile Forms of Communication

KEY CONCEPTS IN THIS CHAPTER

- **Common tactile reading and labeling systems used by individuals with visual impairments**
- **The history of tactile reading systems**
- **Six tactile systems that utilize the braille cell**
- **The Fishburne Alphabet and its uses**
- **Methods of determining labeling and reading media**
- **Methods of assessing braille reading potential**
- **Major braille textbooks**
- **Proper braille reading methods**
- **Affective aspects of teaching braille**

When an individual experiences a loss of vision that has a significant impact on the way in which he or she performs activities and obtains information, finding alternate ways of performing activities is essential for independent living. The rehabilitation teacher's role in helping the individual develop such alternatives is critical.

As significant methods of communication in our society, reading and writing are cornerstones of an independent life for clients and thus are among the primary activities that the rehabilitation teacher must address. Because these tasks ordinarily are so dependent on visual input, it is essential for the rehabilitation teacher to help the client determine whether visual, auditory, or tactile methods or a combination of all three are appropriate alternatives. Much of the literature regarding choice of reading medium relates to the education of children, but Caton (1994), Koenig and Holbrook (1991, 1993), and Rex, Koenig, Wormsley, and Baker (1994) offer discussions relevant to teaching adults.

Low vision devices are key components of a reading system for many clients, as are braille and tape recorders. When helping clients make decisions about appropriate media for reading, rehabilitation teachers should bear in mind that reading can be classified into two categories: spot reading, used to read labels, address lists, or thermostat settings; and extensive reading, or reading of longer texts, such as books or magazine articles. Although an adaptation may work well for spot reading, another may be needed for extensive reading. For example, one 80-year-old woman with low vision and no color perception, who lives alone, uses recorded books to read for pleasure, her low vision magnifier to read food labels, and braille labels to identify her clothing.

Determining which form to use for spot reading is a matter of observing which method is most effective. If a client can read canned-goods labels with a low vision adaptation, the choice to use vision is simple. However, determining media for extensive reading is more complex, involving consideration of the client's reading speed with a low vision adaptation, how long he or she can tolerate visual reading, the stability of his or her eye condition, the client's tactile sensitivity, and his or her adjustment to sight loss. The average braille reader reads at a rate of 90 to 100 words per minute (Nolan, 1966), and auditory readers read approximately two times faster (Foulke, 1980). Therefore, the rehabilitation teacher can compare these rates with the client's reading speed using a low vision adaptation to see which would produce a better result. Someone who can read from 100 to 200 words per minute using a low vision device would likely do extensive reading with sight. However, if the client cannot tolerate reading more than a few minutes at a time, or additional loss of sight is imminent, an alternative to visual reading is indicated.

Because rehabilitation teaching clients are usually adults and accustomed to making their own decisions, they should be thoroughly involved in the choice of reading medium. Even if all indications point to the need for an alternative to visual reading, clients who have not adjusted well to their loss of sight may be resistant to braille or even auditory reading. The rehabilitation teacher may need to continue work with visual reading while introducing braille in order to help the client make the transition.

If vision is not an option for extensive reading, a choice must also be made between recordings and braille. Once the decision is made to pursue an alternative to sight reading, the rehabilitation teacher will conduct an assessment of the client's potential for reading braille to help make that decision. In the case of older adults, an alternative to visual reading usually involves a combination of extensive reading with recordings and spot reading with braille. The occasional adventitiously blind client who learns to read extensively in braille usually starts by using recordings to read immediately following the loss of sight and continues to work on braille reading until he or she is proficient enough to read well tactilely.

HISTORY AND BACKGROUND

The development of tactile methods for reading and writing, beginning in the late 1700s, was a monumental achievement that changed the lives of people with severely limited vision, providing for the first time an independent means of literacy, communication, and education. Numerous forms of tactile reading and writing modes have been introduced over the past 200 years, but only a few have survived.

The early educators Valentin Haüy of Paris and Samuel Howe of Boston (see Chapter 2) both favored raised conventional letters as the basis of a tactile system for communication. Haüy's system, called "negative typecasting," produced impressions on paper by striking the paper with much force; Howe's system was a blocky modification called Boston line type (Lowenfeld, 1973). Dr. William Moon, the first home teacher, subsequently developed a modification of raised capital letters in the mid-1800s that became known as Moon type. In his efforts, Moon eliminated parts of some letters and added new ones to enhance their tactile legibility (Koestler, 1976). The use of identifiable forms of raised print received strong support from school administrators, since sighted teachers of blind children did not require any special training to work with raised print, and it was also more familiar to sighted benefactors who might be willing to donate money for raised-print teaching materials (Dixon, 1990).

Simultaneous with the development of the raised-print systems, several systems of raised dots were being developed, based on the works of Louis Braille. These systems ultimately resulted in two forms, including New York Point, which was utilized in the early days of teaching but is no longer in common use, and braille, the medium known by modern-day rehabilitation teachers (National Library Service for the Blind and Physically Handicapped, 1983).

The version of braille used in the United States and Canada is English braille, American edition. Although Moon type is still popular in the United Kingdom, where it is distributed through the

Royal National Institute for the Blind (Harris, 1981), only the tactile systems that remain in popular use in North America will be addressed here. These are braille, the Fishburne Alphabet, raised block letters, and tactile symbols. Although all of these systems have important uses for people with visual impairments, only braille is widely used for extensive reading and writing; hence, the instructional methods presented in this chapter focus on the teaching of braille.

TACTILE SYSTEMS

Braille

Braille has been in use for more than 150 years, has survived a verbal and financial battle for support termed "the War of the Dots" (Irwin, 1955/1970; Lowenfeld, Abel, & Hatlen, 1974), and has been shown to be more effective than other tactile systems (Burklen, 1932; Dixon, 1990; Maxfield, 1928; Zickel & Hooper, 1957).

Braille is a punctiform system based on a "cell" composed of six dots arranged in two columns and three rows (see Figure 7.1). The dots are numbered from 1 to 3 down the left side of the cell and from 4 to 6 on the right. Combinations of these six dots represent alphabet letters and other symbols. Teaching the braille code is beyond the scope of this book. The National Library Service for the Blind and Physically Handicapped (NLS), Braille Development Section, and other sources (see Resources section) have instructional materials suitable for teachers.

Because the braille dot system allows much flexibility, it has been used as the basic unit in six braille "codes," including:

- grade 1 braille, composed of the alphabet letters, numbers as used in literature, and punctuation marks
- grade 2 braille, including all of grade 1 plus nearly 200 "contractions" that are representations of groups of letters or whole words
- grade 3 braille, containing even more contractions than grade 2, generally used for personal notetaking
- the Nemeth Code of Braille Mathematics and Scientific Notation (see Chapter 11), a special form designed to be used in science and mathematics
- the braille music code, representing musical notation
- braille computer code, which reflects characters used by computers and is used primarily by computer programmers and users of assistive computer technology (see Chapter 9).

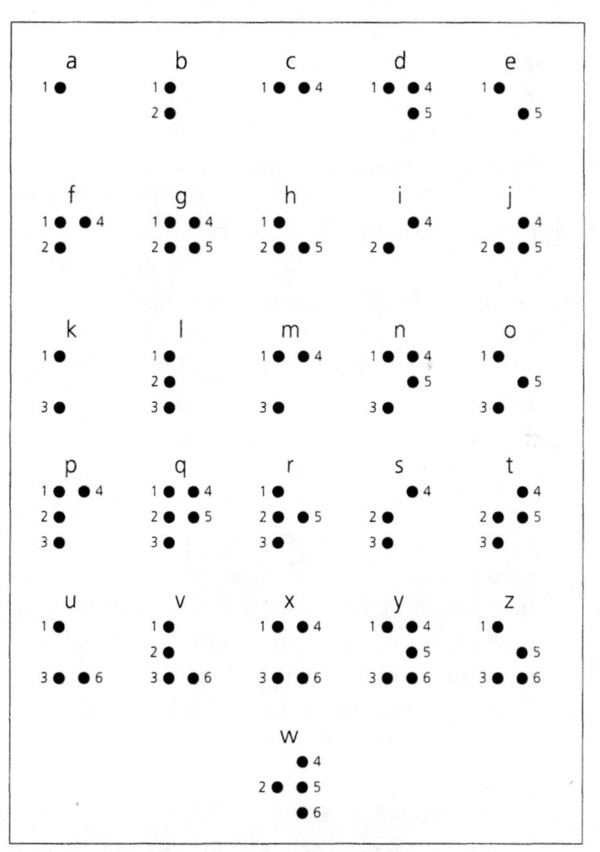

Figure 7.1. The Braille Alphabet
The first 10 letters (*a–j*) are formed by dots in the upper part of the cell. The next 10 (*k–t*) are identical, except that dot 3 is added. The final 5 letters (skipping *w*) follow the same pattern, but add dots 3 and 6. Because *w* is not in the French alphabet, it was added later for English braille.

Grades 1, 2, and 3 are literary codes. Although all six braille codes are extremely useful, only the first two are commonly taught by rehabilitation teachers because adults with acquired severe visual limitations seldom use the others (youngsters who need to learn braille codes are generally taught in the education system rather than in the rehabilitation system).

Braille is produced in three sizes, including standard, jumbo, and large cell. Jumbo braille uses both an enlarged cell and an enlarged dot, whereas large-cell braille uses standard-size dots in an enlarged cell, with increased spacing between dots, cells, and lines. The enlarged forms were developed to meet the needs of learners with decreased tactile sensitivity. Large-cell braille provides a high degree of tactile sensation, and it may be destined to phase out jumbo braille for those with impaired tactile ability because it appears to be more readable (Baskerville, 1989).

Braille has proven to be a useful tool in the rehabilitation process. Clients who are unable to read print efficiently can utilize braille to store and retrieve information such as telephone numbers, addresses, and recipes. Braille can also be used to label clothing, medication bottles, or cans in the cupboard. It is used for leisure and job-related reading purposes as well, as shown in the following example:

> Fifty-two-year-old George M. operated a greenhouse before losing nearly all of his sight in an automobile accident. His daily routine at the greenhouse included keeping an inventory of fertilizer and pesticides, taking orders from customers by telephone, calling suppliers of the materials he needed, and controlling temperatures in each room of the greenhouse to meet the needs of several varieties of plants. He also interacted with the customers in the office. Although he had discovered that he could meet some of these needs, such as keeping a telephone list of suppliers and customers, with his tape recorder, he had not been able to think of a way to identify personal articles such as his clothing or work-related items such as the chemicals used in the greenhouse, and he could no longer set the thermostats in the greenhouse. After learning the first 10 letters of the alphabet and the braille numbers, he immediately designed braille labeling systems for each of these needs, and he discovered that brailled lists were superior to the recorded ones he had used previously.

Although the usefulness of braille has been questioned by some (see, for example, Mack, 1984), in recent years the importance of braille for the literacy of people with visual impairments has been affirmed (Ponchillia & Kaarlela, 1986; Rex, Koenig, Wormsley, & Baker, 1994; Spungin, n.d.). Although braille has some drawbacks, such as its bulkiness, the limited number of book and magazine titles available, and the slow reading speeds users generally attain, it provides clear benefits. When compared to auditory reading (the use of recorded reading materials, discussed in Chapter 10), braille provides readers with the ability to scan pages quickly, go back to review passages in detail, and be an active rather than passive learner. Braille is the most widely used and accepted of all tactile systems (Etheredge, 1992).

Fishburne Alphabet

The Fishburne Alphabet is an embossed system designed to meet the needs of people with tactile limitations. The Fishburne system uses four basic symbols in a simple repetitive pattern (see Figure 7.2) that is designed to make the alphabet easier to memorize (see Sidebar 7.1). The system is based on five lines consisting of six symbols each (except for the last incomplete line). The symbols on each line utilize an identical pattern. The first letter on a line is a single symbol placed above an imaginary midline; the second letter is a single symbol below the midline; the third letter is represented by the same symbol both above and below; the fourth is a double symbol above; the fifth is a double symbol below; and the sixth is double symbols both above and below. The so-called A line uses dots and represents the

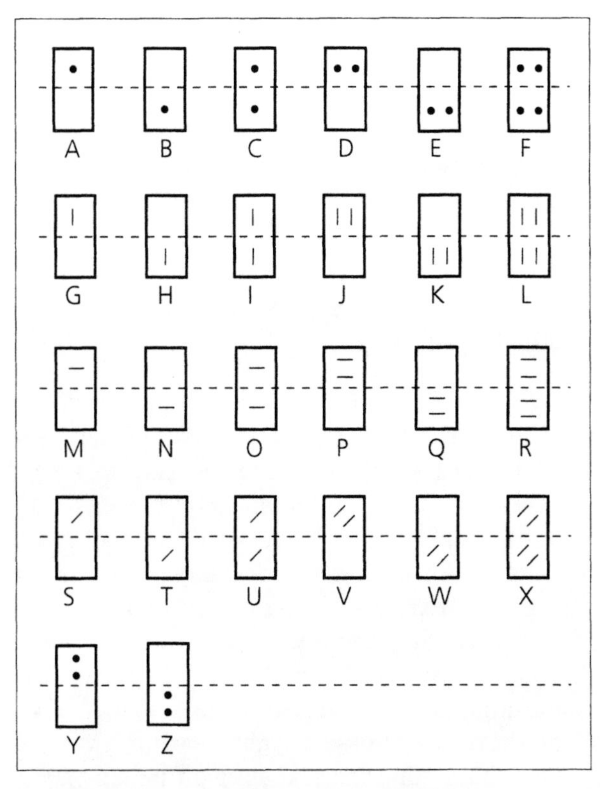

Figure 7.2. The Fishburne Alphabet

Source: Reprinted, by permission of the publisher, from S. E. Newman and A. D. Hall, "Ease of Learning the Braille and Fishburne Alphabets, *Journal of Visual Impairment & Blindness, 81* (1988), p. 148. Copyright © 1988, American Foundation for the Blind.

letters *a* through *f*; the G line uses vertical lines to represent letters *g* through *l*; the M line uses horizontal lines for letters *m* through *r*; the S line uses diagonal lines for letters *s* through *w*; and the Y line uses two dots placed vertically to represent *y* and *z*.

The Fishburne Alphabet is designed only for personal communication; there are no books or other materials published in Fishburne. It provides a useful alternative for labeling and personal communication for adults with limited vision who are unable to learn braille (Shafrath, 1986). Its use is somewhat limited, however, by the manner in which it is produced. The Fishburne embosser is designed for producing individual letters on plastic tape, not for embossing whole words on sheets of paper.

The individual letters can be adhered to 3" x 5" cards to "write" labels, addresses, or messages, or they can be attached to magnetic craft tape to create reusable labels for cans. A kit with embosser, tape cutter, metal slates, instructional tapes, and a complimentary copy of the Fishburne code is available from the supplier, Fishburne Enterprises (see Resources section).

To be independent, Fishburne Alphabet users must possess the fine motor ability to cut 1" x ½" strips of plastic tape, then insert them into the ap-

Learning Fishburne

SIDEBAR 7.1

The systematic structure of the Fishburne Alphabet is said to make the task of learning it easier than learning braille. This assumption was supported by a study comparing the ease of learning braille and the Fishburne Alphabet. Newman and Hall (1988) found that sighted college students performed significantly better in memorizing the symbols of the Fishburne Alphabet than they did with braille symbols. The study raises more questions than it answers (the subjects memorized the symbols visually, not tactilely, for example), and further research is suggested. However, Newman and Hall noted that a number of rehabilitation teachers reported that some of their students who had tactile difficulties and were discouraged about attempts to read braille were sufficiently reinforced by their progress in reading Fishburne that they were more successful when they were later switched back to braille. Newman and Hall suggested that learning Fishburne may be a helpful preliminary task for people who find learning braille difficult.

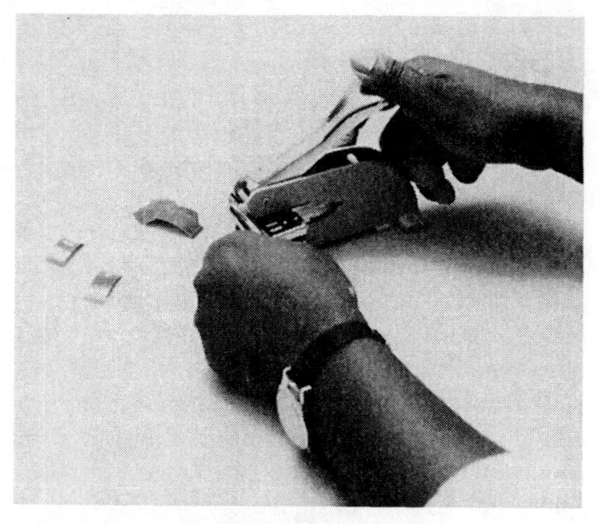

The Fishburne embosser.

propriate area of the embosser to imprint each symbol. Some rehabilitation teachers suggest that individuals who have difficulty with the tactile and fine motor task of writing with the Fishburne Alphabet can still use the system if someone else manages the task of producing a variety of the raised symbols for later use, as was done for Carmen G.

> Carmen G. was a former nurse disabled by complications of diabetes which included total loss of sight. She lived alone and when contacted by a rehabilitation teacher, expressed a need for instruction in adaptive insulin measurement, adaptive kitchen skills (see Chapter 13), and labeling methods. She needed to label clothing and food items and wanted a system for storing telephone numbers and addresses. Braille was introduced, but severe neuropathy affected her tactile sensitivity, hampering her ability to discriminate symbols in either standard or large-cell braille. When the Fishburne Alphabet was introduced as an alternative, Carmen G. was able to discern individual symbols easily. She was able to identify clothing, cans, prescription bottles, and 3" x 5" index cards with names and telephone numbers affixed to them using the Fishburne Alphabet. However, she was not able to successfully manipulate the Fishburne embosser to create the individual letter symbols, so the rehabilitation teacher and a volunteer worked together to emboss a supply of symbols, which were stored in a compartmentalized box of the type used for crafts. Carmen G. could then locate letters to create new labels independently as needed.

Raised Letters

Raised alphabet letters, usually in block form, can also be read tactilely. Their use is especially advantageous because alphabet letters are nearly universally known, particularly by persons with adventitious sight loss. Thus, raised letters require no significant degree of additional learning for those who are already literate in print and can be used for labeling immediately after an individual has lost his or her vision. Raised letters have the same limitations as the Fishburne Alphabet, however: the only embossers available cannot be used for anything other than labeling on 1-inch plastic tape. Even if convenient writing instruments were available, the usefulness of raised letters for extensive reading is questionable, because reading speed is slow since it must be read letter for letter and uses no contractions.

Tactile Symbols

The earliest tactile form of communication for people with severe sight limitations was in all likelihood some form of nonliterary symbols. Today, such systems are generally used by visually impaired people for labeling clothes and other items. The labeling systems used today are as diverse as the people who have invented them. Examples include notches in clothing labels to identify color and style, rubber bands placed around medicine containers in various numbers to identify their contents, plastic models of different foods to indicate the contents of cans or boxes, and the removal of a print label to distinguish identically shaped bottles, such as one of shampoo and another of conditioner. As in the cases of the other nonbraille systems, these special markings are used only for labeling. Labeling and identification systems are discussed in more detail in Chapter 12.

TEACHING BRAILLE READING AND WRITING

Research on braille has demonstrated that braille and print reading are functionally identical, except that the finger is used rather than sight and that the unit of perception is narrower in tactile reading (Kusajima, 1974). Therefore, readers using the tactile sense are less efficient at recognizing characters, scanning documents, tracking lines, or viewing a full of page than readers using the visual sense. As with visual reading, braille reading involves both a sensory and a cognitive component. That is, reading ability is dependent on braille readers' tactile sensitivity and their intellectual capabilities.

The major skills involved in braille reading are (1) the ability to perceive braille characters and to recognize combinations as words (Nolan & Kederis, 1969); (2) linguistic knowledge (Nolan & Kederis, 1969); and (3) efficient use of reading hands and fingers (Foulke, 1991; Rex, Koenig, Wormsley, & Baker, 1994; Wormsley, 1981). Linguistic knowledge allows the reader to predict words and phrases, thus eliminating the need to read all the letters of familiar words. Foulke (1991) reported that strong evidence points to the use of hands and fingers as the most important factor in determining braille reading speed. Having to track lines, move from one line to the next, and preview the reading material tactilely all lead tactile reading to be slower, in general, than visual reading. Whereas sighted readers read an average of 250 to 300 words per minute, Nolan (1966) found the mean reading speed of high school braille readers to be 90 to 120 words per minute, and Lowenfeld, Abel, and Hatlin (1974) found mean braille reading speeds of 116 words per minute for eighth graders in mainstream classes and 149 words per minute for the same grade in residential schools.

In the case of people who have recently lost their vision, reading speed in the early stages of learning braille is tediously slow—perhaps 10 words per minute or less. This initial loss of reading speed, coupled with the painstaking process of training the fingertips to recognize letter shapes, often results in frustration for the learner. These factors contribute to failure rates among would-be braille readers. However, much of the frustration inherent in learning braille can be alleviated if the learner utilizes the most efficient reading methods. It is essential, therefore, that the rehabilitation teacher be familiar with those methods in order to provide the best possible learning situation. There are at least six areas or issues to consider when teaching braille, including assessment, instructional materials, reading skills, speed building, writing skills, and affective aspects of learning.

Assessment

Print-reading skills depend on both the ability of the individual's visual system to discriminate among graphic representations and his or her cognitive capacity to understand what they represent. The basis of braille-reading skills is similar, but the tactile sense replaces the visual one. Therefore, when the rehabilitation teacher conducts an assessment of the client's potential for reading braille, both tactile and conceptual aspects must be assessed separately.

The conceptual assessment generally utilizes a model of a braille cell, which can be purchased or homemade from egg cartons or muffin tins. Tennis balls, ping pong balls, or similar items can be used to illustrate the concept of dot arrangement to a new learner. Regardless of the model used, the assessment consists of a brief explanation of the layout of the braille cell, a description of the first few letters of the braille alphabet, and an evaluation of the learner's ability to read randomly presented letters and to formulate letters on the model. Because the vast majority of clients will have learned to read print as children, few will have difficulty conceptualizing what the braille letters represent.

The medium for tactile assessment is generally the braille cell itself, but other tactile discrimination materials, such as different textures of sandpaper or fabric, could be used. The use of actual braille cells is most practical, however, because use of actual braille provides a direct measure of what is to be learned, which leaves less chance for error. Furthermore, using the braille cell makes more efficient use of instructional time because the assessment also serves to introduce the braille system.

Assessment using braille cells is best accomplished by using symbols with three dots or less, because reading errors increase significantly when cells contain four or more dots (Nolan & Kederis, 1969). Increasing the space between dots also increases reading efficiency. The rehabilitation teacher presents the individual with these cells, and asks him or her to describe the features of the cell, such as number of dots and their relative positions. For example, an *e* can be described as "two dots forming a diagonal from top left to bottom right."

No standardized measures yet indicate the level of accuracy an individual must achieve during an assessment that would predict later success in learning braille. However, it can be assumed that those who are able to read 7 or 8 out of 10 letters during an initial assessment will be able to utilize the system. Readers who perform at lower levels might be given tactile training until they reach such levels. The *Read Again* program (Caton, Pesler & Bradley, 1990), which helps to instill proper reading skills before actual instruction in braille reading begins, is ideal for such purposes.

If the client's tactile ability is limited to an extent that precludes the use of standard braille, similar assessments utilizing the larger forms of braille, the Fishburne Alphabet, or raised letters should be undertaken. However, because these systems are of limited usefulness, every effort should be made to remediate tactile limitations so that standard braille can be utilized before proceeding to the alternatives.

In addition to considering learning ability and tactile ability, a full assessment of braille reading potential will also include consideration of the learner's age, previous reading level, and goals with regard to braille. All five factors are taken into account when selecting instructional materials.

Selection of Instructional Materials

The teacher's selection of the proper instructional materials affects the client's ultimate success in learning braille. A number of texts and reading systems have been published to teach braille, and each has useful and unique qualities that differentiate it. Braille textbooks are typically written to suit particular ages, reading levels, and learning abilities. Their content, use of repetition in exercises, and even the material on which the book is embossed can vary from text to text. In addition, some texts begin their initial lessons with contracted braille rather than with the braille alphabet. It is important for the rehabilitation teacher to match the characteristics of the text to the needs and characteristics of the learner. Rehabilitation teachers will also want to consider whether a text provides such useful features as a teacher's manual in print or braille and other additional teaching materials such as writing exercises on tape and whether extra spacing is used in the early lessons, which is especially helpful for individuals with tactile deficits (Baskerville, 1989). Table 7.1 presents a listing developed by the Adult Braille Literacy Empowerment Project (1995) of the American Foundation for the Blind of the most commonly used textbooks and their characteristics that can assist the rehabilitation teacher in making the most appropriate choice.

If a person's goal is to learn only grade 1 braille, all textbooks are not appropriate. In general, it would appear that for learners whose assessments and ultimate goals clearly indicate a need for grade 2 braille, the rehabilitation teacher might choose a text that introduces grade 2 symbols early on interspersed with alphabet letters. However, those whose goals are not yet clearly de-

Table 7.1. Commonly Used Textbooks for Teaching Braille to Adults

Title	Author	Publisher	Latest Publication Date	Target Population	Medium	Levels of Braille Code Covered	Comments
ABCs of Braille	Bernard M. Krebs	American Printing House for the Blind	1982	Children and beginning adult learners	Braille and print (line by line)*	Grades 1 and 2 interspersed	Provides initial tracking and tactile training practices
ABLK Method of Teaching Braille	Bernice G. Robins	Canadian National Institute for the Blind	1994	Deaf-blind adults	Braille text; braille and print manual	Grade 1 only	
Beginning Braille	Michael Tobin	Royal National Institute for the Blind	1987	Independent adult learners	Braille text; print manual; taped instructions	Grades 1 and 2	In British braille.
Beginning Braille for Adults	Mabel Nading and Romona Walhof	National Federation of the Blind	1986	Independent adult learners	Braille text; taped instructions	Grades 1 and 2	
Braille: A Different Approach (Arkansas Materials)	Johnette B. Weiss, and Jeff Weiss	American Printing House for the Blind	1985	Adult learners	Braille (student and teacher's manuals); cassette (writing exercises)	Grades 1 and 2	
Braille in Brief	Bernard M. Krebs	American Printing House for the Blind	1983	Advanced adult learners; review learners	Braille and print (line by line)	Grades 1 and 2	
Braille Series 1992 (Illinois Series)	Illinois Braille Committee	American Printing House for the Blind	1992	Adult learners	Braille and print	Grades 1 and 2 interspersed	All of grade 1 introduced before grade 2 contractions. Some words shown uncontracted. Additional practice volumes available.
Braille Too	Nancy Lake Hepker and Sharon Cross Coquillette	Grant Wood Area Education Agency	1995	Secondary students and young adults	Braille; print teacher's manual; IBM-compatible disk (text); cassette (writing exercises)	Grade 2	
Brushing Up on Braille	Pat Robertson	Canadian National Institute for the Blind	1990	Review learners	Braille, grade 1 only	Review of Grade 2	
English Braille in 40 Lessons	Mary Lou Archer	Mary Lou Archer Communications Center	1982	Adult learners	Thermoform braille	Grades 1 and 2	No teacher's guide available.

*Line by line indicates that the text of the print matches that of the braille lines.

(continued on next page)

Table 7.1. Commonly Used Textbooks *(continued)*

Title	Author	Publisher	Latest Publication Date	Target Population	Medium	Levels of Braille Code Covered	Comments
Getting in Touch with Reading	Margaret M. Smith	American Printing House for the Blind	1982	Adult learners	Braille text; print (teacher's manual)	Grades 1 and 2	Practice passages are informative and provide good repetition.
Manual for Spanish Braille	Dorothea Goodlin	Lehigh Valley Braille Guild	1978	Spanish-speaking adults	Braille and print (line by line); print English translation	Grade 1 only	
McDuffy Reader	Sharon L. M. Duffy	National Federation of the Blind	1989	Adult learners	Braille and print (text and teacher's manual); taped guidelines	Grades 1 and 2	
Modern Methods of Teaching Braille (Kansas Materials)	Claudelle S. Stocker	American Printing House for the Blind	1979	Adult learners	Braille (text and teacher's manual); print (teacher's manual)	Grades 1 and 2	
Read Again	Hilda Caton, Eleanor Pester, and Eddy Jo Bradley	American Printing House for the Blind	1990	Adult learners	Braille and print (text and teacher's manual); taped instructions	Grades 1 and 2	All of grade 1 taught before grade 2; some words shown uncontracted. Tactile training practices also included.
Reading with Feeling (Oregon Materials)	Anne V. Strauss	Multiple Services Media Technology	1988	Poor readers	Braille and print combination	Grades 1 and 2	Extended grade 1 reading practice. Grade 2 passages include famous quotes.
Step-by-Step Braille (Hadley Materials)	Bernard M. Krebs	Hadley School for the Blind	Volume 1,1988; Volumes 2–4, 1990	Independent adults	Braille exercises; taped instructions	Grades 1 and 2	Self-study program. No teacher's guide available.
Teaching Braille Reading to Adventitiously Blinded Individuals	Grace D. Napier	Napier Publications	1987 (under revision)	Former print readers	Braille and print (text and teacher's manual) (line by line)	Grades 1 and 2	
The World at My Fingertips	Norma L. Schecter	Beach Cities Braille Guild	1983	Learners with reduced tactile sensitivity	Thermoform jumbo braille; braille and print text planned	Grade 1	

Source: Adapted with permission from Adult Braille Literacy Empowerment Project, "Review of Braille Curriculum Materials," *Guidelines for Model Braille Literacy Programs, The ABLE-G* (Atlanta: American Foundation for the Blind, 1995). Based on research by Cheryl Richesin.

termined might best start with a text that presents grades 1 and 2 separately, in sequence.

Choice of a text may also depend on the type of material on which the braille is embossed. Some books are produced on paper and others on thermoform sheets. Thermoform braille is easily produced on plastic sheets using heat and vacuum and is durable. However, the plastic sheets cause significant tactile friction, which in turn causes the fingers to stick in humid weather or when the reader is perspiring. Also, thermoform dots sometimes appear blurred or smooth rather than crisp, which might make braille learning more difficult. Finally, some readers become confused because they can discern dots from the following page through the thermoform page, although a sheet of paper inserted between pages may alleviate this difficulty.

Learners who have experienced sensory loss that resulted in diminished tactile discrimination may read better with larger braille. However, few texts are produced in the larger sizes, and the instructor may need to reproduce one of the standard texts in large-cell braille by hand.

Some braille texts available for teaching adults are also appropriate to use with children who have already learned to read. However, instructors who teach beginning reading skills to young children will want to utilize either a transcribed version of the child's classroom reading series or a specially designed reading series for blind children. (For more specific information about teaching braille reading to children with visual impairments, see Harley, Henderson, & Truan, 1979; Heinze, 1986; Olson, 1981; and Rex et al., 1994).

Reading Skills

A number of skills are crucial to impart to new learners of braille reading. This section discusses some of the reading skills and important considerations, such as posture, book position, finger and hand position, letter recognition, scanning, and tracking. The reader can also refer to the detailed Lesson Plan 7.1 for an initial braille reading lesson covering letters *a* through *e*; and for further information, besides the references mentioned in the text, the reader can consult Erin and Sumranveth (1995) and Pester (1993).

Proper sitting position and book position help make reading more comfortable and efficient. As in typing or keyboarding, the individual will find fatigue setting in quickly if he or she does not sit upright. The book to be read should be placed on a table low enough to allow the elbow to be held at an angle of 90 degrees or more. If the angle is less than that, the reader's hands cannot lie flat on the book. In addition, the book should be pushed far enough away from the reader to allow the forearms to rest on the table. Arm fatigue will occur rapidly if only the hands contact the book. By the same token, the reader should push the book farther away as he or she moves to the bottom of the page, rather than moving the hands down until the arms no longer make contact with the table. Readers accustomed to writing by hand may be tempted to angle their book slightly, but it is probably more efficient to keep the book consistently at right angles to the forearm of the reading hand because reading the letters accurately depends on their position; for example, the letter *e* can appear to be the letter *c* if the book is rotated too far counterclockwise.

The correct use of hands and fingers is also important. There appears to be no real difference in reading efficiency between the left and right hands, but the placement of the finger on the braille cell appears to be crucial (Nolan & Kederis, 1969). A common misunderstanding new braille readers have is that they should use the tips of their fingers to read braille. They say: "I can't read braille because I have calluses," or "My fingernails are too long." Neither of these circumstances interferes however, since reading is done with the pad of the finger—the soft part of the finger above the first joint—not the tip. The pad is more sensitive and also offers two to three times more surface area. If a reader is using the fingers correctly, the palm will be less than an inch off the reading surface. The use of finger tips only may lead readers to miss the lower two dots in the braille cell.

Learning to recognize grade 1 braille generally takes at least 15 to 25 hours. Most new readers

LESSON PLAN 7.1

An Initial Braille Lesson

I. Objective: When presented with randomly chosen words composed of the letters from *a* to *e*, the learner will read them with 90% accuracy.
II. Materials: Beginning level braille textbook, braille cell model.
III. Assessment:
   A. Does the learner have any knowledge of or experience with braille?
   B. Does the learner have the ability to conceptualize the symbolism of the braille cell?
   C. Does the learner have the tactile ability to identify various dot combinations?
IV. Procedure
   A. Uses (reasons for learning braille)
      1. Information storage and retrieval for such items as telephone numbers, recipes, and instructions
      2. Labeling of such items as canned goods, clothing, medicines, and records
      3. General reading
   B. Conceptual Assessment
      1. Give the learner the braille cell model with all six dots up.
      2. Have the learner describe the layout of the dots in the cell; explain if he or she is unable to.
      3. Explain the dot numbering system.
      4. Have the learner identify random dot combinations set on the braille cell model.
      5. Ask the learner to set specified dot combinations.
      6. Describe and show the first five letters of the alphabet.
      7. Have the learner identify randomly set letters from *a* through *e*.
      8. Ask the learner to set randomly selected letters.
   C. Tactile Assessment
      1. Show the learner which part of the finger is used for reading.
      2. Present the learner with two widely spaced lines of braille characters that have three dots or less per cell.
      3. Have the learner identify dot positions.
      4. Determine the best or preferred hand for reading.
      5. Proceed with the lesson plan if the learner is 70–80% accurate.
      6. If the criterion is not reached, remediate with the *Kansas Braille Reading Readiness Book* (Stocker, 1983), or other tactile skills training material.
   D. Pre-reading instruction
      1. Present the learner with the braille textbook.
      2. Open the book to a page with a centered heading, paragraph indentations, and some blank areas.
      3. Explain the tactile methods for investigating the page format.
         a. Have the learner use most of the surface areas of the fingers on the palm side of both hands to investigate the surface of the page.
         b. Discourage the use of the fingertips only.

(continued on next page)

An Initial Braille Lesson (continued)

c. Have the learner move both hands down the page in an *S* pattern, noting the blank spaces in the text.
d. Have the learner find the centered heading, indentations, blank spaces, and other landmarks until he or she is competent.
e. Use this exercise as a warmup in future lessons.

4. Reading comfort.
    a. Describe the proper sitting position.
    b. Describe the proper book position.
    c. Describe the placement of forearms on the table.
    d. Explain why horizontal movement is important in braille reading.
        (1) Horizontal movement establishes a tactile baseline on the finger where the bottom of braille letters passes and provides a consistent presentation of the letters.
        (2) Optimal braille reading speed is not possible with vertical movements.
        (3) Explain that vertical movement is called *scrubbing*.

E. Braille reading and character recognition.
1. Turn to the beginning lesson in the textbook.
2. Have the learner identify the letters presented in the first two or three lines of the lesson.
3. Explain the concept of the *leading* and *trailing* edges of letters.
    a. Letter *C* has a leading single dot at the top and a trailing single dot at the top.
    b. Letter *D* has a leading single dot at the top and trailing two dots at the top.
    c. Letter *E* has a leading single dot at the top and a trailing single dot in the middle.
4. Have the learner continue reading in the first lesson of the textbook until the criterion is reached; they proceed to the next lesson.

V. Memoranda
A. Be sure to give rest breaks after approximately 20 minutes; have the learner let his or her hands hang down and allowing the muscles to relax.
B. Be sure to constantly reinforce the idea of leading and trailing edge; when learners make mistakes, ask them to investigate the leading or trailing edge, depending on where the mistake was made.
C. Assuming this is the first braille lesson, pay attention to the emotional state of the learner and stop to discuss feelings about braille when indicated.
D. Introduce the idea of tracking lines and moving from line to line after three to four more lessons in the textbook.
E. Although it will be difficult, constantly reinforce horizontal movement of the reading finger.

VI. Evaluation
A. Have the learner read ten lines of braille words containing the letters *a* to *e*; note errors.
B. Pay attention to proper reading behaviors and record performance.

VII. Assignment
A. Have the learner read practice pages with words formed with letters *a* through *e*

learn the letters by the shapes the dots form. The teacher can easily reinforce this learning with explanations such as "The letter *f* points up and left and *d* points up and right." Perhaps the most helpful way to present letters is by using the concept of leading edge and trailing edge. Because the finger moves from left to right, dots 1, 2, and 3 are encountered first, and these are termed the leading edge; dots 4, 5, and 6, which are noted as the finger leaves the cell, constitute the trailing edge. Thus, the letter *f* can be described by saying, "the leading edge is two dots in the upper part of the cell and the trailing edge is a single dot at the top of the cell." If the learner misidentifies a letter during instruction, it is recommended that the teacher ask the learner to identify the leading and trailing edges. If the learner is still confused, the instructor can then describe these two edges to clarify the shape of the letter. Simply telling the learner the correct letter does not reinforce letter recognition as well as this approach does.

Most clients learn the early alphabet letters quickly, but slow down as letters with similar shapes and those with four or more dots are introduced. The letters *d, f, h,* and *j* are similar in shape, as are *e* and *i, m* and *n,* and *o* and *n.* Confusions can be overcome by comparing letters. For example, if the learner is confusing *m* and *n,* the teacher can present groups of three or four letter *m*'s in which there is one *n* and have the learner identify the letter that is different. Other than giving the learner a lot of reading experience, little can be done to overcome the confusion caused by cells with many dots, but the teacher should keep in mind that learning tends to be slower when these letters are encountered in the alphabet.

Even before instructors begin to teach letter shapes, they should train learners to find their way around the page quickly. Good practice exercises are counting the number of lines of braille, locating the shortest and longest braille line, and locating a line that differs in length from the others. After this skill is mastered, it should be reinforced at the beginning of each new lesson. Although scanning (searching for a given point on a braille page) is not a reading skill per se, readers become frustrated when they are unable to move around easily on the reading material. Novice tactile readers generally use one finger to search for paragraph indentations or page numbers or to count lines. However, the finger pad is so small that it covers only about one-half of 1 square inch. Thus, only one or two characters are touched at any one time. The instructor should emphasize during initial lessons that scanning is considerably more effective if the surfaces of all four fingers or even the entire hand are utilized because the area is increased to as much as 50 square inches. The additional surface area yields more information, such as the relative position of the beginning of two or more lines or the format of the page. Thus, experienced braille readers will move both hands lightly over a braille page to locate areas of space that indicate paragraph divisions, exercise numbers, or subject headings.

The ability to track—to follow a line tactilely from left to right and locate the beginning of the next braille line—is also a basic skill in braille reading. At least two factors related to tracking appear to affect reading speed. Lowenfeld, Abel, and Hatlen (1974) demonstrated that smooth left to right movement with a minimum of vertical movement (scrubbing) is best; yet continuous left to right reading is one of the most difficult braille reading skills to teach. Nearly all new braille readers seem to scrub; that is, they move their reading finger up and down to help identify letters. Scrubbing helps identification at first, but is a habit that later interferes with building reading speed. If readers do not scrub, they soon establish a place on the finger that eventually becomes a sort of baseline. Each time a line is read, that point on the finger is placed on dots 3 and 6 of all the cells on the line. In this way, consistency in letter shape is established. Scrubbing should be politely discouraged. Exercises such as tracking lines of symbols without actually reading them can help establish the baseline. Along with the scanning exercise described earlier, such tracking exercises are good warmup lessons for braille reading.

Lowenfeld, Abel, and Hatlen (1974) also found two-handed readers to be superior to those using only one hand. Mangold (1982) described how the learner should read the first half of the line with the left hand and the remainder with the right. As the right hand is finishing the previous line, the left is dropped to the beginning of the next.

Many adult learners will probably be one-handed readers, however, since most clients receive only a few weeks of braille instruction, and the ultimate goal may not be extensive reading. For these readers, locating the next line can be a major tracking problem because it requires backtracking across the line. This is best accomplished by dropping the fingers below the line just read and following the space or trough between lines back to the left, rather than by tracking the braille characters themselves. However, the teacher should strongly encourage the reader to use his or her other hand to hold the place or to locate the next line. Teachers should also encourage advanced braille students to use both hands, since it virtually guarantees increased speed.

If only one hand is used, the preference of which one appears to be best left to the learner, since research about this point is inconclusive (Kozel, 1995). In early studies of braille reading, Burklen (1932) and Hermelin and O'Connor (1971) reported that the left hand was more effective for reading, while Maxfield (1928) determined that the right hand was more effective. In any case, these data were collected on readers with congenital visual impairments and may not be applicable to those with adventitious vision loss.

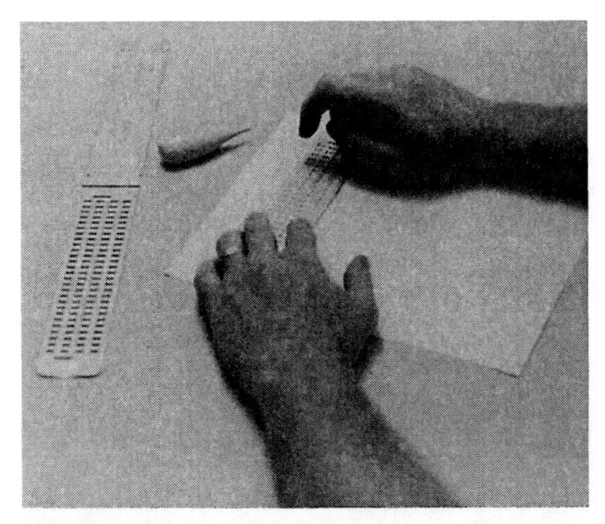

Writing with the slate and stylus. A braille eraser (left center) is used to flatten dots embossed by accident. Orientation marks are also visible—the raised line between the second and third row of cells and raised dots separating every fifth cell.

Braille Writing

Writing instruction is probably best initiated after a few reading lessons so that the concept of the braille cell and the system is clearly understood. There appears to be no uniformity among braille instructors in this regard, however (Ponchillia & Durant, 1995). Indeed, few of the major textbooks on braille contain extensive guidelines for teaching writing, and little is published in the general literature regarding the subject.

The two basic braille-writing instruments are the slate and stylus and the brailler or braillewriter. The slate and stylus is a relatively inexpensive portable device designed to be used more or less as a note pad. Slates are especially handy for taking classroom notes, jotting down addresses, embossing recipe cards, and the like, but they are also useful for more extensive writing. Teaching the use of a slate and stylus is perhaps a logical first braille-writing lesson for adults, since only a minority will have access to the more costly brailler, a device similar to a typewriter. Because the brailler is usually the preferred writing instrument for lengthy documents, both teachers and clients are sometimes reluctant to teach or learn the use of the slate and stylus (Ponchillia & Durant, 1995). However, as noted, the slate meets specific needs that the braillewriter does not. It is the most practical method of writing braille for the majority of people who will use braille for labeling and brief notetaking. In addition, braillers are expensive, and there often may be a lengthy waiting period to receive braillers from the manufacturer. Client and teacher should take these considerations into account when determining which instrument to use, and every effort should be made to teach the slate and stylus to those who need it.

Slate and Stylus

A typical slate consists of a metal template containing four rows of 28 cells. This basic or pocket slate is attached by a hinge at one end, so that it opens like a book to insert a sheet of paper. The front side contains windows into which the stylus is placed for embossing. Each window has six notches that correspond to the dot positions of the braille cell and to the indentations in the back (or bottom) plate of the slate. As the stylus is pushed into the paper, it causes the paper to expand into the indentations, forming the braille dot. The slate has a raised line between the second and third row of cells and raised dots separating every fifth cell. These are orientation marks designed to help the writer formulate columns or keep his or her place while writing. The four pointed pegs at the corners of the back of the slate when it is opened hold the paper firmly inside. These parts vary slightly among the different styles of slates designed to meet specific needs, such as labeling, postcard embossing, and performing mathematical calculations.

Because the dots are formed on the back side of the paper, the numbering system for writing is the mirror image of that for braille reading. For example, the top left corner of the cell being read is position 1, but it is position 4 on the braille slate. As a result, slate writing is a right-to-left process, rather than left to right as in reading. Although many people suggest that slate writing is "reversed" or "backwards" when compared to braille reading, this description gives use of the slate a negative connotation and makes it sound especially difficult. Most teachers prefer to simply point out that while writing from right to left, the learner encounters dots 1, 2, and 3 first, just as in braille reading, and then dots 4, 5, and 6. The only difference is the direction from which the hand approaches the cell.

There appear to be at least three choices as to how the learner conceptualizes braille characters when learning to write with the slate and stylus:

- memorizing the numbers of the dot positions as read and transposing them to the slate cell
- referring to each letter by the position of dots in the top, middle, and bottom of the first side and top, middle, and bottom of the second side (Mangold, 1977)—for example, *d* is a "top, top, middle" letter
- reversing the mental image of the letter that has been memorized for reading as it is written.

There is apparently no research relevant to this topic, but in the authors' experience, the last method is the most commonly used. If the rehabilitation teacher determines that a learner is using this method, perhaps teaching slate writing through reciprocal characters such as *f* and *d* or *e* and *i* could enhance learning.

Stocker (n.d.) suggests using an enlarged braille cell model to teach slate writing and having the student use a forefinger to trace the dot positions, based on the idea that whatever the forefinger is trained to do, the hand can replicate with a tool. The specific sequence and methods for teaching the slate and stylus are presented in the sample lesson plan that accompanied Chapter 4, and readers can also consult Mangold (1985) for more information.

The Perkins brailler.

An Initial Braillewriter Lesson

I. Objective: When presented with a Perkins brailler and 11" x 11½" braille paper, the learner will emboss braille with 90 percent accuracy.

II. Materials: Perkins brailler, braille paper

III. Assessment
   A. Does the learner know braille?
   B. Does the learner type or understand the operation of the typewriter?

IV. Procedure
   A. Uses: Extensive writing, like that done with a typewriter
   B. Parts
      1. Have the learner describe the machine, being sure to cover the primary components.
         a. Keys: embossing bar, line space, backspace, space bar
         b. Paper mechanism: release, rubber roller, grooved roller, paper feed knobs
         c. Return mechanism
         d. Margin sets
      2. Have the learner compare the braillewriter with the typewriter if he or she is already familiar with typing.
   C. Paper insertion
      1. Point out the dimensions of the paper, noting that brailling should be horizontally across the 11½" width of the paper.
      2. Have the learner pull the paper release forward.
      3. Have the learner turn the right paper-feed knob clockwise until it stops; explain rewinding.
      4. Have the learner hold the paper with the long side horizontal.
      5. Have the learner insert the paper over the paper support bar, sliding it under the embossing head and grooved roller until it stops at the bottom paper stop. Tell the learner to hold the paper straight and flat, then push the paper release levers away from him or her to clamp the paper.
      6. Have the learner roll the paper in, turning the right paper feed knob counterclockwise until it stops.
      7. Have the learner strike the line space key to engage the line-spacing mechanism and create the correct top margin.
         a. Demonstrate improper insertion; point out the "crunching" sound.
         b. Explain reasons: bent edge, crooked insertion, improper paper removal.
         c. Explain remedies: turning paper to another edge; pressing down on the paper and pushing it into the machine while turning the paper feed knob counterclockwise; pressing on the line spacer until it locks, then inserting the paper.
   D. Embossing
      1. Have the learner emboss the alphabet, or the portion he or she knows, until he or she is competent.
      2. Have the learner emboss words, phrases, sentences, paragraphs until he or she is competent.
      3. Have the learner adjust margins for indentation, centering, and small paper.

(continued on next page)

An Initial Braillewriter Lesson (continued)

4. Have the learner correct mistakes while the paper is in the brailler.

V. Memoranda
   A. Many new learners strike the keys with too much force.
   B. Point out the risk of damage if liquid spills on the brailler.
   C. Stress the importance of using the dust cover.
   D. Depending on the learner's need, mention adaptations such as the electric brailler, extension keys, the Dymotape attachment, and the narrow-paper adapter.

VI. Evaluation: Have the learner emboss 10 lines of dictated material, and check for the quantity and types of errors made.

VII. Assignments: The learner can practice known characters and words repetitiously to reinforce hand movement and build speed.

Braillers

The brailler, which in the United States is nearly synonymous with the Perkins brailler is much like a typewriter and is used in much the same way for more extensive writing chores. (Other braillers, such as the Mountbatten brailler, may be available as well, but they are similar to the more common Perkins model.) The brailler keyboard consists of nine keys. The center one is the space key, and the three to its immediate left and three on the immediate right are embossing keys. The far left key is the line spacer, and the one on the far right is the backspace key. The embossing keys are numbered 1, 2, and 3 moving to the left of the space key and 4, 5, and 6 to the right. The embossing keys are struck in combination to form braille characters. For example, to emboss the letter *c*, the user strikes keys 1 and 4 simultaneously. The other parts of the brailler are the carriage return, embossing head, paper release levers, rubber roller, fluted roller, and margin sets.

Because of its similarity to the typewriter, the brailler is relatively simple to use for those who have previously typed. Efficient use is taught through practicing the motor memory skills, much like learning to play a musical instrument. The details of the instructional sequence are presented in Lesson Plan 7.2 for an initial braillewriter lesson in this chapter. The major drawbacks of the instrument are its bulkiness, weight, and cost.

Affective Considerations

Learning braille may touch on significant psychological issues for some individuals. Perhaps the most noteworthy of these stems from the fact that the word *braille* is so closely associated with total blindness. The first lesson can be traumatic, because the learner confronts his or her association with blindness, regardless of the actual degree of vision loss. Consequently, the instructor should be prepared to accept the initial behaviors that may result from the fear and anger provoked by the situation. For example:

> George M., the greenhouse owner described earlier, was still in the early stages of adjustment to his sight loss when he was scheduled for his first braille class at the rehabilitation center. When he did not appear in class, the instructor found him in his room and asked if he knew he was late. He answered in a flat, unemotional voice: "Yeah, I know, but braille and canes are for blind people like Helen Keller, not for me. I don't want to be like them." The teacher responded, "I know it is hard. I have

> had many students who have lost their reading vision just like you, and they nearly always have difficulty at first. I won't try to force it on you, but because I know your abilities and needs, I know it would help you a lot. How about letting me show you the first few letters here in your room?" In response, Mr. M. shouted, "Just go away and leave me alone!" Later in the day, he came to the instructor's office, apologized for his behavior, and then asked if he could come to braille class the following day.

Learning braille can also be a slow process, sometimes taking as long as 100 hours of instruction to complete grade 2. Often, students master grade 1 quickly but are discouraged to learn that there are many more symbols to encounter before completing grade 2 braille. New learners may also be disappointed by a drop in their reading speed with braille as compared to print or auditory reading. In addition, most instructional textbooks begin with lessons reminiscent of first-grade primers. New learners may be frustrated to the point of quitting, and new teachers may be reluctant to broach the subject of teaching or continuing braille lessons in the face of a client's negative response.

However, the instructor will find that such feelings generally pass quickly as the learner begins to recognize the benefits of learning the tactile code and experiences successes in the lessons. The teacher can use information gleaned from the initial assessment to reinforce braille learning and counter negative feelings by incorporating the client's interests into the lessons with concrete examples, such as hobby-related words, telephone numbers, or practice that relates to the client's vocational goal.

Objective Measures of Performance

Progress in reading and writing braille must be measured objectively, both to give the learner maximum reinforcement and to allow the instructor to plan appropriately for future lessons. The number of symbols or words the learner reads or writes per minute is a good indicator of daily progress. In addition, the rehabilitation teacher should note any specific repetitive reading problems, such as scrubbing, losing the place while returning to the left margin, or slow speed. The learner may gain sufficient reinforcement from knowing that he or she read another two pages of braille in the lesson. However, the concrete knowledge that he or she has increased the number of words read correctly per minute since the last lesson will not only add to the reinforcement, but will also demonstrate once again that the learner and teacher are partners in achieving their goals.

BEYOND BRAILLE

Learning braille and other tactile methods of reading and writing will open up new opportunities for reading and for written communication for an individual with a vision loss. However, for larger tasks, for written communications with sighted people, and for vocational uses, other methods are required. Moreover, the rapid developments in microcomputers have made their use a virtual necessity in today's world and at the same time have created the adaptations that make them an easily accessible means of communication for people with visual impairments. The results of George M.'s experience with braille illustrate how a combination of braille and other methods may be useful:

> Three years after George M. left the rehabilitation center, he was keeping his braille address list in a well-organized card file, he had chemical names brailled on plastic tape to be placed on containers with elastic bands, his thermostats were all marked with braille, he kept his brailled planting records in brailled folders in a file cabinet, and he used braille labels in his clothing. He had even begun to use braille outlines for the many speaking appearances he made as the local plant and gardening expert. In addition, he had plans to purchase a braille-input/voice-output microprocessor so that he

would have random access to his planting records while out at the greenhouse.

Chapter 9 covers the keyboarding and other skills required to use both typewriters and computers for word processing and other purposes. Nevertheless, even people with access to this technology will need to write or draw by hand at times—sometimes only to sign their name to a check or document; at other times, to write a shopping list, letter, or other personal document. For these instances, the rehabilitation teacher needs to teach handwriting skills, which are covered in the next chapter.

CHAPTER 8

Handwriting and Drawing

KEY CONCEPTS IN THIS CHAPTER

- **The importance of script writing to an individual's self-image**
- **The difficulties encountered by individuals with visual impairments when attempting to write by hand**
- **Types of handwriting guides**
- **Methods for making script-writing guides that are specific to the learner's needs**
- **Types of tactile drawing boards**
- **Methods for instructing individuals who lost their vision after learning to write**
- **Methods for instructing those who are learning to write for the first time**

Handwriting is a skill so common that the average person takes it for granted. Reading and writing are traditionally linked together as the cornerstones of personal literacy. The previous chapter examined adaptations for reading for persons with visual impairments; the present chapter explores writing modifications for people who have experienced vision loss.

Writing is learned by individuals in early childhood and is used virtually every day to sign legal and financial papers, write notes to family members or colleagues, or write informal letters to friends. A significant loss of sight does not change the need to execute such tasks, but it does interfere with the ease with which writing can be accomplished. In spite of a vision loss, there are still voter registration forms to fill out, paychecks to endorse, and charge card receipts to sign, and friends continue to expect the handwritten letters they have always received.

Although some people may accept the idea of scratching an *X* instead of a signature, correspondence is often assumed to lack validity or authority without a proper signature, and losing the ability to write their signature may cause some people to feel that they personally have lost that validity or authority (McGillivray, 1980). The association of being unable to sign one's name with illiteracy may have a debilitating effect on an individual's self-image as well (Carroll, 1961). Therefore, it is important for the rehabilitation teacher to emphasize that numerous adaptive techniques and devices are available to allow people with impaired vision to resume or learn printing or writing script as well as the production and monitoring of graphic representations. The effects on self-esteem of losing writing skills and of renewing them through adaptive techniques can be seen in the following example:

> Walter M. was an elderly retired postman who became legally blind as a result of macular degeneration. He lived alone on the family farm,

and, before his vision was affected, he had corresponded regularly with elderly relatives and friends by mail. He had always prided himself on his beautiful, flowing script and was severely discouraged and depressed by the effect of his vision loss on his previously enjoyable skill. He complained that he could not write in a straight line or monitor what he had written, and was resigned to giving up writing checks and paying bills to a nephew by marriage. Unfortunately, the nephew could not assist him regularly, so Mr. M. was also concerned about making sure his bills were paid on time.

During the initial assessment, his rehabilitation teacher had to persuade him to attempt a writing sample. His high standards for the appearance of his handwriting seemed to interfere with his willingness to demonstrate it. During that and subsequent visits, Walter M. was shown a variety of handwriting guides for letter writing, check writing, and signatures, He sampled a few different bold markers and found one he liked. He became more animated during lessons and began to participate in developing solutions to his handwriting problems. When a black plastic template was created to fit over his unique checks, he devised an adaptation to secure the template to his checkbook. Later, he proudly reported to friends in a support group on the various adaptations he had begun to use, and smiled when explaining that some of the elderly friends with whom he corresponded had even thanked him for using a bold marker, since they themselves had difficulty seeing.

As the example of Walter M. illustrates, the nature of the instruction in handwriting that an individual needs depends on both his or her prior experience with handwriting and goals in that area. People who were used to writing before they lost their sight are usually able to continue as before, perhaps with the assistance of an adaptive aid. Congenitally blind adults who have never learned to write may wish to learn no more than their signature or may master the entire alphabet. Handwriting instruction for various needs and goals is discussed in more detail later in this chapter.

ADAPTIVE HANDWRITING AIDS

Individuals who need to write and sign documents after they have experienced a loss of sight need assistance in accomplishing the following:

- finding the line on which to sign or write
- knowing the proper amount of space to sign or write in
- keeping the bases of the letters on the base line
- know where to cross *t*'s and dot *i*'s
- maintaining proper letter spacing
- in some cases, remembering how the letter shapes were made.

People who are newly visually impaired may be overwhelmed by these difficulties, and some may simply assume that handwriting is no longer possible. Some evidence confirms that handwriting does deteriorate among the visually impaired population (Schropp, 1990; Ziebarth, 1989). But all of these difficulties can be overcome. This section describes devices that make handwriting easier, and adaptive techniques are discussed in the section on teaching handwriting.

Handwriting guides provide users with assistance in such areas as determining the space in which to write. Broadly speaking, there are four main types of handwriting guides: rigid guides, flexible guides, bold-line guides, and tactile surface guides (McGillivray, 1980). The characteristics of each are described, along with some examples, in the following sections. For information on obtaining the products mentioned, see the Resources section.

Rigid Guides

In general, handwriting guides classified as rigid hold a piece of paper in place while the line spaces in which the user writes are delineated by

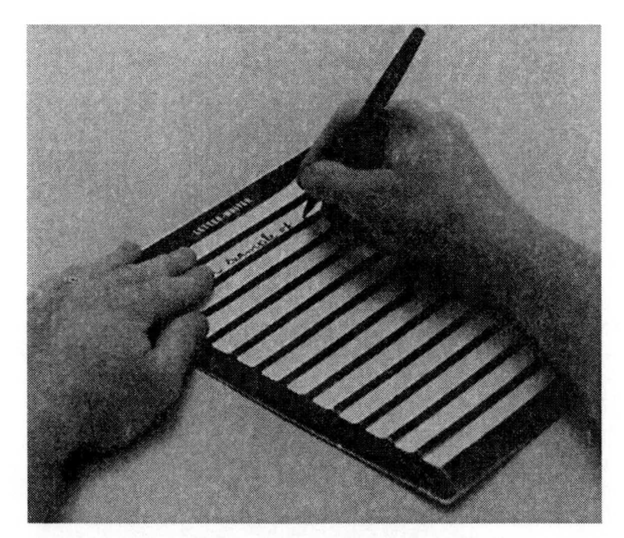

The Hewitt Letter-Writer Guide.

rectangular, cut-out spaces formed by solid, unbending boundaries made of plastic, cardboard, or metal. These guides are the most confining, particularly because the rigid base does not allow the writer to make the descenders found in letters such as *y* or *g*. They are helpful, however, because they instill confidence in the novice that his or her writing is truly within the line space. They are also helpful to people who have difficulty with spatial concepts or who have orthopedic problems.

One of the better-known rigid handwriting guides is the Marks Writing Guide, a modified clipboard to which a metal rectangular rod attaches, serving as a line-space border. The Marks Writing Guide holds a sheet of unlined paper under the clip. The metal line-space border clicks into line positions vertically along the paper. It also provides a metal tab that slides horizontally between the guide rods as the user writes to indicate that the end of the line is coming up or to mark the place where the writer left off.

The Hewitt Letter-Writer Guide is a commercial template made of a thin folded cardboard sheet with line spaces cut out of one side and the paper held in place inside the folder. It has end-of-line indicators at the right side. The Moxon Guide, often used in Canada, is similar to the Hewitt, but is made of both plastic and cardboard.

Flexible Guides

Flexible guides differ from rigid ones only in that they utilize an elastic baseline material that allows the writer to make the tails of letters. They require more skill to use than the rigid guides, however.

The stringboard is an example of a flexible guide. It holds the paper under a frame that is hinged at the top. The line spaces are delineated by elastic strings. Each string contains a bead that serves the same purpose as the metal tab on the Marks Guide. A similar guide used in Canada, the

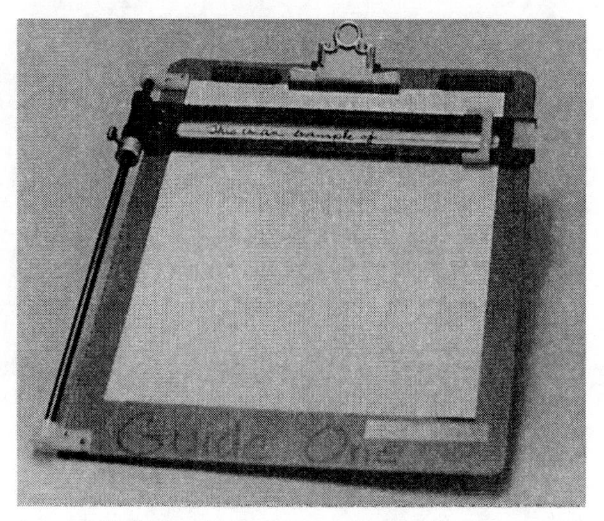

Flexible full-page handwriting guides: Garrett stringboard (left) and Guide One (right).

Tactile writing guides, such as this fiberboard guide, have ridges that can be felt when they are placed under plain paper.

Millard, uses elastic for flexible guidelines but does not have beads for line markers. The Guide One is essentially a hybrid of a rigid and a flexible guide. It combines elastic guides that permit writing below the baseline with a rigid outer border.

Bold-Line Guides

Bold-line guides are tablets of paper with lines that are denser in color or wider than on normal lined paper. They are useful for people with enough remaining vision to see the lines.

Tactile Surface Guides

Tactile surface devices may be paper with raised lines or boards with raised ridges designed to be placed under a piece of paper through which the ridges of the aid can be felt. The ridged board allows users to write on plain paper placed on top of the raised lines. Users with a light touch perform well with tactile surface guides, and some prefer the more natural-looking handwriting these guides allow.

Commercial and Homemade Guides

Other guides designed for specific uses, such as writing checks, addressing envelopes, and signing one's name, are available commercially. These are usually but not always rigid guides. Check-writing guides come ready-made for standard designs or can be ordered custom-made for unusual checks. Envelope guides are generally templates with spaces for inserting each line of an address. Many financial institutions now offer checks with bold

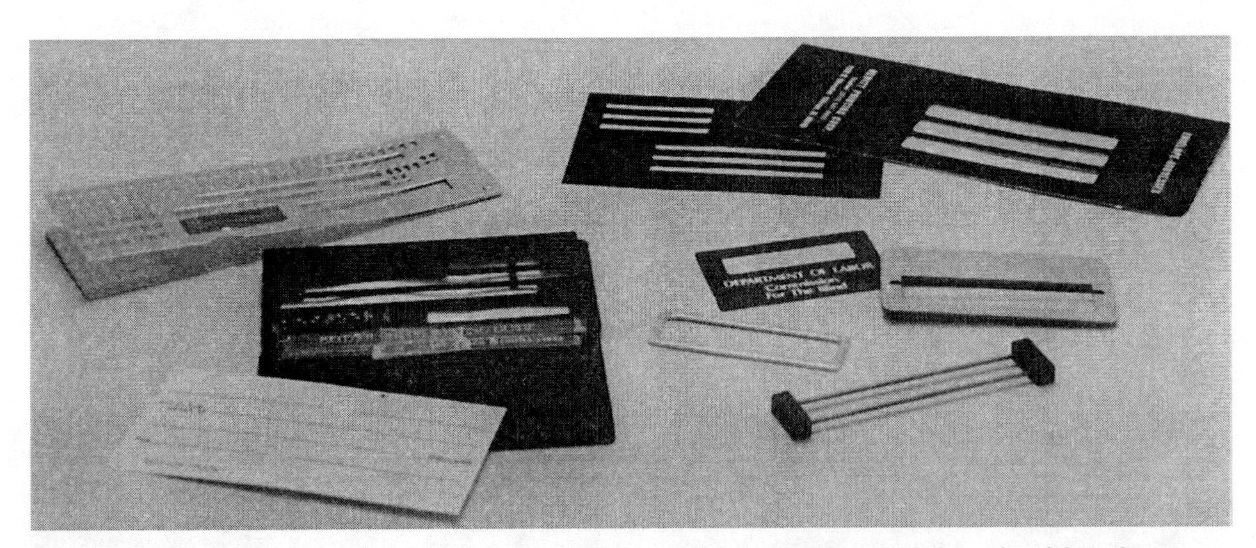

Examples of guides for writing checks (left), addressing envelopes (top right), and writing signatures (bottom right).

and/or raised black lines on a yellow background and large bold-lined ledgers.

Homemade guides may be created that have the characteristics of any of the types of handwriting guides described. They can be as simple to make as rolling a piece of paper around a pencil and then flattening the paper when the pencil is removed to create rows of creases that can be used like the raised ridges of a tactile surface guide. Homemade templates can be created for specific purposes such as filling out a commonly needed form. A simple method for making a homemade template for filling out checks or other forms is presented in Sidebar 8.1 (McGillivray, 1980).

Script-writing guides for people with useful vision should be made of a dark material such as overexposed X-ray film (which can often be obtained at no cost from radiologists who are discarding mistakes) or black cardboard. If this is not possible, the edges of the openings or the entire guide can be darkened with a black felt marker. Shiny or reflective surfaces, which cause glare, can be abraded with sandpaper or an ink eraser to eliminate the problem.

SIDEBAR 8.1

Instructions for Making a Homemade Check-Writing Guide

MATERIALS

- Copy of check (or other form) to be filled out
- Piece of plain paper
- Tracing or carbon paper
- Pen or pencil
- Plastic sheet such as exposed X-ray film or acetate (black is preferable)
- Cutting tool such as matte knife or X-Acto knife
- Metal ruler
- Permanent black marker

METHOD

1. After deciding how the template guide will fit over the check or form, make a paper template. Cut a piece of paper as wide as the check or form, but twice the height. (It is best to have a template with backing cut out of the same piece, then folded at the bottom.)
2. Trace the appropriate openings for the information to be filled out onto the paper with the pencil. The horizontal areas between the openings will be the part of the template that will guide the user and should be as wide as possible for durability. For example, on most checks, the opening for "payable to" may need to be higher up than the actual line on the check, but will still look appropriate.
3. Cut openings on the paper template.
4. Lay the paper template on the plastic sheet, which has been cut to size, and attach with tape or paper clips.
5. Draw the openings on the plastic sheet with the marker or a sharp tool.
6. Use the knife to cut the openings by making several light passes along the lines. Greater pressure increases the chance of overcutting the desired openings.
7. Fold the guide to form an envelope or pocket to hold the check being written in place, using the metal ruler to make a sharp crease.

Source: Adapted with permission from R. McGillivray, Ed., "Handwriting Guides," *Aids and Appliances Review* (1980), p. 13 (Newton, MA: Carroll Center for the Blind).

RAISED-LINE DRAWING BOARDS

Another type of aid useful to persons with severe visual impairments is the raised-line drawing board, which enables visually impaired people to tactilely investigate linear graphics, such as maps, line drawings, and statistical graphs. Raised-line drawing boards are invaluable to anyone enrolled in statistics, economics, or science classes, but they are also useful at any point in the instructional process when words are not sufficient to describe certain spatial or graphic concepts, such as the shape of a cursive letter.

In general, raised-line drawing boards consist of a thin sheet of rubber fastened to a firm backing of cardboard, plastic, or wood, over which a disposable sheet of plastic is attached. Writing on the plastic with a ballpoint pen, pencil, or stylus produces raised lines that can be perceived tactilely, rather than the indentations that would be formed by writing with firm pressure on paper.

There are two distinct types of raised-line drawing boards: one provides a raised image on the surface of the paper on which it is drawn; and the other raises images on the back of the page. Boards of the latter type are awkward, because they require whoever is drawing on them to draw or write backwards; that is, to flip the figure 180 degrees from the way it would normally be created. For example, an upper-case *D* would be written with the straight line on the right rather than the left.

The Sewell Raised Line Drawing Kit, a commonly used drawing board, is a clipboardlike device on which a dense rubber pad has been affixed. A clear plastic sheet to be written on is placed on the pad under two screw-driven clips. The graphic representations are drawn on the plastic using slightly more pressure than one would use when writing on a standard clipboard. Although the commercial Sewell board is sold with a supply of plastic sheets, paper can be used on it effectively.

A homemade screen drawing board can be easily made by fastening a sheet of aluminum or steel screen onto the flat surface of a thin masonite-type board or a commercial clipboard. The edges of the screen are folded under and sandwiched between the front board and a backing board. It can be used with either a plastic or paper sheet.

The following are some primary rules to bear in mind when using raised-line boards to represent linear graphics:

- The figure should only be drawn in two planes, since attempts to add depth, as in visual representations, can confuse tactile users.
- The drawing instrument should be held at a more slanted angle to the paper than when writing.
- The writing instrument used on the screenboard should have a broader writing head than a standard pen.

Rehabilitation teachers often use raised-line drawing boards when they are first familiarizing students with letters in handwriting lessons. These boards are particularly useful in demonstrating the shapes of letters to students and providing concrete feedback when students use them as their writing surface. This use of raised-line drawing boards should be discontinued as soon as students are able to form letters properly, however, since the surface is not a natural one for writing.

HANDWRITING INSTRUCTION

As noted earlier, people with visual impairments vary in their need and desire to write by hand. Usually, the most basic need is for a method to sign checks or other documents. The possible goals of handwriting instruction fall along a continuum, starting with the simplest adaptation for creating a signature and continuing through complete competence in handwriting. Thus, the aim of handwriting instruction might include any of the following:

- use of signature stamp
- stylized signature

- initials
- full last name plus first initial
- full signature
- signature plus selected words (such as "love," or "sincerely")
- numbers
- full alphabet (the remaining letters).

In addition, as in many areas of rehabilitation teaching, rapidly advancing technology has provided another possible avenue of approach to the handwriting needs of visually impaired individuals: the possibility of "handwriting" by computer (see Sidebar 8.2 and Resources section).

As with most areas of rehabilitation teaching, the client's needs, and therefore the teaching approach, will tend to differ depending on whether the client's vision loss is recent or long-standing. People with useful vision also will need different adaptations than those who will not use any vision for writing.

People with Useful Vision

It is imperative to conduct a thorough assessment to determine whether visual or tactile methods for writing or some combination are best for each individual who has some remaining vision. The deciding factor is whether the individual can write more quickly and legibly using residual vision or without it.

The two primary problems with writing faced by those with limited but useful vision are locating where to write and staying on the line while writing. The visual challenges involved in writing are more complex in certain ways than those involved in reading, however, since the learner must visually follow the movements of the hand, not just lines of static letters.

Writing is best accomplished with two hands, one for steadying the material and one for writing. Therefore, a headborne low vision aid is most helpful for writing for people with useful vision. The major skill involved is keeping the tip of the pen in focus as it moves across the paper. When using a bioptic telemicroscope while writing script, for example, the writer locates the place to begin writing with the regular eyeglass, then brings the pen tip into the visual field of the telemicroscope and follows it from left to right as letters are written (Watson and Berg, 1983). Other suggestions for writers with low vision include:

- writing loops, points, and circles rather than words until the writer is comfortable with the lens in his or her device
- writing script rather than printing, because the pen needs to be lifted from the paper less frequently

SIDEBAR 8.2

Computerized Handwriting

Probably anyone—with or without vision—would appreciate computer software that is designed to print text in any one of more than 300 different handwriting fonts. The T-Maker company gathered samples of handwriting from around the United States, analyzed them, and created software that is compatible with either Apple Macintosh or Microsoft Windows (Lewis, 1995). Disability Accommodation Services has devised Sign It Yourself, software that works with word processors to add one's personalized signature at the end of letters, using a sample sent to the company. Greg Mark, a visually impaired computer consultant in Indianapolis, Indiana, uses both a formal and an informal signature sample to create the computerized signature resource.

- writing larger
- tracking back along the line just written to locate the next writing space on the line below
- using bold-lined paper and felt-tipped markers for writing.

People with Adventitious Impairments

For those who have lost their sight after having written in script for some time, the major problem in continuing to write is one of orientation. The motor skill of drawing letters is largely unaffected by the loss of sight. Except for dotting *i*'s and crossing *t*'s, most people can write individual script letters as they did before their vision loss—unless they have stopped practicing the skill for several years. Therefore, teaching handwriting to people with adventitious vision loss is basically a matter of orienting them to writing guides and perhaps reviewing letter shapes (see Lesson Plan 8.1 for teaching the use of handwriting guides in this chapter).

A significant variable in the teaching of handwriting is the rigidity of the writing guide used. Among people who cannot see well enough to read what they are writing, novices or people who need a lot of concrete reinforcement generally prefer the more structured guides, such as the Marks, Moxon, or Hewitt, while those with more experience might be comfortable with other types. Thus, the teaching sequence generally moves from the more rigid guides to the more flexible ones, until the learner determines the guide with which he or she is most comfortable. Some evidence (Cronheim, 1992) indicates that learners perform as well with less rigid guides, so rehabilitation teachers may want to experiment with the sequence that works for the individual student.

Beginning lessons introduce the methods of inserting the paper into the guide, the operation of the writing guide if it has moving parts, and orientation to the line space provided by the guide. The learner can get a feel for the space available for writing with the guide by making loops, points, circles, and, finally, letters until he or she develops a proprioceptive awareness of the vertical writing space (see Figure 8.1).

When the writer joins letters to form words and sentences, the instructor should pay attention to their horizontal spacing, because many people have a tendency to crowd them (see Figure 8.2). Overcoming this is a matter of practice with immediate feedback from the instructor.

The problem with dotting *i*'s and crossing *t*'s or *x*'s is remediated in the same way. However, some learners may not be able to master this skill by utilizing the traditional method of completing the letters by going back to finish them at the end of the word. Instead, they may need to stop to complete a

Figure 8.1 Writing Loops, Points, and Circles
This exercise helps the learner develop an awareness of the line space available for writing.

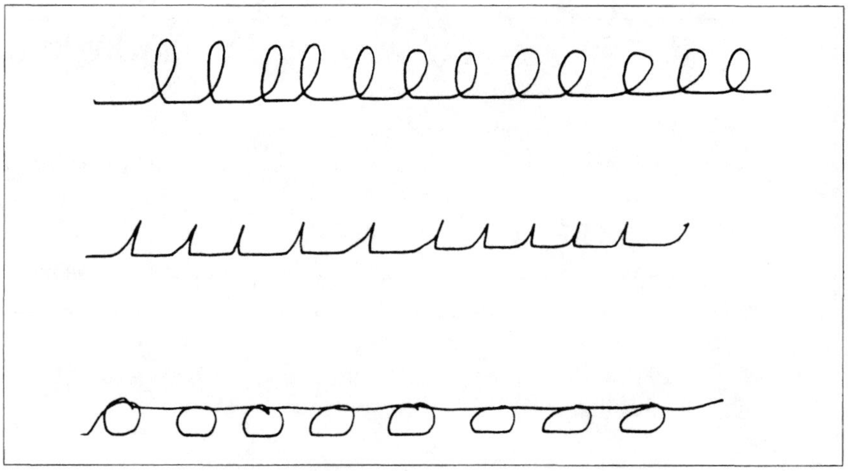

Teaching the Use of Handwriting Guides

I. Objective: When presented with a full-page writing guide, the learner will write a one-page letter in script that is legible enough to allow a reader to understand the content.

II. Materials
- A. A rigid guide
- B. A flexible guide
- C. A tactile surface guide
- D. A bold-line guide
- E. Writing tools (ballpoint pen, felt-tip pen, pencil)
- F. Unlined paper

III. Assessment
- A. Can the learner write his or her signature?
- B. Has the learner written script since experiencing vision loss?
- C. How long has it been since the skill was last used?
- D. Can the learner monitor his or her writing visually?
- E. Can the learner physically grasp the writing tool?

IV. Procedure
- A. Introducing types of guides and their uses
  1. Full-page guides
  2. Envelope guides
  3. Signature guides
  4. Check guides
- B. Determining guide preference
  1. Have the learner investigate the overall design of a rigid guide.
  2. Have the learner investigate the line spaces of a rigid guide.
  3. Have the learner use the guide to make four lines of loops, points, mounds, or letters.
  4. Repeat steps 1–3 with the flexible guide.
  5. Repeat steps 1–3 with the tactile surface guide.
  6. Repeat steps 1–3 with the bold-line guide if appropriate.
  7. Have the learner select his or her guide of choice.
- C. Orienting the learner to the guide
  1. Have the learner point out the parts of the guide.
  2. Describe any parts that were missed.
     - a. End-of-line indicator
     - b. Last-word marker
     - c. Mechanism for moving the metal line space bar down the page
     - d. Mechanism for holding the paper in place
- D. Writing with the guide
  1. Have the learner insert the paper.
  2. Have the learner write four lines of text.
  3. If letters are not formed properly,
     - a. describe improperly formed letters, demonstrating them on a raised-line board.

(continued on next page)

Teaching the Use of Handwriting Guides (continued)

b. have the learner practice writing the letters in one line space or in an enlarged form if necessary.

4. If horizontal spacing is not adequate,
   a. describe the spacing problem or demonstrate it on a raised-line board.
   b. have the learner practice writing in one line space or in an enlarged form if necessary.
5. If *t*'s and *i*'s are not properly formed,
   a. describe the problem and have the learner practice.
   b. if the learner is unable to correct the problem, have him or her cross *t*'s and dot *i*'s at the top of the writing stroke.

V. Memoranda
   1. Slowing the learner's writing speed sometimes remediates problems with letter formation.
   2. Using black or darkened guide edges increases the visibility of the line space.
   3. Totally blind learners may need positive feedback from more than one staff member or family member to verify the instructor's evaluation.

VI. Evaluation: Have the learner write a one-page letter to a friend and read it for content.

VII. Assignment: Have the learner use his or her preferred guide daily to write an informal note, make a grocery list, or write a friendly letter.

letter while it is being written. In this method, as the writer makes the upstroke for the lower case *i*, he or she then makes the dot before completing the downstroke portion of the letter. Similarly, the writer crosses the *t* as the upstroke is being completed (see Figure 8.3). Many people find that the index finger of the other hand can be used to follow the pen to help with spacing and also to hold the place while lifting the pen to cross *t*'s or dot *i*'s.

In summary, to suit the needs of learners with adventitious loss, the rehabilitation teacher determines which guide the writer prefers and also writes most legibly with, offers feedback on legibility, and, perhaps, provides remediation of minor problems with letter formation.

People with Congenital Impairments

Facility with writing is related to the age at which the vision impairment occurred. In general, those who have never seen the smooth, flowing shapes of cursive letters have difficulty reproducing them.

Figure 8.2. An Example of Letter Crowding

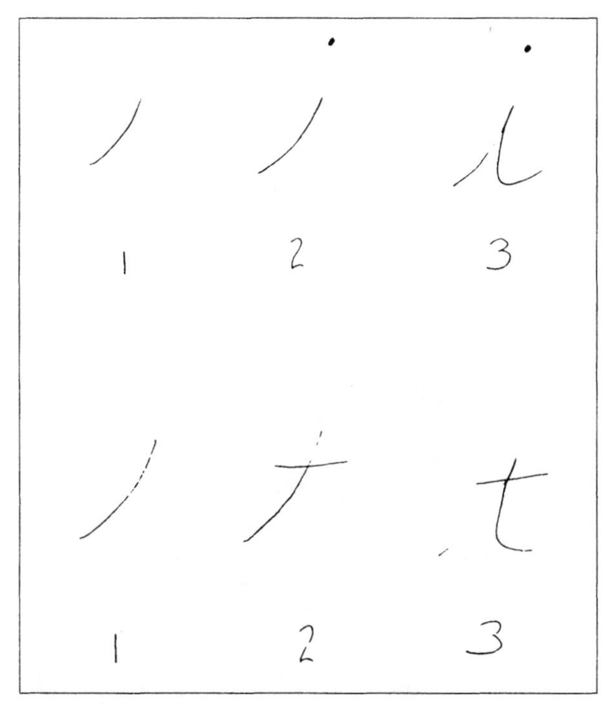

Figure 8.3. Dotting *i*'s and Crossing *t*'s

Whereas those with adventitious impairments retain a kinesthetic memory for drawing letters, those with congenital vision loss must repeatedly practice the mechanical movements of forming each letter, based on nonvisual feedback, until motor memory is established. As a result of this difficulty, adults with a congenital visual impairment commonly use handwriting only for writing their signature, rather than for writing checks, notes, or friendly letters (Ponchillia & Kaarlela, 1986).

Although the authors would strongly encourage offering children with congenital vision loss extensive instruction in writing script while they are in elementary school, when such learning is reinforced through peer pressure, they have found that adults must be extremely motivated to pursue competency in a skill that offers no immediate concrete reinforcement. Signing one's name is usually a priority, however, since everyone will ultimately need to use a signature whether or not he or she pursues advanced scriptwriting skills. Therefore, this discussion will focus on instructional methods required for signature writing (see Lesson Plan 8.2 in this chapter for teaching signature writing to someone who is congenitally blind). If the client is interested in pursuing extensive instruction in handwriting, the rehabilitation teacher can refer to the work of Huckins (1965) and Marks and Marks (1954).

The major steps in the teaching sequence for signature writing are:

- familiarizing the writer with letters and their formation
- connecting letters
- decreasing letter size.

Familiarizing the Writer with Letters

Numerous techniques have been utilized to introduce the learner to letter shapes. The staff of Community Services for the Visually Handicapped (1974) accomplished this introduction by having the learner trace the shape of a raised cursive letter with his or her finger. Huckins (1965) used task analysis to determine how to provide a combination of verbal cues and raised letters produced on a screen board. Stocker (1963) and later Freund & Nagano (1966) utilized engraved letters into which the learner could place a writing instrument, repeatedly tracing their shapes to gain kinesthetic memory of the letter forms. Harrison (1968) had learners visualize the face of a clock and described the formation of letters by beginning at the center of the circle and proceeding from one number to another until the letter was drawn.

Weiss and Weiss (1978) suggested a technique, commonly referred to as the braille cell method, which uses the six dots in each of four adjacent braille cells (designated as the original cell, left cell, right cell, and lower cell) to describe each letter (see Figure 8.4). Letters are formed by connecting the numbered dots in the braille cells in a specified order in a manner similar to "connect-the-dots" pictures. Letters may look square and awkward initially, but practice leads to a more rounded appearance. Weiss and Weiss (1978) provide a full listing of dot sequences to form script and print upper- and lowercase letters. People

LESSON PLAN 8.2

Teaching Signature Writing to Someone Who Is Congenitally Blind

I. Objective: When presented with a signature guide, paper, and pencil, the learner will write a legible signature 9 out of 10 times.

II. Materials
- A. Raised-line drawing board
- B. Freund writing kit
- C. Plastic template writing guide with bars removed between four horizontal line spaces
- D. Plastic template writing guide with bars removed between three line spaces
- E. Plastic template writing guide
- F. Clipboard
- G. Unlined paper and writing tools

III. Assessment
- A. Does the learner currently write a signature?
- B. Is the learner familiar with the linear shapes of any letters in his or her name?
- C. If the learner had previous training in signature writing, what method or materials were used?

IV. Procedure
- A. Orientation
  1. Have the learner describe the template with three line spaces.
  2. Have the learner describe the clipboard and place the paper and guide in it.
  3. Have the learner demonstrate the way he or she holds a pencil.
  4. Have the learner demonstrate the proper method of holding a pencil.
  5. Have the learner draw loops, points, and mounds utilizing the full line space. (If needed, show these shapes with the raised-line drawing board.)
  6. Describe the concept of one-half line space.
  7. Have the learner draw loops, points, and mounds in one-half line space.
- B. Letter familiarization and connecting letters
  1. Demonstrate the shape of the first letter in the learner's last name.
     - a. Draw the letter on the raised-line board.
     - b. Have the learner draw the letter in a full line space on the clipboard-held guide.
     - c. If the learner is unable to do so,
       - (1) have him or her trace the Freund letter several times with the index finger.
       - (2) have him or her hold the pointed dowel rod like a pencil and trace the engraved letter several times.
       - (3) have him or her draw the letter on the clipboard.
  2. Familiarize the learner with the second letter in his or her last name by repeating the procedure for the first letter.
  3. Familiarize the learner with the third letter in his or her last name by repeating the procedure for the first letter.
     - a. Introduce the letter in the form used in the name; if it follows *b, o,* or *w* it will be formed differently than if it follows any other letter.

(continued on next page)

Teaching Signature Writing (continued)

b. Use the drawing board to demonstrate if necessary.
4. Have the learner draw the second and third letters with the connecting stroke, using the drawing board to demonstrate if necessary.
5. Repeat the procedure for the remaining letters of the learner's last name.
6. Familiarize the learner with the first letter of his or her first name and have him or her draw it.
7. Repeat the familiarization and connecting procedure for the remaining letters of the learner's first name.

C. Size reduction
1. Reduce the available line space by replacing the guide with one that utilizes two line spaces for the writing area.
2. Have the learner write in this size space until he or she is proficient.
3. Replace the guide with one that utilizes the standard one-line space for the writing area.
4. Have the learner use this space until he or she is proficient.
5. Replace the guide with a standard signature guide.
6. Have the learner use the guide until he or she is proficient.

V. Memoranda
A. Be aware of the implications of learning handwriting for the individual's self-image.
B. Although the Sewell board is not the ideal writing surface, it can be used in combination with the writing template as a practice tool for the learner. Write the correct form of the letter at the beginning of a line and have the learner repeat it on his or her own.
C. If not utilized, a signature will not be maintained at a highly legible level.
D. If the learner is making letters incorrectly, compare his or her letters with the correct versions by presenting them on the drawing board.

VI. Evaluation
A. Have the learner write his or her signature 10 times using a standard signature guide.
B. Repeat this evaluation after several days have passed.

VII. Assignment: The student can practice repetitious writing of new letters or words as they are successfully mastered.

who learn letter formation through the Weiss and Weiss method may be able to practice independently using taped or brailled instructions that give the dot and cell descriptions of each letter.

All of these methods have proved effective, but the degree of success varies with the learner's abilities. In many cases, it is necessary to use combinations of these methods as well as facets of traditional methods used to teach sighted children to write script, such as the Palmer Method (King, 1987) and D'Nealian writing (Thurber, 1987). As is usually the case, however, it is best to use the least amount of instruction necessary to reach the student's goal. For example, most learners will be able to reproduce letters after examining raised letters, such as those available in the American Printing House for the Blind's Freund Handwriting Kit (see the Resources section), so that is likely to be the main familiarization technique used. Other techniques can be used for supplementary instruction if more information is needed. Complex letters, such as *z*, might best be illustrated in an engraved form. The braille cell method might be used to motivate someone who is especially fond of braille.

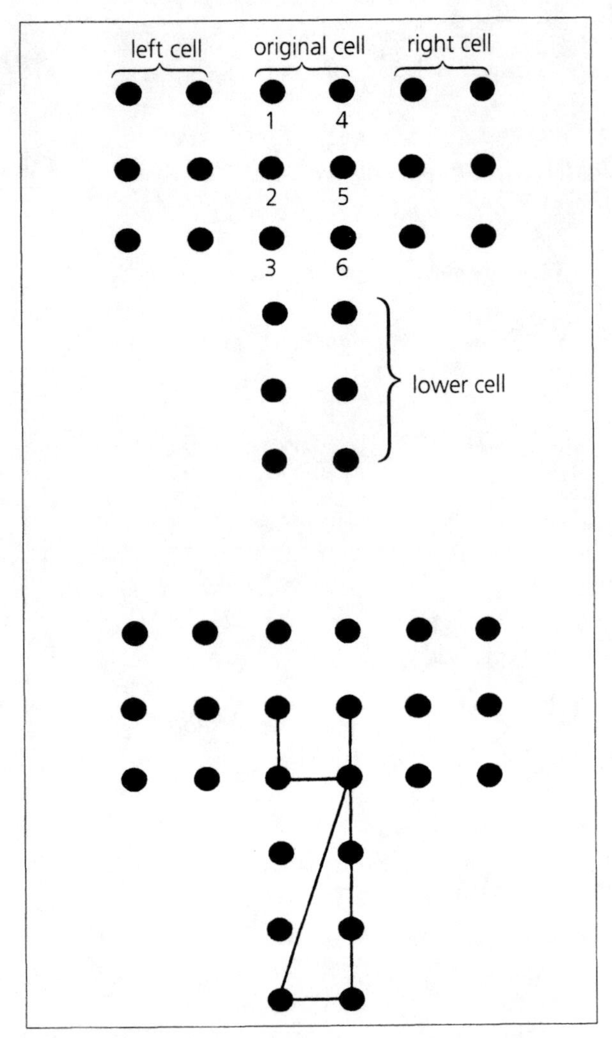

Figure 8.4. The Braille Cell Handwriting Method

In the braille cell method of teaching handwriting, every letter is formed by following a series of dot numbers in four adjacent braille cells, as shown here. This lowercase *y* is formed by placing the pen at dot 3 in the original cell and following the sequence 2, 3, 6, 5, 6, lower cell 6, 3, original cell 6.

The elaborate descriptions of task-analyzed movement proposed by Huckins (1965) might be advantageous in teaching individuals who need smaller units of learning, since they break down the writing of each letter into its basic components.

Regardless of which method of familiarization is used, the letters that are introduced should be presented through oversized models so that they are easily discernible tactilely. When the learner begins to reproduce letters, they will also be enlarged—generally in the range of 1 to 2 inches—but he or she can work at reducing the size after achieving consistency in reproducing the letters correctly.

If an individual's goal is to write a signature, the only letters to be learned are those necessary for his or her name. Later, if the learner is successful and is motivated enough to pursue the whole alphabet as a result of having learned his or her signature, the letters learned while mastering the signature can serve as building blocks for learning the rest. When the learner's goal is to master his or her signature, the sequence in which the letters are presented is probably not important from a learning standpoint, but if the last name is presented first, followed by the first initial and eventually the full first name, a legal signature can be attained more quickly. "J. Doe" is mastered more quickly than "Jonathan Doe."

After Mr. Doe is familiar with the upper-case *D*, he must transfer that knowledge to the action of drawing it on paper. As is the case with anyone learning to write with a pencil or pen, he must be shown the proper way to hold the writing instrument—although this skill would have already been taught if letters were introduced with engraved models. If Mr. Doe has difficulty in forming the *D*, at least two types of remediation can be used. The simplest is to present the learner with tactile comparison of his version and the correct one on a raised-line drawing board. Another alternative is to substitute a block print capital letter for the cursive one. The more elaborate letters, such as the upper-case *F* or *Z*, are likely to require such a substitution.

A writing guide with an opening of 1 to 2 inches in height is generally used during the initial writing phase so that the concept of line space can be introduced. After Mr. Doe masters the mechanical motion of writing the *D*, the *o* is introduced, along with the concept of the half-line space for lower-case letters between the topline and baseline.

Connecting Letters

Introducing Mr. Doe to the lower-case *e* brings with it the concept of connecting letters. The *e* is connected to the *o* by a flowing line at the half-line level, and it should be presented in that form, rather than in its basic form, in which it rises from a connector along the baseline. However, if Mr. Doe is working toward the more complex goal of learning all the cursive letters, he would need to know both forms. It should be borne in mind that letters also vary in shape when they follow *b, v* and *w*. Marks and Marks (1954) provide good verbal descriptions of how to connect letters.

Decreasing Letter Size

After learning all the letters in his or her name and connecting them to produce a complete signature, the learner must then reduce the signature to a usable size. The simplest method for accomplishing this is to gradually reduce the size of the line space provided by the writing guide. A series of homemade guides can be created with progressively decreasing line spaces using X-ray film or black cardboard, as described earlier.

The final product of all this hard work is a legible signature that may appear somewhat blockier than that produced by most sighted individuals. However, the degree of blockiness would appear to be a function of the methods used to familiarize the learner with letter shapes. For example, learners who use engraved letter guides will probably have more curvilinear writing than those using the braille cell method.

As is the case with any motor skill, signature writing must be used frequently, or the ability is lost over time. Moreover, writers who are totally blind cannot easily monitor their own performance. Therefore, they must make a special effort to elicit feedback from sighted friends or to practice on a raised-line drawing board so they can monitor the legibility of their writing.

HANDWRITING AND SELF-IMAGE

Rehabilitation teachers should be aware of the implications of learning skills such as handwriting for the self-image of people who are visually impaired. Literate people who find themselves in the role of a student attempting to master a skill that many learn in early elementary school can be easily frustrated and discouraged. Both learner and instructor should bear in mind the many hours, days, and weeks that young children spend learning and practicing the kinesthetic skill of handwriting. One is not likely to master or remaster that level of expertise and dexterity in only a few hours of lessons. Therefore, handwriting instruction is a skill best addressed when lessons can occur regularly for a substantial length of time. A new learner might need 40 to 50 hours of instruction to complete the goal of writing all the alphabet letters.

Occasionally, people in positions of temporary authority, such as bank tellers and cashiers, may question the legibility of a signature produced by a person with a visual impairment. It is easy to be daunted by the opinion of a sighted person who says he or she cannot accept a check because the signature is not readable, and such an incident may threaten the enhanced self-esteem an individual has won by learning or relearning signature writing.

> Sonia N., a totally congenitally blind woman, experienced an embarrassing incident at a drugstore when she paid for some purchases by check. After she took her purchases to the checkout counter and was told the amount owed, she had her friend fill out her personal check for the exact amount. Then she signed her rather long name to the check using a signature guide, while the clerk watched her slow and deliberate movements. Ms. N.'s cheeks burned with embarrassment when the clerk announced that he could not accept her check because he couldn't read the signature. She asked to speak to the manager, stating that her signature was probably no more or less readable than anyone else's and that it was a legal signature. The manager immediately apologized to Sonia N., explaining that the clerk was new. After approving the check, he told her that although the experience was not pleasant for

her, it had alerted him to something that should be covered when orienting employees. Ms. N. never had any other difficulties while shopping at the drugstore.

Recognizing that the slowness of writing her long signature legibly tended to draw attention to her and perhaps hold up other customers, Sonia N. asked her rehabilitation teacher to work with her on a more stylized signature that could be produced quickly and with a flourish. The end result was an artistic-looking stylized signature, based on recognizable cursive forms of her initials *S* and *N* followed by wavy lines, that could be produced in just seconds. Her signature was never again questioned, despite its departure from standard-looking letters.

It is important and empowering to the individual to include in handwriting instruction a discussion about what to do if one's signature or ability to write is questioned. The rehabilitation teacher can emphasize that many times even people who are experienced with handwriting have signatures that are not fully legible. In fact, many people in the general population adopt stylized signatures that scarcely approximate legibility. Students with visual impairments should have the option of choosing a traditional-looking signature or a stylized signature that would require fewer hours of instruction, be quicker to produce, and might even be somewhat more sophisticated looking, which could enhance self-image. In either case, the client should feel confident that his or her signature is a perfectly legal one.

CHAPTER 9

Keyboarding and Computer Skills

KEY CONCEPTS IN THIS CHAPTER

- **Adaptive methods utilized in typewriting with low vision or no vision**
- **Methods used to teach adaptive typewriting**
- **Uses of personal computers for individuals with visual impairments**
- **The components of personal computer systems**
- **Voice output systems for personal computers and their characteristics**
- **Nontechnical adaptations and screen enlargement output systems for computer users with low vision**
- **Braille output systems for personal computers**
- **Braille or standard keyboard input/speech output notetakers**
- **Methods of teaching word processing**

The tactile communications systems discussed in Chapter 7 are primarily used by people with visual impairments to communicate with themselves or with other people who are visually impaired. These methods are not generally useful for communicating with people who have normal vision because, for the most part, they consist of codes or symbols that are unfamiliar to most sighted people. To present ideas and information in a written form to readers who are sighted, people who are blind usually use printed or typed materials. Thus, a knowledge of typing or word processing is a virtual necessity for any visually impaired person who has a need to create formal written documents.

The manner in which written documents are created has changed dramatically since 1980. At that time, mechanical and electric typewriters allowed users to type very quickly and to make machine-based corrections. However, these gave way in rapid succession to electronic typewriters and to computers. Computers are especially helpful to people with visual impairments because of the ease of access made possible by adaptive devices and software. The rapidity of the development of accessible microprocessors has been astonishing, and it is all but impossible for this or any other text to present completely current technical information because new products and technological developments appear daily.

The first commercially available device to give visually impaired people access to computer technology, introduced by a Maryland-based company in the late 1970s (Ponchillia & Mark, 1988), was a dedicated microcomputer that had been modified to produce speech. It was designed for word processing and as a talking telephone directory for operators with visual impairments. Because it was manufactured exclusively for blind users and not produced on a large scale, it cost in excess of $20,000. During the early 1980s, innovative blind persons or their advocates developed software and hardware that could be used with mainstream personal computers. The earliest attempts resulted in Apple computer software packages that combined word-processing programs designed specifically for visually impaired users with voice-output programs.

In recent years, the emphasis has shifted from specially designed word-processing packages to adaptive output devices that allow visually impaired users access to a variety of more powerful mainstream software applications. Today, as a result of specially designed devices and software (computer programs), virtually all computer applications are available to people with visual impairments. They are made accessible through the media of speech, large print, and refreshable braille displays (a device connected to a computer in which plastic pins pop up to form braille characters one line at a time), or hard copy braille (Leventhal, Uslan, & Schreier, 1990; Lowry, 1985; Luxton, Gerber, & Henry, 1985; Schreier & Uslan, 1991; Story & Kuyk, 1988).

Access to electronic word processing has provided a tool for people with visual impairments that allows them to overcome most of the problems described by Father Carroll (1961) as limitations to written communication (see Sidebar 9.1). Unlike the standard typewriter, an accessible computer allows people with visual impairments to review the material that has been keyboarded so that they can easily set margins, compose documents, and detect and correct mistakes. Database software has also improved the ability of visually impaired persons to store and retrieve information. Whereas people with limited vision once stored address lists, recipes, checkbook data, and classroom notes on cassette tapes or in large braille files, they now can locate specific information immeasurably more quickly using a personal computer. Similarly, information contained in

SIDEBAR 9.1

Father Carroll's View of the Effects of Vision Loss on Ease of Written Communication

Among the 20 losses Father Carroll (1961) specified as resulting from blindness, he considered the loss of ease of written communication—"the writing and reading of language symbols," including "signs, cartoons, and pictures,"—as "one of the most widely known of the losses." Within this category he noted such examples as:

- The loss of the ability to read books
- The loss of the ability to read magazines, trade publications and journals, and the daily papers, including the funny pages
- The loss of the ability to accomplish such diverse tasks as reading, advertisements, finding numbers in a telephone book, or watching television (which Carroll considered a recreational activity equivalent to reading)
- The loss of the ability to read one's own mail, to write one's own letters, to keep up one's personal correspondence without the intrusion of another party
- The "grave" loss of the ability to write one's own signature
- The loss of the ability to write such varied items as checks, a grocery list, notes to one's self, and messages on greeting cards.

such sources as newspapers and catalogs can be reached through telecommunications networks in addition to reading machines (discussed in Chapter 10). Many people use their computers to gain access to their bank accounts—checking balances, transferring funds, and paying bills—and to communicate with others through electronic mail. Computer games have increased recreational possibilities as well. The keyboard can also be used to manipulate the environment—for example, to set oven timers, thermostats, and bathwater temperatures.

The key to this world of electronic word processing, computers, and telecommunications is the basic typing skill that allows individuals with visual impairments to use typewriters and computer keyboards to communicate and otherwise manipulate data. Therefore, this basic skill will be considered first, and then examination of the adaptations that make computers accessible to visually impaired users will follow. Finally, an overview of the basics of word-processing programs and the fundamentals of teaching word processing will be presented because it is the area most commonly taught by rehabilitation teachers.

KEYBOARDING SKILLS

The skill most basic to entering data into a computer is keyboarding—that is, using the panel of keys to operate the machine and to enter text or data. Since typewriters are less expensive than personal computers and are easily utilized by persons with visual impairments, the specific skills involved in typing are important as well. Although few retail vendors of typewriters still carry a selection of mechanical machines, the machines remain in use (Page, 1990). Many clients still use them, particularly elderly people who use them to write letters and are not interested in making use of the power of personal computers. For example,

> Lucy E., an 83-year-old woman who is totally blind, had difficulty using handwriting because of difficulties with fine-motor coordination. Several years after completing her rehabilitation program, she uses an electronic typewriter to write letters to relatives, compile her grocery lists for the neighbor who shops for her, and leave notes for her housekeeper. She stores most information, such as telephone numbers, recipes, and addresses, on cassette tape. When asked about switching over to computers, she states that she is meeting her needs nicely with her present system and would have a difficult time finding the money to upgrade.

Because of their current importance to many individuals, the adaptive skills involved in using both electronic and mechanical typewriters will be covered in detail here. Keyboarding skills for the computer are essentially identical, although there are additional keys to learn.

The inability to monitor visually the layout of the machine or what is being typed changes the usual sequence for typewriting in several ways, and affects the following:

- initial orientation
- inserting the paper
- setting margins and tabs
- detecting and correcting mistakes
- detecting the end of the paper
- signing letters
- composing documents
- typing the text in the proper place on the page.

Each of these aspects of typewriter use will be considered in turn (see Lesson Plan 9.1 for teaching keyboarding in this chapter).

Initial Orientation

Proper seating and posture should be stressed when introducing the learner to keyboarding, particularly if he or she plans to spend long periods of working at the machine. This would apply regardless of the type of machine—mechanical,

Teaching Keyboarding

I. Objective: When presented with an electronic typewriter and paper, the learner will type a business letter with less than one mistake per page.

II. Materials
- A. Electronic typewriter with dictionary, correction feature, and automatic paper loading
- B. Standard typing paper
- C. Tape recorder with foot pedal control
- D. Typing drills on tape

III. Assessment
- A. Has the learner typed in the past and to what degree?
- B. Does the learner remember his or her typing speed if formerly measured?
- C. Can the learner see typewriter markings or standard typed print?

IV. Procedure
- A. Uses of typewriting
    1. Probably the best method of corresponding with friends
    2. Inexpensive method of producing formal documents for business or education
- B. Orientation to the machine and its parts
    1. Have the learner investigate and describe the machine as a whole.
    2. Have the learner locate and name the parts of the typewriter if he or she is not new to typing.
    3. If the learner has never typed, have him or her describe the major parts.
    4. Point out the following parts if missed:
        - a. cord and on/off switch
        - b. paper insertion mechanism
        - c. paper line advance mechanism
        - d. typewriter keyboard
        - e. number keys
        - f. special function keys
        - g. ribbon mechanism
- C. Paper insertion
    1. Have the learner investigate the paper insertion mechanism.
    2. Have the learner describe the paper insertion process, if possible; if not, explain it.
    3. Have the learner insert paper into the typewriter.
    4. Explain how to determine if paper is in straight.
        - a. Have the learner match the top and bottom edges of the paper.
        - b. Have the learner line up the top edge of the paper on a straight edge of some machine part.
        - c. Have the learner practice until he or she demonstrates consistent ability to insert the paper straight.
- D. Keyboard orientation
    1. Introduce the keys of the home row (*a, s, d, f, g, h, j, k, l, ;*) and have the learner drill until those keys are learned.

(continued on next page)

Teaching Keyboarding (continued)

2. Introduce the other keys controlled by the right index finger (*y, u, m, n*) and have the learner drill until those keys are learned.
3. Introduce the character correction key and have the learner drill until that key is learned.
4. Introduce the other keys controlled by the left index finger (*t, r, v, b*) and have the learner drill until those keys are learned.
5. Introduce the other keys controlled by the second fingers (*e, c, i*, comma) and have the learner drill until those keys are learned.
6. Introduce the whole word correction feature and have the learner drill until that feature is learned.
7. Introduce the other keys controlled by the third fingers (*w, x, o*, period) and have the learner drill until those keys are learned.
8. Introduce the other keys controlled by the fourth fingers (*q, z, p*, slash) and have the learner drill until those keys are learned.
9. Have the learner drill, correcting mistakes, until he or she reaches a proficiency of eight mistakes or less per page.
10. Numeric keyboard
    a. Have the learner use the "organ method" (that is, lifting the hand and setting all the fingers down on the top row of numeric keys, rather than extending them from the home row), until all the number keys are learned.
    b. Have the learner use the touch method until all the number keys are learned.
11. Setting margins and tabs
    a. Explain margins and tabs, if necessary, and explain how to set them by counting the number of spaces to equal the desired width.
    b. Describe the method of setting the margins and tabs.
    c. Have the learner set margins and tabs until the method is learned.
12. Letter format
    a. Explain the spacing for friendly and business letters.
    b. Explain that there are six line spaces per vertical inch.
    c. Have the learner type friendly letters until there are less than eight mistakes per page after correction.
    d. Have the learner type business letters until there is less than one mistake per page after correction.
13. Envelopes
    a. Explain envelope spacing and format.
    b. Have the learner type long and short envelopes until there is less than one mistake per envelope.
14. Special adaptations
    a. Explain the methods for detecting the bottom of the typed page.
        (1) Some machines emit a warning signal.
        (2) A shorter backing sheet can be used that falls out before the typed page.

(continued on next page)

Teaching Keyboarding (continued)

(3) Crease the page about 1 inch from the bottom and monitor tactilely to determine when that point is reached.

b. Explain that prerecording the text eliminates the frustration of trying to type and compose at the same time.

c. Explain that the line for signing the letter can be monitored tactilely if the name is typed over several times.

d. Have low vision learners experiment with reading stands and lighting.

V. Memoranda

A. It is generally best to discourage the use of vision in making sure the correct keys are being struck, but encourage its use for reviewing the document.

B. It is generally helpful to have the learner do a survey of available machines at the end of the instruction period to determine the best buy.

VI. Evaluation

A. Have the learner type a one-page friendly letter with less than eight mistakes per page.

B. Have the learner type a business letter with less than one mistake per page.

C. Have the learner type a business envelope with less than one mistake.

VII. Assignment: Have the learner practice independently, typing each type of document as it is taught.

electronic, or computer. Tactile investigation of the machine is as adequate for initial orientation as visual inspection. When learners have typed previously, they should be allowed to explore the machine in order to identify its parts, and new typists need to investigate to find out how the parts are related to one another. It is not important for the learner to know the function of all the parts at this stage, since he or she will be able to remember them more easily as they gain relevance during subsequent lessons.

After tactile exploration, the next step is learning the keys on the keyboard. The usual method is to introduce the home row—the set of keys (*a, s, d, f, j, k, l, ;*) on which the typist's fingers rest and to which they return between strokes—and then teach the proper fingering for one or two keys at a time. The sequence of keys to be taught will vary with the typing manual that is used. The instructor can follow the lessons of any well-known mainstream typing text or make use of other products, such as typing instruction software that is usable on voice-output computers. The advantage of voice output is immense, given the need for immediate feedback on the part of both the learner and the instructor.

As the client is learning the keys and becoming tactilely oriented to the keyboard, the instructor can reinforce proper stroking by marking the key or keys to be learned with a raised symbol or a large print letter. When a keystroke is mastered, the instructor removes the symbol and places it on the next key to be learned. This method is especially helpful when teaching keys that require reaching away from the home row, such as *y* or *t*. Many commercial typewriters and computers contain raised symbols permanently affixed to the *f* and *j* or the *d* and *k* keys to enhance rapid placement of fingers on the home row, but other markers can be added if necessary. Stroking can be reinforced by modeling: The instructor places his or her hands on the keyboard and the learner lays his or her hands on top to allow monitoring of the proper finger movement.

Occasionally, learners with visual impairments may also be limited to the use of only one hand. In that event, teaching is modified to use whichever hand is functional. In *Type with One Hand* (Richardson, 1959), the main objective is to provide a functional keyboard approach, with a primary emphasis on hand position—that is, operating from a smaller home row that is in the center of the keyboard. This text provides methods and exercises for either hand. Other resources, such as modified computer keyboards for one-handed keyboarding, can be located in *Closing the Gap*, a bimonthly publication covering technology for people with disabilities (see Resources section).

Paper Insertion

In general, the correct insertion of the paper into the machine requires simple adaptations for people with limited vision. The paper must be placed in the carriage at a 90-degree angle to the roller, and some typists have difficulty inserting it straight. Some electronic typewriters insert the paper mechanically, but they, too, need to be monitored for straightness. The solution is to tactilely compare the edge of the paper with a straight edge and straighten it, if necessary, with the platen lock released. The typist can compare the top edge of the paper with a straight surface on the typewriter, such as the cover over the roller, insert the paper halfway, and pinch the top and bottom edges together over the roller to make sure they are even.

Setting of Margins and Tabs

Because the number of spaces per inch on typewriters is uniform, margins and tabs can be set by counting spaces. Typewriters with pica print contain 10 spaces per inch, and elite machines have 12 per inch. To set the standard margins of 1 inch on the left and 1/2 inch on the right requires 10 pica spaces from the paper's left edge, or 12 elite spaces, and 5 pica or 6 elite spaces from the right edge (Lennon, n.d.). The process of setting margins or tabs by counting spaces is dependent on setting the paper guide properly so that the left edge of the paper lines up with the leftmost margin setting. Therefore, it is recommended that the zero point for the paper guide be marked so that the typist can reset it at zero if it is accidentally moved.

Electronic machines generally have preset margins for standard typing tasks. Changing them is usually accomplished through sequential keyboard input, the specifics of which vary greatly among brands of machines. In most cases, the procedure must be recorded in an accessible form or memorized by the typist with a visual impairment.

Correction of Mistakes

Perhaps the major shortcoming of typewriters in the past for people with visual impairments has been the inability of the typist to detect mistakes. Although skilled blind typists can produce flawless documents because they often realize immediately after striking an incorrect key that they have made an error, new learners cannot be expected to be as efficient unless they have enough vision to reread their work. Some electronic typewriters contain dictionaries of words that the device constantly scans. When the typist makes a typographical error, an auditory signal indicates a misspelled or repeated word, thus virtually eliminating the error detection problem.

Once the typist recognizes an error, there are several ways to make corrections. Electronic machines are the most user-friendly in this regard. Models that include "spell checkers" generally also hold text in memory, which allows the user to command the machine to erase a character, a word, or an entire line with a single keystroke. For example, at the sound of the beep indicating the error, the typist strikes the erase-character key and retypes the letter correctly.

Correcting mistakes made with mechanical machines is also possible, but requires more effort. Unless the user possesses sufficient vision to see the typed characters, standard correction fluids are virtually useless, since it would be difficult to "white out" only the incorrect character without using sight. Correction papers are more useful for typists with vision loss. There are two types in common use. The first has one surface covered with a white powder to cover up incorrect letters and is used with ink ribbons; the second contains a sticky surface designed to actually remove characters typed with a carbon ribbon by lifting them off the page. In either case, the typist backspaces to the incorrect character, places the correction paper between the document and the ribbon, strikes the incorrect letter key again to cover or remove that letter, removes the correction paper, backspaces, then types the correct letter. The powdered or sticky surfaces of the correction paper can be easily detected tactilely, but touching them may interfere with their effectiveness, and the powder can easily be spread from fingers to clothing. To avoid this problem, the typist can fold over about one-half inch of the nonfunctional side of the paper, providing a safe place for handling and making it easier to recognize the functional side.

Detecting the End of the Paper

Detecting the end of the paper on which one is typing can also be difficult for a person with a visual impairment. Many visually impaired typists are familiar with the maddening sound of the typing paper sliding to the floor while they are still diligently typing away.

As with correcting mistakes, electronic typewriters can be especially helpful, since some models provide a warning signal that enables the user to stop before the paper falls out. Methods for alerting the typist on a mechanical machine that the end of the paper is approaching include the following:

- using a shorter backing sheet that is inserted into the roller along with the top sheet and falls away when the typing head is near the end of the page
- crimping the paper 1 inch from the bottom before beginning to type and then monitoring it tactilely to determine when that point is reached.

Signing Letters

Typists who are totally blind may also have difficulty locating the proper place to sign letters that they have typed. On a mechanical machine, the user can type a line, using the underline key, that is four spaces below the closing and just above his or her typed name. If the line is struck over several times, it becomes tactilely discernible.

Composing Documents

Composing documents on a typewriter is especially difficult for people with limited vision who are unable to read what they have typed. The writer is required to recall the exact wording of what has already been written, know the exact point at which the typing ceased, and, at the same time, deal with any interruptions to his or her train of thought. It is usually advantageous to separate the composing chore from the typing; that is, to compose the document first in braille, in enlarged handwriting, or on tape, thus providing a means of review, and then to keyboard it later. A good habit for typists to develop in the event of an interruption while typing is to complete the sentence, punctuate, and space twice before attending to the interruption. That will ensure that a document does not have confusing changes in topic or spacing errors within sentences where the typing stopped abruptly and restarted.

Placement

To place the typed text in the proper location on the page or on an envelope without using vision, the typist can count spaces from the edges of the paper, as when setting margins. For example, knowing that there are 66 lines per typed page and 6 typed lines per inch allows the typist to leave a 1-inch margin at the top and bottom of a business letter. The typist can also count spaces in a typed line to determine its midpoint so the text can be centered.

If electronic typewriters are superior to mechanical ones for most users, they are especially helpful to those with visual impairments. Not all electronic typewriters contain all the features discussed, however, and there is considerable range in functional characteristics between the least and most expensive models. Rehabilitation teachers should constantly survey the major brands to be able to make appropriate recommendations to clients.

COMPUTER ADAPTATIONS

The adaptations that give people with visual impairments access to computers allow them to utilize all their recreational, data-management, and networking functions, as the example of Brenda H. illustrates:

> Brenda H., a 40-year-old woman who is totally blind, makes her living as a medical transcriptionist at a hospital. For years she transcribed her dictated work flawlessly, using a typewriter. However, when the hospital converted to a computer-based transcription system a few years ago, Brenda H. was forced to learn the system, using a voice synthesizer (discussed later in this section) as her access device. Since that time, she has purchased her own personal computer, voice synthesizer, book scanner, and braille printer. Brenda is now able to do freelance transcription in her own home. She reads print leisure books daily with her scanning device and also frequently uses her computer for more advanced functions, such as programming, networking with on-line bulletin boards, shopping, and banking. In fact, she is well-known in her community as the one to call when someone is stymied by a computer problem.

As a tool for written communication, computers function mainly through the medium of word-processing programs—programs that make the computer operate essentially as a highly sophisticated electronic typewriter. To be able to teach clients word-processing skills, rehabilitation teachers need to have an overview of computer use so that they can introduce new users to the computer and help them learn the necessary adaptations, as well as teach a specific word-processing program. Therefore, this section will examine computers and adaptations for visually impaired users, and the next section will present word-processing skills. (Chapter 10 includes discussion of some other computer applications for communication, including computer reading systems that convert printed text into electronic files or directly into speech and "computerized" books that are available on disk or on line.)

Teaching Introductory Computing

Teaching beginning computer skills to a student with a visual impairment is not difficult, but the task of deciding the content and sequence of lessons is often complicated by the fact that many instructors either have had no formal training in computers or know a vast amount about the realm of computing and find it difficult to limit and condense lessons. However, the key to introducing accessible computing for people with visual impairments using adaptive technology seems to be to discuss the potential uses with the student, briefly introduce the parts of the computer, and then provide sequential instruction in a more-or-less rote manner that leads toward a specific goal—for example, use of a word-processing program with a voice synthesizer or use of a household budget program with screen-enlargement software. Thus, the user is taught just those commands necessary to

- load the access software
- load the application software
- complete the desired task
- save the information or print it out, if necessary
- "exit" the software properly.

When the learner has mastered these basics and is ready for more information and options, the additional details are likely to be more meaningful because they will be based on concepts that are already familiar.

> Kai Q. was a young adult who had central scotomas in both eyes which interfered with reading and other near tasks. He had learned to type, and he was eager to learn to use a computer, but was intimidated by it since he had never seen one before. His first lessons on a computer with voice output were simple. His instructor let him explore the various parts while they discussed possible uses for the new student. During the first lessons, the instructor turned the system on and loaded the voice synthesizer and word-processing software, and Kai typed a letter. He was ecstatic to hear his keystrokes announced, even when he accidentally hit the wrong keys. The cursor control, backspace, and delete keys were introduced only as he needed to use them to review or correct his writing, when the information would make sense to him. A short time later, when he was accustomed to the synthesizer, he asked if he could turn off the feature that made it "talk when I type" (keyboard announcement), and asked how to make it talk faster. The instructor decided it was the opportune time to introduce the speech control commands.
>
> As Kai Q. became more sophisticated in his use of computers, the instructor added more information to assist him in becoming an independent computer operator. For example, after Kai was shown how to create speech windows, using game software as an example, he wanted to know how to make a duplicate of the non-copyrighted game for a friend, so the instructor used the situation as a basis for introducing operating system commands.

Orienting a client who has never used a computer before involves explaining the basic components of the computer, including the following:

- *Central processing unit* (CPU)—the "brain" of the computer
- *Keyboard*—the arrangement of the keys used to operate the computer, similar to that of a typewriter, with additional keys
- *Disk drives*—part of the computer that can read information stored on magnetic *disks.* Computers commonly have "hard" drives installed inside the CPU and one or more "floppy" disk drives.
- *Monitor*—a screen similar to that of a television, through which the user accesses the data stored in the computer
- *Peripheral devices*—auxiliary devices that perform additional functions, such as *printers, braille devices,* and *speech synthesizers,* which plug into their corresponding receptacles or *ports* found on the back panels of most machines
- *Cards*—special circuit boards that allow the computer to communicate with the peripheral devices.

(For more detailed information, see Espinola and Croft, 1992.)

Adaptations such as speech synthesizers, braille displays, and screen magnifiers that allow people with little or no vision access to most computer functions do so by modifying the way in which the information on the computer screen is

A typical computer.

presented. These tools allow the operator to review one part of the screen, usually one line or less, at a time. That section can be heard, read tactilely, or scanned visually.

Speech Output

Speech synthesis is probably the adaptive medium most widely used by people with visual impairments to gain access to computers. A synthetic speech system is composed of two parts: the synthesizer that does the speaking and the screen access program that tells the synthesizer what to say. The synthesizer can be either a card (a circuit board) that is installed in the computer or a separate box attached to one of the computer's ports by a cable.

When the user types letters or reads through computer text using cursor movement keys, a voice synthesizer provides auditory equivalents of what is shown on the screen. The synthesizer converts the electronic signals that are being transmitted to the screen as text into spoken units. This is possible because the rules contained in the software allow the computer to recognize phonemes, the letter combinations unique to a language that constitute distinct sounds. For example, a speech synthesizer program for English identifies the *shun* sound of the letter combination *tion* or the long *e* sound of the *ea* combination and speaks them appropriately. The minimum number of rules required for this process is approximately 400 (Williams, 1983). The more sophisticated synthesizers require far more rules, and the cost increases proportionally with the amount of time required to develop the software, but the present range of choices makes use of a synthesizer within reach of the average consumer. (The actual methods of using the keyboard to control the speech synthesizer and to read the screen are usually taught along with word processing and are discussed under Teaching Speech Synthesizer Commands later in this chapter.) Scanning devices that are capable of translating written text into computer files that can then be converted into speech by the synthesizer are discussed in Chapter 10.

Commercially available speech devices are diverse and vary greatly in usefulness. Therefore, anyone interested in purchasing one should know the more desirable characteristics. Two essential capabilities are *screen review* and *keyboard announcement* (Morford, 1983). Many software packages on the market claim to be useful to blind users simply because they speak. Many of these verbalize what is on the screen, but do not allow the user to review the content of specific lines or of the spelling of specific words without using the cursor to move through the document character by character or line by line. Screen review freezes the document; gives the user access to the voice configurations (explained later in this chapter) that control how it's being read; and allows the user to move rapidly through the document, reading only the desired information, without altering it. Since synthesizers do not reproduce speech perfectly, screen review is a much-utilized feature, and without it synthesizers are of little use. For example, the synthesizer may pronounce the word *ocean* as "oh-seen," so the operator will need to listen to it again, character by character, to hear "o-c-e-a-n." Likewise, a single word spoken aloud out of context, as in a spelling game such as Hangman, may not be understood. Keyboard announcement, the feature that speaks the name of a key as it is struck, is, of course, especially helpful to new learners since they can receive immediate feedback while typing.

Other desirable characteristics of speech synthesizers include the ability to:

- stop the voice instantly at the strike of a key
- spell out unusual letter combinations, such as acronyms
- adjust the rate of speech
- pronounce computer code symbols, such as those used by word-processing software for underlining or boldface type
- suppress or limit announcement of a series of repeated characters, such as a series of asterisks used to make a box on the screen for sighted users

- view windows or columns, rather than the full screen (Alliance for Technology Access, Morford, 1983; Meyers & Schreier, 1990).

The last characteristic allows the user to strike a specified key to read any part of the screen aloud. This is important because the instructions or questions that are displayed on the screen do not always appear on the same line; they may appear anywhere on the screen, from the first half of line 1 to the last half of line 25. Once users are familiar with specific software, they can set fixed review windows at any desired location on the screen. When a window is established, the user can avoid having to listen to the full screen to find a small bit of information, such as which page of a document he or she is working on.

Generally, vendors that sell adaptive computer products for visually impaired individuals have included these features to make their products competitive. The rehabilitation teacher needs to be most concerned when purchasing from a mainstream company with little experience in serving the needs of visually impaired persons.

One family of adaptive computer devices combines braille or standard keyboard input with speech output. They are small, portable microprocessors, often referred to as *notetakers* (Leventhal, Schreier, De Witt, & Myers, 1988; Leventhal & Uslan, 1992). The braille input notetakers have a seven-key brailler keyboard and output through a speech synthesizer only; some have limited braille displays. These keyboard-input/voice-output devices are advantageous to people who do not need visual displays because the devices are so small and portable. Although keyboard-input/voice-output microprocessors are often not equipped with disk drives, their files are easily transferable to optional disk drives or other computers. They can also be used as modular speech synthesizers for mainstream computers.

Braille Output

Braille output devices produce either *refreshable* braille on a shifting display or *hard copy* braille embossed on paper. The refreshable braille display is

A refreshable braille display.

A braille printer.

formed by a series of pins that can be read tactilely when raised. The pins are arranged in six-holed cells, corresponding to the dots of the braille cell. Each pin in each hole is activated by a switch. When the computer activates the switch, the pin is forced up through the hole, representing one braille dot. One line is usually displayed at a time, with subsequent lines displayed at the touch of a key.

Braille printers are embossing devices that can be attached to microcomputers in the same fashion as are standard printers to produce braille output on paper. Reasonably priced models are available for personal use (Leventhal, 1994), while more expensive ones are marketed for mass production of braille documents.

Screen Magnification

In addition to using devices that provide auditory or tactile computer output, people with visual impairments can use adaptations to make the characters on the computer monitor more visible. Increasing the visibility of the screen can be approached in several ways, based on the same principles used to increase the visibility of any reading medium (see Chapter 6). One or more of the key variables must be manipulated:

- lighting
- contrast
- glare
- size.

These variables can be manipulated either by modifying the working environment or by more elaborate electronic means. In general, environmental modifications are preferable because electronic enlargement limits the amount of information available on the monitor at one time to as little as one line or even a few characters at a time. In addition, the computer-based adaptations are significantly more expensive.

Environmental Adaptations

All four environmental variables can be modified without special software interventions. Lighting, contrast, and glare are, to some degree, functions of ambient room lighting. As the room light is decreased, the contrast of the display with the rest of the room increases and glare from the monitor screen surface decreases. Contrast can also be ad-

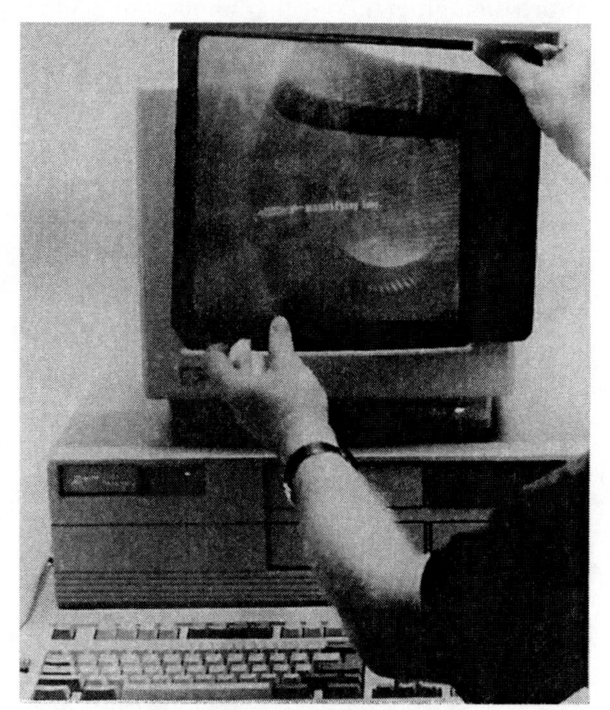

An attachable screen-magnifying lens.

justed by experimenting to find the best setting of the contrast control on the monitor and by altering the color of the letters and the background used for display. The availability of amber, green, yellow, or full-color displays also allows the user to choose the one that is most visible. Character size can be increased by purchasing a larger monitor, changing default settings of the software, moving the monitor closer, or adding one of several magnifying lenses that cover the entire screen and are available through vendors of adaptive equipment (see Resources).

Computer-Based Electronic Adaptations

If simple mechanical solutions do not increase the visibility of the monitor enough to make it accessible to an individual with limited vision, the rehabilitation teacher should investigate a computer-based magnification system. These systems, which electronically enlarge the characters displayed on the monitor, may work through software only, hardware only, or combinations of both.

Screen enlargement software is loaded into a standard personal computer prior to the word-processing program or other applications and is stored in the computer's memory. This type of software allows the user to magnify the displays of many types of programs (see, for example, Shragai & Uslan, 1995b). Because it is more versatile, more portable, and often less expensive than other electronic forms of magnification, screen enlargement software is especially useful to individuals with low vision. Users need only insert a disk into a compatible machine to magnify their work. However, screen enlargement software is not always completely compatible with mainstream machines or software. Therefore, anyone contemplating such a purchase should investigate thoroughly to be sure a given program works with his or her hardware and applications software.

Combined Outputs

Each adaptive output medium has its advantages and disadvantages. Therefore, many users choose combinations of devices and adaptations that maximize their efficiency. Although such an approach costs more, some situations, particularly those related to an individual's vocation, may warrant the extra expense. For example, if a person who is totally blind needs to turn out a large quantity of highly accurate documents for his or her job, he or she may need a speech synthesizer for rapid production and quick review, and a braille output device to ensure accuracy. By the same token, someone with limited but useful vision who had a similar job would find the combination of a speech synthesizer and a large-print device most efficient (De Witt, Schreier, Leventhal, & Meyers, 1988). The programmer in the following example combined speech output with screen magnification:

> Brad T. makes his living as a computer programmer, but also uses the computer to meet his personal needs, such as word processing, keeping track of his finances, and communicating on computer networks. He uses both screen-enlargement and voice-output systems. On the job, he generally uses his screen-enlargement software because accuracy is extremely important in programming, and he can best monitor the accuracy of what appears on the screen visually. However, he uses voice synthesis for most other applications because it increases his screen reading speed more than twofold. He opts for the speed of voice output over the accuracy of enlarged visual screen reading, since he can monitor spelling in his written documents with his word processor's spell-check function, and accuracy is not as important in most of his networking applications.

WORD-PROCESSING PROGRAMS

Word processing can be defined as the act of creating a document that is stored in machine memory. It is much akin to typing, but the document is not being produced as the keys are being struck. Rather, it appears in its electronic form on the computer's screen and is stored in the computer's memory. After all corrections have been made and it is in its final form, the document can be printed.

The numerous existing word-processing programs vary greatly in complexity, but most share some common functions and commands to execute them. Commands associated with keyboarding the written document and making alterations in its text or appearance will be referred to here as the *editing* commands; those that instruct the computer on what to do with the completed document will be termed *system* commands.

Editing Mode

The editing commands of most word-processing programs typically include the following:

- *Cursor movement.* The cursor is a blinking symbol on the computer screen. In word processing it is analogous to the typewriter head in that it indicates where the next character to be entered will appear and moves to the next space to the right after a character is typed.

  The movement of the cursor is controlled by four keys marked with arrows. The right arrow moves the cursor one character to the right, the left arrow moves it one to the left, the up arrow moves it up one line, and the down arrow moves it down one line. The backspace key also moves the cursor back one space, but usually performs the function of erasing the last character typed as well. The cursor can also be moved from one page to another or to the beginning or end of a multipage document.
- *Searching.* The cursor can also be moved through the use of a search command, which locates a given word or string of characters anywhere in the current document.
- *Deleting.* Various delete functions allow the operator to eliminate single characters, single words, groups of words, entire lines or larger blocks of text, depending on the command used.
- *Inserting.* The insert function gives the operator the power to place one or more characters within existing text. For example, if during proofreading the operator notes that a word was inadvertently omitted, the operator can insert it, and the computer will automatically push the remainder of the text ahead, thus eliminating the need for retyping the document.
- *Centering.* The centering function automatically places all the text on a single line at the midpoint of that line.

System Mode

When a document is finished, the computer must be instructed what to do with the information. The system mode allows the user to perform the following commands with entire documents, known as text files:

- *Saving.* Saving a document in the form of a text file is the process of transferring it to a storage disk. When saving to a disk, the save command sends the data from the memory through a circuit board, through a port, and to a disk drive, where it can be stored on the computer's hard disk or on a removable floppy disk in much the same fashion as material is recorded on an audiocassette tape.
- *Retrieving.* The user can retrieve a saved document from the computer's hard drive to edit it further. Or, the user can insert a disk containing the text file into the disk drive, load the text file back into the computer, and make alterations to the document.
- *Deleting.* The delete command functions much as it does in the editing mode, but in the system mode it eliminates entire

text files from the disk, rather than characters or words from the text file.

- *Printing.* The print command sends the text file to a printer to produce a paper, or "hard copy," document.
- *View directory.* The directory command instructs the computer to display the names of all the text files stored on either the particular disk placed in the disk drive or in the hard drive (or a specified subdirectory of either). This display is analogous to the table of contents of a textbook, but it contains additional information, such as the size of the file and the date when it was produced.

Most word-processing programs provide other powerful functions that allow the operator to move text from one file to another, check for spelling errors, look up synonyms, print portions of files, and the like. There are also useful system commands to perform such operations as formatting disks, copying disks, or copying files from one disk to another. As the operator's skills increase, the need for such tools also increases. However, the basic functions already described allow the user to produce a perfectly credible document. Therefore, learning initially to use a complex word-processing program is not as monumental a task as it might appear when a novice opens the user's manual for the first time. By the same token, it is not especially difficult for an experienced user to produce a simple document even with unfamiliar word-processing programs.

TEACHING WORD PROCESSING ON ADAPTED COMPUTERS

The instructional sequence utilized to teach word processing to someone who has a visual impairment is complicated by the fact that the learner must be taught not only to use a word-processing program and the computer's operating system commands required of visual learners, but must also learn additional commands to control speech, braille, or large-print output. Since speech synthesis is the most common output tool for computer users who are visually impaired, it will be used as the example here.

Because there are actually three distinct bodies of information to be taught—the word processor, the speech synthesizer, and advanced system commands—the instructor must determine the sequence in which they would best be introduced. Experience has led the authors to conclude that the word processor should be presented using the speech output, but without teaching the detailed operation of the speech synthesizer. Knowledge of speech commands is unnecessary in the beginning if the instructor configures the speech output software in such a way as to allow the user to read any part of a document with the cursor keys, and advanced system commands have little relevance until much later. The instructional sequence is also important within each of these three subdivisions. The sequence that appears to work the best is as follows (see Lesson Plan 9.2 for teaching word processing in this chapter):

- word processor with speech output
  - uses of a personal computer
  - major parts of a personal computer system
  - keyboard and typing skills
  - cursor movement
  - basic editing commands
  - basic system commands
  - advanced commands
- speech commands
- advanced system commands.

Teaching the Word Processor

Uses and Parts

As is the case with any lesson that introduces a new topic, the uses or benefits of the skill—word processing—should be presented first. In this way

Teaching Word Processing

I. Objective: When presented with a speech-enhanced IBM-compatible computer and word-processing software, the learner will produce a one-page document containing fewer than five mistakes per page.

II. Materials
   A. A computer system with speech synthesizer
   B. Word-processing software

III. Assessment
   A. Can the learner touch type in the proper manner?
   B. Does the learner hear well enough to understand the synthesizer?
   C. What experience has the learner had using computers or word processing?

IV. Procedure
   A. Practical uses of personal computers
      1. Have the learner describe those uses with which he or she is familiar.
      2. Be sure the following are discussed:
         a. Word processing
         b. Information storage and retrieval
         c. Recreation
         d. Telecommunications
         e. Control of devices and appliances in the home environment
   B. Orientation to parts of the microcomputer
      1. Have the learner identify those parts with which he or she is familiar.
      2. Be sure the following are introduced:
         a. central processing unit
         b. keyboard
         c. monitor
         d. disk drives, including hard drive
         e. disk
         f. printer
         g. ports
         h. mouse
      3. Have the learner investigate the keyboard.
      4. With the speech synthesizer on, have the learner identify the remaining keys.
      5. Be sure the following are covered:
         a. function keys
         b. alt and control keys
         c. escape key
         d. back space, number lock, and scroll lock keys
         e. capitals lock, insert, and delete keys
         f. number pad and cursor keys
         g. back-slash key
         h. enter key

(continued on next page)

Teaching Word Processing (continued)

6. With the word-processing and speech synthesizer software loaded and the synthesizer configured so the keyboard voice is on, the cursor keys allow the user to read text, and the voice automatically speaks menu choices, have the learner type 10 lines of text using the backspace key to correct errors.
7. Explain the use of the cursor keys to read characters, words, and lines, and have the learner read what he or she has typed.
8. Repeat until the learner is comfortable.

C. Basic editing commands
   1. Explain deleting; have the learner use it to remove characters, words, parts of lines, and lines.
   2. Explain inserting; have the learner use it.
   3. Explain centering; have the learner use it.

D. Basic systems commands
   1. Explain the concepts of saving and retrieving.
   2. Analogy with cassette tapes is useful.
   3. Introduce the learner to disk and disk drives.
   4. Explain the status line and speech windows.
   5. Have the learner use a window to read the present status line.
   6. Explain the concept of naming text files.
   7. Have the learner save and retrieve his or her text file with the appropriate commands.
   8. Explain exiting the program and have the learner do so.
   9. Explain loading the speech and word-processing programs.
   10. With the speech software set up to load the default configuration being used during training, have the learner load the word-processing and speech programs.
   11. Explain the concept of printing
       a. Demonstrate the proper placement of the paper into the printer and have the learner insert paper.
       b. With the printer set at default parameters, have the learner load his or her text file and print it.
   12. Explain the concept of a directory and have the learner view one.
       a. Explain types of files and their designations.
       b. Explain file size designations.
       c. Explain date designations.

E. Advanced commands
   1. Explain the following and have the learner perform them:
      a. Search forward and backward.
      b. Spell check a portion of text.
      c. Move a block of text.
      d. Merge text.
      e. Set up the printer at other than default parameters.

V. Memoranda

(continued on next page)

Teaching Word Processing (continued)

A. If the learner needs remediation in keyboarding, see the lesson plan for typing.
B. Analogies with the typewriter and the tape recorder are usually useful.
C. The learner may reject the voice completely at the beginning, but will generally pick it up in 4 to 6 hours of use.

VI. Evaluation
A. Have the learner sit in front of the computer with it turned off.
B. Have the learner complete all the operations it takes to produce, print, and save a full page of text.

VII. Assignments: The learner can practice at each level of skill gained:
A. turning the system on and loading software.
B. loading software and typing sentences for review of key location.
C. loading software and typing and printing a document.
D. loading software and typing, printing, saving, and retrieving documents.

the learner will understand the learning objectives and will be more likely to put forth a significant effort to achieve them. Also, as in other initial lessons involving equipment, the instructor should give only simple explanations of the parts of the computer, keeping in mind that the objective at this stage is merely to orient the learner.

Keyboard and Typing Skills

Keyboarding skills for word processing are virtually identical to the skills for touch typing, so the methods for teaching typing described earlier in this chapter should be consulted if the learner has never typed. Regardless of whether the learner is new to typing or simply needs a keyboard review, however, the instructor should engage the keyboard voice when the keys are introduced, since the computer's announcement of the key being struck is an outstanding feedback mechanism.

Cursor Movement

After the student becomes familiar with the keyboard, the instructor can introduce the use of the cursor movement keys for correcting mistakes and for screen reading. If the instructor configures the speech software to speak when the cursor keys are used, the learner will be able to use those keys to read characters, words, lines, and sentences as the cursor moves along them. This is a particularly effective way to introduce the pronunciation idiosyncracies of the speech synthesizer gradually, because the learner is familiar with the text that he or she is in the process of typing.

Editing Commands

If the learner has typed previously, the computer skills learned to this point differ little from those used previously on the typewriter. The introduction of the search, delete, insert, and centering commands are the first entirely new concepts to be introduced. Because they demonstrate vividly the advantages of word processing over conventional typewriting, they serve to motivate the learner.

Basic System Commands

The commands for saving, retrieving, and printing are also new concepts. However, saving and retrieving are so akin to storing and retrieving recorded material on cassette tapes that few people have difficulty with these notions. Special attention should be paid to describing the difference between temporary storage in the computer's CPU and storage on a floppy disk or the hard disk drive. Students sometimes have difficulty with the idea that the document remains in the computer's memory even after it has been saved to a disk, viewing the document as if it were water flowing from one place to another.

The act of printing causes little difficulty if default formats are used, but the instructor needs to demonstrate the proper placement of the paper in the printer, since procedures vary. The commands for viewing the list of files in the directory are relatively simple, but the information other than the file name, such as date and file size, must be explained.

Advanced Commands

If time permits, advanced functions such as spell checking and moving blocks of text can be added to the initial instructional program. However, a learner who has mastered basic word-processing skills should be able to learn the advanced functions on his or her own by using the word-processing system's manual or its computer-readable "Help" files.

Teaching Speech Synthesizer Commands

As already noted, speech software must provide the user with more than simple speech reproduction of text. Complex format situations exist, and the user may want to alter such features as the speed of the voice output or its pitch. Most speech programs offer what will be termed application and speech-command modes. In the application mode, the speech synthesizer simply provides a voice for the application software being used. The application mode would be used during the word-processing lessons or to utilize other application software, such as a database or to play a computer game. If the operator needs to alter the voice or the manner in which the synthesizer operates, he or she switches to the speech-command mode, which is usually accomplished with a single keystroke.

The speech-command mode allows the manipulation of parameters in three broad categories:

- voice characteristics setup
- menu setup
- windows setup.

Voice Characteristics Setup

Voice characteristics setup is usually taught first, because it requires the least amount of learning, but the instructional sequence does not appear to be important. Most speech software allows the user to alter the rate, pitch, tone, and volume of the voice, and some programs offer a choice among different voices as well.

Menu Setup

The speech synthesizer menu setup usually provides choices relating to the screen voice, which reads the document on the screen, and the keyboard voice, which echoes keystrokes. (These voices may or may not actually sound different.) Setting these parameters is a more complex task than voice setup and varies considerably among programs. However, typical menu options for the screen voice include:

- capital letters noted by a change in pitch or by announcement
- symbols noted or not
- repeated characters spoken once or as many times as they occur
- words appearing in unusual colors announced or not
- letters pronounced in the usual manner or phonetically
- blank spaces or lines announced or not.

For example:

> Brad T., the computer programmer, was playing Spellbinder, a computer spelling game. The opening screen of the game was completely sur-

rounded by a row of asterisks. The first time he played this game, his voice synthesizer read all 80 asterisks found on line 1, which was unnecessary and irritating, so he entered the speech-command mode to change the voice command to announce the asterisk only twice. By hearing the asterisk spoken aloud twice, Brad was alerted that there were multiple asterisks, but he did not have to listen to all of them. Spellbinder also displayed the incorrect spelling of the word to be spelled by highlighting it with red, so Brad used the speech-command mode to have the screen voice announce "red" when it was encountered. The game indicated a correct answer on the screen by displaying a dollar sign, but in its default setting, the voice synthesizer read only the most common symbols such as periods and question marks. Brad had to change the speech command to tell the screen voice to read most symbols, which included the dollar sign. To be able to play a spelling game, Brad had to be able to understand the voice when it announced single letters. For example, the letter *b* is often indistinguishable from *v*, when spoken aloud. Therefore, Brad set the synthesizer to provide phonetic assistance, so that, for example, it announced "bravo" rather than *b*.

The options for the keyboard voice are similar to those for the screen voice, but also include:

- turning the voice off for typing
- speeding up the voice response for quicker typing
- turning on an audible click to indicate when a key is struck properly
- speaking either characters or whole words as they are typed.

Numerous other features may be available, depending on the particular brand of synthesizer.

Windows Setup

The "windows" of a speech program have no connection to the Windows operating systems used by some computers. Rather, a window is a defined area of the computer screen in which a certain type of information is displayed. There are many types of windows, but the most important are what will here be termed *speech* windows, *active* windows, and *silent* windows.

Speech windows allow the user to "read" any part of the screen with a single keystroke. This saves time and many keystrokes because the operator who is blind cannot view the entire screen at once to find the one area or piece of information he or she wants to read—frequently a menu of options or program instructions. If not for speech windows, the operator would have to use the cursor keys to read through the entire screen just to find that one line. For example, if an operator had just completed typing a full page of information in the word-processing program WordPerfect, the status line, which appears on line 25 of the computer screen, at this point would read: "Doc 1 Pg 1 Ln 9.83 Pos 7 (identifying the document, page number, and the cursor's position on the page and line). A speech window could be set in the speech-command mode so that at one keystroke, the synthesizer would speak the contents of the status line, skipping all the other information on the screen.

Active windows can also be set that constantly monitor a specified portion of the screen and, when a change occurs there, automatically command the computer to speak the contents of that window. Using the example of WordPerfect again, when a user wants to save his or her document and strikes the "save" key, the status line changes. An active window can be set to continually monitor line 25 for changes, which in turn trigger the speech window to automatically announce what is displayed—in this case, "Save document? **Y**es (**N**o)."

Silent windows are the opposite of speech windows. They can be linked to active windows to silence unneeded information that is displayed on a computer screen and is ordinarily announced. After a user becomes familiar with specific application software and its menus, for example, it may be more expedient not to have the information in such menus spoken aloud.

> Brad T. uses all three types of windows when he plays a favorite computer game, Computer Poker, an electronic version of the popular card game five-card stud poker. Both Brad and the computer get five cards, one face down and four face up. The cards shown on the screen look just like playing cards, with the value and suit of the face-up cards displayed at the top as well as the bottom. As the cards are dealt one at a time, the values of the dealer's (computer's) face-up cards are displayed on lines 10 and 14 of the computer screen, and Brad's cards are all displayed on line 20 and 24. Brad could listen to all 25 lines of the game screen to get the information he needs to play the game, but he would hear unnecessary information, including repetition of each card value when the voice synthesizer read the top and bottom lines on each card. So Brad has set active and speech windows on lines 10 and 20, so that each time a new card is added to either player's hand, the speech synthesizer automatically announces all the cards in both players' hands. He also set several active and silent windows to stop the computer from speaking the instructions shown on the remainder of the screen because he has memorized them.

Fortunately, nearly all speech programs are sold with preset voice and windows configurations for commonly used application software. For example, WordPerfect users hear automatic messages every time the status line changes, any incorrectly spelled words detected by the spell checker are announced and spelled automatically, and the choices listed in the thesaurus are spoken. Learning and teaching tasks are simplified when such configurations are supplied and users need only learn how to load the configuration in the speech-command mode. Unfortunately, there are myriad application programs for which preset configurations are not available, so that the instructor and the learner must understand the process of setting windows. Because procedures differ among voice-synthesizer software packages, the user's manuals, which are generally available in recorded or brailled form or on computer disk, should be consulted.

Teaching Advanced System Commands

Once a client has learned how to perform a task on the computer, such as word processing a letter or playing a game using alternative output such as a voice-synthesizer or screen-enlargement program, the stage has been set for more advanced instruction. The client will probably be motivated to learn more, and the instructor can allude to the application and access software with which the learner has become familiar when explaining advanced system commands.

Advanced system commands can include any additional commands necessary to operate a computer independently, including those needed to install programs and copy, delete, or move files. They may also include the commands necessary to change the default settings that control various peripherals, such as the print quality of a printer or the braille format of a braille printer. Visually impaired computer operators may also find it useful to learn the commands that write or change the "batch" files—files that contain a batch of operating system commands and can control such functions as automatically loading both the voice synthesizer and the word processor with a single typed command (see Espinola & Croft, 1992).

In general, all operating system commands fall into the category of advanced system commands. Operating systems can be considered as the set of instructions to the computer that manage its memory; manage the hard disk, disk drives, and files; control the means of interacting with the user, such as the monitor, keyboard, mouse, and the like; and communicate with peripheral devices, such as printers and other computers. At this time, visually impaired computer users are able to use either Microsoft DOS or Windows operating systems (Leventhal, 1995). Those who use DOS systems have nearly complete access to software, because DOS is a text-based operating system and is compatible with most methods of access for visually impaired computer users, such as voice synthesizers and screen enlargement software.

However, the trend today is for computer operating systems and the software applications they run to be based on what is known as a graphical user interface—that is, the user must select a graphic icon (picture) or other visual data on the monitor screen using an input device known as a mouse. The mouse is moved manually to control a pointer on the screen rather than using a keyboard to control a cursor. Although this type of system can give a sighted user a considerable amount of information all at one glance, it causes some difficulties for users of speech software. Efforts to develop synthetic speech software that can translate these visual operating systems and make them accessible to blind and visually impaired users have resulted in useful products, but still lag behind the quality of access to DOS-based systems. However, the sophistication of the access software producers has made the task of using computers with graphical user interface less daunting. A keyboard rather than a mouse can be used to operate the computer and its software, a feature especially helpful to people who use a voice synthesizer; and visual symbols are not a barrier to independent computer usage, since the text descriptors paired with the icons are spoken aloud by the voice synthesizer (Shragai, 1995; Shragai & Uslan, 1995a).

Using computer technology in combination with appropriate adaptive aids, an individual with impaired vision is able to utilize computers for the wide range of functions of which they are capable, from writing letters to playing games to maintaining complex databases. With enormous rapidity, computers and electronic networks have also become the source for the most current information on every imaginable topic. The next chapter covers electronic methods that people with visual impairments can use to gain access to information that is usually presented visually, including computer-based methods and more traditional listening and recording devices.

CHAPTER 10

Access to Information: Electronic Listening, Recording, and Reading Devices

KEY CONCEPTS IN THIS CHAPTER

- **The uses and parts of standard tape recorders**
- **The proper maintenance of tape recorders**
- **Features of adapted tape recorders produced for individuals with visual impairments**
- **Methods of indexing tape recordings to aid in locating material**
- **Methods and devices for increasing the listening speed of tape recordings**
- **Systems used to increase the storage capacity of cassette tapes used for reading**
- **Talking book programs and reading machines**
- **The basic components and operation of reading machines and optical character recognition systems**
- **Other audible and electronic sources of information**

Gaining access to printed information is one of the major needs of individuals with visual impairments. It is so important that Father Carroll (1961) considered the loss of the ability to read magazines, newspapers, and trade publications and journals among the 20 major losses suffered by persons with adult-onset vision loss (see Chapter 9). Information that is readily accessible to the general public through newspapers, magazines, catalogs, textbooks, and the like is not as available to those who cannot see well enough to read. This lack of access can lead to inconvenient gaps in awareness of current information, interfere with education, block employment, and generally cause a great deal of personal frustration. Reading braille alleviates the problem to some degree, particularly in regard to education, but since not everyone can make use of braille and not all information is available in this medium, it has by no means eliminated the information deficit experienced by many visually impaired persons.

People who are visually impaired have also turned to electronic devices, such as tape recorders and computers, to meet some of their reading needs. They may read novels and textbooks in recorded form, and printed materials are now directly accessible through optical character recognition (OCR) systems and computer-based reading machines. This chapter reviews a number of aids and adaptive devices and methods used to help visually impaired people obtain information, including regular and adapted cassette recorders; talking books on audio disc or cassette; computer reading devices; computerized books; and other audible or electronic resources such as the radio and the telephone.

TAPE RECORDERS

Uses of Tape Recorders

Because cassette tapes are useful storage units for information and because recordings are easily produced, they have become an important adaptive tool for those who cannot read print with ease. More than 80 percent of former rehabilitation clients surveyed in one Michigan study used them (Whitten, 1986), and they are used more by such persons than by those in the general population (Schropp, 1990). Cassettes are especially handy for storing such information as addresses and telephone numbers, recipes, bank transactions, and detailed instructions. Cassette recorders outfitted with a telephone pick-up patch cord (a cord that can plug into both recorder and telephone) allow the user to record directly from the telephone information obtained from directory assistance operators; bus, train, or airline schedules; directions to stores or offices; business or personal appointments; and the like.

Cassettes are also well suited for storing literary works that have been read aloud. As a result, large repositories of textbooks and leisure reading materials have been compiled by such agencies as Recording for the Blind and Dyslexic and the Library of Congress National Library Service for the Blind and Physically Handicapped (NLS) in the United States and, in Canada, the Canadian National Institute for the Blind for primarily English materials or Institute Nazareth et Louis Braille for primarily French reading materials (see Resources section).

The tape recorder's popularity is a result of the ease with which it can be used. Whereas it takes a good deal of time to become proficient in reading braille or using an optical magnifier, most people can master the tape recorder in a single session or two. The tape recorder is thus especially helpful to the rehabilitation teacher in working with people who cannot read print, because it makes available teaching tools, such as cookbooks, that clients could not otherwise use until they had extensive lessons in other reading methods.

People who have both hearing and visual impairments can also make use of recorders, although mainly as a means for expressive communication. For example, someone who is unable to speak can keep a prerecorded message to play to the fire department or emergency operator over the telephone in the event of a fire or other emergency, giving the location of the person's house and other information. Another use of tape recorders by deaf-blind persons is to solicit assistance at busy street crossings. A continuous-loop tape can be used to relay the appropriate message, such as "Hello, my name is __________. I am deaf-blind. Can you please assist me across the street?" Deaf-blind people can also use recorders to tape lectures or other lengthy communications, which can be transcribed or interpreted at a later time.

The tape recorder has some distinct disadvantages, despite its usefulness. It is not good for teaching beginning reading skills, because it gives a young student less concrete information about spelling and punctuation than either print or tactile reading systems. Also, users must contend with the difficulty of locating specific information on a tape, the relatively slow speed at which humans are able to read aloud, and the limited amount of material that can be stored on a cassette tape. Although these drawbacks have not been completely solved as yet, a number of adaptations and techniques have considerably improved the functioning of tape recorders for people with visual impairments. Before presenting these adaptations, however, it will be helpful to review the basic operation of cassette recorders.

Parts of Cassette Recorders

Standard cassette recorders generally contain some common features, including the following:

- The *keyboard* generally consists of either mechanical or pressure-sensitive switches for the functions of play, rewind, fast forward, record, pause, stop, and tape eject.

- The *cassette well* contains the parts that move the tape and make the recorder play or record.
- The *input and output jacks* are where connections can be made to other equipment; one allows for direct input of sound to be recorded through a microphone or a patch cord, and one outputs sound to an earplug.
- The *volume* and *tone controls* are usually slide or pressure-sensitive switches.
- A highly sensitive and omnidirectional *condenser microphone* is usually built into the case; a hand-held microphone plugged into the input jack increases the quality of the recorded material.

Because the rehabilitation teacher will inevitably be faced at times with tape malfunctions related to the working of the cassette well, a thorough knowledge of the parts of this component is important. For example, tape sometimes gets caught and pulled into the parts in the cassette well. Knowing the direction of rotation and the interrelationship of the parts can assist the rehabilitation teacher or the client in correcting the problem. Figure 10.1 presents an illustration of a standard cassette receptacle. However, the following discussion will be clearer if the reader also examines an actual cassette recorder and cassette case. At the back left of the cassette well is the anti-record device. It corresponds to the "knock-out tabs" on the back of the case that houses a cassette tape. When the tab on the case is intact, it

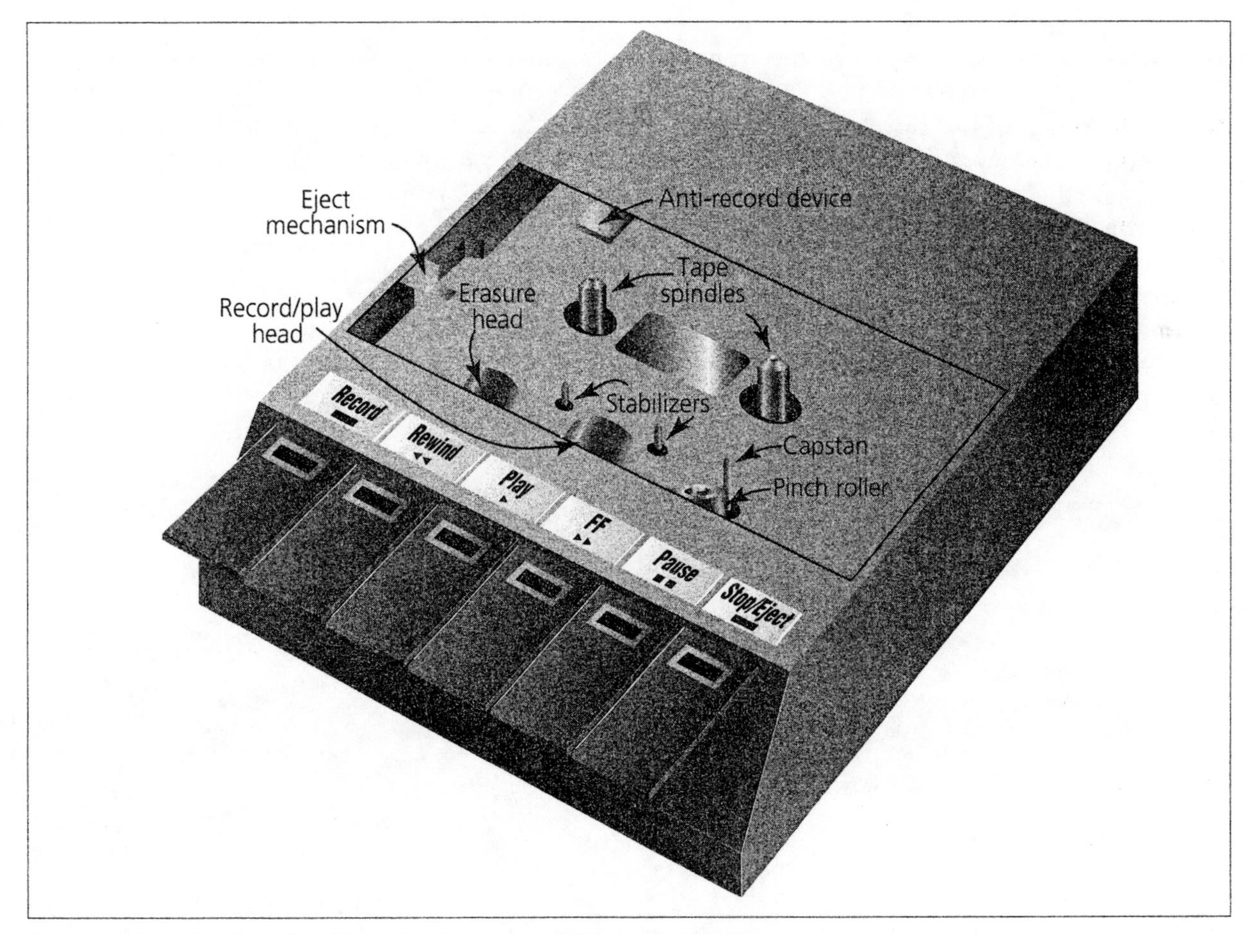

Figure 10.1. Parts of a Standard Cassette Tape Recorder

depresses the anti-record device as the cassette is inserted into the well, which in turn releases the machine's record key. When the tab is knocked out of the cassette case to prevent recording over a tape, the anti-record device will not be depressed when the tape is inserted and the record key remains locked and unusable. This protects valuable recorded materials. Each cassette tape has two such tabs, one for each side of the tape case (see Figure 10.2).

Along the front of the cassette well are the two convex metal heads that are responsible for creating the magnetic field that allows the machine to record. The head on the left receives the magnetic tape first and erases it when the record function is engaged. The head on the right is responsible for both the play and record functions. On the sides of the heads are one or two stabilizer brackets, which hold the cassette firmly in place during play and record modes. The stabilizer brackets correspond to two small slots on the front (or working) edge of the cassette case. The stabilizer pins on the floor of the cassette well perform a similar function; they correspond to the stabilizer pin holes on the top of the cassette case.

Between the heads in most players is the automatic shut-off switch. When the cassette tape has played completely through, the tape tightens, putting pressure on this switch and causing the play or record key to be disengaged. The tape-eject mechanism, shown on the side of the well floor in the diagram accompanying this discussion, pushes the cassette case out of the well when the eject key is depressed.

Immediately to the right of the record/play head are the capstan and the rubber pinch roller. The capstan is a metal pin that turns during all machine functions. When the recorder is in either the play or the record mode, the pinch roller is pushed against the capstan, causing it to turn in a counterclockwise direction. Although the two tape spindles are primarily responsible for pulling the tape through the machine, the rubber pinch roller assists them during recording and playing by maintaining a constant speed as the amount of tape on the spindles varies.

The erase head, play/record head, and the rubber wheel contact the magnetic tape through the three larger windows or holes on the front working edge of the cassette case during record and play functions. Thus, erasing is accomplished through the first window on the left, playing and recording is done through the middle window, and the rubber wheel helps to pull the tape across the heads through the right-hand window.

Cassette Tapes

In addition to the features of cassettes tapes already mentioned, it is important to be aware that most cassettes have several inches of nonmagnetic

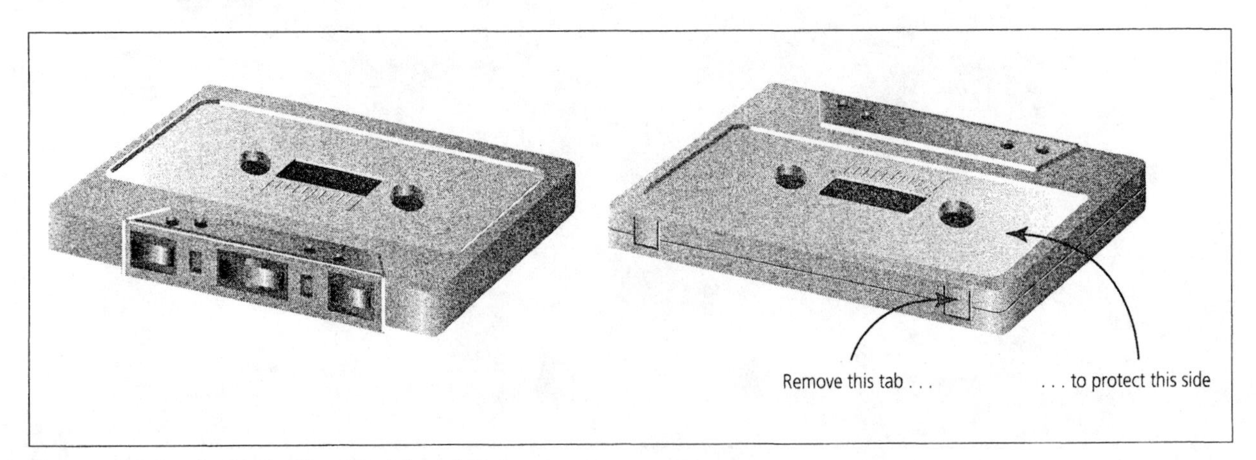

Figure 10.2. A Cassette Knockout Tab

"leader tape" that connects each end of the magnetic tape to the tape spools and on which nothing can be recorded. New listeners may be confused by the 10 to 20 seconds of silence at the beginning of a new cassette while the leader tape runs past the heads and may wrongly assume something is wrong with the recording or with their operation of the machine. Users should count to 20 before starting to record at the beginning of a cassette to make sure that all the leader tape has passed the heads. Sometimes the leader tape is specially designed to clean the machine heads, simplifying maintenance duties. Individuals should check brands to determine which ones have this feature.

Cassette tapes come in several lengths, including 15, 30, 45, 60, 90, and 120 minutes (see Sidebar 10.1 for ways to determine tape length). Longer tapes of 90 or 120 minutes as well as microcassette tapes are made of thinner magnetic tape to reduce the bulk (Utrup, 1979), and if the user constantly stops and starts or reverses the direction of play, these tapes are more liable to break. Generally, therefore, longer tapes are most useful for class lectures and recorded books, whereas shorter tapes come in handy for organizing addresses, budget information, recording messages, and the like, both because the shorter length makes it easier to find specific items and because the stronger tape is less likely to break. It is also useful to know that, although the two halves of some cassette cases are glued together, many cassettes are fastened together with small screws, which makes it easier to disassemble them for repair when necessary.

RECORDING ADAPTATIONS

As noted earlier, the tape recorder has three main disadvantages as a vehicle for reading and storing information: the difficulty in locating desired information on a tape, the slow speed of reading aloud, and the limited storage capacity of tapes. Specially adapted techniques and machines have been developed that minimize each of these difficulties.

Locating Information

Locating specific information efficiently on a recorded cassette tape can be time consuming and sometimes difficult. If one cannot read the tape number on the recorder's tape counter at the beginning of each recorded segment, finding information recorded with a standard tape recorder can be a frustrating experience. Three indexing systems exist to overcome this problem:

- passive indexing
- tone indexing

SIDEBAR 10.1

Hints for Determining Cassette Tape Length

Cassettes are frequently reused, particularly by individuals who receive many publications on tape, and it is helpful to know how long the tape is before starting to record something new. When the length of the tape is not apparent from the label, there are several other places to look for that information.

- The tape length may appear somewhere on the front label as a simple number or as part of a code, such as C-60 or C-92.
- The tape length may be stamped on the narrow edge of the cassette case where the knock-out tabs are located. Occasionally, cassettes have an extra 2 to 4 minutes, so this number may be 62 for a 60-minute cassette (30 minutes on each side).
- The tape length may be printed on the leader tape at the beginning of the recording tape. The tape must be fully rewound to check the clear leader tape for that information.

- voice indexing.

All rely on a feature of some cassette recorders known as "preview and review" or "cue and review." This feature allows the tape to contact the play/record head while in the fast-forward or rewind modes. As a result, the recorded material on the tape is audible during these functions. The listener can quickly learn to recognize the differences among types of recordings played at high speed. For example, sections of voice recording can be readily distinguished from music, and blank sections are easy to recognize.

Passive Indexing

In passive indexing, periods of silence are left to mark the beginning of a new topic. For example, if the user is recording daily classroom lectures, he or she can leave 15 seconds of blank tape to indicate the beginning of each new day's recording. Later, when searching for a particular day's lecture on the tape, it is simply a matter of counting the number of blank spaces as the tape is previewed in the fast-forward mode to find the right day.

Tone Indexing

Tone indexing is similar to passive indexing but offers the user more information. A tone of extremely low frequency is recorded and used on the tape to mark the beginning of new material instead of a section of blank tape. The tones produced by most adapted machines with tone index controls are of such a low frequency that they are nearly inaudible when the tape is played at normal speed, but when the fast-forward (cue or preview) and rewind (review) functions are used and the tape speed is increased, the frequency of the tone increases to an easily audible level. The resulting "beep" tones can be used singly to mark the beginnings of sections, such as the daily lectures mentioned before, or they can be combined into more elaborate systems. For example, commercially recorded books often indicate new chapters with a series of three tones and new pages with a single one. Recorded cookbooks often use double tones to indicate sections, such as breakfast, lunch, or dinner, and single tones to label the beginning of each recipe within the section.

Although an adapted machine or tone index attachment is needed to create tones in this way, a little creativity with an over-the-counter machine that has a preview or review function can produce a less-sophisticated but equally usable tone. Humming into the microphone at a low frequency in the record mode creates a similar beep tone that will be audible at fast speeds. Since some clients will not be able to afford the more expensive adapted recorders, it is important for the rehabilitation teacher to explain the role of the preview and review function in creating the user's own indexing system before he or she purchases a machine.

Voice Indexing

The inherent drawback of tone indexing is that the user must later remember the coding system he or she designed when recording a tape. If the user picks up the tape a year or two after its creation, it may be difficult to recall what three tones or two tones within the narrative mean. James Chandler, promoter of voice indexing and creator of Voice Indexing for the Blind, recommended voice indexing—replacing the beep tone with a descriptive word—as a solution to this problem (Voice Indexing for the Blind, 1984). For example, an indexing term such as "breakfast," rather than three tones, would be used to indicate the beginning of a section of a cookbook, and single tones marking recipes would be replaced with index terms such as "pancakes" or "biscuits."

The indexing term is produced by recording it in the fast-forward mode. Thus, the record, fast-forward, and play keys must all be depressed almost simultaneously. Not all recorders will function in this manner, but most adapted machines and many standard ones will. The sequence in which the three recorder function keys must be depressed varies among machines. When experimenting with different recorders, the rehabilitation teacher should try first pressing the record key, followed by the play and fast-forward keys. If that does not work, the order of the last two should be reversed.

Voice indexing has two drawbacks. First, the indexing phrase may produce a disconcerting high-pitched squeal when played at normal speed, although this does not occur in professionally produced recordings. The squeal is not generally a significant problem, however, because there is no reason to listen to indexed sections of tape at normal speed. Second, the index phrases use up more space on the tape than do tone indexes. However, the advantages of voice indexing appear to overshadow these minor inconveniences.

Efficiency in using any form of indexing will be improved by following a standard format for recording information. For example, recording the title and table of contents for the tape at the beginning, including the indexing label and track for each segment, will make it easier for the listener to find the information he or she is looking for.

Listening Speed

Although the slow verbal reading speed of humans who record materials might seem an immutable fact of life, it can be increased by utilizing two different adaptations: variable speed control and speech compression.

Variable Speed Control

Variable speed control allows the user to increase or decrease the listening speed selectively. Speed reduction is especially helpful in improving comprehension of people studying text materials or individuals with hearing impairments, but more listeners take advantage of the ability to increase listening speed. In general, the rate of play can be comfortably increased about one-and-a-half times the actual speed. Unfortunately, as the speed of the tape is increased, both the distortion of the signal and the pitch increase, producing what might be termed a "chipmunk" effect. Increasing the speed more than two times normal causes a great deal of difficulty for listeners (Foulke, 1980). If they can understand the recording, however, auditory readers quickly become accustomed to the pitch distortion, and the benefits of the increased listening speed generally outweigh the disadvantages. Novice listeners can be taught to increase the speed gradually, stopping to listen at each increased speed until they are comfortable before proceeding to the next level.

Speech Compression

The distortion caused by increasing the speed not only affects listening comfort, but can also decrease comprehension (Foulke, 1980). Speech compressors were developed to overcome these significant problems. A speech compressor is an electronic device that reads cassette recordings in the same fashion as does the head of a tape recorder, but instead of reading the entire tape, the compressor repeatedly switches the head on and off within a brief period of time so that it samples the recorded material as it is played at an increased speed. By eliminating portions of the recording, the frequency—the number of sound waves produced per second—is returned to normal. Because pitch—the highness or lowness of a sound—is based on frequency, this procedure produces a time-compressed output that effectively corrects the pitch and distortion. Thus, the quality of the output signal is maintained, pitch is corrected, and speech sounds are still understandable.

Both a speed adapter and a speech compressor are required for speech compression. The variable speed control adjusts the speed, while the speech compressor adjusts the pitch. The degree of compression needed is directly proportional to the increase in recording speed: The more the listening speed is increased, the greater the degree of compression needed.

Adaptive devices that contain built-in speech compressors generally have two adjacent slide controls, one to adjust the speed and the other the pitch (through the degree of compression). Compressors are also available as separate modules that are attached by patch cords to machines that have only variable speed controls. Speech compressors commonly emit fluttery sounds, somewhat reminiscent of a motorboat, during play. Although the problem is less severe with the more expensive speech compressors, it is also less evident when playing good-quality recordings, and it is not usually of much consequence to experienced listeners.

Increasing Storage

Adapted recorders also have features designed to increase the storage capacity of cassette tapes. Two built-in features enable users to increase capacity by as much as four times. The first adaptation relates to tape recording speed, and the second relates to the number of recording tracks.

Speed Adaptation

Standard recorders play and record at a tape speed of $1\frac{7}{8}$ inches per second (ips), but in 1974 NLS began recording at half that speed, $\frac{15}{16}$ ips, to allow more information on the same amount of tape (Leventhal, Schreier, De Witt, & Meyers, 1989). When a recording is made at $\frac{15}{16}$ ips and replayed at that speed, most listeners cannot detect any loss of sound quality. A 60-minute cassette that would allow one hour of recording (30 minutes per side) at the standard $1\frac{7}{8}$ ips speed will allow twice as much to be recorded (one hour per side) when the recorder speed is switched to $\frac{15}{16}$ ips.

Adapted tape recorders have a dual speed control that can be set at either $1\frac{7}{8}$ ips to listen to commercial recordings recorded at that standard speed or set at $\frac{15}{16}$ ips to listen to adapted recordings. (The dual speed control should not be confused with the variable speed control described in the previous section that is adjusted on a continuum for individual listening comfort.)

Four Tracks

The other method for increasing the storage capacity of cassette tapes, known as the four-track format, was also popularized when NLS adopted a configuration that differed from the commercial standard (Leventhal, Schreier, De Witt, & Meyers, 1989). The special head configuration helped NLS avoid copyright problems for its recorded books because they could not be played on standard tape players. More important, however, it increased the number of places on the face of the tape onto which recorded materials are placed.

The location of the recorded material on a tape is generally referred to as a track. In actuality, recordings are placed only on the front surface of the tape. The "side" of the tape refers only to the plastic cassette case. When the case is turned from side A to side B, the front surface of the tape still faces the heads of the recorder; it simply receives the magnetic recording along a different area or track. Standard nonstereophon-

A built-in speech compressor (left) and an external speech compressor (right).

ic cassette tape recorders record on one track at a time per side, resulting in two tracks per cassette. Normally, the user records track 1 on side A of a cassette tape and turns it over to side B to record track 2. Stereo tape recorders have two tracks per side, but both tracks are recorded and played together. Adapted recorders, however, enable the user to record separately on two tracks per side, or four per tape, doubling the length of tape available for recording. Thus, after track 2 is recorded on side B of a cassette tape, the user simply turns the tape back over to side A, changes the setting of the track selector switch to tracks 3 and 4, and records track 3. After track 3 is recorded, the user turns the tape back to side B again to record track 4.

The number of tracks on the surface of a magnetic tape is a function of the recorder, not the tape, and any blank tape can be made into a multiple-track tape. Although the recording head is approximately as wide as the tape, the point at which each track is recorded is a narrow band on the front of the magnetic tape akin to the groove placed on a record during its production—so narrow, in fact, that recording devices used in professional recording studios are capable of placing more than 16 tracks on a single tape. The heads of the recorder can be changed at the flip of the track-selector switch. The adapted machines used by persons with visual impairments generally record on four tracks.

An adapted cassette recorder.

Teaching Adaptive Tape Recording Skills

Many vendors of products for people with impaired vision sell adapted recorders (see Resources section). These machines are generally mainstream devices to which one or more adaptations are added (Leventhal, Schreier, De Witt, & Meyers, 1989). In addition to the dual-speed switch, the track selector switch, the tone index button, and the speed adapter, adapted machines may also have raised symbols on the keys and a cassette door with a motion sensor window. This window exposes the top of the right sprocket, so the user can use a finger to check tactilely that the machine is running.

Teaching someone to use adapted recorders can be complex, and learners will vary greatly in their knowledge of machine use. Some will have no background in using tape recorders, but many will have at least used the simpler Talking Book players (which are discussed later in this chapter) and will be somewhat familiar with the adaptations.

Assuming the learner has little experience, the instruction begins with an introduction to the recorder's uses and an orientation to its parts. When the track switch or other adaptive functions are encountered, complex explanations are delayed until the learner is ready for them. Much as reading is taught before writing, playback functions should be taught before recording so that the learner understands the practical uses of recordings before having to produce them. For example, it is easier for someone to understand how to record and tone or voice index a list of addresses and telephone numbers once he or she has heard a prepared example. A detailed sequence for teaching the use of adapted tape recorders is found in Lesson Plan 10.1.

LESSON PLAN 10.1

Teaching the Use of an Adapted Tape Recorder

I. Objective: When presented with a blank tape and the adapted tape recorder, the learner will perform the following operations quickly and efficiently:
   A. Listen to a ten-minute segment of recorded material and manipulate variable speed and speech compressor, if available.
   B. Produce a segment containing one minute of recorded material at 15/16 ips and one at 1 7/8 ips.
   C. Produce a recorded tape of one-minute segments at the beginnings of each of four tracks.
   D. Produce a tone-indexed segment containing at least three subsections.
   E. Produce a voice-indexed segment with at least three subsections.

II. Materials: Adapted cassette recorder, blank cassette, National Library Service (NLS) Cassette Talking Book, commercially produced tone- and voice-indexed recording

III. Assessment
   A. Has the learner used a cassette machine before?
   B. Can the learner describe the machine he or she used?
   C. Can the learner describe the uses of cassette recorders?
   D. Does the learner understand the concepts of tracks, speed, and indexing?

IV. Procedure
   A. Uses: Explain and demonstrate specific information and storage uses, including notetaking, recordkeeping, correspondence with others, leisure reading, and dubbing telephone information.
   B. Orientation to parts
      1. Have the learner point out known parts.
      2. Point out the following if missed:
         a. individual keys of the keyboard
         b. motion sensor window
         c. track and dual speed switches
         d. variable speed adapter and speech compressor
         e. tone-indexing button
         f. multiple input/output jacks
   C. Simple operation for new learners
      1. Point out the eject button and have the learner insert a recorded cassette.
      2. Point out and have the learner use the play and pause buttons.
      3. Point out and have the learner use the rewind and fast-forward buttons.
      4. Point out and have the learner use the record button.
         a. Explain the tape leader.
         b. Have the learner record a one-minute segment.
         c. Explain rewind with the play button depressed to identify different segments on the tape at high speed.
         d. Have the learner practice until comfortable.
      5. Operation of adaptive functions
         a. Using track and speed functions

(continued on next page)

Teaching the Use of an Adapted Tape Recorder (continued)

(1) Have the learner listen to a commercial four-track tape.
(2) Have the learner locate the beginnings of several tracks until he or she is confident.
(3) Have the learner experiment with the two-speed switch.
(4) Have the learner determine the speed of unknown tapes until he or she is confident.
(5) Have the learner record one-minute segments at two speeds at the beginning of several tracks until he or she is confident.

b. Using indexing systems
(1) Explain the need for indexing.
(2) Demonstrate indexing with a prerecorded tape.
(3) Explain passive indexing.
(a) Demonstrate the preview and review functions.
(b) Demonstrate how the fast-forward or rewind key can be depressed when the play key is depressed to identify different segments on the tape at high speed.
(c) Demonstrate passive indexing with a prerecorded tape.
(d) Have the learner locate specified sections using preview and review.
(4) Explain tone indexing.
(a) Have the learner locate specified tone-indexed sections on the tape.
(b) Have the learner produce a single tone index, then a set of two distinct tones.
(c) Help the learner design a tape format for an address file.
(d) Have the learner produce an address file with at least four sections separated by tone indexes.
(5) Explain voice indexing and its advantage.
(a) Have the learner locate specified voice-indexed sections on the tape.
(b) Demonstrate the creation of a voice index by pressing the record, play, and fast-forward buttons together.
(c) Have the learner create several voice indexes until he or she is confident.
(d) Have the learner modify his or her address file to combine voice and tone indexing.
(6) Explain how to design an indexing sequence in a standardized format for ease of use.
(a) Record a title.
(b) Record a table of contents.
i) Explain the indexing system to be used.
ii) List the sections contained on the tape and their indexing label and track.
iii) Leave adequate space for additions to the table of contents.
(c) Record each section, being sure to leave an adequate pause between the index and the beginning of the entry.
(d) Leave adequate space for additions to each section.
(e) Label the cassette tape.

(continued on next page)

Teaching the Use of an Adapted Tape Recorder (continued)

(7) Demonstrate speed adaptation.
   (a) Have the learner gradually increase the listening speed of a commercially recorded tape until the maximum practical speed is achieved.
   (b) Demonstrate the compressor.
   (c) Explain the relationship between increased speed and the need for increased compression.
   (d) Have the learner change speed and compression several times until he or she is confident.

V. Memoranda
   A. Be sure to discuss the many types and the price range of cassette recorders.
   B. Be sure the learner is aware of maintenance requirements.
   C. Be sure to explain that the compressor will drain the battery quickly.
   D. Inform the learner of sources of recorders.

VI. Evaluation: Have the learner produce a tape that includes at least two storage files on parts of at least three tracks and that contains both voice- and tone-indexed segments.

VII. Assignments
   A. Have the learner record and play back a tape containing a series of items, such as a list of telephone numbers or several recipes, using both voice and tone indexing and including a table of contents.
   B. Have the learner record a program from the radio, using a patch cord.

MAINTENANCE AND REPAIR

Tape Recorder Maintenance

As with any electromechanical device, proper maintenance of a tape recorder is crucial for optimum performance and prolonged operating life. The rehabilitation teacher should be prepared to teach the client how to

- protect the recorder from dust
- clean the tape heads
- demagnetize the tape heads.

The presence of dust between the tape and the machine heads is like fine sandpaper rubbing on the heads and, in time, will affect these smooth surfaces. In addition, dust can clog the moving parts of the recorder, causing them to wear out more quickly. Protecting the tape recorder from dust is a simple matter of keeping the machine covered when it is not being used. Itinerant teachers who travel dusty rural roads should be especially aware of this.

In addition, because of the properties of magnetic tape, a residue from dust and the tape surface builds up on the heads over time that can become thick enough to prevent proper erasing and cause poor performance in recording and playback. If the heads are never cleaned, a machine will eventually become nonfunctional. Therefore, it is recommended that the heads be cleaned at least every six months (Utrup, 1979). This can be accomplished by using one of the special cleaning cassettes that are commercially available, which are placed in the cassette well and run through the machine like a regular tape. These cassettes contain a tape with an abrasive surface that removes the residue, but with prolonged use they can affect the surface of the heads. Cleaning solutions, generally a combination of rubbing alcohol and detergent, can also be used. The solution is applied to a small cloth or cotton swab, which is rubbed against the erase and play/record heads and the pinch roller. Rubbing alcohol alone is also effective and less expensive. The user should be sure that both recorder heads are carefully cleaned and that they are dry before the machine is used again.

Another consequence of the constant tape movement across the heads is a buildup of static electricity that can affect recording quality over time. Rather than losing clarity, as with residue buildup, sound affected by static buildup becomes distorted. The static charge should be removed with a demagnetizer after each 10 hours of use (Utrup, 1979).

Tape Repair and Erasure

People who make frequent use of cassettes for storing important information should know how to repair tapes and how to erase used tapes efficiently for reuse. Clients who are unfamiliar with methods of tape repair should be shown how to use a tape splicer in case they find themselves with an important tape that has gotten partially inhaled by a recorder and is torn or crumpled. Cutting out damaged sections of tape eliminates only about six seconds of sound on both sides (depending on the speed) for every foot of tape removed. One method is to cut out the crumpled part with scissors, connect the ends with transparent tape, and trim the excess tape. An easier method for people with severe vision loss or dexterity problems is to use an inexpensive cassette tape splicer and magnetic repair tape, available from audio and electronic stores, which can be recorded over, because the splicer holds both ends of the broken tape securely while the repair tape is applied and automatically trims the excess tape.

There are three ways to erase a cassette tape: (1) record directly over previously recorded material, (2) record with the condenser microphone off to produce blank tapes, or (3) use a bulk eraser. The first two methods are slower than the last since they both require real-time recording—that is, running the entire tape through the player at regular speed. Bulk erasers, magnetic or electromagnetic devices that quickly and completely erase tapes (Utrup, 1979), can be purchased at electronic or office supply stores.

TALKING BOOK PROGRAMS

The National Library Service for the Blind and Physically Handicapped (NLS) of the United States Library of Congress and the National Library Service for Canadians operated by the Canadian Na-

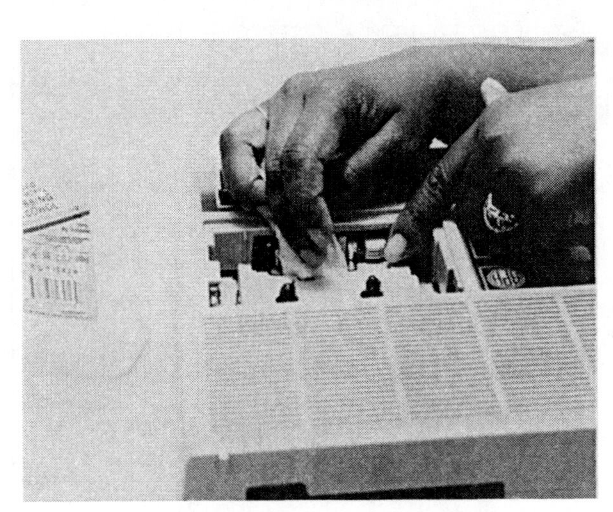

Cleaning the heads of a cassette recorder.

Demagnetizing the heads of a cassette recorder.

tional Institute for the Blind (CNIB) both administer what are commonly referred to as talking book programs, which provide braille and recorded books and magazines free of charge to people with visual, physical, or other reading disabilities.

The "talking book" concept dates back to 1877, when Thomas Edison listed "books for blind people" as a possible use on his patent application for the tin-foil phonograph. However, lacking the appropriate technology (a standard phonograph record could only play for five minutes), the talking book did not become a realistic option until 50 years later (Koestler, 1976).

The American Foundation for the Blind (AFB) launched the talking book program in 1932, by establishing an in-house laboratory to develop the long-playing record and playing machine as well as a studio to produce master recordings. One year later, AFB launched a campaign to obtain funds for the distribution of talking book machines to blind people nationwide. A 1933 amendment to the Pratt-Smoot Act of 1931 allowed the Library of Congress to purchase and distribute recorded books for blind people in addition to books in braille. The CNIB program stemmed from private efforts.

SIDEBAR 10.2

Free Matter Mailing Privileges for People Who Are Blind or Visually Impaired

Certain material sent by or to people who "cannot read or use conventionally printed material because of a physical impairment" may be mailed free of charge. Generally covered under the regulation, known as Free Matter for the Blind and Other Handicapped Persons, are reading or listening matter and letters sent by eligible individuals. Printed material in smaller than 14-point type or handwritten letters are not eligible. The rules apply to domestic mail; check with the local post office for international mail and to establish an individual's eligibility for the privilege.

ACCEPTABLE MATTER

- Books; magazines; musical scores; sound reproductions; and letters in braille, large print, or recorded form for the use of eligible individuals. The material cannot include advertising.
- Paper, equipment for producing adaptive reading materials (such as braillewriters) or sound reproduction, or other equipment and devices for eligible individuals
- Letters prepared in raised or large type, only if sent by a visually impaired or handicapped individual

QUALIFIED INDIVIDUALS

- People who are blind or cannot read conventionally printed materials as a result of a physical impairment

PROCEDURES

Eligible individuals may need to submit a statement from a physician, optometrist, or other "competent authority" certifying that they are unable to read conventional material.

- Materials must be available for inspection purposes.
- The upper right-hand corner of the envelope or parcel must contain the words: "Free Matter for the Blind or Handicapped" (in the United States) or "Literature for the Blind" (in Canada).
- Bills, regular print materials, and other materials sent to an eligible person from a noneligible person must be sent postage paid.

By the spring of 1934, AFB had orders for 600 record players, and in October, the distributing library at the Library of Congress's Service for the Blind began operations. Today, several nonprofit and commercial firms contract with the Library of Congress to record and duplicate talking books, including AFB and the American Printing House for the Blind (APH).

Although some differences may exist between the U.S. and Canadian programs, both generally offer recorded versions of novels and popular periodicals on either recorded discs or cassette tapes as well as in braille versions. The books are distributed by mail through a system of regional libraries. In the United States, books are mailed at no cost under federal mailing privileges known as "free matter for the blind and other handicapped persons" (see Sidebar 10.2). The large NLS holdings are listed in annual general catalogs as well as catalogs on special topics. In addition, registered borrowers learn of new books added to the collection through the NLS's two bimonthly magazines, *Braille Book Review* and *Talking Book Topics.*

NLS also loans the devices on which the recordings are played, as well as special accessories for them. These currently include the Talking-Book Machine, the Talking-Book Cassette Machine and the Easy Cassette Machine. The Talking-Book Machine is a record player that plays records and flexible discs, known as flexidiscs, that have been recorded at the slow speed of $8\frac{1}{3}$ rpm, at $16\frac{2}{3}$ rpm or at $33\frac{1}{3}$ rpm. The Cassette Machine is a nonrecording playback machine that has four-track, dual speeds ($1\frac{7}{8}$ and $\frac{15}{16}$ ips), variable speed control, and preview and review functions. The Easy Cassette Machine is a simplified cassette playback device that automates some of the control functions, such as turning the cassette over and switching the track button. There is also a Combination Machine, which combines the disc and cassette player functions.

Because use of these machines is so widespread, they will be described here in considerable detail, including a lesson plan for instruction. NLS typically provides information on their use in braille or recorded media only, and further instruction is often necessary for a client to be able to use the machines successfully.

Disc Player

The Talking-Book Machine, once popular but now being phased out, remains the choice of some users because it is simple and also because certain reading materials, such as periodicals, were available only on discs. Although the disc player is simple to use, some aspects commonly require instruction, such as placing the needle on the edge of the record, setting the playback speed, and replacing damaged needles. On older machines, the needle is placed by using the middle finger as a guide to locate the edge of the turntable. Record

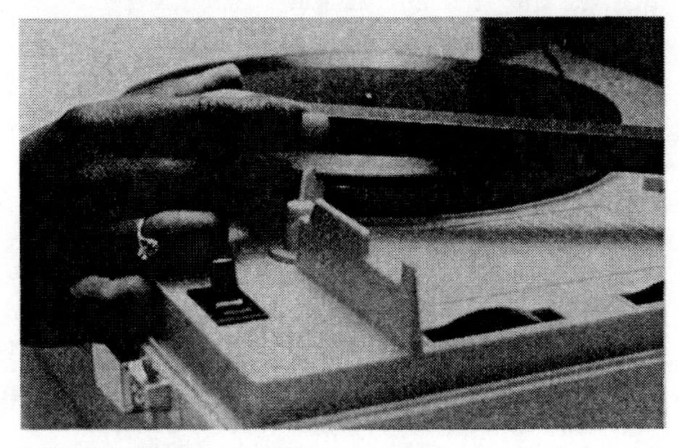

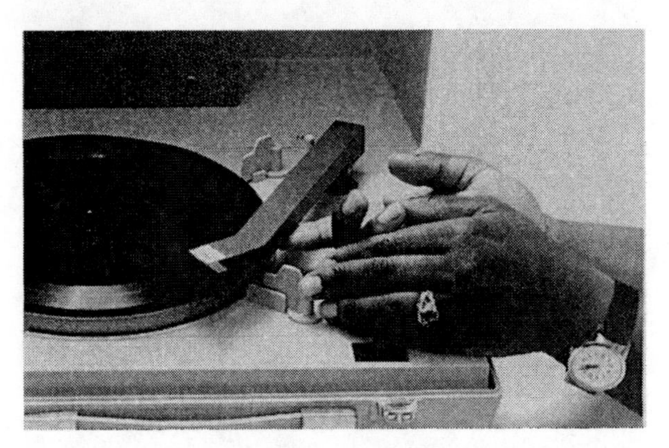

The Talking-Book Machine disc player: Using the finger to guide the needle onto a record (left); using record guides (right).

guides are also placed around the turntable to aid in this procedure.

A more recent model, the A-1, has a modified mechanism for placing the arm and needle. The user moves the playing arm to the left, applying downward pressure until a guide on the arm makes contact with the edge of the disc. When the user releases the downward pressure, the playing needle moves downward until it makes contact with the playing surface.

Setting the proper play speed is usually just a matter of keeping the lever set at 8⅓ rpm, since virtually all NLS disc books are recorded at that speed. If it is necessary to change the speed, the user can be taught to move the lever through the three speed settings until the playback sounds correct.

The needle on the Talking-Book Machine is housed in a rod-shaped plastic cartridge that fits into a collar on the play arm. The cartridge actually contains two individual needles located on the top and bottom surfaces. When muffled sound or the needle sliding across the disc indicates that the needle is worn out, a lever on the side of the play arm can be rotated to switch to the spare needle. To be fully independent in the use of the disc player, the user should be able to both rotate and change needle cartridges. Therefore, instruction should include how to detect needle problems, how to change the cartridge, and how to contact the regional library to get replacements. Rehabilitation teachers who work in itinerant settings should never be without a supply of cartridges, because they are relatively short-lived. Despite the phaseout of disc players, rehabilitation teachers are likely to encounter the need to instruct new learners in their use for some years to come.

The A-1 Talking-Book Machine.

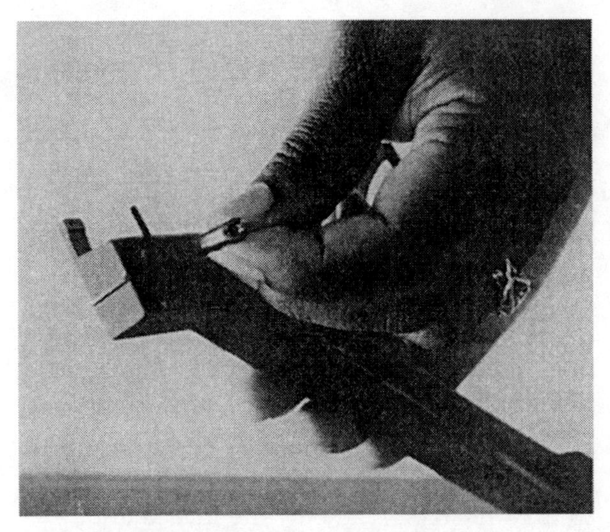

Changing the disc player needle.

Cassette Player

The Talking-Book Cassette Machine is nearly identical to the specially adapted cassette recorders used by people with visual impairments, except that it does not record. The keyboard contains, from left to right, a red stop key marked by a raised *X*, a rewind key marked by a left-pointing arrow, a green play key marked by a circle, a fast-forward key marked by a right-pointing arrow, and an eject key with no marking. The controls on the right are from top to bottom, speed adapter, dual speed function, four-track function, tone control, and volume control.

Instruction in the Talking-Book Cassette Machine is similar to teaching any adapted cassette player (see Lesson Plan 10.1). Any difficulties gen-

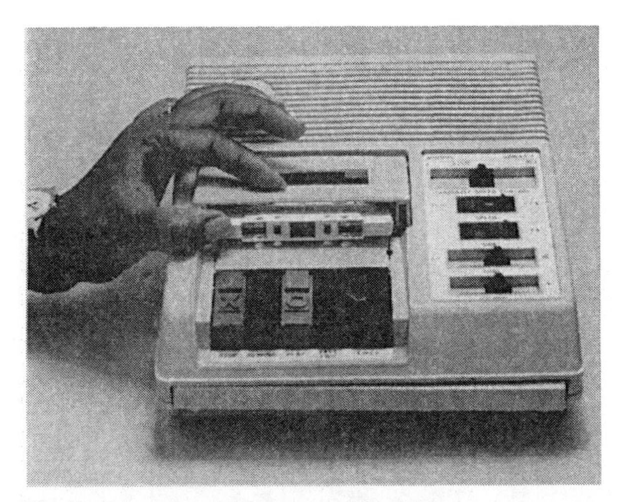

The Talking-Book Cassette Machine.

erally stem from understanding the adaptive functions, particularly the track selector switch. Tapes produced by NLS or CNIB can make this process easier because the narrator instructs the listener to "Turn the cassette over" at the end of the first track and "Turn the cassette over and change the side selector switch" at the end of track 2. After tracks 3 and 4 are played, the last track ends with the instruction: "Change the side selector switch. This book is continued on the next cassette." Because the concept of tracks is difficult for some users, materials produced by NLS use the terms "side" and "track" synonymously.

The Easy Cassette Machine

The Easy Cassette Machine was designed for those who have difficulty with the Talking-Book Cassette Machine. Some users, particularly those with no former experience with recorders, cannot master or are not comfortable with all the controls of the standard machine. People with physical disabilities who are unable to remove cassettes and turn them over must depend on others to do it for them with the standard Talking-Book Cassette Machine. In order to increase access to recorded library materials for such persons, NLS designed the Easy Cassette Machine, which is simple to use and incorporates automatic track switching.

The Easy Cassette Machine can be operated with only two controls: an on-off/volume switch and a rewind key. (It also has hidden controls for manual operation.) The door of the cassette well slides back and forth for easier use, rather than opening from the front on a hinge as does the Talking Book Cassette Machine. The tape is placed into the well by pushing it straight down with the braille label up, the door is pulled forward, and the tape is played by moving the on-off/volume switch about two-thirds of the way to the right. The tape can be rewound to review material, but it otherwise plays through all four tracks automatically. The cassette well is spring-loaded, so the cassette is removed by opening the door and pushing down on the cassette case. However, the user must be cautioned not to remove the cassette until it is completely read, because the device is programmed to rewind automatically when a new cassette is loaded, and a partially read tape would be rewound to the beginning if it was removed and then replaced. (See Lesson Plan 10.2 for teaching the Easy Cassette Machine.)

LISTENING, RECORDING, AND READING: THE FUTURE

As the development of all forms of technology proceeds rapidly, the adaptive technology available to enable people with visual impairments to

The Talking-Book Easy Cassette Machine.

LESSON PLAN 10.2

Teaching the Use of the Talking-Book Easy Cassette Machine

I. Objective: When presented with the Easy Cassette Machine, the learner will read two sides of a book recorded by the National Library Service (NLS) quickly and efficiently.

II. Materials: Easy Cassette Machine, NLS Talking Book cassette

III. Assessment
- A. Has the trainer used a cassette machine before?
- B. Does the learner know the concept of a talking book?

IV. Procedures
- A. Uses
- B. Have the learner describe the parts. If missed, point out:
  1. Carrying handle
  2. Cord and plug
  3. Cassette well, door, and spindles
  4. On/off/volume and rewind controls
  5. Side 1 of the cassette book
- C. Machine operation
  1. Have the learner plug the machine into an outlet.
  2. Have the learner open the cassette door.
  3. Have the learner place the cassette in the well facing away.
  4. Have the learner turn on the player by moving the slide switch three-quarters of the way to the right.
  5. Have the learner adjust the volume for comfort and listen for a few minutes.
  6. Explain that the NLS narrator's instructions ("turn tape over, change side switch") do not apply to this machine.
  7. Have the learner use the rewind switch to review short segments.
  8. Have the learner remove the cassette and replace it and determine the result of that action.
  9. If necessary, explain that the cassette should not be removed from the well until finished, or it will be rewound to the beginning.
  10. Have the learner listen through 1½ sides.

V. Memorandum: The importance of not removing the cassette case from the well and of ignoring the NLS narrator may need to be reinforced.

VI. Evaluation: Hand the learner a cassette book and have him or her listen to 1½ sides, performing all operations independently. Be sure the rewind key is used in this process.

VII. Assignment: Have the learner select a book and read it.

gain access to information of all sorts is changing equally as fast. Although there will no doubt have been innovations even since the publication of this book, this section briefly reviews some of the most recent developments and trends in listening and recording technology.

Recording Equipment

People with severe visual impairments now have many more options related to adaptive notetaking and writing and are not limited to standard or adapted cassette recorders. One device, the Voxcom, is a small recorder that can record on individual cards that have magnetic recording tape affixed along the edge. These cards can then be used as messages or affixed to products as labels to be read back with the Voxcom whenever needed. The Voxcom, available from distributors of adaptive products (see Resources section), is an excellent resource to use for short messages, to label foods, or to record short recipes such as those found on box mixes.

Other simple recorders are manufactured to record and play back one or more messages of 20 to 60 seconds in length. The user records while pressing the single operation button; then the message is played on an endless loop tape or from a memory chip when the device is activated. Such message recorders are useful for busy family members who need to leave important messages; for example, "Please wash the dishes before I get home. Love, Mom." They can also be useful for other purposes, such as recording telephone numbers from directory assistance.

Given today's rapid pace of change, it is possible that analog cassettes and cassette recorders will become obsolete and that people with visual impairments may soon be utilizing different technology to meet their listening and recording needs. Digital media, optical disks, CD-ROM access, and compact disks are all being examined to determine their usefulness to people who need alternatives to reading and writing print. It is difficult to predict which type of future media will solve needs most efficiently and be adopted by the majority of the countries that provide library services to people with visual impairments, but greater random access capabilities can in all likelihood be anticipated, thus eliminating the problems of searching for and locating information that are inherent in analog recording.

Computerized Books and On-Line Resources

Computer-based methods now provide access to reading material through "computerized" books. Since the metal type of previous eras has been replaced by computer files as the basis for the printing process, textbooks and other published material can be read directly on a microcomputer if the electronic versions are available.

Several types of services are now providing reading materials in this manner as of this writing. Recording for the Blind and Dyslexic in Princeton, New Jersey (see the Resources section), joined forces with Computerized Books for the Blind, which pioneered the development of books and manuals for use with personal computers and adaptive software. Recording for the Blind and Dyslexic negotiates with individual copyright holders to provide books on computer disks, in a form known as "E-text," which are sent using free matter for the blind mailing privileges to individuals with severe visual impairments.

Another computer-based reading resource, the Reader Project, based in Washington, DC (see Resources), provides access to electronic books via online telecommunications. Users purchase the book files, which are downloaded into personal computers equipped with a modem via telephone lines. The files are electronically "fingerprinted" so they cannot be copied and can only be read by the devices to which they are downloaded. Another source of electronic text is the Internet. A number of universities and other providers presently offer access to the complete or abridged text of some books (see On-Line Resources in the Resources section). Of course, the text of books is only a small part of the information available on the Internet to those who have the capabilities, including the adaptations described in Chapter 9, to make use of it. Users of all these systems use the adaptive devices of their personal computers to read the computerized book files in whatever accessible format they prefer. The number of titles available from suppliers is relatively small at present, but will no doubt one day surpass the holdings of conventional recorded books.

OCR Systems and Reading Machines

Recorded and brailled books, and now computerized books, have made the printed word accessible to a large extent, but these media require intermediate processing, either in the form of a human reader or a transcriber. Ideal access would enable the person with a severe visual impairment to read printed information directly. Attempts at creating electronic devices for that purpose date back to 1911, when the Optaphone was introduced, which emitted six tones relating to letter shapes (Gissoni, 1990). The Optaphone was followed by other electronic devices, including the Optacon, introduced in 1971 and now obsolete, which converts visual images into tactile ones, and the Kurzweil Reading Machine, a computer-based reader that reproduced printed text in a spoken form, in 1978. The Kurzweil Reading Machine, which consisted of an automatic scanner, a keyboard, and a software-driven microprocessor, was originally a large, stationary device, and the initial cost was approximately $50,000. The latest stand-alone systems can usually be carried in one hand, and their cost has been reduced dramatically.

Reading systems may or may not be designed specifically for visually impaired users. In general, optical character recognition (OCR) systems are able to convert print material into an electronic form, which is then made accessible using adaptive equipment such as a personal computer with voice output capability (Schreier & Uslan, 1991) (see Chapter 9). An OCR system contains a scanner that moves down a page of printed material and sends the electronic equivalent of each character to a computer, where it can be stored in a text file. The files can then be printed in hard copy or, for users who are visually impaired, read with a voice synthesizer or translated with braille translation software and read with a refreshable braille device (see Chapter 9). Some OCR systems are self-contained, and others require a personal computer.

With electronic readers designed specifically for use by people who are visually impaired, users can read most printed documents, review what has been read by line, word, or character, determine the punctuation marks in the text, and perform many other functions. To teach a client to use such a reading system, the functions can be divided into four groups:

- reading commands
- simple controls
- review commands
- special function commands.

For the user to be efficient and to solve problems that arise, he or she must be able to use the simple controls to adjust such features as volume, tone, and degree of speed adaptation and compression; to go back and review the content of the materials; and to utilize the device's special func-

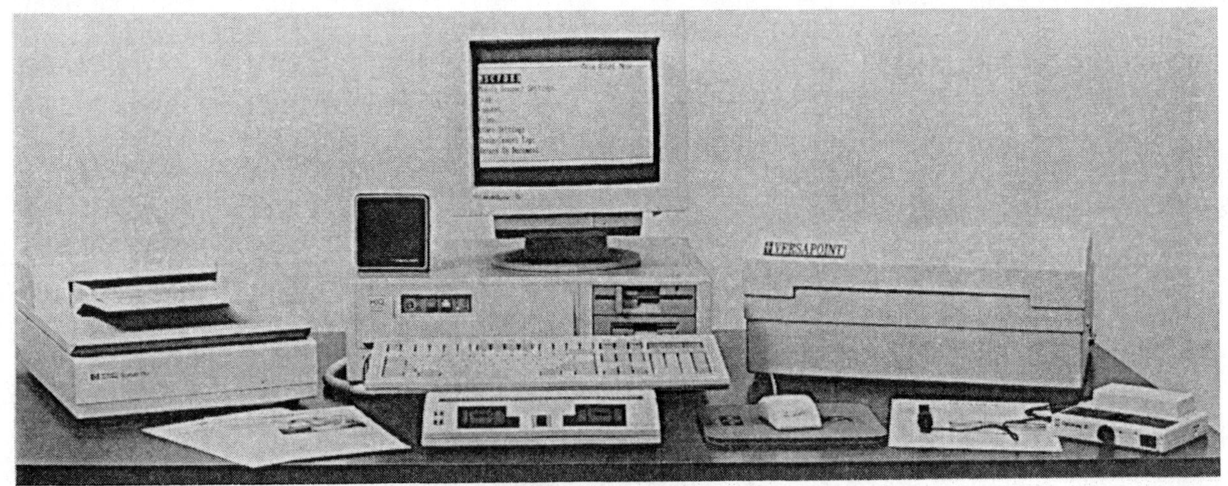

A computer-based optical character recognition system.

tions. The review functions are similar to those for microcomputers with voice output devices (see Chapter 9).

No reading machine or OCR system is perfect in its ability to recognize print because print styles are so varied and because the degree of print contrast may not be sufficient. In an evaluation of six OCR systems, Schreier and Uslan (1991) found they all did a reasonably good job of optical character recognition, though the length of time to accomplish the reading task varied. They also found a variety of features, including braille translation software that allows braille users to convert the print directly to braille; portable hand scanner capability; and a "sound picture" feature that uses various tones to represent blank areas, text, and pictures to help the user interpret the contents of a document.

Audible Information Resources

A variety of auditory resources have become available to people with visual impairments in recent years and should be an integral part of the listening and recording curriculum. Perhaps the oldest and best-known is the radio reading service. Radio reading services are aimed at persons whose visual, physical, or reading disabilities hamper their access to current and pertinent information. Programs vary from place to place but often provide the kind of information that is not easy for visually impaired people to obtain, such as newspaper articles; commentary; advertisements; best-sellers not yet available in adapted form; consumer information; and discussion of issues of interest, such as jobs, access, and transportation. Most radio reading services operate on unused radio frequencies and require special receivers (often distributed free of charge), although Audio Newsstand in Canada is primarily transmitted through local cable television companies on a designated channel as well as on some radio frequencies (Sokol, 1991).

Another helpful resource available through the telephone to the general public as well as people with visual impairments in some parts of the United States is what might be referred to as a dial-in information data bank. One such service, known as the Talking Telephone Directory, offers such information as current weather, headline news, sports, astrology, local attractions, soap opera updates, and fashion trends. Other dial-in resources such as Talking Newspapers for the Blind in Michigan and Newsline for the Blind in the Washington, DC, area enable the visually impaired user to read articles of choice from newspapers via telephone. These data banks are typically free or low cost to users; require Touch-tone telephones; and have

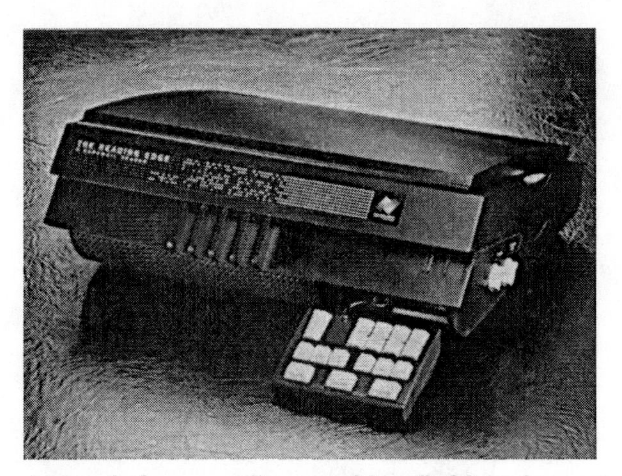

A stand-alone reading machine (left) and a system with a built-in computer (right), which can also be plugged into a standard keyboard.

sophisticated systems for making selections that allow the user to move quickly to other sections, read selectively, conduct word searches, and fast forward through the information using the telephone keypad. Information about locally available radio reading services and dial-in services can be obtained from regional Libraries for the Blind and Physically Handicapped, from local blindness organizations, and from the *AFB Directory of Services* (American Foundation for the Blind, 1993).

Teaching clients about using information data banks is a matter of providing practice and devising systems for keeping the required code numbers in an accessible medium. Specific skills and adaptations involved in using the telephone to gain access to such information, as well as for its everyday communication and personal uses, are covered in Chapter 14 on personal management.

MATHEMATICAL INFORMATION

This chapter has focused on methods of gaining access to information that is usually found in printed form. Another type of information that is essential to nearly every individual in our society is presented in numbers. Whether needed for school, job, or everyday personal finances, the ability to manipulate figures and statistics and perform calculations is a basic skill. Although people who are visually impaired sometimes perform calculations in the same media used for reading and writing—for example, in braille—mathematical notation frequently does not lend itself gracefully to these methods. Thus, alternate means have been developed, which are discussed in the next chapter.

CHAPTER 11

Mathematical Calculation

KEY CONCEPTS IN THIS CHAPTER

- **Adaptive methods used by people with visual impairments to calculate mathematical problems**
- **Adaptive devices used for calculating mathematical problems**
- **Methods for teaching the use of an adaptive calculator**
- **The uses and parts of a Cranmer abacus**
- **The method of teaching addition using a Cranmer abacus**
- **The method of teaching subtraction using a Cranmer abacus**

The average consumer, whether sighted or visually impaired, makes use of mathematical calculation in his or her daily life for such routine tasks as balancing a checkbook, creating a family budget, making decisions about purchases, monitoring expenses while shopping, and so forth. People engaged in occupations such as sales, vending stand operation, teaching, and banking have an even greater need to do calculations on a regular basis.

The evolution of adaptive tools that people who are visually impaired can use for such mathematical calculation has followed a course similar to the evolution of mainstream methods. Just as the mathematical tools used by the general population have advanced from pencil to calculators to sophisticated computer systems, so have adaptive methods moved from braille to talking calculators and on to computers.

ADAPTIVE METHODS OF CALCULATION

Early braille methods of mathematical calculation utilized the literary braille code, but this method is not only slow, it also requires large amounts of paper. Use of the literary braille code for calculation is extremely cumbersome because the code has no special symbols for numbers; nor does it contain any symbols for the common mathematical operational signs, such as addition or subtraction. Instead, a symbol called the number sign is used to precede the letters *A* through *J* to indicate the numbers 1 through 0. This requires the writer to make the number sign repeatedly.

In response to this need, Abraham Nemeth devised the Nemeth Code of Braille Mathematics and Scientific Notation, which was adopted by the American Association of Instructors of the Blind and the American Association of Workers for the Blind in 1952. (It was subsequently revised in 1965 and is updated periodically [Nemeth Braille Code of Mathematics and Scientific Notation, 1987, 1991]). The Nemeth code provided symbols for basic mathematic operations as well as technical scientific notation, reduced the need for inserting the number sign, and streamlined braille calculation significantly.

Mathematical problems are generally embossed on paper for braille users with a braillewriter in much the same fashion as paper-and-pencil calculations. Just as paper-and-pencil calculations require erasing and rewriting, however, so do calculations in Nemeth code. Over the years, several slates were devised to make calculations in braille easier. The Brannan cubarithm slate, or cube slate, looks like a small tray with a series of square receptacles into which can be inserted small blocks that contain braille numbers and mathematical signs. Rather than erasing braille on paper to make corrections in calculations, the user can remove the incorrect blocks and substitute the correct ones. Although the cube slate solves the problem of erasing and rewriting in braille calculations, it is no longer used much in schools because the slate is somewhat clumsy to manipulate, and the small blocks are somewhat difficult to read and are easily spilled if the slate is accidentally bumped.

The development of the Nemeth code and braille slate-and-paper methods of calculation made mathematics vastly more accessible to children with visual impairments. Because the use of such methods requires good braille skills and special tools, however, they do not meet the everyday needs of adults who have recently become visually impaired. The slowness of calculation with these methods is especially frustrating to these individuals because of the stark contrast to the speed of calculators that are so widely accessible to the general population. To respond to the needs of visually impaired persons for prompt access to mathematical information and ways of performing mathematical operations, calculators have been modified to provide output in braille, large print, or speech. For more complex computations, the development of voice output for computers (see Chapter 9) has made spreadsheet, statistical, and other types of software readily accessible to people with vision loss.

Adapted calculators virtually eliminated difficulties with everyday calculations for people of all ages with visual impairments. However, because calculators provide answers without teaching or reinforcing mathematical concepts, they are not useful for students who are learning basic concepts, regardless of their degree of vision.

The solution to the need for a portable, erasable, inexpensive way of performing possibly complex calculations was the abacus. Terrance V. Cranmer, director of the Kentucky Division of Services for the Blind and himself blind, was aware of the awkward nature of braille mathematical calculation. He was also familiar with the speed and power of the Japanese soroban abacus in per-

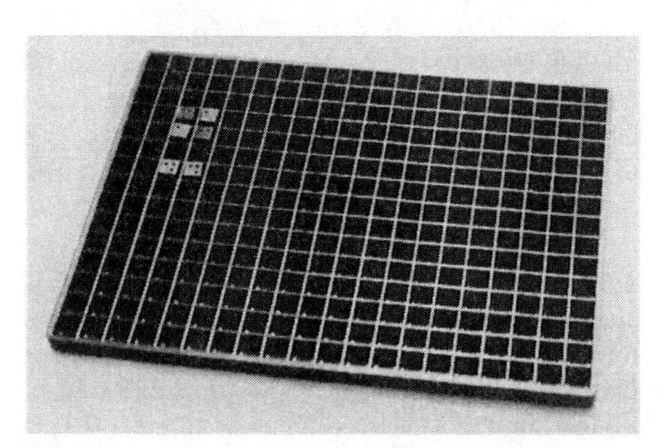

Brannan Cubarithm Slate holding the calculation 31 + 13 = 44.

A talking calculator.

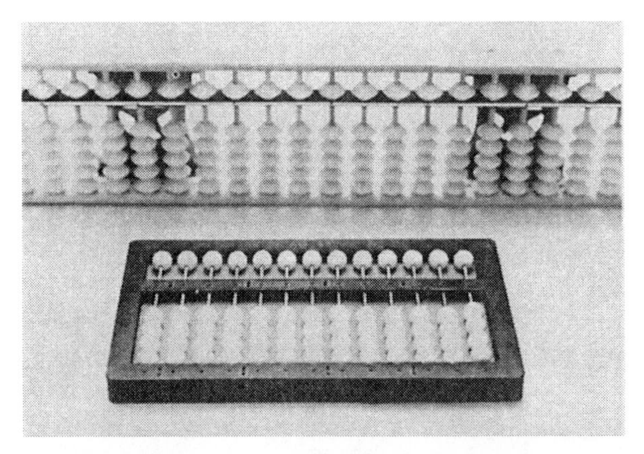

The Cranmer abacus (bottom) compared with the traditional Japanese abacus (top). The round shape of the beads and the orientation marks along the separation bar differentiate it.

forming similar functions, and in 1962, he developed a modified version of the abacus for tactile use (Becker & Kalina, 1975). The major modifications were replacing the traditional chip-shaped beads with round ones and adding a cushion behind them. These adaptations were designed to hold the beads in place firmly enough to prevent them from moving inadvertently. The Cranmer abacus is now used with visually impaired children in schools throughout the United States to teach and reinforce computational skills. The abacus allows the tactile learner to write, change, and "erase" problems directly.

The portability and low cost of the abacus brought it to the attention of rehabilitation teachers beginning about 1964 (personal communication, Fred Gissoni, March 1995), who began to introduce it to adults who were newly visually impaired. The low cost of the abacus—under $10—was especially significant when contrasted with the price of voice output calculators, which first became available in the early 1970s at approximately $500 each. Over time, the cost of talking calculators has dropped to as low as $10 to $15, while the cost of an abacus has risen. Consequently, for most clients the abacus is not particularly practical.

Teaching the Cranmer abacus.

Interestingly, although adapted calculators and abaci are both now widely available, it appears that most people with visual impairments seldom use either one to a great extent. Surveys of people who received rehabilitation services demonstrated that less than 10 percent of those questioned used either device (Ponchillia & Kaarlela, 1986; Schropp, 1990). The reasons for this phenomenon are unknown, but perhaps the difficulty of learning to use the abacus, the lack of access to instruction in its use, or the fact that many clients had enough vision to solve problems on paper were factors. Also, it is possible that the number of severely visually impaired individuals who have sole responsibility for household bookkeeping—and thus a strong need for such devices—is relatively small.

If the determination of whether or not to teach abacus skills to aspiring rehabilitation teachers was based solely on the current use of the device, abacus instruction would not be part of the curriculum. It is important for rehabilitation teachers to be familiar with the abacus for other reasons, however, including the lack of alternative tactile calculation tools for clients who have both severe visual and hearing impairments. In addition, blind adults enrolled in remedial math classes, where students are often not permitted to use calculators, must have an alternative to solving problems with paper and pencil or a talking calculator, as Taylor P., a young community college student, discovered.

Taylor P. lost her vision from diabetic retinopathy when she was 18 years old and became severely visually impaired. After completing personal adjustment training at a rehabilitation center, she moved to her own apartment in a new town in order to attend the community college.

Taylor realized that she could use a talking calculator to help her with personal household accounting, and she also assumed that she would need one for her community college courses. She had been shown a talking calculator during personal adjustment training, but had received no instruction. She telephoned the local blindness agency to inquire about obtaining a calculator and perhaps receiving some instruction in its use. The agency rehabilitation teacher helped her purchase a calculator, and lessons were begun. They first discussed the uses of the device; then the teacher introduced her to its keyboard and other parts and taught her the basics of addition, subtraction, multiplication, and division. Practical problems relating to her real-life situation were used to develop efficient skills. Instruction in the basic functions was followed by a lesson in the use of the more advanced functions, such as the percent key and the memory, reinforced with math problems that might be encountered in her college mathematics courses. Finally, Taylor learned to operate another advanced function to change the voice settings from word output, such as "nine-hundred-fifteen," to digit output: "nine, one, five." Taylor met her personal accounting needs and completed most of her college classroom assignments with the talking calculator.

Taylor's course work included a remedial math class during her second semester. When she met with the instructor prior to the beginning of the class, he made her aware that students were not allowed to use calculators, so that they would absorb the basic mathematical concepts presented in the class. Taylor spoke to the rehabilitation teacher, who suggested that they immediately begin instruction in the use of the abacus.

Because rehabilitation teachers must be prepared for situations such as these, a simple step-by-step introduction to teaching abacus skills to adults follows the section on teaching adapted calculators.

ADAPTED CALCULATORS

Adapted calculators range from simple electronic devices with output in braille, large print, or speech to elaborate software-based devices capable of virtually any mathematical calculation. The simpler ones are generally available from mainstream distributors, but scientific calculators capable of advanced functions can be purchased from Science Products, a company specializing in the adaptation of scientific instruments for consumers with visual impairments (see the Resources section).

Teaching the use of a calculator to people with visual impairments differs little from teaching it to sighted people, as shown in the previous example of Taylor P. Once the client understands the functions of a calculator, he or she needs only to memorize the keyboard, using a "home row"—a consistent set of keys on which to position the fingers as one would do with the typewriter or push button telephone. Becoming efficient is a matter of practice. Learning the more elaborate functions of a computer-based scientific calculator is more complex, but once the user knows how to work with the speech synthesizer, the process is little different than it is for sighted users. Therefore, the rehabilitation teacher who needs to teach an adapted calculator should consult the product manual for specific information on the functioning of a particular model.

THE CRANMER ABACUS

Several methods have been proposed for teaching the abacus (Davidow, 1979; Gissoni, 1962; Hanson, 1977). The one described here and used in Lesson Plan 11.1 for teaching the abacus in this chapter is a modification of the one proposed by Davidow (1979). As in previous chapters, the sequence used for teaching an unfamiliar tool is to introduce it by discussing its uses and giving a general orientation to its parts and then to proceed to an explanation of its operation. Readers will find it helpful to obtain an abacus so that they can follow the explanations of its use as they work through this chapter.

Teaching Addition with the Cranmer Abacus

I. Objective: When presented with a Cranmer abacus, the learner will add three-digit numbers with 90 percent accuracy.

II. Materials: Cranmer abacus

III. Assessment

   A. Can the learner add numbers up to 9 mentally?

   B. Does the user's tactile sensitivity and ability require an enlarged abacus?

IV. Procedure

   A. Uses of the abacus: general calculator, bookkeeping aid, calculating prices or purchases when grocery shopping, tool for remedial math classes

   B. Parts and nomenclature

      1. Parts: separation bar, orientation marks
      2. Terminology: clear, set, add

   C. Reading and setting numbers

      1. Explain bead values.
      2. Explain column values.
      3. Explain pinching reading action and searching technique.
      4. Have the learner read one-, two-, and three-digit numbers until he or she is efficient.
      5. Explain how to determine the proper column for setting and the pinching action for doing so.
      6. Have the learner set one-, two-, and three-digit numbers until he or she is efficient.

   D. Direct addition

      1. Explain the method of direct addition.
      2. Have the learner calculate the following problems until he or she is efficient:

3 + 1	5 + 2	6 + 3
5 + 1	6 + 2	7 + 2

      3. Explain left-to-right addition of multiple-digit numbers.
      4. Have the learner calculate the following problems until he or she is efficient:

21 + 13	25 + 12	51 + 35
123 + 21	206 + 72	526 + 312

   E. Indirect addition using 5

      1. Have the learner attempt to add 3 + 2 and explain the need for borrowing.
      2. Explain the equation 2 = 5 – 3 and demonstrate the simultaneous manipulation of the abacus.
      3. Reinforce the need to use the abacus, rather than mentally calculating and setting the answer.
      4. Explain the equations for adding 1, 3, and 4 using 5.
      5. Have the learner calculate the following problems until he or she is efficient:

4 + 3	3 + 3	4 + 1
4 + 2	32 + 13	34 + 11
31 + 14	35 + 23	43 + 35

(continued on next page)

Teaching Addition with the Cranmer Abacus (continued)

123 + 31	134 + 121	325 + 253
421 + 134	432 + 324	

F. Indirect addition using 10

1. Have the learner attempt to add 8 + 2 and explain the relationship to borrowing 5.
2. Explain or have the learner explain the equation 2 = 10 – 8.
3. Explain or have the learner explain the equations for adding 1, 3, 4, 5, 6, 7, 8, and 9 using 10.
4. Have the learner calculate the following problems until he or she is efficient:

9 + 2	7 + 4	6 + 5
8 + 3	9 + 7	9 + 5
8 + 5	8 + 7	8 + 8

5. Explain that the equation and manipulation are identical in any column.
6. Demonstrate how to solve the problem 81 + 25.
7. Have the learner calculate the following problems until he or she is efficient:

68 + 51	76 + 52	92 + 67
86 + 55	62 + 48	123 + 91
678 + 501	751 + 428	589 + 541
627 + 431	805 + 365	987 + 245
789 + 489	899 + 599	

G. Indirect addition using subtraction

1. Explain direct subtraction.
2. Have the learner calculate the following problems until he or she is efficient:

7 – 2	8 – 2	16 – 11
28 – 13	54 – 52	

3. Have the learner attempt to calculate 6 – 4.
   a. If he or she is unsuccessful, explain indirect subtraction using 5.
   b. Explain the reversal of signs compared to indirect addition.
   c. If necessary, explain the following equations:

– 1 = – 5 + 4	– 2 = – 5 + 3
– 4 = – 5 + 1	– 3 = – 5 + 2

4. Have the learner attempt to calculate 7 + 6.
   a. If he or she is unsuccessful, explain the two-step process.
   b. Demonstrate the manipulation of 6 = 10 – 4 and – 4 = – 5 + 1.
5. Have learner calculate the following problems until he or she is efficient:

18 + 6	27 + 16	57 + 6
67 + 27	126 + 58	165 + 75
678 + 169	857 + 626	678 +667

H. Indirect addition over 4

1. Have the learner attempt to add 43 + 8.
2. If he or she is unsuccessful, explain addition over 4.
3. Have the learner practice the following problems until he or she is efficient:

(continued on next page)

Teaching Addition with the Cranmer Abacus (continued)

42 + 9	41 + 7	36 + 19
32 + 18	127 + 229	514 + 339
507 + 345	281 + 256	816 + 437

I. Indirect addition over 9
1. Have the learner attempt to add 99 + 2.
2. If he or she is unsuccessful, explain addition over 9.
3. Have the learner calculate the following problems until he or she is efficient:

98 + 3	92 + 9	94 + 7
87 + 18	76 + 29	69 + 38
63 + 39	654 + 347	765 + 254

V. Memoranda
A. If there is doubt about the learner's knowledge of simple mathematical facts, addition should be reviewed before beginning instruction on the abacus.
B. Learners with previous knowledge of the abacus should be assessed to determine how they were taught.

VI. Evaluation: Have the learner add the prices of 20 items from a grocery shopping list and subtract the value of 5 coupons with 90% accuracy.

VII. Assignment: Have the learner solve 20 addition problems utilizing three-digit numbers.

Uses

The abacus is a calculator, which, like the electronic versions, can be used for addition, subtraction, multiplication, division, determining square roots, and other mathematical functions. Some people also use it for temporary storage of a telephone number obtained from directory assistance. The abacus is often used for common household bookkeeping chores such as recording how much is being spent at the grocery store, balancing a checkbook, or adding up charges on an invoice. However, as pointed out earlier, it is also useful in learning situations in which electronic calculators are not permitted, and it is probably the only alternative for people with both severe visual and hearing impairments.

Parts

The abacus consists of beads, rods, separation bar, rubber pad, and raised orientation marks. There are 13 columns of beads, each containing a single bead above the separation bar and four beads below. On both the separation bar and the lower front edge are a series of raised dots and lines that help to identify the columns tactilely. The dots correspond to the rods or columns of beads, and the lines separate each group of three columns, just as the commas do in numbers of 1,000 or above. In theory, the user counts the raised dots on the separation bar to determine in which column to set each number. However, counting the rods instead simplifies the process because the hands need not be moved again to set the beads, and the rods or the beads themselves are larger and more tactilely discernible than the raised markings.

Reading and Setting Numbers

The abacus has its own specific terminology. When the beads are placed against the separation bar, they are *set*; when they are moved away from

Setting (left) and clearing (right) numbers on the abacus.

it, they are *cleared*. Setting is like writing numbers on paper, and clearing is like erasing.

The numeric value of each single bead above the separation bar is 5, and those below it have the value of 1 each. Therefore, if all five beads in one column are pushed against the bar (set), the column is meant to be read as 9. If one bead from the top and one from the bottom are set, the value is 6 (see Figure 11.1).

As in numbers written on paper, each column on the abacus represents an increase in value by 10, beginning with the rightmost column and moving left. In other words, the first column on the right is the units column, the second is the tens, the third is the hundreds, and so forth. Therefore, if a 1 is set in column one, it has the value of 1; if a 1 is set in column 2, it is equal to 10; and if it is set in column 3, it is equal to 100. Consequently, if the abacus contains a 4 in column 2 and a 3 in column 1, it reads 43. If there is a 5 in column 2 and an 8 in column 1, it reads 58 (see Figure 11.2).

After introducing the learner to the parts of the abacus and the basic principles of its operation, the rehabilitation teacher should give the client practice, starting with reading numbers and proceeding to set them. The learner should probably be able to read and set at least five-digit numbers correctly and consistently before moving on to addition. As with braille, learning to use one's hands correctly on the abacus will increase the speed with which one functions, and this ability may make it more likely that a client will continue to use the skill after instruction is complete. When numbers are being read, the bead settings are investigated with the dominant hand while the instrument is held in the other hand. When beads are being set, the nondominant hand is placed on the rod on which the dominant hand is working so that the user will be less likely to lose his or her place or set beads in the wrong column.

There are two different ways to begin reading numbers. First, since the user knows that the number will appear on the right side of the abacus, one suggestion is to pinch the separation bar at approximately column 10 and move to the right until beads are found. Then the index finger and thumb are used to determine how many beads are in that column and in each succeeding column to the right, until the number is read completely from left to right. The second way to read numbers is to start from the right, sliding the fin-

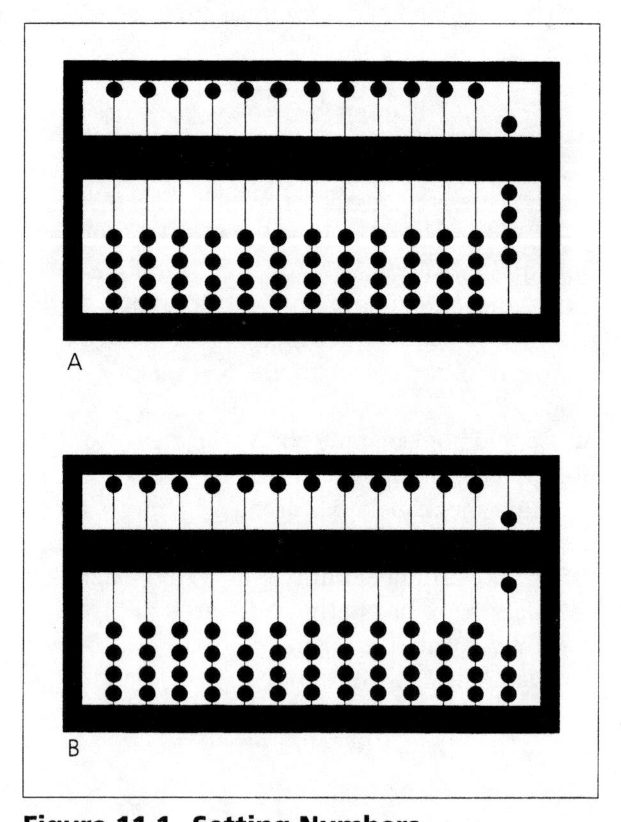

Figure 11.1. Setting Numbers
The number 9 set on the abacus (top); the number 6 set on the abacus (bottom).

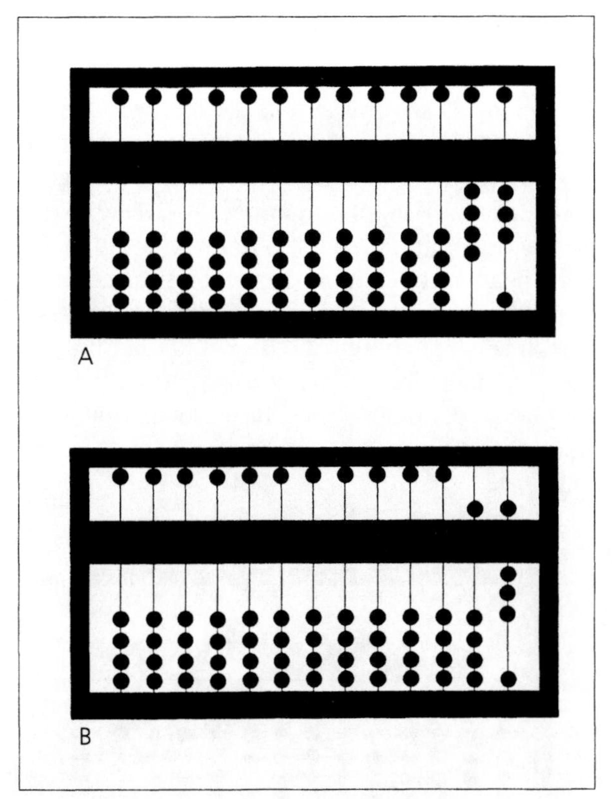

Figure 11.2. Two-Column Numbers
The number 43 set on the abacus (top); the number 58 set on the abacus (bottom).

ger pad to the left flat along the separation bar, until the finger feels the last rod on which beads have been set against the bar; then the number can be read with the thumb and forefinger from left to right. The user soon learns to recognize the number of beads in the column by the distance between index finger and thumb as they pinch the beads. This tactile action becomes a function of motor memory and is more efficient than counting the beads one by one.

The pincher action can also be helpful in setting numbers. For example, to set the number 645, the user would pinch the separation bar at column 1 and count the rods over to column 3 by touching them with finger above and thumb below the separation bar. Then the index finger pulls the upper bead down and the thumb pushes the lower beads up to set the 6 there in column 3 and the 4 and 5 in columns 2 and 1, respectively.

Addition

Addition is the most important skill to teach because it entails all the basic concepts of operating the abacus. In fact, it generally takes less time to learn all the other basic mathematical functions than it does to learn addition alone. As a calculator, the abacus is not necessarily the right tool for teaching basic number or mathematical concepts. The learner should already know how to add numbers up to 10 before beginning instruction on the abacus.

There are six steps or levels of addition, in the following sequence:

- direct addition
- indirect addition using 5
- indirect addition using 10
- indirect addition using subtraction
- indirect addition over 4
- indirect addition over 9.

Direct Addition

Direct addition is simply the process of adding numbers that require no carrying over to other columns; that is, when each column is added, the sum will be 9 or less. For example, if 7 is set in column 1, and 1 is to be added, the user simply pushes one bead up, resulting in a sum of 8. The same process is followed for problems containing multidigit numbers, but contrary to the usual pencil-and-paper method of calculation, the individual numbers are added left to right. (The reason for this relates to the mechanics of multiplication, and so is not discussed here.) For example, if 31 is set on the abacus and 12 is to be added, the operation requires two steps. First, a single bead is pushed up in column 2, resulting in a 4, and then two beads are pushed up in column 1, resulting in a 3. The abacus then reads 43 (see Figure 11.3).

It should be noted that the larger of the two numbers to be added was set on the extreme right side of the abacus and the smaller number was

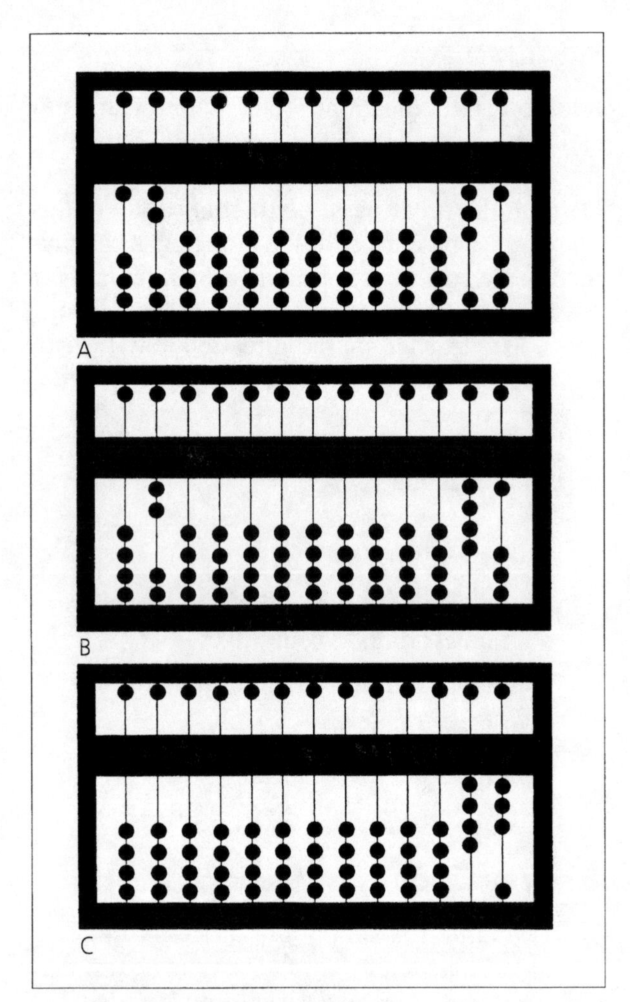

Figure 11.3. Direct Addition
Direct addition on the abacus: 31 + 12 = 43.

set on the left. Placing the number on the left is helpful in case the user forgets it while performing the calculation on the right. Although it doesn't matter in solving the problem which number is placed on which side, it helps to maintain consistency between teacher and learner when both are using abaci.

The learner should master the following problems before proceeding to the next section:

65 + 23 =	56 + 32 =	76 + 21 =
325 + 152 =	207 + 172 =	567 + 321 =
521 + 278 =	560 + 328 =	631 + 156 =
6,418 + 551 =		

Indirect Addition Using 5

Direct addition is not possible in all cases. For example, if 4 is set on the abacus, the user cannot add 2 directly because all available beads have been used below the separation bar (see Figure 11.4). However, in this situation, the 5 bead found above the separation bar has not been used. But if the 5 bead is added, then 3 must be subtracted so that the net result is adding 2. The user mentally calculates the equation 2 = 5 – 3 and manipulates the abacus as the calculation is made. First, the user adds 5 by pulling the 5 bead down, then subtracts 3 from that total by moving 3 single beads

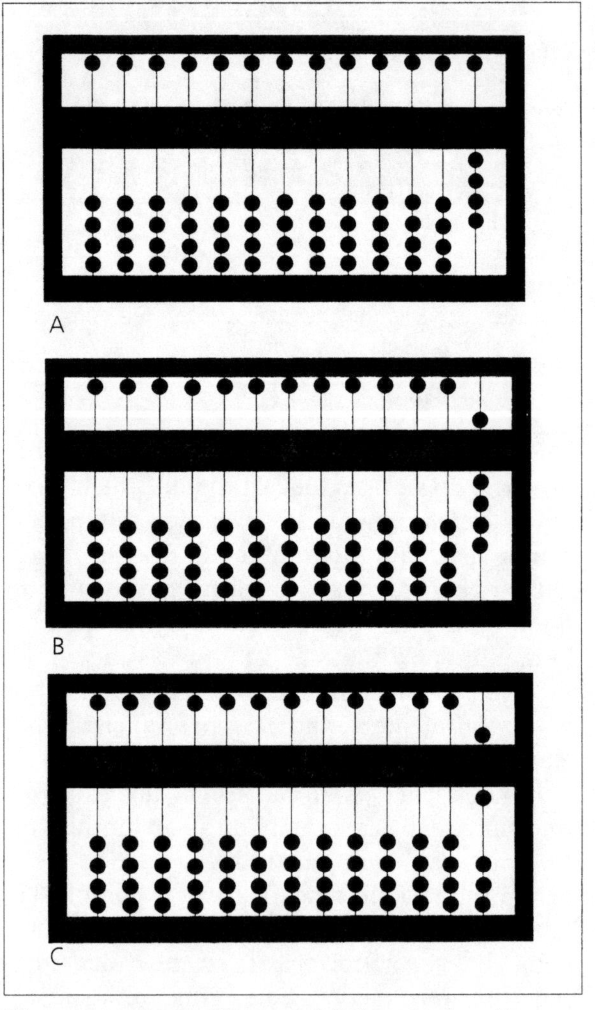

Figure 11.4. Indirect Addition Using 5
Indirect addition using 5 on the abacus: 4 + 2.

away from the separation bar. The number that is originally set on the abacus is inconsequential in this equation, and the user would do well to ignore it. Every time a 2 must be added and only a 5 bead is available, the manipulation of the abacus is always the same, regardless of the number set on it. Thus, if 2 is to be added to a 3, the operation is exactly the same as it was when 4 was set: 2 = 5 – 3.

Learners must resist the temptation to add the numbers in their heads and then set the answer on the abacus. It is easy to add 4 and 2 mentally and set a 6, but the concept of indirect addition will not be established for the individual, and when calculations become more complex, the learner will be unable to do them. The instructor must encourage the novice to work in a rote manner until he or she grasps the concept. When adding indirectly using the 5 bead, the learner should recite the following equations and simultaneously perform the stated operations:

1 = 5 – 4   2 = 5 – 3   3 = 5 – 2   4 = 5 – 1

Thus, every time a user wants to add 1 when no more beads are available below the separation bar, he or she adds 5 and subtracts 4. Adding 2 requires adding 5 and subtracting 3; adding 3 requires adding 5 and subtracting 2; and adding 4 requires adding 5 and subtracting 1. Again, having the learner verbalize the formula as he or she makes the manipulations will reinforce the concept.

The instructor should teach the learner to always check first to see if direct addition can be done, and then, if no beads are available to add directly, use indirect addition. Indirect addition using 5 is possible in any column on the abacus. It makes no difference if the 4 to which 2 will be added is in column 1, 2, 3, or even 13. The manipulation is always the same.

The learner should master the following problems before proceeding to the next section:

12 + 4 =	14 + 4 =	43 + 41 =
45 + 32 =	35 + 23 =	123 + 45 =
345 + 132 =	234 + 143 =	321 + 134 =
432 + 234 =	321 + 231 =	

Indirect Addition Using 10

The next step in learning comes when the user attempts to add beads to a column in which there are neither sufficient single beads nor a 5 bead to use. For example, when a 9 is set in column 1 and the user wants to add a 1, neither direct nor indirect addition using 5 is possible (see Figure 11.5). In this case, the 10 bead is used for borrowing instead of the 5 bead. Again, the user verbalizes the appropriate equation, substituting the number 10 for 5. Thus, when adding 1, the equation is 1 = 10 – 9. The learner recites this aloud while pushing up a single bead in column 2—whose value is 10—and subtracting 9 from column 1.

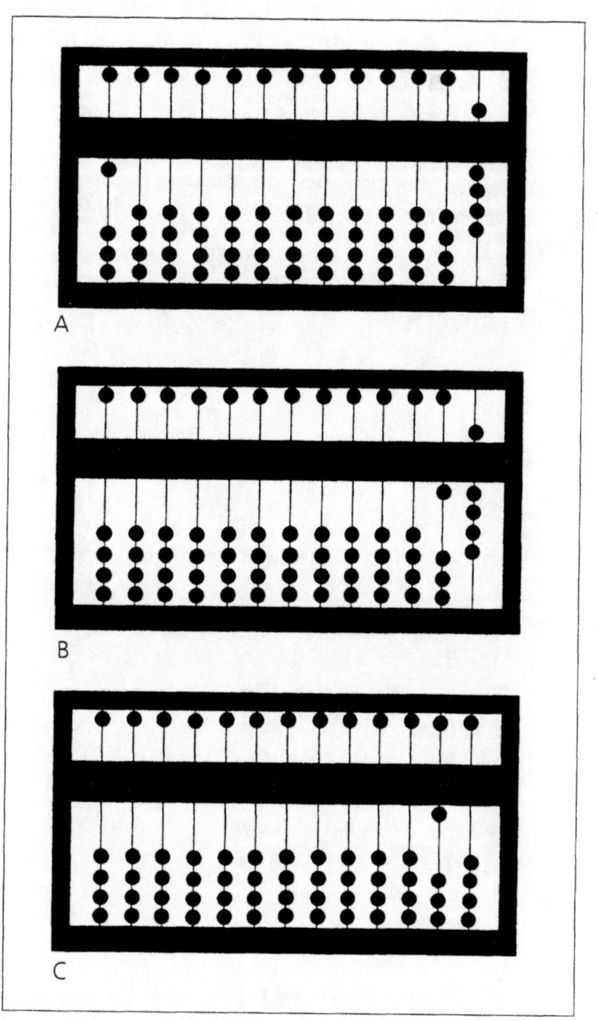

Figure 11.5. Indirect Addition Using 10
Indirect addition using 10 on the abacus: 9 + 1.

Indirect addition using 10 can only be used if direct addition or indirect addition using 5 are not possible. In each case, the user must first look below the separation bar for sufficient 1 beads and then check to see if a 5 bead is available. Only if neither is available can indirect addition using 10 be utilized. Thus, in the example of 9 + 1, neither the 1 nor the 5 is available. If the problem was 8 + 1, however, a single bead would be available, and the problem could be done directly. If the problem was 4 + 1, a 5 bead would be available, and it would be used rather than the 10 bead.

It is also important to understand that the 10 bead to be used comes from the column to the immediate left of the one in which the number is to be added. In the example given, this was column 2. Even if the addition is being made in a column other than the first, the bead is still taken from the next column to the left. Therefore, adding 1 to 9 is virtually the same operation as adding 10 to 90, but the single bead is borrowed from the third column. The verbalized equation is still 1 = 10 – 9.

The following equations are used when indirectly adding using 10:

1 = 10 – 9	2 = 10 – 8	3 = 10 – 7	4 = 10 – 6
5 = 10 – 5	6 = 10 – 4	7 = 10 – 3	8 = 10 – 2
9 = 10 – 1			

The following problems should be mastered before proceeding to the next section:

9 + 8 =	8 + 4 =	7 + 5 =
9 + 5 =	8 + 5 =	16 + 9 =
37 + 8 =	72 + 9 =	63 + 18 =
72 + 53 =	63 + 29 =	59 + 23 =
32 + 29 =	123 + 59 =	919 + 217 =
58 + 57 =	567 + 249 =	823 + 795 =
345 + 275 =	843 + 276 =	678 + 552 =
456 + 451 =	7,789 + 589 =	

Indirect Addition Using Subtraction

The need for indirect addition with subtraction arises when the numbers to be added require the removal of beads in the column, but they cannot be subtracted directly—that is, the beads cannot simply be pulled away from the separation bar. For example, if the problem is adding 6 to 7, sufficient beads are not available to add directly or to add using 5. If one attempts to add using 10, with the equation 6 = 10 – 4, the 10 is pushed up, but when the user attempts to subtract 4 in the first column, it cannot be done directly because only two beads are available (see Figures 11.6A and B). As a result, the manipulation requires one more step for the subtraction of the 4. However, this operation now entails using the 5 bead, or indirect subtraction using 5, which requires abacus manipulations similar to those used in indirect addition using 5. In the case of subtraction, the signs of the numbers are reversed in each verbalized equation. Thus, to subtract 4 (–4) the equation is –4 = –5 + 1. As the user states "minus five," the 5 bead is pushed up (Figure 11.6C), and as he or she states "plus one," one bead is pushed up from below (Figure 11.6D). Thus, the complete equation for adding 6 is 6 = 10 – 4, and –4 = –5 + 1. The need for this kind of manipulation occurs with the following number combinations: adding 6, 7, 8, or 9 to 5; adding 6, 7, or 8 to 6; adding 6 or 7 to 7; and adding 6 to 8.

The following problems should be mastered before proceeding to the next section:

16 + 7 =	28 + 16 =	57 + 27 =
66 + 28 =	165 + 26 =	256 + 128 =
267 + 175 =	586 + 162 =	725 + 655 =
756 + 168 =		

Indirect Addition Over 4

Indirect addition over 4 is necessary when the user attempts to borrow a 10 bead from the column to the left, but all four 1 beads are used. For example, if one wants to add 8 to 43, the equation is 8 = 10 – 2. Because there are no single beads available in column 2 to use for the 10, the user must resort to indirect addition using the 5 bead in that column. Therefore, the user pulls a 5 bead to the bar and subtracts the four 1 beads in column 2 (1 = 5 – 4).

The learner should master the following problems before proceeding to the next section:

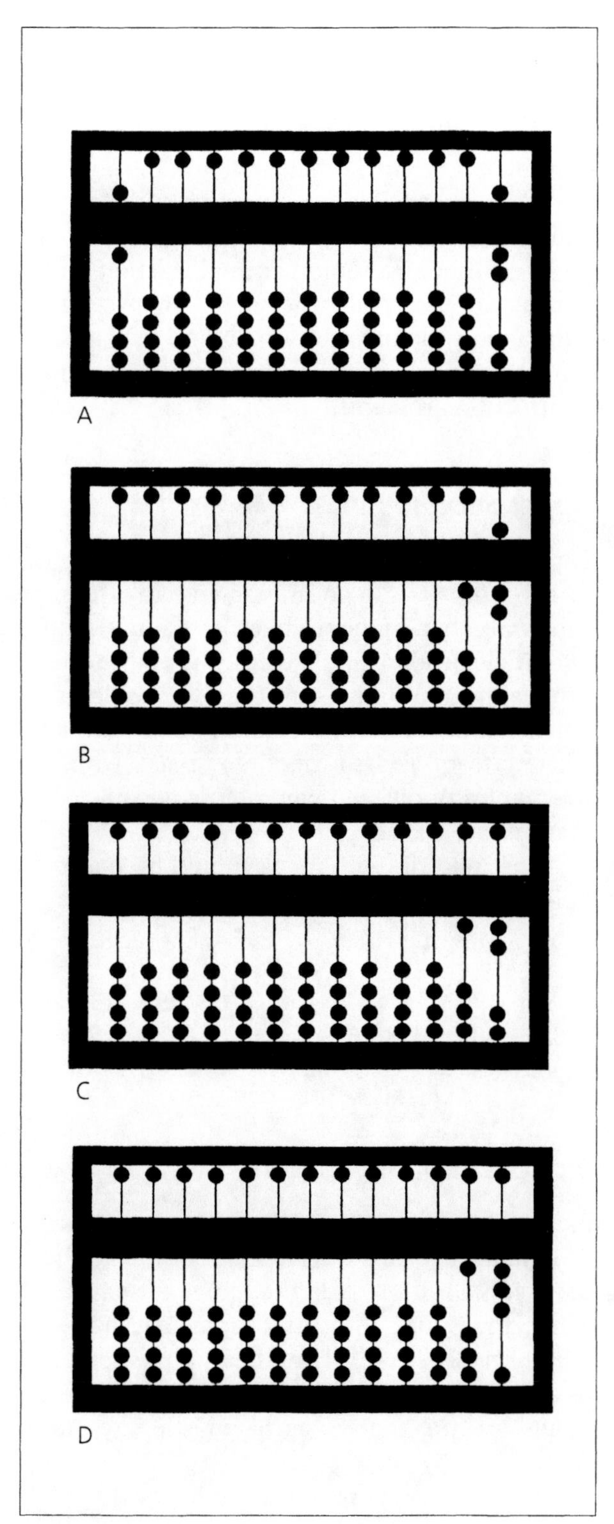

Figure 11.6. Indirect Addition Using Subtraction
Solving an indirect addition problem using subtraction: 7 + 6.

42 + 9 =	37 + 15 =	29 + 22 =
214 + 137 =	308 + 143 =	321 + 129 =

Indirect Addition Over 9

A similar situation exists when one attempts to borrow a bead from a column in which all the beads are already used. If the problem is adding 2 to 99, the user would try the equation 2 = 10 – 8, but the second column contains a 9, so no bead is available for the 10 (see Figure 11.7A). In this case, the user must pass over the 9 and borrow from the third column, so the 10 is pushed up in column 3 (Figure 11.7B), and the 8 is removed from column 1 as usual (Figure 11.7C). In order to get the correct answer, however, the 9 that was passed over must be removed, which leaves column 2 empty (Figure 11.7D). A similar operation would be required if 2 was to be added to 9,999, the only difference being that three 9s would be passed over, and all three must be removed after borrowing from the fifth column.

The following problems should be mastered before proceeding to the next section:

92 + 8 =	98 + 7 =	173 + 128 =
765 + 235 =	567 + 435 =	706 + 299 =
876 + 125 =		

After completing instruction up to this point, the learner should be able to use the abacus to calculate any addition problem. The instructor's role is then to provide enough practice to increase the user's confidence.

Subtraction

By the time the learner reaches this point in studying the abacus, he or she will have already learned several of the steps in performing subtraction on the abacus because they are integral to the methods of doing addition. In fact, using the abacus to perform subtraction is nearly identical to performing addition, but the manipulations are done in the opposite direction. Learners will have already learned direct subtraction and

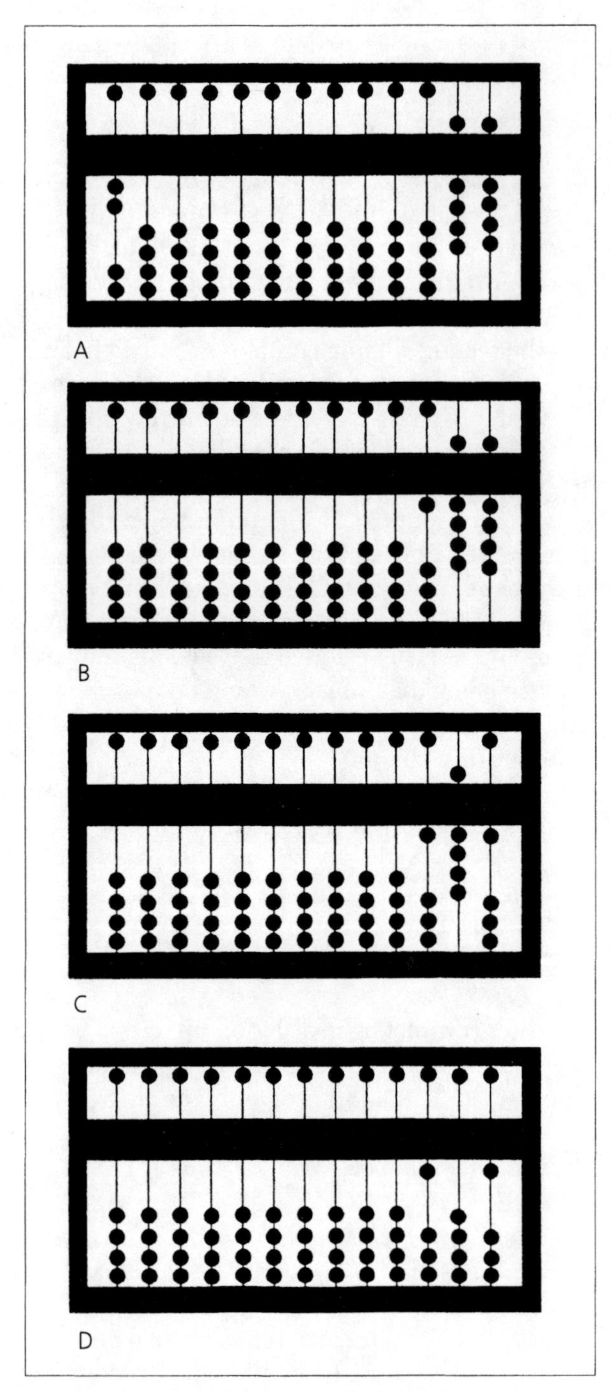

Figure 11.7. Indirect Addition Over 9
Indirect addition over 9: 99 + 2.

indirect subtraction with 5 when faced with problems requiring indirect addition. Thus, in direct subtraction, the beads are pulled away from the separation bar rather than pushed toward it, as in addition. If indirect subtraction is necessary, the signs for the numerals in the equations are reversed. For example, when adding 4, the equation $4 = 5 - 1$ is used. When subtracting 4, the end result is -4, so the reversed equation becomes $-4 = -5 + 1$. Although addition and subtraction on the abacus are essentially the same, when teaching subtraction the instructor may find it helpful to refer to the following sections, and the sample subtraction problems.

Direct Subtraction

Direct subtraction is accomplished by pulling the number of beads to be subtracted away from the separation bar. In the problem $4 - 2$, for example, two single beads are pulled away from the separation bar in column 1. As in addition, problems involving more than one column should be subtracted from left to right, to assist with the mechanics of division when more advanced operations are learned.

The following problems should be mastered before proceeding to the next section:

9 – 4 =	8 – 2 =	17 – 5 =
36 – 21 =	98 – 45 =	287 – 135 =
889 – 688 =	789 – 234 =	678 – 157 =
567 – 516 =		

Indirect Subtraction Using 5

As noted, indirect subtraction using 5 makes use of equations based on the number 5, like those used for addition, but the signs are reversed. Thus, the subtraction of 2 from 5 utilizes the equation $-2 = -5 + 3$. The 5 bead is pushed away as the user says "minus five," and the three lower beads are pushed up as he or she says "plus three."

The following problems can be used to reinforce indirect subtraction using 5:

7 – 3 =	8 – 4 =	5 – 2 =
26 – 4 =	26 – 14 =	67 – 42 =

76 – 43 =	175 – 142 =	256 – 131 =
567 – 423 =	678 – 564 =	

Indirect Subtraction Using 10

Indirect subtraction using 10 is used when direct subtraction is not possible and no 5 bead is set. A 10 bead is used instead. For example, to subtract 9 from 23, the equation $-9 = -10 + 1$ is used. A 10 bead in column 2 is cleared, and a single bead is added to column 1 (see Figure 11.8).

The following problems should be mastered before moving to the next section:

18 – 9 =	27 – 19 =	42 – 28 =
123 – 89 =	264 – 193 =	678 – 439 =
607 – 579 =	235 – 194 =	678 – 589 =
987 – 899 =		

Indirect Subtraction Using Addition

Indirect subtraction using addition is required when the final step of the equation involves the addition of a 5 bead. For example, subtracting 7 from 14 involves using the equation $-7 = -10 + 3$. However, none of the single beads in column 1 are available for adding the 3. Instead, to achieve the desired 3, the equation $3 = 5 - 2$ is used. The 5 bead is pulled down and two single beads are cleared.

The following problems can serve as practice for indirect subtraction using addition before proceeding:

12 – 7 =	15 – 9 =	23 – 8 =
64 – 58 =	31 – 16 =	236 – 185 =
248 – 197 =	534 – 483 =	824 – 569 =
514 – 389 =		

Indirect Subtraction Over Zero

Indirect subtraction over zero is needed when one attempts to remove a 10 bead from the column to the left of the one in which subtraction is being performed, but there are no beads in that column. In this case, the user borrows 10 from the next available column to the left, and, in a manner similar to that used in adding over 9, sets a 9 in every empty column passed over. For example, when subtracting 5 from 100, one cannot subtract directly from the first or second column, so the single bead in column 3 is borrowed, the 5 is subtracted from column 1, and a 9 is set in column 2. Because the borrowing is done from the hundreds column, the equation $-5 = 100 + 95$ would be used. Because this concept can be confusing, teachers often find it simpler to point out, "Since you skipped over some columns with zeros in them to borrow from the next column, always set a 9 in the columns that were skipped."

The following problems will allow the learner to practice indirect subtraction over zero:

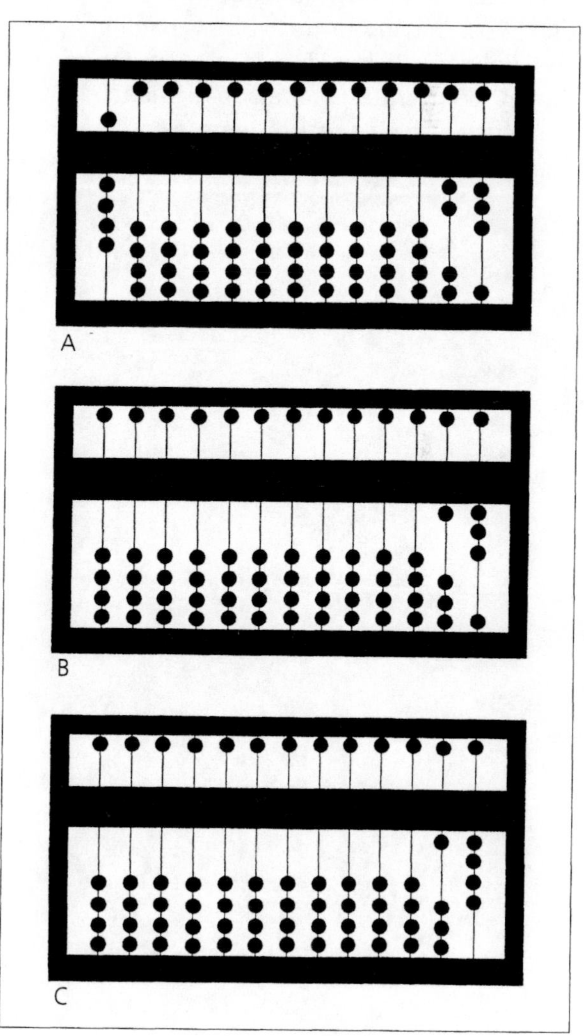

Figure 11.8. Indirect Subtraction Using 10
Indirect subtraction using 10: 23 – 9.

102 – 6 =	203 – 9 =	312 – 18 =
435 – 336 =	876 – 578 =	786 – 588 =

The calculation of multiplication and division problems are beyond the scope of this chapter, but the addition and subtraction skills learned to this point are the basis for both. Readers can consult Davidow (1979) for the specific methodology.

CALCULATION AND DAILY LIVING

Mathematical skills are incorporated into different areas of our daily lives, but most frequently into those having to do with managing money and finances. Being able to manage one's own money contributes to personal financial independence as well as self-esteem. Some of the financial areas in which rehabilitation teachers can offer instruction are identifying different monetary units, keeping financial records, conducting personal banking, and using appropriate behavior when making purchases. Since these tasks involve not only mathematical skills but also organizational and adaptive methods for the individual with impaired vision, money management will be discussed as an activity of daily living in Chapter 14 of this book.

The communication skills that were addressed in Part 3, although separated for the purposes of instruction, are not used in isolation. Rather, they are all incorporated into the countless activities each individual does every day, whether balancing a checkbook, brailling or recording a recipe to prepare for dinner, or reading the label on an item of clothing to be washed or worn. These everyday tasks, known as activities of daily living, are covered in the following section of this book, Part 4.

PART FOUR

Activities of Daily Living

CHAPTER 12

Basic Daily Living Skills

KEY CONCEPTS IN THIS CHAPTER

- **The effect of instruction in basic daily living skills on an individual's adjustment to loss of vision**
- **Safety precautions suggested for persons with visual impairments**
- **Sighted guide technique**
- **Other techniques for safe indoor movement**
- **Techniques for locating dropped objects**
- **Methods of organizing the home environment and personal effects to facilitate the location and identification of one's belongings**
- **Adaptive labeling methods and materials**
- **Principles of monitoring and preventive cleanup**

The activities of daily living are the daily tasks required to get along in life. They encompass an enormous range of behaviors, from brushing one's teeth, to dressing, to walking around one's home, to preparing a meal, to fixing a leaky faucet. The skills used to carry out these activities are known as daily living skills. In the process of teaching them to people who have experienced a loss of sight, rehabilitation teachers help their clients recover self-confidence and self-esteem that may also have been lost.

The chapters in Part 4 describe the means by which persons with visual impairments accomplish the tasks encountered in daily life and the ways in which the rehabilitation teacher can best teach the requisite skills. This broad subject will be divided into four areas—adaptive kitchen skills, personal management skills, home management and home mechanics skills, and leisure-time pursuits—which will be covered in the succeeding chapters. This chapter will discuss some concepts that are common to all instruction in daily living skills.

SPECIAL CONSIDERATIONS

Activities of daily living (ADL) pose a different set of challenges for people with visual impairments than do communications skills. Each specific aspect of communications—such as the use of braille, computers, and so forth—is relatively technical in nature and requires a great deal of specific adaptation or special knowledge for which a sequential program of instruction is readily available. For example, using Grade 2 braille requires learning nearly 200 contractions; using a computer requires learning word-processing software as well as voice-output programs. These communication skills have a specific, predetermined goal for which a set of specific intermediate steps must be mastered. However, nearly everyone routinely learns daily living skills as a part of growing up, so the skills the rehabilitation teacher is presenting in this area may appear to be common knowledge. Yet, individuals with long-term visual impairments may not have had experience with or instruction in daily living skills; and others who had previous experience while they were fully sighted may be daunted by the thought of performing daily living tasks with low vision or no vision. Thus, even though these skills may not require technical or specialized knowledge, they are no less crucial, and many adaptations, including both techniques and devices, can be taught to make daily living skills easier for persons with visual impairments to perform. Indeed, the ease with which many adaptations can be learned and the resulting increase in self-image and motivation to learn other adaptive skills makes instruction in daily living skills an especially important part of the overall rehabilitation process.

Because many newly visually impaired persons hold on to attitudes about blindness that they had before their loss of sight, they may not attempt even simple tasks on their own. For example, some individuals who become blind as a result of a sudden accident often gladly accept unnecessary care from others, for instance, being fed by hospital personnel when they could easily feed themselves. Sometimes attitudes of helplessness can be modified by instructing clients in one or two simple adaptive techniques. Many times the result is the dramatic first steps toward rehabilitation. A case in point is the example of Patricia L., the woman described in Chapter 5 who was proud of her cooking ability before she lost her vision, but who was terrified of climbing the stairs at the rehabilitation center. After spending one week in the adaptive kitchen skills class learning adaptive techniques that would help her to once again prepare the foods she had made for many years, she was whistling, smiling, and eager to begin cooking again and had lost all fear of the stairs. Tom H. had a similar experience:

> Tom H., age 42, did not show up at his scheduled home mechanics class at a rehabilitation center because he thought it was impossible for him to regain his wood-working skills after losing his sight in an industrial accident, and he did not want to face disappointment. After a great deal of encouragement from the rehabilitation teacher, he agreed to come to class. A simple successful lesson in hammering nails prompted tears of happiness and the realization that blindness was not as limiting as it once had appeared to be.

People with congenital impairments often need different kinds of instruction in daily living skills than do people who lose their sight later in life, because those with congenital impairments may not have learned basic skills as youngsters. Their vision may have been too limited to allow them to observe their parents performing routine tasks, or they may have been overprotected because of their parents' fear of accidents. For example, many adults developed an interest and ability in the kitchen from having helped their parents prepare food during childhood, but many parents of congenitally blind children may be less likely than other parents to involve their children in food preparation because they may be afraid their youngsters will get cut or burned or make a mess. However, a failure to involve visually impaired children in everyday activities affects the acquisition of skills in later years. Freyberger (1971) and Morrison (1974) both noted that years of overprotection and lack of learning experiences as children in the kitchen can cause adults great anxiety about being burned or being cut on a sharp object.

In addition, as noted in Chapter 5, some people with congenital visual impairments have difficulties with concepts relating to space, size, and shape relationships (Cratty, 1971; Freyberger, 1971; Hill & Blasch, 1980). In an extreme instance of this, one woman who was totally congenitally blind had difficulty judging the height of the flame on a gas stove because she could not hold her hand out from her body consistently at chest height over the flame. She also had the misconception that the flame was supposed to be high enough over the sides of the pot to somehow enter it and cook the food directly. Another example of a behavior that results from misconceptions about space relationships—in this case, not being able to judge distance—is attempting to sweep the floor by standing in one spot and turning in a circle. Most learners who are congenitally visually impaired will not have such significant difficulties, but rehabilitation teachers need to be prepared to teach basic daily living skills to some students in addition to teaching simple adaptations to all. Thus, a detailed assessment of basic skills is indicated (see Chapter 3), including an examination of abilities that might normally be taken for granted, such as plugging in electrical appliances, cutting with scissors, opening and closing wire twist ties, opening and closing packages, and removing bottle caps and lids.

COMMON PRINCIPLES FOR DAILY LIVING SKILLS

Many of the adaptive concepts or techniques that assist day-to-day functioning are common to all the areas of daily living. For example, abilities to organize materials and to identify items tactilely are helpful in food preparation, in personal and home care, and in craft activities as well. These common principles can be grouped under the following categories:

- safety
- orientation and mobility (O&M)
- organization
- identification
- monitoring.

Safety

The inability to see potential hazards creates dangerous situations and may understandably cause much anxiety for people with impaired vision. The rehabilitation teacher needs to emphasize safe practices in every technique he or she teaches. Proper use of the O&M techniques discussed in the next section will also promote safety.

Individuals who have lost some vision will need to think more about accident prevention than was previously necessary. Sharp objects such as razors or knives cannot be left where they might be accidentally contacted; drawers and doors cannot be left open; and nothing can be left on the floor in frequently traveled routes. Knives are particularly hazardous, so it is a good idea to have a system for their use and storage. For example, they can be stored in a knife rack or in a drawer in commercial or homemade sheaths made of cardboard. When knives are used and ready to be washed, they should not be dropped right into the sink, but instead can be placed in an established location, for instance, immediately behind the water faucets, where they will not accidently be encountered. Then, when the individual is ready to wash them, he or she can easily locate, wash, and place the knives point down in the dish drainer to dry before returning them to the knife sheath or rack.

Orientation and Mobility

The ability to move around safely and get from place to place in one's own home is central to virtually every other daily activity. A number of specific techniques are available to help those with severely limited vision move about safely and remain oriented; that is, understand their location in a particular environment.

The rehabilitation teacher is often called on to teach basic indoor O&M techniques, especially if the client is not receiving O&M services. These include sighted guide technique; self-protective techniques (upper hand and forearm technique, and lower hand and forearm technique); systematic search; trailing and indoor direction taking (aligning and squaring off); and basic self-familiarization to an area. These techniques can improve a client's confidence and efficiency in moving about in his or her home, as Carol A. discovered.

Carol A., a homemaker who lost all her vision as a result of diabetic retinopathy, was referred for itinerant teaching services. During the initial assessment, she complained that although she did not have many problems doing everyday activities such as cooking, she was frustrated by getting lost in her spacious kitchen and by misplacing ingredients and utensils, so learning basic indoor O&M skills was made part of her service plan. Her rehabilitation teacher began by showing her how to navigate safely in the house. Carol quickly grasped the value of squaring off with her back to the stove to walk to the refrigerator, rather than setting out on an uncertain path to where she thought the refrigerator should be. She was also more efficient in moving about to prepare meals when she trailed back and forth across the fronts of the counters and appliances. The rehabilitation teacher demonstrated how to use systematic search patterns to locate dropped or misplaced items. She reinforced this by having Carol drop a piece of silverware on the floor, listen in order to locate the sound of the object and turn toward the sound if she was not already facing it. Then, squatting and using protective techniques to guard against bumping her head on counters or appliances. Carol could "sweep" the floor gently with her hand to locate the object.

After Carol was successful at safely and efficiently maneuvering around her home, she felt encouraged to ask the rehabilitation teacher to show her how to walk to the neighborhood grocery store, two blocks away. Since this was a task that required using a long cane and crossing a street, Carol A. was referred to an O&M instructor.

Clients who need instruction in advanced O&M techniques, including use of the long cane, independent outdoor travel, use of public transportation, and other travel skills, should be referred to O&M instructors. O&M instructors are prepared to provide instruction in these areas, and also are called upon to orient clients to new neighborhoods or job sites, and frequently provide follow-up orientation for dog guide users who return home after training with a new dog. Although the roles of rehabilitation teachers and O&M instructors overlap in regard to instruction in such areas as sighted guide techniques, practical application of these techniques should be conducted under the direction of an O&M instructor (Hill & Ponder, 1976).

Sighted Guide Technique

When a sighted person assists a visually impaired individual in traveling, the sighted guide technique is used. With his or hand in a *C* position (the thumb to the outside and the four fingers to the inside of the guide's arm), the visually impaired person grasps the sighted guide just above the elbow (see Figure 12.1). The guide keeps his or her guiding arm tucked close to the body, and the visually impaired individual walks alongside a half-step behind the guide (see Figure 12.2). This position enables the individual who is visually impaired to detect changes in pace or direction. Communication is key in the sighted guide technique: A potential guide should first ask the visually impaired person if he or she would like assistance and then keep him or her informed about changes in direction or obstacles that lie ahead.

Protective Techniques

Many visually impaired individuals use the long cane (taught by the O&M specialist) to detect dangerous obstacles in the environment, but it is not always practical to use a cane in such situations as working in the kitchen, cleaning, or using tools to make repairs, when individuals need their hands

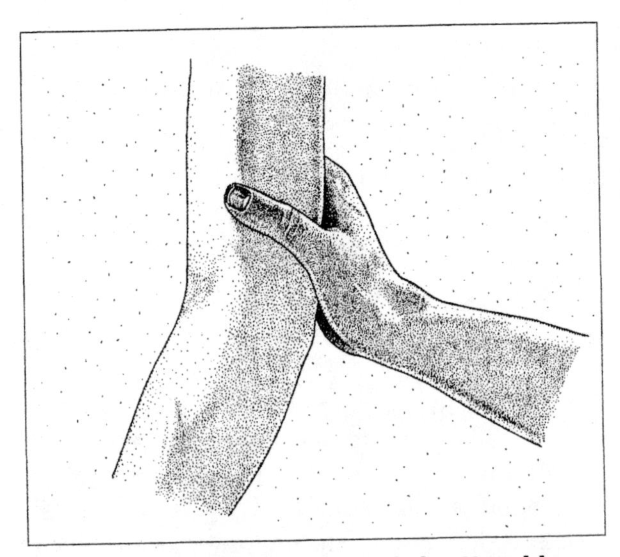

Figure 12.1. The Position of the Hand in the Sighted Guide Technique

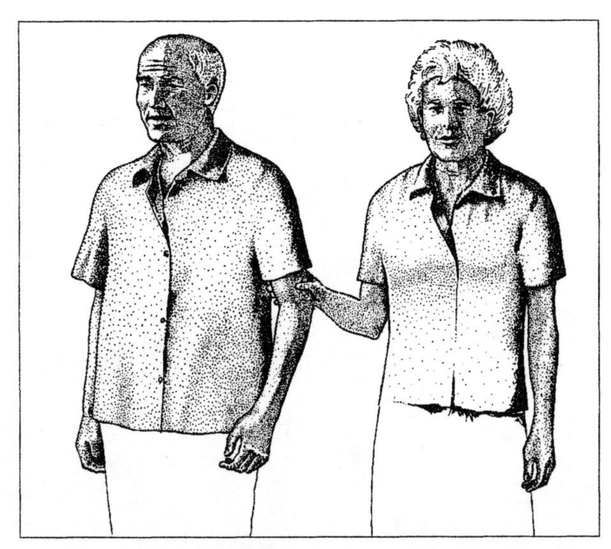

Figure 12.2. Sighted Guide Technique
The visually impaired individual walks a half-step behind the guide.

free for other tasks. Any rehabilitation teacher who has seen a client catch his exploring fingers in a closing door or bend at the waist to pick something up from the floor and smash her face into a countertop is all too aware of the need to teach protective techniques that serve to prevent injury.

The *upper and lower hand and forearm techniques* are especially useful for preventing unexpected body or facial contacts and locating desired items in a room, such as a kitchen table or counter. In the upper hand and forearm technique, the forearm is placed diagonally in front of and across the body, with the arm bent at the elbow, the palm turned outward at neck height, and the fingertips in line with the opposite shoulder to prevent or absorb any collision with obstacles that might come in contact with the body from the waist up. In the lower hand and forearm technique, the arm is extended diagonally down, across and away from the body, with the inside of the upper arm maintaining contact with the side of the chest and the palm of the hand facing in just below the waist to protect against contact with or to locate chairs, tables, and other low objects (see Figure 12.3).

Thus, when the individual using this technique moves toward a counter, workbench, or open door, there is a buffer between the person and the object that prevents injury and provides information about items in the environment. The upper hand is also used to protect the face from sharp corners, counter tops, and the like whenever an individual bends down. This technique frequently comes into play when an individual is retrieving a dropped object, such as a kitchen utensil.

Search Patterns

The use of systematic patterns is useful in performing nearly any type of searching activity, such as searching on a countertop for ingredients, looking for items inside cupboards, or reaching down to locate a dropped object. A commonly described search pattern is the grid pattern, in which the individual utilizes a left-to-right, front-to-back movement of the hand or hands to ensure full coverage of the area. Another pattern, often used when searching for a dropped item, is the circular pattern, in which the individual squats, bending at the knees and using protective techniques to avoid collisions, and makes a fanlike motion of the

Figure 12.3. Protective Techniques
Upper and lower hand and forearm techniques protect against collision.

hand to "sweep" the floor in first small and then progressively larger circles until the object is located. The use of systematic tactile search patterns is especially helpful for people with severe vision loss, but rehabilitation teachers will also find it useful to teach tactile search patterns to individuals with useful vision who have field losses that interfere with successful visual locating techniques.

Despite the use of search patterns, students and clients frequently overlook searching one or more sections of an area such as a floor, countertop, or drawer, so that they fail to locate the needed or lost item. An individual's mistakes are often consistent, however, although the location of the overlooked section varies from person to person, so overcorrection (double checking the lower-left corner of an area, for example) may solve the problem.

Trailing and Indoor Direction Taking

Becoming reoriented to a familiar area such as one's home after vision loss is usually not difficult. Since the overall layout of the place is already known, the person primarily needs to take time to identify his or her present location within it. For example, when a rehabilitation teacher was orienting a new client to his kitchen, identifying the stove was sufficient to alert him to the location of the sink.

However, moving from one place to another in the home can present more of a challenge. The mobility techniques of *trailing, squaring off,* and *alignment* can help. *Trailing* is a technique in which the fingers are kept in constant contact with a surface such as along a wall or other object to afford protection and aid orientation as one moves (see Figure 12.4). It is generally done with the back of the hand closest to the wall or other surface. Injury to fingers or hands can be prevented by approaching objects with the backs of curled fingers rather than directly with fingers extended (see Figure 12.5). If there is a continuous surface between the stove and the sink in the client's kitchen, for example, he can use the back of his curled fingers to trail or follow along the counter from the stove until he reaches the sink.

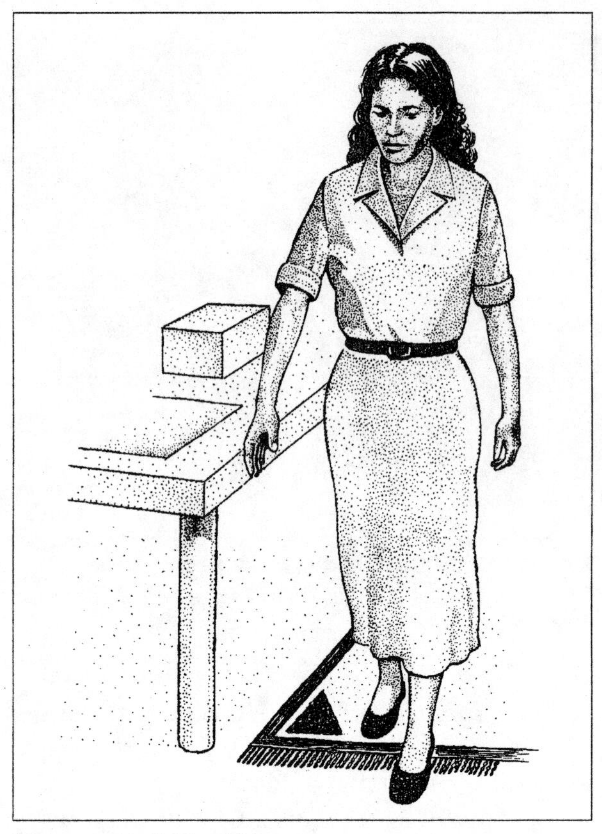

Figure 12.4. Trailing
Trailing along furniture using the backs of the fingers.

When the route does not follow a continuous surface, the client can utilize alignment or squaring-off. If the client is continuing in a straight line when there is a gap—say, she needs to cross an open space between the refrigerator and a kitchen counter where the dining alcove is located—she aligns herself to the initial surface, making sure she is parallel with the refrigerator to establish a line of travel, continues across the open area, and resumes trailing on the other side. In the squaring off technique, the individual places his or her back "squared" against an object to determine a line of direction away from (perpendicular to) that object. Thus, if the client squared off against the stove to determine which direction was straight forward from there, she could locate any other object in the room. Rehabilitation teachers can have their students practice these techniques by having them first orient themselves, then point to a spec-

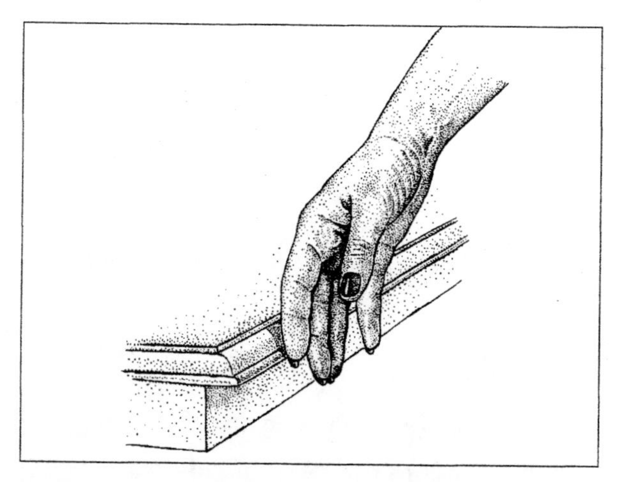

Figure 12.5. The Position of the Hand in Trailing
This position prevents injury to the fingers, which are curled toward the palm.

ified object, and then use protective techniques to move toward that object.

Familiarization

If the environment is not familiar to the person, orientation and movement are more complex. In such cases, the instructor first needs to show the client how to become oriented to a new environment, and familiarization techniques are useful in this regard. The instructor has the client stand at the entrance to the room—a bathroom, for example. This point serves as the "home base" or reference point for exploring the rest of the room. The client then either scans the room visually, if that is possible, or uses auditory skills to try to gather information about the environment—for example, listening for street noise from the window or the sounds of appliances. Then the client trails the perimeter of the room and, for instructional purposes, simultaneously describes it. Finally, the individual returns to the doorway and describes the room as he or she experienced it.

After this familiarization process, individuals with well-developed spatial concepts will generally be able to use the O&M techniques already described to move about safely in the new environment. For those clients who have less well-developed spatial concepts and are familiar with braille, the braille cell locating technique may be a useful method of orientation. This method involves using the client's knowledge of the dot positions of the braille cell to help him or her relate specific objects to one another. Graduate students at Western Michigan University have been successful in teaching clients to superimpose an image of a braille cell on their mental map of a room to organize the information about the location of doorways and furniture. To help a client visualize his kitchen, for example, the rehabilitation teacher might say, "On the left side of this room, the stove is at dot 1, the sink at dot 2, and the dish drainer at dot 3. On the right side, you'll find the refrigerator at dot 4, the canned goods cupboard at dot 5, and the kitchen table at dot 6." Other methods that can be used with clients who are not learning braille include using the numbers on a clock as reference points or naming walls or areas by their function or landmarks.

Through the use of systematic O&M techniques, clients can be helped to move safely through their environments. For further information on the basic techniques taught by rehabilitation teachers, readers can consult Blasch, Wiener, and Welsh (in press), Hill and Ponder (1976), Jacobson (1993), and LaGrow and Weessies (1994).

Organization

Losing items such as tools, keys, and personal belongings is a frustrating experience that everyone undergoes at some time. When working on a faucet repair project, for example, there may be nothing more inconvenient than not being able to find the screwdriver you had in your hand just moments ago. For people with severe visual impairments, such situations are also common in the kitchen, when working on craft projects, while applying makeup, and in countless other tasks.

As with safety issues, prevention is the best approach to deal with lost objects, and organization is the key element for prevention in this strategy. For example, a cafeteria tray can be used to organize ingredients and utensils for a certain recipe; tools and materials for a home repair job can be placed in a carpenter's apron; and all materials required for makeup application can be assembled in a basket or box. Some suggestions for ways to organize some commonly used items are found in Sidebar 12.1.

SIDEBAR 12.1

Principles of Organization

- **For frequently used items such as keys, eyeglasses, and writing instruments,** establish rules about where they can be left. For example, house keys are always returned to a purse or the keyrack next to the door; eyeglasses are always placed on the nightstand.
- **Small items, such as earrings, craft supplies, and miscellaneous household items,** can be sorted in various sized multidrawer storage units of the type sold in hardware departments for nuts and bolts. Large-print, braille, or other tactile labels can be affixed to the fronts of the drawers.
- **Items in a purse, backpack, or briefcase** can be grouped together with clips or rubber bands or can be placed into pockets or smaller containers. For example, a slate and stylus and index cards on which to braille can be retained in a small, zippered makeup case; and important papers can be stored in a briefcase in accordion files rather than standard file folders.
- **Zipper-type plastic food storage bags** of various sizes are helpful organizers or separators for such items as mail to be read, cosmetics, or socks and hose, especially since they are flexible and reusable.
- **Low vision devices, such as magnifiers or typoscopes,** can be stored near the location where they are typically used. For example, fixed-focus magnifiers used to read food labels can be stored in a kitchen drawer, and pocket magnifiers used to read price tags at the grocery store can be stored in a purse or hung on a neck chain.
- **Medications can be grouped on a small tray or banded together** according to the time of day they must be taken. Or, morning medications can be placed in the kitchen and evening medications on the nightstand. Inexpensive medication organizers with individual compartments (morning, midday, suppertime, and bedtime) labeled with large numbers and/or with braille markings can be purchased from drugstores and specialty catalogs.
- **A grocery-shopping list can be created**, based on the order in which products are locate in the store, so that shoppers will not need to traverse the store repeatedly to located needed items (see Chapter 13). A master list of foods and other items arranged in the order in which they are found in the local grocery store can be recorded on tape, typed into a computer file, or brailled and then consulted when planning a shopping trip. Or, reusable food labels (miniature plastic replicas, large-print or braille index cards, or brailled tape labels) can be removed from food items and clipped together as the food is used up. Then, the clipped-together labels can be taken to the store to use as the shopping "list." The reusable labels can be attached to the purchases as they are placed in the grocery cart.

Identification and Labeling

Another form of organization is required to make it possible for people with visual impairments to be able to identify easily such items as canned goods, clothing, medicine bottles, or compact disks by a favorite musician. In the case of persons with useful vision, the rehabilitation teacher might teach the locating techniques described in Chapter 6, coupled with various labeling methods described in this section that are appropriate for individuals with low vision. In the case of those who have no useful vision, instruction should focus on tactile discrimination and labeling methods. In either case, it should be noted that identification does not necessarily mean attaching a label. Many individuals will be able to identify familiar clothing items from memory by a distinctive feature or feel, such as a texture of a shirt or style of sweater, and some items are so unique that they need no label. Nevertheless, many types of items cannot be distinguished without a label, canned goods and medicine containers among them. (Labeling of clothing is covered in Chapter 14.)

An important way to simplify the identification process is to organize items by their placement. For example, canned fruits can be placed on a shelf separate from canned vegetables; medications meant to be taken with meals can be stored on the dining room table, while nighttime medications are kept by the bedside; shampoo can be placed at the front of a tub or shower and conditioner kept at the rear. Labels may still be used for objects that are stored together, but the identification process will be shorter.

Methods of labeling include:

- special symbols or markings
- raised-print letters
- enlarged print letters
- tactile codes (braille or Fishburne).

Special symbols might include varying numbers of rubber bands placed around medicine bottles, different numbers of notches made in the caps of two sizes of fuses, or specific numbers of raised-glue dots on labels to identify different colors of yarn. Such symbols or markings are only useful for differentiating two or three items from one another, since elaborate memorization schemes

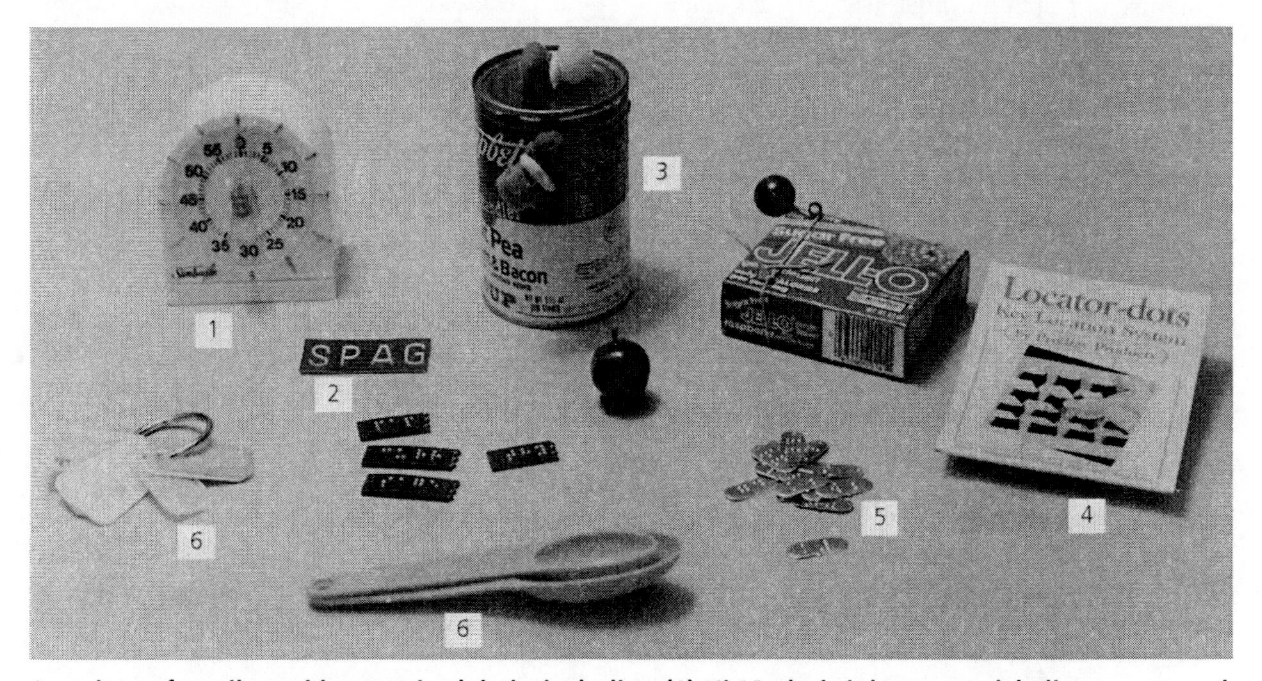

A variety of tactile and large-print labels, including (1) Hi Marks bright orange labeling compound; (2) Loeb braille and large-print labels; (3) Loeb miniature fruit and vegetable labels; (4) single-dot Locator-dots; (5) brailled aluminum clothing tags; and (6) brailled and large-print labeling tape.

would be required to deal with more items. It would be cumbersome for identifying a large assortment of canned soups, for example. In the case of food, small plastic replicas of fruits, vegetables, and other products on elastic bands to be affixed to food items are available from the Gladys Loeb Foundation and other sources of adaptive aids (see Resources).

Raised-print letters are useful for differentiating large numbers of items, but unless they are relatively large, they may be difficult to read tactilely. Raised-print letters are generally used one at a time. For example, a large magnetic letter might be used to represent the first letter of the type of soup contained in a can, with N for noodle, V for vegetable, and so forth. A single letter made from Puff Paint, a latex-like material that expands when heated, can be placed on clothing labels in a similar way. If a person has some vision, large words or letters made with felt-tip markers on index cards can be attached to canned goods with rubber bands or to clothing with twist ties and used in the same way as tactile letters (Loeb, 1982; McGillivray, 1981).

Braille or Fishburne labels (see Chapter 7) are especially useful if the item to be identified has more than one characteristic, such as a shirt that is brown and white plaid or a can of tomato rice soup. Fishburne labels are somewhat limited in that they must be produced on 1" x ½" pieces of plastic labeling tape, which are then affixed to an item, but braille can be placed on an item in several ways. These include brailling on plastic labeling tape or on pieces cut from file cards, discarded talking book flexidiscs, or even light aluminum strips or aluminum duct tape. Braille or Fishburne labels should be placed on the item in a way conducive to reading with the fingertips, not the eyes. For example, if compact discs or records are stored vertically in holders, the label would be placed upside down on the back upper edge, so that it would appear right side up to the fingers reaching down between the records. Otherwise, if the labels were placed right side up on the front, all but the first record would have to be removed from the holder to make room for the hand to touch the label and read it tactilely. Similarly, if a waist-high shelf is to be labeled, the tactile label would be placed on the top rather than on the front edge so that the reader does not have to stoop low to read it. Loeb (1982) and McGillivray (1981) both provide thorough coverage of various labeling principles and methods.

Monitoring and Preventive Cleanup

Completing most household tasks entails creating some measure of mess or dirt. The best ways to deal with this challenge are through monitoring and preventive cleanup. Monitoring here refers to the ability to determine either tactilely or visually the appearance of a given area. This kind of activity is particularly important in maintaining a clean and hygienic household environment. Most foreign substances, such as dust or sticky spills, are easily recognized tactilely, which in turn makes cleanup relatively simple. However, stains in clothing or on carpets may be more difficult to detect. Therefore, as with safety and organization, preventive techniques are advisable. Examples include working over a sink or cafeteria tray in the kitchen, polishing shoes on paper towels or old newspapers, or applying wood stain over a drop cloth.

"Preventive cleanup" refers to the concept of overcleaning. In overcleaning, people with visual impairments are taught to clean well beyond the area in which they had been working to ensure that any undetected messes are also cleaned. Cleaning is treated in more detail in Chapter 15 on home management.

The various activities of daily living are covered in the chapters that follow. For each area, the discussion will include descriptions of specific tasks to be performed, general adaptive methods, specific instructional methods, special considerations for first-time learners, and tables of specific adaptations.

CHAPTER 13

Adaptive Food-Preparation Skills

KEY CONCEPTS IN THIS CHAPTER

- Some of the common problems of cooks with visual impairments and solutions to those problems
- The types of food-preparation skills that may require special instruction for learners with congenital visual impairments who have never cooked before
- Adaptive skills used to pour, cut, peel, spread, mix, and measure
- Methods used by people who are visually impaired to detect when cooked food is done
- Methods of familiarizing learners with stoves and ovens
- Modifications that learners with low vision can make in the kitchen to enhance visibility
- Eating techniques that learners with visual impairments can use to locate food, cut items, and transfer food from a serving container onto the plate
- Ways to make recipes available in accessible media

The ability to prepare food to be eaten is an important daily living skill because of the basic role food and eating have in our lives. Being able to provide sustenance for themselves will be a significant step toward self-sufficiency for many newly visually impaired individuals. For those who have been used to cooking for their families, the restoration of this skill will be a meaningful part of rebuilding their self-image.

Food-preparation skills can be viewed on a continuum ranging from simple to complex, beginning with pouring cold liquids; opening cans and packages; spreading and slicing foods; dicing or peeling fruits; and progressing to preparing elaborate hot meals involving many ingredients, varied cooking techniques, and multiple preparation steps. Related skills are washing dishes and kitchen cleanup; locating and following recipes; and shopping, including preparing grocery lists, traveling to the market, soliciting assistance, using prescribed low vision devices to locate items, making selections, identifying foods or packages, and making purchases. Once the food is prepared, most clients will be able to serve it to others appropriately (to cut it into appropriate sizes or spoon portions from a serving bowl, for example); know proper food storage techniques; and demonstrate acceptable eating skills.

An individual's preferences, abilities, and living situation will dictate how many of the skills involved in the continuum will be accomplished. Some who live with others may need or want to learn only the skills required to prepare a simple snack; people who live alone will probably need at least simple hot food-preparation skills; and those who were used to having a major role in food preparation for themselves or their families may want to learn a more comprehensive and complex set of skills.

SPECIAL CONSIDERATIONS

Clients usually learn adaptive kitchen skills best when they are taught a combination of skills that leads to a finished product or tangible result—particularly if it is one the client has selected him- or herself. Rather than pouring plain tap water into a variety of vessels during a pouring lesson, for example, it is more reinforcing to prepare instant iced tea or fruit drink from a powdered mix. In addition to requiring the ability to pour, preparing an actual drink involves the ability to be oriented in the kitchen, the ability to organize utensils and ingredients, the ability to measure a dry ingredient, and the ability to mix—and the student has a finished beverage to enjoy or share with classmates or family.

Because of the need to plan an appropriate lesson for teaching new skills, the rehabilitation teacher must be familiar with a variety of recipes and food-preparation techniques. An appropriate lesson should include a goal—usually preparing a food product that the client would enjoy making, the achievement of which

- involves reviewing previously learned skills
- teaches one or more new skills
- does not require skills that are beyond the learner's present abilities.

For example, Anne L., who has never cooked before, is progressing well through the adaptive kitchen skills sequence and is ready for her first lesson in using the oven. If she and her teacher choose the preparation of a traditional cake or cookie recipe as a first goal, Anne will be faced with complex tasks that might include using an electric mixer, reading an adapted recipe, measuring a number of ingredients, separating eggs, transferring cake batter to a pan or placing cookies evenly on a cookie sheet, and timing or testing the doneness of items for which an extra minute or two of baking time can be significant. Perhaps a more appropriate lesson for Anne's first introduction to the oven might be a baked stew or casserole that only requires gathering ingredients and peeling and slicing them. This is a simpler goal and set of tasks, although new, and the result should be rewarding to Anne, particularly if she can share a delicious main dish with her family or colleagues.

Experienced cooks will probably have their own ideas about which foods they wish to be able to prepare again, so it is advisable to have them choose their own recipes to meet lesson objectives. Novice cooks, such as most teenagers, can benefit from lessons that also reinforce balanced nutrition.

Rehabilitation teachers will occasionally find it necessary to seek out new recipes to meet clients' needs for special diets or other preferences, such as low-sugar dishes for clients with diabetes. In addition, they may be called on to instruct their students in adaptive techniques for unfamiliar cooking methods that may not coincide with their own culture, habits, or preferences, including deep frying, stir frying, canning or preserving fruits and vegetables, preparing pastries and desserts, and cooking various meats. To learn unfamiliar cooking techniques, instructors can consult cookbooks, and the U.S. Department of Agriculture Cooperative Extension Service found in each county and many foreign countries provides research-based printed information on nearly every homemaking skill.

Clients with Adventitious Impairments

The majority of adult clients learning kitchen skills will have previously learned to cook. People who were used to working in the kitchen before they lost some or all of their sight can in general be expected to regain their previous level of skill, unless additional impairments intervene. Such individuals might typically need instruction only in the following areas:

- becoming oriented in the kitchen
- locating, labeling, and organizing food items and utensils
- measuring, transferring, and pouring foods
- using the stove and other appliances safely and effectively
- using adapted recipes and cookbooks
- determining when food is properly cooked.

Rather than following a set of lessons dictated by the rehabilitation teacher that proceed from the simple to the complex, the sequence of instruction is often based on helping the individual who is visually impaired relearn to prepare the foods he or she cooked before the loss of sight. Thus, the teacher can use a familiar food preparation task to teach and reinforce a variety of adaptive skills. For example, Mario H. often used to make a tuna casserole for his family's supper. He remembers how to open cans, chop vegetables, boil pasta, stir the mixture, and move oven racks for proper placement, but he needs to be shown how to orient himself to the kitchen; locate, identify, and measure the food items using low vision or tactile methods; mark and set the stove and oven dials; and test for doneness using adaptive methods. The rehabilitation teacher can expect that the client will generalize the adaptive kitchen skills acquired when learning to prepare one food to the preparation of similar foods.

Clients with Congenital Impairments

For people who have been visually impaired since birth and have had little or no previous kitchen experience, learning adaptive kitchen skills can be complicated by the potential conceptual limitations discussed in Chapter 12, such as excessive fears about safety, difficulties with spatial relationships, or misconceptions about the nature of cooking itself. Thus, the rehabilitation teacher not only needs to teach standard adaptations formulated for visually impaired cooks (discussed later in this chapter), but may also be required to teach basic kitchen skills themselves. Because most rehabilitation clients with congenital impairments have in all likelihood already acquired sufficient skills in the communications areas during their school years, kitchen skills may be one of the major foci of rehabilitation teaching for these individuals. In addition to the skills previously listed that need to be taught to those who have cooked before, inexperienced cooks will usually need instruction beginning at a more basic level in:

- pouring from and into a variety of vessels
- cutting, slicing, dicing, and peeling
- spreading
- measuring concepts, including liquid, dry, and semisolid foods
- identifying food and food packaging (see Chapter 12)
- transferring foods
- mixing
- working on the stove top (including centering pans, gauging temperature, and turning foods during frying)
- cleanup (see Chapters 12 and 15).

One such client was Tina P.

> Tina P., a 17-year-old high school senior, was referred in the fall to a rehabilitation teacher at a private rehabilitation agency for evaluation and training. The primary focus was to be on personal management and adaptive cooking and related food-preparation skills in anticipation of her impending high school graduation and entry into a state university. When the rehabilitation teacher completed a case file summary form, he discovered a narrative report by a counselor from the State Commission for the Blind indicating that Tina's parents were very

protective of their totally blind daughter. For example, her mother typically drove her to school instead of letting her walk to the curb in front of her house to take the school bus. A report from the school O&M instructor documented Tina's progress during lessons, but also indicated that Tina received no reinforcement outside of lessons because her parents were afraid to allow Tina to walk alone.

When the rehabilitation teacher began the assessment interview and observation, he found that Tina had no experience in performing even basic kitchen skills, such as pouring milk into a cereal bowl, spreading butter on toast, or spreading peanut butter or condiments on bread. Tina said that she usually studied or watched television after school. She did not prepare foods for herself and had never made a sandwich. If she wanted a snack or drink of water, her mother always got it for her. She had never been asked to set the table, pour family beverages, or help make a batch of cookies. In fact, Tina admitted that she did not know where food, dishes, or tableware were kept in the kitchen; and she had never felt curious about exploring the kitchen, since her mother had always cautioned her to stay away because of the possibility of accidents, burns, or cuts.

Since Tina was planning to live in a dormitory with a weekly meal plan, the initial emphasis of instruction was on the skills required to eat in the cafeteria, including pouring liquids; filling glasses and cups from soda and cocoa or coffee dispensers; spreading foods such as condiments, jelly, and butter; applying salad toppings from a salad bar; and so forth. In addition, an introduction to food preparation was begun, with an emphasis on simple cold and hot foods that Tina could prepare in a dorm kitchenette for snacks or meals when the cafeteria was closed. Food familiarization and packaging were covered, and she was shown how to open and close various packages, use a bottle and can opener, and use twist ties and plastic tabs to close plastic bags. Because she was so inexperienced in the area of food preparation, the teacher also covered basics of food storage and preservation. Tina learned how to use a toaster, microwave, and instant hot water heater and was introduced to stovetop cooking.

The rehabilitation teacher found it necessary to provide basic information about every aspect of every lesson. Tina's lack of any previous knowledge in this area affected her ability to make use of the new information she was gathering. She had no previous practical experience to which she could relate what she was learning or that could help her figure out, for example, whether she might have measured too much or too little of an ingredient in a recipe that failed or whether a dish was under- or overcooked. Therefore, repetition of newly learned skills was important to give her a foundation of experience that could then be built upon. For example, once she learned to make a sandwich, she was encouraged to make one at the beginning of every after-school lesson—a task that also provided her with a snack.

The lessons continued each day after school until graduation and for longer periods during summer vacation. By the time college started, Tina was able to walk confidently and independently through a cafeteria line and select meals as well as to prepare a variety of nutritious cold and simple hot dishes. At the last lesson before Tina's classes began, Tina made cookies from scratch with the assistance of the rehabilitation teacher, in part so that Tina could determine whether she might wish to continue instruction the following summer. The lesson was deemed a success by Tina and her parents, who agreed that she would pursue further lessons and vowed to encourage more such experiments in the family kitchen.

Length of Lessons

Many rehabilitation programs and agencies follow a rigid schedule allowing only one hour per lesson, but particularly in cooking one hour may not be long enough to accomplish the objective of a lesson without interruption. New cooks or peo-

SIDEBAR 13.1

Common Kitchen Adaptations

MONITORING POURING LEVEL

1. Place a fingertip over the edge of the glass.
2. Listen to the sound of filling.
3. Use an electronic liquid level indicator.
4. Use the weight of the filled container to estimate fullness.
5. Use the temperature on the outside of the vessel as a clue.
6. Use light, contrast, or magnification, if possible.

SLICING, DICING, AND PEELING

1. Monitor tactilely if necessary.
2. Use a broad-bladed knife.
3. Use a commercial appliance or knife with an adjustable guide.
4. Use the fingers as guides for the width of slices: Place the knife at the edge of the item to be sliced, move it away from the edge to the desired width, place fingers on either side of the knife from above to avoid accidental injury.
5. Establish a standard location in which to place knives when not in use; place dirty knives behind the faucet until ready to wash them; dry them with point down; store them in a knife holder or homemade sheath.

MEASURING

1. For people with useful vision, use color contrast, improve lighting, and enhance or enlarge markings on measuring tools.
2. Use graduated (dry) measuring cups, which have a separate scoop for each amount to be measured, so that dry ingredients can be leveled off at the top and cups can be dipped into liquids.
3. Label measures with braille, tactile marking compounds, or notches filed on the handle.
4. Bend measuring spoons into ladles that can be dipped into a liquid stored in a wide-mouth container.
5. Measure ingredients over a larger container to catch spills, instead of over the mixing bowl, and use a funnel to return the excess to the original container.

SPREADING SEMISOLIDS

1. Spread outward from a central deposit.
2. Spread in an organized pattern, left to right, top to bottom, or center to outside.
3. Monitor tactilely if necessary.

CENTERING PANS ON STOVETOP BURNERS

1. Center the pan tactilely or visually while the burner is cold, comparing the edges of the pan with the edges of the burner.
2. Tactilely monitor the evenness of heat above and around a pan by holding the hand palm down at chest height and circling the hand to determine the location of the heat source.
3. Check the alignment of the pan on the burner with a wooden spoon, using the 3 o'clock, 6 o'clock, 9 o'clock, and 12 o'clock positions.

TURNING FRIED FOODS

1. Fry one item at a time.
2. Use a double-bladed spatula to hold the item securely and to get tactile feedback about doneness and location.
3. Push the item against one side of the pan to stabilize it on the spatula.
4. Carefully touch the item on top while using the turner underneath.
5. Rotate the wrist fully toward the inside to make sure that the food is turned over completely.

BAKING

1. Check the placement of the oven rack before turning the oven on.
2. Use long, fire-resistant oven mitts.

(continued on next page)

Common Kitchen Adaptations (continued)

3. Pull the oven racks out for loading and unloading.
4. Stand to one side when opening the oven door to avoid steam burns.

DETERMINING DONENESS

1. Establish cooking times for commonly prepared items.
2. Monitor the peak smell of properly cooked items.
3. Check the firmness of meat by "pinching" with a double spatula.
4. Listen for the sound of frying items to change from sizzle to quiet.

TIMING

1. Use large-print timers.
2. Use tactile timers from specialty suppliers.
3. Create tactile timers with Hi Marks or glue dots on commercial timers.
4. Use voice-output timers from specialty suppliers.
5. Record a "timing tape" with verbal announcements of time at specific intervals.

ADAPTING COOKBOOKS AND RECIPES

1. Purchase brailled, recorded, or large-print books from suppliers.
2. Record, braille, or enlarge favorite recipes and books.
3. When recording recipes, repeat the amount of each ingredient when it is mentioned in the directions section and leave moderate pauses between the ingredient and the direction.
4. Voice indexes are bothersome if used within a recipe and are unnecessary.
5. Large (5" x 7") index cards can be used for brailled recipes.
6. Braille recipes last longer when brailled on durable plastic, enclosed in plastic page protectors, or enclosed in a three-ring binder.
7. Recipes can generally be made accessible to cooks with reading vision by printing them out from a computer in a large type font, photocopying them with an enlarging copy machine, or hand printing them with a large, bold marker.

ple who have recently lost their vision often need more time than cooks who are sighted or those who have had experience with cooking since having lost their vision. Therefore, it is helpful to schedule two-hour blocks of time to complete lessons in adaptive kitchen skills. Whereas students may get tired when typing or reading braille for more than 30 to 40 minutes at a time, most will not show fatigue during a longer period in the kitchen. However, students who are older or who have multiple disabilities may need shorter lessons or need to sit rather than stand.

If lessons are strictly limited to one hour, the teacher will need to choose foods that either can be prepared quickly or whose preparation can be divided neatly into two or more lessons. For example, the stew that Anne made in her first lesson on using the oven can be made over a period of several days, with peeling, slicing, and dicing tasks being covered in one session and cooking done in the next.

ADAPTIVE COOKING SKILLS

Since not every client will need to learn all the adaptive techniques mentioned here for cooking and working in the kitchen, the rehabilitation teacher can choose the ones that are most appropriate to teach according to a particular client's needs and interests. Sidebar 13.1 summarizes the adaptations commonly used by people with visual impairments for a variety of kitchen skills.

Pouring

Pouring liquids (such as cold and hot beverages or ingredients for recipes) is one of the first daily living skills usually assessed and taught, as it is simple to learn, frequently utilized, and can easily remedy the chagrin caused by spills. The main pouring skill to be taught is filling a vessel to the appropriate level. The variety of methods to detect levels of liquids include:

- placing a finger over the edge of a glass or cup to detect the level of the liquid tactilely as it reaches the finger
- holding the glass or cup as it fills and determining the level of the liquid by the weight of the vessel
- attending to the temperature change on the outside of or above the vessel as it is filled with a hot or cold liquid
- listening to the change in the sound that the liquid makes as it fills the vessel (the pitch rises as the container fills)
- using an object that floats above the liquid (such as an ice cube) to detect the liquid tactilely as it approaches the rim of the glass
- using an electronic level indicator (ELLI).

An ELLI is a device with 1-inch-long prongs that are hooked over the rim of a container. The device beeps when the liquid inside the container reaches the prongs. Teachers may wish to use the ELLI as a training tool, even if the learner prefers to use other methods for detecting liquid levels. Pairing an ELLI with any of the other techniques during initial pouring lessons may provide sufficient feedback for the learner to develop great accuracy in using the other technique without the device (Kikkeri, 1989; Lariccia, 1986).

Learners who have never poured before may need detailed sequential instruction on pouring first cold and then hot liquids from a variety of vessels—such as 2-liter bottles, syrup containers, milk cartons of different sizes, pitchers, and coffeepots—into a variety of vessels—such as drinking glasses, coffee cups and mugs, graduated measuring cups, and measuring spoons. Pouring cold liquids into a large glass works well for initial lessons in detecting liquid levels. Lesson Plan 13.1 for teaching pouring appears in this chapter.

Cutting

Cutting can be difficult for some people because of a fear of knives, but more commonly the difficulty relates to the ability to slice fruits and veg-

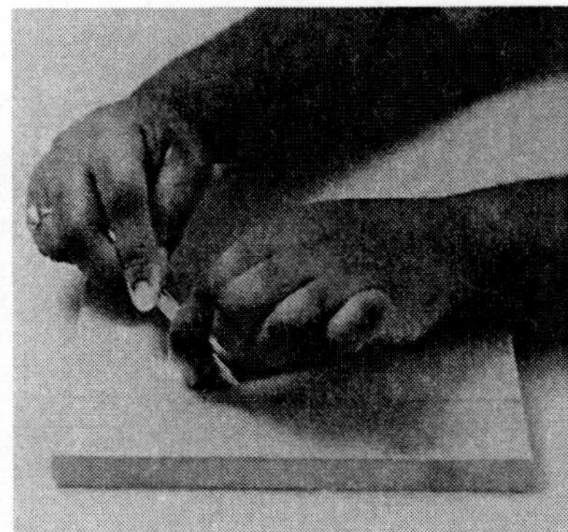
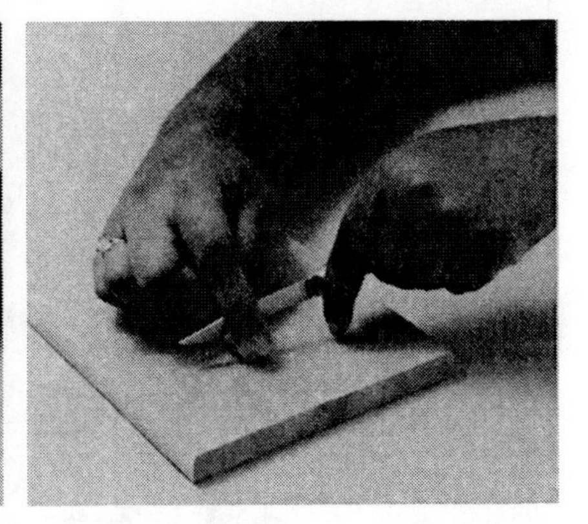

Safe cutting techniques. Curled fingers serve as a "backstop" for the knife (left). The thumb and forefinger are placed over the top of the knife like a bridge to gauge the width of the cut from above (center and right). The cutter in the right-hand photo is left handed.

Teaching Pouring

I. Objective: When presented with a variety of pitchers, glasses, and cups at a sink, the learner will pour liquid into the containers to within 1 inch of the top without spilling with 90% accuracy.

II. Materials
   A. Dinner glass, juice glass, and coffee cup
   B. Two-quart pitcher with pouring lip
   C. Cafeteria tray
   D. Electronic liquid level indicator
   E. Cold and hot drink mixes of the learner's choice

III. Assessment
   A. Has the learner attempted to pour hot or cold liquids since sight loss?
   B. If so, has the learner discovered any adaptive pouring techniques?

IV. Procedure
   A. Orientation to materials
      1. Have the learner describe the sink area.
      2. Point out any items that are missed.
      3. Have the learner identify the pitcher, tray, and containers.
      4. Point out the pouring spout of the pitcher if the learner missed it.
   B. Pouring cold liquids using the index finger
      1. Have the learner fill the pitcher about half full with cold tap water.
      2. Have the learner place the tray holding the dinner glass just to the left of the sink (or to the right if he or she is left-handed).
      3. Have the learner hold the glass near the top, with the index finger placed in the glass up to the first joint.
      4. Have the learner hold the glass on the tray and as near to the sink as possible.
      5. Have the learner pick up the pitcher, holding it in the sink below the level of the counter, and find the edge of the glass with the pitcher spout.
      6. Have the learner pour the water into the glass.
      7. Have the learner note when the glass is properly filled by feeling the water as it reaches the index finger.
      8. Have the learner practice until comfortable.
      9. During the practice pourings, have the learner note changes in the sound of the water and the temperature of the glass when the glass is properly filled.
      10. Have the learner measure the proper amount of cold drink mix, place it in the glass, pour in the proper amount of water, and stir.
      11. Have the learner pour water into a juice glass and a coffee cup, noting the differences with filling the dinner glass.
   C. Pouring hot liquids
      1. Explain that the finger need not actually touch the hot liquid, but can feel the heat rising just below it.
      2. Have the learner pour hot tap water from the pitcher into the cup, following the steps for pouring cold water.

(continued on next page)

Teaching Pouring (continued)

3. Have the learner pour tea, coffee, or other hot liquids.
4. Have the learner prepare an instant hot drink.

D. Pouring with an electronic liquid level indicator (ELLI) by listening, and by weight
1. Have the learner describe the ELLI.
2. Point out any missed parts.
3. Have the learner practice pouring into the dinner glass, the juice glass, and the cup and ask him or her to predict when the ELLI will sound off.
4. Have the learner describe the different sounds of the three containers filling.
5. Have the learner fill each container while holding it over, but not touching, the tray and ask him or her to note the weight of each when filled.
6. Have the learner practice filling the containers, preferably using only sound, temperature, and weight, until the objective is met.

V. Memoranda

A. Reinforce pouring by sound, temperature, and weight as much as possible because it is necessary in social situations, such as pouring refreshments at a party.

B. If none of these techniques work because of a tactile or hearing loss, have the learner place a clean Ping-Pong ball in the glass and monitor fullness with the palm of the hand over the glass until the ball touches the hand.

C. If the learner is reluctant to pour hot liquids, use warmer and warmer tap water to develop confidence.

D. If the learner is a coffee or tea drinker, it is usually a good idea to practice filling a cup with coffee or hot water from the spigot of a large urn.

E. Learners who use an ELLI during training may develop accurate pouring ability that persists even without using the ELLI because the feedback from the device during the initial lessons reinforces their accuracy with other methods.

VI. Evaluation: Have the learner prepare one or more instant cold and hot drinks.

VII. Assignments

A. Have the learner practice at home with a variety of vessels at least five times a day for a week.

B. Have the learner note sound, weight, and temperature clues while pouring a variety of liquids, such as soda, milk, water, and juice.

etables uniformly. This challenge may be further complicated for some learners by a lack of an overall concept of uniformity. However, a good deal of practice with reinforcement is usually sufficient to produce satisfactory slices, or the learner can use a food processor or similar appliance or a knife with an adjustable cutting guide, which can be found in both adapted products catalogs (see Resources section) or stores that sell kitchen gadgets.

One technique for safe cutting involves keeping the fingers of the hand that is not holding the knife resting slightly curled on the item to be cut. The knife is positioned against the backs of the curled fingers, which move back out of the way as more of the item is sliced. In another cutting technique, the thumb and forefinger are placed over the top of the knife like a bridge, and the forefinger can move back and forth to help the cook judge the size of the slices from above while remaining out of the way of the blade.

Dicing and Peeling

Techniques for dicing (cutting food into small cubes) and peeling used by persons with visual impairments do not necessarily differ from ordinary methods. Persons with low vision can make use of adjustments in contrast, lighting, or magnification (see Chapter 6) to dice and peel with ease. New learners who have never diced items such as vegetables will benefit from basic instruction on how dicing is accomplished by hand. Although many people may hold items such as potatoes in the hand to dice them, it is safer to slice the item in half on a cutting board, lay it flat side down to stabilize it, continue slicing in one direction, and then rotate the item to slice in a perpendicular direction (monitored tactilely), forming the cubes. Alternatives to dicing by hand include handheld food choppers and food processors.

Learning to peel foods such as vegetables, fruits, and boiled eggs may require instruction on how to hold a paring knife or vegetable peeler as well as feedback from the teacher about whether skin or peel remains on the item. Cooks who must depend on tactile ability to determine whether an item such as a potato is completely peeled will find that frequently rinsing both the food item and their fingers will help them to detect any unpeeled areas.

Measuring

The techniques used to measure foods and ingredients typically require little modification for people with limited vision, but there are a number of suggestions that can make the task of measuring easier. In general, it is a good idea to review measurement techniques with all clients who will be using them, since many people with or without vision are unfamiliar with some of the specifics of following measuring instructions in recipes, such as the use of measuring spoons rather than tableware or the necessity of packing brown sugar into the measuring cup. Also, individuals who have never seen may have a tendency not to fill measuring cups up to the top.

Cooks with low vision may find the information in Chapter 6 on enhancing visibility, such as utilizing color contrast and better lighting, particularly helpful for measuring. Dickman (1983) suggested using gooseneck lamps or fluorescent lights over the counter for the best illumination. Contrast can be utilized by using dark utensils for measuring flour and by working with dark ingredients on light-colored plastic sheets or boards and with light ingredients on dark surfaces.

The markings on clear or light-colored measuring instruments can be enhanced or enlarged with dark permanent markers. Cooks with no useful vision might prefer measuring utensils such as cups or scales labeled in braille. Graduated or "dry" measuring cups, which provide a separate cup for each amount (usually in units of 1 cup, ½ cup, ⅓ cup, and ¼ cup) may provide the easiest means of accurately measuring both dry and liquid ingredients. The different sizes of graduated cups are easy to identify when stored as a set. Also, if necessary, the individual cups can be identified with braille labels or a tactile or visual

Measuring can be done most accurately with graduated measuring cups. Spills can be controlled by holding the measuring spoon or cup over a larger container.

Liquid can be measured from a wide-mouth jar by bending a measuring spoon into a ladle.

marking compound such as Hi Marks, or notches can be filed on the handles (two notches for ½ cup, three for ⅓, and so forth). Dry measures allow cooks to determine the amounts of ingredients accurately because they can be filled flush with their top edges. The cook can also hold the cup over a larger one as he or she pours, to catch any overflow and avoid wasting spilled ingredients. A funnel can be used to return the overflow to the original container. It is important for cooks with or without vision to be cautioned to avoid measuring over their mixing bowls, since it is difficult or impossible to remove excess powder or liquids if they spill into the bowl. Ingredients can be measured over a sink, tray, or pan.

Some liquids, such as vanilla, are easier to measure if they are stored in wide-mouth containers and then measured with aluminum measuring spoons bent into the shape of a dipper or ladle that can be dipped down into the liquid. Cooks who follow recipes that depend on measuring food by weight may wish to consider using cookbooks that are based on measurement of volume—although voice-output food scales that are within the purchasing range of the average consumer are now available from specialty catalogs (see Resources section).

Spreading and Mixing

Spreading semisolid foods, such as peanut butter, involves using an organized pattern to spread the food outward from a central point—for example from left to right, top to bottom, or center to outside. The food can be monitored tactilely if necessary to make sure the desired area is covered.

Because some people who have never seen may not have a completely developed sense of size relationships, they may have a tendency to underestimate the amount of food to be spread or the area to be covered. For example, some people may place too little peanut butter on a piece of bread and spread it over too limited an area when preparing a peanut butter sandwich. A tendency to underestimate various tasks in mixing is also not uncommon. For instance, when some individuals mix pancake or other batter with a spoon, their stirring motion is frequently too small to incorporate all the ingredients into a smooth whole, and a portion of the mix that sticks to the sides of the bowl may also be missed.

Hand-over-hand modeling of spreading and mixing skills by the rehabilitation teacher and frequent practice sessions accompanied by verbal reinforcement generally suffice to instruct most students. However, if more in-depth instruction is necessary, the use of task analysis (see Chapter 4) and hand-over-hand demonstrations of how to hold spoons, rubber spatulas, or other utensils may be helpful. It may also be effective to practice mixing foods that provide more noticeable contrast between mixed and unmixed versions, such as a muffin batter with raisins added.

Using the Stove

Many rehabilitation teachers automatically assume that stove-top cooking should be introduced before oven cooking; and when asked about their preference, many learners, regardless of past experience, would agree. Because the stove coil or burner is a relatively small heat-producing source and because pots and pans are placed on top of it, it seems safer than the larger hot, cavernous space of an oven into which a cook must reach. In reality, there are probably more safety concerns related to stove-top cooking than oven baking, because of the possibility of contact with the direct heat source, because food can be accidentally dropped onto the heat source, and because people sometimes fry with grease that can spatter. Thus, even though learners are more likely to readily accept stove-top cooking as the initial lesson in using the stove, teachers are urged to consider teaching the use of the oven before the stove top. In addition, there are many convenience or homemade foods that can be prepared cold, placed into the oven to bake unattended for a period of time, and then removed ready for the table. Use of a standard or microwave oven instead of a stove top is particularly useful for those who cannot stand at the stove for long periods or for people who have difficulty using the stove because of motor or cognitive difficulties.

No generalization can be made about whether a gas or an electric stove is better for someone with a visual impairment. Most people develop their own preference based on previous experience. Moreover, few people actually have a choice of which kind of appliance to use, unless they are building a new kitchen or replacing a worn-out range. Since people without vision can cook safely on wood-burning stoves and with campfires, on electric and on gas ranges, and in microwave ovens, it is apparent that if safe techniques are taught and followed, in general visually impaired persons are able to use either gas or electric ranges.

Cooking on the Stove Top

Because stove-top burners cannot be monitored tactilely when in use, they are frequently unfamiliar to individuals who have congenital vision losses and who cannot monitor them up close visually, and the prospect of working with them may therefore cause anxiety for many clients. However, familiarity with the workings of an appliance usually helps to reduce fear. Special attention should be paid to explaining how the burners function on electric and gas ranges. In addition, clients should have the opportunity to examine the stove top while the burners are cold and should be shown how to remove and replace the electric coils or gas rings and the burner pans for cleaning. Thorough instruction would also include discussion of the different-sized coils and their locations on the stove top, how to match pan size to coil or burner size, and how to ensure that pans are centered, as well as simple cooking techniques, such as boiling water. Lesson Plan 13.2 is a lesson plan for stove-top cooking.

Learners with useful vision can make use of the modifications discussed in Chapter 6 to enhance the visibility of range controls, pan and food location, and color (for detecting when food is done). However, cooks with low vision may tend to lean too close to the stove top to set temperatures and monitor foods. If using vision to complete a task is risky because of the need to get close, alternative techniques are recommended.

Centering Pans. Learners with no usable vision should be taught a variety of ways to center pans on the stove top. When the coil is known to be

Checking if the stove is on and the pot is centered.

An Initial Lesson for Stove-Top Cooking

I. Objective: When presented with a package of instant soup mix and a sauce pan, the learner will detect boiling and prepare the soup safely, two out of three times, without intervention from the teacher.

II. Materials
   A. Electric or gas stove top
   B. Saucepan
   C. Package of instant soup mix
   D. Soup bowl that is large enough to make pouring easy
   E. Soup spoon and crackers if soup is to be eaten

III. Assessment
   A. Has the learner ever cooked on a stove top?
   B. If the sight loss was adventitious, has the learner used a stove top since the loss?
   C. If the stove top has been used, was it electric or gas?
   D. Has the learner attempted to boil anything since the sight loss?
   E. Does the learner express any fear of the stove top?

IV. Procedure
   A. Orientation to materials
      1. Have the learner describe the stove top while it is cold.
      2. Point out burner controls, oven controls, and burner sizes, if missed.
      3. Have the learner investigate the sauce pan and soup mix package.
   B. Stove top familiarization
      1. Discuss the safety issues regarding burners, particularly loose hair and clothing.
      2. Have the learner operate the burner controls until he or she is comfortable with setting them.
      3. Being sure the burners are cool, have the learner remove the burner grates or the electrical element and briefly discuss cleaning.
   C. Centering on the burners
      1. Have the learner center the pan, containing a cup of water, on a cold burner, using touch or vision.
      2. Have the learner move the pan around on the cold burner to feel the balance when it is centered.
      3. Ask the learner to describe how the pan might be centered when the burner is already hot.
      4. Explain any methods the learner has not thought of:
         a. Holding the palm over the pan and burner at chest height to feel the center of the heat.
         b. Using a wooden spoon to check.
         c. Checking whether the pan feels balanced on the burner.
   D. Preparing the soup
      1. Have the learner fill the pan with cold water, following the directions for the instant soup mix.

(continued on next page)

Stove-Top Cooking (continued)

2. Have the learner center the pan on a cold burner.
3. Explain the need to turn the pan handle to a specified location, rotated either left or right 90 degrees, both for safety and for ease in locating it.
4. Have the learner locate the pan handle with the backs of curved fingers (the instructor can hold the the pan to stabilize it during the first attempts).
5. Have the learner set the burner control on "high."
6. Have the learner practice moving the pan off center and using one of the methods described to recenter it until he or she is competent.
7. Ask the learner to explain how boiling might be detected.
   a. Point out the sound of boiling water, if necessary.
   b. Point out the feel of boiling (the vibration of the pan handle), if necessary.
8. Have the learner attempt to determine when the water is boiling.
9. While waiting for the water to boil, have the learner place the soup mix in the bowl and place the bowl on a tray near the stove.
10. Have the learner pour the hot water into the soup bowl, stir the soup, and wait the amount of the time specified on the soup mix package before eating it.

V. Memoranda
   A. If the learner shows fear of the stove, more time can be spent practicing on the cold stove top.
   B. If the learner is a novice, time should be spent on cleaning the burners following this and other stove-top lessons.
   C. If the learner is especially fearful or inexperienced, extra time should be spent on relating movements to stove parts. For example, the pattern for finding the handle of a pan on a left burner is to locate the left edge of the stove, then trail along the side toward the back of the stove until the wrist or forearm touches the pan handle.

VI. Evaluation: Have the learner prepare foods such as jello or instant hot chocolate until the criterion is met.

VII. Assignments
   A. Have the student prepare tea or cocoa using the stove top to heat water at least once a day for a week.
   B. Have the student visit an appliance store (perhaps on a mobility lesson) to investigate other brands of ranges to see the layout of burners, controls, and landmarks.

cold, the cook can locate the correct size burner for the pan, place the pan on the burner, and then cup both hands around the base to feel whether the pan covers the area evenly.

Once the burner has been turned on, other clues besides the tactile ones must be used, either singly or in combination. A commonly used method is circling the hand above the burner to locate the center of the hot coil before placing the pan on it. (This method also works with stove tops that have smooth—not raised—burners or grills.) Once the pan has been placed on the burner, the cook can grasp the handle to feel if the pan is level or unstable, and a wooden spoon can be used to feel whether the burner is surrounding the pan bottom evenly.

Learners should develop a personal rule about which way to point the handle of a pot once it is on the stove, so that he or she can find them again easily. Leaving pan handles jutting out toward the front of the stove is unsafe, particularly if there are children in the house, because of the chances of accidentally knocking into them. Some people turn pan handles toward the center of the stove top and locate them by reaching down from above or backwards from a front and center landmark, such as the oven door lock on self-cleaning stoves. Others prefer to place the handles of pans on the left burners facing left (toward 9 o'clock on a clock face) and right side pan handles facing right (toward 3 o'clock) because they can relocate the handle by trailing along the outside edge of the stove top until the handle is encountered.

Rehabilitation teachers may need to approach instruction regarding the stove top slowly with some learners, and items whose cooking requires moderate or low heat should be presented first. Instructors should also be aware that teaching techniques such as centering a pan by holding one's hand above the hot burner might be complicated by some clients' inexperience with heat or by conceptual problems. For example, it is difficult for some novice cooks to estimate how high above the coil they should hold their hand to feel the heat. In that event, the learner can practice by using a landmark on the body, such as the front of the chest, or the chin for a shorter person, to determine the height above the stove at which to extend the hand. Some learners who are just learning to center pans have been confused because once they place a cold pan on the hot coil, they feel the diffused heat coming from around the perimeter of the pan rather than from the center. Explaining and demonstrating the notion of "covering up the heat with the pan" may help the client to grasp the concept.

Gauging Temperature. The dials on electric stoves have indications of temperature that are reasonably accurate. Most gas stoves do not have such markings, and when they do they are not always reliable, so clients with gas stoves need to develop other methods for judging whether the flame is low, medium, or high. A method similar to that of circling the hand to center pots can be used. The learner extends a hand at chest height while the teacher turns on the burner and demonstrates what a high heat feels like, then medium, and low. Once the learner has become acquainted with the different sensations, the teacher can vary the temperature and let the learner practice determining whether it is high, medium, or low.

Once a client is familiar with the stove top, he or she can try preparing a simple mix that only requires boiling water, such as instant soup. The learner can be taught to detect when the water in the pan has boiled by the sound it makes or the feel of the handle vibrating.

Turning Foods. Fear of hot burners can interfere with an individual's ability to turn foods like hamburgers in a pan. This task may also be complicated by a client's lack of knowledge concerning the fragility of the food to be turned. Turning an egg, for example, is a different task from turning meat.

Some learners may attempt to rotate their wrists and the utensils they are holding toward the outside. For example, a right-handed person may try to turn a grilled cheese sandwich over by picking it up and rotating the wrist to the right. Outside rotation is not as controllable as turning the wrist toward the inside, and the sandwich may slide sideways off the spatula or other utensil (and fall apart) or land outside the pan. Such habits must be assessed and addressed as food-turning exercises begin. For example, the teacher can model the movement necessary to flip a sandwich successfully, and the learner can practice this with cold foods before turning on the stove.

Double spatulas—tong-like food turners similar to barbecue tools, but smaller—are especially useful to cooks with visual impairments. These utensils are helpful for frying and turning such foods as grilled sandwiches, sausages, and hamburgers. While being secured in the pincer-like grip, food items can be lifted, squeezed to test for doneness, or turned over. Double spatulas are particularly useful for inexperienced cooks, who may tend to flip foods too slowly so that, with a conventional single turner, the food would slide off the utensil onto its original cooked side.

Teaching Frying

I. Objective: When presented with a premade hamburger patty and a skillet, the learner will fry the hamburger safely and to the proper level of doneness two out of three times or until deemed competent.

II. Materials
   A. Uncooked hamburger patties
   B. Heavy skillet (a large one is preferable)
   C. Food turner and double-bladed spatula
   D. Plate, paper towel, hamburger bun, and desired condiments

III. Assessment
   A. Has the learner used a stove top for frying, either before or following sight loss?
   B. If so, have the learner describe the extent of his or her experience.
   C. Has the learner had beginning stove top lessons since sight loss?

IV. Procedure
   A. Preparation for frying
      1. Have the learner describe the stove top, if necessary; point out any missed parts.
      2. Have the learner investigate single- and double-bladed spatulas.
         a. If the learner has no experience with these implements, demonstrate the use of each.
         b. If the learner's sight is very limited and he or she has never turned food before, demonstrate how to turn with each implement, using the learner's hand as if it were the item to be turned.
      3. Place a paper towel on a plate near the stove and prepare the bun and condiments.
   B. Determining doneness in frying
      1. Ask the learner if he or she can think of ways to determine doneness with limited sight.
      2. If not included, discuss the following:
         a. The feel of doneness
         b. The sound of doneness
         c. The smell of doneness
   C. Frying
      1. Have the learner center the skillet with the handle to the side on a cold burner of the proper size.
      2. Have the learner center the patty in the skillet.
      3. Have the learner set the burner control to "medium high."
      4. Have the learner cook the patty for about five minutes on one side.
      5. Have the learner turn the patty with the spatula of choice.
         a. Have the learner push the patty to the far left side of the skillet (if he or she is right handed).
         b. Have the learner slip the spatula under the patty and move it back to center of skillet.
         c. If the learner is using the single-bladed turner, he or she can carefully touch the top of the patty with a finger and hold it down against the blade.
      6. Have the learner determine doneness by touching the patty with a fork or with fingertips.

(continued on next page)

Teaching Frying (continued)

a. If the learner has low vision, point out the possible dangers of getting close enough to see.
b. Point out peak smell and doneness sounds as they occur.

7. Have the learner remove the patty with a spatula and place it on the plate.
8. Have the learner prepare the sandwich.

V. Memoranda
   A. Experienced cooks will usually be confident enough to monitor the patty with fingertips. New learners will likely want to use utensils in initial lessons.
   B. Be sure to monitor safety in centering, handle placement and movements over the burners and correct the techniques if they are unsafe.
   C. If the learner is especially fearful, turning practice can be done with cold items.

VI. Evaluation: Have the learner fry sausage patties, pancakes, or another item of his or her choice until the criterion is reached.

VII. Assignment: Have the learner read a cookbook to learn common cooking times for items he or she would like to to prepare.

The following sequence is a helpful outline for new learners of the steps in turning food:

- Use a systematic search pattern to gently tap around inside the pan with the food turner to locate the food item to be turned.
- Slide the item to the side of the pan to stabilize it as the food turner is slipped underneath. Lift the food turner to feel whether the food is stable.
- Move the turner and the item toward the center of the pan before flipping it over.

Lesson Plan 13.3 covers teaching frying, and determining when food is done is covered in a later section.

Oven Use

Introducing oven use to experienced and inexperienced cooks alike should start with a thorough inspection of the appliance while it is cold. Learners should know where the controls are as well as the location of the racks, thermostat, coils, and the pilot light housing. Other skills, such as adjusting racks, using a broiler pan, and cleaning the oven, may be taught later. Since opening the door of a hot oven and reaching in to locate the rack or a pan is frightening for most new cooks, patient and careful instruction should be provided. The teacher should reinforce the importance of using long, ovenproof mitts to protect both hands rather than small, square potholders.

The following sequence of steps summarizes the process of oven baking, and Lesson Plan 13.4 on oven baking appears in this chapter:

- Check the position of the oven racks before turning on the oven.
- Preheat the oven approximately one minute for every 100 degrees of heat desired.
- When the food is ready to be placed in the oven, put the pan near the range or on top of the stove if the burners are cold.
- Open the oven door without leaning over the opening, since the heat blasting out of

Teaching Oven Baking

I. Objective: When presented with an unfamiliar stove and a package of brown-and-serve rolls, the learner will consistently bake the rolls safely and to the proper level of doneness.

II. Materials: Oven, brown-and-serve rolls, baking sheet, oven mitts, cooling rack, hot pad, and timer

III. Assessment
   A. Has the learner used a stove or oven before?
   B. How much does the learner know about baking?
   C. Has the learner used some form of timer previously?

IV. Procedures
   A. Parts of the oven
      1. With the oven door closed, have the learner identify parts.
      2. If they are missed, point out stove controls, burners, oven door, and handle.
      3. With the oven door open, have the learner identify parts.
      4. If they are missed, point out oven heating elements, thermostat, burners, racks, rack guides, depth and width, movement of racks.
   B. Baking
      1. Preparation
         a. Have the learner open the package of rolls and place them on the baking sheet.
         b. Have the learner preset the oven temperature to 250 degrees.
      2. Placing food in the oven
         a. After the oven warms, have the learner move to the side of the oven door opposite his or her dominant hand.
         b. Have the learner don oven mitts.
         c. Have the learner open the oven door with his or her dominant hand.
         d. Have the learner pull the lower rack out of the oven.
         e. Have the learner place the baking sheet on the rack, being sure it is in the middle and square with the rack.
         f. Have the learner push the rack back in the oven.
         g. Have the learner close the oven door.
         h. Have the learner set the timer for the appropriate time.
      3. Removing food from the oven
         a. Have the learner set the hot pad and cooling rack on a counter near the stove.
         b. Have the learner repeat the door-opening procedure with oven mitts on.
         c. Have the learner pull the rack out, remove the baking sheet, and place the sheet on the hot pad.
         d. Have the learner replace the rack and close the door.
         e. Have the learner turn the oven control to the "off" position.
      4. Removing rolls and testing for doneness
         a. Have the learner touch the tops of the rolls with the spatula, keeping an oven mitt on the nondominant hand to check their firmness while giving feedback about doneness.

(continued on next page)

Teaching Oven Baking (continued)

b. Have the learner remove the first row of rolls, then the second, and so on, placing them on the cooling rack.
c. Instruct the learner to allow rolls to cool on the cooling rack before serving.

V. Memoranda
  A. If the learner is confident, have him or her check doneness with bare fingers, being careful not to touch the baking sheet.
  B. Slow this lesson down if the learner shows considerable of fear of oven temperatures.
  C. If the learner is extremely fearful of getting burned, have him or her spend time manipulating the cold oven with mitts before using heat.
  D. Many foods work well for this lesson, so consider preparing a favorite food of the learner.
  E. Preheating takes approximately one minute for every 100 degrees of temperature desired.

VI. Evaluation: Have the learner prepare slice-and-bake cookies or another favorite food without instructions.

VII. Assignment: Have the learner review cookbooks to select recipes for future lessons.

the oven into the face can be uncomfortable and frightening.

- Use a mitted hand to move downward in an arc from the top of the oven opening to the desired rack.
- Pull out the rack.
- Place the pan in the center of the rack. Gauge the correct distance from the edges of the oven by feeling with mitted hands.
- Push the rack in and reach down for the door handle to close the oven.
- When checking for doneness or removing food, pull the rack out, rather than reaching into the oven.

Testing for Doneness

Many recipes instruct the cook to "bake until brown" or "cook until juice runs clear," but cooks with visual impairments usually need to know alternatives to visual inspection for testing whether food is done. Three adaptations are particularly helpful:

- peak smell
- timing of cooking
- tactile or auditory inspection.

Peak smell is the odor a food emits when it is done. For example, chocolate brownies start to emit a smell when they begin to bake, emit a peak smell when they are done, and then, if left in the oven too long, will progress from smelling over-

Examples of commercially available and modified kitchen timers. From left, a specially modified braille timer, a tactilely adapted commercial timer, and a large-print timer.

cooked to smelling burned. Novice cooks may need reinforcement to learn to identify peak smells by initially being told when the peak smell of certain foods is occurring.

Since timing is an important way for people with visual impairments to monitor food for doneness, consistency in preparing foods is critical so that cooking times will be consistent as well. As a cook begins to use the same pans in the same oven with a specific recipe, he or she can establish exact cooking times for frequently prepared foods. The actual timing can be accomplished by using talking or tactile timers or clocks; cassette timing tapes that contain recorded indicators of both short and long time periods; or even by counting songs played on the radio, which are three to four minutes long on average.

Tactile and auditory clues can also be helpful indicators of doneness. The individual can learn to note the texture or sounds of different foods as they progress through cooking. For example, french-fried potatoes stop sputtering when they are done; and pasta can be bitten to see if it is soft but still "al dente" (firm to the tooth). Sidebar 13.2 provides a sample list of doneness clues for specific foods.

Putting Recipes in Accessible Formats

Cooks with visual impairments can make use of recipes and cookbooks made available through brailling, recording, or, for those who can read print, enlarging or other modification. Although modifying recipes is not difficult, there are several helpful hints that can be of considerable assistance to cooks.

Braille recipes will usually be produced in grade 2 braille, but the braillist can save space and avoid confusion in the ingredients section in several ways. Placing the abbreviated measurement unit immediately before the number sign relating to the ingredient and avoiding capitalization both save space. For example, "2 cups of flour" is often brailled as "c2 flour," and "8 ounces of chocolate chips" is "oz8 chocolate chips." This practice allows the letter *c* to be used as the abbreviation for "cup," as is common in print, when it is found immediately before a number, without confusing it with the braille *c* standing alone, the usual short form of the word "can." Recipes reproduced in braille will fill more than the usual 3" x 5" index card, but functional alternatives include brailling on larger index cards joined together, on braille transcription paper, or on durable media such as Thermoform, Labelon, or Con-Tact type self-adhesive paper, which can be stored in a recipe notebook.

Recorded recipes will suit the needs of the majority of cooks with visual impairments. One or more recipes can be placed on standard cassettes, while Voxcom cards and continuous-loop tape devices (see Chapter 10) are useful for short recipes or instructions for preparing convenience foods. A variety of recorded cookbooks are available on loan from public and private libraries and for purchase from private organizations, but rehabilitation teachers frequently produce their own recorded recipes to suit a client's needs. The format for recorded recipes is somewhat different from the usual print format. Pauses should be left between ingredients and between sections of the recipe. Most important, in addition to listing all the ingredients at the beginning of the recipe, as is usually done in print so the cook can gather and organize them, the recipe should repeat the amount as the item is mentioned in the directions section. Thus, a taped recipe will first list ingredients (for example, "Ingredients: 2¼ cups butter, 1 tablespoon soda, 2 eggs, 1 cup white sugar"), and then provide a reminder of how much of each ingredient is necessary when the cook follows the directions ("Directions: Combine the 2¼ cups butter with the 1 cup of white sugar"). Repeating the ingredient amounts helps avoid unnecessary rewinding to locate the information and saves the cook time.

Voice indexing and tone indexing (see Chapter 10) are helpful when creating a tape that will contain several recipes and allows users to scan to specific recipes. Voice indexing within recipes is unnecessary, however, and the loud squeals that indexing produces when played at normal speed can be irritating when the cook is occupied or has sticky hands and cannot fast-forward past the indexed terms.

SIDEBAR 13.2

Examples of Nonvisual Clues for Telling When Cooked Foods are Done

Bread, yeast—The loaf sounds hollow rather than dull when removed from the pan and tapped on the bottom.
Bread, quick—A toothpick inserted into the center comes out clean, with no sticky dough on it.
Cake—A toothpick inserted into the center comes out clean, with no sticky dough on it, and the top surface of the cake is firm and cake springs back when pressed. Use a toothpick or utensil to locate the surface; press the surface lightly and quickly, then move fingers lightly over the surface to detect any depressions that would show that the cake is not yet done.
Cookies—When touched, the cookie is soft and does not spring back. If it is not soft, it is overcooked. Peak smell is an important indicator.
Custard—A knife inserted into the custard comes out clean, with no sticky substance on it.
Eggs—The white is firm. A knife inserted into the white comes out clean, without slippery liquid on it.
Fish—It flakes easily with a fork.
Fruits—The largest or toughest part is tender and pierces easily when a fork is inserted.
Gelatin—The gelatin quivers when moved; it is not rigid and does not have a liquid feeling.
Liver—The meat feels tender when pierced with a fork. If it feels tough, it is overcooked.
Meat, beef or pork—The meat feels dry to the touch, unless cooked with moist heat. If it is a cheaper, tougher cut of meat, it will feel tender and fall apart when pierced with a fork. Better cuts will feel firm when cooked to well done, and will feel soft but will spring back when cooked to medium rare. The feel of rare, medium, and well-done meat can be compared to the feel of the soft fleshy area of a hand between the thumb and forefinger, the padded areas of the palm just below the fingers, and the firm center of the palm.
Pancakes—The bottom edge of the first side is gently lifted with a spatula, and then let drop. If it "thuds," it is ready to be flipped to cook the other side for one more minute. If it makes a wet slap, it is not yet ready to turn.
Pasta—It feels soft but slightly resistant when bitten.
Potato, baked—There is no resistance when the potato is pierced deeply with a knife or fork.
Potatoes, french fried—All sputtering of hot fat ceases.
Potatoes, hash brown—When a spatula is slid underneath the potato as if to turn it, it feels crisp, not soft.
Poultry—The hip joint of a whole roasted bird feels loose when the drumstick is moved back and forth. Avoid piercing the skin if possible, as it causes juices to run out and dries the meat.
Sautéed food—It can be pierced with a fork or put between the teeth to test for the desired firmness.
Soufflé—The soufflé is firm and set, and a knife inserted comes out uncoated.
Vegetables—The largest or toughest part is tender and pierces easily when a fork is inserted. A kernel of corn on the cob no longer tastes milky.
Waffles, homemade—Steam stops flowing out of the side of the waffle iron, and the top of the iron is no longer resistant to a gentle pull.
White sauce—The sauce feels thick and smooth. To ensure a thick and lumpless sauce, place it in a 350-degree oven for 20 minutes instead of stirring it constantly over a burner.

Modifications of recipes for those who read print are not standardized but are based on the needs and abilities of the individual. Recipes can be enlarged using a copy machine with a magnification feature or a computer program or printer that produces large print or by copying them in large print with a felt marker. In addition, the visibility of recipes can be enhanced by placing yellow acetate over them to provide more contrast and reduce glare (this acts as a sheet protector as well), adjusting lighting, or using low vision devices such as stand magnifiers in combination with magnetic or stick-on clips to hold the recipe at eye level (see Chapter 6).

EATING SKILLS

Many people who are visually impaired have difficulty feeling comfortable while eating, particularly in public places (Huebner, 1986; Mangold, 1980).

> Sadie B., an 82-year-old woman with a central field loss, was a former rehabilitation client who moved from her own house to a retirement center because of poor health. At her new residence, she dined at a table with four or five of her peers. When living in her own home, she had a good appetite, was able to prepare her meals, and felt comfortable eating in her own dining room. However, soon after moving to the senior facility, she called the rehabilitation teacher who had worked with her in her home and requested an appointment, asking if the teacher could arrange for her to have all meals brought to her room. After a short assessment, the rehabilitation teacher realized that Sadie was embarrassed about eating in the presence of others. She said: "I can't stand being seen touching my food all the time, and I just know I'll spill my drink in front of everyone." The teacher was able to convince Sadie that a few lessons on eating skills would help her, and after a couple of weeks she felt at ease enough while eating that she began to take part in the table conversation.

Some individuals have eating habits that are not socially acceptable, usually because of a lack of either training or experience. If someone has been made to feel in the past that his or her eating skills were inappropriate to his or her age and that he or she had to be given assistance usually reserved for young children, the act of eating can become imbued with feelings of inadequacy, apprehension, and guilt (Mangold, 1980).

The teacher might begin instruction in the area of eating skills by reassuring clients with visual impairments who are reluctant to eat in restaurants or other public places. The rehabilitation teacher can explain that few if any restaurant diners closely observe the eating skills of fellow diners. Usually, minor problems such as occasionally bringing an empty fork to the mouth are disconcerting only to the person who bites the empty fork.

Initial instruction in eating skills generally should not be offered during mealtimes. Learners may not be as interested in details of technique if they are hungry; if the food becomes cold, neither appetite nor learning needs will be satisfied. Rather, instructional information and practice should be scheduled at another time, using real or substitute foods.

The extent or depth of the instruction needed in eating skills may relate to whether the student has adventitious or congenital vision loss. Generally, those with adventitious or partial loss of sight may only need to learn a few adaptations, whereas individuals with a congenital loss frequently require more detailed information about the subtleties of eating various foods, methods of holding the fork, spoon, knife, and so forth.

The adaptations used in eating include techniques to assist with

- locating the items in a place setting
- locating the food items on a plate
- cutting meat and other foods
- spreading butter
- using condiments
- getting food onto forks or spoons
- keeping the food on the plate.

SIDEBAR 13.3

Common Eating Adaptations

LOCATING PLACE SETTING

1. Find edge of the table with the backs of curled fingers; then move both hands over the edge and forward, maintaining contact with table surface.
2. To avoid tipping over glasses and bowls, do not move the hands above and across the table surface.
3. Use knowledge of standard place settings to visualize where items should be:
   A. Fork on left, spoon and knife on right
   B. Glass and cup and saucer at upper right of plate
   C. Butter plate at upper left
4. At home, use contrasting tablecloth and dishes to make locating items easier.

ORIENTATION TO CONTENTS OF PLATE

1. Get a description of the contents that relates the food to the top, right, bottom, and left of the plate or to the positions of the numbers on the clock face.
2. Explore the contents of the plate by tapping lightly with a fork to identify foods.
3. Be aware of or ask about nonconsumable items served with various types of foods, such as lemon wedges with fish, parsley with many foods, or syrup containers placed next to a stack of pancakes.
4. Ask the server to leave off the plate any foods the diner wishes to avoid, such as butter, sour cream, or onions.

CUTTING

Meats

1. Determine the cutting edge of the knife by dragging an edge along the edge of a plate and listening or feeling for serrations.
2. Slide a finger or thumb down the handle to touch the junction of the knife and handle; the cutting edge of the blade will usually extend slightly outward.
3. Measure the size of slices of meat to be cut by placing a fork 1 inch from the edge of the piece.
4. Determine the size of the cut meat by its weight on the fork.
5. Drag the cut portion away from the rest of the meat; the amount of resistance will give feedback such as whether the piece is too big or still attached; then stab the piece with the fork to pick it up.
6. Request that awkward meats be cut by companions or by chefs in restaurants.
7. In formal situations, base menu selections on ease of cutting; prepare or order boneless meat if feasible.

Lettuce Salad

1. Place a fork into the nearest part of the lettuce and cut with a knife beyond it. Keep placing the fork a step farther and cut beyond that spot.
2. Anchor the salad bowl during the cutting with the pressure of the fork.
3. Anchor the remaining lettuce with the knife while pulling the fork away.

SPREADING BUTTER

1. Locate the proper edge of the knife (see Cutting).
2. If the butter is in a stick, estimate the size of a slice by placing the flat edge of the knife at the end of the stick and sliding it along the stick.
3. Place the pat of butter in the center of a piece of bread and spread out to the edges.
4. Monitor coverage by feeling the slickness of the surface with a finger or the knife.

SALT AND PEPPER AND OTHER CONDIMENTS

1. Distinguish salt from pepper by shaking the container— salt is louder and usually heav-

(continued on next page)

Common Eating Adaptations (continued)

ier—or by taking a careful sniff.

2. Shake salt or pepper into the hand, then apply to food.
3. Determine the shaker's rate of flow and estimate the amount to be applied; conservative estimates are safest.
4. To apply catsup or other condiments, place a finger at the spot where it is to be applied to feel the amount; avoid touching the bottle opening.
5. Identify packets of powdered creamer, sugar, and sugar substitute by their characteristics: sugar packets are heavier and bulkier than sugar substitutes; creamer comes in smooth, foil-lined packets. Partially tear the top and leave the torn paper attached to the packet to avoid accidentally dropping it into the food or beverage.

PLACING FOOD ON FORKS OR SPOONS

1. Use a slice of bread in the nondominant hand to help push the food onto the utensil.
2. Discreetly use the third finger hidden under the bread to monitor food and stabilize it.
3. Use a knife to push the food onto a fork or spoon, as is commonly done in Europe.
4. Place mashed potatoes or other heavy foods at the back of the plate to act as backstops for loading the fork or spoon.
5. Eat foods, such as chicken or french fries, with the fingers when it is acceptable. Hold pie by the crust to stabilize it.
6. Request assistance with foods, such as Cornish hen or whole duck, that are difficult to eat without handling.
7. Grasp a small salad dish or dessert dish around one edge, as if it were a glass, to act as a backstop and prevent knocking the food off the plate.

CAFETERIAS, SALAD BARS, AND BUFFETS

1. Ask for assistance from a sighted person to avoid accidents or food contamination.
2. Ask a sighted helper to describe the foods before beginning to serve so that requests can be planned accordingly.
3. Hold a plate or tray while having a sighted helper load it. Slide the tray along the cafeteria rail or maintain elbow contact with the sighted assistant, who walks ahead.
4. Stabilize drinks at the edge of the tray with one of the hands that is holding the tray, or ask the sighted helper to carry them.
5. To avoid bumping one's head, be aware of protective overhangs above salad bars and buffets.

Suggestions for common eating adaptations are listed in Sidebar 13.3.

The place setting can be investigated by finding the table edge with the backs of curled fingers and moving both hands up over the edge and forward, maintaining contact with the table top (Widerberg & Kaarlela, 1976). If the individual reaches out above the tabletop, it is easy to knock over tall glasses or other items that are precariously balanced. Knowledge of standard place settings—with forks usually on the left, spoons and knives on the right, glasses at the upper right of the plate, and the bread plate at the upper left—will help the diner anticipate the location of items.

To identify the foods on a plate that someone else has placed on the table, the individual might ask for a description of the plate. The location of the food on a plate is normally described in relation to the top, right, bottom, and the left of the plate or by comparing it to the positions of the numbers on a clock face. If a visually impaired individual feels comfortable identifying the food himself or herself, or if it is not convenient to ask someone else, a fork can be used to identify the food. Lightly tapping or probing with the fork can give feedback about which item on the plate is the meat, vegetable, or dinner roll, for example. Restaurant patrons who are totally blind should be aware that nonconsumable items or decorative foods often appear on serving plates. Garnishes can be expected with certain foods, for example, lemon wedges with fish, parsley or decorative cabbage leaves with entrees, butter pats or jelly packages with eggs and toast, and syrup containers with pancakes.

Cutting meat and other items at the dinner table can also be managed with a few simple adaptations. The cutting edge of a serrated knife can be detected by dragging one edge along the plate or another piece of silverware and listening or feeling for the "buzz" of the uneven surface, or simply by carefully touching the knife blade. Many knives have a slight outward flare at the junction of the handle on the blade side; sliding the thumb carefully toward the blade may help detect the proper side for cutting. The size of the cut to be made for meat can be determined by placing a fork in the meat about an inch from the edge and cutting parallel with the edge. The size of the piece can be judged by the weight of the fork, but this determination takes some practice. Some foods, such as Cornish game hen or whole duck, are difficult to eat without handling. Requesting assistance with them may be less embarrassing than tearing them apart bit by bit with a fork. Also, many people routinely ask companions or the restaurant staff to cut difficult-to-handle meats, such as steak with bones. In extremely formal situations, menu selections can be based on how easy the food is to cut.

As with spreading foods in cooking, spreading butter at the table is usually accomplished by placing the butter in the center of a piece of bread and working it toward the edges in a specific pattern. If the butter is in a stick, the flat side of the butter knife can be used to locate the end, from which the proper width of the slice can then be estimated. The slickness of the surface of the bread indicates where it is covered. With practice, most people can detect coverage with their knife.

Seasoning, such as salt and pepper, can be managed with a few simple hints. For example, salt and pepper shakers can be distinguished by shaking them, since shaken salt usually makes a louder sound than does pepper; it also is heavier than pepper. A careful sniff will also serve to identify the pepper. Many people apply salt and pepper by shaking a little into the palm of the hand and sprinkling it onto the food. Once the person dining determines how fast the spice is flowing out of the shaker, he or she can estimate how much to apply, but conservative estimates are safest. Condiments such as catsup, mustard, steak sauce, and the like are usually best monitored tactilely while pouring them onto the food or the side of the plate.

Getting food onto forks or spoons can be one of the more difficult eating tasks when sight is limited. However, a slice of bread held in the nondominant hand can be used to push food onto the eating utensil. When this technique is used, the diner can discreetly tuck the third finger under the bread to monitor and stabilize the food. A knife can also be employed to push food onto a fork or spoon, as is customary in European dining. It is acceptable to eat many foods, such as chicken or french fries, with the fingers, and some, such as pie, can be held by the crust to stabilize them.

Strategic placement can also help to keep food on the plate and out of one's lap. For example, if the plate is rotated so that mashed potatoes or other heavy foods are at the back of the plate, they can serve as a backstop to keep troublesome, mobile foods such as peas or beans from rolling off. In addition, grasping a small salad plate or dessert plate around the edge with the thumb and forefinger spread can also provide an emergency backstop for the food.

The skill of transferring foods when serving oneself from a container to a plate (or when preparing recipes) requires both knowing how much is being transferred and understanding spatial relationships between the container and plate or two containers. Some foods, such as string beans, spaghetti, or gelatin dessert, are particularly tricky to serve, because they are slippery and/or long and tend to slide off the serving spoon. Some helpful hints that may be employed to make transferring foods more successful include:

- moving the containers next to each other
- learning how to judge amounts of different foods by weight
- using a ladle, tongs, or measuring cup
- counting spoonsful.

Young adults with congenital vision loss and who have little experience with social eating skills may need extensive instruction in such details as the following:

- how to hold eating utensils properly and efficiently
- how to use different techniques for cutting various foods such as meat, pie, pancakes, or lettuce salad, including how to cut with a knife as well as with the side of a fork
- how to spread butter, honey, or jam on bread, rolls, or muffins in various forms from various containers such as bulk containers or fast-food packets
- how to serve oneself and others from family-style platters and bowls, and how to determine how much to serve.

Teenagers, in particular, may not want to look different from their friends and will probably be interested in the subtle nuances of eating snack and fast foods. For example, fast-food pancakes are often served in styrofoam containers accompanied by squeeze-tube butter and syrup in small tear-back packets that they must learn to manipulate. Also, teenagers would want to know that one commonly eats a slice of pizza or pie point first until it is roughly rectangular, then rotates the food to eat the crust edge from side to side.

Other common needs that clients may have for teachers to assess include

- eating spaghetti and other awkward pasta dishes
- eating other special foods such as tacos or fajitas
- opening cartons or boxes of milk and juice
- pouring beverages such as coffee, milk, juice or soda from large dispensers such as those found in fast-food restaurants and cafeterias

and mastering any other special foods or eating techniques the client may commonly encounter.

GROCERY SHOPPING

In order to be able to prepare food, an individual first has to be able to obtain the ingredients. The majority of newly visually impaired learners will probably already have a basic understanding of grocery shopping techniques, purchasing information, and food products, but some less-experienced clients may need assistance with basic information. For example, one novice shopper, upon moving into her own apartment, began purchasing milk by the gallon since she was accustomed to seeing that size container at her family's home. Since she used up so little milk by herself, a large amount spoiled. This client benefited from instruction in estimating amounts of food to buy and information about food spoilage and the common volumes and sizes of the packaging of different products. Such incidents emphasize the importance of assessing the detailed knowledge that clients have beyond the basics of knowing how to get around the store and make purchases.

Students with adventitious impairments may have experience in grocery shopping but might need instruction in

- developing strategies for locating items
- soliciting assistance from volunteers or store employees
- labeling purchased items
- transporting groceries home—for example, in a grocery cart or on public transportation.

Novice shoppers will need extensive instruction that also includes the following:

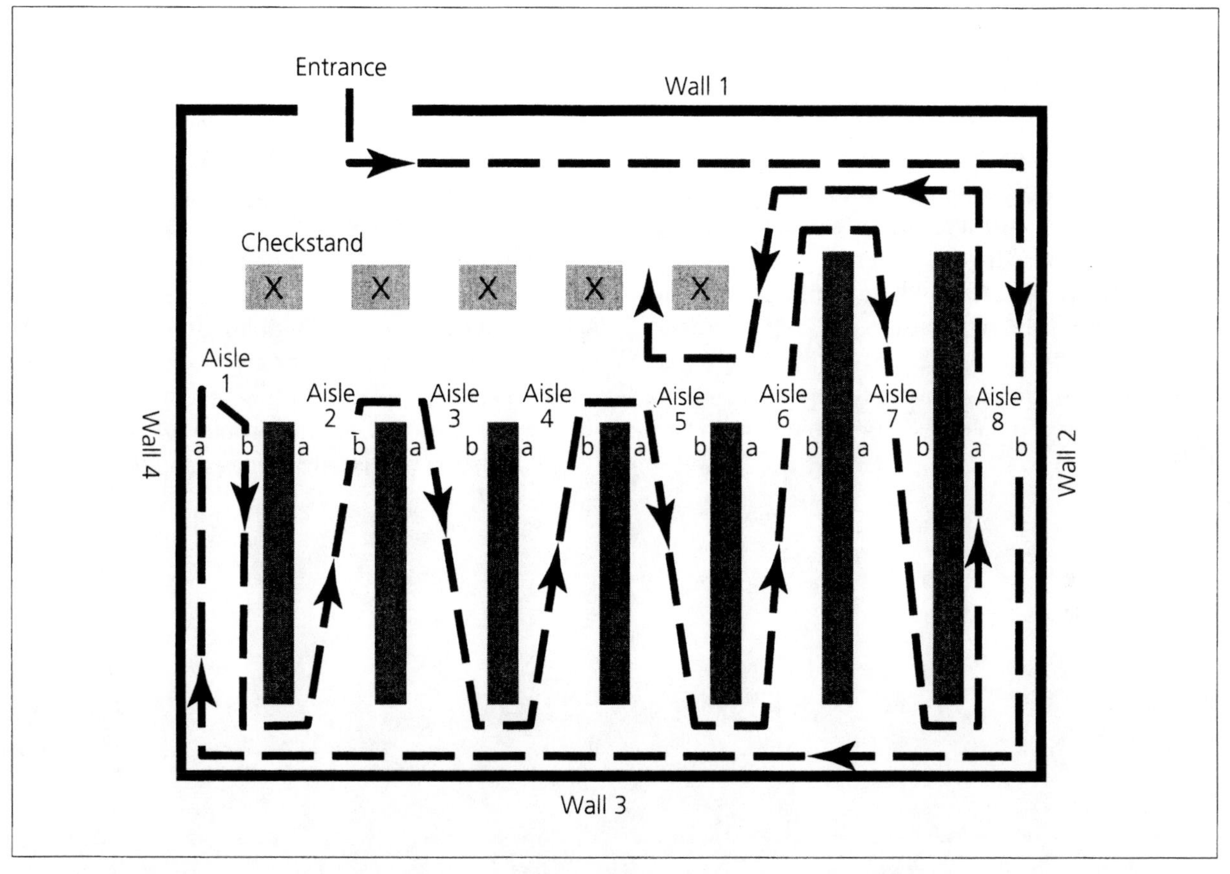

Figure 13.1. Diagram of a Grocery Store Layout with a Planned Route
Sample diagram of a grocery store. The arrows show a patterned route of travel. Each wall and aisle is identified by a number.

Source: Adapted with permission from Robert C. Savage, "A Grocery Shopping Technique for the Blind and Partially Sighted," *Long Cane News* (Michigan Commission for the Blind Training Center), *10*(1) (1977), p. 5.

- the typical layout of grocery stores: checkout lanes in front, featured sales items placed prominently, meat coolers and delicatessen along the perimeter
- familiarization with various foods and food packages
- selection of appropriate sizes and amounts for personal needs
- use of tactile or visual clues to identify product locations (including use of low vision devices to locate signs and items)
- adaptive methods for making grocery lists and tallying purchases
- negotiation of checkout lanes and the various ways to pay for purchases.

Inana (1980) described a comprehensive nine-step program that included basic principles of grocery shopping as well as information on nutrition, planning meals, saving money, and organization and storage of food at home.

Savage (1977) provided specific suggestions for teaching people with visual impairments to shop for groceries independently. He suggested that orientation to the grocery store be accomplished in two stages, using a sighted guide to help the shopper first learn a route around the peripheral walls of the store and then learn a patterned route through the aisles, using the store's numbering system to identify different areas (see Figure 13.1). During this process, the shopper can map the products within the store by recording an auditory list of items as he or she walks the route with a guide or instructor. Savage also suggested using a long cane to ensure that the pathway is clear while pulling the cart through the aisle, rather than walking behind it, to avoid pushing the cart into objects or people. The latter can be easily adopted by experienced long cane users or can be taught to novices by an O&M instructor.

Alternative methods of grocery shopping, such as home-delivery companies and telephone-ordering services, can be explored in each individual's community to meet the needs of those with transportation difficulties, time constraints, or physical limitations. New opportunities to do grocery shopping and pay bills using telecommunications technology or bar code readers and credit or debit cards will soon be widely available, offering all visually impaired individuals alternatives to traditional grocery shopping as well as providing new challenges for rehabilitation teachers, who can work with people who are visually impaired to design workable ways to utilize these opportunities.

CHAPTER 14

Personal Management Skills

KEY CONCEPTS IN THIS CHAPTER

- **The role of the rehabilitation teacher in the teaching of personal management skills**
- **Adaptive methods used to accomplish personal grooming tasks such as shaving, toothbrushing, bathing, caring for feminine hygiene, applying makeup, and caring for hair**
- **Adaptive skills used in such tasks of caring for clothing as washing, drying, and ironing clothing and polishing shoes**
- **The basics of caring for prosthetic eyes**
- **Adaptive methods of telling time**
- **Adaptive methods of using a telephone**
- **Adaptive methods of identifying money and managing finances**
- **Methods of managing medications, including insulin, and glucose monitoring**

Personal management refers to the activities required to meet one's personal needs, including grooming, clothing care, keeping time, using the telephone, managing money, and medication management. The role of rehabilitation teachers in regard to personal management skills varies considerably from client to client, depending on the individual's background and previous experience, amount of vision, and whether he or she needs to learn any unfamiliar personal management skills. Thus, the teacher's task can range from presenting a brief lesson to an adventitiously visually impaired adult about how to label and organize products and medications for easy access to teaching a teenage girl with total congenital vision loss a comprehensive unit on makeup application, including what the products are, where they are applied, how to select and label them, and how to make sure that makeup is evenly and properly applied.

Perhaps the most important consideration in teaching personal management skills is the manner in which the rehabilitation teacher approaches this subject. Because these skills are so personal, they need to be presented with the utmost respect for the client's feelings. Since the importance of one's appearance varies so much among individuals, there is no one good way to approach the topic. It is probably best to discuss the intimate nature of this subject area at the outset of working with a particular client, which will give the rehabilitation teacher some idea of how sensitive the client is about his or her appearance and how important it is to him or her.

In general, concerns relating to appearance and hygiene are best introduced in a matter of fact manner, as part of the overall assessment process at the beginning of personal adjustment training. However, in some cases the client may be reluctant to even discuss personal management issues. If such personal topics appear to be too delicate for the student to deal with comfortably, the teacher can delay further discussion until the client feels more at ease. If the teacher is of the opposite sex, the client may feel more comfortable discussing personal management topics with an instructor or peer of the same sex. Sometimes clients deny having any difficulties accomplishing personal management tasks, yet their appearance contradicts their response. Such clients may simply not realize that their appearance or cleanliness is not similar to that of those around them. Whether the underlying cause is lack of knowledge, cultural differences, upbringing, or another factor, however, the teacher has the responsibility of informing clients about any disparity between their perception of their personal appearance and that of people around them, because it may affect their prospects for employment and personal relationships.

Specific grooming chores that people deal with daily are bathing, shaving, applying makeup, hair care, feminine hygiene care, and toothbrushing. Rehabilitation teachers may be called upon to help clients with the care and cleaning of artificial (prosthetic) eyes and to deal with related questions of the client's appearance. Tasks related to clothing are washing and drying, ironing, shoe care, and identifying the color and styles of articles of clothing. Medication management includes the identification of different medications, and the rehabilitation teacher frequently assists people who have diabetes with their special needs regarding insulin measurement and glucose monitoring. There is no set sequence in which these skills should be taught. Rather, the order depends on the client's preferences, concerns, and needs. Sidebar 14.1 presents some common adaptations in grooming, clothing care, and other personal management areas that may be helpful to clients.

Many personal management skills will be well established in clients who previously had vision, and, in fact, many clients will discover ways of dealing with them with little or no instruction. However, the more complex skills of makeup application and management of diabetic needs generally require a good deal of teaching, and the use of items such as adapted watches can be complex if the construction of the item itself is complex. Therefore, more attention will be paid to these areas in this chapter.

Individuals who have never seen face the additional difficulty of not being able to monitor their own appearance and may need special help in understanding the relationship of colors and styles and utilizing appropriate amounts and shades of makeup. Therefore, learning skills such as applying makeup, matching clothing, purchasing clothing, sorting clothing for washing, and ironing clothing is especially important for these clients. In addition, rehabilitation teachers may occasionally need to assess and remediate such basic skills as tying shoes; buttoning clothing; opening and closing zippers; buckling belts; and manipulating safety pins as a prerequisite to using them to label clothes.

GROOMING

Toothbrushing and Flossing

Individuals who have previously brushed and flossed their teeth before losing their sight do not lose that skill, but will often have difficulty just in measuring out the right amount of toothpaste or length of floss or in aiming the toothpaste onto the brush. Several simple adaptations are available to address these concerns (see Sidebar 14.1) such as placing a finger alongside the bristles of the brush to monitor the application of the toothpaste. However, rehabilitation teachers will find it challenging to teach an individual who has never brushed or flossed by himself or herself. Although the mouth is a very familiar place to an individual, a novice may need some very basic instruction about how and where to brush or floss. The rehabilitation teacher may need to model the actions involved in toothbrushing or give a hand-over-hand demonstration.

Teaching an individual to floss for the first time involves several steps, including:

Adaptive Methods for Personal Management Tasks

SIDEBAR 14.1

GROOMING

Toothbrushing

1. Place a finger alongside the bristles to monitor the amount of toothpaste application.
2. For those with neuropathy or other conditions that might hinder the ability to monitor the toothpaste tactilely, place the toothpaste directly into the mouth.
3. Monitor coverage with the tongue.

Hair Care

1. Mark products for identification.
2. Use contrast, such as hanging a dark towel on the wall behind a fairhaired person's head, to help improve visibility in the mirror.
3. Use tactile or visual landmarks, such as the nose, to determine where a part or barrette should be placed.

Shaving

1. Use landmarks, such as a point on the ear, to indicate where to shave.
2. Use overlapping strokes.
3. Repeat coverage at a 90-degree angle from the first set of strokes.
4. Monitor coverage tactilely.

Makeup

1. Label products such as eye shadow for color identification.
2. Use facial landmarks to locate areas to apply cosmetics such as blush and eye shadow.
3. Organize cosmetics in a basket or on a tray to allow easy access and location.
4. Choose cosmetics that are less likely to spill or cause messes.
5. Protect clothing by placing a towel in the lap.
6. Use subtle shades of cosmetics to make uneven or inconsistent application less noticeable and to decrease the visibility of any mistakes.
7. Count the number of brush strokes on the cake of blusher or eyeshadow to control the amount to be applied.
8. Stabilize the hand against the face or with the other hand when applying such cosmetics as mascara, eyeliner, or lipstick.
9. Use preventive cleanup, such as wiping the bridge of the nose with a tissue to remove any mascara that may have touched it.

Nail Care

1. Use polish pens that are similar to felt-tip markers to apply polish.
2. Nail buffers or clear polishes provide sufficient "shine" for some people.
3. Stabilize the nail enamel brush with the middle finger while holding the brush between thumb and first finger.
4. Cool the polish in the refrigerator to make it easier to feel coverage on the nail.
5. Practice preventive cleanup. Trace around the nail with manicure sticks dipped in polish remover or polish "correcter pens" to remove any polish from skin.
6. Explore alternatives, such as a professional manicure.

CLOTHING

Washing and Drying Clothing

1. Memorize the position of preferred control settings or mark dials tactilely or in a contrasting color.
2. Use a one-cup dipper for measuring detergent.
3. Separate clothing using labeling or memory to prevent discoloration in the wash.
4. Wash clothes after each wearing to ensure cleanliness.
5. Mark known stains with a laundry pin so that stain remover can be applied before washing.

Ironing Clothing

1. Use a funnel for filling a steam iron.

(continued on next page)

Adaptive Methods for Personal Management Tasks (continued)

2. Use a cord holder to prevent setting the iron down on the cord and to aid in locating the handle.
3. Monitor the water level in the iron by shaking it.
4. Follow the cord to locate the iron safely.
5. Use a heat-proof pad for resting the iron to prevent accidentally touching a hot surface or knocking over the iron.
6. Monitor wrinkles tactilely if necessary.
7. If the iron is knocked over, put clothing over the hand to protect it while locating the iron.

Shoe Care

1. Use labeling methods to identify polish colors.
2. Use wax polish in preference to liquids, since it cannot spill.
3. Use preventive measures, such as always organizing shoes and supplies on newspaper and removing shoelaces before polishing shoes.
4. Apply paste in two directions to ensure complete coverage.
5. Use low vision or tactile techniques to monitor coverage.
6. Practice preventive cleanup of containers, shoe soles, hands, and the work area to avoid staining other surfaces.
7. If a protective shoe spray is used, aim the nozzle by touching it to the surface of the shoe and then moving the can straight back 12 to 15 inches.

USING THE TELEPHONE

1. When using a push-button telephone, place the first, second, and third fingers on the 4, 5, and 6 keys and reach from there to dial other numbers.
2. When using a rotary telephone, to dial the numbers 1 through 5, place the first, second, third, and fourth fingers in the 4, 3, 2, and 1 holes and reach for the 5 hole with the first finger; to dial 6 through 0, place the first finger in the 7, the second in the 8, the third in the 9, and the fourth in the 0 and reach for the 6 with the first finger.
3. If dialing is not possible within the time constraints of the telephone company, obtain speed-dialing service through the telephone company, purchase a telephone that can be programmed to dial a number by keying a short code or ask the operator to dial.
4. Consider a voice-dialing telephone for people who have difficulty dialing.
5. Obtain free directory assistance by applying at the local telephone company.
6. Conduct a survey of the information banks available through the telephone in your local area.

MONEY IDENTIFICATION

1. Identify coins by size and edge serrations.
2. Fold money in different ways according to the denomination.
3. If residual vision is present, use it to identify denominations by investigating the backs of paper money. Gross differences in the frame or central picture can provide important clues to identifying denominations.
4. If independent identification is crucial, use an electronic money identifier.
5. To exercise extra caution, pay with the denomination or bill just above the cost of a purchase or ask for change in one-dollar increments.

- showing the client how to locate the end of the floss and cut a portion away from the dispenser
- demonstrating how to hold floss taut around fingers on both hands and then wind it from one hand to another to expose a clean length of floss
- orienting the learner to the areas to be flossed (the spaces between the teeth)
- demonstrating how to hold the hands and floss so that the floss enters the spaces between the teeth.

A thorough lesson on dental care for a novice would also include—perhaps during a trip to a drugstore—introduction to the varied assortment of products available and information on how to select toothbrushes, floss, dental tape, and toothpaste.

Hair Care

Hair care is not particularly problematic for persons with visual impairments, although individuals with low vision may benefit from suggestions on how to use lighting, contrast, or magnification to enhance their view of their hair appearance. For example, an elderly white-haired lady with low vision may find that installing a high towel bar across from the mirror in the bathroom and hanging a dark towel on it provides enough contrast to allow her to satisfactorily discern the appearance of her hair. Persons without sufficient vision to monitor the appearance of their hair may need some basic instruction on how to use tactile landmarks and techniques to properly part or section the hair and to place barrettes, bows, or other hair accessories. The teacher may need to provide orientation to new hair care products and appliances, such as curling irons, and teach such adaptations as how to label the settings on the device. Adolescents who are learning about independent hair care for the first time as well as those concerned with staying "in fashion" will benefit from occasional consultations with hair stylists who can provide helpful information about current styles and trends. Having a hair stylist speak to a group of clients who are interested in fashionable hairstyles while the rehabilitation teacher provides suggestions for any needed adaptations in techniques is a good way to get expert input.

Shaving

The idea of shaving without being able to see may be frightening to sighted individuals who depend on vision for feedback. In reality, shaving without normal vision poses few problems to most people. Much of the task (such as determining where whiskers are or whether a nick has occurred) is tactile. Good coverage can be ensured by using overlapping strokes and by shaving the area over again at a 90-degree angle to the original strokes. Those who have not shaved before need the same kinds of information as anyone else, including what types of products to use, which direction of hair

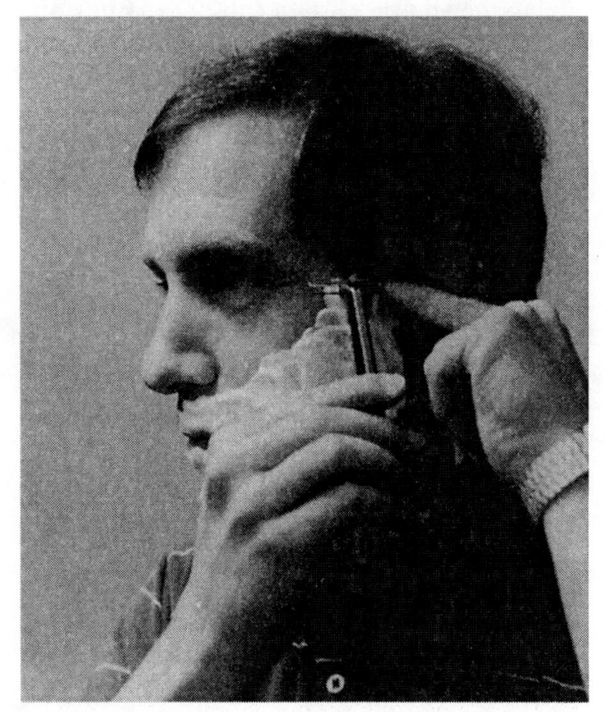

Using a landmark to determine where to begin shaving.

growth and strokes to follow, and so forth. Locating landmarks, such as a point on one's ear, with the hand that is not holding the razor can assist with determining where to shave (or not shave).

Bathing

It is unusual for most rehabilitation teachers to have to give instruction in the area of bathing because nearly all clients have had a good deal of experience with it, and lack of sight poses no real obstacles. Such routine adaptations as distinguishing shampoo from conditioner or identifying other bath products may need to be addressed. An occasional client will not have had experience with bathing independently—generally those with multiple impairments or developmental disabilities or those who have been overprotected. Such a client would need instruction in setting the water temperature, activating the shower, using the washcloth properly, selecting and using bathing products, and maintaining safety in the tub or shower. Practical tips, such as pulling the shower curtain shut when adjusting the water temperature before entering the tub, may need to be addressed, as well. Novices who have not bathed independently before may also benefit from an orientation to a variety of faucet and shower control configurations so that they are able to operate them independently in such situations as staying in a motel or visiting friends.

Feminine Hygiene

Most female clients with whom the rehabilitation teacher works will already be familiar with products used for menstruation, and loss of vision has little effect on the ability to use them. However, there will occasionally be a few clients, particularly young women with congenital impairments, who have been overprotected and have had little opportunity to learn about such topics. Such clients require comprehensive basic instruction, including information about the menstrual cycle and its physical manifestations, familiarization with the management of menstruation and feminine hygiene products, methods of utilizing and disposing of these products, and ways to detect the start of menstruation. A thorough lesson would also include information about what to do in case of "accidents," how to remove blood stains, and how to locate and operate sanitary product vending machines in public washrooms. Male rehabilitation teachers or those not comfortable teaching these topics might work with an agency nurse or a local human service agency, such as Planned Parenthood, to deliver instruction.

Makeup and Nail Care

Marylee H., a college student with no usable vision, requested instruction on makeup application. She explained that she had previously

Using a landmark such as the bottom of the nose or base of the cheekbone can assist with the application of cosmetics such as blush. Stabilizing the hand against the face helps avoid accidents or smudges.

learned how to use mascara, but wanted to know about other products. Since the male rehabilitation teacher had other clients who were interested in make-up application and a number of female members of the local consumer organization for persons with visual impairments had expressed interest in the topic, he contacted a self-employed cosmetic sales representative to arrange for a workshop on skin care and cosmetic application.

The representative was pleased to be invited to demonstrate her products and explained that she saw the opportunity as a challenge and public service, rather than a sales opportunity. She admitted that she was nervous and expressed concern about her ability to explain techniques, but the rehabilitation teacher assured her that he would assist with adaptations if any were necessary. In fact, when the cosmetic representative demonstrated a new product such as blush or eye shadow, the participants exchanged their own suggestions for monitoring coverage, such as counting brush strokes, and for ways to label the various colors. They also discussed helpful hints. Marylee mentioned that she always had a damp washcloth ready to wipe her hands during mascara application, and when she finished, she gently wiped the area on either side of the bridge of her nose since it frequently got bumped by the mascara wand—an example of the principle of preventive cleanup. Everyone, including the cosmetic representative, admitted learning much from the group session.

Applying makeup may be tedious for someone with limited or no vision, but it can be mastered with practice. Cosmetics can be labeled in braille or with some other system so that the visually impaired individual can identify the makeup colors without assistance. Facial landmarks can be used to determine where to apply products such as eye shadow or blush. For example, the edge of the eyebrow is a good landmark to use in deciding how far out toward the side of the face eye shadow should go. The bottom of the nose or the base of the cheekbone can form a boundary for applying blush.

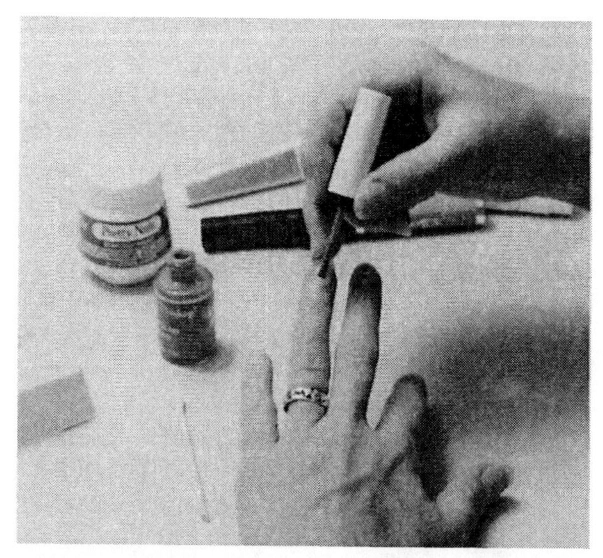

The middle finger can be used to stabilize the hand holding the brush for the application of polish to nails.

Stabilizing the hand during tasks such as applying mascara, eye shadow, lipstick, or nail polish by resting it on the face or body at a point other than where the makeup is being applied results in better fine motor control and provides the user with a point of reference as well. For example, when applying mascara, the individual can place the hand holding the brush against the cheek to keep the hand steadier and find the eyelashes more easily. In general, people who have had little practice in applying makeup would do well to get feedback from a trusted friend during the first few attempts.

Counting the number of strokes needed to apply a specific item or noting specific amounts necessary to ensure appropriate and adequate coverage can offer a mathematical solution to the vagaries of nonvisual makeup application. For example, a woman may determine that a single drop of foundation applied to each cheek, the nose, the chin, and the forehead will provide sufficient coverage. Similarly, she can count the number of brush strokes needed on the cake of eye shadow to get enough on the brush or the number of strokes to make over the eyelid. Feedback from a sighted observer will help to determine how much is enough. If the individual selects subtle shades of cosmetics such as eye shadow, foundation, and blush, observers are more likely to overlook slight flaws in application.

A little forethought will help to prevent spills and accidents. Cosmetics can be organized on a tray to allow easy access. Choosing cosmetics carefully can prevent some messes. For example, cream-based cosmetics will not fall off the applicator or finger and onto clothing as powder-based products do. Washing hands frequently during the application process is suggested to prevent accidentally rubbing some makeup residue off on the face or clothes. Overcleaning or preventive cleaning of nearby areas—for example, tracing around the cuticles with a cotton swab dipped in nail polish remover after polishing the fingernails—will increase the likelihood of a neat appearance. Protecting clothing by placing a towel in one's lap during any makeup application is a useful preventive measure as well.

CLOTHING CARE

Clothing care skills are usually familiar to people who previously had vision. They are usually accomplished with simple adaptations such as marking the controls of laundry machines with tactile or highly visible substances, using adaptive techniques for measuring out laundry soap (see Chapter 13), learning to monitor the general appearance of clothing tactilely, and identifying items of clothing through labeling systems.

Identification and Selection of Clothing

Although labeling was discussed in general terms in Chapter 12, the identification skills required to maintain an appropriate appearance involve not only labeling clothing to be able to identify items, but also being able to match items to each other and select appropriate clothes. In general, the simplest method is usually best, and reducing the number of items to identify may work well for some people. For example, a man may choose to purchase only one color of dark dress socks for winter, switching to a lighter color of socks for warmer months when he is likely to wear fewer dark items. This method eliminates the need for any labeling system for this item, since the out-of-season socks can be put away until they are needed again.

People with low vision who are unsure of their ability to identify colors may need to have their ability to discriminate color evaluated. Perhaps improving lighting conditions in the closet or bedroom will be sufficient to help someone with low vision discriminate colors.

Physical characteristics other than color can be used to identify many items (the blouse with the lace collar is the white one, the coarse slacks are the navy blue ones), but other systems may be necessary. Labeling with braille or large print markings is relatively simple, using a variety of products such as metal clothing tags, plastic hanger tags, or Voxcom recording cards (see Chapter 10) with holes for hooking on the hanger along with the item of clothing. Other labels can be affixed to a standard place, such as on the label of a blouse or shirt. Braille labels can be easily made on half-inch Teflon skived tape available from specialty catalogs (see Resources section) and sewed to clothing.

Systems that use special symbols require some thought and planning. One system utilizes small brass laundry pins to specify garment style and color (Utrup, 1977). This system uses identified positions on the garment to establish a sequential placement of pins that corresponds to alphabetized colors. For example, the system for blouses or shirts might be set up as follows:

- Positions for placing the pins are established using the buttons and the space between them, so that position 1 is behind the top button, position 2 is between the top and second button, position 3 is behind the second button, and so forth.
- Colors are alphabetized and assigned in order to the numbered positions, for instance:

- black—position 1
- blue—position 2
- brown—position 3
- gray—position 4
- green—position 5
- pink—position 6
- red—position 7

- The direction of the pin can indicate the pattern; for example, the head of the pin can face up for solid colors, right for stripes, down for plaid, and left for print styles.

Thus, a green plaid blouse would be marked with a pin placed behind the third button (position 5), with its head facing down. Belt loops and the spaces between them work well for establishing positions for the pins on slacks, and on pullovers the front, right, back, and left of the collar or waistband can be used. A number of commercial clothing-labeling systems have been developed to date, including Do Dots (clear plastic snap-together buttons that have braille symbols to tell color and design of the garment), Match Makers (safety pins bonded to plastic covers with varying numbers of raised dots), Identi-Buttons (variously shaped buttons to indicate the color of garment), and Say What (shoe-horn shaped pieces with braille descriptions attached), all available from the specialty catalogs listed in the Resources section. No one system is ideal for everyone, as variables such as cost, ease of use, durability of the product, and number of color choices can affect the efficacy of an identification system for people with visual impairments.

Matching the colors of clothing items is not an exact science, even for people with good vision. The rehabilitation teacher can recommend that certain colors usually go well together—for example, blue and pink—but there are certain shades of these combinations that may clash. As a result, some people who do not have enough sight to identify colors keep file cards in braille or large print to describe which clothing items go well together and which do not. A typical entry might read: "The green striped blouse goes well with the yellow slacks, the green shorts, and the yellow plaid pullover, but not with the green plaid skirt." The initial clothes-marking session in which colors are matched would, of course, require some assistance from a sighted person whose judgment is valued.

Persons with visual impairments are often understandably concerned about keeping up with current clothing styles, which can be difficult for anyone in our ever-changing society, but the salespeople in clothing stores or the personal shoppers employed by some stores are generally helpful. Also, such special publications as *Dialogue: The Magazine for the Visually Impaired,* (a quarterly published by Blindskills in braille, on four-track cassette, and in large print), and the *Matilda Zeigler Magazine for the Blind* (a monthly general-interest magazine published in braille and on disk), often print helpful articles in this regard (see Resources section). Those who have little experience with selecting their own clothes may need more detailed instruction that includes how to choose clothing appropriate for their age, size, and shape and the occasion, as well as for the weather and method of travel. Different types of clothing will be appropriate for work, leisure, and dress wear, and someone who stands outside waiting for public transportation in inclement weather will want to invest more in weatherproof clothing than someone who rides to work in a car each day.

Doing Laundry

Although doing the laundry is no more or less tedious for a person with a visual impairment than for anyone else, some simple adaptations are particularly helpful to assist people with limited or no vision in:

- setting the washer and dryer controls
- sorting items to avoid discoloration of clothing from fabrics that bleed
- measuring cleaning products
- removing stains.

Methods used to set the controls of washing machines and dryers are similar to those used to set and mark other appliances (see Chapter 12). The simplest method is always the easiest; for example, memorizing the position of a dial or switch when it is pointing to the preferred setting is easier and safer than depending on an applied label. This principle is particularly helpful when using the laundry facilities in an apartment complex or a commercial laundry, since labels are easily tampered with. Moreover, people generally use just one or two different settings on a washer or dryer, so it is relatively easy to determine and remember the positions of a dial by comparing them to the numbers on a clock face or the directions on a compass. If dials must be marked, it is best to use a labeling system such as clear plastic labeling tape that does not interfere with the visibility of the controls. For example, large dots made of Hi Marks (available from the catalogs listed in the Resources section) or liquid solder (available from hardware stores) can be placed next to, rather than on top of the word indicating "permanent press."

Organization and planning can assist with sorting clothes to prevent discoloration during laundering. Soiled items can be sorted into separate containers for light clothes, dark clothes, cold wash only, and so forth as they are removed at the end of the day. Clothing labels will assist with that task, if the individual does not have enough vision to detect color.

Measuring laundry products such as detergent, fabric softener, or bleach can be accomplished easily by using either the measuring cups that are often enclosed with these products or a vessel of the correct size, such as a graduated measuring cup or a plastic drinking cup cut to size. A relatively new product, known as activated ceramic laundry discs and sold through ecology-minded outlets, easily solves the measuring problem, since no detergent is necessary.

Stain removal is a common concern of individuals with visual impairments, who often complain that they seem to get more than their fair share of clothing spots. If an individual is aware of having gotten a stain, he or she can mark the location of the spot with a small laundry pin before removing the clothing item, using the part of the body on which, say, the spaghetti sauce landed as a landmark. Then, later, stain remover can be applied to the pinned area before washing. Women who are not sure whether they have menstrual stains can use the principle of preventive cleaning and treat all items as though they might possibly have bloodstains—washing them in cold water and using chlorine or color-safe bleach during the wash cycle. Although it is difficult to deal with stains one doesn't know are there, many people with visual impairments say they have explained to friends or co-workers that they would prefer to be alerted to clothing stains. Most people are reluctant to ask about whether they look okay when they go out in public or whether their clothing is stained, but the rehabilitation teacher can explain that making use of someone else's eyes is, in its own way, an independent living skill.

Use of public laundry rooms or laundromats not only requires O&M skills, but also necessitates greater organization than washing clothes at home to prepare clothes, laundry products, and money in advance. Use of a large laundry bag, backpack, or cart will allow the individual to transport the clothes and laundry products while keeping the hands free for opening doors; using a low vision device, a cane, or dog guide; and locating washers, dryers, and vending and change machines. To help lighten the load, only the needed amount of detergent or fabric softener can be transferred to smaller containers such as zipper-type plastic storage bags or plastic jars.

Clients who are learning to do laundry for the first time will need to be taught basic information about choosing laundry products, selecting the appropriate water temperature, and sorting clothes. The necessity of removing lint from the lint trap of a dryer is easy to overlook, so developing a habit of cleaning it each time the dryer is loaded is a helpful safety suggestion. Lessons for people who have never used public laundries before should include information about the types of machines typically available, their cost and the way coins are inserted, types of products sold at laundromats, and the existence of rolling carts to transport items from the washers to the dryers and folding tables. Lessons such as the use of a laundromat make good use of teamwork between the rehabilitation teacher, O&M instructor, low vision specialist, and client, since so many skills taught by all three vision professionals are involved in meeting the needs of the client.

Ironing

Ironing can be a difficult skill to teach and to learn because of the fear of being burned by the hot iron. For those who were used to ironing clothes before losing their sight, instruction focuses on the adaptations necessary for safety and avoiding burns, but for those with no experience, it is necessary to teach the basic concepts of ironing as well.

The hot iron can be safely located by placing it with the cord hanging off the front edge of the ironing board. That way, the iron can be located by trailing along the front of the ironing board until the cord is contacted, then following the cord to the handle. The user can avoid knocking the iron over or touching the hot surface when reaching for it by using a Teflon or other heat-resistant resting pad on which the iron can be set with the hot surface face down. A cord holder that attaches to the edge of the ironing board can assist with keeping the cord out of the way of the iron. Individuals with low vision can make use of the principles of visibility by selecting a cover for the ironing board that contrasts with the iron.

An introduction to the basics of ironing for those who need it should start with a discussion of the concepts of wrinkles and ironing and proceed to familiarization with ironing tools and products. Instruction would also generally include detection of wrinkles, how to arrange different types of clothing flat on the ironing board, proper use of the iron, setting the iron to the proper temperature, filling the iron with water for steam ironing, folding clothing, and hanging clothing.

Ironing with no usable vision is typically accomplished by smoothing the area to be ironed with the hands, ironing the area, examining the ironed area with the iron held up out of the way to feel for any cold spots that were missed and to detect remaining wrinkles, and then reapplying the iron if necessary. Then, with the iron replaced on the resting pad, the clothing is rearranged to place the next unironed section flat on the board. New learners in particular will benefit from going through these motions first using a cold iron.

Shoe Care

Caring for shoes when vision is limited involves techniques for thorough coverage and for preventing messes resulting from highly pigmented shoe care products. Coverage can easily be assured by applying the polish in two directions, since the surface area to be covered is small, and can be monitored tactilely since polished and unpolished surfaces are readily distinguished by touch. Preventive cleanup strategies are especially critical to keep shoe care products from staining carpets, tabletops, and clothing—for example, always working on newspaper, removing the laces from shoes before beginning, and washing hands thoroughly when finished. Wax polishes or cleaning products are preferable to liquids since they can't spill.

PROSTHETIC EYES

Rehabilitation teachers will eventually encounter clients who wear artificial eyes, or prostheses, which are plastic inserts that have been individually fitted for the wearer and have been hand painted to look like the user's natural eyes. The two major types are prosthetic shells and full-bodied prostheses. The former is like a contact lens that is worn over an unsightly or misshapen eye, and the latter is used when the natural eye was enucleated (removed). Eye removal is accomplished either by complete removal of the globe or by removing the inner viscera and keeping the outer tunic intact. When the tunic is saved, a plastic ball is sewn into it to act as a base of support for the artificial eye. Since the muscles attached to the tunic are intact, eye motility in such cases is nearly normal.

The rehabilitation teacher's role in regard to eye prostheses is usually to assist the wearer with care and cleaning. Proper care is especially important because these devices can cost a thousand dollars or more. Guidelines for care and cleaning include the following:

- Wash the eye only with soap and water.
- Keep the eye moist when it is removed by soaking it in water or contact lens solution.
- Always wipe the eye away from the nose to avoid dislodging it.
- Never place the eye in a tissue, as it can be easily lost.
- Protect the eye from cold, heat, and dry weather and wind, as they all are irritants.
- Always practice extreme cleanliness when handling the eye. It should not be left on a shelf or unprotected.
- Have the eye checked and polished once a year.

Occasionally, the rehabilitation teacher may be required to assist a client in inserting or removing an artificial eye. The eye is inserted by pulling out the upper eyelid, pushing the artificial eye up and under it, and then pulling the lower lid down. The eye will automatically slide into place. The prosthesis is removed by pulling the lower lid down until the prosthetic device falls out. This process can be aided by using a small suction cup specially devised to attach to the surface of the prosthesis for this purpose.

As part of personal management instruction, the rehabilitation teacher monitors the appearance of artificial eyes worn by clients for straightness of gaze, clarity, and overall cleanliness. If the gaze is not centered, the eye may have been placed in the socket incorrectly or may need to be adjusted by a prosthetist, a technician who creates and maintains prosthetic eyes. If the surface is dull, it should be polished by the prosthetist. If the artificial eye causes secretions or excess mucus, it may need to be cleaned or polished, or the client may have an infection. If the secretions persist, the client should be referred to an ophthalmologist.

Personal management instructors are often asked to help clients make the decision about whether or not to wear prostheses. It is common to hear such questions as "How do my eyes look?" "Should I wear sunglasses?" and "Do my eyes look bad enough to need artificial eyes?" Knowing that one's appearance is a deeply personal issue and that every individual has his or her own view of the importance of appearance, the rehabilitation teacher must be both discreet and honest in answering such questions.

> Allen L., a totally blind 18 year old who had just graduated from high school, was enrolled in a college preparatory program held at the state rehabilitation center that included a personal skills assessment in communication and daily living skills and two freshman-level college classes given at a local university. During the initial assessment, Allen's personal management instructor noticed that his eyes had become badly misshapen, had lost their color, and had some unusual growths on them. She brought her observations up at Allen's first staffing conference, and it was decided that the counselor assigned to manage Allen's case at the center would raise the issue with him.
>
> A few days later, Allen asked his personal management instructor, "Do you think my eyes look bad?" Knowing that her response would have considerable emotional ramifications, she queried "Why do you ask?" Allen replied, "My counselor has told me that my eyes don't look very good and may cause me some trouble socially. I guess I just wanted someone else's opinion. Are they really that bad?" The rehabilitation teacher then responded, "I'm glad that you trust me enough to ask me such a personal question, and I know it must be a difficult one for you to ask. Your eyes have lost their shape and their color and because of that, they look a lot different from the average person's eyes. I guess I would agree with your counselor's opinion that they might cause you some problems, particularly when it comes time to go to a job interview." Obviously troubled,

Allen finally said, "My counselor suggested that I consider wearing sunglasses, but I hate that idea. And the thought of having my eyes removed and getting fake eyes is more than I can bear. What do you think? What would you do? The teacher responded, "I don't really know what I would do, but those are both good alternatives. Perhaps the best approach would be to have you talk to other clients here who have had to make this decision. You can also talk with Ms. Sutter, the person who fits prosthetic eyes here in town."

After several consultations with other clients, the prosthetist, and his ophthalmologist, Allen finally decided to get prosthetic eyes—a decision made easier because the deterioration of his eyes caused him frequent pain. He left the rehabilitation center to have enucleation surgery in which the globes were removed and plastic implants were placed within the outer covering of both eyes. After the surgery and recuperation, just before the process of fitting the prosthetics was to begin, Allen's itinerant rehabilitation teacher resumed visits to his home. Still not completely comfortable with the idea of the prostheses, Allen told him, "I'm not sure what will happen when I go to the eye doctor to get my new eyes. Can you tell me about it?" The teacher responded, "I'd be glad to tell you, but I'd also be glad to go with you on your first visit if you'd like. I know the doctor well and I've been there before with other clients. Would you like me to go with you?" Allen immediately accepted the offer.

During the first visit, Ms. Sutter made latex impressions of Allen's eye sockets, in much the same way that impressions are taken for false teeth, and later would make molds from the impressions. At the second visit, the prosthetic eyes that had been made from the molds were fitted, and Allen brought an old picture of himself that showed his original eye color. Before the third visit, Ms. Sutter made the required adjustments to the newly made prostheses, and they were painted to resemble Allen's own eyes. Allen left after the third visit looking great. His rehabilitation teacher later helped him read through the care and cleaning literature that Ms. Sutter had provided.

In attempting to serve the client most effectively, the instructor needs to consider the consequences of unsightly eyes and the reactions of the general public. For example, a recent study suggested that members of the general public viewed a person whose eyes were slightly disfigured and was not wearing prostheses more negatively than they did the same person wearing them (Pratt, 1992). In addition, people with managerial jobs had a more negative view of the person without prostheses than did other respondents. If these preliminary results are an accurate measure of public attitudes, it appears that unsightly looking eyes could have an effect on the individual's ability to obtain employment and to interact with others in social situations. Therefore, it is important for rehabilitation teachers to be objective and truthful in advising clients in this regard. The option of prosthetic eyes, cosmetic shells, or slightly tinted eyeglasses can be explained to individuals with disfigured or irregular eyes. (In general, dark sunglasses recall the stereotypic appearance of blind people and seem out of place when worn indoors). A side benefit of wearing eyeglasses is that they protect the face from undetected objects.

TELLING TIME

Telling time is just as important to a person with a visual impairment as it is to anyone else, although accurate time telling may be especially important to people who depend on public transportation. Telling time is generally accomplished through the use of adaptive timepieces, which include raised-dot, large print, and talking clocks and watches, available through specialty catalogs (see Resources section). The front of a raised-dot watch opens, allowing the user to read the watch with the fingers. Such timepieces usually have three raised dots at the 12 o'clock and 6 o'clock positions, two dots at the 3 o'clock and 9 o'clock positions, and a single dot at all others.

When teaching clients how to read raised-dot watches, the instructor begins with a relatively large watch. The learner first reads easily discerned times such as 12:00, 3:00, 6:00, and 9:00, and then progresses to times at the half hour, quarter hour, and so forth. Times at which the hands of the watch are placed nearest to one another are the most difficult to interpret. To avoid dislodging the hands on a braille watch, tactile reading is best accomplished by having the learner find the center point of the watch face, lightly and repeatedly touch the center to discern the direction of the hands, and then gently trace the hands out from that point. Setting a watch should be taught after instruction on reading a watch. This teaching sequence works for large-print watches as well, which usually have larger numbers placed on a highly contrasting background.

Talking timepieces come in a variety of sizes and styles and are read by the simple push of a button, but setting them is more complex than turning a watch stem. They generally contain at least two sets of buttons or switches. One is for selecting the mode, such as the mode for setting either the current time or an alarm. The second set may consist of three buttons, one for selecting the hour, a second for selecting the minute, and another for entering the setting into memory. Thus, a sample sequence for setting an alarm for 6:15 a.m. would be as follows:

- Place the mode switch at the alarm set position.
- Push the hour button until 6:00 a.m. is announced.
- Push the minute selector until the clock says 6:15 a.m.
- Push the set button to lock the time into memory.
- Return the mode switch back to the "read" or neutral position.

The rehabilitation teacher will probably not be able to determine the actual teaching sequence for a client until he or she examines the particular clock involved.

Adaptive timepieces are available from nearly any supplier of products for persons with visual impairments (see Resources section), and the large-print and talking versions are now commonly available through mainstream retailers. Not all talking timepieces will announce the time while the time and alarm are being set, however, which leaves the visually impaired individual unable to monitor the time and dependent on a sighted person or on trial and error to set the clock or watch. Therefore, it is important to remind clients to check for that and other desirable features before purchasing any talking timepieces.

TELEPHONE SKILLS

The telephone has for decades linked people with visual impairments to others. Even though accessible transportation to reach friends or obtain services is often hard to obtain, the telephone is always there to call friends, summon a taxi, or get product information from a local retailer. The advent of computer-controlled information banks has made it an even more vital tool. The person with a visual impairment in Father Carroll's day was in danger of slowly losing contact with the events of the day because he or she had only limited access to current information such as local news, announcements of special events, and fashion trends (see Chapter 9). Today, however, telephone news services and other telecommunications innovations help solve the problem of keeping up to date for people who are blind or visually impaired.

Dialing

The two main challenges encountered by blind and visually impaired persons in using the telephone are usually dialing and recording telephone numbers, but these can be met with relative ease. Although specific methods for recording telephone numbers will not be described in detail, solutions will be found in the techniques covered in other chapters for keeping track of information—such as making a large-print list with a dark marker on bold-lined paper (Chapter 8) or recording on Voxcom cards (Chapter 10).

When people have difficulty dialing, frequently either they get disconnected because they take longer than 10 seconds to dial the next digit of the number or they reach a wrong number. Some visually impaired people devise their own systems for dialing, but others who are unaware of simple adaptive devices or dialing techniques may become discouraged by their first attempts. If an individual has sufficient vision, enlarged number rings (for rotary telephones) or enlarged stick-on numbers (for push-button models) can be affixed to the telephone. Some telephone companies will provide these free of charge for people with certified visual disabilities; alternatively, telephones can be purchased with large buttons or numbers. However, a disadvantage of depending on large numbers is that people find themselves unable to use other telephones without them. Thus, alternative dialing techniques are important.

Tactile dialing techniques focus on training the fingers to operate specific sections of the telephone dial or keypad and using a "home row," as in typing.

Dialing a rotary telephone. The fingers are positioned to dial one of the higher numbers. Large numbers on the dial assist individuals with useable vision.

Using a push-button telephone. The 4, 5, and 6 buttons are treated as a "home row" from which to dial.

When the individual uses the rotary telephone dial that is still found most often in rural areas, the four fingers of the right hand are placed, in order, in the holes. Thus, to dial one of the first four numbers, the little finger is placed in the 1 hole and the other fingers in 2, 3, and 4, successively. Then all fingers are removed but the correct finger for the digit to be dialed. If a 5 is needed, the dialer reaches over with the index finger. Then the fingers are replaced before dialing the next digit. To dial the higher numbers, the little finger is placed in the 0 hole and the others in the 9, 8, and 7 holes, respectively. Some users prefer to use only three fingers in a similar manner. Some simply count the holes to reach the desired number; however, this method is slow, akin to the hunt-and-peck method of typing, and, as noted, the dialer will be disconnected if he or she takes longer than 10 seconds to locate and dial the next digit. To help in locating the correct numbers without having to count forward from 1 or back from 0, one or two tactile placemarkers, such as raised dots or small pieces of yarn, can be fastened to the rotary dial at the 5 and 8 positions.

Rotary telephones are somewhat difficult to use for older persons with arthritis. If finances allow it, the purchase of a push-button telephone may make it easier for some people to dial. The push-button keypad can be mastered by treating one row as the home row to which the fingers always return. If the user is right handed, the index finger is placed on the 4 button, the middle finger on the 5, and the ring finger on the 6. The other keys are reached from that home-row position.

Alternatives to Dialing

Several alternatives are available for dialing telephone numbers. First, voice-input telephones are now available. The caller need only say aloud the name of a person whose number has been previously programmed into the telephone, and it is automatically dialed. Although the advantages are evident, these telephones can be expensive, and the voice dialer only works for a limited group of numbers that have been preprogrammed. Unprogrammed numbers can be dialed from the keypad, as usual.

A second alternative, known as speed dialing, is available from the local telephone company for a small monthly charge. After arranging for speed-dialing service, the user must first preprogram frequently called numbers paired with short speed-dialing codes. Once the programming is done, the caller dials only the short code number to reach friends, family, or other frequently called numbers. It is not necessary to purchase a different telephone to use the telephone company's speed-dialing service.

A similar alternative that does require purchase of a different telephone or attachment is usually referred to as a "memory" or "programmable" telephone. Programmable telephones or dialing attachments use either the regular keypad or an additional set of buttons to dial preprogrammed numbers. At least one device even allows the caller to place visual identifying material under the programmed dialing button, such as a family member's photograph, a picture of emergency personnel in uniform, or a name written in large print.

As an alternative for those with special dialing problems, local telephone companies also generally offer a "dial Operator" service that allows qualified users with special needs to obtain free dialing assistance from the operator. Another service for people with visual impairments or other disabling conditions is the directory assistance waiver. People who are unable to consult a print telephone directory may make many more calls for directory assistance than telephone companies typically allow without charge. Telephone companies will waive extra charges for people who have been granted a waiver for directory assistance calls from their home telephone within their local calling area. Rehabilitation teachers are qualified to certify a person's eligibility for such services; for information on how to apply, the local telephone company can be contacted.

Because there are a variety of alternatives available for persons who have difficulty making telephone calls, and because many older people are virtually isolated unless they can make use of the telephone, telephone use and the individual's skills and needs in this regard are an important area for rehabilitation teachers to assess early in the provision of services.

MONEY AND FINANCES

Getting and spending money has many overtones relating to adulthood and autonomy, particularly in our society. Therefore, learning skills to help manage their own money helps people who are visually impaired increase their self-esteem as well as their personal independence. Rehabilitation teachers can teach specific methods for identifying money as well as help with general financial organization and appropriate habits when dealing with money in public.

Money Identification

The need to differentiate among the various denominations of paper currency can arise many times in the course of a day—any time one makes a purchase, receives change, or does banking. This routine aspect of everyday transactions can be difficult for people with limited vision, particularly in the United States, where bills are not easily identifiable by color, texture markings, or size, and it is not likely that this will change anytime in the near future. However, there are a number of ways that money can be identified.

Coins can usually be differentiated by their size and the texture on their edges. For example, U.S. and Canadian quarters and nickels are larger than dimes and pennies, but the quarters can be differentiated from the nickels because quarters have serrated edges. The Canadian one-dollar coin has eleven flat spots along a smooth edge; the two-dollar coin is smaller and has serrated edges. Different denominations of bills can be folded in different ways to aid later identification before being inserted in a wallet or pocket. For example, dollar bills can be kept flat, the five-dollar bill folded in half crosswise, the ten-dollar bill folded in half crosswise twice, and the twenty-dollar bill folded in half lengthwise (Kurpis, 1977). People with some useful vision may be able to read the numbers on bills, and sometimes the back of a bill offers information about its value (Kurpis, 1977). Gross differences in the frame of engraving around the perimeter of a bill and in the contrast between the perimeter and center figures make identifiable clues that can be learned by those who are able to detect these differences. For example, the back of a one-dollar bill appears dark, except for a circle of light in the center. The back of the five-dollar bill is lighter than any other bill, with a darker center and two large light patches on either side (Kurpis, 1977).

People without usable vision can invest in paper currency identification equipment, which is now available through specialty catalogs. Although moderately expensive, these voice output scanners, similar to those used in vending and change machines, allow the user to identify bills independently. Individuals can also ask for information about the denomination of bills when they receive cash at banks and checkout lanes. To be extra cautious when using cash to make purchases in unfamiliar stores, people can pay with the smallest possible denomination of bill or ask for change in one-dollar increments.

Organization for Financial Independence

Although many visually impaired individuals may be able to see well enough to record personal financial information using traditional means, others may need to learn alternative ways. These include brailling account balances and keeping records in braille or recording the information on cassette or adapted computer. Bold-line and raised-line checkbooks are available for those who desire them, as are a variety of check-writing guides (see Chapter 8). Furthermore, many people use computer-based budget and banking software to record balances and print checks. Software is now available that prints a personal signature on command, eliminating the need to locate the proper spot for signing a check, but checks must be used that are compatible with one's printer.

Technology is enormously helpful to individuals with visual impairments. Most people now have access to telephone banking, 24-hour automatic teller machines with accessible features, automatic debit cards, and brailled credit cards. Telephone banking allows complete independence in determining checking account balances, transferring funds among accounts, paying bills, and obtaining other services. Rehabilitation teachers should become acquainted with local resources so that they can explain specific services or adaptations that are particularly useful to individuals who are visually impaired.

Although few people will need specific information about procedures when checking out at a store, some young people who have had little life experience may not be aware of such points of etiquette as being prepared with one's wallet out or signing a check while grocery charges are being totaled. In addition to pointers like these, the rehabilitation teacher can also cover other topics such as the existence of check-writing counters, courtesy pens, debit card swipe machines, and the like at the checkout counter. Without dwelling on dishonesty or danger, teachers should caution novices not to display money in public. If money must be folded according to denomination, it should be done quickly to avoid exhibiting it to others.

MANAGING MEDICATION

An itinerant rehabilitation teacher who serves primarily elderly persons recently remarked:

> It usually takes me at least three months of visits to get new clients' medications straightened out. I start by asking them if they have difficulty identifying and keeping track of medications, but because I am often the only person who sees them in their own homes, I feel compelled to go beyond just assisting them with labeling. They often have multiple medical problems and several different doctors, each of whom is unaware of other medications they take. Many of these clients tend to save unused medication, and as a result of these circumstances, they are sometimes taking dangerous combinations of medications. Many of my clients have a whole shoebox full of various prescription and over-the-counter medications.

These comments illustrate the range of concerns rehabilitation teachers are called upon to address in regard to medications. In addition to suggesting ways that people with vision problems can label and identify medications, rehabilitation teachers may need to help clients identify the purpose of each medication and clarify the instructions for its use, devise adaptive methods for clients to measure medicine or break pills accurately, and provide consultation on adaptations to nurses who are teaching visually impaired individuals to operate peritoneal dialysis equipment for kidney failure or catheter equipment.

It is helpful if the rehabilitation teacher is familiar with common medications for hypertension, glaucoma, diabetes, heart, or circulatory problems in order to notice whether a client is taking two kinds of medication for the same problem and consultation with the client's physician, pharmacist, or county health resource service might be indicated. Overmedication is common in elderly persons, who may not realize that they are having medication-induced difficulties, and an itinerant rehabilitation teacher may be in a position to notice such problems.

Labeling medication for identification can be as simple as placing different numbers of rubber bands around each bottle. However, some clients will need additional information, such as how many times a day a particular medication must be taken, so the rehabilitation teacher works with each individual to develop a system that works best for him or her. Clients with enough vision can ask their pharmacist to print out their prescription label and instructions in large print or may be able to use a CCTV or other prescribed low vision devices to read the label. Other suggestions for medication management offered by veteran teachers include organizing medications together based on time of day they must be administered (for example, morning medications go on the kitchen table lazy susan; nighttime medications are placed on the night stand); applying distinctive tactile labels to identify different medications by number, shape, and color (specially devised labels are available from catalogs of adaptive products); and using a commercially available seven-day pill holder with 28 compartments (4 per day for each day of the week) identified with raised-print and braille symbols, which can be filled either by the client or family member or visiting nurse. Other labeling suggestions are offered in Chapter 12.

Diabetes Management

Over 16 million people, or about 6 percent of the U.S. population, have either Type I (insulin-dependent) or Type II (non-insulin dependent) diabetes (American Diabetes Association, 1996). Diabetes is a chronic disease affecting the metabolism of carbohydrates in which the body either does not produce insulin or does not use it effectively. Control of diabetes involves maintaining near-normal blood glucose levels through control of diet; exercise; and, for many, medication, including insulin. Long-term diabetes can cause a variety of complications, including peripheral vascular disease, kidney disease, nerve complications, and diabetic eye disease (retinopathy). Nearly 98 percent of those who have had diabetes for more than 15 years will experience some vision loss, and many will become severely visually impaired (American Diabetes Association, 1996).

Because the number of persons with diabetes-related vision loss is increasing, rehabilitation teachers are more frequently being called on to assist such individuals with the tasks involved in managing their condition. The rehabilitation teacher most often works as a member of a team with physicians, nurses, diabetes educators, and others.

A collaborative effort by nurses, diabetes educators, and rehabilitation teachers has resulted in a comprehensive manual entitled *Diabetes and Visual Impairment: An Educator's Resource Guide* (Cleary, 1994), funded by the Education and Research Foundation of the American Association of Diabetes Educators. Rehabilitation teachers are encouraged to read this publication and subscribe to the *Diabetes Forecast*, the bimonthly publication of the American Diabetes Association, to become more familiar with diabetes and diabetes management. *Diabetes Forecast* compiles an annual consumer's guide to diabetes management products in the October issue, which now includes a section on devices for those with visual impairments.

One of the areas addressed by rehabilitation teachers is insulin measurement, since nearly 43 percent of adults with diabetes use insulin (American Diabetes Association, 1996). Persons with insulin-dependent diabetes mellitus must inject one or more types of insulin one or more times daily to treat the disease. They also need to test the level of glucose in their blood, often several times a day. Although it is the role of the physician, nurse, or diabetes educator to provide treatment and instruction about controlling diabetes, rehabilitation teachers are often the source of information and instruction regarding techniques and adaptive devices for measuring insulin and blood glucose levels (Ponchillia, 1993a; Ponchillia & LaGrow, 1988; Ponchillia, Richardson, & Turner-Barry, 1990) for persons with diabetes and visual impairments.

Insulin Measurement

The rehabilitation teacher frequently provides resources and instruction to assist those who have difficulty seeing well enough to measure insulin. His or her role may range from providing the medical team with information about adaptive devices to actually teaching the client to measure insulin accurately using adaptive methods or devices in collaboration with the medical team.

A variety of products are available (see Resources section) to assist persons who have little or no usable vision with insulin measurement (Petzinger, 1992; 1993). Most are considered extremely accurate, but people who have difficulty with fine motor movements or other problems as a result of their diabetes may not always achieve precise measures (Ponchillia, Richardson, & Turner-Barry, 1990). Typically, rehabilitation teachers will introduce the client to a variety of adaptive insulin measurement devices to assess his or her ability with each. The client and teacher can then decide together which device best meets the client's needs and provides the most successful and accurate independent measurement.

Specific needs addressed by various devices include measuring insulin accurately with low or no vision, getting the syringe needle into the insulin vial without blunting or bending it, managing two types of insulin in one dose, and preventing air bubbles in the syringe. The devices available from specialty catalogs that help with accurate measurement usually include some form of holder for the syringe and/or vial to make it easier to direct the needle into the vial. Some hold two vials at once to facilitate mixed doses, and others allow the vials to be changed without disturbing the syringe for the same purpose. These devices often include needle guides; measurement mechanisms, such as a click wheel that gives tactile and auditory feedback for each unit of insulin; and magnifiers that allow the scales on the barrel of the syringe to be seen more easily. Often, however, the magnification of commercial syringe magnification devices is low (2X–3X), and few clients who are legally blind can make use of them unless they use additional magnifiers in combination with the syringe magnifier. Clients with low vision can also be encouraged to apply information about lighting, contrast, and illumination to improve the visual environment where insulin will be drawn. For example, use of a free-standing lighted magnifier intended for craft projects may improve an individual's ability to measure insulin.

Preventing air bubbles in the syringe is an important part of measuring insulin. Air bubbles need to be avoided not so much because of the danger they present, since it would take a very large air bubble injected directly into a vein to cause significant problems, but because air in the syringe replaces the prescribed dose of insulin that is necessary to control the diabetes. There are a number of techniques to avoid air bubbles and ensure that the full amount of insulin is in the syringe:

- Holding the vial of insulin upright, inject air into the vial with the syringe, pressing the plunger in firmly. Then invert the vial and withdraw the full amount of insulin.
- Withdraw a small amount of insulin into the syringe and then return it to the vial before withdrawing the full dose. Expelling a small amount from the syringe will eject any small bubbles that have collected at the tip.
- Discard the vial when the amount of insulin is no longer sufficient to guarantee that a dose can be withdrawn without exposing the tip of the needle to air in the vial. The appropriate time for this is determined by calculating the precise number of safe doses contained in a new vial and using a careful recordkeeping system to keep track of the number of doses withdrawn. Standard vials hold 10 cc's of insulin, equivalent to 1,000 units, and at least 60 units must remain in a 1,000-unit vial to avoid withdrawing air instead of insulin. This leaves 940 units of insulin available for safe withdrawal.

Depending on the number of units the client withdraws for each dose, he or she can calculate how many syringes can be safely filled before he or she must discard the vial. For example, Kathy G. uses 30 units of regular insulin once daily and 10 units of long-acting insulin twice daily. She can withdraw from the regular vial a full month (940 units ÷ 30 units/injection = 31.3333 injections). Because she injects the long-acting insulin twice a day, she uses 20 units each day (10 units/injection x 2 = 20 units/day). Therefore, she can use the vial of long-acting insulin for nearly six weeks before discarding it (940 units ÷ 20 units/day = 47 days).

If avoiding air bubbles in the syringe is based on calculating the number of safe doses in the vial,

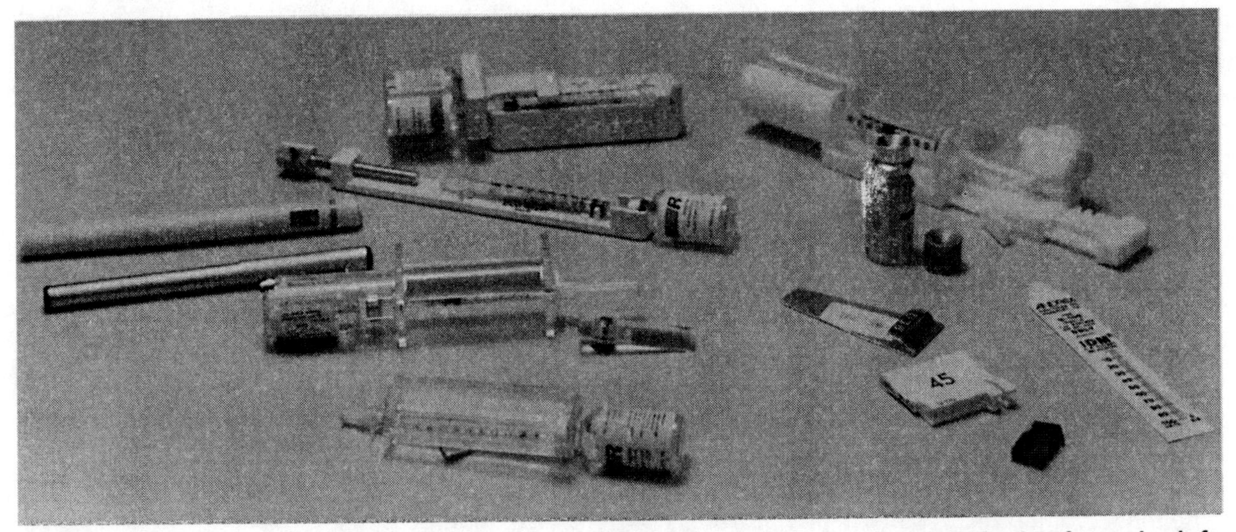

Adaptive insulin measurement devices for persons with low or no vision. Clockwise from the left: pen injectors, tactile insulin measurement devices and needleguides, and syringe magnifiers.

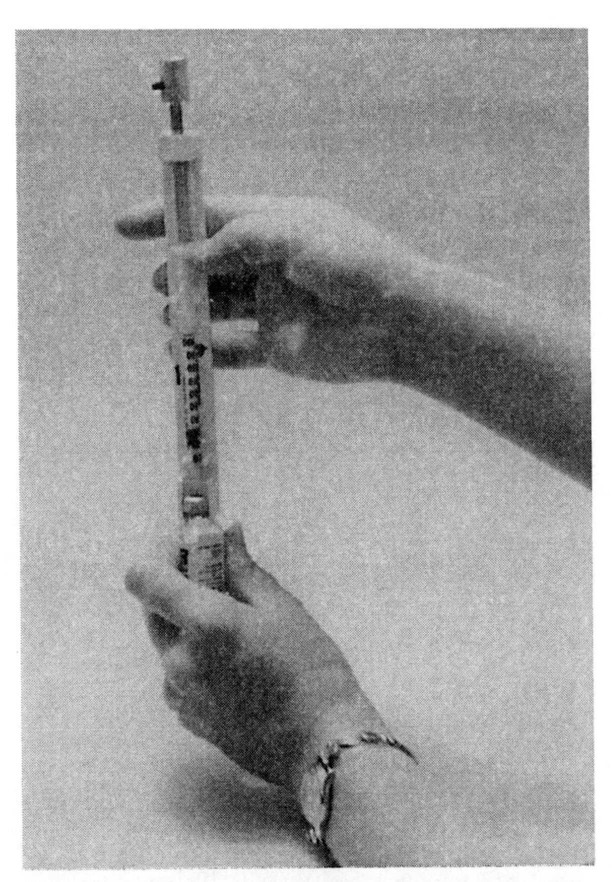

Injecting air into the insulin vial while it is right side up helps to avoid bubbles in the syringe.

then recordkeeping must be foolproof to avoid potentially dangerous situations. Disposable syringes make good counters for measuring how many injections to withdraw from a vial. They can be counted out as a new vial is started, and when they are gone, the vial is considered unusable. Or, the client can keep track of the number of days a vial can be safely used, rather than the number of doses. In the previous example, Kathy could begin a new bottle of regular insulin on the first day of each month, since the maximum of 31 dosages allows her a month's use. For her long-acting insulin, she could set aside 47 disposable syringes when beginning a new bottle, which would be discarded when all the syringes were used up.

Some rehabilitation teachers and agency administrators are concerned about the possibility of litigation arising as a result of a client or family member contending that the instruction provided in adaptive insulin measurement led to problems. Potential liability can be avoided through careful practice and documentation, including the following:

- Work as part of the team providing services to the individual, so that the physician, diabetes educator, or nurse can each provide his or her own expertise.
- Set a goal for accuracy within 1 unit of the desired dosage.
- Document the client's progress and performance levels.
- Make sure the client's performance is consistent by monitoring it over time and having the client periodically demonstrate continued accuracy to a spouse, partner, or physician (Berkowitz et al., 1993).

Observance of these suggestions will help ensure accurate and successful insulin measurement by clients who wish to do this independently.

Performance during insulin measurement lessons can be documented through two measures: the percentage of accuracy and dosage safety. Percentage of accuracy can be calculated by comparing the desired dosage with the actual dosage that was drawn into the syringe by the client. If they are exactly the same, the client's accuracy was 100 per cent for that draw. If the actual dosage is not the same as the desired dosage, the percentage is calculated by dividing the smaller number by the larger number and multiplying by 100 (Ponchillia, Richardson, Turner-Barry, 1990):

$$\text{Accuracy} = \frac{\text{smaller dosage}}{\text{larger dose}} \times 100$$

The measurement of dosage safety is more subjective, but should include whether the client is able to verbalize the method he or she is using to ensure that there is sufficient insulin in the vial; whether the needle remains straight rather than bent while the syringe is filled; and whether the client identifies the correct vial of insulin. If an error is made in any of these steps, then the dose would be considered unsafe, even if it had been measured with 100 per cent accuracy.

The percentage of accuracy can be recorded or graphed and included in the client's progress notes together with the determinations of safe or unsafe dosages. This record can be used by the teacher and client in making a joint decision about which device provides the greatest accuracy and safety for that client. If a client has difficulty following the prescribed techniques for accurate measurement, the rehabilitation teacher should caution the client not to measure his or her own insulin independently until he or she achieves adequate safety and accuracy through further instruction or alternate methods.

Not every visually impaired individual with diabetes is capable of measuring insulin independently. Occasionally, diabetic hand syndrome, neuropathy, or other multihandicapping conditions interfere with successful measurement (Davidson, 1991; Ponchillia, 1993a). In that event, the rehabilitation and medical team can work together to provide alternate solutions. These may include employing a visiting nurse to draw insulin daily and perhaps perform other related tasks; having a family member or visiting nurse draw a number of syringes several days ahead; or using premeasured syringes. The rehabilitation teacher may need to devise a labeling system if premeasured syringes or syringes drawn ahead of time have to be separated according to the size of the dosage.

Glucose Monitoring

Individuals with diabetes need to monitor the level of glucose in the blood to make sure that the insulin and other health measures are properly regulating the amount of sugar in the blood. Monitoring this may need to be done up to several times daily and is accomplished at home using chemically treated strips that are compared to a color chart or using an electronic glucose monitor. The availability of glucose monitors with speech output now allows individuals with diabetes who have limited vision to be independent.

Most glucose monitors require a drop of blood (usually referred to as a "hanging drop") to be placed on a reagent strip. Small pen-sized spring-loaded lancet devices are used to prick the side of the fingertip between the fingernail and pad of the finger. The accuracy of readings may be reduced if the finger itself touches the reagent pad, so most manufacturers suggest dropping the blood over the target area or gently touching the drop only to the target area. The reagent strip is inserted somewhere in or on the machine. The machine scans the strip to analyze the color change caused by the blood glucose on the reagent pad and displays the result digitally, in milligrams per decilitre.

It is possible for persons with visual impairments to measure accurately and independently their own blood glucose levels using speech-output machines, standard glucose monitors with speech output attachments (see Resources section), or machines that have large, contrasting color displays. Some people with low vision can make use of their prescribed low vision aids to monitor the digital display of a standard glucose monitor. However, people with little or no useful vision may need assistance with several aspects of glucose monitoring, including obtaining a sufficient blood sample and placing the blood in the proper location on the reagent strip. Ponchilla and LaGrow (1988) and Cleary (1994) suggest following specific sequential procedures to ensure success with independent nonvisual glucose monitoring:

- Arrange equipment and supplies on a tray.
- Wash the hands in warm water just prior to the test.
- Keep hands below the heart to increase the blood flow.
- Use a preestablished location on the distal (outward) side of the finger for lancing. This makes it easier to locate the target area because the thumb is not in the way and the hand does not have to rotate inward to touch the blood to the strip.

- Gently apply pressure to or milk the finger down its length toward the tip to encourage formation of a sufficient blood droplet, counting the number of strokes. Have a sighted observer note how many times the finger must be milked before an adequate blood sample (a "hanging drop") forms.
- Lance the finger near the monitor so the blood sample is not likely to be bumped or jolted off while moving the finger toward the target area.
- To avoid awkward gestures, angle the machine so that the hand can reach out at its natural angle to deposit the blood on the strip placed in the machine. This is the same principle as angling a piece of paper to make it easier to write.
- Locate the target area by using landmarks on the machine, such as straight or curved parts, or raised dots or other tactile or contrasting markings.

Although clients may not be successful during the first lesson or two, most will eventually be able to monitor their glucose levels independently if they work with the rehabilitation teacher or diabetes educator to control any variables that interfere with success. For example, if the client has trouble knowing whether sufficient blood is available for an accurate sample, the teacher would, over a number of attempts, identify the minimum number of gentle "milkings" the client would need to give the finger to be sure that a hanging drop of blood would form after lancing the finger. Using small plastic pipettes to gather blood and disperse it onto the target area may also assist those who have difficulty getting the blood on the strip. In addition, some glucose monitors can be fitted with attachments to help aim the blood onto the strip.

Noninvasive means of testing blood glucose levels are currently awaiting approval, and these may solve the difficulties involved in glucose monitoring. Although no such methods are currently available, the equipment will most likely be adapt-

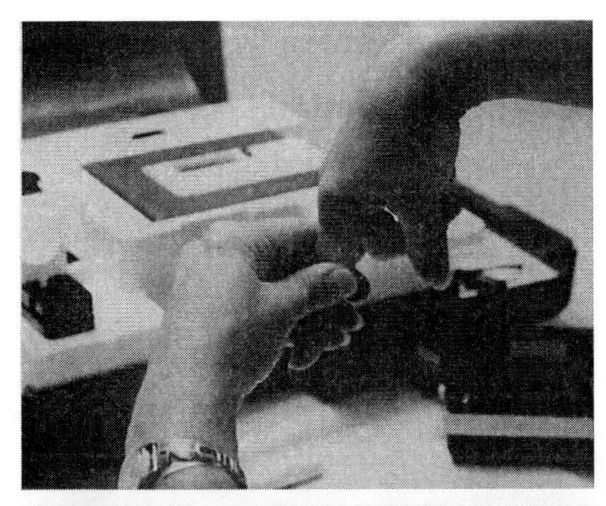

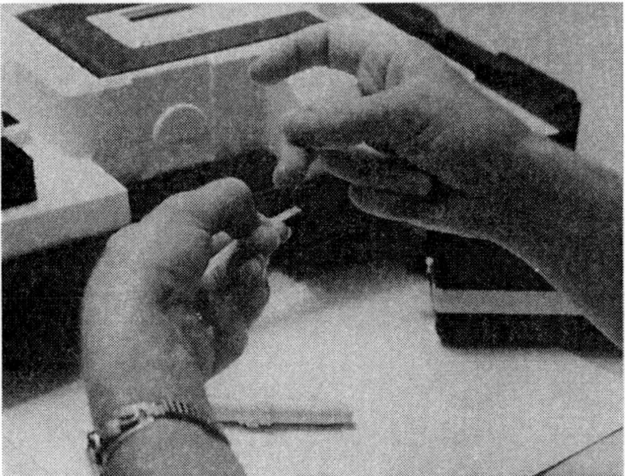

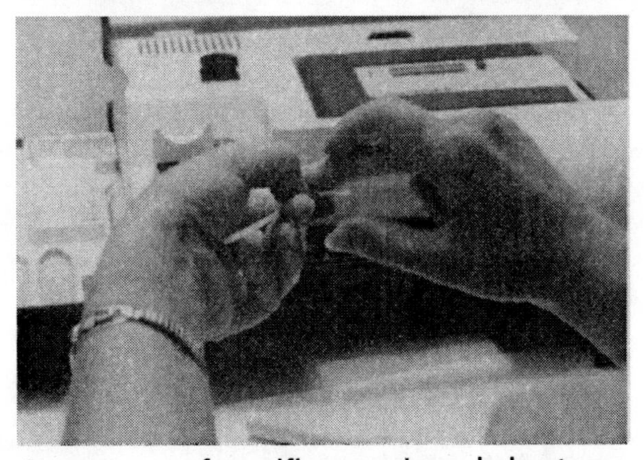

A sequence of specific procedures helps to ensure accurate glucose monitoring, including (from top to bottom), counting the number of times the finger must be "milked" to produce a "hanging drop," lancing the finger on the outside, and touching only the drop of blood, not the finger, to the strip.

ed with voice output when it is fully developed.

As is evident from the scope of this chapter, personal management skills cover an enormous range of activities. Mastering these skills is of the utmost importance to people who are blind or visually impaired because it allows them to care independently for their most personal needs. Therefore, the rehabilitation teacher needs to focus considerable attention on this area. Similarly, home management skills are significant because they make it possible for people who are visually impaired to function independently in their home environment. These skills will be considered next.

CHAPTER 15

Home Management Skills

KEY CONCEPTS IN THIS CHAPTER

- The role of the rehabilitation teacher in teaching home care and home mechanics skills
- The importance of organization in the completion of home care and home mechanics tasks
- Ways of adapting living quarters to make them safer and more livable for a person with low vision
- Adaptive techniques utilized to accomplish home cleaning tasks
- Differences in teaching home care skills to those who learned these skills before vision loss and those who had little or no previous experience in this area
- The unique role of home mechanics in the self-image rebuilding process
- Adaptive methods used in accomplishing home mechanics tasks

Home management skills allow an individual who is visually impaired to maintain a clean and safe living environment. Being able to take care of one's home or living space is an essential part of being independent. Even someone who is not the primary caretaker should be familiar with home care skills so that he or she can contribute equitably to the household. Home management is therefore an important part of the endeavor to build or restore the individual's self-esteem and independence in rehabilitation teaching.

Home management skills include the ability to detect soiled surfaces; to dust, wash, mop, polish, and wax; to make beds; and generally to care for one's home. Thus, household safety and home repair, also called home mechanics, are part of home management as well. The adaptations required for home care are relatively simple and are based on two main ideas: organization and overdoing of cleaning tasks. Sidebar 15.1 summarizes some common adaptations for home management tasks.

ORGANIZATION

Organizational skills are presented in detail in Chapter 12. In general, organization of the tools and products needed for a particular job is essential for people with severely limited vision, whether the task relates to cleaning or to home mechanics. For example, while cleaning house it is all too easy to set the furniture polish down somewhere and then misplace it while the dustcloth or feather duster is being used. Thus, wearing an apron with pockets containing furniture polish,

SIDEBAR 15.1

Common Adaptations for Home Management

CLEANING SMALL FLAT SURFACES (DUSTING TABLETOPS, WASHING WINDOWS OR MIRRORS)

1. Use a consistent pattern for coverage, for example, from top left to bottom right.
2. Use overlapping strokes, repeating, if necessary, at a right angle to the original strokes.
3. Monitor tactilely if necessary.

CLEANING FLOORS (SWEEPING, VACUUMING, MOPPING)

1. Use the perimeter of the room to maintain orientation.
2. Use overlapping strokes away from the perimeter toward the center.
3. Monitor cleanliness with a stockinged foot if necessary.
4. Subdivide the area with strategically placed items of furniture.
5. Overclean and perform preventive cleanup.

MAKING A BED

1. Determine the correct side of bedclothes by finding the seams.
2. Monitor neatness tactilely if necessary.
3. Use safety pins at the midpoints of the bedding to mark the center of linens so the ends hanging over are even.
4. Stand at the center of the foot or the head of the bed to center bedding.

dust cloth, and feather duster will prevent a great deal of frustration, since each item can be placed back into its compartment when not being used.

Organization of home furnishings can also be of benefit. In general, people who are already familiar with their living quarters adapt quickly to moving around without vision and have little difficulty. However, minor injury can be prevented by making simple changes, such as placing a nonskid throw rug to act as a tactile warning near a low table or at the head of a staircase. Injuries caused by running into the edges of doors or drawers can be prevented for the most part by following a practice of always closing cupboard doors or drawers after use and always opening or closing doors fully.

Manipulation of furnishings can be especially helpful to those who have low vision. Dickman (1983) described many beneficial modifications based primarily on increasing visibility by adding lighting or making use of contrast in the living environment. Increased lighting in danger areas, such as staircases, and in work areas, such as the kitchen or workshop, and nightlights in the bedroom and bathroom can make it safer and easier to move around the house and accomplish the necessary tasks.

In the living room or bedroom, throw rugs or furniture covers that contrast with the surroundings can make nearby objects more visible and make it easier for people with low vision to judge distances. In the kitchen, increasing contrast by using dark- or light-colored mats, work surfaces, or trays can make food preparation easier and may decrease glare from the kitchen counter. Readers can consult Dickman (1983) for a more thorough discussion of this subject.

CLEANING

Many individuals who previously took care of their own homes when they had full vision give up their cleaning responsibilities after losing sight because they feel it is no longer possible to do them effectively. The rehabilitation teacher can assure such clients that they will be able to resume these chores with just a few simple adaptations.

House cleaning involves determining the appearance of an area and either preventive or remedial methods for maintaining cleanliness. Dirty surfaces can be detected by touch in most cases, since, for example, soiled countertops are not slick, fine dust on a tabletop is gritty, and dirty

Cleaning small areas is most efficient if small objects are cleared away first, and then a systematic pattern of coverage is followed.

stovetop burners are usually sticky. Preventive cleaning, which is discussed in Chapter 12, is based on the assumption that, even if one does not feel or see dirt, grease, or spills, a surface might be soiled nonetheless. Routine wiping of all countertop surfaces after food preparation, cleaning a microwave after each use, and a weekly mopping of the kitchen floor are examples of preventive cleaning. The process of cleaning—whether dusting, washing, or sweeping—is accomplished by using systematic patterns and essentially overdoing the job. The most commonly used system is a pattern of overlapping strokes in one direction, followed by a series of overlapping perpendicular strokes. Instruction follows a sequence from small surfaces, such as mirrors and windows, that can be be cleaned all at once without moving, to areas such as countertops and tabletops that might require one move to complete, to larger areas, such as floors, in which a visually impaired individual can become disoriented.

Performing tasks involving large areas—for example, vacuuming a carpet or mopping a vinyl floor—is more difficult than cleaning small surfaces, particularly for people who are totally blind, because of the need to maintain one's orientation. People without vision have a tendency to turn in a circle without knowing it when they do not keep in contact with a stationary object. Therefore, to maintain orientation, it is helpful to make contact with a sofa or wall. One technique for vacuuming a room is to place one's heels against a sofa, wall, or cabinet along the perimeter of the room and then vacuum with overlapping strokes at a 90-degree angle away from the wall. When the area of a floor to be cleaned is so large that strokes made from the perimeter will not reach the center of the room, the rehabilitation teacher can show the client how to place a

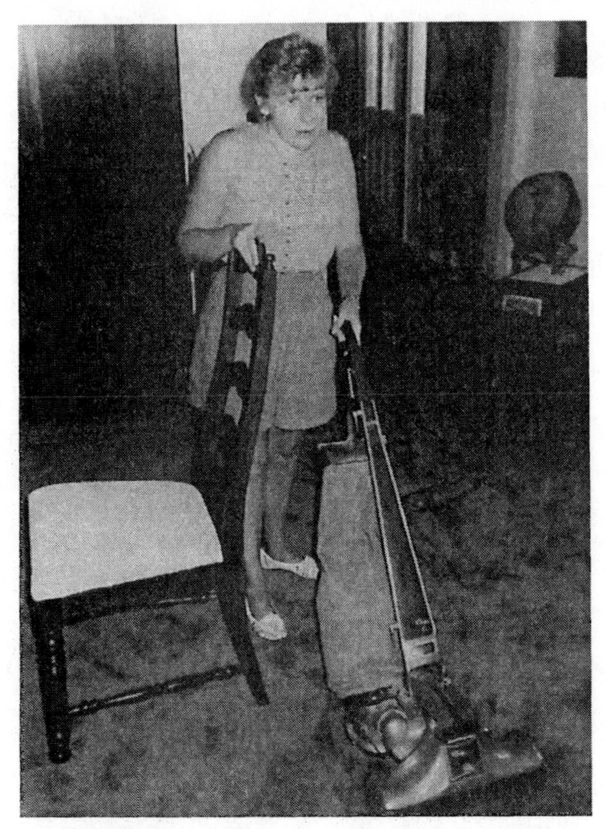

Cleaning larger areas is most efficient if a landmark is established for orientation and a systematic pattern of coverage is followed.

chair or other large object strategically in the room to serve as a landmark that subdivides it into manageable segments. As the area beside the landmark is cleaned, the landmark can be moved over to mark off the next section. In general, if the room can be divided into areas approximately 8 feet square, they can be cleaned one at a time until the entire surface area is done. Even a large area such as a lawn can be subdivided with lawn furniture or trash receptacles in this manner for raking leaves, or possibly for mowing grass.

As is the case with other daily living skills, clients who have never had usable vision may not have had previous experience with cleaning tasks and may need to learn the meaning of such concepts such as clean and dirty, full coverage, scrub, sweep, and mop, before going on to cleaning skills and adaptations. Establishing the concept of clean and dirty is usually not a complicated matter, unless a client has developmental disabilities or has been extraordinarily overprotected. However, a significant number of clients will have had little or no experience with scrubbing, mopping, and other cleaning jobs. The movements required to accomplish such tasks can usually be taught by modeling them. However, the rehabilitation teacher might need to pay particular attention to such details as keeping a broom in the proper sweeping position, using the proper amount of liquid or granular cleaning products, moving a broom back and forth the necessary degree and slowly enough to avoid blowing dust around the room, and reaching out an adequate distance with a broom or mop to complete the task effectively.

The cleaning process itself can be used to dictate the teaching sequence for those who need to learn the basics. Once the concept of clean and dirty is understood, the teacher might progress to dusting; scrubbing and polishing or waxing small flat surfaces; washing mirrors and windows; sweeping, mopping, and polishing or waxing floors; and vacuuming carpeted areas.

Clients who are learning to vacuum for the first time should have a chance to investigate the machine and its attachments. The rehabilitation teacher should point out such features as the on-off switch; height controls for different types of rugs; carpet beater bar, floor, and brush attachments; belts; and disposable or reusable vacuum bags. The rehabilitation teacher might even include a visit to an appliance store as part of the lesson so the student can examine the variety of vacuum cleaners he or she might encounter. A complete lesson would include a discussion of troubleshooting and how to check for problems if the machine makes an unusual sound, which might indicate a large object or carpet strands tangled in the beater bar or a broken belt. At least one client who had not been told to watch out for unusual sounds or smells left burned streaks in the carpet everywhere she pushed the vacuum when the belt came loose and the motor overheated. Finally, the teacher may consider deliberately scattering something "noisy" around the room as part of a lesson, before the student vacuums, as a novice cleaner can learn much from the reinforcing sound of bits of cereal being sucked into the vacuum.

MAKING BEDS

Making a bed is relatively simple to do by touch. The proper side of the sheet or blanket can be determined by feeling the side where the seam is sewn, which is nearly always the underside. Sheets normally have a larger seam at the head and a smaller one at the foot. Since bedclothes are supposed to fit symmetrically, the evenness of the overhang of sheets or blankets on either side of the bed can be used to monitor their positioning. Some people find it easier to center the sheet on the bed by pinning a safety pin in the middle of the sheet at the bottom, standing at the foot of the bed halfway between the sides, and placing the pinned area of the sheet at that spot. The pin can be left in permanently to assist with folding the sheet after laundering.

HOME MECHANICS

Living independently also entails managing minor home mechanics tasks such as replacing screws, repairing leaky faucets or toilets, changing fuses, or hanging pictures. The inability to accomplish chores such as these can cause inconvenience; expense, if a repairperson must be employed; and frustration, to say the least. Most people feel a sense of satisfaction and independence when they are able to make their own home repairs. According to Utrup (1974), if these skills were important to an individual before sight loss, they usually play a significant role in the process of rebuilding the self-image, as was the case with Tom H., an accomplished woodworker and handyman who was mentioned briefly in Chapter 12.

Tom H. arrived at the rehabilitation center on Sunday afternoon and was assigned to classes on Monday. Because he had been quite a handyman before his sight loss—in fact, he had built his own cabin in the north woods—one of his first scheduled classes was home mechanics.

When Tom did not come to the home mechanics class at the assigned time, the rehabilitation teacher went to his room to check on him. Visibly upset, Tom said he did not want to go to class because he couldn't do any handywork without vision. The teacher discussed the problem until Tom calmed down and agreed to come to the home mechanics class the following day. The next day, however, Tom again did not show up and the instructor again had to visit his room, where he finally persuaded the distraught Tom to come to the workshop.

After a long time spent trying to convince Tom that he could use tools with no vision, the instructor managed to begin a nailing lesson, and he showed Tom how to hammer nails. Tom had a little trouble at first, but after five or six nails, he was hammering away with ease. Tom was overjoyed to the point of tears, and for the rest of the class period he pounded nails nonstop. New possibilities for a life without sight had clearly opened up for him, and his self-esteem was considerably bolstered.

Home mechanics is often considered the introduction to advanced woodworking, metalwork, and other industrial arts skills. Because the major purpose of teaching advanced home mechanics skills is to restore self-image, they are usually taught only to those who enjoyed doing home repairs before sight loss, such as Tom H. Skills relating to home safety, such as changing fuses or resetting circuit breakers, shutting off the main water supply in case of emergency leaks, using fire extinguishers, and changing batteries in smoke alarms, are important for anyone who plans to live independently. Therefore, home safety skills are taught to clients more often than other, more advanced home mechanics skills. Skills such as repairing doorknobs or hinges, wiring an electric plug, changing washers in the faucets, unplugging drains, and repairing a toilet mechanism are all easily accomplished by touch or with low vision, for the most part using standard, traditional tools. Most of the adaptations required to perform home repair chores are organizational, such as separating tools according to type, always storing them in their designated place, and using a carpenter's apron to hold the tools and parts needed to accomplish a specific task. For those with low vision, the organizational schemes would include making use of increased lighting and contrast as well. Three home repair tasks—hammering, sawing, and sanding—require more elaborate adaptations than do most others, and they will be discussed in more detail. Sidebar 15.2 outlines some adaptations commonly used in home mechanics.

Home Safety

If clients are to live independently or are to be alone for long periods, they must know how to handle common emergencies. If a water pipe bursts because it is frozen, the main water supply must be shut off; if a fuse blows or a circuit breaker is tripped, it must be replaced or reset to restore power; and if a kitchen fire ignites, it must be extinguished. Home environmental monitors, such as smoke or carbon monoxide detectors, must also be kept in working order. If a client has lived in the home or apartment before sight loss, he or she probably already knows how to find the water shut off, deal with the circuit breakers, and maintain the detectors. If a client is not familiar with

Common Adaptations for Home Mechanics

SIDEBAR 15.2

NAILING

1. Hold the nail near the head, not against the wood or other surface.
2. Strike the nail with two strokes, the first a tap to locate it and the second the driving stroke.
3. Hold the hammer nearer the head for added control when learning how to use it.

SAWING WOOD

1. Use a large print, raised-dot, or click ruler.
2. Drive a scratch awl into the wood to mark the measured length.
3. Use the scratch awl and a try square to scratch a line along which to saw.
4. Saw along the engraved line or use a C-clamp and a small board to make a saw guide along the engraved line.
5. Use a mitre box if an exact cut is crucial.

SANDING WOOD

1. Determine the direction of grain tactilely (usually lengthwise on a board).
2. Apply a little water to the surface of the board to raise the grain.
3. Determine grit size of sandpaper tactilely.

any of these simple skills—usually the case only if someone has been blind since childhood—a rehabilitation teacher can generally teach them in a few minutes. The only special instruction required would be basic adaptive techniques such as labeling; the use of tactile clues; and low vision adaptations to improve visibility such as improving contrast or using a flashlight to increase visibility.

Most individuals are less familiar with the use of fire extinguishers than they are with other safety measures and will likely require some instruction and adaptation. Utrup (1974) made the following suggestions:

- Dry fire extinguishers are probably best for home use by individuals with visual impairments because they are effective in fighting a broad range of fires.
- Clients should be taught to point the extinguisher nozzle not at the flames but at the base of a fire, where the actual combustion is taking place; this can be determined tactilely by the source of the heat.
- The fire extinguisher should be moved in a back-and-forth sweeping motion, using the arms rather than the wrists.
- General safety measures that should always be taken in case of a fire include:
  - Always stay between the fire and an exit.
  - Fight the fire only for the life of the extinguisher; then leave the scene if it is not out.
  - Call the fire department about a fire of any size, even if you think it is extinguished.

Hammering

Hammering nails can be accomplished without sight, and most clients could undertake this task with little instruction if they had sufficient confidence. However, many newly visually impaired persons would probably not attempt it. The rehabilitation teacher might approach the teaching of hammering by initially using short, stout nails and by teaching two adaptive techniques (Utrup, 1974). The first involves the manner in which the nail is held. Typically, the nail is grasped between the first finger and thumb near its point and against the board or other surface into which it is to be driven. Holding it near the nailhead is actually safer, however, because if the fingers are struck with the hammer, they are then knocked aside rather than smashed against the board. The second technique is to use a two-stroke hammering method. The hammerer locates the nail on the first stroke by lightly tapping it, then follows with a more forceful stroke to sink it into the wood. The index finger touches the side of the nailhead to locate it during the first tapping stroke, but is removed before the second forceful stroke. The resulting sound pattern is tap-bang, tap-bang, tap-bang, rather than the familiar bang, bang, bang.

Sawing

The major adaptations needed for sawing relate to measuring, marking a sawing line, and maintaining a square cut. Tactile or enlarged adaptations are available for each of the tasks (Utrup, 1974). Measuring is one aspect of home mechanics in which adapted tools are used: these include raised-dot rulers, click rulers, and large-print rulers; the choice of which to use will depend on the individual's needs and amount of usable vision. Raised-dot rulers are similar to any other, but the lines marking the inch, half-inch, and quarter-inch increments are made by various numbers of raised dots, with the inch line the longest and containing the most dots. The ruler is also marked with braille numbers, but it is not necessary to know braille to use it. The click ruler is set up so that a rod pulled away from the ruler's main body clicks once for each sixteenth-inch it is extended. Both tactile rulers, as well as large-print rulers, are available from vendors of adaptive aids (see the Resources section).

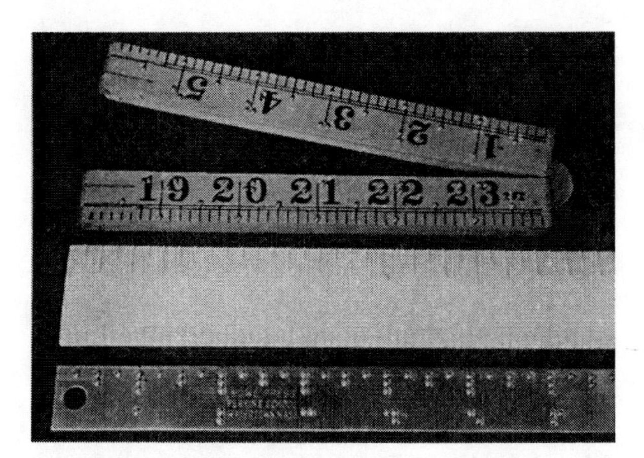

Examples of adapted rulers: large print with braille numbers (top); raised lines (center); raised dots with braille numbers (bottom).

After the desired length of board to be cut has been measured, the spot is marked by sinking a common scratch awl into the wood at that point. A try square is then slid along the board, using the awl as a stop. With the try square held tightly in place, the awl is removed and used to make a deep scratch along the edge of the square. The awl, in this case, becomes the adaptive replacement for a pencil. A felt marker can also be used for this purpose if the user has enough vision to see the marking.

The actual cut can be made in several ways, but all are easier when the board is placed in a vice. To make freehand sawing easier, the saw can be placed in the scratch awl gouge and moved back and forth a few times to deepen the mark. Sawing can then be monitored by pausing occasionally to check the straightness of the cut with the fingers. A saw guide, created by attaching a small piece of wood onto the board with a C-clamp so that its edge lines up with the scratch awl line, will guide the saw along the mark to ensure a square cut. If the cut must be made at an exact angle, the carpenter can use a mitre box, a commercially available tool designed for this purpose.

Sanding

Like most other tasks, sanding wooden surfaces can be accomplished without sight. However, because sanding must be done in the direction of the wood grain, one adaptation is required. Usually, the direction of the wood grain can be determined tactilely, but if the wood is old or has paint on it, the grain cannot be felt. Since the grain generally runs in the direction of the longest dimension of the board, sanding lengthwise will usually give the desired result. If the correct direction is in doubt, however, applying a small amount of water to a piece of wood and waiting a few minutes will nearly always cause the grain to rise enough to make it tactilely discernible.

When sanding woodcrafts or repairing wood surfaces, it is necessary to know the grit size of the sandpaper being used, which indicates its coarseness, because it affects the texture of the finished product. Individuals with low vision may be able to read the grit numbers on the back of the sandpaper using low vision devices or strategies. People with no usable vision can depend on tactile ability to discriminate between coarse-, medium-, and fine-grit paper.

The learning of home management and home repair skills frequently starts out as a way of maintaining a household independently. For many individuals, both with and without visual impairments, however, the satisfaction of producing a finished piece of work and developing advanced skills evolves into a hobby and a form of relaxation as well. As such, it contributes to both the enjoyment of a full life and the reinforcement of self-confidence and self-esteem. An endless assortment of activities can serve the same important functions for other individuals. Methods of adapting a variety of leisure-time activities to the needs of people who are visually impaired are discussed in the next chapter.

CHAPTER 16

Leisure-Time Pursuits

KEY CONCEPTS IN THIS CHAPTER

- **The role of leisure and craft activities in the rehabilitation process**
- **The role of the rehabilitation teacher in teaching recreation and leisure-time skills**
- **The adaptive techniques needed to perform craft hobbies, including sewing**
- **The adaptive techniques used to modify games and playing cards for persons with visual impairments**
- **Resources for recreation, leisure, and sports activities**

Leisure-time activities make up an important component of personal adjustment training. Personal interests and ways of spending spare time that are enjoyed and valued play a vital part in everyone's life. Moreover, the leisure-time pursuits of people who are blind and visually impaired are as varied as are the individuals themselves (Ludwig, Luxton, & Attmore, 1988). It is therefore essential for the rehabilitation teacher to help individual clients find ways of adapting such valued activities so that they can be enjoyed, despite a loss of vision.

Because a large majority of the caseloads of many rehabilitation teachers are made up of elderly retired persons with low vision, crafts are likely to be an important focus of instruction. Ponchillia and Kaarlela (1986) found that at least 35 percent of the visually impaired persons in their study who had undergone rehabilitation participated in some form of crafts or hobbies. Furthermore, participating in a pleasurable manipulative activity is an effective way for persons who recently have become visually impaired to develop their fine and gross motor tactile skills and to increase their self-esteem, thereby assisting in rebuilding their own self-image.

This chapter addresses the craft hobbies that traditionally have been taught by rehabilitation teachers, sewing, commonly played games, and other leisure and recreational activities. As with other daily living skills, those who were previously accustomed to participating in crafts, hobbies, or leisure activities are likely to continue them with a few adaptations, whereas those who first learn these skills when they have a visual impairment may need additional instruction.

CRAFTS AND HOBBIES

Unless the client is a novice, no particular teaching sequence is generally followed for the skills involved in pursuing crafts or hobbies. In such circumstances, prepackaged kits (such as those for leatherwork or building a wooden birdhouse) provide a helpful way to learn beginning activities. As with personal care in areas such as grooming and hygiene, the individual client's preferences, desires, needs, and interests determine which activity is the first focus of instruction. In addition to the client's preference and prior experience, an assessment of the client's gross and fine motor skills is necessary, because those with limited experience in performing tasks requiring fine motor skills, as well as those with new vision loss, may have difficulty when first beginning craft activities. Many individuals find it helpful to start with large items, such as a large crochet hook or knitting needles, thicker yarn or thread for knitting or sewing, and big beads or wooden pieces for beadwork or woodcrafts, until they develop more tactile sophistication. In the beginning, patterns selected for sewing, leatherwork, or woodcrafts should have straight lines or gentle curves, and they will be easier to handle if they are made of thick paper, cardboard, or recycled X-ray film.

Most skills to be learned for crafts and hobbies are accomplished tactilely with relative ease by the majority of people, but to become competent takes practice. It is important for the rehabilitation teacher to remember that individuals who were once experts at a complex hobby may experience frustration and disappointment when reintroduced to it. For example, someone who used to produce fine needlework but is not able to perform at the same level after experiencing vision loss might become discouraged; however, as clients become more familiar with the appropriate adaptations, they may return to the previous level of skill. Even if they do not, over time they may become more comfortable with their degree of competence as part of their overall adjustment, as was the case with Almina L.

> Almina L., an 87-year-old woman with low vision, indicated that she wanted the rehabilitation teacher to help her learn to crochet fine lace collars and cuffs as she used to before her sight loss. Although the teacher did not wish to discourage Almina from her goal, it became apparent during the teacher's assessment that Almina had always been a meticulous craftswoman and would not be pleased with a less than perfect product. She had already tried a variety of adaptive methods, such as improving illumination, using a contrasting background behind her crocheting, and using a magnifier, but she still was unhappy with the results because they did not match up to her exacting standards. Almina could not see or discern tactilely whether the needlework was done properly. She and her rehabilitation teacher continued to work together on ways to achieve that goal, but in the meantime, the teacher introduced Almina to a different form of needlework called rake knitting, a craft done on a wooden or plastic loom with rakelike projections. Almina was delighted with rake knitting, which was easier for her to master because the yarn was larger and thus easier to feel and see. Soon, Almina was showing her friends at a peer-support group how to knit scarves and stocking caps, and she and several others initiated a project to donate their completed products to a local children's shelter.

Thus, providing success and encouragement in initial lessons may be the most important aspect of teaching crafts skills.

Some of the more important adaptations necessary to pursuing leisure-time activities, as with many other endeavors, involve organization of materials. The frustration that comes from not being able to find the proper knitting needle or the correct craft tool is a strong disincentive to continuing work on a project. It is therefore a good idea to review the principles of organization in Chapter 12 before teaching crafts and hobbies. Trays or shallow boxes may assist clients with corralling errant tools and pieces of a craft project, and other individualized storage vessels will help as well. For example, a multidrawer storage unit designed for nuts and bolts, or simply a number of different envelopes or zipper-lock plastic bags can help organize embroidery floss or beads.

Low vision adaptations also are important when clients are working on crafts and other projects. People who are visually impaired may need special instruction in the use of lighting, contrast, and magnification; for example, using contrasting yarn and needles for knitting, a chestborne or lamp magnifier to free the hands for close work such as gluing small parts, and contrasting tools and pegboards to store woodworking tools. (Teachers may wish to review the principles for increasing visibility discussed in Chapter 6.)

SEWING

Although sewing for clothing construction as well as for crafts may not be as necessary a skill today as it once was, most individuals still find a need for basic hand-sewing skills—such as threading needles, mending ripped seams, and replacing buttons—to make simple clothing repairs or to affix clothing labels. A variety of crafts also require needle-threading ability and stitching skills.

When an individual wants or needs to sew, whether by hand or by machine, the first step is to thread the needle. A variety of devices exist to help with this task, but following some general principles will make it simpler, regardless of the method used.

To start, a tray or other shallow container helps keep materials together and organized. Inserting the point of the needle into a stabilizer, such as a bar of soap, a cork, or a styrofoam block, keeps the needle secure and upright while it is being threaded. Holding the needle closer to the end with the eye, and holding the thread close to its end also makes the task easier. Knowing which direction the opening is facing helps increase success in threading the needle.

To locate the eye of the needle, clients should be told to hold the blunt end gently between thumb and forefinger and rotate it. The sides of the needle's eye flare out, while the flat surfaces that can be perceived indicate the opening. Thick thread and a large needle facilitate ease of handling, although various adaptive devices require various sizes of needles. Polyester thread frays less than does cotton, so it will be easier for most people to use. Coating the end of the thread with beeswax helps also. Finally, repetition is extremely important in learning this task. Clients should not expect success with their initial attempts. They should continue to practice until they are able to thread a needle consistently.

A simple device to help with needle threading is the wire loop threader, which is available where conventional sewing supplies are sold. This small tool consists of a collapsible wire loop designed to be poked through the eye of the needle. Once through the eye, it opens up to accept the end of the thread, and then it is used to pull the thread back through the eye. Hitting the eye hole with the threader is easier if the hole is first located with the rotation method previously described. While holding the eye gently between the finger and thumb, one slides the wire loop between the fingers and thumb through the needle's eye. Threading with wire loop threaders is easier if needles with large eyes are used. To make sure that the loop is through the eye, the sewer can pull up on the threader to determine if the needle follows along. Some sewers may not be able to feel whether they have successfully aimed the end of the thread through the wire loop. To control the thread going through the loop, the end of the thread can be compacted by rolling it between thumb and forefinger or it can be wrapped gently around a straight pin (dressmaker pins with large ends are useful), and the straight pin used to aim the thread through the wire loop. The straight pin is removed before the loop with the thread is pulled back through the eye.

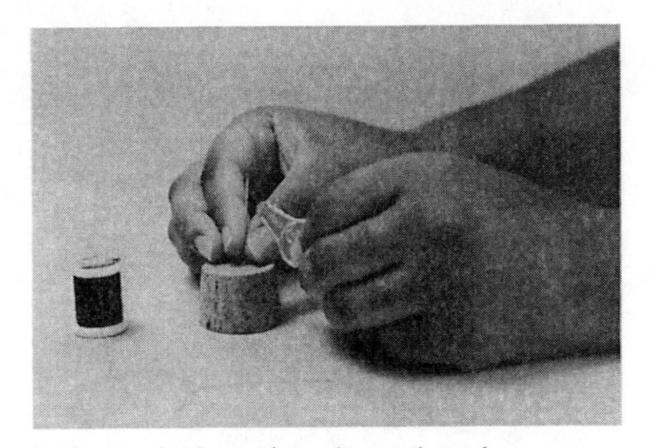

Using a wire loop threader to thread a conventional needle. A cork is used as a stabilizer to hold the needle steady during threading.

A dental floss threader also makes a good needle threader. This is a plastic string with a loop at the end (designed to get dental floss into small spaces such as between braces or dentures). It can be used in the same way as a wire loop threader and may also require needles with large eyes. Dental floss threaders can be found in the dental products section of grocery and drug stores.

Some threading devices hold a needle in place in a chimneylike receptacle (usually with the eye down); when the user pushes a button, a small metal prod inside the device pushes the thread through the needle's eye. Many people find such devices frustrating to use, but there are several measures that can increase the chances of success:

- Use a needle that is large enough to accept the prod and thread but small enough to fit into the receptacle of the device.
- First locate the eye of the needle and place it in the chimney or receptacle with the hole facing the prod.
- Drape the feeder thread gently over the opening in the threading device where the prod catches it; if the thread is too taut, the prod will not catch it properly.
- Pull up on the needle while the prod is inserted in the eye to check that the prod has actually entered the eye. This technique will prevent the frustration of continuing the procedure or attempting to sew when the thread is not engaged.
- Continue pushing the button to keep the prod engaged while feeling the front of the device to determine if the thread has been pushed through the needle's eye and out the front of the device.

Self-threading needles are similar to regular sewing needles, but in addition to a small regular eye, they have a V-shaped opening in the end into which thread can be pulled. The opening of a self-threading needle can be located by feeling for the two blunt points that form the "V" into which the thread is slipped. Once the thread is slipped past the narrow "V" opening, it is secured. The general principles already mentioned for stabilizing the needle, reducing the distance from the end of the

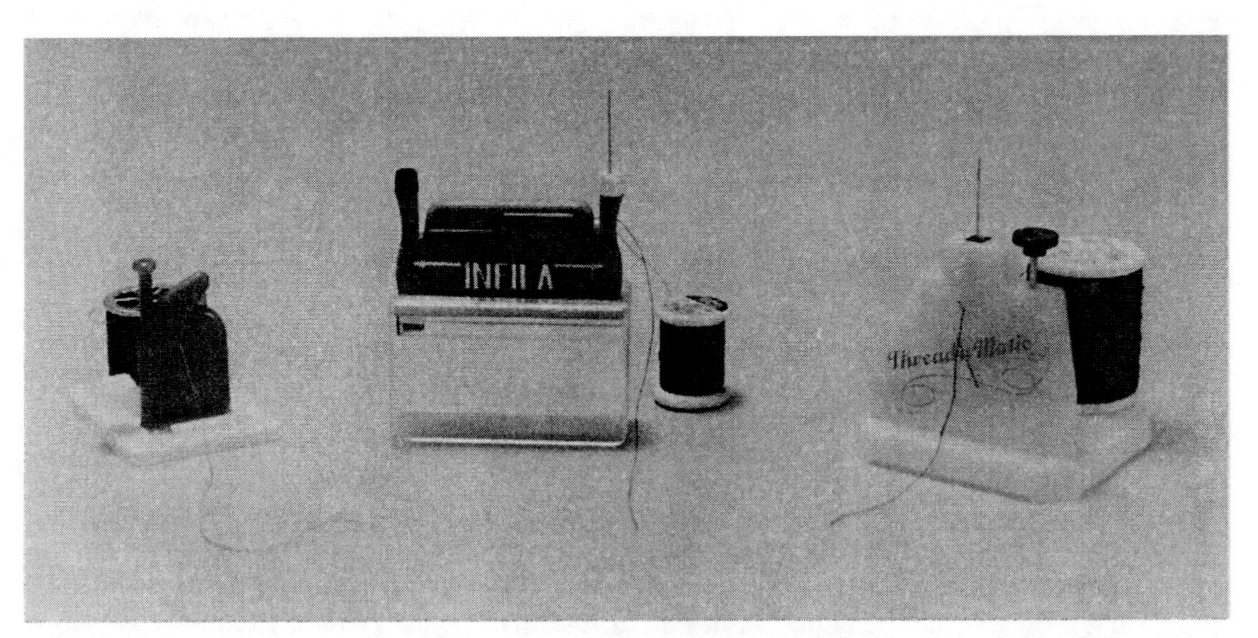

Devices to help thread needles include (left to right) the Hexe, the Infila, and the ThreadaMatic. These devices hold the needle while the user pushes the thread through with a small metal prod.

Teaching Basic Hand Sewing

I. Objective: When presented with the necessary supplies, the learner will perform basic hand stitches with 80 percent accuracy.

II. Materials
   A. Variety of needle threaders
   B. Needles and thread
   C. Straight pins and dressmaker pins
   D. Pincushion, small block of styrofoam, cork, or bar soap to stabilize pins and needles
   E. Scissors
   F. Adapted tape measure
   G. Thimble
   H. Swatches of fabric or garments to be mended
   I. Magnifiers, if necessary

III. Assessment: Determine the learner's knowledge and experience in the following areas:
   A. Use of needle and thread
   B. Sewing stitches
   C. Terminology
   D. Familiarity with other sewing equipment

IV. Procedures
   A. Uses
      1. Labeling garments
      2. Mending ripped seams or tears
      3. Replacing buttons
   B. Threading a needle
      1. Threading a needle with a wire loop threader or dental floss threader
         a. Explain that wire loop threaders have a lightweight metal handle to which a diamond-shaped wire loop is attached that collapses when inserted into the eye of a needle and that opens into a loop again on the other side.
         b. Present the learner with a needle in a pincushion and have the learner locate the eye by rotating the needle until he or she feels a bulge near the top (away from the point).
         c. Have the learner hold the needle by placing the thumb on one side of the bulge and the index finger on the other side, with the eye between the fingers.
         d. Have the learner pass the needle threader between the thumb and index finger through the eye.
         e. Have the learner leave the needle standing in the pincushion with the threader inserted, locate a spool of thread, and unravel approximately 18 inches of thread (from the tips of the finger to the elbow).
         f. Have the learner wind the free end of the thread several times around a straight pin with a large head (dressmaker's pin).
         g. Have the learner pass the straight pin through the wire loop, pulling the thread with it, and then remove the straight pin and put it away.

(continued on next page)

Teaching Basic Hand Sewing (continued)

h. Have the student pull the wire loop back through the eye of the needle, pulling the thread with it.

2. Threading a self-threading needle
    a. Present the learner with a self-threading needle stuck in a pincushion with the eye uppermost.
    b. Have the learner measure out 18 inches of thread.
    c. Have the learner grasp the thread between the thumb and index finger of each hand, several inches from one end, leaving about 1 inch of thread between the hands.
    d. Have the learner locate the opening at the top of the needle by feeling with an extended index finger the twin points that form the "V," which guides the thread into the eye; this "V" can then be used as a guide for the thread.
    e. Have the learner bring the 1-inch section of thread to rest on the top of the needle.
    f. Have the learner pull the thread through the slit of the "V" into the eye of the needle with firm downward pressure.
    g. Have the learner check that the thread is through the eye by lifting the thread to see if the needle lifts with it.
3. Tying a knot in the end of the thread
    a. Have the learner hold the thread between thumb and index finger, and wrap it around the index finger several times.
    b. Have the learner rub the index finger against the thumb toward the thumb joint to create a snarl of thread.
    c. Have the learner grasp the twisted thread, and pull it toward the end of the thread until a tight knot is formed.

C. Sewing the backstitch

1. Describe the backstitch as a strong stitch with which to repair seams or zippers.
2. Have the learner pin fabric together in a seam, placing pins along the seam line and measuring to ensure a consistent seam width.
3. Have the learner hold the area to be stitched in the left hand.
4. Have the learner insert the needle from the back of the fabric to the side facing him or her and place left thumbnail against the needle to mark the position of the stitch.
5. Have the learner pull the thread through until the knot lies against the seam.
6. Have the learner insert the point of the needle back into the fabric ⅛ inch to the right of the thumbnail by sliding the needle along the thumbnail to the fabric and moving it slightly to the right.
7. Have the learner advance the point of the needle ¼ inch to the left along the back of the fabric until the point is felt under the ball of the thumb, then insert the point through the fabric, moving the thumb to facilitate this.
8. Have the learner place the left thumbnail against the needle as it comes through the fabric to mark the stitch and then pull the needle and thread all the way through.

(continued on next page)

Teaching Basic Hand Sewing (continued)

9. Have the learner continue sewing the seam in like manner, removing the pins as they are reached.
10. At the end of the seam, have the learner fasten the end of the work by making a small stitch, catching the loop formed over the finger, inserting the needle through it twice in the same direction and cutting the thread about ½ inch from the knot.

V. Memoranda
   A. Experienced sewers may have an established method for performing certain stitches; encourage the use of their own methods.
   B. The use of beeswax on self-threading needle eyes may assist with threading and avoid thread breakage.

VI. Evaluation: Have the learner sew at least 10 stitches independently, knotting the thread when finished.

VII. Assignment
   A. Have the learner mend a garment with a ripped seam.
   B. Have the learner sew on a button.

needle, and locating the direction of the eye also are helpful with self-threading needles.

One method of using a self-threading needle is to hold a section of the thread taut between both hands while lowering the thread into the crosswise points of the needle, whose point is imbedded in a stabilizer. Another method is to hold the thread taut in one hand by winding it around the thumb and forefinger, which are held approximately 1½ inches apart, then lowering the upside-down self-threading needle (held close to its eye) onto the thread. The sensation of the thread snapping into place as it enters the eye may indicate that the needle has been successfully threaded; the user also can check by pulling up on the needle to determine whether the thread pulls back up with it.

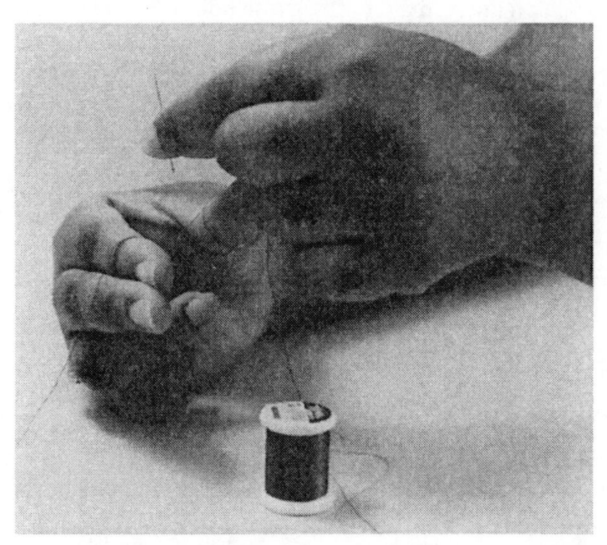

Threading a self-threading needle by holding the thread taut in one hand and lowering the opening of the needle onto the thread.

Some clients may want to consider the various alternatives to doing their own sewing. Tailors can perform alterations, repairs, and button replacement; most dry cleaners also provide button-replacement services. Friends or neighbors may be willing to help or may barter sewing services for other favors. Iron-on patches and repair material and fabric glue are other ways to solve minor clothing repair problems. For sewing on buttons, commercially available products such as the Buttoneer attach buttons through the use of short plastic threads similar to those that hold price tags to clothing.

Basic instruction in hand sewing is based on the use of adaptive techniques and equipment to thread needles, reattach buttons, and mend tears or ripped seams (see the lesson plan on teaching basic hand sewing in this chapter). Those who are interested in making their own clothes may need more advanced adaptive techniques for tasks such as the following:

- using patterns to cut clothing pieces
- marking seams, darts, and stitching lines
- threading sewing machines
- adjusting sewing machine tension nonvisually
- sewing seams of the appropriate width.

Rehabilitation teachers seldom need to teach clothing construction. Rather, their role is to be the adaptive expert who can assist the novice during the lessons provided by a sewing teacher or who can provide adaptive instruction to the experienced sewer who has lost vision. The type of assistance provided by the rehabilitation teacher may include showing the student how to substitute thick paper pattern pieces for the thin tissue used in clothing and craft patterns, teaching the student or the sewing instructor how one would nonvisually thread a particular sewing machine and adjust its tension, using adapted seam guides (either contrasting colors or tactile magnetic guides), and making use of magnifiers to see the work area in clearer detail.

GAMES

Brailled and large-print playing cards and board games are among the most common products sold by vendors of adaptive aids (see Resources section). Many popular games, such as Scrabble and Monopoly, are available in special editions. These may feature clear plastic braille overlays for board games, spaces with raised outlines to keep pieces from slipping (as on Bingo cards), oversized dice with tactile markings, and game pieces (such as checkers) distinguished by shape. Myriad electronic and computer-based games are also available, and computers equipped with voice output or screen-magnification software make such games accessible to nearly anyone with a visual impairment. Therefore, rehabilitation teachers generally do not need to provide much instruction for playing games, but it is important that teachers be familiar with sources of adapted products and methods of adapting commercial games, as Scott H. discovered:

> Scott H., a totally blind lawyer with a wife and two young children, had almost completed personal adjustment training when he and the rehabilitation teacher met to discuss recreation and leisure skills. Scott was especially eager to learn about resources that are available for activities that he and his family could enjoy together, such as adapted games, combination braille and print children's books, and descriptive videos. He also wanted specific information about how to modify some of the children's games, such as Candyland, that his family already had at home. Scott and the rehabilitation teacher discussed how game boards could be modified. The teacher showed Scott clear 8½-by-11-inch plastic sheets that could be brailled on and affixed to the game board. Scott ordered

The discs in this adapted Othello game are marked for tactile identification, and the raised ridges around the squares on the board keep the discs from sliding.

a brailled Scrabble game, Hi Marks raised-marking paste, and tactile dice from a special catalog, and got the addresses of the companies that produce descriptive videos and the adhesive plastic sheets.

The manner in which a particular game is modified is, naturally, dependent upon the needs of the individual. Some people who have no usable vision and read braille may wish to have instructions, game cards, or parts of the game board brailled and/or have tactile markings added to assist them in locating playing areas. Use of clear labeling tape or clear adhesive sheets is recommended, in addition, so that sighted players can continue to see the information on the game board. The players may wish to add tactile markings to the playing pieces or to substitute more identifiable objects. Hi Marks raised marking compound, household glue, or thick fabric paints in tubes can be used to create raised lines to delineate areas or boundaries.

Rehabilitation teachers may also find it necessary to teach students how to braille playing cards. The usual method of brailling playing cards is to use a slate and stylus or brailler to place symbols on top of the print numbers at top and bottom, so that players can read the cards whichever way they are turned. Either regular or large-dot braille can be used.

These adapted playing cards have both large numbers and braille dots.

The brailled markings are limited to two symbols only: the card value in the first cell and the card suit in the second cell. Because a number is expected in the first cell, the number sign is unnecessary; thus, the first cell holds a number from 2 through 10 (without a number sign) or the initial of a face card: J, G, K, or A for jack, queen, king, or ace. The number 10 is abbreviated to X to keep it in one cell. The second cell holds the initial of the suit: H, D, S, or C for hearts, diamonds, spades, or clubs. The only exception is the joker, which is brailled JO; this takes up both cells, but jokers have no suit.

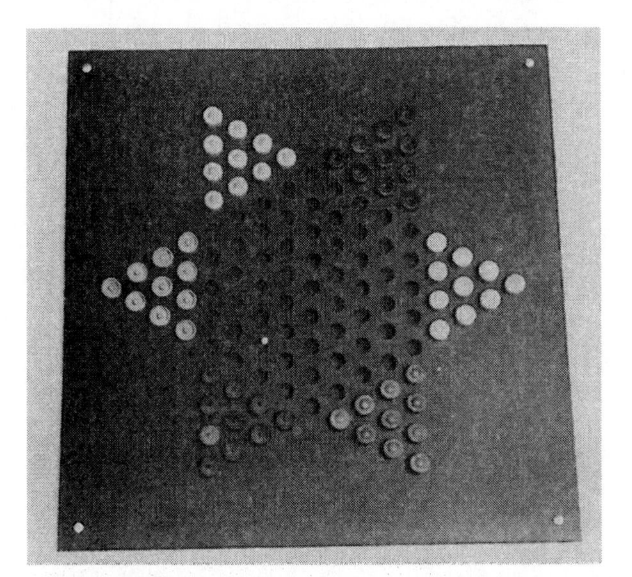

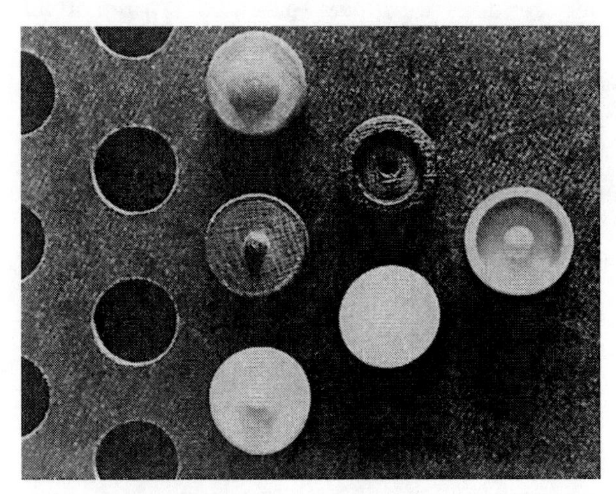

The pegs of this adapted Chinese Checkers game can be identified both visually, by their different colors (left), and tactilely, by the different shapes on the tops (right).

OTHER LEISURE AND RECREATIONAL ACTIVITIES

As mentioned earlier, there is no specific teaching sequence for leisure and recreational activities because the needs, interests, and abilities of the individuals whom rehabilitation teachers serve can vary widely. The role of the rehabilitation teacher in this area can vary from simply providing information about resources—for example, modified equipment such as bowling rails—to teaching specific skills—the game of bowling itself.

An important resource that persons who are visually impaired may not be aware of is audiodescription, which addresses the problem of not being able to see the action on television programs or in videotaped movies (McCarville, 1996). The best-known service, Descriptive Video Service (DVS) (see Resources section), makes television programs and movies on video accessible to people with visual impairments by providing narrated descriptions of key visual elements without interfering with the dialogue. DVS videos can be viewed with any videocassette recorder (VCR), but DVS broadcast television programs require either a stereo television set or VCR with the Second Audio Program (SAP) feature or an SAP adapter. Similar services available at some theaters provide narration of stage plays. Knowledge of such services does not appear to be all that widespread among persons with visual impairments, and rehabilitation teachers may be the primary source of such information (McCarville, 1996).

It is beyond the scope of this text to discuss in detail leisure and recreation for persons with visual impairments, but there are a multitude of resources for equipment, instruction, and networking in a variety of sports and activities (see Resources section). The Hadley School for the Blind provides several free correspondence courses related to health, fitness, participation in local recreational programs, and outdoor recreation. A national organization, Blind Outdoor Leisure Development (BOLD), promotes a variety of outdoor activities for persons with visual impairments, including downhill and cross-country skiing, hiking, rock climbing, and horseback riding. The United States Association for Blind Athletes promotes participation in competitive sports at the local, state, national, and international levels in activities such as wrestling, gymnastics, track and field, tandem cycling, swimming, and goal ball (a game specially designed for people who are blind). The American Blind Bowling Association, the National Beep Baseball Association, and Ski for Light, also promote opportunities for competition in their respective sports.

CONCLUSION

With this chapter, all the skills that rehabilitation teachers commonly teach in personal adjustment training have been covered. In light of the new knowledge gained from the study of specific areas of rehabilitation teaching, readers may now want to return to Part 2 and review the process of rehabilitation teaching presented there. With a more in-depth understanding of clients' needs, the skills and adaptations that will meet these needs, and what is required to teach these skills and adaptations, the information presented in the chapters on assessment, planning, and teaching and learning will take on new significance. Readers can then begin to apply this information to specific teaching situations discussed in the chapters on communications skills and activities of daily living.

Now that they have a broader overview of the work of the rehabilitation teacher, readers may also find themselves wondering how professionals in the field manage the many and varied tasks the job entails and how they organize their time and their responsibilities. Part 5 first examines these questions and then goes on to look at the changes that rehabilitation teachers may anticipate in their field in the future.

PART FIVE

The Practice of Rehabilitation Teaching

CHAPTER 17

Managing a Rehabilitation Teaching Caseload

KEY CONCEPTS IN THIS CHAPTER

- **Management duties of an itinerant rehabilitation teacher**
- **Methods for determining when referrals are necessary and identifying appropriate human services agencies in the community**
- **The purposes and benefits of a peer-support group**
- **The difficulties sometimes encountered when teaching in a client's living quarters and the methods for managing the teaching environment**
- **Contents of an itinerant teaching kit**
- **The process of setting priorities among clients' needs**
- **Techniques for planning travel to and from clients' homes**
- **Techniques for encouraging clients to be reliable in keeping appointments**
- **The purpose of and techniques for documenting the outcome of lessons in progress notes and final reports**
- **Methods of supervising paraprofessionals and volunteers**
- **Methods for training other personnel who work with blind and visually impaired clients**

Although the responsibilities of today's rehabilitation teachers are less broad than were those of their predecessors, who, as described in Chapter 2, undertook everything from teaching braille to collecting chairs for caning, they still involve a good deal more than the teaching of the specific adaptive skills outlined in Parts 3 and 4 of this book. This chapter will examine the functions that generally fall under the rubric of case management. As defined here, these additional tasks include the following:

- determining the services to be offered (discussed in Chapters 3 and 4)
- making referrals to agencies that provide services not directly related to blindness and visual impairment
- keeping records on clients' progress
- providing informal counseling
- advocating for clients
- managing time and materials.

In addition, rehabilitation teachers frequently perform professional and administrative functions, such as public education and in-service training and supervision of teaching aides or volunteers, which will also be discussed in this chapter.

RANGE OF TASKS

The wide variety of tasks performed by rehabilitation teachers was examined and classified in a study by Leja (1990), who asked practicing rehabilitation teachers to estimate the frequency with which they performed various tasks in the course of their jobs. Using the responses of 209 rehabilitation teachers to his Job Task Inventory, he found that activities fell into three broad categories. These are (from most to least frequently performed) (1) various teaching tasks, (2) case management, particularly tasks related to scheduling, client counseling, and contacting other community agencies, and (3) professional or administrative duties.

The most common activities within each category are listed in rank order in Table 17.1. Nearly all the activities were performed an average of one to three times per week, and none were performed an average of four or more times per week. Only four tasks—developing an individual plan of instruction, formulating lesson plans, teaching home management, and scheduling appointments with clients—had average frequencies that fell in the range of two to three times per week; and only a few activities, all of them in the area of professional or administrative tasks, were performed an average of less than once a week. However, the differences from one task to the next in how often on average they were performed was slight. Moreover, there was considerable variation in the frequencies reported for each activity, so that in all likelihood individual rehabilitation teachers differed considerably in how often they performed each task.

Leja's study thus confirms that a significant portion of the rehabilitation teacher's time is spent in tasks other than direct teaching. Some of these case management functions are important because, particularly in a field-based or itinerant teaching setting, they may meet needs of the client that are even more immediate and pressing than learning specific skills. For example, a person who has no food or heat at home must have those needs met before instruction can begin. Efficient management of a caseload and of an individual's case is also important, given the large caseloads—sometimes exceeding 100 clients—of many rehabilitation teachers, because it allows for the most effective use of the teacher's time. This, in turn, allows the teacher to spend more time in direct contact with clients and to work with more of them.

Leja's (1990) study of rehabilitation teachers' job roles showed that teachers based in field offices tend to perform case management functions more frequently than do those who work in residential rehabilitation centers. This difference is basically a result of the larger itinerant caseloads plus the lack of ancillary services (such as occupational therapy or specialized computer or industrial arts instruction) in the field. Rehabilitation centers tend to have larger staffs with a more strictly defined division of labor. Clients who obtain services in state-operated rehabilitation centers are referred by field-based rehabilitation counselors or rehabilitation teachers who have determined their eligibility for services and written an IWRP that includes personal adjustment training at a center. On arriving at the center, the client is assigned to a center-based counselor who determines which classes will be included in his or her program. Subsequently, the client is met in classroom settings by rehabilitation teachers who are generally assigned to specific curricular areas. For example, some teachers may teach only one subject, such as communication or kitchen skills. The only significant case management role for rehabilitation teachers in such a setting is record keeping.

In contrast, rehabilitation teachers carrying an itinerant caseload in a state vocational rehabilitation or private agency or in the Canadian system must attend to a wide variety of tasks. For example, they may be responsible for all case management tasks other than determination of eligibility, including writing the IWRP or IPP. However, most teachers must perform these additional tasks in a limited amount of time. In fact,

Table 17.1 Most Common Activities Performed by Rehabilitation Teachers, in Rank Order of Average Frequency

Teaching

1. Developing instructional plans
2. Developing lesson plans
3. Teaching home management
4. Evaluating client needs in areas of daily living
5. Teaching kitchen skills
6. Teaching labeling
7. Teaching personal management
8. Teaching money management
9. Teaching writing guides
10. Teaching adaptive timepieces
11. Teaching eating skills
12. Teaching listening equipment
13. Teaching tape recording
14. Teaching telephone skills
15. Teaching about recording services
16. Teaching handwriting
17. Teaching spatial concepts
18. Teaching clothing identification
19. Teaching household personal shopping education skills
20. Teaching interpersonal skills
21. Teaching hygiene skills
22. Teaching adaptive social skills
23. Teaching personal health skills
24. Teaching diet management

Case Management

1. Scheduling appointments
2. Discussing clients' eye condition
3. Counseling client about adjustment to blindness
4. Interpreting eye medical reports
5. Instructing small groups
6. Contacting other community agencies
7. Teaching sighted guide technique
8. Counseling family about adjustment to blindness
9. Providing information about benefits
10. Teaching home site orientation
11. Interpreting eye reports to determine eligibility for services
12. Helping to modify or eliminate architectural barriers
13. Case finding
14. Handling contracts or authorizations for services
15. Performing follow-up services
16. Providing consultation to medical and paramedical personnel
17. Arranging for medical services
18. Helping to locate attendant care services

Professional/Administrative Activities

1. Participating in staff meetings
2. Consulting for other agencies
3. Participating in continuing education
4. Attending conferences
5. Participating on professional committees or boards
6. Participating in support groups
7. Participating in research
8. Interviewing volunteers
9. Writing grants

Source: Adapted from J. A. Leja, "The Job Roles of Rehabilitation Teaching," *Journal of Visual Impairment & Blindness, 84,* (1990), p. 158.

because the caseloads of itinerant teachers are often large and they must perform more case management tasks than those in center-based jobs, they often see individual clients as infrequently as once per month (Splear, 1986).

The time that a rehabilitation teacher can devote to direct service is further limited by the additional tasks of making referrals, controlling the teaching environment, and managing instructional materials (Olmstead, 1991). Clients whose needs cannot be completely met by the rehabilitation teacher must be referred to one or more of the myriad other agencies in a given geographic area; the interruptions encountered in the client's home during teaching sessions must be minimized or controlled; and the materials needed for teaching must be at hand when the teacher is many miles away from the office. In addition, many rehabilitation teachers supervise aides or volunteers, coordinate peer-support groups, and devote time to giving presentations on blindness to other professionals and community organizations. Thus, rehabilitation teachers who work in itinerant settings need to be skillful planners and time managers (see Sidebar 17.1). Although much of the information in this chapter on managing the various aspects of a rehabilitation teaching caseload will be helpful for teachers based either in rehabilitation centers or in the field, the focus will be on the itinerant teacher, for whom such tasks are more significant.

MANAGING REFERRALS

As noted, the ongoing process of refining rehabilitation teaching as a profession has led to a more narrowly defined role for rehabilitation teachers than that of earlier home teachers. Tasks considered simple enough that they do not require professional training or those requiring technical expertise beyond that of the rehabilitation teacher are now referred to others. Therefore, rehabilitation teachers must be able to recognize when a referral is called for and must have a sound knowledge of the resources available in community agencies. Most important among the services requiring a referral are those that meet acute survival needs of new clients. These needs include:

- food
- heat
- transportation
- administration of insulin and other medication
- crisis intervention
- medication counseling.

It is important for rehabilitation teachers to know the sources of assistance that exist in their community to meet such immediate needs. For example, food may be available through Meals on Wheels programs. Funds for home heating fuel are provided to many who cannot afford it through Community Chest organizations. Most communities offer some type of door-to-door transportation service for disabled residents. Telephone hot lines for dealing with suicide or other crises are common. County-based nursing services are usually available for assisting persons with diabetes and other medical conditions, and some health care agencies provide information relating to over-the-counter drugs or prescription medications and contraindications for their use.

Other important services that clients might require are family counseling, economic assistance, educational services, AIDS support, legal aid,

SIDEBAR 17.1

Tips for Managing Time

- **Build sufficient travel time into the schedule** to avoid a domino effect of late appointments.
- **Establish a definite time frame for lessons** so that both teacher and client are aware of the need to accomplish specific goals during each visit.
- **Establish a regular meeting time for long-term clients**; they are less likely to forget and therefore be away or otherwise occupied.
- **Keep a detailed map** in the car.
- **Schedule lessons to avoid traveling at peak traffic times**, if possible.
- **Schedule clients according to their geographic proximity** to keep travel efficient.
- **List necessary materials for each day's lessons in a daily planner** and gather all materials before leaving the office.
- **Ask the client for directions to his or her home** when the initial appointment is made, including landmarks; ask what you'll see if you've gone too far; call the client for directions if you get lost on the way.
- **Make referrals to other professionals with differing expertise** when appropriate to reserve more time for direct teaching.
- **Verify appointments** the day before or have clerical or volunteer staff do so to prevent missed appointments and wasted trips to clients' homes.

health care services, bereavement counseling, domestic abuse shelters, literacy instruction, sexual or domestic assault crisis intervention, substance abuse services, consumer education, and services for seniors, such as Alzheimer's support groups.

Recognizing one's professional limitations is often difficult. Most people who have chosen to be rehabilitation teachers have dedicated their lives to service and many would like to be able to provide all the assistance necessary for the rehabilitation of each client themselves. For caring professionals, it is usually not easy to pass up a request for assistance with a simple but time-consuming task such as driving a client to an appointment or picking up a few groceries on the way to the house. Many teachers may also be tempted to try to provide more technical services, such as teaching literacy skills along with typewriting instruction or counseling the families of clients. Regardless of the teacher's ability to teach literacy or to counsel, however, the time spent on such efforts is difficult to justify when other clients are waiting for the rehabilitation teacher's specialized services. Furthermore, technical services such as instruction in literacy can usually best be provided by those who specialize in them.

Counseling

Counseling has frequently been reported as one of the major functions actually performed by rehabilitation teachers (Leja, 1990; Young, Dickerson & Jacobson, 1980). However, the term is defined differently by different people; in actuality one might differentiate at least three distinct types of counseling: informal counseling, advice giving, and psychotherapy.

Because the rehabilitation teacher works with clients one or a few at a time and because clients are commonly in the process of adjusting to sight loss, there is a great deal of opportunity for the sharing of ideas and opinions, particularly about the client's sight loss. Emotional discussions of the difficulties of adjustment are, in fact, common topics of conversation during lessons, and when emotions are extreme, these discussions sometimes supplant the planned lesson. A rehabilitation teacher who did not respond to these obvious calls for help by clients would be remiss, because this type of informal counseling is an important part of the personal adjustment process.

Discussions with clients also commonly lead rehabilitation teachers into situations in which they are called on to give advice. Indeed, teaching a client to perform a skill is, in some ways, itself a form of advice giving. Advice relating directly to instructional areas—such as where clients might buy a particular adaptive aid, how to improve control of their personal appearance, whether braille or large print might be their primary reading medium, or where they might obtain a specific service—is legitimate because it falls within the teacher's area of expertise.

However, the rehabilitation teacher needs to carefully consider the extent to which advice is given. Because persons adjusting to new vision loss are commonly in a rather emotional state, they may tend to form overly dependent relationships with their rehabilitation teacher and put a great deal of trust in the teacher's opinions. An individual in this type of relationship might ask for advice on any number of topics, such as a pending divorce, career choices, or how to deal with an unruly teenager. This type of advice giving, as well as the third level of counseling—psychotherapy—are generally beyond the expertise of most rehabilitation teachers. Rehabilitation counselors or professional counselors from a community agency are better prepared to provide professional counseling.

Locating Community Agency Resources

To be able to recognize that a referral to an outside resource is needed and to be able to locate the appropriate source handily, a rehabilitation teacher must have a thorough knowledge of the types of services that are available in the community. Cities, even small ones, may contain hundreds of agencies, however, and in rural areas agencies may be located in the county seat, possibly miles from the people who need services. Therefore, the rehabilitation teacher needs a systematic method for learning about community agencies and their services.

Community agencies are generally listed in local telephone directories, often in a separate community agency resource section near the front or back of the book. They may also be found in the Yellow Pages under the appropriate heading (such as Mental Health or Senior Citizens' Services) if the specific agency name is not known. More useful for gathering information are directories of community agencies, which offer more detailed descriptions, commonly including an agency's goals and services, instructions for making referrals, eligibility requirements, the costs of services, and the length of any waiting list. These directories are usually available from United Way or its equivalent or from such community sources as the public library or the local chamber of commerce. However, such directories can be so large as to be overwhelming. Therefore, rather than attempting to memorize the functions of all the agencies listed, it is generally more useful to identify specific services that will be needed by an individual and then to consult the directory for the names of agencies offering them. Each state also has a state agency, department, or office responsible for state programs for older people funded by the Older Americans Act, and each county or group of counties has an area agency on aging that will know about the availability of such programs as home-delivered meals, door-to-door transportation and escort services, and other services for elderly persons.

The listing of Sources of Information and Services in the Resources section of this book provides a sampling of federal government agencies and national organizations that may either themselves provide services or may function as sources of information about where to obtain needed services. The AFB *Directory of Services for Blind and Visually Impaired Persons in the United States and Canada* (1993) provides extensive listings of services and sources of information that will be of use to rehabilitation teachers and their clients.

Following Up

Although an agency's referral procedure is easily learned from an agency directory or from the agency itself, the rehabilitation teacher should understand that making a referral does not necessarily ensure that a client will obtain needed services. Many clients who are referred for services often have difficulty actually securing services, perhaps because they are uncomfortable about accepting help from people or organizations they do not know or because fear of an unknown situation makes it difficult to follow through. It is, therefore, important for the rehabilitation teacher to take action to ensure the success of a referral. Such action may entail either arranging for transportation to the initial agency visit or actually accompanying the client, or it may mean being present when the worker from the referral agency makes his or her initial visit to the client's home.

Using Peer-Support Groups

Peer-support groups composed of people with visual impairments constitute a helpful community resource that may easily be overlooked. These groups meet periodically to discuss the common problems of people experiencing a loss of vision; and they are a significant source of information and emotional support for clients. Byers-Lang (1984; Byers-Lang & McCall, 1993) and her colleagues demonstrated the value of such groups. They trained former clients to serve as friendly visitors, listeners, teacher's aides, and providers of resource information, and then set up regularly scheduled meetings for clients in the community. These peer-support groups provided the mutual support among clients that is usually a natural and significant consequence of serving persons in residential centers and demonstrated that such support can also be provided in a community setting. The rehabilitation teacher's role in the formation of groups usually involves organizing the group, training peer supporters, and making new referrals to the group. When people are trained to serve as peer supporters and teacher's aides, it also reduces some of the rehabilitation teacher's work load.

In addition, telephone networks set up among rural clients may be helpful in providing support to far-flung clients who may be in isolated settings. An example of a successful rural telephone peer-support system in northern Indiana is known as the Buddy System. A local rehabilitation teacher organized this program in which clients and former clients call other clients on a biweekly basis and share helpful hints and emotional support (D. Horner, personal communication, 1996).

MANAGING THE TEACHING ENVIRONMENT

Successful lessons depend to some degree on the quality of the teaching environment. Managing a center-based teaching environment is much akin to managing a classroom in an educational setting. A classroom in a rehabilitation center tends to be a teacher-centered situation. That is, the instructor is familiar with the classroom and can keep it organized, clean, and relatively protected from interruptions.

In contrast, when instruction occurs in the learner's home, the teacher knows little about the environment, which may or may not be organized or clean, and may be prone to innumerable interruptions. Being unfamiliar with the surroundings and the organizational system of a kitchen can make the teacher less efficient and can be especially difficult for a rehabilitation teacher who is visually impaired. This difficulty can be handled by having the client describe the surroundings, which in any case is a part of the usual assessment process; teachers who utilize drivers can train them to make critical observations and provide feedback. However, all rehabilitation teachers in the field, regardless of their visual status, have to confront the issues of cleanliness—a health concern—and interruptions. If lack of cleanliness in a client's home stems from the client's lack of vision, modifying the situation may require instruction in relevant adaptive skills, but if it is a result of the client's personal practice, making changes may be more difficult. The teacher must generally respect a client's beliefs, but as lessons proceed and trust is built between teacher and client, the teacher can sometimes make suggestions about changes and share information about cleaning practices if necessary.

Managing Interruptions

The management of interruptions is one of the more challenging aspects of delivering services in the home setting. During instructional visits, family members may want to take part in the client's activities, children may need attention, friends may telephone, and salespeople may even attempt to peddle their wares. It is virtually impossible to stop such interruptions, but they can usually be controlled sufficiently to accomplish the goals of rehabilitation. For example, some people are so accustomed to having their television on that it never occurs to them to turn it off. The rehabilitation teacher can simply be assertive about turning off the television during lessons if no one else is watching it.

Clients are usually the key to controlling interruptions. If they understand the problem that disruptions present to effective instruction, they can ask family members and friends to visit or call at other times, place children in the care of others, and use their rehabilitation teaching appointments as the perfect excuse to discourage salespeople. If a client is not able to help, the teacher must either intervene or, in extreme cases, discontinue services in the home setting. If lessons in the home are restricted by conditions there, then a center setting or other locale may be more beneficial. For example, adaptive cooking lessons might be moved to the kitchen of a local church, and handwriting or braille lessons could be held in a public library or senior center.

Gender-Related Issues

When the client and the rehabilitation teacher are of different sexes, either one may become uncomfortable with the situation, and this feeling may be likely to develop when instruction occurs in the client's home. Male rehabilitation teachers should be aware that a visit to the home of a female client who will be alone during the teaching session may be perceived as threatening. It is therefore generally a good idea to address the issue at the time of the first telephone contact. A male instructor can provide a female client with his agency's telephone number and a supervisor's name so that she can verify his employment and legitimacy, or he can invite the client to have someone else in the home during the visit.

Female rehabilitation teachers sometimes face the reverse situation when going to a male client's home: They may occasionally receive sexual overtures from male clients or family members. These circumstances can often be avoided by formally maintaining a professional teacher-student interaction, which subtly reminds the client of his position as a student during lessons. If such subtle reminders are not sufficient, the teacher can consider arranging for a team (a rehabilitation teacher and an O&M specialist, for example) to work together at the client's house, having the client transferred to a male co-worker, arranging for lessons to be held in a different location, or threatening the loss of agency services unless the inappropriate behavior ceases.

Table 17.2. Contents of a Sample Kit for an Itinerant Rehabilitation Teacher

Area	Materials
Assessment, planning, and case management	Agency forms, talking book program applications, transportation applications, directory assistance waiver forms, referral forms for other agencies
Braille	Braille cell model, beginning braille textbook, slate and stylus, paper, plastic labeling tape
Handwriting	Assorted signature, envelope, check, and full-page writing guides; X-ray film; razor blade knife; paper; felt-tipped pens; pencils; raised-line drawing board
Recorders	Adapted recorder, cassette tapes, headset, catalog of talking books, disc player needles, cleaning supplies
Low vision	Assessment tools, tracking and scanning exercises, sun filters, yellow acetate sheets for contrast, portable lamp with rheostat, sun visor
Home management and leisure	Cafeteria tray, adapted timer, adapted cookbooks, measuring cups and spoons, adapted ruler, raised marker (Hi Marks), labeling tape
Personal management	Clothing tags, laundry pins, adapted timepieces, assorted coins and paper currency, insulin measuring device, scissors, simple sewing kit (assorted needles, thread, needle threaders, buttons, and fabric pieces)
Miscellaneous	Super glue, paper clips, cellophane tape, plastic or fabric tape, permanent markers, small three-corner file for engraving notches and lines
Personal use	Prepackaged disposable cleansing towelettes, paper towels, plastic bags for items requiring disposal or cleaning, insect spray

MANAGING TEACHING MATERIALS

Field-based instructors must make a special effort to have appropriate instructional materials on hand when they are needed. If a rehabilitation teacher sees 15 to 20 persons in a given week, he or she must either drive a van that can carry all the supplies that might be needed or take time each morning to go to the office to gather them—neither of which is particularly practical. Itinerant rehabilitation teachers usually overcome this difficulty by organizing the most commonly needed materials into a portable itinerant teaching kit and by taking larger and less frequently used items, such as typewriters, only as needed (Olmstead, 1991).

The contents of the itinerant teaching kit will include a variety of items to use in teaching and demonstrations. Instructional materials can be placed in a compartmentalized box that can be sealed to protect its contents from dust and that fits conveniently into the trunk of a car. The compartments can correspond to particular teaching areas to make locating items easier. Some teachers also store frequently needed paperwork, such as agency forms, in this kit, but often-used papers

A well-organized car trunk.

may be handier when carried in a separate briefcase. Teachers who travel on public transportation may want to organize a large carryall or backpack to keep their hands free.

The contents of the itinerant teaching kit will vary from teacher to teacher and from agency to agency. New field-based instructors will want to plan such a kit before their employment begins. Table 17.2 contains a list of materials that might be included in a relatively large kit, including some unusual items recommended by veteran teachers that are not specifically related to any curriculum.

MANAGING A SCHEDULE

Scheduling is a complex task for a field-based teacher. In order for time to be managed efficiently and services to be provided to those who need them most, scheduling entails setting priorities among clients' needs; utilizing maps to plan a route; estimating travel time, and operating a car, following public transportation schedules, or supervising a driver.

Setting Priorities

Setting priorities in regard to clients is a process of determining who should be seen soonest and most often. Clients who would be considered high priority to receive services include individuals who

- are at risk because they have no support systems
- have an IWRP with a high number of planned personal adjustment training hours
- have a need to gain certain skills to qualify for a training program
- have others who are dependent on them.

For example, a single mother who lives in a rural home with no support, has a vocational goal of becoming a medical transcriptionist, and has shown outstanding rehabilitation potential would in all likelihood be classified as a top priority service recipient. Someone in a supported living situation who needed to develop leisure skills only would in all probability be given a lower priority and might be seen less frequently.

Occasionally, assigning a client a level of priority may be complicated by other factors, for example, the development of minimal AIDS-related vision loss. Even though a client with this condition might be currently employed or have vision that is not yet significantly reduced, the rapid progression of the disease often warrants assignment of a higher priority and the provision of immediate services (Kiester, 1990).

Planning a Route

Planning the day's schedule based on clients' geographic locations when possible will help the itinerant rehabilitation teacher to minimize travel time and costs and increase the amount of time available for direct contact with clients. A map of the area to be covered can be placed on the office wall to aid in scheduling, and the location of clients' homes can be marked with colored pins to represent the service sites so that clusters of clients can be easily seen. The color or size of the pins can be varied to indicate clients' priority for receiving services. Travel routes from site to site can be easily plotted if a detailed county or city map is used.

Some types of maps are more useful than others. Although city or highway maps contain streets and roads, some maps available from county governments provide additional information, with special symbols indicating the location of churches, cemeteries, small streams, and the like. Such landmarks are helpful for planning travel routes and especially for getting reoriented if one gets off track en route, and it is worth the effort to learn to use them.

Estimating Travel Time

Estimates of travel time are based primarily on the distance between sites but must also take into consideration the amount of traffic to be expected, the weather conditions that may prevail, and other local conditions on the basis of the rehabilitation teacher's familiarity with the area. However, the client is often the best source of this estimate, especially if the rehabilitation teacher does not know an area well. In general, the novice should allow more time than that estimated until he or she is more skilled at estimating travel time or traveling a particular route. Also, those who are new at travel planning should not forget to include time for lunch stops, required visits back to the office, and the like. Even if the rehabilitation teacher has a driver, learning the layout of the service area is the teacher's responsibility, and drivers are not necessarily skilled at finding locations or using maps. When an instructor makes contact with the potential client before the initial appointment, it makes sense to request precise directions, including the location of landmarks, and to ask questions such as, "Is that road marked?" "What color is the building?" "What will I pass if I've gone too far?" It is time consuming, not to mention unsafe, for the teacher or the driver to attempt to read every street sign as well as the map while looking for an unfamiliar home. In rural areas, post offices and postal carriers are reliable sources of assistance in finding clients' homes.

Promoting Clients' Cooperation

In addition to creating a schedule that is workable, efficient, and serves clients' needs, another aspect of time management involves encouraging the cooperation of clients in adhering to their part of the schedule. It is not only a waste of valuable time but frustrating when a rehabilitation teacher travels 20 miles to an appointment site only to find that a client forgot the appointment and no one is home. Such situations are less likely to occur if the teacher makes it easy for clients to remember appointments or to notify the teacher if it is necessary to cancel, for example, by setting a standard meeting time from week to week, having office staff call clients the day before to confirm appointments, and providing clients with a business telephone number in case of last-minute changes.

The rehabilitation teacher can also maintain a communications link with his or her office by providing a daily travel itinerary, calling in periodically, and perhaps using a pager or car telephone to receive messages about cancellations. Cellular telephones are also useful for calling ahead to confirm appointments, as well as for the rare instance when it is necessary to call for help in case of trouble. It is also a good idea always to bring paperwork along as a backup activity so that time is not wasted in case a client does miss an appointment. In addition, the teacher might have large-print and braille business cards made in case they need to be left with a note stating that he or she was at an absent client's home.

FREEDOM AND FLEXIBILITY

Although an itinerant caseload is generally more difficult to manage than a center-based one, it provides some advantages to both client and teacher. Clients are frequently less anxious when they receive services in their homes than if traveling to an unfamiliar rehabilitation center. A client's familiarity with the equipment and the layout of the learning environment also eliminates the need for him or her to transfer skills learned in a classroom to his or her own kitchen or home. In addition, family members or close friends can be called upon to reinforce learning when provided with appropriate instruction or materials. For example, a client's spouse can observe the client testing blood glucose levels with a voice-output monitor during initial training and provide feedback if necessary. The home setting is often comfortable for the teacher as well. The one-on-one situation and its location in the community in some cases may foster rapport between teacher and client more quickly than the environment of a rehabilitation center.

Although an itinerant caseload requires considerable flexibility on the part of the rehabilitation teacher, it also offers a good deal of freedom. For example, if some clients can only be seen after normal work hours, the teacher can usually begin his or her work day a bit later to compensate for the late appointments. If a client does not show up for an appointment, the teacher can use the time for planning, writing reports, or making telephone calls regarding referral sources, appointment verification, and so forth. Many itinerant teachers operate out of their homes most of the time and visit the office once only or twice a week for such tasks as completing reports, finding cases, and meeting with supervisors.

MANAGING REPORT WRITING

Maintaining formal written documentation of clients' progress is an essential part of case management for the rehabilitation teacher. Record keeping and report writing are seldom a teacher's favorite tasks, but they are crucial for documenting the success of both the client and the agency's services. A succinct but detailed report can also provide a measure of the outcome of a lesson or of an entire program of services from which later services can be planned. These reports will be consulted by the rehabilitation counselor who is serving as the client's overall case manager, as well as by other rehabilitation teachers who may be called upon to work with that client in the future. In addition, these records may be required by the agency's funding source for accountability purposes. Daily progress notes are usually quick evaluations that assist the teacher in documenting progress and preparing for subsequent lessons, while interim reports (if required) and final reports summarize the subjects that were taught and the client's performance on evaluation. In addition, as noted, measuring and documenting the outcomes of teaching provide agencies with a means of evaluating their overall service program.

Formats for reports vary from agency to agency. Some use standard forms listing the long-term and short-term goals that appear on the service plan, which the teacher can simply check off when the student achieves those particular skills, whereas others require written narratives of a client's performance. The Blind Rehabilitation Centers of the U.S. Department of Veterans Affairs utilize an on-line system with a standardized report format, and some state vocational rehabilitation systems use similar computer-based report formats. Users of these network systems have the benefit of almost immediate access to case information about clients from any location.

When a reporting system is already in place, it usually simplifies the task of completing clients' reports for the rehabilitation teacher after a short period of training in the required format. However, some agencies use neither report forms nor standard formats for narratives; in that case, teachers may follow whatever format they wish, but it is up to them to devise a method of record keeping that works well for them. The criteria portion of the behavioral objective for the lesson (see Chapter 4) lends itself nicely to a report on the outcome of that lesson. For example, if the criterion for a lesson reads, "The client will be able to read grade 2 braille at 20 wpm, . . ." the outcome statement might be, "The client is able to read grade 2 braille at 16 wpm."

Although it may suffice for a progress or final report to note tersely "objective reached," more information is desirable. Several key points are important to include when reporting on clients' progress, regardless of the type of report in question:

- Make the report as succinct as possible to save time on paperwork, both in writing the reports and reviewing them later.
- Describe briefly what was done during the lesson or lessons being documented.

- Note the final outcome in both quantitative and qualitative terms.
- Make recommendations for future lessons, if warranted.
- In the case of daily progress notes, make note of any commitments made to the client, such as promising to bring a descriptive video to preview at the next lesson.

The description of what was presented during the lesson or a series of lessons should be brief. It is preferable to avoid writing in the first person, since the report should focus on the client and his or her performance, not the teacher's. For example, rather than "I showed Ms. Newman the Marks Guide, the Guide One, and the string board, and then I asked her to write several lines on each," a more objective statement is suggested, such as, "A variety of handwriting guides (string board, Marks Guide, Guide One) were presented, and the client wrote several lines using each."

Including both quantitative and qualitative descriptions or evaluations of clients' performance should provide the rehabilitation counselor or other teacher who may be reading the report with a clear understanding of lesson outcomes. A quantitative statement, as the term implies, relates to a numerical measure of outcome, such as the number of times the client performed an activity successfully; the number of words or lines read, typed, or written; or the number of items correctly labeled or identified. A quantitative evaluation provides an objective score achieved during a lesson or series of lessons. Some examples are:

- Reads 30 words per minute in grade 2 braille.
- Correctly identified 9 out of 10 compact discs labeled in grade 1 braille.
- Using the Count-a-Dose, was able to measure 10 different dosages of insulin with 100 percent accuracy.
- Poured cold liquids to the proper level in a tumbler 9 out of 10 times without spilling.

Sometimes a quantitative description of performance may not in and of itself reflect the full outcome of lessons. Moreover, many times, it is impractical for a client to perform an activity multiple times—for example, when drawing blood for glucose monitoring—or it may be difficult to quantify performance—as when preparing a recipe. Therefore, it is always a good idea to also include a qualitative description of performance as well. This type of evaluation is more subjective, but still describes observable behaviors—or the absence of observable behaviors—that reflect the client's mastery of the skills in question. Examples of qualitative descriptions or evaluations are:

- Performed all steps in the blood glucose monitoring sequence in the correct order with no hesitation.
- Ms. Newman was able to follow the recipe, gather ingredients, and prepare the salad without assistance. She moved quickly about the kitchen and appeared confident.

Qualitative descriptions are also used in combination with quantitative descriptions to provide important details about specific errors or behaviors. For example, the report that a client reads 15 words per minute (wpm) in grade 2 braille is not complete unless the teacher also notes such details as whether he uses one or both hands, that he reads slowly because he tends to "scrub" (see Chapter 7), or that he consistently misreads symbols with more than three dots.

PROVIDING SUPERVISION AND EDUCATION

Other nonteaching functions of rehabilitation teachers that are becoming more and more common are the provision of supervision and education or training. Because the large caseloads of field-based rehabilitation teachers sometimes limit their ability to serve their clients, some agencies have been shifting some of the rehabilitation teacher's work load to teacher's assistants, volunteers, or personnel in other community human service agencies. In fact, most agencies have a volunteer coordinator who actively recruits volunteers from the community. Koenig (1989) found that 34 percent of the private blindness agencies in the United States employed paraprofessionals or teaching aides, and an even greater number (77 percent) reported that they were in favor of doing so.

It is likely that the number of persons requiring rehabilitation services will increase in the coming decades, particularly as the percentage of older people in the population grows, while budget constraints often dictate maintaining rather than increasing the number of staff, so that caseloads may become less and less manageable (see Epilogue). Thus, the need to distribute the rehabilitation teacher's workload will only increase, and with it the role of rehabilitation teachers in supervising and training teaching aides and volunteers.

Such assistants may perform noninstructional chores, such as collecting crafts for resale, making friendly visits, distributing supplies, and doing clerical or custodial work. They may also teach food preparation, home care, listening and recording devices, personal management, clothing care, and crafts under the direction of the rehabilitation teacher. Other examples of assistive roles might range from monitoring keyboarding lessons and dictating sentences for braille writing practice to traveling to client's homes to assist with labeling microwave and stove controls.

As noted, the two major tasks faced by a rehabilitation teacher who is assisted by paraprofessionals or volunteers are training and supervising them. Although training programs may be available in some locations, rehabilitation teachers are likely to be responsible for training volunteers and paraprofessionals as well as for giving in-service education to the personnel of community human service agencies that are providing services to rehabilitation clients but do not have experience in working with people who are blind or visually impaired. In addition, public education about blindness for community groups is also an important role that has many similarities to that of training teaching assistants and will also be discussed in this section.

Supervising Teaching Aides and Volunteers

As teaching aides, paraprofessionals, and volunteers increasingly take on teaching tasks, it is likely that the rehabilitation teacher's role will shift to a certain degree away from direct teaching and more toward assessment and planning, teaching of highly technical areas, and supervision of paraprofessionals and volunteers. Therefore, it is important for rehabilitation teachers to understand some basic principles of supervision. (For a more in-depth discussion of supervision, see Emener, Luck, & Smits, 1981).

As when any two people are interacting, good communication is vital to success. Supervisors, whether of employees or volunteers, are generally expected to provide a precise definition of the job responsibilities, provide ongoing guidance, evaluate job performance and give feedback, and reward good performance (Learn, 1988; Emener, Luck, & Smits, 1981; von Schlegell, 1992).

Defining the paraprofessional's or volunteer's job responsibilities includes providing a detailed, written job description and, for each client, specific directions about the subjects to be taught and the methods to be used. Ongoing guidance is generally provided in weekly or biweekly supervisory meetings or client reviews. At such meetings, the supervising rehabilitation teacher might suggest ways of overcoming any problems encountered by the teaching assistant, help with writing upcoming lesson plans, or work on improving written progress notes.

Performance evaluation comes from direct observations of the assistant, feedback from clients, and review of the assistant's written reports. When such evaluations indicate a need to improve some aspect of performance, the supervisor must be willing to provide suggestions in a supportive and objective manner. Any suggestions for improvement should be made in a private setting away from clients. If an assistant's teaching errors occurred in part due to lack of supervision or were caused in some way by the supervisor, the supervisor should be willing to share the responsibility (von Schlegell, 1988).

Giving meaningful reward for good performance is as important as giving suggestions for improvement. Rewards take many forms, ranging from verbal compliments to salary increases. Providing appropriate recognition for volunteers differs slightly from rewarding employees, since increasing their salary is not an option. For volunteers in particular, rewards for good performance are often relegated to recognition at an annual awards banquet. But other, ongoing rewards provided on a day-to-day basis that demonstrate a respectful professional regard are frequently the strongest motivators. For example, provision of office space or a staff mailbox, inclusion in staff meetings or discussions of clients, invitations to professional training workshops, and acknowledgement by other staff members all give volunteers a feeling of being valued members of a team.

Education and In-Service Training

Training those who will ultimately work directly with visually impaired individuals requires longer and more thorough education than do one-time public education workshops. However, many of the guidelines to follow when planning an in-service workshop are the same, whether the purpose is providing general information to the public or educating those who will work directly with persons with visual impairments. In either case, the rehabilitation teacher should consider the following pointers:

- In-service workshops are, in essence, lessons and require the same degree of planning as do lessons for clients, including lesson plans complete with objectives, lists of materials, assessment questions, and procedures. (Lesson Plan 17.1 for teaching an in-service workshop appears in this chapter.) The objective can be specifically tailored to the group being addressed by assessing the group's needs and desires before the plan is written. For example, the objective of an in-service workshop for a group of preschool teachers might be designed around the specific needs of a particular blind child who attends the preschool.
- The content of the presentation should fit the amount of time available as well as the audience's needs and interests. Because rehabilitation teachers are often eager to share the not-so-commonly-known facts about visual impairment, it is easy to overwhelm the audience by cramming too many facts, figures, and adaptive devices into the space of a short workshop. As when instructing a client, the speed of presentation can be monitored by asking a few well-placed questions to evaluate what the group has learned.
- Just as when teaching a lesson to a client, learning during an in-service training session will be enhanced by involving the learners in the process. Although it may be easier to present a workshop in a lecture format, participants will be more attentive if the teacher asks them to suggest their own solutions to situations that vision loss might present or has them perform tasks, such as writing or identifying coins, without vision.
- Since the emphasis of many in-service presentations is on changing people's perceptions of blindness and blind persons, the focus of the presentation should be on the abilities rather than the limitations of visually impaired individuals. For example, signing one's name, identifying coins, or pouring a cold beverage would be better choices of activities during a short workshop than having participants attempt to read braille tactilely, which might only appear frustrating during a brief first experience, or walk up and down stairs, which could be frightening or even dangerous for novices. And, although it is important and entertaining to demonstrate adaptive aids such as talking devices or low vision devices, an overemphasis on them could lead participants to believe

Teaching a Public Education In-Service Workshop

I. Objective: After presentation of information about blindness and visual impairment and after performing several tasks with occluded vision or simulated low vision, the participants will be able to perform sighted guide assistance, verbally identify problems associated with various eye conditions, and state the name of the state agency that provides services to persons with visual impairments to a level that indicates understanding.

II. Materials

  A. Workshop outlines in accessible media

  B. Communications: braille and large-print reading materials, handwriting guides, bold-lined paper, bold felt-tip markers, brailler, slate and stylus, talking book materials, etc.

  C. Activities of daily living: braille clothing tags, talking calculator, big-button telephone, liquid level indicator, folding cane, etc.

  D. Eyeshades (occluders) and low vision simulation goggles

III. Assessment

  A. Ask members of the audience if they know anyone who is visually impaired.

  B. Ask participants what kinds of things their visually impaired acquaintances do in their daily lives, and how they read, get around, go to work, and so forth.

IV. Procedure

  A. Review the types of vision loss that people experience (acuity loss, peripheral field loss and night blindness, central field loss, mixed scotomas, etc.)

  B. Provide brief facts about the causes of visual impairment, statistics, legal blindness, and the availability of services to those with problems related to vision loss.

  C. Demonstrate how people can retain skills despite vision loss by having participants sign their name while occluded.

  D. Demonstrate how adaptive techniques are sometimes necessary to continue to perform certain skills by having participants identify coins, while occluded, by their size and edges; and, while simulating low vision, by viewing them in better light, by holding them closer to the eye, or by viewing them from a different angle.

  E. Briefly present an overview of the effects of congenital and adventitious vision loss.

  F. Demonstrate sighted guide technique and ways to guide or assist a person with a visual impairment.

  G. Have participants pair up and practice guiding their partners.

  H. Briefly describe some adaptive equipment, which can be displayed.

  I. Ask participants if they have any questions.

V. Memoranda

  A. Remind participants that they should not make assumptions about a person with visual impairment—for example, they should always ask an individual whether he or she needs assistance.

  B. Remind participants that many legally blind individuals may not need or use any of the materials or techniques demonstrated and that the ones shown are only examples.

VI. Evaluation

  A. Ask participants whom they should contact if they have questions about vision loss or if they have a referral.

  B. Ask other questions as a review of the material presented.

that the device, rather then the client's efforts, are the reasons for a client's success.

- Reinforcing learning by providing the information in print or accessible media is generally helpful, particularly if sources of information or devices are presented or participants are to be tested on the information.

In-Service Training for Aides or Other Professionals

Whereas public education sessions usually involve providing general information about blindness, the abilities of people with visual impairments, and blindness resources, future teaching assistants would need, in addition, a knowledge of the factors affecting clients' behavior, the factors affecting visibility, and the principles of communicating with people who have limited vision. If the workshop participants are concerned with specific areas—for example, a paraprofessional assigned to teach daily living skills or a volunteer reading teacher from a literacy organization—training would necessarily require specific instruction related to those subjects as well.

Explaining the factors affecting clients' behaviors—particularly the age at which the impairment occurred, the length of time since the impairment occurred, and the specific functional limitations of certain eye disorders—is of paramount importance in a training program for teaching aides or other professionals who work with visually impaired clients. For example, such knowledge as why unusual head movements are common in those with limited visual fields, that denying the permanance of sight loss is common immediately following the loss, or that the tactile abilities of those blinded early in life are generally outstanding, is basic to working with visually impaired individuals. Since most clients have some functional vision, teaching assistants or other professionals will also need a thorough understanding of the factors that affect the ability to see objects and the ways vision can be enhanced. In addition, understanding the limitations imposed by vision loss on communications between teacher and client is a prerequisite to any lessons with visually impaired individuals. Finally, since the rehabilitation teacher will probably depend on the paraprofessional or volunteer for input on clients' progress, those individuals should have instruction on how to document their work with clients.

The objective for the written plan used with this type of workshop is usually based on the type of client the participants will encounter. For example, if the in-service workshop is being delivered to nursing home personnel, its objective need only address the information and skills needed to work with elderly persons who have visual impairments. Although the special needs of people with congenital impairments might be discussed in the workshop, it would probably be counterproductive to spend a great deal of time on the subject.

Direct assessments of the participants' needs can be gathered through questioning, either prior to or at the beginning of the session. Having participants describe anyone they have encountered or with whom they have worked who had a visual impairment is especially helpful, since many of the behaviors that might be discussed in the workshop would already have been noted by anyone who had spent a significant amount of time with someone who was visually impaired. For example, participants are likely to mention that the blind person they know is able to see quite a bit, a point that can be used to explain that many people considered blind actually have some useful vision.

Suggested topics to cover that might serve as headings for the procedure portion of a lesson plan for an in-service training workshop include:

- facts about vision loss: definitions, statistics, and causes
- factors affecting behavior: age at onset of vision loss, degree of adjustment, and types of functional vision loss and their effects
- adaptive skills: reading, writing, mathematics, daily living, orientation and mobility, leisure-time activities
- low vision: factors affecting visibility and increasing visibility

- instructional communications: barriers and methods for overcoming them.

General Workshop for Community Groups

Providing information about blindness to community groups not only increases public awareness of the needs and abilities of people in the community who have a visual impairment, but may also result in additional referrals of people experiencing new vision loss for services. Public education may also have the added benefit of identifying community groups or individuals that are willing to assist with clients' transportation or donate funds to purchase adaptive equipment for clients with financial need.

As in training sessions with professionals, a general audience's knowledge and attitudes about blindness can be readily assessed by asking how many of them know someone with a visual impairment and then asking those who respond to describe that person. There are innumerable ways to deliver this type of public workshop, but regardless of format, presentations generally include the following information:

- facts about vision impairment, such as definitions, causes, and statistics
- information about how people with visual impairments conduct everyday tasks
- resources for further information.

A presentation of how everyday tasks are accomplished can address frequently asked questions, such as: "How do blind people read, write, or do math?" "How do they know how to identify the cans in their cupboards, the money in their billfolds, or the clothes in their closets?" How do they know when to cross the streets and how to get to specific locations in their neighborhoods?" Audience participation can be increased by posing these questions, letting participants attempt to come up with their own solutions individually or in groups, and then filling in the missing information. Examples of some direct-participation activities that can be done under occlusion include:

- writing a signature on a chalkboard or paper
- identifying well-known items by touch
- reading the time on a large tactile watch or clock
- walking with a sighted guide
- using a talking calculator
- using a beeper or other sound source to find a specific item in the room.

CONCLUSION

As a rehabilitation teacher gains experience, managing a rehabilitation teaching caseload becomes second nature. But, as the profession of rehabilitation teaching continues its process of growth and development, many changes will occur that may affect what rehabilitation teachers do, who their clients are, and even what they are called. The epilogue examines some of the forces that are affecting rehabilitation teaching today and the opportunities that new teachers entering the profession are likely to encounter in the future.

EPILOGUE

The Future of Rehabilitation Teaching: Challenges and Opportunities

The profession of rehabilitation teaching has come a long way since Dr. William Moon began his pioneering work in the late 1800s. It survived the growing pains of the expansion phase in the early part of the 20th century; delineated its chief characteristics, strengths, and weaknesses during the definition phase of the mid-20th century; and has been improving the provision of rehabilitation services and education during the refinement phase of the last four decades of the century (see Chapter 2).

There is no single point at which it can be said that rehabilitation teaching became a profession, but it is clear that it has. Rehabilitation teachers have, to a significant degree, assembled a body of professional knowledge that is passed along through training, gained autonomy, demonstrated commitment, achieved a professional identity, developed professional ethics, and maintained standards—all the components of a profession as described by Raelin (1985). But professional development never ends, and rehabilitation teachers must be prepared to meet the challenges and the opportunities that the future will bring as they move into the 21st century.

CHALLENGES

Meeting the Future

Perhaps the greatest challenge that rehabilitation teaching must face is the global challenge of changing with the times, staying current with new developments in areas such as technology and medicine, and moving into the future with confidence. Just in the past 30 years, simple mechanical typewriters have been replaced by complex computers, and, for many families, evening meals have evolved from elaborate home-cooked affairs to often-hurried dinners that make use of many convenience foods. Such changes affect the content of lessons and the methods used to teach them. It would be wrong of a rehabilitation teacher to deny clients the power of new technology and developments because he or she is ignorant of computers, just as it would be unrealistic to continue to teach food preparation as if most meals were prepared by stay-at-home housewives. As the coming years bring even more significant changes, rehabilitation teachers must be prepared to learn and to teach the requisite skills.

The preceding chapters have hinted at some of the other transformations that have been underway even as this book was being written: major changes in the ways we communicate and exchange information through computer-based networks (Chapter 10), in the ways we shop and pay for purchases (Chapter 13), and in devices that can help people who are blind or visually impaired to read (Chapter 10) and to write (Chapter 8). Many of the devices that help with the activities of daily living—such as talking scales and other measuring devices—are constantly being altered and updated. Each of these new developments requires rehabilitation teachers to make adjustments in the way they practice their profession.

The Changing Nature of Clients

The profession must also be aware of the challenge posed by the ever-changing nature and needs of the people it serves. As the population ages—particularly the large group of post-World War II "baby boomers"—there are more elderly clients (Goodrich, 1991). As a result, teachers will increasingly be working with service providers in what is termed the "aging network" to ensure that older persons who are blind or visually impaired have the services and benefits provided through this network, such as Meals on Wheels and transportation. And, since over two-thirds of older individuals who are blind or visually impaired have at least one other chronic health problem or disability (Orr, 1992), rehabilitation teachers will be spending more time working collaboratively with other rehabilitation professionals in the health care system, such as occupational therapists and physcial therapists, particularly when vision loss results from a stroke. Finally, with the marked growth in the number of people in the category of "oldest of the old" (those 85 and over), teachers will spend more time in efforts to keep clients out of long-term care facilities and more time providing services within such institutions and working in concert with allied health professionals who also care for clients there, such as nurses, occupational therapists, and physical therapists.

Current epidemiological changes are likely to alter caseloads to include more individuals with HIV infection and closed-head injuries as well. In these areas, too, rehabilitation teachers will be facing the challenge of becoming part of a medical-social service team and working with greater numbers of terminally ill clients. They will also have to learn the varied needs of individuals with traumatic brain injuries (as advanced medical and emergency techniques allow more people to survive more devastating accidents) and the best methods for instructing such clients. The increasing number of persons with AIDS or HIV infection and other infectious diseases has already affected caseload management and the role of rehabilitation teachers (Kapperman, Matsuoka & Pawelski, 1993; Kiester, 1990). The delivery of services for all individuals is now affected by the necessity of using universal precautions for disease control during lessons, regardless of whether AIDS or other diseases have been diagnosed.

Loss of Financial Support

A major challenge to the future of the profession is the threat that existing financial support from government sources will be lost, both for the provision of services to persons with visual impairments and for the training of new rehabilitation teachers to work with them. The loss of government support for training, which has sustained university programs since the 1960s but has steadily decreased in the 1980s and 1990s, would be devastating, because support funds have been instrumental in attracting talented people to the profession. Indeed, the profession already suffers from an inability to produce the number of university-trained teachers that are required. Agency directors commonly hold jobs open for a year or more in the hope of finding a rehabilitation teacher who has been professionally trained. Many administrators feel that they are forced by this lack of personnel to hire individuals trained in related fields, such as education or psychology, and then attempt to teach them about visual impairments along with the adaptive skills on the job.

Decreased funds for services would cause teachers to see clients even less frequently than they do now and would create added strain in efforts to meet the needs of an expanding client population. Funding cuts for services would also result in personnel cuts and the combining of jobs at state vocational rehabilitation agencies in attempts to economize. Remaining personnel would likely be expected to take on more generalized roles, which in turn might lead to the assignment of rehabilitation teaching functions to other professionals.

Professional Identity

Although rehabilitation teachers are sometimes asked to perform roles traditionally done by others—particularly the case management functions of rehabilitation counselors—there is a much greater trend toward others performing some of the roles traditionally undertaken by rehabilitation teachers. The professional identity of rehabilitation teachers is strong within the field of those who work with visually impaired persons, but in the general field of health and human services, their name and function are less well known. Thus, agency directors who are combining direct service positions to save money are more likely to look elsewhere, for example, to vocational rehabilitation counselors, to fulfill rehabilitation teaching tasks.

Indeed, in the United States at this time, revolutionary changes whose outcomes are yet to be determined are affecting the quality and delivery of health care and related services. As concerns relating to cost cutting and managed care come to the fore, every profession involved in health-related fields is being forced to examine service delivery. Issues of cost containment and reimbursement have gained prominence along with questions of quality of service. For example, agency directors are motivated by financial considerations to look outside the rehabilitation system to find allied health service providers, such as occupational therapists, who can receive reimbursement from third-party health insurance companies for vision-related services. Rehabilitation teachers, along with every other provider of services to people who are blind and visually impaired, are faced with questions of what services they will provide, where, when, how, with which other professionals, and how they will get paid. Thus, in an effort to ensure that clients can continue to receive high-quality services focused specifically on the needs of people with visual impairments, rehabilitation teachers and other blindness professionals are directing considerable energy into refining professional qualifications. Moreover, as increasing collaboration with other allied health professions becomes a reality, the definition of rehabilitation teaching will have to be refined still further in debate and discussion throughout the profession in order to resolve questions of professional mission and autonomy.

OPPORTUNITIES

In the face of this description of the challenges confronting the profession, it is reassuring to note that the list of opportunities for its development in the coming decades is longer than the list of its challenges. Rehabilitation teachers are already taking the opportunity to take an active role in the Association for Education and Rehabilitation of the Blind and Visually Impaired (AER), the professional organization (see Chapter 2), in order to maintain visibility, keep abreast of new developments in the field of blindness, and exchange information with other rehabilitation teachers and blindness professionals. In fact, rehabilitation teaching and independent living services has become one of the larger divisions in AER. This connection will be particularly useful in helping teachers to stay abreast of current information and learn future skills through AER's continuing education efforts.

The pervasiveness of computer-based communications and the use of the Internet provide opportunities for rehabilitation teachers to communicate more frequently with one another. Several bulletin board services and list servers focus on rehabilitation teaching and related matters (including RT-L, an Internet forum initiated in 1996) and are fully accessible to anyone with access to a computer (see Resources section). This burgeoning of communication options will allow rehabilitation teachers who are not in geographical proximity to each other to discuss issues within the profession and will also provide a forum for teachers to offer solutions to questions posed by other vision professionals. The creation of World Wide Web pages offers a new avenue for promoting the profession, boosting awareness of employment possibilities, and informing others about the services that rehabilitation teachers provide. Many of the problems of limited service provision to people in their homes could be solved through the Internet as well. For example, a teacher at a computer in Reno, Nevada, might now interact with four or five rural clients, all separated by several hundred miles of roads.

Taking technology one step further, virtual reality created by computers will soon give us the power to simulate nearly any teaching environment, perhaps even to bring a virtual rehabilitation center right into clients' homes. As this book is being published, a tactile glove is under development that can simulate a variety of tactile sensations. The ability to teach braille with such a device is probably just a few years away. Clients can already use computers to control the temperature of their apartments, prepare food, and do other tasks. Artificial intelligence will increasingly be used to help clients with impaired cognition to make everyday decisions, particularly if computer-based decision making would be sufficient to keep them living safely in their own homes or in assisted living environments instead of in an institution. For example, a voice-output computer programmed with information about a client's abilities, needs, and daily schedule could use artificial intelligence capabilities to provide reminders to take medications; prepare a grocery list and send an order for delivery via telecommunications; and provide related support to help the individual remain independent. Another ideal opportunity is the creation and use of so-called artificial intelligence expert systems that would use compiled knowledge of seasoned rehabilitation teachers and data from case files to assist with planning and teaching. Such a system could, for example, prescribe low vision training exercises based on a client's eye condition, acuity, low vision devices, and other variables.

As Roberts (1995) has pointed out, rehabilitation teachers have an abundance of opportunities to enhance their professional image, particularly by focusing their efforts on each of Raelin's (1985) six components of a profession. Better training and more knowledge through research, better public relations, greater identification with the technologies of low vision and communications, perhaps a name change to a more recognizable one, enforcement of the code of ethics, and a test-based certification or licensing program would all represent significant opportunities for professional growth. Thus, a program of development for the next stage of the profession might include all the following:

- pursuing licensing and becoming more closely associated with the medical and allied health professions
- enhancing the professional visibility of rehabilitation teaching through increased national leadership roles, research, and publication
- exploring the idea of changing the name rehabilitation teacher to a more identifiable one that would reinforce the identity of the profession; some possibilities include *visual rehabilitation therapist*, *vision therapist*, or *visual impairment therapist*
- increasing efforts to recruit new students for university training programs
- providing children with daily-living skills instruction *before* they leave the educational system
- redoubling efforts to certify all rehabilitation teachers
- actively encouraging federal requirements for certification of rehabilitation teachers as a prerequisite for an agency's receipt of funding

The 21st century brings new opportunities to strengthen both the practice and the professional status of rehabilitation teaching. In the pursuit of these challenges, moreover, lies the greatest opportunity of all to ensure the growth and survival of this still-young profession: the opportunity to serve clients more efficiently in the unique relationship of teaching, guidance, and advocacy that defines the role of the rehabilitation teacher.

REFERENCES

Acton, J. (1976). Establishing and maintaining a therapeutic environment in a residential rehabilitation center for the blind. *New Outlook for the Blind, 70,* 149–152.

Adult Braille Literacy Empowerment Project. (1995). *Guidelines for model braille literacy programs, The Able-G.* Atlanta: American Foundation for the Blind.

AFB National Technology Center. (n.d.). *Closed circuit television systems.* New York: American Foundation for the Blind.

Agency for Health Care Policy and Research. (1993). *Cataract in adults: Management of functional impairment.* Clinical Practice Guideline No. 4 (AHCPR Publication No. 93-0542). Rockville, MD: U.S. Department of Health and Human Services.

Alliance for Technology Access. (1994). *Computer resources for people with disabilities: A guide to exploring today's assistive technology.* Alameda, CA: Hunter House.

American Diabetes Association, (1996). *Diabetes 1996 vital statistics.* Alexandria, VA: Author.

American Foundation for the Blind. (1993). *AFB Directory of Services for Blind and Visually Impaired Persons in the United States and Canada* (24th ed.). New York: Author.

Anderson, J. W. (1965). Home teachers are teachers. *New Outlook for the Blind, 59,* 169–172.

Anderson, S. (1988). *Self-monitoring of blood glucose for the functionally blind diabetic.* Unpublished manuscript, Western Michigan University, Department of Blind Rehabilitation, Kalamazoo.

Arenberg, D. (1974). A longitudinal study of problem solving in adults. *Journal of Gerontology, 29,* 650–658.

Asenjo, J. A. (1975a). *Rehabilitation centers for the blind and visually impaired: The state of the art, 1975.* Final report of the National Workshop on Rehabilitation Centers. New York: American Foundation for the Blind.

Asenjo, J. A. (1975b). *Rehabilitation teaching for the blind and visually impaired: The state of the art, 1975.* Final report of the National Workshop on Rehabilitation Teachers. New York: American Foundation for the Blind.

Aslanian, C. B., & Brickell, H. M. (1980). *Americans in transition: Life changes as reasons for adult learning.* New York: College Entrance Examination Board.

Baltes, P. B., Dittmann-Kohli, F., & Dixon, R. (1984). New perspectives on the development of intelligence in adulthood: Toward a dual process conception and a model of selective optimization with compensation. In P. B. Baltes & O. G. Brim (Eds.), *Life-span Development and Behavior* (Vol. 6). Orlando, FL: Academic Press.

Bailey, I. L., & Hall, A. (1990). *Visual impairment: An overview.* New York: American Foundation for the Blind.

Barraga, N. C. (1976). *Visual handicaps and learning.* Belmont, CA: Wadsworth.

Barraga, N. C. (1986). Sensory perceptual development. In G. T. Scholl (Ed.), *Foundations of education for blind and visually handicapped children and youth* (pp. 83–98). New York: American Foundation for the Blind.

Baskerville, L. (1989, Spring). Large-cell braille: Improved reading for the touch-impaired. *NBA Bulletin,* p. 3.

Bauman, M. K. (1973). *The social competency of visually handicapped children.* Paper presented at the Conference on the Blind Child in Social Interaction: Developing Relationships with Peers and Adults. New York.

Becker, C., & Kalina, K. (1975). The Cranmer abacus and its use in residential schools for the blind and in day school programs. *New Outlook for the Blind, 69,* 412–415, 417.

Beliveau-Tobey, M., & de l'Aune, W. (1991). *Identification of roles and functions of rehabilitation teachers: Executive summary.* Mississippi State: Mississippi State University Rehabilitation Research and Training Center on Blindness and Low Vision.

Benjamin, A. (1981). *The helping interview* (3rd ed.). Boston: Houghton Mifflin.

Berkowitz, K., Bernbaum, M., Bryant, E., Cleary, M., Davis, J., Evers, C., Kiger, D. G., Koenig, P. J., Luxton, L., Martin, R. D., Petzinger, R. A., Ponchillia, S., Schulz, J. M., Taft, S. H., Teasley, M. L., Thom, S. L., & Williams, A. S. (1993). Guidelines for the practice of adaptive diabetes education for visually impaired persons. *Journal of Visual Impairment & Blindness, 87,* 378–382.

Blasch, B. B. (1978). Blindism: Treatment by punishment and reward in laboratory and natural setting. *Journal of Visual Impairment & Blindness, 72,* 215–230.

Blasch, B. B., Wiener, W. R., & Welsh, R. L. (in press). *Foundations of orientation and mobility* (2nd ed.). New York: AFB Press.

Bledsoe, W. (1972). History of philosophy of work for the blind. In R. Hardy & J. Cull (Eds.), *Social and rehabilitation services for the blind* (pp. 5–68). Springfield, IL: Charles C Thomas.

Borden, P. A., Lubich, J. L., & Vanderheiden, G. C. (1996). *Trace resource book: Assistive Technologies for Communication, control, and computer access, 1996–97.* Madison: Trace Research and Development Center.

Bringle, B. (1987). *The effect of a "Driver Alert" motion detector upon the reduction of stereotypic rocking behavior.* Unpublished manuscript, Western Michigan University, Department of Blind Rehabilitation, Kalamazoo.

Brodwin, M. G., Tellez, F., & Brodwin, S. K. (1995). *Medical, psychosocial and vocational aspects of disability.* Athens, GA: Elliott & Fitzpatrick.

Brokenleg, M. (1987, August). *Values in Native American cultures.* Paper presented at the North Central Regional Conference Association for the Education and Rehabilitation of the Blind and Visually Impaired, Sioux Falls, SD.

Brookfield, S. (1987). *Developing critical thinkers.* San Francisco: Jossey-Bass.

Bruner, J. (1965). In defense of verbal learning. In R. C. Anderson & D. P. Ausubel (Eds.), *Readings in the psychology of cognition.* New York: Holt, Rinehart & Winston.

Burklen, K. (1932). *Touch reading of the blind.* New York: American Foundation for the Blind.

Byers-Lang, R. (1984). Peer counselors: Network builders for elderly persons. *Journal of Visual Impairment & Blindness, 77,* 193–197.

Byers-Lang, R. E., & McCall, R. A. (1993). Peer support groups: Rehabilitation in action. *RE:view, 25*(1), 32–36.

Canadian Council of the Blind. (1993). *Active living through physical education: Maximizing opportunities for students who are visually impaired* (2nd ed.). Ottawa, Ontario: Author.

Carroll, T. J. (1961). *Blindness: What it is, what it does and how to live with it.* Boston: Little, Brown.

Carter, K. (1983a). Assessment of lighting. In R. T. Jose (Ed.), *Understanding low vision* (pp. 403–414). New York: American Foundation for the Blind.

Carter, K. (1983b). Comprehensive preliminary assessments of low vision. In R. T. Jose (Ed.), *Understanding low vision* (pp. 85–104). New York: American Foundation for the Blind.

Carter, K. D., & Carter, C. A. (1981). Itinerant low vision services. *New Outlook for the Blind, 75,* 255–260.

Caton, H. (Ed.). (1994). *TOOLS for selecting appropriate learning media.* Louisville, KY: American Printing House for the Blind.

Caton, H., Pester, E., & Bradley, E. J. (1990). *Read again.* Louisville, KY: American Printing House for the Blind.

Cattell, R. B. (1987). *Intelligence: Its structure, growth and action.* Amsterdam: North-Holland.

Chiang, Y., Bassi, L. J., & Javitt, J. C. (1992). Federal budgetary costs of blindness. *Milbank Quarterly, 70*(2), 319-340.

Cholden, L. (1958). *A psychiatrist works with blindness.* New York: American Foundation for the Blind.

Cleary, M. E. (Ed.). (1994). *Diabetes and visual impairment: An educator's resource guide.* Chicago: American Association of Diabetes Educators.

Coe, D. W. (1993). *The effectiveness of the Aqualert on a blind swimmer's turn during competitive swimming.* Unpublished manuscript, Western Michigan University, Department of Blind Rehabilitation, Kalamazoo.

Commission on Standards and Accreditation for the Blind. (1966). *The COMSTAC report: Standards for strengthened services.* New York: National Accreditation Council for Agencies Serving the Blind and Visually Handicapped.

Community Services for the Visually Handicapped. (1974). *Handwriting manual: A reference manual for rehabilitation teachers working with the adult blind.* Kalamazoo, Michigan: Western Michigan University.

Coopersmith, S. (1967). *The antecedents of self-esteem.* San Francisco: Freeman.

Cosgrove, E. (1961). *Home teachers of the adult blind: What they do, what they could do, and what will enable them to do it?.* Washington, DC: American Association of Workers for the Blind.

Cratty, B. (1971). *Movement and spatial awareness in blind children and youth.* Springfield, IL: Charles C Thomas.

Cronheim, A. H. (1992). *A comparison study of two handwriting guides used with blindfolded subjects.* Unpublished manuscript, Western Michigan University, Department of Blind Rehabilitation, Kalamazoo.

Cull, J. G. (1972). Psychological adjustment to blindness. In J. G. Cull & R. E. Hardy (Eds.), *Social and rehabilitation services for the blind* (pp. 174–186). Springfield, IL: Charles C Thomas.

Culturgram '92: Taiwan. (1992). Provo, UT: David M. Kennedy Center for International Studies, Brigham Young University.

Cutsforth, T. D. (1951). *The blind in school and society: A psychological study.* New York: American Foundation for the Blind.

Davidow, M. (1979). *The abacus made easy.* Louisville, KY: American Printing House for Blind.

Davidson, J. K. (1991). *Clinical diabetes mellitus: A problem-oriented approach* (2nd ed.). New York: Thieme Medical.

De Witt, J. C., Schreier, E. M., & Leventhal, J. (1988). A look at closed circuit television systems (CCTV) for persons with low vision. *Journal of Visual Impairment & Blindness, 82,* 151–162.

De Witt, J. C., Schreier, E. M., Leventhal, J. D., & Meyers, A. M. (1988). A guide to selecting large print/enhanced image computer access hardware/software for persons with low vision. *Journal of Visual Impairment & Blindness, 82,* 432–442.

Dickey, T. W., & Vieceli, L. (1972). A survey of the vocational placement of visually handicapped persons and their degree of vision. *New Outlook for the Blind, 66,* 38–42.

Dickinson, R. M. (1956). The discipline of home teaching. *Proceedings of the Thirtieth Convention of the American Association of Workers for the Blind,* Los Angeles (pp. 21–28). New York: American Foundation for the Blind.

Dickinson, R. M. (1963). Why do we need home teachers? *New Outlook for the Blind, 57*(7), 263–267.

Dickman, I. R. (1983). *Making life more livable: Simple adaptations for the homes of blind and visually impaired older people.* New York: American Foundation for the Blind.

DiFrancesco, A. (1980). Kinesiology. In R. L. Welsh & B. B. Blasch (Eds.), *Foundations of orientation and mobility* (pp. 37–41). New York: American Foundation for the Blind.

Dixon, J. M. (1990). The braille system: An evolution of literacy. In *World braille usage* (pp. 1–2). Washington, DC: United Nations Educational, Scientific and Cultural Organization and the National Library Service for the Blind and Physically Handicapped, Library of Congress.

Dodds, A. G. (1987). NAOMI mobility officer survey. *New Beacon, 72,* 71–73.

Dodds, A. G., Bailey, P., Pearson, A., & Yates, L. (1991). Psychological factors in acquired visual impairment: The development of a scale of adjustment. *Journal of Visual Impairment & Blindness, 85,* 306–310.

Emener, W. G., Luck, R. S., & Smits, S. J. (1981). *Rehabilitation administration and supervision.* Baltimore: University Park Press.

Erikson, E. H. (1950). *Childhood and society.* New York: Norton.

Erin, J. N., & Sumranveth, P. (1995). Teaching reading to students who are adventitiously blind. *RE:view, 28,* 103–111.

Espinola, O., & Croft, D. (1992). *Solutions: Access technologies for people who are blind.* Boston: National Braille Press.

Etheredge, P. (1992). *Identifying methods of teaching braille to adults with adventitious visual impairments.* Unpublished manuscript, Western Michigan University, Department of Blind Rehabilitation, Kalamazoo.

Farrel, G. (1956). *The story of blindness.* Cambridge, MA: Harvard University Press.

Felps, J. N., & Devlin, R. J. (1988). Modification of stereotypic rocking of a blind adult. *Journal of Visual Impairment & Blindness, 82,* 107–108.

Ferraro, J., & Jose, R. T. (1983). Training programs for individuals with restricted fields. In R. T. Jose (Ed.), *Understanding low vision* (pp. 363–376). New York: American Foundation for the Blind.

Ferrell, K. A. (1986). Infancy and early childhood. In G. T. Scholl (Ed.), *Foundations of education for blind and visually handicapped children and youth* (pp.119–137). New York: American Foundation for the Blind.

Field, D., Schaie, K. W., and Leino, V. E. (1988). Continuity in intellectual functioning: The role of self-reported health. *Psychology and Aging, 3*(4), 385–392.

Finn, W. A., Gadbaw, P. O., Kevorkian, C. A., & De l'Aune, W. R. (1975). Increased field accessibility through prismatically displaced images. *New Outlook for the Blind, 69,* 465–467.

Foley, K. M. (1919). The re-education of the adult blind. *New Outlook for the Blind, 13,* 47–52.

Foulke, E. (1980). Reading by listening to time compressed recorded speech. *Aids and Appliances Review* (Carroll Center for the Blind, Newton, MA), *4,* 1–2.

Foulke, E. (1991). Braille. In M. Heller and W. Schiff (Eds), *The psychology of touch* (pp. 219–234). Hillsdale, NJ: Lawrence Erlbaum Associates.

Freeman, M. H. (1990). *Optics* (10th ed.). Newton, MA: Butterworth-Heineman.

Freund, E. C., & Nagano, P. (1966). *Longhand writing for the blind, based on the Marks method.* Louisville, KY: American Printing House for the Blind.

Freyberger, P. E. (1971). Comparative methods in teaching cooking to the congenitally vs. the adventitiously blind adult. *New Outlook for the Blind, 65,* 149–151, 154.

Gardner, H. (1983). *Frames of mind.* New York: Basic Books.

Gardner, H. (1990, September). *Art and intelligence: A personal perspective.* Keynote address presented at a workshop entitled The Human Spirit: The Arts in Education, Greeley, CO.

Gissendanner, S. V. (1955). Report: A study to determine standards for the home teaching profession. In *Proceedings of the Twenty-Ninth Convention of the Association of Workers for the Blind. Quebec City, Quebec* (pp. 97–104). New York: American Foundation for the Blind.

Gissoni, F. L. (1962). *Using the Cranmer abacus for the blind.* Louisville, KY: American Printing House for the Blind.

Gissoni, F. (1990). Where did it begin: A history of reading machines. *TACTIC, 6*(2p). Cincinnati: Clovernook Publishing House for the Blind.

Goldberg, S. (1986). *Ophthalmology made ridiculously simple.* Miami: MedMaster.

Goodrich, G. L. (1991). *The legally blind veteran popuation: Estimates and characteristics.* Washington, DC: Blind Rehabilitation Service, U.S. Department of Veteran Affairs.

Gould, R. L. (1972). The phases of adult life: A study in developmental psychology. *American Journal of Psychiatry,* 129(5), 521–531.

Gould, R. L. (1978). *Transformations: Growth and change in adult life.* New York: Simon & Schuster.

Greenblatt, S. L. (Ed.). (1989). *Providing services for people with vision loss: A multidisciplinary perspective.* Lexington, MA: Resources for Rehabilitation.

Greig, D. E., West, M. L., & Overbury, O. (1986). Successful use of low vision aids: Visual and psychological factors. *Journal of Visual Impairment & Blindness, 80,* 985–988.

Griffin, H. C. (1981). Motor development in congenitally blind children. *Education of the Visually Handicapped, 7*(4), 107–111.

Hanson, T. (1977). *The 1, 2, 3's of the abacus.* Kalamazoo: Western Michigan University, Department of Blind Rehabilitation.

Harley, R. K., Henderson, F. M., & Truan, M. B. (1979). *The teaching of braille reading.* Springfield, IL: Charles C Thomas.

Harris, E. M. (1981). *In touch: Printing and writing for the blind in the nineteenth century.* Washington, DC: Smithsonian Institution Press.

Harrison, L. M. (1968). *Scriptwriting for the blind: A status survey and a new method.* Unpublished master's thesis, Colorado State College, Greeley.

Heinze, T. (1986). Communication skills. In G. T. Scholl (Ed.), *Foundations of education for blind and visually handicapped children and youth* (pp. 301–314). New York: American Foundation for the Blind.

Hergenhahn, B. R. (1988). *An introduction to theories of learning* (3rd ed.). Englewood Cliffs, NJ: Prentice-Hall.

Hermelin, B., & O'Connor, N. (1971). Functional asymmetry in the reading of braille. *Neuropsychologia, 9,* 431–435.

Hill, E. W., & Blasch, B. B. (1980). Concept development. In R. L. Welsh & B. B. Blasch (Eds.), *Foundations of orientation and mobility* (pp. 265–290). New York: American Foundation for the Blind.

Hill, E. W., & Ponder, P. (1976). *Orientation and mobility techniques: A guide for the practitioner.* New York: American Foundation for the Blind.

Hoshiyama, T. (1989). *The effect of tactile models on teaching origami to blindfolded persons.* Unpublished manuscript, Western Michigan University, Department of Blind Rehabilitation, Kalamazoo.

Huckins, A. P. (1965). Teaching handwriting to the blind student. *New Outlook for the Blind, 59,* 63–65.

Huebner, K. (1986). Social skills. In G.T. Scholl (Ed.), *Foundations of education for blind and visually handicapped children and youth* (pp. 23–33). New York: American Foundation for the Blind.

Huebner, K. M., Prickett, J. G., Welch, T. R., & Joffee, E. (Eds.). (1995). *Hand in hand: Essentials of communication and orientation and mobility for your students who are deaf-blind.* New York: AFB Press.

Huxley, A. (1975). *The art of seeing.* Seattle, WA: Montana Books.

Inana, M. (1980). Grocery shopping: Principles and techniques for the blind consumer. *Journal of Visual Impairment & Blindness, 74,* 329–332.

Irwin, R. B. (1970). *The war of the dots.* New York: American Foundation for the Blind. (Originally published in R. B. Irwin, *As I saw it,* 1955, New York: American Foundation for the Blind.)

Jacobson, W. H. (1993). *The art and sciences of teaching orientation and mobility to persons with visual impairments.* New York: American Foundation for the Blind.

Javal, E. (1905). *On becoming blind.* London: Macmillan Company.

Joffe, L. S., & Vaughn, B. E. (1982). Infant-mother attachment: Theory, assessment, and implications for development. In B. B. Wolman & G. Stricker (Eds.), *Handbook of developmental psychology.* Englewood Cliffs, NJ: Prentice-Hall.

Jones, H. E., & Conrad, H. S. (1933). The growth and decline of intelligence. *General Psychological Monographs, 13.*

Jose, R. T. (1983a). The eye and functional vision. In R. T. Jose (Ed.), *Understanding low vision* (pp. 3–42). New York: American Foundation for the Blind.

Jose, R. T. (1983b). The low vision rehabilitation service. In R. T. Jose (Ed.), *Understanding low vision* (pp. 67–71). New York: American Foundation for the Blind.

Jose, R. T. (1983c). Minimum assessment sequence: The optometrist's viewpoint. In R. T. Jose (Ed.), *Understanding low vision* (pp. 75–83). New York: American Foundation for the Blind.

Jose, R. T. (1983d). Optics. In R. T. Jose (Ed.), *Understand low vision* (pp. 187–248). New York: American Foundation for the Blind.

Jose, R. T. (1983e). Treatment options. In R. T. Jose (Ed.), *Understanding low vision* (pp. 211–248). New York: American Foundation for the Blind.

Jose, R. T. (Ed). (1983f). *Understanding low vision.* New York: American Foundation for the Blind.

Jung, C. G. (1933). The basic postulates of analytic psychology. In H. M. Ruitenbeck (Ed.), *Varieties of personality theory.* New York: Dutton.

Kaarlela, R. (1966). Home teaching: A description. *New Outlook for the Blind, 60,* 80–83.

Kapperman, G., Matsuoka, J. C., & Pawelski, C. E. (1993). HIV/AIDS prevention: A guide for working with people who are blind or visually impaired. New York: American Foundation for the Blind.

Keating, M. P. (1988). *Geometric, physical, and visual optics.* Newton, MA: Butterworth.

Kelly, V. (1908). Home teaching in Maryland. *Outlook for the Blind, 1,* 151–152.

Kennedy, C. (1991). A guide to low vision services and aids. *TRACES: Teaching research assistance to children and youth experiencing sensory impairments, 1*(4), 6–7.

Kidd, J. R. (1973). *How Adults Learn.* New York: Cambridge.

Kiester, E. (1990). *AIDS and vision loss.* New York: American Foundation for the Blind.

Kikkeri, P. (1989). *The effect of training in the use of the electronic liquid level indicator on pouring accuracy of visually impaired persons.* Unpublished manuscript, Western Michigan University, Department of Blind Rehabilitation, Kalamazoo.

Kimball, F. A. (1908). Home teaching in Rhode Island. *Outlook for the Blind, 1,* 152–153.

King, F. M. (1987). *Palmer method transition to cursive, Grade 2.* Schaumburg, IL: A. N. Palmer.

Koenig, A. J., & Holbrook, M. C. (1991). Determining the reading medium for students with visual impairments via diagnostic teaching. *Journal of Visual Impairment & Blindness, 85,* 61–68.

Koenig, A. J., & Holbrook, M. C. (1993). *Learning media assessment of students with visual impairments: A resource guide for teachers.* Austin, TX: Texas School for the Blind and Visually Impaired.

Koenig, P. J. (1989). A survey of private agency directors regarding rehabilitation teaching paraprofessionals. Unpublished manuscript, Western Michigan University, Department of Blind Rehabilitation, Kalamazoo.

Koestler, F. A. (1976). *The unseen minority: A social history of blindness in America.* New York: David McKay.

Kohlberg, L. (1990). Stage and sequence: The cognitive-development approach to socialization. In D. A. Goslin (Ed.), *Handbook of socialization theory and research.* Chicago: Rand McNally.

Kozel, R. J. (1995). Consideration of hand in the reading of braille. *RE:view, 28,* 78–82.

Kübler-Ross, E. (1970). *On death and dying.* New York: Macmillan.

Kurpis, J. S. (1977). People with low vision can distinguish paper currency. *Journal of Visual Impairment & Blindness, 71,* 75–77.

Kusajima, T. (1974). *Visual reading and braille reading: An experimental investigation of the physiology and psychology of visual and tactual reading.* New York: American Foundation for the Blind.

LaGrow, S. J. (1992). *The rehabilitation of visually impaired people.* Auckland: Royal New Zealand Foundation for the Blind.

LaGrow, S. J., & Ponchillia, S. V. (1989). Children with visual impairments. In A. F. Rotatori & R. A. Fox (Eds.), *Understanding individuals with low incidence handicaps: Categorical and noncategorical perspectives* (pp. 133–186). Springfield, IL: Charles C Thomas.

LaGrow, S. J., & Repp, A. C. (1984). Stereotypic responding: A review of intervention. *American Journal of Mental Deficiency, 88,* 595–609.

LaGrow, S. J., & Weessies, M. J. (1994). *Orientation and mobility: Techniques for independence.* Palmerston North, New Zealand: Dunmore Press.

Lariccia, P. (1986). *The significance of teaching visually impaired persons to pour using a liquid level indicator.* Unpublished manuscript, Western Michigan University, Department of Blind Rehabilitation, Kalamazoo.

Lasker, H. M., & Moore, J. (1980). *Current studies of adult develoment: Implications for education, adult development, and approaches to learning.* Washington, DC: National Institute of Education.

Lasker, H. M., Moore, J., & Simpson, E. (1980). *Adult development and approaches to learning.* Washington, DC.: National Institute of Education.

Learn, R. L. (1988). *Supervision of paraprofessional workers in special needs vocational education* (ED296154). Paper presented at Pennsylvania Vocational Education conference.

Leja, J. A. (1990). The job roles of rehabilitation teachers of blind persons. *Journal of Visual Impairment & Blindness, 84,* 155–159.

Lennon, E. M. (n.d.). *Typing techniques for the visually impaired.* Unpublished manuscript, Western Michigan University, Department of Blind Rehabilitation, Kalamazoo.

Leventhal, J. D. (1994). A review of an inexpensive interpoint braille printer. *Journal of Visual Impairment & Blindness, JVIB News Service, 88,* 18–21.

Leventhal, J. D. (1995). Accessing Microsoft Windows with synthetic speech: An overview. *Journal of Visual Impairment & Blindness, JVIB News Service, 89*(3), 14–18.

Leventhal, J., Schreier, E. M., De Witt, J. C., & Meyers, A. (1988). A guide to paperless braille devices. *Journal of Visual Impairment & Blindness, 82,* 290–296.

Leventhal, J. D., Schreier, E. M., De Witt, J. C., & Meyers, A. (1989). A comparison of portable adapted cassette players and recorders. *Journal of Visual Impairment & Blindness, 83,* 258–263.

Leventhal, J. D., & Uslan, M. M. (1992). A comparison of the two leading electronic braille notetakers. *Journal of Visual Impairment & Blindness, 86,* 258–260.

Leventhal, J. D., Uslan, M. M., & Schreier, E. M. (1990). A review of technology-related publications. *Journal of Visual Impairment & Blindness, 84,* 127–130.

Levinson, D. J. (1978). *The seasons of a man's life.* New York: Knopf.

Levinson, D. J. (1986). A conception of adult development. *American Psychologist, 41*(1), 3–13.

Lewis, P. H. (1995, September 19). Putting that handwritten touch on your mail. *New York Times,* p. C10.

Locust, C. (1990). *Hopi beliefs about unwellness and handicaps.* Tucson: University of Arizona Native American Research and Training Center.

Loeb, G. E. (1982). *What, where, when: A resource handbook for the blind and visually impaired, their families and friends, and the general public.* Silver Spring, MD: Gladys E. Loeb Foundation.

Loevinger, J. (1976). *Ego development: conceptions and theories.* San Francisco: Jossey-Bass.

Lowenfeld, B. (1973). *The visually handicapped child in school.* New York: John Day Company.

Lowenfeld, B., Abel, G. L., & Hatlen, P. H. (1974). *Blind children learn to read.* Springfield, IL: Charles C Thomas.

Lowry, S. (1985). *Speech resources.* Houston: Speech Enterprises.

Ludwig, I., Luxton, L., & Attmore, M. (1988). *Creative recreation for blind and visually impaired adults.* New York: American Foundation for the Blind.

Luxton, K., Gerber, J., & Henry, L. (1985). *Computer equipment and aids for the blind and visually impaired.* New York: Baruch College.

Mack, C. (1984). How useful is braille? Reports of blind adults. *Journal of Visual Impairment & Blindness, 78,* 311–313.

Magers, R. F. (1962). *Preparing instructional objectives.* Palo Alto, CA: Fearon.

Magill, A. N. (1959). Report of board of certification of home teachers. In *Proceedings of the Thirty-Third Convention of the American Association of Workers for the Blind, Detroit, MI* (pp. 7–8). Washington, DC: American Association of Workers for the Blind.

Mangold, P. N. (1980). *The pleasure of eating for those who are visually impaired.* Castro Valley, CA: Exceptional Teaching Aids.

Mangold, P. N. (1985). *Teaching the braille slate and stylus: A manual for mastery.* Castro Valley, CA: Exceptional Teaching Aids.

Mangold, S. (1977). *The Mangold developmental program of tactile perception and braille letter recognition.* Castro Valley, CA: Exceptional Teaching Aids.

Mangold, S. S. (Ed.).(1982). *A teacher's guide to the special educational needs of blind and visually handicapped children.* New York: American Foundation for the Blind.

Mangold, S. (1994). *Teaching signature writing to those who are visually impaired.* Castro Valley, CA: Exceptional Teaching Aids.

Mangold, S., & Mangold, P. (1989). Selecting the most appropriate primary literacy medium for students with functional vision. *Journal of Visual Impairment & Blindness, 83,* 294–296.

Marks, A. S., & Marks, R. A. (1954). *Teaching the blind scriptwriting by the Marks method: A manual.* New York: American Foundation for the Blind.

Maslow, A. H. (1970). *Motivation and personality* (2nd ed.). New York: Harper & Row.

Maxfield, K. E. (1928). *The blind child and his reading.* New York: American Foundation for the Blind.

McCarville, T. L. (1996). *The use and knowledge of talking books and descriptive videos by visually impaired older adults.* Unpublished manuscript, Western Michigan University, Department of Blind Rehabilitation, Kalamazoo.

McGillivray, R. (Ed.). (1980). Handwriting guides. *Aids and Appliances Review* (Carroll Center for the Blind, Newton, MA), *3.*

McGillivray, R. (Ed.). (1981). Alternative labels: Aids for independent living. *Aids and Appliances Review* (Carroll Center for the Blind, Newton, MA), *5.*

McKay, E. (1965). The historical role of the home teacher. *New Outlook for the Blind, 59,* pp. 167–168.

McMullen, R., & Kellis, T. (1982). Educating visually handicapped students at the secondary level. In S. S. Mangold (Ed.), *A teacher's guide to the special educational needs of blind and visually handicapped children* (pp. 102–110). New York: American Foundation for the Blind.

McNeil, J. M. (1993). Americans with disabilities: 1991-92: Data from the Survey of Income and Program Participation. *Current Population Reports, Household Economic Studies* (pp. 70–33). Washington, DC: U.S. Bureau of the Census.

Merriam, S. B., & Caffarella, R. S. (1991). *Learning in adulthood: A comprehensive guide.* San Francisco: Jossey-Bass.

Meyers, A., & Schreier, E. (1990). An evaluation of speech access programs. *Journal of Visual Impairment & Blindness, 84,* 26–38.

Michaels, D. D. (1993). Ocular disease in the elderly. In A. A. Rosenbloom & M. W. Morgan (Eds.), *Vision and aging* (2nd ed., pp. 111–159). Boston: Butterworth-Heinemann.

Morford, R. A. (1983). How to select a talking terminal. *Aids and Appliances Review* (Carroll Center for the Blind, Newton, MA), *9 & 10,* 6–10.

Morrill, K. (1986). *The effect of age on the provision and use of rehabilitation training and the desire for further training.* Unpublished manuscript, Western Michigan University, Department of Blind Rehabilitation, Kalamazoo.

Morrison, M. (1974). The other 128 hours a week: Teaching personal management to blind young adults. *New Outlook for the Blind, 68,* 454–459.

Moss, G. S. (1992). Considerations on dispensing low vision devices. *Journal of Visual Impairment & Blindness, 86,* 86–88.

Mund, S. (1978). Vocational rehabilitation; employment; self-employment. In R. M. Goldenson (Ed.), *Disability and rehabilitation handbook* (pp. 67–87). New York: McGraw-Hill.

National Center for Health Statistics. (1995). Current estimates from the National Health Interview Survey, 1994, *Vital and Health Statistics* (Series 10, No. 193). Washington, DC: U.S. Department of Health and Human Services, Centers for Disease Control and Prevention.

National Library Service for the Blind and Physically Handicapped. (1983). *That all may read: Library service for blind and physically impaired people.* Washington, DC: Author.

Nelipovich, M., Godley, S., & Vieceli, L. (1982). Job descriptions of rehabilitation teachers and orientation and mobility specialists in state agencies. *Journal of Visual Impairment & Blindness, 76,* 191–194.

Nelson, K. A., & Dimitrova, G. (1993). Severe visual impairment in the United States and in each state, 1990. *Journal of Visual Impairment & Blindness, 87,* 80-85.

Nemeth Braille Code of Mathematics and Scientific Notation. (1987). Louisville, KY: American Printing House for the Blind.

Nemeth Braille Code of Mathematics and Scientific Notation: Addendum. (1991). Louisville, KY: American Printing House for the Blind.

Newman, S. E., & Hall, A. D. (1988). Ease of learning the Braille and Fishburne alphabets. *Journal of Visual Impairment & Blindness, 82,* 148–149.

Nolan, C. Y. (1966). *Perceptual factors in braille word recognition.* Paper presented at the Forty-eighth Biennial Conference of the American Association of Instructors of the Blind, Washington, DC.

Nolan, C. Y., & Kederis, C. J. (1969). *Perceptual factors in braille word recognition* (Research Series, No. 20). New York: American Foundation for the Blind.

Olmstead, J. E. (1991). *Itinerant teaching: Tricks of the trade for teachers of blind and visually impaired students.* New York: American Foundation for the Blind.

Olson, M. R. (1981). *Guidelines and games for teaching efficient braille reading.* New York: American Foundation for the Blind.

Orr, A. L. (1992). Aging and blindness: Toward a systems approach to service delivery. In A. L. Orr (Ed.), *Vision and aging: Crossroads for service delivery* (pp. 3–33). New York: American Foundation for the Blind.

Osman, S. A. (1987). *Biofeedback in controlling stereotypic behavior in blind adults.* Unpublished manuscript, Western Michigan University, Department of Blind Rehabilitation, Kalamazoo.

Page, J. (1990). Writing got a lot easier when the old "manual" was new. *Smithsonian, 21*(9), 54–65.

Perry, W. G. (1968). *Forms of intellectual and ethical development in the college years: A scheme.* New York: Holt, Rinehart & Winston.

Pester, E. (1993). Braille instruction for individuals who are blind adventitiously: Scheduling, expectations, and reading intrests. *RE:view, 25,* 15–22.

Petzinger, R. A. (1992). Diabetes aids and products for people with visual or physical impairment. *Diabetes Educator, 18,* 121–138.

Petzinger, R. A. (1993). Adaptive blood glucose monitoring and insulin measurement devices for visually impaired persons. *Journal of Visual Impairment & Blindness, 87,* 341–345.

Piaget, J. (1981). *Intelligence and affectivity: Their relationship during child development.* Palo Alto, CA: Annual Reviews.

Ponchillia, P. E. (1988). *Common broadleaf trees of the upper midwest: An identification tool designed especially for the blind.* Unpublished manuscript, Western Michigan University, Department of Blind Rehabilitation, Kalamazoo.

Ponchillia, P. E., & Durant, P. A. (1995). Teaching behaviors and attitudes of braille instructors in adult rehabilitation centers. *Journal of Visual Impairment & Blindness, 89,* 432–439.

Ponchillia, P. E., & Mark, G. P. (1985). Computers: Are They for You? *Tactic, 1*(l), 31–37.

Ponchillia, P. E., & Kaarlela, R. (1986). Post-rehabilitative use of adaptive skills. *Journal of Visual Impairment & Blindness, 80*, 665–669.

Ponchillia, S. V. (1993a). Complications of diabetes and their implications for service providers. *Journal of Visual Impairment & Blindness, 87*, 354–358.

Ponchillia, S. V. (1993b). The effect of cultural beliefs on the treatment of native peoples with diabetes and visual impairment. *Journal of Visual Impairment & Blindness, 87*, 333–335.

Ponchillia, S. V., & LaGrow, S. J. (1988). Independent glucose monitoring by functionally blind diabetics. *Journal of Visual Impairment & Blindness, 82*, 50–54.

Ponchillia, S. V., Richardson, K., & Turner-Barry, M. M. (1990). The effectiveness of six insulin management devices for blind diabetic persons. *Journal of Visual Impairment & Blindness, 84*, 364–369.

Potok, A. (1980). *Ordinary daylight: Portrait of an artist going blind.* New York: Holt, Rinehart & Winston.

Pratt, H. M. (1992). *The effects of ocular prosthetics on the public's opinion toward people with disfigured eyes.* Unpublished manuscript, Western Michigan University, Department of Blind Rehabilitation, Kalamazoo.

Raelin, J. (1985). The basis of the professional resistance to managerial control. *Human Resource Management, 2*, 147–176.

Raftary, A. (1977, July). *Initial client assessment and teacher effectiveness.* Paper presented at the meeting of the Greater Detroit Society for the Blind, AAWB Biennial Convention of the American Association of Workers for the Blind, Detroit, MI.

Resources for Rehabilitation. (1993). *Living with low vision.* Lexington, MA: Author.

Rex, E., Koenig, A. J., Wormsley, D. P., & Baker, R. L. (1994). *Foundations of braille literacy.* New York: AFB Press.

Richardson, N. K. (1959). *Type with one hand* (2nd. ed.). New Rochelle, NY: Southwestern Publishing Company.

Roberts, A. (1995). Enhancing public support of rehabilitation teaching. *Journal of Visual Impairment & Blindness, JVIB News Service, 89*(2), 20–22.

Roessler, R. T., & Rubin, S. E. (1992). *Case management and rehabilitation counseling: Procedures and techniques* (2nd ed.). Austin, TX: Pro-Ed.

Rogers, C. R. (1983). *Freedom to learn for the 80's.* Columbus: Merrill.

Rosenthal, B. P. (1991). Low-vision devices are based on ancient principles and modern technology, materials. *Lighthouse National Center for Vision and Aging: Aging and Vision News, 4*(1), 1, 5–6.

Rubin, S. E., & Roessler, R. T. (1995). *Foundations of the vocational rehabilitation process* (4th ed.). Austin, TX: Pro-Ed.

Ryder, B. E., & Kawalec, E. S. (1995). A job-seeking skills program for persons who are blind or visually impaired. *Journal of Visual Impairment & Blindness, 89*, 107–111.

Savage, R. C. (1977). A grocery shopping technique for the blind and partially sighted. *Long Cane News* (Michigan Commission for the Blind Training Center), *10*(1), 3–8.

Schaie, K. W., & Labouvie-Vief, G. F. (1974). Generational versus ontogenetic components of change in adult cognitive behavior: A fourteen-year cross sequential study. *Developmental Psychology, 10*, 305–320.

Schaie, K. W., & Stroether, C. R. (1968). A cross-sectional study of age changes in cognitive behavior. *Psychological Bulletin, 70*, 671–680.

Schaie, K. W., & Willis, S. L. (1991). *Adult development and aging.* (3rd ed.). Boston: Little, Brown.

Schlossberg, N. K. (1987). Taking the mystery out of change. *Psychology Today, 21*(5), 74–75.

Schlossberg, N. K., Lynch, A. Q., & Chickering, A. W. (1989). *Improving higher education environments for adults.* San Francisco: Jossey-Bass.

Scholl, G. T. (1986a). Growth and development. In G. T. Scholl (Ed.), *Foundations of education for blind and visually handicapped children and youth* (pp.65–81). New York: American Foundation for the Blind.

Scholl, G. T. (1986b). What does it mean to be blind? In G. T. Scholl (Ed.), *Foundations of education for blind and visually handicapped children and youth* (pp. 23–33). New York: American Foundation for the Blind.

Scholl, G. T., Bauman, M. K., and Crissey, M. S. (1969). *A study of the vocational success of groups of the visually handicapped.* Ann Arbor: College of Education, University of Michigan.

Schreier, E. M., & Uslan, M. M. (1991). An evaluation of PC-based optical character recognition systems, *Journal of Visual Impairment & Blindness, 85*, 131–135.

Schropp, A. J. (1990). *Comparing skills of post-rehabilitated visually impaired adults with sighted adults.* Unpublished manuscript, Western Michigan University, Department of Blind Rehabilitation, Kalamazoo.

Schulz, P. J. (1980). *How does it feel to be blind?* Los Angeles: Muse-Ed.

Shafrath, M. R. (1986). An alternative to braille labeling. *Journal of Visual Impairment & Blindness, 80*, 955–956.

Shragai, Y. (1995). Access to Microsoft Windows '95 for persons with low vision: An overview. *Journal of*

Visual Impairment & Blindness, JVIB News Service, 89,(6).

Shragai, Y., & Uslan, M. M. (1995a). Low vision access to Microsoft Windows: An overview. *Journal of Visual Impairment & Blindness, JVIB News Service, 89*(5), 17–21.

Shragai, Y., & Uslan, M. (1995b). A review of Telesensory's Vista screen-magnification system. *Journal of Visual Impairment & Blindness, JVIB News Service, 89*(5).

Silver, J., & Fass, V. H. (1977). Closed circuit television as a low vision aid: Development and application. *Ophthalmic Optician, 17*(16).

Skinner, B. F. (1974). *About behaviorism.* New York: Knopf.

Smith, M. M. (1982). *Getting in touch with reading.* Louisville, KY: American Printing House for the Blind.

Sokol, A. (1991, September 6). A voice for the blind: Audio newsstand opens up a world of information for the visually impaired, disabled, and people who have trouble reading. *Toronto Star,* pp. F1–2.

Splear, J. E. (1986). *The effect of rehabilitation service setting on post-rehabilitation outcomes.* Unpublished manuscript, Western Michigan University, Department of Blind Rehabilitation, Kalamazoo.

Spungin, S. J. (n.d.). *Braille literacy: Issues for blind persons, families, professionals, and producers of braille.* New York: American Foundation for the Blind.

Spungin, S. J. (1987). Preface. In R. Swallow & K. M. Huebner (Eds.), *How to thrive, not just survive: A guide to developing independent life skills for blind and visually impaired children and youths* (p. vii). New York: American Foundation for the Blind.

Statistics on blindness in the model reporting area, 1969–1970. (1973). Washington, DC: U.S. Department of Health, Education & Welfare.

Sternberg, R. J. (1985). *Beyond I. Q.: A triarchic theory of human intelligence.* Cambridge, England: Cambridge University Press.

Sternberg, R. J. (1990). Understanding adult intelligence. In R. A. Fellenz & G. J. Conti (Eds.), *Intelligence and adult learning.* Bozeman, MT: Center for Adult Learning.

Stocker, C. (1963). A new approach to teaching handwriting to the blind. *New Outlook for the Blind, 57,* 208–210.

Stocker, C. (1983). *Kansas braille reading readiness book* (Teacher's ed.). Louisville, KY: American Printing House for the Blind.

Stocker, C. S. (n.d.). *Modern methods of teaching braille writing simplified.* Unpublished manuscript.

Stolov, W. C., & Clowers, M. R. (1981). *Handbook of severe disability: A text for rehabilitation counselors, other vocational practitioners, and allied health professionals.* Washington, DC: U.S. Government Printing House.

Storti, C. (1994). *Cross-cultural dialogues: 74 brief encounters with cultural difference.* Yarmouth, ME: Intercultural Press.

Story, S. M., & Kuyk, T. K. (1988). First time recognition of synthesized speech: A comparison of three systems. *Journal of Visual Impairment & Blindness, 82,* 28–29.

Sugarman, L. (1986). *Life-span development: Concepts, theories, and interventions.* New York: Methuen.

Swallow, R. M., & Huebner, K. M. (1987). *How to thrive, not just survive.* New York: American Foundation for the Blind.

Thorndike, E. L. (1932). *Fundamentals of learning.* New York: Skinner-Crofts.

Thurber, D. N. (1987). *D'Nealian handwriting* (2nd ed.). New York: Harcourt, Brace, Jovanovich.

Tielsch, J., Sommer, A., Witt, K., et al. (1990). Blindness and visual impairment in an American urban population: The Baltimore Eye Survey. *Archives of Ophthalmology,* 108, 286–290.

Tuttle, D. W. (1984). Self-esteem and adjusting with blindness. Springfield, IL: Charles C Thomas.

Tuttle, D. W. (1986). Educational programming. In G. T. Scholl (Ed.), *Foundations of education for blind and visually handicapped children and youth* (pp. 239–253). New York: American Foundation for the Blind.

U.S. Department of Labor. (1991). *Dictionary of occupational titles* (Vol. 1, 4th rev. ed.). Washington, DC: U.S. Government Printing Office.

Uslan, M. M. (1993). A review of two low-cost closed-circuit television systems. *Journal of Visual Impairment & Blindness, 87,* 310–313.

Uslan, M. M. (1994a). A review of Acrontech's "Executive" series of closed circuit television systems. *Journal of Visual Impairment & Blindness, JVIB News Service, 88*(1), 14–20.

Uslan, M. M. (1994b). A review of Humanware's "Viewpoint" series of closed-circuit television systems. *Journal of Visual Impairment & Blindness, JVIB News Service, 88*(3), 13–17.

Uslan, M. M., & Shen, R. (1996). A review of three low cost stand-mounted closed-circuit television systems. *Journal of Visual Impairment & Blindness, JVIB News Service, 90*(3).

Uslan, M. M., & Shragai, Y. (1995a). A review of high-powered screen-magnification software for IBM-compatible computers. *Journal of Visual Impairment & Blindness, JVIB News Service, 89*(2), 14–19.

Uslan, M. M., & Shragai, Y. (1995b). Screen-magnification software for IBM-compatible computers: An overview. *Journal of Visual Impairment & Blindness, JVIB News Service, 89*(1), 19–22.

Utrup, R. G. (1974). *Home mechanics for the visually impaired.* Kalamazoo: Western Michigan University Department of Blind Rehabilitation.

Utrup, R. G. (1977). *Basic personal management for the congenitally blind man.* Unpublished manuscript, Rehabilitation Center for the Blind, Michigan State Department of Social Services, Kalamazoo.

Utrup, R. G. (1979). *The tape medium and the visually impaired: An introduction for the rehabilitation teacher.* Little Rock: University of Arkansas at Little Rock.

Vaughan, D. G., Asbury, T., & Riordan-Eva, P. (1995). *General ophthalmology* (14th ed.). Norwalk, CT: Appleton & Lange.

Voice Indexing for the Blind. (1984). *Voice indexing manual.* College Park, MD: Author.

von Schlegell, A. J. (1992). Who should ask for the gift? Volunteers. *Currents, 18*(1), 20–23.

Wagg, H. J. (1932). *A chronological survey of work for the blind.* London: Sir Isaac Pitman & Sons.

Warren, D. H. (1984). *Blindness and early childhood development* (2nd ed.). New York: American Foundation for the Blind.

Watson, G., & Berg, R. V. (1983). Near training techniques. In R. T. Jose (Ed.), *Understanding low vision* (pp. 317–362). New York: American Foundation for the Blind.

Weiss, J., & Weiss, J. (1978). Teaching handwriting to the congenitally blind. *Journal of Visual Impairment & Blindness, 72,* 280–283.

Whitney, D. B. (1975). The optical design of spectacle magnifiers. In E. E. Faye & C. M. Hood (Eds.), *Low vision* (pp. 51–59). Springfield, IL: Charles C Thomas.

Whitten, L. L. (1986). *The effect of the amount of vision on the use of post-rehabilitative skills.* Unpublished manuscript, Western Michigan University, Department of Blind Rehabilitation, Kalamazoo.

Widerberg, L., & Kaarlela, R. (1976). *Techniques for eating: A guide for blind persons.* Kalamazoo, MI: Western Michigan University, Department of Blind Rehabilitation.

Wiener, W. R., & Luxton, L. (1994). The development of guidelines for university programs in rehabilitation teaching. *RE:view, 26*(1), 7–14.

Williams, J. M. (1983). Speech synthesis—How it works. *Aids and Appliances Review* (Carroll Center for the Blind, Newton, MA), *9 & 10,* 17.

Wormsley, D. (1981). Hand movement training in braille reading. *Journal of Visual Impairment & Blindness, 75,* 327–331.

Yeadon, A. (1974). *Toward independence: The use of instructional objectives in teaching daily living skills to the blind.* New York: American Foundation for the Blind.

Young, P. S., Dickerson, L. R., & Jacobson, W. H. (1980). A study of the job responsibilities of the field rehabilitation teacher. *Journal of Visual Impairment & Blindness, 74,* 386–389.

Zickel, V., & Hooper, M. S. (1957). The program of braille research: A progress report. *International Journal of Education of the Blind, 6,* 79–86.

LEARNING ACTIVITIES

The learning activities included in this section are designed to help readers deepen their understanding of the material contained in this text. These assignments for the most part can be carried out by readers either independently or as assigned by an instructor in a classroom setting. As noted in Chapter 5, most people learn best by doing, and readers will find that working through the exercises for each chapter as they finish the reading will help them analyze and synthesize the information presented, assimilate the concepts, practice the techniques, and fully integrate all they have learned.

Many of these learning activities require that sighted individuals occlude their vision or simulate low vision to attempt to replicate some of what their clients experience when they attempt various skills for the first time. Total blindness can be simulated by using sleep shades, which are commonly available in the travel and luggage section of department stores. Low vision can be simulated using homemade or commercially available modified lenses in welders' goggles. DAAS Consulting (see Resources) sells low vision simulator kits. It is recommended that students always practice with a partner, both for safety reasons and to obtain feedback on their techniques.

Chapter 1. An Introduction to the Profession

1. Call the local vocational rehabilitation, private, or Veterans Affairs blindness agency to request an interview with a rehabilitation teacher or to observe a teacher on the job to get information about his or her job tasks and roles.
2. Interview a current or former client rehabilitation teaching with a visual impairment to gain insight from the client's perspective about the services he or she received. (Arrange this by asking a local agency to give a willing client your telephone number, because confidentiality requirements prevent agencies from sharing clients' names.)

Chapter 2. The Evolution from Home Teaching to Rehabilitation Teaching

Complete these supplementary readings and then consider the questions that follow:

James A. Leja, "The Job Roles of Rehabilitation Teachers of Blind Persons," *Journal of Visual Impairment & Blindness, 84* (4) (1990) pp. 155-159.

R. B. Irwin, *The War of the Dots* (New York: American Foundation for the Blind, 1970; originally published in *As I Saw It,* American Foundation for the Blind, 1955).

Frances A. Koestler, "The Three-Wheeled Cart," Chapter 18 (pp. 287–301) in *The Unseen Minority: A Social History of Blindness in the United States* (New York: David McKay, 1976).

1. What do rehabilitation teachers do today that differs from the activities described in the early accounts of home teachers?

2. How does the perception of the public today regarding blindness and rehabilitation and education of people with visual impairments differ from that circa 1875? Are there similarities?

Chapter 3. The Assessment Process

1. Examine the case file of a rehabilitation client that has all identifying information deleted. Complete a Case File Summary Form based on the information found in the file.
2. Work with a partner or friend who will portray a new rehabilitation client who has recently lost his or her vision. Conduct an initial interview with this simulated client and complete the skills assessment portion of the Rehabilitation Teacher Interview assessment form.

Chapter 4. The Planning Process

1. Using the information gathered from the assessment interview completed in the learning activity for Chapter 3, complete a service plan for your fictitious client, setting priorities for his or her needs, based on a limit of approximately 30 hours of instruction.
2. Using the sample lesson plans provided throughout the text as models, develop an original lesson plan to teach another skill with which you are familiar.
3. Select an everyday task such as toothbrushing or tying shoes. Develop a task-analyzed lesson plan, listing each individual step necessary to complete the task. Work with a partner to test your task analysis by having your partner attempt to follow the instructions to complete the task as you read each step.

Chapter 5. Learning and Teaching

1. Work with a partner who has a visual impairment or who will simulate a visual impairment. Develop a lesson plan to teach an activity that requires gross motor movement, such as bowling or using a broom. Then teach your partner the skill, utilizing the principles of teaching persons with visual impairment outlined in the text.
2. Work with a partner who has a visual impairment or who is simulating a visual impairment. Develop a lesson plan to teach a fine motor skill with which your partner is not familiar, such as a craft activity or nail care technique. Then teach your partner the skill, utilizing the principles of teaching persons with visual impairments outlined in the text.
3. Working with a partner, who is occluded if sighted, verbally describe a variety of objects, if possible, choosing things with which your partner is not familiar. Do not allow your partner to inspect an item visually or tactilely until the description is compete. Then have your partner compare the verbal description with the actual object and provide feedback about the description. Discuss ways to enhance the verbal picture offered initially.

Chapter 6. Low Vision Skills

1. Interview someone who has received low vision services. Attempt to discern the person's perception of his or her experience. Determine which low vision devices were prescribed, which devices are typically used and for what tasks, and which if any devices are seldom or never used.
2. Visit a low vision clinic and, if, possible, observe an appointment with a patient who has low vision. Note which equipment and tests are used by the clinician and which low vision devices are prescribed and for what tasks.
3. Practice using a variety of low vision aids, if available to you. Attempt to perform near-vision tasks, such as reading, dialing a telephone, and threading a needle, as well as

viewing distant objects such as street signs and house numbers. (Avoid moving while using distance aids.) Notice how the use of landmarks such as the margins of pages or signposts help you to locate the desired objective. Also note how long you are able to use the devices effectively before you experience visual fatigue.

4. Study your home environment and consider how it might be enhanced to improve visibility if you had difficulty with such factors as glare, lighting, or contrast. Note which tasks might be difficult for you to accomplish unless you made changes in the visual environment.

Chapter 7. Braille and Other Tactile Forms of Communication

1. If you do not know the braille code, contact the National Library Service for the Blind and Physically Handicapped (see Resources section) to obtain materials for learning braille. Use the remaining learning activities for this chapter as practice exercises for your study of the braille code.
2. Obtain the first book of a braille teaching series. With vision occluded if sighted, scan the pages using both hands. Determine the location of page headings, page numbers, paragraph indentations, and section divisions. Do not attempt to read the braille characters initially.
3. Simulate tracking by following braille lines with the right hand while keeping place with the left.
4. Practice reading and writing labels, such as those for cassettes, compact discs, or canned foods, to reinforce the use of braille for labeling.
5. Work with a partner to trade brailled index cards with names and telephone numbers; take turns reading the cards aloud to each other.
6. Practice writing familiar names or phrases repetitively on both a brailler and a slate to reinforce the kinesthetic movements used to write or type braille.
7. Create a sample brailled address file with index cards and dividers. Note that both the index tabs of the dividers and the names on the cards must be placed upside down and facing the back of the box in order for a tactile braille reader to read the information by slipping his or fingers between the cards without having to take the cards out of the box.

Chapter 8. Handwriting and Drawing

1. Gather a variety of writing guides, such as full-page, signature, check-writing, and envelope-addressing guides. Write several lines or a signature with each to gain an understanding of the characteristics of each guide, using an eyeshade to simulate total blindness or low vision simulators if sighted.
2. Order a variety of adaptive aids catalogs (see Resources section) to determine which guides are currently available.
3. Consult with the service desk at local banks to determine whether they offer bold- or raised-line checks.
4. Make your own writing guide for a personal check or another type of form that people frequently have to fill out.

Chapter 9. Keyboarding and Computer Skills

1. Consult adaptive computing resources such as the Closing the Gap *Resource Directory*, the *Trace Resource Book* (Borden, Lubich, & Vanderheiden, 1996), or the American Foundation for the Blind National Technology Center (see Resources). Compare and contrast adap-

tive products designed to provide computer access to people with visual impairments.

2. Practice using the various features on a computer with voice output if one is available. Simulating blindness with an occluder, if sighted, manipulate voice parameters and set speech windows. Word process a letter, performing simple editing tasks.
3. Practice using the various features on a computer with screen enlargement, if one is available. Simulating reduced visual acuity or field loss, if sighted, manipulate the features that improve visibility, such as contrast and font size, and the viewing windows. Word process a letter, performing simple editing tasks.

Chapter 10. Electronic Listening, Recording, and Reading Devices

1. Obtain a Talking-Book Cassette Machine and a Talking-Book cassette and listen to all sides of the Talking Book.
2. Listen to a recorded version of *Talking Book Topics*, keeping in mind methods that a client can use to keep track of the information needed to make book selections, such as titles and order numbers.
3. Using an adaptive recorder, practice using all indexing methods by creating a tape that is recorded on all four sides. For example, record 5 to 10 addresses with tone indexing between the name and address and voice indexing before each person's name.
4. Examine the cassette well of a standard or adaptive recorder. Use a demagnetizer and cleaning products to clean and demagnetize the heads.

Chapter 11. Mathematical Calculation

1. Practice solving addition, subtraction, multiplication, and division problems using a speech-output calculator, simulating blindness with an occluder if sighted.

Obtain an abacus and complete the following exercises, using an occluder to simulate blindness if sighted:

2. Solve the sample problems in the addition section of the chapter.
3. Solve the sample problems in the subtraction section of the chapter.
4. As a final exercise to practice all levels of addition, work through the following progressive addition problem: Set 1 on the abacus. Add 1. Then add 2 to the sum. Add 3 to the sum; then add 4; add 5; and continue adding the next higher number until you have added 50 to the sum.

Chapter 12. Basic Daily Living Skills

1. After you have received an introduction to sighted guide technique, practice with a partner. Begin in large spaces, then move to narrow areas, then to ascending and descending stairs. Keep in mind the needs and abilities of elderly persons.
2. Practice indoor safety techniques while exploring parts of your home nonvisually. Consider how you would describe the area to someone else who cannot see.
3. As you go about your daily activities for the rest of the day, make a mental note of which items (for example, appliances, food, or personal management products) you could not identify or operate if you had low vision or no vision. Consider how you might label those items.
4. Practice locating objects nonvisually by dropping a set of keys nearby, then using proper search techniques.

Chapter 13. Adaptive Food-Preparation Skills

1. With a partner, perform a variety of basic skills such as pouring liquids, spreading, peeling vegetables, and opening cans while fully occluded or simulating low vision, if sighted.
2. Eat a full meal while fully occluded, if sighted, making use of techniques to locate, cut, and eat several different food items. If possible, eat at a conventional sit-down restaurant, a buffet-style restaurant, and a fast-food restaurant. Repeat one or more of these visits while simulating low vision and manipulating the factors that affect visibility by, for example, using a high-intensity lamp or changing position in relation to the light source; using contrasting dishes, placemat, or tray; and using magnification.
3. Make a resource list of currently available cookbooks that have been produced in braille, in large print, on computer disk, or in recorded format.
4. Research local grocery stores to determine if home delivery is available, if the store provides a map or list of products according to their location in the store, and if on-line grocery ordering is possible.
5. With a partner, travel to the local grocery store to examine visual landmarks and clues that may be helpful to shoppers with low vision. Practice locating aisle signs with a telescopic low vision aid.

Chapter 14. Personal Management Skills

1. Work with a partner to practice a variety of personal management tasks, simulating low vision or total blindness if sighted. The partner can monitor performance and give feedback. Include practice using telephone dialing and coin identification techniques. Troubleshoot and modify techniques, if necessary.
2. Enroll in local diabetes education courses to learn more about the basics. (Students and professionals in the field of blindness can often enroll free of charge as a professional courtesy.)
3. Consult a directory of community agencies to determine which agencies might offer consultation in such areas relating to personal management as women's health, basic birth control education, and child care education. Consult with local home health care and visiting nurses agencies to learn about their services.

Chapter 15. Home Management Skills

1. Working with a partner and while occluded or simulating low vision, if sighted, complete a variety of home management activities, including cleaning a tabletop, washing a window or mirror, sweeping, and vacuuming. Use preventive cleanup techniques and a grid pattern to make sure that surfaces are thoroughly clean.
2. Write one or more lesson plans for accomplishing home management activities, such as vacuuming a room or changing a fuse with no vision or low vision. Then discuss with a partner what changes, if any, are necessary.
3. Practice hammering nails or other home mechanics tasks with a partner, while occluded or simulating low vision, if sighted. Keep in mind techniques that someone with low vision could use to enhance the visual environment while performing these tasks.

Chapter 16. Leisure-Time Pursuits

1. Analyze a craft project to determine how it can be adapted for persons with low vision or

no vision. Write a lesson plan that includes suggestions for any modifications that must be made for those with limited vision.

2. Practice threading needles using one or more of the methods described in the chapter.
3. Braille a deck of playing cards.
4. Contact the sports and recreational organizations listed in the chapter to obtain information about various recreational activities and find out which ones might be available in your area.

Chapter 17. Managing a Rehabilitation Teaching Caseload

Develop a daily schedule over a two-week period for an itinerant teacher who works from 8:00 a.m. to 5:00 p.m. and has a caseload of 10 clients. Consider the needs of the clients as identified in the following summaries, and set priorities for services that are reflected in the number and length of visits scheduled for each client during the two-week period. Present your schedule in the form of a matrix, showing the times when lessons begin and end; allowing time for lunch breaks, office hours, and an average of 20 to 30 minutes travel time for each appointment.

1. Mr. Arnold

Address: 710 North Vankal, Kalamazoo
Age: 73
Vision: 20/200 both eyes, macular degeneration
Living situation: Lives in a farmhouse 2 miles from town. Gets one visit from daughter per day and gets meals delivered from an elders program once per day. Operates a small chicken egg business.
Goal: To be able to live alone with support from his daughter.
Personal adjustment training needs: Handwriting guides; introduction to Talking Book Program; training with near-vision reading devices; simple housecleaning tasks.

2. Mr. Brown

Address: 208 West Clinton, Augusta
Age: 23
Vision: Totally blind
Living situation: Lives in a group foster home with five others.
Goal: To be able to care for his clothing and dressing needs in group home situation.
Personal adjustment training needs: Hanging, folding, marking, and identifying clothes.

3. Mrs. Corbin

Address: Bronson Place, 1700 Bronson Way, Kalamazoo
Age: 71
Vision: Good acuity, 6-degree fields, recent loss from glaucoma
Living situation: Lives in a retirement complex with maid service and one hot meal per day.
Goal: To continue to live in the retirement complex.
Personal adjustment training needs: Simple hot food preparation skills; introduction to talking book program tape recorder skills, crafts.

4. Ms. Dixon

Address: 912 North Edwards, Kalamazoo
Age: 45
Vision: Light perception
Living situation: Lives with her 3-year-old son. Just lost her sight after working as a word processor/receptionist for 10 years. Has no family support.
Goal: To return to employment as soon as possible.
Personal adjustment training needs: Nearly all daily living areas; keyboarding; braille; recorders; handwriting.

5. Mr. Elsinga

Address: 7114 Leawood, Portage
Age: 68

Vision: Macular degeneration, 20/200
Living situation: Lives with his wife in a well-kept home and works part-time at his old job as a consultant. Needs to keep up with the latest professional literature in his field.
Goal: To continue his work and to regain his skill as a woodworker.
Personal adjustment training needs: Reading with an OCR; working with his table saw and other power tools.

6. Mrs. Wong

Address: 12236 East T Avenue, Scotts
Age: 81
Vision: 20/600 from failed cataract surgery
Living situation: Lives with her grown son and his family of four.
Goal: To continue in the same living situation but take over some of the household chores for her daughter-in-law, who works full time.
Personal adjustment training needs: Homemaking skills; food preparation; tapes for cookbooks; labeling.

7. Mrs. Goodman

Address: 6136 Avon, Portage
Age: 71
Vision: No measurable acuity, but is able to count fingers following an accident 4 months ago
Living situation: Lives alone in a relatively dangerous neighborhood known to have many muggings and break-ins. Has no one close to help her.
Goal: To live independently in her present home.
Personal adjustment training needs: Virtually all communications and ADL areas.

8. Mr. Hanson

Address: Alamo Nursing Home, 8290 West C Avenue, Kalamazoo
Age: 67
Vision: 20/200; loss of right hemisphere from stroke
Living situation: Lives in a nursing home as a result of a stroke about 6 months ago. He has been in the nursing home only a few weeks and gets lost frequently.
Goal: To be able to find important locations in the nursing home.
Personal adjustment training needs: Orientation to the nursing home; protective and trailing techniques.

9. Ms. Inman

Address: 7264 North 30th, Richland
Age: 18
Vision: Totally blind
Living situation: Lives at home with her parents. She is attending community college for the first time next fall.
Goal: Wants to be a physical therapy assistant.
Personal adjustment training needs: Notetaking skills; computer word processing skills.

10. Mr. Gomez

Address: 10407 Woodlawn Drive, Portage
Age: 38
Vision: 20/800 as a result of optic atrophy
Living situation: Lives with his wife and two young children.
Goal: To return to his job teaching history in local high school.
Personal adjustment training needs: This client was just referred for a personal adjustment assessment. This will be his first visit.

APPENDIX A

PROFESSIONAL STANDARDS

REHABILITATION TEACHER JOB DESCRIPTION

(Approved by Division XI and Division XVII, Association for Education and Rehabilitation of the Blind and Visually Impaired [AER], and the AER Board of Directors.)

Job Title

Rehabilitation Teacher
Independent Living Specialist
Rehabilitation Instructor

Qualifications

It is recommended that an individual have a degree in rehabilitation teaching and Association for Education and Rehabilitation of the Blind and Visually Impaired (AER) Rehabilitation Teaching certification. Otherwise, it is recommended that the individual possess a minimum of a bachelor's degree in a related discipline: special education with an emphasis in visual handicaps, home economics education, rehabilitation counseling, human services and be AER certifiable.

Roles

The Rehabilitation Teacher's roles may include:

- assessment and evaluation of clients' needs in home, community, educational, and vocational environments
- teaching adaptive independent living skills
- case management and record keeping
- identification and utilization of community and national resources
- utilization of community support services
- facilitation of psychosocial adjustment to vision loss.

Specific Responsibilities

The Rehabilitation Teacher may be responsible for:

- assessing and evaluating the independent living needs and abilities of individuals with impaired vision for meeting immediate and lifelong goals
- developing individualized rehabilitation teaching plans in conjunction with the client
- teaching adaptive skills needed for independent living in the areas of personal management, household management, communication, education, leisure activities, orientation and movement in the immediate environment, and use of low vision devices and techniques
- coordinating the implementation of the rehabilitation teaching service plan
- teaching problem solving and resource utilization, including adaptive equipment
- facilitating the individual's and family's psychosocial adjustment to impaired vision

- case management and case recording
- providing consultation, public education, and inservice training.

REHABILITATION TEACHER CERTIFICATION PROCESS

Initial Professional Certification, Type AA

Type AA certification is for graduates of university training programs in rehabilitation teaching.

1. Instructions and applications for rehabilitation teaching certification are obtained from the Association for the Education and Rehabilitation of the Blind and Visually Impaired (AER).
2. Application form is submitted with certification fee and the following required documents:
   - Official university transcript showing completion of a rehabilitation teaching program
   - Letter of reference from a certified university educator in the program attended
   - Field Placement/Internship Reference Form completed by the placement/internship supervisor
   - Statement of having read and endorsed the Code of Ethics for Rehabilitation Teachers
   - Proof of membership in AER or other related professional organization (such as the Council for Exceptional Children or the National Rehabilitation Association).
3. Completed materials are distributed to the members of the Rehabilitation Teaching Certification Committee, which meets quarterly (after March 1, June 1, September 1, and December 1) to review applications.
4. Certification approval is granted for a period of five years, at which time the rehabilitation teacher is eligible for Renewable Professional Certification.

Initial Professional Certification, Type A

Type A certification is for individuals who have a degree in a related field and are employed as rehabilitation teachers. These individuals need to provide specific information about their on-the-job training or other training in the following knowledge/skill areas:

1. Interpersonal Relations and Environmental Influences
2. Principles of Teaching and Learning
3. Principles of Adult Education
4. Concepts of Rehabilitation
5. Dynamics of Blindness
6. Physiology and Function of the Eye
7. Major Physical and Mental Disabling Conditions
8. Gerontology
9. Knowledge and Practical Application of Rehabilitation Teaching Skills
10. Orientation and Utilization of Community Agencies and Resources
11. Legislation and Services Related to Blindness
12. Case Management Skills
13. Personal Management
14. Communication Skills (including abacus, braille, handwriting, listening and recording devices, and typing)
15. Home Management Skills
16. Therapeutic and/or Leisure-Time Activities

Renewable Professional Certification

Applicants seeking renewal of their AER professional certification as rehabilitation teachers must complete regular professional activities during the five-year period of their certification, for which points are assigned toward certification renewal. Points must be accumulated from at least three of the following areas:

- college credit
- continuing education
- peer observation
- publication of article
- publication of book
- mentorship/supervision
- educational project
- professional presentation
- professional conference
- curriculum development
- professional service.

Information about the allocation of points for various activities is available from AER. The individual must accumulate a total of 200 points if the teacher has completed 2,500 hours of direct service, or 400 points if the teacher has provided between 800 and 2,500 hours of direct service.

CODE OF ETHICS FOR REHABILITATION TEACHERS OF INDIVIDUALS WITH VISUAL IMPAIRMENT

(Adopted by Division XI, Association for Education and Rehabilitation of the Blind and Visually Impaired [AER], Washington, DC, July 23, 1990. Approved by AER International Board, April 1991.)

Preamble

We, the rehabilitation teachers of Division XI of the Association for Education and Rehabilitation of the Blind and Visually Impaired (AER), recognize our commitment to provide the highest quality of services to those individuals whom we serve. The purpose of our profession is to instruct individuals with visual impairments in the use of those compensatory skills and aids that will enable them to live safely, productively, interdependent, and up to each person's maximum potential. Our primary obligation, as rehabilitation teachers, is to our clients. In all of our relationships, we will protect our clients' welfare and will diligently seek to assist our clients toward achieving their goals. While fulfilling this commitment, we rehabilitation teachers become responsible to our clients and their families, to our employers and the community in which we work, to our profession and other professionals in the field of human services; and to ourselves. We recognize that both our actions and in-actions affect the lives of those whom we seek to serve and we accept the responsibility and consequences of our actions and/or in-actions. Defined by this Code of Ethics a rehabilitation teacher is a professional practicing in the public or private sector who evaluates, instructs, and guides a person with visual impairment through an individualized plan of rehabilitation instruction designed to help that person carry out daily activities. These competencies encompass specific, identifiable evaluation and teaching skills and knowledge to enable the person with the visual impairment to develop and/or enhance sensory and kinesthetic capabilities, personal management skills, communication skills, indoor orientation, low vision utilization, and home management skills. In addition to the instructional areas listed, the rehabilitation teacher will be involved with assisting the client to understand their vision loss, and to facilitate the development of appropriate coping mechanisms.

1. Commitment to the Client

1.1. The professional rehabilitation teacher shall respect the worth, culture, and dignity of each individual. This includes exhibiting courtesy and temperance in situations of conflict.

1.2 The role of the rehabilitation teacher as an advocate is to protect and promote the welfare of persons with visual impairments for the purpose of assisting them to achieve their desired levels of independence.

1.3 The purpose of confidentiality regarding

client information is to safeguard facts, data, and professional judgments that are obtained in the course of practice. Disclosures of information are restricted to what is necessary, relevant, and verifiable with respect to each client's right to privacy. Professional files, reports, and records shall be maintained under conditions of security.

1.4 The rehabilitation teacher shall obtain the informed consent of the client before inviting others to observe a lesson, having the client photographed or recorded, or involving the client in a research study in which personal identifying information would be gathered and disseminated.

1.5 The rehabilitation teacher shall take all reasonable precautions to ensure the safety of the clients and will seek to provide an instructional environment that is conducive to learning.

1.6 Prior to the commencement of instruction, the rehabilitation teacher will seek to obtain and evaluate information that is relevant to the client's rehabilitation program.

1.7 Decisions regarding the continuation or discontinuation of instruction shall be made with each client, respecting the rights of the clients to participate in decisions regarding their instructional programs, and shall be based upon objective evaluation of the clients' needs and abilities to benefit from defined services.

1.8 The rehabilitation teacher shall seek, where appropriate, the support and involvement of the client's support system in promoting an individual client's instructional objectives and in advancing continued success. This includes sharing information with the family, or others, that will facilitate the client's welfare and independence, but not communicating information which violates the principles of confidentiality.

1.9 The rehabilitation teacher will relate to all clients in a professional manner during the clients' rehabilitation program and not engage in personal or private relationships that would jeopardize the rehabilitation process.

2. Commitment to the Community

2.1 The rehabilitation teacher, when using any specialized knowledge or abilities to contribute to community education, seeks to exhibit the highest standard of rehabilitation practices and client services, avoiding exaggeration, sensationalism, superficiality and other misleading activities; and to indicate how the community can become involved in the educational and/or rehabilitation process.

2.2 The rehabilitation teacher shall not engage in any public education activity that results in exploitation of the client and/or the client's family.

3. Commitment to the Profession

3.1 The rehabilitation teacher should seek full responsibility for the exercise of professional judgment related to instruction.

3.2 The rehabilitation teacher has the responsibility to contribute to the growing body of knowledge, expertise, and skills of the profession.

3.3 The rehabilitation teacher is encouraged to support individual and public efforts to advance services to disabled persons through education, legislation, personal commitment, and improved agency practices and procedures. This includes promoting understanding and acceptance of current rehabilitation programs and past achievements in the fields; and participation in local, state, regional, and national organizations that are directly related to the profession of rehabilitation teaching.

3.4 The rehabilitation teacher should strive to provide fair treatment and support to all members of the profession.

3.5 The rehabilitation teacher shall make reasonable effort to oppose incompetent, illegal, or unethical behavior, and report such behavior to the proper regulatory bodies.

4. Commitment to Colleagues and Other Professionals

4.1 The rehabilitation teacher is expected to facilitate and enhance team efforts, on a professional level, and to share specialized knowledge, resources, experience, concepts, and skills. In situations where team decisions are made, the rehabilitation teacher is expected to contribute relevant information and abide by the team decision.

4.2 The rehabilitation teacher should avoid assuming responsibilities which are better provided by other professionals. Referrals to other professionals shall be done in agreement with the client and the client's service plan.

4.3 The rehabilitation teacher responds factually when requested to write a letter of recommendation for a colleague seeking a professional position.

5. Commitment to Professional Employment Practices

5.1 The rehabilitation teacher should adhere to the policies and regulations of the employer and should abide by the terms of a contract or agreement, whether verbal or written, unless the job duties include behavior which violates the Code of Ethics. The rehabilitation teacher should not accept a position where proven principles of rehabilitation teaching practices are compromised or abandoned.

5.2 The rehabilitation teacher should demonstrate concern and appreciation of the heritage, values, and principles of the employing agency.

5.3 The rehabilitation teacher providing additional professional services through private contracts shall avoid engaging in outside employment or other outside activity which is incompatible with the full and proper discharge of job duties and responsibilities, or which constitute a conflict of interest.

5.4 The rehabilitation teacher may not solicit or directly accept a gift, subscription, advance, rendering, or deposit of money, gratuity, favor, entertainment, loan, or anything of significant value from a person, business, or organization with whom they have official relationships. This does not preclude normal business practices which enable the rehabilitation teacher to maintain ongoing services.

5.5 The rehabilitation teacher shall avoid distributing, or cause to be distributed, any advertisement, materials, or samples aimed at soliciting referrals for personal profit.

6. Commitment to Private Business Practice

6.1 The rehabilitation teacher in private practice will adhere to all applicable federal, state, and local laws which establish and regulate business practices and shall refuse to participate in practices that are inconsistent with the rules or standards established by regulatory bodies regarding the delivery of rehabilitation teaching services to clients.

6.2 No persons shall be refused service by the rehabilitation teacher on the basis of race, color, religion, national origin, gender, age, sexual orientation, or disability.

6.3 The rehabilitation teacher shall avoid causing misrepresentation of professional credentials or competencies.

6.4 The rehabilitation teacher in private contracting is encouraged to carry professional liability insurance protection.

6.5 No rehabilitation teacher shall effectuate or participate in the wrongful removal of professional rehabilitation files or other materials.

6.6 When asked to comment on cases being actively managed by another rehabilitation practitioner and/or agency, the reviewer shall make every reasonable effort to conduct an in-person evaluation before rendering a professional opinion.

6.7 Competitive advertising of services and products shall be factually accurate. The rehabilitation teacher shall promise or offer only those services or results which there is reason to believe can be provided.

6.8 The rehabilitation teacher shall establish a fee for private contracting in cooperation with the contracting agency that is consistent with the reasonable and customary rate of that particular geographic region.

6.9 The rehabilitation practitioner shall not enter into fee arrangements which would be likely to create a conflict of interest.

6.10 The individual rehabilitation teacher shall not behave in such a manner as to use the position to influence or cause the recipient of services to name them as a beneficiary of a will, insurance policy, or other assets as compensation for services or personal profit.

APPENDIX B

ADDITIONAL DISABILITIES OR CONDITIONS

This appendix describes some of the examples of additional disabilities or conditions that rehabilitation teachers may encounter among clients and explains how these conditions may affect the teacher's work with the client.

AIDS (Acquired immunodeficiency syndrome)

AIDS is a virus that, over time, causes progressive deterioration of the body's immune system, making the affected individual susceptible to many different types of life-threatening infections and tumors. Many of the opportunistic infections common with AIDS affect vision, most commonly cytomegalovirus, as well as Kaposi's sarcoma, toxoplasmosis, and cryptoccocal meningitis. People who have AIDS-related vision loss typically are ill with one or more additional opportunistic infections. Dementia is common. In addition, a client may experience confusion, depression, or forgetfulness. Half the people who experience the vision problems common to AIDS also have chronic and severe diarrhea. The side effects of medication may include anemia, neutropenia (low white blood-cell count), muscle fatigue and aches, sleep difficulties, severe headaches, and mental confusion.

Visual impairment is usually a late complication of the disease, when impending death may be combined with blindness to have a doubly severe impact. Blindness may be the final blow in a series of losses, including loss of loved ones from the same disease, rejection by friends and family, and impending death (Kiester, 1990). Because of the poor prognosis for people with AIDS at present, personal adjustment training is needed immediately, but a full program may not be necessary; approximately 75 percent of clients with AIDS-related blindness may need only in-home orientation and mobility training or sighted guide techniques, plus basic daily living skills such as pouring, eating techniques, and personal labeling methods. Teachers who are ill with infectious diseases—even a common cold—should avoid lessons with clients who have weakened immune systems.

Amputation

Amputations of upper extremities such as fingers, a hand, or an arm affect an individual's ability to pick up, grasp, and stabilize objects. Rehabilitation teachers may need to assist such clients with alternate methods of stabilizing objects (for example, securing a mixing bowl in a drawer) and selecting alternate tools to accomplish tasks (such as a bowl with suction cups on the bottom or a one-handed device for dental flossing), and may also need to teach alternate methods for keyboarding (see Chapter 9) or brailling, if necessary. Lower-extremity amputations of toes, feet, or legs can affect balance, gait, and ability to stand. Rehabilitation teachers may need to teach such clients adaptive solutions for performing daily living skills, such as preparing food while seated or cleaning house while using a wheelchair.

Arthritis

Arthritis is one of a group of rheumatic diseases that affect the supporting structures of the body, including the joints and tissues. People with arthritis tire easily and have pain, decreased energy, stiffness, and loss of motion of their joints. Their endurance is affected, and mobility and activities of daily living may also be impaired. Rehabilitation teachers working with clients who have arthritis need resources on adaptive techniques or tools to assist students who have difficulty performing physical tasks, such as a jar-opening tool for the kitchen or extension keys for the brailler or tape player. Teachers should consider modifying lessons if a student becomes easily fatigued.

Burns

Severe burns can cause tissue and nerve damage, and amputation of severely affected body parts may be necessary. Although burns do not themselves cause damage beyond the initial event, scarring or nerve damage can affect a client's ability to detect heat extremes in the affected parts and therefore may increase his or her risk of future burns. Range of motion may be limited in severely burned joints. Implications for rehabilitation teachers include the need to determine the client's ability to detect differences in texture and temperature and, if necessary, to teach alternative methods for tactile adaptations such as nonvisual reading, testing for food doneness, and the like. Clients also may benefit from adaptive devices that alleviate difficulties caused by a limited range of motion.

Cerebral palsy (CP)

Cerebral palsy (CP) is a disorder of movement resulting from damage to the brain during its period of growth and development (prenatal through about 8 to 12 years of age). CP affects muscle control and can cause rigidity, ataxia (lack of muscle control), athetosis (involuntary purposeless movement), and dystonia (abnormally increased muscle tone); it may affect short-term memory and attention span, and it is associated with seizures in as many as 60 percent of those affected. Persons with motor difficulties benefit from adaptive devices to help them accomplish tasks such as kitchen skills, and they may need to use compensatory skills to deal with short-term memory deficits. Repetitive lessons may be helpful for people with this condition.

Developmental disability/mental impairment

Visual impairment is frequently found secondary to conditions that cause developmental delays or mental impairments. Definitions of an impairment in an individual's mental state are usually based on the individual's mental and functional limitations, as in the following definition: "Significantly subaverage general functioning existing concurrently with deficits in adaptive behavior, and manifested during the development period" (Grossman, 1977, p. 5). Mental impairment causes a slower rate of learning and difficulty in generalizing or transferring information learned in one situation to another. Cerebral palsy and epilepsy frequently accompany mental impairments. The rehabilitation teacher who works with a client who is mentally impaired may need to utilize highly structured lessons and task analysis (teaching smaller increments of a skill) for teaching a specific skill (see Chapter 5), rather than assuming that the client is able to generalize from another skill already mastered.

Diabetes

Diabetes encompasses a variety of conditions, but it usually refers to a metabolic disorder of the pancreas in which production or efficient use of insulin by the body is affected, which in turn affects the body's ability to metabolize carbohydrates.

Diabetes produces elevated blood sugar and excessive urine production. Physical complications from long-term diabetes may include vision loss, peripheral and autonomic neuropathy, heart disease, stroke, circulatory insufficiency, frequent infections, hearing loss, and gastrointestinal difficulties such as nausea, vomiting, or diarrhea. Some individuals have frequent episodes of hypoglycemia (low blood sugar), whose symptoms include dizziness, sleepiness, sweating or clammy skin, disorientation, and unconsciousness. Hypoglycemia can be treated by ingesting something containing carbohydrates, such as a sandwich or milk; by consuming glucose preparations for hypoglycemia; or by injecting glucagon to increase blood sugar levels. Individuals with diabetes also may have dietary restrictions.

Since there are different types of diabetes, a rehabilitation teacher who has a diabetic client must be aware of the client's specific needs. This may entail allowing flexibility in scheduling; providing adaptations for those with tactile deficits caused by neuropathy; paying attention to symptoms of hypoglycemia, which may occur frequently during initial rehabilitation programs as a result of increased activity; keeping sources of glucose on hand; and placing priority on lessons that assist with independence in control of blood glucose levels (such as adaptive insulin measurement and glucose monitoring). The teacher also should give special attention to proper foot and toenail care in personal management because of the risk of infection from reduced circulation and reduced sensation of pain. See also Neuropathy, autonomic; and Neuropathy, peripheral.

Epilepsy

Epilepsy, or seizure disorder, is a neurological disorder in which normal brain activity is disrupted by excessive electrical discharge. Epilepsy can cause either tonic-clonic (formerly known as grand mal) seizures or absence (traditionally known as petit mal) seizures. Tonic-clonic seizures cause the body to become rigid, then convulsive for two to three minutes, after which the individual may be disoriented or fatigued. Absence seizures are less visible and cause momentary disruption of consciousness lasting about 10 to 20 seconds. Medications to control seizures may cause drowsiness. The rehabilitation teacher working with clients who have epilepsy should be aware of the need for safety measures if a client has seizures while performing certain tasks, and for flexibility in scheduling lessons in the event that the client is too fatigued to attend.

Hearing impairments and deafness

Hearing impairments are the most common form of chronic physical disability in the United States today. Hearing loss can be mild or severe, and primarily it affects communication. Rehabilitation teachers working with clients who have hearing loss as well as vision losses must pay attention to reducing noises that might interfere with communication during lessons and must use alternate communication methods, such as sign language, palm printing, braille, or messages written in large print with bold markers. Rehabilitation teachers may be called on to assist clients in locating adaptive devices, such as amplifier headsets for talking book machines, smoke alarms for persons with hearing impairment, vibrating alarm clocks, and flashing or vibrating doorbells. (For more information, see Huebner, Prickett, Welsh, and Joffee, 1995.)

Heart disease (cardiovascular disease)

Among the various causes of damage to the heart or decrease in blood flow, the most common is coronary artery disease, which affects a person's endurance and strength. The psychological implications of heart disease can be strong enough to affect a client's motivation and willingness to engage in activity. The rehabilitation teacher must consult with the client's physician to learn the client's specific limitations, such as limits on the amount of lifting or exertion, which may affect the client's personal adjustment training. Lessons may need to be shortened, or the client may wish to be seated to perform activities such as cooking.

Multiple sclerosis

One of the most common neurological diseases in North America, multiple sclerosis is an adult-onset, chronic, sometimes progressive disease of the central nervous system that interferes with nerve function. Symptoms come and go unpredictably and can include fatigue, weakness, numbness, impaired vision, and difficulty with coordination, gait, and balance. The client also may experience cognitive dysfunction including short-term memory loss and difficulty with problem solving. Stress, illness, and extremes of temperature can affect the client's functioning. Rehabilitation teachers working with clients who have multiple sclerosis may need to reschedule or modify lessons if fatigue or illness occur. Teachers can also provide alternatives and teach compensatory skills if short-term memory or problem-solving ability are affected; examples include carrying a tape recorder to make lists of things to do; learning procedures by rote memorization; and using a recorded or brailled list of steps to follow for procedures.

Neuromuscular diseases

Impairments caused by neuromuscular diseases, such as Huntington's disease, Parkinson's disease, Guillain-Barré syndrome, and muscular dystrophy, are limited mainly to the motor system and cause weakness or difficulty in controlling motion. Some diseases cause involuntary movements. Clients with such disorders may need to perform tasks from a seated position, to be shown adaptive tools or techniques to complete tasks (such as extension keys for a cassette player or brailler), and to use alternative methods for performing tasks of daily living, such as using a microwave oven to avoid accidents with a conventional stove or oven.

Neuropathy, autonomic

Although neuropathy, disease of the nerves, can affect any part of the nervous system, the effects on the gastrointestinal system can be devastating. Symptoms may include nausea, constipation, stomach cramps, vomiting, and uncontrollable diarrhea. Although rehabilitation teachers will not necessarily be involved with the treatment of these symptoms, they may need to assist with special dietary preparations, including teaching adaptive techniques for self-administration of intravenous nourishment. Scheduling and length of lessons may be affected. Although autonomic neuropathy is common in people with diabetes, many clients may not be aware that their intestinal difficulties are related to their condition and can be controlled; thus, rehabilitation teachers may need to suggest that clients discuss this possibility with their physician.

Neuropathy, peripheral

Peripheral neuropathy is a disease of the peripheral nervous system in which sensations from the extremities, such as hands and feet, are either hindered from reaching the brain or send incorrect sensory information, including pain, tingling, or increased sensitivity. This condition is frequently found in people with diabetes. Clients with peripheral neuropathy may have difficulty detecting tactile clues such as braille or raised markings; they also may be at risk of injury because of an inability to detect temperature extremes. Rehabilitation teachers may need to devise alternative systems for labeling and information storage and be aware of safety considerations.

Stroke and cerebral trauma, traumatic brain injury

Injuries to the brain, such as those that result from stroke or injury, can cause problems with motor coordination and emotional, behavioral, or cognitive functioning. Injuries to one side of the brain typically affect the opposite side of the body. The effects vary tremendously from individual to individual, but they may include speech difficulties, short-term or long-term memory loss, and inappropriate social behavior. The rehabilitation teacher working with a client who has had a stroke or brain injury first must determine the effect that the injury has had on a client's ability to learn or perform the requisite skills for personal adjustment training and then devise adaptations to meet the client's needs. Structured and task-analyzed lessons may be useful for clients with cognitive disabilities.

REFERENCES

Brodwin, M. G., Tellez, F., & Brodwin, S. K. (1995). *Medical, psychosocial and vocational aspects of disability.* Athens, GA: Elliott & Fitzpatrick.

Grossman, H. J. (Ed.). (1977). *Manual on terminology and classification in mental retardation.* Washington, DC: American Association on Mental Deficiency.

Huebner, K., Prickett, J. G., Welch, T. R., & Joffee, E. (Eds.). (1995). *Hand in hand: Essentials of communication and orientation and mobility for your students who are deaf-blind.* New York: AFB Press.

Kiester, E. (1990). *AIDS and vision loss.* New York: American Foundation for the Blind.

Stolov, W. C., & Clowers, M. R. (1981). *Handbook of severe disability: A text for rehabilitation counselors, other vocational practitioners, and allied health professionals.* Washington, DC: U.S. Government Printing Office.

APPENDIX C

BLANK FORMS

Case File Summary Form

Name ______________________________

Address ______________________________

Date ____________ **Age** ____________ **Gender** ____________

Education ______________________________

Visual impairment history

Cause ______________________________

Age of onset ______________________________

Prognosis ______________________________

Acuity ______________________________

____

____

Field ______________________________

Comments ______________________________

____

Medical history

Disabilities ______________________________

Medications ______________________________

Comments ______________________________

____

Vocational history

Present ______________________________

Past ______________________________

Goal ______________________________

Comments ______________________________

____

____

____

(continued on next page)

Social history

Marital status ______________________________

Living situation ______________________________

Living situation goal ______________________________

Client support ______________________________

Family/group support ______________________________

Testing history

____

____

Rehabilitation history

Past year ______________________________

Number of weeks of previous training ______________________________

Setting ______________________________

Activities of daily living training ______________________________

Communication ______________________________

____

Other ______________________________

____

Rehabilitation Teacher Interview Assessment Form

Name ______________________ **Date** ______________

Address ______________________ **Interviewer** ______________

Other disabilities ______________________

Living situation ______________________

Immediate dangers ______________________

____

Accuracy of knowledge of eye condition ______________________

____

COMMUNICATION

Reading

A. Current reading ability ______________________

____

B. Past reading interests ______________________

____

C. Use of tape recorder ______________________

____

D. Knowledge of talking books ______________________

____

Writing

A. Present handwriting skills ______________________

____

B. Keyboarding (typewriter and/or computer; past and present experience)______________________

____

C. Use of tape recorders (past and present experience) ______________________

____

Mathematics (past and present abilities and responsibilities)

____

____

(continued on next page)

ACTIVITIES OF DAILY LIVING

Home Management (all past and present methods, responsibilities, and experiences)

A. Food preparation ______________________________

____

B. Cleaning ______________________________

____

C. Home repairs ______________________________

____

Personal Management (all past and present abilities)

A. Grooming/makeup ______________________________

____

B. Medicinal management ______________________________

____

C. Clothing identification and care ______________________________

____

D. Money identification ______________________________

____

E. Telling time ______________________________

____

F. Telephone use ______________________________

____

Leisure Pursuits (past interests and present use)

____

____

Indoor Mobility

A. Present difficulties ______________________________

B. Knowledge of sighted guide techniques ______________________________

C. Visibility in living situation (lighting and contrast) ______________________________

____

Individualized Written Rehabilitation Program

CLIENT DESCRIPTION

1. **Name and Address**

2. **Case Number**

3. **Case Status**

4. **Date**

5. **Type** ☐ Original ☐ Amendment ☐ Annual ☐ Closure

SECTION I—VOCATIONAL OBJECTIVE

DOT Number

Plan Justification

Deficits

SECTION II—PLANNED SERVICES

Service

(continued on next page)

Objective

Description

Service dates **Begin** **End**

Cost

Total cost

Funding source

Progress evaluation

Service

Objective

Description

Service dates **Begin** **End**

Cost

Total cost

Funding source

Progress evaluation

(continued on next page)

Service

Objective

Description

Service dates **Begin** **End**

Cost

Total cost

Funding source

Progress evaluation

Service

Objective

Description

Service dates **Begin** **End**

Cost

Total cost

Funding source

Progress evaluation

(continued on next page)

SECTION III—CLIENT'S RESPONSIBILITY

Client will

Client's view of objectives and services

SECTION IV—CLIENT'S UNDERSTANDING AND AGREEMENT

I have discussed this plan with my counselor, have a copy of it, and I understand and accept the provisions outlined.

I understand that the planned employment outcome and the financial support provided for it by the rehabilitation agency are dependent upon my meeting the responsibilities outlined in the previous section. I further understand that failure to meet these responsibilities may result in termination of my program.

I understand that I may discuss problems or disagreements with the IWRP with my counselor. If I am dissatisfied, I may request an informal review with my counselor's supervisor for administrative review. I understand that if, after review, I continue to be dissatisfied, I will be assisted with application for a Fair Hearing with the Agency.

I understand that the Client Assistance Program is available to assist and/or represent me in the administrative review and fair hearing. I have been informed that the CAP worker is ____________________ and he can be reached at ____________________.

I understand that all services of this agency are provided on a nondiscriminatory basis without regard to race, color, creed, gender, age, national origin, or disability.

I further understand that services provided under this IWRP are subject to change on the basis of circumstances such as available funds or educational programs, and is not a binding contract.

____________________	____________________
Client's Signature	**Date**
____________________	____________________
Counselor's Signature	**Date**

Individual Program Plan

Client Name:

Client Short-Term Goal:

Client Long-Term Goal:

Client's Goals	***Implementation Process***	***Target Date***

Additional Information

____

____

____

____

I have reviewed the above information and agree with the program plan outlined.

____________________	____________________	__________
Client's Signature	**Case Manager's Signature**	**Date**

Service Plan

Instructions

Place a check mark on the line in front of each of the objectives that are required to meet the client's program goals. If additional objectives are needed, please write them in the space provided at the end of this form.

Name

Date

Instructor

COMMUNICATION SKILLS

I. Low Vision

A. At the completion of the unit describing environmental visibility, the learner will modify his or her environment to a level that maximizes his or her visual performance.

___ 1. When asked, the learner will describe the effects of size, contrast, and illumination on environmental visibility to a level that demonstrates an adequate knowledge.

___ 2. When given a location in his or her living quarters, the learner will modify it to achieve maximum visibility.

B. At the completion of the vision training unit, the learner will perform reading and other functions to a level sufficient to meet his or her daily needs.

___ 1. When asked, the learner will describe his or her best eye placement for eccentric viewing to a level that demonstrates adequate knowledge.

___ 2. When presented with a hand-held magnifier, the learner will read labels, dial settings, etc., with 90% accuracy.

___ 3. When presented with a stand magnifier, the learner will read and describe the material with 90% accuracy.

___ 4. When presented with a headborne microscope, the learner will read and describe material with 90% accuracy.

___ 5. When presented with a telemicroscope, the learner will read and describe material with 90% accuracy.

___ 6. When presented with a closed-circuit television system, the learner will read and describe material with 90% accuracy.

___ 7. When presented with a telescope, the learner will use it to view television and for other indoor purposes at a level sufficient to meet daily needs.

II. Braille and Other Tactile Systems

A. Upon completion of the grade 1 braille training unit, the learner will read grade 1 braille at a level sufficient to meet his or her information-storage, reading, and labeling needs.

___ 1. When presented with a braille training manual, the learner will read letters A through E with 90% accuracy.

___ 2. When presented with a braille training manual, the learner will read letters F through J with 90% accuracy.

(continued on next page)

___ 3. When presented with a braille training manual, the learner will read numbers with 90% accuracy.
___ 4. When presented with a braille training manual, the learner will read letters K through O with 90% accuracy.
___ 5. When presented with a braille training manual, the learner will read letters P through T with 90% accuracy.
___ 6. When presented with a braille training manual, the learner will read letters U through Z with 90% accuracy.
___ 7. When presented with a braille training manual, the learner will read necessary braille punctuation signs with 90% accuracy.
___ 8. When presented with a braille training manual, the learner will read necessary composition signs with 90% accuracy.
___ 9. When presented with a braille training manual, the learner will read two pages of uncontracted braille with 90% accuracy.

B. Upon completion of the grade 2 braille training unit, the learner will read grade 2 braille at a level sufficient to meet his or her information-storage and reading needs.
___ 1. When presented with a braille training manual, the learner will read alphabet word signs with 95% accuracy.
___ 2. When presented with a braille training manual, the learner will read short form word signs with 95% accuracy.
___ 3. When presented with a braille training manual, the learner will read the signs for *and, with, for, of,* and *the* with 95% accuracy.
___ 4. When presented with a braille training manual, the learner will read part word signs with 95% accuracy.
___ 5. When presented with a braille training manual, the learner will read lower signs with 95% accuracy.
___ 6. When presented with a braille training manual, the learner will read initial letter signs with 95% accuracy.
___ 7. When presented with a braille training manual, the learner will read final letter signs with 95% accuracy.
___ 8. When presented with a braille training manual, the learner will read cookbook units of measure with 95% accuracy.

C. Upon completion of the braille writing training unit, the learner will emboss braille at a level sufficient to meet his or her information-storage and labeling needs.
___ 1. When presented with a standard slate, paper, and a stylus, the learner will emboss two pages with 95% accuracy.
___ 2. When presented with a braillewriter and paper, the learner will emboss two pages with 95% accuracy.
___ 3. When presented with vinyl labeling tape and other materials, the learner will emboss braille labels with 95% accuracy.
___ 4. When presented with braille writing materials, the learner will write the descriptions and addresses of four sources of braille materials with 95% accuracy.

D. At the completion of the Fishburne Alphabet training unit, the learner will read and write it at a level sufficient to meet his or her needs.
___ 1. When presented with letters A through E, the learner will read them with 90% accuracy.

(continued on next page)

___ 2. When presented with letters F through M, the learner will read them with 90% accuracy.
___ 3. When presented with letters N through Z, the learner will read them with 90% accuracy.
___ 4. When presented with labels, the learner will read them with 95% accuracy.
___ 5. When presented with the embossing device, the learner will produce the letters of the alphabet with 95% accuracy.

III. Handwriting

A. Upon completion of the handwriting training unit for those who have congenital visual impairments, the learner will write words that are legible to a degree sufficient to meet his or her daily needs.
___ 1. When presented with the letters in his or her name, the learner will identify them with 90% accuracy.
___ 2. When presented with the letters of his or her last name and shown how they are connected, the learner will write them until 90% are legible.
___ 3. When presented with the letters of his or her first name and shown how they are connected, the learner will write them until 90% are legible.
___ 4. When presented with a standard signature guide and pencil, the learner will write his or her signature legibly in 90% of attempts.
___ 5. When presented with the remaining letters in the alphabet and given a full-page writing guide, the learner will write them until 90% of the attempts are legible.
___ 6. When presented with a full-page writing guide, the learner will write a one-page letter with 90% of the words legible.

B. Upon completion of the script-writing training unit for those with adventitious impairments, the learner will use handwriting devices at a level sufficient to meet his or her daily needs.
___ 1. When presented with the more rigid and structured writing guides, the learner will write 90% of his or her words legibly.
___ 2. When presented with the flexible baseline and other less structured guides, the learner will write 90% of his or her words legibly.
___ 3. When presented with bold-line writing guides, the learner will write 90% of his or her words legibly.
___ 4. When presented with the writing guide of choice, the learner will write a two-page document with 90% of the words legible.
___ 5. When asked, the learner will write the names, addresses, and descriptions of two major sources of handwriting aids legibly.

C. Upon completion of the raised-line drawing board training unit, the learner will use a raised-line drawing board to read and produce graphic representations to a level sufficient to meet his or her graphic needs.
___ 1. When presented with tactile drawings, the learner will describe them at a level demonstrating that the graphics are recognized.
___ 2. When presented with a raised-line drawing board, the learner will produce drawings that can be recognized visually in four out of five attempts.

IV. Typewriting/Keyboarding

A. Upon completion of the informal typing training unit, the learner will type documents at a level sufficient for such correspondence.

(continued on next page)

___ 1. When presented with a typewriter, the learner will identify the parts necessary for paper insertion and keyboard input with 90% accuracy.
___ 2. When presented with a typewriter and paper, the learner will insert the paper and use the letters of the home row with 90% accuracy.
___ 3. When presented with a typewriter and paper, the learner will insert the paper and use the remaining keys utilizing the first fingers with 90% accuracy.
___ 4. When presented with a typewriter and paper, the learner will insert the paper and use the remaining keys utilizing the second fingers with 90% accuracy.
___ 5. When presented with a typewriter and paper, the learner will insert the paper and use the remaining keys utilizing the third fingers with 90% accuracy.
___ 6. When presented with a typewriter and paper, the learner will insert the paper and use the remaining keys utilizing the fourth fingers with 90% accuracy.
___ 7. When presented with a typewriter and paper, the learner will insert the paper and perform the following adaptive skills at a level sufficient for informal correspondence: (a) set margins, (b) set tabs, (c) correct known keystroking errors, (d) maintain a bottom margin, and (e) mark the closing for subsequent signature.
___ 8. When presented with a typewriter, paper, and envelope, the learner will type an informal letter with 90% accuracy.

B. Upon completion of the business typewriting training unit, the learner will type formal documents at a level sufficient for business correspondence.
___ 1. When presented with a typewriter and paper, the learner will type a three-page document with less than three mistakes per page.
___ 2. When presented with a typewriter, paper, and a business envelope, the learner will type a three-page business letter in the proper formats with less than three mistakes per page.

V. Computer Technology

A. Upon completion of the computer literacy training unit, the learner will describe the uses and major parts of computers at a level sufficient to allow him or her to draw conclusions regarding their usefulness to him or her personally.
___ 1. When asked, the learner will, from memory, describe the major uses of computers to a level indicating an overall understanding.
___ 2. When asked, the learner will, from memory, describe the major parts of a computer to a level indicating an overall understanding of their interrelationship and functions.
___ 3. When asked, the learner will, from memory, define computer terminology to a level indicating an overall understanding.

B. Upon completion of the computer utilization training unit, the learner will perform the necessary functions at a level sufficient to meet his or her word-processing and information-storage needs.
___ 1. When presented with a word-processing program and a voice, large-print, or braille output microcomputer that has been configured by the instructor, the learner will type 60 lines with less than five mistakes.
___ 2. When presented with a word-processing program and a voice, large-print, or braille output microcomputer, the learner will save, retrieve, and print a file and review the directory with 90% accuracy.
___ 3. When presented with a word-processing program and a voice, large-print, or braille output microcomputer, the learner will perform the editing functions (delete, insert, block, search, etc.) with 90% accuracy.

(continued on next page)

___ 4. When presented with a microcomputer, a word-processing program, and a speech synthesizer, the learner will produce and read a two-page document with 95% accuracy.

___ 5. When presented with a microcomputer, a word-processing program, and a braille output system, the learner will produce and read a two-page document with 95% accuracy.

___ 6. When presented with a microcomputer, a word-processing program, and an electronic screen magnification system, the learner will produce and read a two-page document with 95% accuracy.

___ 7. When presented with a computer and an optical character recognition system (scanner), the learner will read documents and store them as text files that contain fewer than 10 mistakes per page.

___ 8. When presented with an adapted microcomputer and the appropriate software, the learner will perform utility functions (copy, format, etc.) with 90% accuracy.

___ 9. When presented with an adapted microcomputer and database software, the learner will store and retrieve information with 90% accuracy.

___ 10. When presented with a braille input–speech output computer, the learner will store and retrieve files with 90% accuracy.

___ 11. When asked, the learner will describe five major sources of computer access devices.

VI. Listening and Recording Devices

A. Upon completion of the tape recorder training unit, the learner will use a tape recorder at a level sufficient to meet information-storage and retrieval needs.

___ 1. When presented with a standard cassette recorder and a blank tape, the learner will record three separate segments on two sides and retrieve them quickly and efficiently.

___ 2. When presented with an adapted cassette recorder and a blank cassette tape, the learner will consistently record information on different tracks at different speeds and retrieve that information quickly and efficiently.

___ 3. When presented with an adapted cassette recorder and a blank tape, the learner will record and locate voice- and tone-indexed segments with 90% accuracy.

___ 4. When presented with a tape recorder, head-cleaning supplies and a demagnetizer, the learner will consistently clean and demagnetize the heads without harming the machine.

___ 5. When presented with a radio or tape player with an output jack, a cassette recorder, a patch cord, and a blank tape, the learner will consistently record information clearly and completely.

___ 6. When presented with damaged cassette tapes and the proper repair materials, the learner will consistently demonstrate the techniques required to restore them to working order.

___ 7. When presented with live lectures, a tape recorder, and a system for condensing and storing notes, the learner will produce outlines of the information presented by the lecturer that contain 95% of the pertinent information.

___ 8. When asked, the learner will describe the Recording for the Blind program to a level that demonstrates a working knowledge of their services.

___ 9. When read a list of recording resources, the learner will record and index those he or she desires and retrieve them quickly and efficiently.

B. Upon completion of the National Library Service for the Blind and Physically Handicapped (NLS) and radio reading service training unit, the learner will utilize the services and products of the programs to a level sufficient to meet his or her pleasure-reading needs.

(continued on next page)

___ 1. When presented with the services of the NLS and radio reading services, the learner will apply for those desired.
___ 2. When presented with a Talking-Book Easy Cassette Machine and a recorded cassette, the learner will consistently play a book without restarting it and demonstrate an understanding of the content.
___ 3. When presented with a Talking-Book Machine disc player and a book on disc, the learner will consistently place the needle in the proper position and demonstrate reading comprehension without scratching the record.
___ 4. When presented with a Talking-Book Cassette Machine and a recorded cassette, the learner will consistently find specific page locations on different tracks and demonstrate an understanding of the book's content.

VII. Mathematics

A. Upon completion of the adaptive calculator training unit, the learner will use a calculator at a level sufficient to meet his or her daily needs.
___ 1. When presented with a large-display calculator, the learner will perform the four basic mathematical functions (addition, subtraction, multiplication, and division) with 95% accuracy.
___ 2. When presented with a talking calculator, the learner will perform the basic mathematical functions with 95% accuracy.
___ 3. When presented with a scientific calculator, the learner will perform the necessary functions with 98% accuracy.
___ 4. When presented with a list of calculator resources, the learner will record those he or she desires.

B. At the completion of the abacus training unit, the learner will perform the four basic mathematical functions at a level necessary to meet his or her daily needs.
___ 1. When presented with a Cranmer abacus, the learner will add three-digit numbers with 95% accuracy.
___ 2. When presented with a Cranmer abacus, the learner will subtract three-digit numbers with 95% accuracy.
___ 3. When presented with a Cranmer abacus, the learner will multiply three-digit numbers with 95% accuracy.
___ 4. When presented with a Cranmer abacus, the learner will divide three-digit numbers with 95% accuracy.
___ 5. When presented with a list of abacus resources, the learner will record those he or she desires.

DAILY LIVING SKILLS

VIII. Orientation and Movement in the Home Environment

A. Upon completion of the orientation and movement training unit, the learner will move through his or her home environment efficiently.
___ 1. When traveling with a sighted guide, the learner will move through his or her environment safely and efficiently.

(continued on next page)

___ 2. When moving through familiar environments, the learner will use searching and trailing techniques to move through his or her environment safely and efficiently.
___ 3. When moving through familiar environments, the learner will use orientation techniques to move through his or her environment safely and efficiently.
___ 4. When moving through familiar environments, the learner will use diagonal cane technique to move through his or her environment safely and efficiently.

B. When presented with the self-protection training unit, the learner will function safely in familiar environments.
___ 1. When presented with a familiar environment, the learner will use protective techniques to a level that ensures minimal risk.
___ 2. When presented with a familiar environment, the learner will describe its safety hazards and suggest ways that it might be modified to minimize risks.

IX. Kitchen Skills

A. Upon completion of the cold foods training unit, the learner will prepare foods that need not be heated to a level sufficient to meet his or her lunch and snack needs.
___ 1. When asked, the learner will consistently describe the kitchen area and its contents to a level indicating a working knowledge.
___ 2. When presented with common kitchen utensils, the learner will describe their functions to a level indicating a working knowledge.
___ 3. When presented with various pouring tasks, the learner will consistently fill containers with hot and cold liquids to a proper level without spilling.
___ 4. When presented with bread and a butter knife, the learner will consistently spread various semisolid foods evenly and with thorough coverage.
___ 5. When presented with various can openers, the learner will consistently open cans safely and efficiently.
___ 6. When presented with various volumetric measuring devices, the learner will consistently measure solids, semisolids, and liquids at a level to meet recipe needs.
___ 7. When presented with kitchen knives, the learner will consistently slice, dice, and peel various foods safely and efficiently.
___ 8. When presented with soiled dishes and work area, the learner will consistently clean them safely and efficiently.

B. Upon completion of the simple hot foods training unit, the learner will prepare snacks, lunches, and simple dinner meals at a level sufficient to meet his or her daily needs.
___ 1. When presented with a hot beverage device, the learner will consistently prepare various instant foods safely and efficiently.
___ 2. When presented with a toaster or toaster oven, the learner will consistently prepare prepackaged foods safely and efficiently.
___ 3. When presented with an electric or gas stove, the learner will consistently perform the following: (a) describe stove dials, (b) describe dial marking methods, (c) detect heat from the burner, (d) center pots and pans on a burner, (e) set stove dial in the correct position, and (f) detect boiling liquid safely and efficiently.
___ 4. When presented with a frying pan and various foods, the learner will consistently fry them safely and to the proper level of doneness.

(continued on next page)

___ 5. When presented with an oven, a timer, and various foods, the learner will consistently bake them safely and to the proper level of doneness.
___ 6. When presented with a microwave oven and various foods, the learner will cook them safely and to the proper level of doneness.
___ 7. When presented with an adapted form of a simple cookbook or list of instructions from food containers, the learner will use it to prepare foods to meet his or her needs.
___ 8. When presented with foods of his or her choice, the learner will prepare a full-course meal efficiently and to the proper level of doneness.

C. Upon completion of the elaborate hot foods training unit, the learner will prepare appetizers, dinners, and desserts, to a level sufficient to meet his or her daily needs.
___ 1. When presented with a cookbook of his or her choice, the learner will adequately describe how it could be adapted to meet his or her needs.
___ 2. When presented with an electric mixer and various foods, the learner will consistently mix them safely and thoroughly.
___ 3. When presented with a food processor and various foods, the learner will process foods safely and efficiently.
___ 4. When presented with a slow cooker and various foods, the learner will prepare them to a proper level of doneness.
___ 5. When presented with a broiler and various foods, the learner will prepare them to a proper level of doneness.
___ 6. When presented with a wok and various foods, the leaner will prepare them to a proper level of doneness.
___ 7. When presented with soufflé equipment, the learner will prepare a soufflé to a proper level of doneness.
___ 8. When presented with the equipment and foods of his or her choice, the learner will prepare a full-course meal (appetizer, entrée, and dessert) efficiently and to the proper level of doneness.

X. Personal Management

A. Upon completion of the clothing care training unit, the learner will maintain his or her desired appearance.
___ 1. When asked, a learner who had no former concept of clothing styles and colors will consistently describe them to a level that indicates understanding.
___ 2. When presented with various articles of clothing and the appropriate materials, the learner will label and later consistently identify them with 80% accuracy.
___ 3. When presented with various articles of clothing and the appropriate materials, the learner will consistently prepare them for storage on hangers, in closets, and in suitcases, so that they are unwrinkled and neat in appearance.
___ 4. When presented with various articles of clothing and the appropriate materials, the learner will consistently sort, wash, dry, and iron them so that they are clean and unwrinkled.
___ 5. When presented with various types of shoeware, the learner will consistently clean and polish them so that they are unsoiled and neat in appearance.
___ 6. When taken to a laundromat, the learner will consistently use the facilities to wash and dry his or her clothing quickly and efficiently.

B. Upon completion of the personal care training unit, the learner will perform hygiene, grooming, and routine health skills at a level sufficient to meet his or her needs.

(continued on next page)

___ 1. When presented with standard bathroom facilities, a learner with multiple handicaps will consistently bathe him- or herself to a level that maintains personal cleanliness.
___ 2. When presented with the materials of choice, the learner will consistently care for his or her teeth at a level sufficient to maintain dental hygiene.
___ 3. When presented with the materials of choice, the learner will consistently care for feminine menstrual needs to a level sufficient to maintain personal hygiene.
___ 4. When presented with the materials of choice, the learner will consistently shave to a desired level of personal appearance.
___ 5. When presented with the materials of choice, the learner will consistently apply cosmetics to a desired level of personal appearance.
___ 6. When presented with the materials of choice, the learner will consistently care for hair to a desired level of personal appearance.
___ 7. When presented with methods of measuring insulin, the learner will choose the one most appropriate and consistently measure it at a level sufficient to ensure adequate and safe administration.
___ 8. When presented with his or her ocular prosthetic devices, the learner will consistently perform the skills necessary to maintain a desired level of personal appearance.
___ 9. When presented with his or her medications, the learner will mark and later consistently identify them at a level sufficient to ensure safe and adequate administration.

C. At the completion of the telephone training unit, the learner will utilize a telephone at a level sufficient to meet his or her daily needs.
___ 1. When presented with a rotary dial telephone and 10 numbers, the learner will successfully contact 9.
___ 2. When presented with a touch-pad telephone and 10 telephone numbers, the learner will successfully contact 9.
___ 3. When presented with a telephone of the learner's choice, he or she will contact local information banks and retrieve information with 90% accuracy.
___ 4. When asked, the learner will describe all the special services of the local telephone company.

D. At the completion of the time and money training unit, the learner will tell time and identify money at a level sufficient to meet his or her daily needs.
___ 1. When presented with a raised-dot or large-print watch, the learner will consistently read the time and set it to within five minutes of the correct time.
___ 2. When presented with a talking watch or clock, the learner will consistently use all its functions to a level sufficient to meet his or her needs.
___ 3. When presented with coins, the learner will identify them correctly with 99% accuracy.
___ 4. When presented with paper money, the learner will describe an identification method and identify random selections with 99% accuracy.
___ 5. When presented with adaptive checking or banking materials, the learner will write checks correctly, enter balances in the ledger, and use an automated teller machine with 99% accuracy.

XI. Home Management

A. Upon completion of the home management training unit, the learner will perform home care skills to a level sufficient to meet his or her daily needs.

(continued on next page)

___ 1. When asked, the learner will describe the following to a level at which training can begin: (a) clean and dirty, (b) dust and dusting, (c) wash and rinse, and (d) polish and polishing.
___ 2. When asked, the learner will describe to a degree indicating adequate knowledge adaptive methods for: (a) maintaining spatial orientation in large areas, (b) thoroughly covering a surface to be cleaned, and (c) monitoring cleanliness.
___ 3. When presented with the proper materials, the learner will consistently dust, wash, and polish various flat surfaces so they are clean and shiny.
___ 4. When presented with a broom, a dustpan and two vinyl floors, the learner will clean them until they are free of dirt.
___ 5. When presented with a dust mop and two vinyl floors, the learner will clean them until they are free of dirt.
___ 6. When presented with a wet mop, water bucket, cleaning fluid, and two vinyl floors, the learner will clean them until they are free of dirt.
___ 7. When presented with vacuum cleaner and two carpeted floors, the learner will clean them until they are free of dirt.
___ 8. When presented with bedclothes, the learner will consistently make a bed neatly and evenly.

XII. Home Mechanics

A. Upon completion of the home mechanics training unit, the learner will perform home repair tasks at a level sufficient to meet his or her daily needs.
___ 1. When presented with a saw, a saw guide and a clamp, the learner will consistently cut boards safely and with minimal veer.
___ 2. When presented with a hammer, nails, and a board, the learner will consistently drive nails safely and with minimal bending.
___ 3. When presented with three grades of sandpaper and a board, the learner will consistently distinguish the grade of the sandpaper and sand a board until smooth.
___ 4. When presented with common hand tools, the learner will consistently use them properly.
___ 5. When presented with a standard faucet, the learner will consistently replace the washers without damaging the mechanism and so that it does not leak.
___ 6. When presented with a standard toilet, the learner will consistently describe the function of each part and consistently disassemble and reassemble the mechanism in such a way that it functions properly.
___ 7. When presented with a standard hinged door, the learner will consistently disassemble and reassemble the doorknob so that it functions properly.
___ 8. When presented with common drain-cleaning tools, the learner will consistently describe their use to a level indicating the necessary knowledge to use them.
___ 9. When presented with an electric wall plug and a disattached cord, the learner will consistently reattach it, so that the wires are not crossed and it will conduct electricity.
___ 10. When presented with a fuse box, the learner will consistently describe its parts and replace fuses safely and effectively.

B. At the completion of the household safety training unit, the learner will demonstrate a knowledge of serious safety issues and their solutions to a level necessary to manage a home independently.
___ 1. When presented with a fire extinguisher, the learner will consistently use it in the proper manner for putting out various types of household fires.
___ 2. When presented with a smoke alarm, the learner will consistently replace the batteries and demonstrate an adequate knowledge of how it is used.

(continued on next page)

___ 3. When presented with a fuse box, the learner will consistently turn it off when asked to do so.

___ 4. When presented with the main shutoff valve for the household water supply, the learner will consistently turn it off when asked to do so.

XIII. Leisure-Time Activities

A. Upon completion of the crafts training unit, the learner will prepare craft items to meet his or her daily needs.

___ 1. When presented with prepackaged craft kits, the learner will consistently produce craft items at a level sufficient to meet his or her needs.

___ 2. When presented with the proper materials, the learner will produce woodcraft items at a level sufficient to meet his or her needs.

___ 3. When presented with the proper materials, the learner will produce tying-craft items at a level sufficient to meet his or her needs.

___ 4. When presented with the proper materials, the learner will produce needlecraft items at a level sufficient to meet his or her needs.

___ 5. When presented with the proper materials, the learner will produce clay, pottery, or dough craft at a level sufficient to meet his or her needs.

___ 6. When presented with the proper materials, the learner will produce paper craft items at a level sufficient to meet his or her needs.

___ 7. When presented with the proper materials, the learner will produce decoupage craft items at a level sufficient to meet his or her needs.

___ 8. When presented with the proper materials, the learner will produce leather craft items at a level sufficient to meet his or her needs.

___ 9. When presented with the proper materials, the learner will produce woven craft items at a level sufficient to meet his or her needs.

B. Upon completion of the sewing training unit, the learner will perform sewing activities at a level sufficient to meet his or her daily needs.

___ 1. When presented with a regular or self-threading needle, thread, and the appropriate needle-threading devices, the learner will thread the needle consistently.

___ 2. When presented with appropriate sewing materials, the learner will consistently reattach buttons.

___ 3. When presented with appropriate sewing materials, the learner will consistently mend seams.

C. Upon completion of the recreation training unit, the learner will perform selected activities at a level sufficient to meet his or her daily needs.

___ 1. When presented with board games, the learner will play them at a level sufficient to meet his or her needs.

___ 2. When presented with card games, the learner will play them at a level sufficient to meet his or her needs.

___ 3. When asked, the learner will consistently describe methods for adapting mainstream recreational or leisure-time activities.

GLOSSARY

This glossary includes terms that are used in this text, and they are defined as they are used in the field of rehabilitation teaching and in working with persons who are visually impaired. Terms may be clarified more fully in the text. Certain additional disabilities or conditions that rehabilitation teachers are likely to encounter are defined and explained in Appendix B.

Abacus A device used for performing mathematical calculation by sliding beads along rods.

Accommodation The ability of the eye to alter its focus to see objects at various distances; accomplished by the action of the ciliary muscle in changing the shape of the lens.

Activities of daily living (ADL) The routine activities that an individual must be able to perform in order to live independently.

Acuity See Visual acuity.

Adapted device An object, such as a talking calculator or a braille ruler, that has been altered to help a visually impaired individual with communication, the activities of daily living, or other activities.

Adaptive skill A technique or method that helps a visually impaired individual with communication, the activities of daily living, or other activities.

Adventitious Occurring after birth; not present at birth. With regard to a visual impairment, it also means occurring after early childhood developmental stages are completed.

Affective domain The emotional realm of a person. Early development in this area may be indirectly affected by interpersonal or social factors related to the effects of a visual impairment.

Alignment An orientation technique in which an individual positions himself or herself alongside an object to establish a line of direction.

Amsler grid A chart consisting of a grid of small boxes used for near-point testing of the central visual field.

Assessment In rehabilitation teaching, the process through which the teacher determines the present needs and skill levels of the client.

Astigmatism A refractive error that prevents light rays from coming to a point of focus on the retina.

Behavioral objective A concisely written statement of the expected outcomes of instruction that is the basic unit of all written rehabilitation plans, consisting of the condition, the behavior, and the criterion; also called instructional or performance objective.

Behaviorism A learning theory based on the notion that learning is measurable in observable behaviors and results from environmental factors.

Binocular vision The ability to use the two eyes together to focus on the same object by fusing the two images into one.

Blind Rehabilitation Centers Residential facilities of the Department of Veterans Affairs that provide comprehensive rehabilitation services to blinded veterans.

Blind Rehabilitation Outpatient Services (BROS) A field service program of the Department of Veterans Affairs that provides adaptive skills instruction to blinded veterans.

Blind spot A physiological blind area in the visual field, corresponding to the point at which the optic nerve leaves the retina to reach the brain.

Blindness Lack of functional vision.

Blood glucose monitoring The periodic estimation of blood sugar level in an individual who has diabetes, usually accomplished with chemically treated strips or electronic glucose monitors.

Bold-line writing guide A handwriting guide for persons with a certain amount of useful residual vision that utilizes highly visible lines to give some measure of visual guidance for writing.

Boston line type A tactile reading mode introduced by Samuel Gridley Howe, consisting of a blocky modification of raised capital letters.

Braille A tactile system for reading and writing, based on a cell composed of six raised dots.

Braille cell locating technique A method of orientation, especially with visually impaired persons who have poor spatial concepts, using the dot positions of the braille cell to help locate specific objects in relation to one another.

Braille cell method A method for teaching handwriting, usually to individuals who are congenitally blind, that utilizes the dots of adjoining braille cells to describe the formation of script and print letters.

Braille printer A computer printer that embosses braille using software to convert from print to grade 2 braille.

Brailler A machine used for embossing braille. Also known as braillewriter.

Bulk eraser A magnetic device that erases cassette audiotapes completely and quickly.

Canadian National Institute for the Blind (CNIB) A rehabilitation agency that serves adults with visual impairments in Canada; it is for the most part private.

Case management A process of overseeing an individual's progress, as in rehabilitation teaching, that includes planning, implementing, and monitoring the service program from assessment through closure.

Cataract An opacity of the crystalline lens of the eye that results in loss of visual acuity.

Central processing unit (CPU) The "brain" of the computer; it stores and operates on data in the form of electronic signals.

Central vision The ability to perceive images to focus on the central area of the retina (macula); used to identify and obtain detailed information about objects.

Client assistance plan (CAP) A federally mandated program to provide information on the available services and benefits to clients under the Rehabilitation Act and Title I of the Americans with Disabilities Act and to provide advocacy in pursuing legal, administrative, or other appropriate remedies to ensure protection of clients' rights.

Click ruler A device used for measuring, which has a rod that is pulled away from the ruler's main body and clicks once for each sixteenth-inch it is extended.

Closed-circuit television (CCTV) A device, used primarily as a reading aid for persons with low vision, that electronically magnifies printed materials and projects the enlarged image on a video monitor.

Cognitive domain The intellectual realm, concerned with the process of knowing, including both awareness and judgment; early development in this area may be profoundly affected by congenital visual impairments.

Cognitivism A learning theory based on the notion that learning is a cognitive process in which the individual considers all information about a problem and actively arrives at a solution.

Commercial template A commercially made handwriting guide that defines the space to be used for writing with cut-out openings in a rigid material.

Computerized books Reading material made available as electronic computer text files.

Confrontation field testing A method of making a rough assessment of the peripheral field by having an individual fixate on the nose of the examiner and indicate when he or she first sees a target that is moved from beyond the seeing area toward the fixation point.

Congenital Present at birth; in the case of blindness or visual impairment, occurring at birth or before early childhood development.

Contrast Dissimilarity in color of adjacent parts; providing appropriate contrast for tasks improves the visual performance of individuals with low vision.

Convergence The ability to focus both eyes at the same time on a near object by directing the visual axes of both eyes inward.

Cornea The clear, transparent covering of the front of the eyeball, which is an important refractive medium.

Cue and review A special feature of cassette recorders that allows the user to auditorily monitor the contents of a tape during the fast-forward and rewind modes; it is essential for the use of certain indexing systems. Also known as preview and review.

Cursor The electronic pointer that is displayed on the computer screen that indicates the position on the screen where data is to be entered.

Denial A psychological defense mechanism characterized by the tendency to ignore problems.

Dental floss threader A device used by persons with visual impairments to thread needles; it has a loop on the end and can be used in the same manner as wire loop threaders.

Diabetes mellitus A systemic metabolic disorder of the carbohydrate metabolism, resulting from inadequate production or utilization of insulin; it results in elevated blood sugar level and presence of sugar in the urine. See also Diabetic retinopathy.

Diabetic retinopathy A complication of diabetes mellitus stemming from changes in the retinal blood vessels, characterized by retinal hemorrhages, neovascularization, and scarring; a leading cause of blindness in the United States.

Dial Operator Service A telephone company service that allows persons with special needs to obtain dialing assistance from an operator free of charge.

Directory assistance waiver A telephone company service offered to people who are unable to use a print telephone directory in which they are not billed for directory assistance calls in their local area.

Disk drive A peripheral device that allows a computer to read information stored on magnetic disks.

Distance vision The ability to see objects from a distance; distance visual acuity is measured using distance vision test charts such as the Snellen chart.

Divergence Deviation of both eyes outward.

Dual speed control A feature of adaptive tape recorders to increase the storage capacity of cassettes by allowing recording and listening to adapted recordings at a slow speed of 15⁄16 inches per second, while also allowing commercial recordings to be played at the standard speed of 1⅞ inches per second.

Easy Cassette Machine A simplified nonrecording cassette playback device for the NLS talking book program; it has some automatic control functions that are easier to operate for persons with physical disabilities than the standard machine.

Eccentric viewing An adaptive low vision skill that involves shifting the gaze to use the functioning areas of the retina when a scotoma interferes with a person's ability to see objects in the central field.

Enucleation A surgical procedure consisting of removal of the entire eyeball.

Evisceration A surgical procedure consisting of removal of the inner viscera of the eye, leaving the outer tunic intact.

Fair hearing An inquiry conducted by an impartial hearing officer to review determinations made by a rehabilitation counselor.

Familiarization A process by which a visually impaired person can become oriented to a new environment.

Field See Visual field.

Fishburne alphabet An alternative tactile reading method consisting of four basic symbols used in a simple repetitive pattern to represent the alphabet; it is utilized mainly for personal communication and labeling by visually impaired people who are unable to learn braille.

Fixation The ability of the eyes to direct and hold the gaze on an object.

Flexible writing guide A handwriting guide that utilizes plastic or elastic strings to define the area for writing; it allows more freedom of motion than rigid guides for formation of letters, especially those with descenders.

Flexidisc Flexible discs used to record talking books.

Focal distance In optics, the distance from a lens to the focal point. Also, the distance from a lens to the object or surface being viewed in order for the object to be in sharp focus.

Focal point The point at which parallel light rays are brought to a focus by a lens.

Full-bodied prosthesis An artifical eye made of silicone or plastic that is substituted for the eye after surgical removal to provide a base for and support a prosthetic shell. Also known as globe prosthesis.

Functional vision A degree of vision sufficient to be of use in performing a given task.

Glare A strong, steady, dazzling light or brilliant reflection.

Glaucoma An ocular disease characterized by an increase in intraocular pressure; it may cause damage to the ocular tissues, including the optic nerve, and loss of visual field.

Grid pattern technique An adaptive method for cleaning, used to ensure full coverage of a surface by moving from top to bottom and from left to right, using overlapping strokes.

Handwriting guide An adaptive device that assists a visually impaired individual in determining the space in which to write.

Homemade writing template A homemade handwriting guide that is designed to fit a specific purpose or item, such as an individual's checks, deposit slips, envelopes, writing paper, or business forms.

Humanism A theory that considers learning from the perspective of the human potential for growth and the individual's affective needs.

Hyperopia (farsightedness) A refractive error in which the light rays from a distant object are brought to focus behind the retina.

Icon A graphic or pictorial representation used by computer software to replace words on the screen.

Illumination The intensity of light per square unit of area.

Independent Living (IL) Program A program administered by the U.S. Rehabilitation Services Administration that offers rehabilitation services to eligible clients who are not candidates for vocational services, such as persons who have multiple disabilities or elderly visually impaired persons.

Individual Program Plan (IPP) A written vocational rehabilitation plan that is used in Canada.

Individualized Written Rehabilitation Program (IWRP) A written vocational rehabilitation plan used in the United States; it is developed jointly by the rehabilitation counselor and the individual with a disability who is eligible for vocational rehabilitation.

Individuals with Disabilities Education Act (IDEA) P.L. 101–476, the new name for the 1990 amendment to the Education for All Handicapped Children Act of 1974 (P.L. 94–142).

Itinerant teacher An instructor who moves from place to place (e.g., from home to home, school to hospital, or school to school) to provide instruction and support to students with special needs.

Keyboard announcement A feature of synthetic speech software that enables a synthesizer to speak the name of any key on a computer keyboard that is struck.

Large print (large type) Print that is larger (14–18 points) than that commonly found in magazines, newspapers, and books (6–12 points).

Leader tape A nonmagnetic segment of tape, usually found at each end of a cassette, that connects the magnetic tape to the tape spools; it is represented by 10 to 20 seconds of silence at the beginning of a cassette because nothing can be recorded on the nonmagnetic strip.

Learning Increased knowledge or skill that results from instruction or experience; in rehabilitation teaching it is measured by observation of behavioral change.

Legal blindness A visual acuity of 20/200 or less in the better eye after correction with conventional lenses, or a visual field of 20 degrees or less in the better eye.

Lens The part of the eye that changes shape to adjust the focus of images from various distances into a sharp image on the retina.

Low vision A degree of vision that is functional but limited enough to interfere with the ability to perform everyday activities and that cannot be corrected with standard eyeglasses or contact lenses.

Low vision assessment A comprehensive appraisal of a visually impaired individual's visual impairment, visual potential, and visual capability.

Low vision devices Various types of optical and nonoptical devices used to enhance the visual capability of persons with visual impairments. See also Nonoptical and Optical devices.

Lower hand and forearm technique A protective technique, used to prevent unexpected contact with low objects, in which the arm is extended diagonally down and across the body with the palm facing in just below the waist.

Macula The central area of the retina, which is the area of best visual acuity and is responsible for fine visual tasks such as reading.

Macular degeneration A degenerative disease of the macula that causes a loss of central vision, resulting in a central scotoma, or a blind or partially blind area in the central visual field; one of the most common causes of visual impairment in elderly people.

Magnification A method of increasing the size of an image on the retina.

Magnifier A low vision device used for short-term near-vision spotting tasks that can increase the size of the image on the retina and can be used at any distance from the eye.

Manipulation A form of demonstration using nonverbal communication in which the instructor manipulates the learner's movements.

Microscope A low vision device, used for near-vision tasks, that uses magnification.

Mobility The ability to move from one's present position to one's desired position in another part of the environment. See also Orientation.

Modeling A form of demonstration using nonverbal communication in which the learner follows the instructor's movements tactilely.

Moon type A tactile system for reading developed by William Moon and still used in the United Kingdom, formed by modifying raised capital letters to enhance tactile legibility.

Myopia (nearsightedness) A refractive error in which light rays from a distant object are brought into focus in front of the retina.

National Library Service for the Blind and Physically Handicapped (NLS) See Talking Book Program.

Near vision The ability to see objects close up. Also known as near-point vision.

Negative typecasts A tactile reading system introduced by Haüy; consists of raised impressions of conventional letters produced by striking the paper with great force.

Nemeth code A braille code system designed for use in science and mathematics.

Neuropathy An abnormal and usually degenerative state of the nervous system or nerves.

Nonoptical devices Low vision devices that do not involve optics, such as lamps, filters, large print, typoscopes, bold-line paper, and writing guides.

Nystagmus An involuntary, rapid movement of the eyeball that may be horizontal, vertical, rotary, or mixed.

Occluder A device used to cover an eye, as when testing the visual acuity or visual fields of each eye.

Ocular Of or pertaining to the eye.

OD Oculus dexter (right eye).

Ophthalmologist A physician who specializes in diseases and surgery of the eye.

Optacon A reading device that converts regular print or computer output into an enlarged vibrating tactile image; now obsolete.

Optic atrophy An ocular condition characterized by degeneration of the optic nerve and resulting in loss of vision and constriction of the visual fields.

Optic nerve The nerve that carries impulses from the retina to the brain.

Optical character recognition (OCR) A system that scans printed text and converts it into an electronic format that can be stored in a text file in computers and accessed by means of adaptive equipment.

Optical devices Low vision devices that incorporate optics, such as magnifiers, microscopes, and telescopes.

Optics The science that deals with light and phenomena associated with it, applied in the prescription of low vision devices.

Optometrist A nonmedical professional trained in the measurement of the refraction of the eye.

Orientation The process of becoming familiar with and establishing one's position and relationship to significant objects in the environment. See also Mobility.

Orientation and mobility (O&M) The field dealing with systematic techniques by which blind or visually impaired persons orient themselves to their environment and move about independently.

OS Oculus sinister (left eye).

OU Oculus uterque (both eyes).

Passive indexing A method of identifying and locating information on recorded tape by leaving a few seconds of blank tape to mark the beginning of each new recording or section; can be detected by using the cue and review feature on a tape recorder.

Patch cord An audio connection cord with plugs at both ends, used to transmit information from an output source (such as a radio, cassette player, or telephone) to an input device (such as a tape recorder).

Peripheral device An auxiliary electronic device that plugs into a computer and performs additional functions, such as a printer, braille device, or speech synthesizer.

Peripheral vision The perception of objects, motion, or color outside the direct line of vision or by other than the central retina.

Personal adjustment training (PAT) The portion of a person's total rehabilitation plan, excluding vocational services, in which adaptive skills training is offered, including communication skills, daily living skills, orientation and mobility, and low vision services; prepares the individual for vocational services.

Photophobia Abnormal sensitivity to light.

Prosthetic shell An artificial eye that is worn like a contact lens over an unsightly or misshapen eye.

Psychological defense mechanisms Subconscious psychological reactions that protect the ego during periods of unacceptable reality.

Psychometric tests Techniques of mental measurement.

Psychomotor domain Motor skills believed to ensue from prior conscious mental activity and visual feedback; psychomotor early development in this area may be affected in children with severe visual impairments.

Radio reading service An auditory information resource, usually operating on unused radio frequencies and requiring a special receiver, that provides persons with visual, physical, and reading disabilities with information such as newspaper articles, commentary, advertisements, best sellers not available in adapted forms, consumer information, and information about issues such as jobs, access, and transportation.

Raised-dot ruler An adaptive device for measuring, with braille numbers and raised dots corresponding to the printed markings.

Raised-line drawing board A device that produces a raised image when the user writes or draws, permitting tactile investigation of linear graphics such as maps, graphs, and line drawings.

Reading machine A computer-based assistive device that converts printed text into speech.

Refraction Deflection in the course of the rays of light; also, determination of the refractive errors of the eye and their correction.

Refractive error An optical defect in the eye that prevents light rays from being brought to a focus on the retina.

Refreshable braille display An electronic device that connects to a computer by a cable and translates information displayed on the computer screen into braille in the form of electronically driven plastic pins that pop up to form braille characters.

Rehabilitation The process of bringing or restoring an individual to a normal or optimum state of health, constructive activity, and so forth by means of medical treatment and physical or psychological therapy; specifically, the relearning of skills already acquired prior to the onset of a visual disability.

Rehabilitation counselor A rehabilitation professional who serves as agency case manager and may provide therapeutic counseling.

Rehabilitation Services Administration (RSA) An agency of the U.S. government, housed in the Department of Education, that administers the provision of vocational services to adults through agencies in every state.

Rehabilitation teacher A professional whose primary goal is to instruct persons with visual impairments to utilize adaptive skills to help them to cope with the demands of everyday life, primarily in the areas of communication, personal management, home management, leisure time, movement in familiar environments, and low vision; other job roles include case management tasks, such as making referrals and advocating for clients' rights, and administrative tasks, such as educating the public about blindness.

Retina The innermost layer of the eye, containing light-sensitive nerve cells and fibers connecting with the brain through the optic nerve that receives the image formed by the lens.

Retinitis pigmentosa (RP) A hereditary degeneration and atrophy of the retina, of unknown etiology; causes night blindness, and results in optic atrophy and constriction of the peripheral visual fields.

Scanner A device that uses a moving electronic beam to convert visual images, such as printed text or images, into an electronic format that can be transmitted or converted into other formats.

Scanning The ability to search systematically for objects in the environment through a coordinated effort of the eyes and head.

Scotoma A blind or partially blind area in the visual field.

Screen-magnification system A computer-based system that electronically enlarges the characters displayed on the monitor; it may work through software only, hardware only, or combinations of both. Also known as screen-enlargement system.

Screen review A feature of speech-synthesizer software that allows the user to review the contents of specific lines or of the spelling of specific words.

Self-threading needle An adaptive sewing needle that has an additional hole in the form of a "v" into which the thread is slipped to increase the ease of threading.

Service plan An outline of all the possible skills taught by the rehabilitation teacher, listing the expected learner outcomes (goals), which is completed for each client.

Sighted guide technique A specific method used by sighted people to guide blind or visually impaired people.

Slate and stylus A portable device for writing braille by hand consisting of the slate, a metal template with a series of braille cells, and the stylus, the implement used to press braille dots into the paper.

Snellen chart A chart used for testing central visual acuity, usually at a distance of 20 feet, containing letters, numbers, or symbols in graduated sizes, labeled with the distance at which each size can be read by the normal eye.

Social learning theory A theory of learning based on the idea that people learn from observing others and that learning is influenced by the individual's environment and by the individual's own inner thought processes.

Speech compression A feature of adapted tape recorders used to make speech understandable; it adjusts the pitch and distortion of sound produced when the tape speed is increased.

Speech synthesizer See Synthetic speech system.

Speed dialing A telephone company service that allows the subscriber to program a standard telephone so that only a short speed-dialing code need be dialed to reach frequently called numbers.

Squaring-off technique An orientation method in which an individual places his or her back against an object or surface to establish a line of direction perpendicular to that object.

Stereotypic behavior Repetitive behavior of extraordinary frequency or intensity, such as rocking, head swinging, and eye poking.

Synthetic speech system A computer-based system that converts the electronic signals that appear on the screen as text into spoken units; it is generally composed of an internal or external synthesizer, which does the speaking, and screen-access software, which tells the synthesizer what to say.

Tactile Related to or experienced through the sense of touch.

Tactile surface writing guide A handwriting guide that uses raised lines or a ribbed or raised surface to define the space for writing.

Talking book A book or other reading material provided in an audible recorded format for the listener to play back.

Talking-Book Cassette Machine An adaptive nonrecording cassette player used for the NLS Talking Book Program.

Talking-Book Machine An adaptive device for playing flexidiscs used for the NLS talking book program.

Talking book program A free national library program administered by the National Library Service for the Blind and Physically Handicapped (NLS) of the Library of Congress for persons with visual and physical limitations, in which books and magazines are produced in braille and on recorded discs and cassettes and are distributed to a cooperative network of regional libraries that circulate them to eligible borrowers; the program also lends the devices on which the recordings are played.

Tangent screen testing An assessment for measuring central field vision in which the client fixates on an X marked on a chalkboard or black screen and reports when he or she perceives a target brought in from the side at various locations.

Task analysis The process of dividing an activity into its simplest parts, providing a step-by-step guide that can be used to teach individuals with learning limitations.

Telemicroscope A low vision device that combines a telescope and a microscope, usually prescribed for tasks to be completed at distances between 20 and 100 cm.

Telescope A low vision device that uses magnification for viewing objects at distances of about 2 feet or greater.

Tone indexing A method of identifying and locating information on recorded tape, on recorders that have the cue-and-review feature, by recording one or more tones or beeps of low frequency to indicate the beginning of each new recording or section, which are heard only when the tape speed is increased.

Track The area of a cassette's magnetic tape on which sounds are recorded; adapted tape recorders record on two tracks per side, or four tracks per cassette, thus increasing the storage capacity of cassette tapes.

Tracking The ability of the eyes to follow a moving object; also, the skill used to follow a line of type or braille across and to locate the next line.

Trailing technique A mobility technique for moving from one place to another along a continuous surface, using the back of one's curled fingers to follow the surface.

Typoscope A low vision device consisting of a piece of black cardboard with a slit in it, used to increase contrast and to help keep one's place when reading printed material.

Upper hand and forearm technique A protective technique used to prevent unexpected body or facial contact, in which the forearm is extended across the body at shoulder height with the palm turned outward at neck height.

Variable speed adaptation A feature of adapted tape recorders that allows the listener to selectively adjust the listening speed.

Veteran's Affairs, U.S. Department of The federal agency that provides services to veterans, including comprehensive rehabilitation services to veterans with legal blindness through the Blind Rehabilitation Service.

Visibility The maximum distance at which an object can be seen under prevailing conditions; the ease with which objects are seen.

Visual acuity The ability to discern form visually; the sharpness or clearness of vision.

Visual disability A limitation in functional ability resulting from visual impairment.

Visual field The area that is visible without shifting the gaze.

Visual handicap The physical, psychological, social, or economic effects resulting from a visual impairment.

Visual impairment Any degree of vision loss, including total blindness, that affects an individual's ability to perform the tasks of daily life.

Visual Impairment Service Teams (VIST) A field service program of the U.S. Department of Veterans Affairs that coordinates comprehensive rehabilitation and other support services to blinded veterans.

Vitrectomy Removal of the contents of the vitreous chamber of the eye and replacement with a manufactured solution.

Vocational rehabilitation The process of preparing an individual for useful employment by means of vocational counseling, training, and so forth.

Vocational Rehabilitation Program A program of vocational rehabilitation services administered by state vocational rehabilitation agencies under the federal Rehabilitation Services Administration and provided to eligible clients who demonstrate significant potential for return to gainful employment.

Voice indexing A method of identifying and locating information on recorded tapes, using a recorder with the cue-and-review feature, by indicating the beginning of each new recording or section with a title or key word that is recorded and played back in fast-forward mode.

Voxcom A small recorder that can record and read individual cards with magnetic recording tape affixed along the edge; used for labeling and for recording brief messages, recipes, and other information.

Wire loop threader An adaptive device for threading needles, consisting of a lightweight metal handle to which is attached a collapsible diamond-shaped wire loop that can be inserted into the needle's eye.

Withdrawal A psychological defense mechanism characterized by a decreased need for social interaction.

Working distance The distance from the eye of the viewer to an object or surface being viewed.

RESOURCES

In providing instruction to clients who are blind or visually impaired, the rehabilitation teacher needs to have at his or her fingertips sources of information and referral for clients as well as a wide variety of products and services. Many of the specialty items used daily by rehabilitation teachers and their clients—such as writing guides, braille paper, and adaptive kitchen or labeling products—are not easily found in local stores. In addition, the needs of clients that rehabilitation teachers may be called upon to address vary widely, and the services available for visually impaired individuals differ considerably from place to place.

This resource guide, although by necessity not an exhaustive listing, is a good place for rehabilitation teachers to start looking for products or services needed for clients or for themselves. Although a complete listing of all sources of information and referral, products, and services is beyond the scope of this book, an effort was made to include some representative examples in all of the important product and service areas.

The first section, Sources of Information and Services, gives descriptive information on some pertinent government agencies and a sizable sampling of national organizations that provide information, consumer education materials, services, and referrals on services for blind and visually impaired individuals either in general or in regard to a specified interest or area. Professional organizations of interest to rehabilitation teachers are also included here. The American Foundation for the Blind (AFB) acts as a national clearinghouse for information about blindness and visual impairment, operates a toll-free national hotline, and is a source of additional information. The National Technology Center at AFB ([212] 502-7642) is a repository of information about assistive technology.

The second section, Sources of Products and Services, is a guide to finding adaptive devices and services. A number of distributors of adaptive devices and products are listed first. These companies sell a wide variety of products that are useful to visually impaired individuals, and rehabilitation teachers might find it worthwhile to keep a number of catalogs from such distributors on hand. The remaining categories of products and services reflect the division of this text into the broad areas of communication and activities of daily living. Teachers looking for a specific product need to consult the category of product that best fits their needs—for example, Communication Aids and Devices in the Communication section or Labeling in the Activities of Daily Living section—and then contact the companies listed to determine the specific products or services they furnish. Some distributors carry a wide range of products and will be listed under many categories, whereas others that are listed only once may provide a very specific product or service and need to be contacted for detailed information.

Readers may find that certain categories overlap considerably; for example, Computer Hardware and Computer Software. The categories of Producers and Publishers of Braille and Large Print and of Recorded Media are also in flux, as organizations and publishers explore electronic formats, such as computerized books (see Chapter 10). Many of these companies also produce videotapes, which may be offered in audiodescribed versions for visually impaired customers. In addition to the producers of alternate media that appear here, a growing number of commercial publishers now publish titles in recorded media. Along with publishers of media, some of the organizations listed also will produce a title in alternate media upon request, frequently for a fee. Readers should bear in mind that names and addresses of companies change frequently and should be verified. BBS numbers are electronic bulletin boards which are accessed by computer through a modem.

Finally, a listing of rehabilitation teacher training programs can also be found here.

More extensive listings can be found in the *Directory of Services for Blind and Visually Impaired Persons in the United States and Canada* published by AFB. Additional information about finding sources for a variety of services within a local community can be found in Chapter 17. Listings of state agencies, such as state departments of vocational rehabilitation and area agencies on aging, which can provide information on available services, are found in the *AFB Directory of Services* as well as in the state and county government sections of local telephone directories. The *Directory* also has listings of such useful services for rehabilitation teachers as regional libraries for the blind and physically handicapped, talking book machine distributors, radio reading services, and phone-in newspapers.

SOURCES OF INFORMATION AND SERVICES

U.S. Government Agencies

U.S. Department of Education

Division of Blind and Visually Impaired
330 C Street, S.W., Room 3227
Washington, DC 20202
(202) 205-9316
Develops methods, standards, and procedures to assist state agencies in the rehabilitation of blind persons. Assists states in developing programs that provide vocational rehabilitation services to blind persons to enable them to become self-supporting and gainfully employed; assists states in analyzing occupations to ascertain their suitability for performance without the use of sight, and demonstrates to employers the suitability for employment of blind persons; promotes and supports institutes and training programs; develops training facilities for blind persons; maintains continuous relationships with other public and private agencies for the blind; cooperates in the development of the Independent Living Services programs for older blind individuals.

Office of Special Education Programs
330 C Street, S.W., Room 3086
Washington, DC 20202
(202) 205-5507
Administers the Individuals with Disabilities Education Act and related programs for the education of disabled children.

Rehabilitation Services Administration
330 C Street, S.W.
Washington, DC 20202
(202) 205-5482
Provides national leadership and technical guidance for the federal-state vocational rehabilitation program. Administers grants to the states for vocational rehabilitation of the disabled. Provides demonstrations, professional training, and independent living grants for disabled persons, including visually impaired persons.

U.S. Department of Health and Human Services

National Eye Institute Information Center
National Institutes of Health
9000 Rockville Pike
Building 31, Room 6A03
Bethesda, MD 20892
(301) 496-5248; (301) 496-2234
Finances and conducts research on the eye and vision disorders; supports training of eye researchers; and publishes materials on visual impairment.

U.S. Department of Veterans Affairs

Blind Rehabilitation Service
531 TECH
810 Vermont Avenue, N.W.
Washington, DC 20420
(202) 535-7637
Oversees programs for blinded veterans within the Veterans Health Administration. Services offered include Visual Impairment Services Teams (VIST) assistance and Blind Rehabilitation Center and Clinic Programs. Visual Impairment Services Teams are diagnostic and treatment agents who provide periodic evaluations of physical, visual, hearing, and adjustment status and ongoing individualized treatment according to needs, goals, and eligibility. There is at least one VIST designated for each state. Blind Rehabilitation Center and Clinic Programs offer comprehensive rehabilitation services.

Veterans Benefits Administration
811 TECH
810 Vermont Avenue, N.W.
Washington, DC 20420
(202) 233-2044
Furnishes compensation and pensions for disability and death to veterans and their dependents. Provides vocational rehabilitation services, including counseling, training, and assistance toward employment, to eligible blinded veterans. Offers and guarantees loans for the purchase or construction of homes, farms, and businesses.

Veterans Health Administration
810 Vermont Avenue, N.W.
Washington, DC 20420
(202) 535-7010
Provides hospital and outpatient treatment as well as nursing home care for eligible veterans in Veterans Administration facilities. Services elsewhere provided on a contract basis in the United States and its territories. Provides nonvocational inpatient residential rehabilitation services to eligible legally blinded veterans of the armed forces of the United States.

Other U.S. Federal Agencies

National Library Service for the Blind and Physically Handicapped
Library of Congress
1291 Taylor Street, N.W.
Washington, DC 20542
(202) 707-5100; (800) 424-8567
FAX: (202) 707-0712
Conducts a national program to distribute free braille and recorded materials of a general nature and braille music to individuals who are blind and who have physical disabilities. Provides reference information on all aspects of blindness and other physical disabilities that affect reading. Conducts national correspondence courses to train sighted persons as braille transcribers and blind persons as braille proofreaders. Provides talking book machines and cassette machines for disc records and cassette tapes. Selects, orders, and distributes materials through a network of 160 libraries nationwide that function as circulating centers, using the mails to serve readers. Materials mailed postage free.

Canadian Government Agencies

National Health and Welfare Disabled Persons Unit
Finance Building, Room 1101
Tunney's Pasture
Ottawa, ON K1A 1B5, Canada
(613) 957-2886; (613) 952-7128
FAX: (613) 941-3550
Under the National Strategy for the Integration of Persons with Disabilities, administers a contribution program to support social, community, and economic integration of disabled persons. Also helps promote and administer independent living center programs.

National Library of Canada
395 Wellington Street
Ottawa, ON K1A 0N4, Canada
(613) 996-1623
Maintains comprehensive information on Canadian libraries and agencies serving people with

disabilities, as well as on special format materials available to disabled persons.

Veterans Affairs Canada
Program Administration Branch
P.O. Box 7700
Charlottetown, PE C1A 8M9, Canada
(902) 566-8114
FAX: (902) 566-8525
Operates programs through which blind veterans are equally eligible with other veterans for a wide range of benefits and services and receive special equipment and supplementary benefits specifically related to their blindness.

U.S. National Organizations

American Council of the Blind
1155 15th Street, N.W., Suite 720
Washington, DC 20005
(202) 467-5081; (800) 424-8666
FAX: (202) 467-5085
Promotes effective participation of people who are blind in all aspects of society. Provides information and referral, legal assistance, scholarships, advocacy, consultation, and program development assistance. Publishes *The Braille Forum.*

American Foundation for the Blind
11 Penn Plaza, Suite 300
New York, NY 10001
(212) 502-7600; (212) 502-7662 (TTY/TDD); (800) AFB-LINE
FAX: (212) 502-7777
E-mail: afbinfo@afb.org
Provides services to and acts as an information clearinghouse for people who are blind and visually impaired and their families, professionals, organizations, schools, and corporations. Maintains a toll-free hotline and a governmental relations department and five field offices across the country. Stimulates research to improve services to visually impaired persons; advocates for services and legislation; maintains the M. C. Migel Library and Information Center and the Helen Keller Archives; provides information and referral services; operates the National Technology Center and the Career and Technology Information Bank; produces videos and publishes books, pamphlets, the *Directory of Services for Blind and Visually Impaired Persons in the United States and Canada,* and the *Journal of Visual Impairment & Blindness.* Maintains the following additional offices:

Governmental Relations
1615 M Street, N.W., Suite 250
Washington, DC 20036
(202) 457-1494
FAX: (202) 457-1492
E-mail: washdc@afb.org

AFB Midwest
401 North Michigan Avenue, Suite 308
Chicago, IL 60611
(312) 245-9961
FAX: (312) 245-9965
E-mail: chicago@afb.org

AFB Southeast
100 Peachtree Street, Suite 620
Atlanta, GA 30303
(404) 525-2303
FAX: (404) 659-6957
E-mail: atlanta@afb.org

AFB Southwest
260 Treadway Plaza, Exchange Park
Dallas, TX 75235
(214) 352-7222
FAX: (214) 352-3214
E-mail: afbdallas@afb.org

AFB West
111 Pine Street, Suite 725
San Francisco, CA 94111
(415) 392-4845
FAX: (415) 392-0383
E-mail: sanfran@afb.org

AFB Office
15 Mechanic Street, #3
Provincetown, MA 02657
(508) 487-5815
FAX: (508) 487-5815
E-mail: lidoff@afb.org

American Printing House for the Blind
1839 Frankfort Avenue
Louisville, KY 40206
(502) 895-2405; (800) 223-1839
FAX: (502) 895-1509
Produces materials in braille and large print and on audiocassette; manufactures computer-access equipment, software and special educational devices for persons who are visually impaired; maintains an educational research and development program and a reference-catalog service providing information about volunteer-produced textbooks in accessible media.

American Rehabilitation Counseling Association
c/o American Counseling Association
5999 Stevenson Avenue
Alexandria, VA 22304
(703) 823-9800; (800) 347-6647
Serves as a professional membership assocation representing rehabilitation counselors. Promotes professional development and effective rehabilitation counseling services.

Association for Education and Rehabilitation of the Blind and Visually Impaired
206 North Washington Street, Suite 320
Alexandria, VA 22314
(703) 548-1884
FAX: (703) 683-2926
Promotes all phases of education and work for people of all ages who are blind and visually impaired, strives to expand their opportunities to take a contributory place in society, and disseminates information. Certifies rehabilitation teachers, orientation and mobility specialists, and classroom teachers. Subgroups include Division 11, Rehabilitation Teaching and Independent Living. Publishes *RE:view, AER Report, Job Exchange Monthly,* and *RT News,* a quarterly newsletter.

Blinded Veterans Association
477 H Street, N.W.
Washington, DC 20001-2694
(202) 371-8880; (800) 669-7079
FAX: (202) 371-8258
Encourages and assists all blinded veterans to take advantage of rehabilitation and vocational training benefits, job placement assistance, and other aid from federal, state, and local resources by means of a field service program. Promotes extension of sound legislation and rehabilitation through liaison with other agencies. Through 38 regional groups and field service offices, operates a volunteer service program for blinded veterans in their communities and provides information and referral services.

Braille Authority of North America
c/o American Council of the Blind
1155 15th Street, N.W., Suite 720
Washington, DC 20005
(202) 467-5081; (800) 424-8666
FAX: (202) 467-5085
Serves as a U.S.-Canadian standard-setting organization whose member agencies strive to promulgate codes regarding the usage of braille and to promote and facilitate its use, teaching, and production. Publishes an *Annual Directory.*

Closing the Gap
P.O. Box 68
Henderson, MN 56044
(612) 248-3294
FAX: (612) 248-3810
Holds conferences and workshops on technology for disabled people. Publishes a bi-monthly newsletter, *Closing the Gap.*

Council for Exceptional Children
1920 Association Drive
Reston, VA 22091-1589
(703) 620-3660 (voice/TTY/TDD); (800) 845-6232
FAX: (703) 264-9494
Acts as the professional organization for individuals serving children with disabilities and children who are gifted. Primary activities include advocating for appropriate government policies; setting professional standards; providing continuing professional development; and helping professionals to obtain conditions and resources necessary for effective professional practice. Publishes numerous related materials, journals, and newsletters.

Council of Citizens with Low Vision International
6511 26th Street West
Bradenton, FL 34207
(941) 742-5958; (800) 733-2258
FAX: (941) 755-9721
Promotes rights of partially sighted individuals to maximize use of their residual vision. Educates the public to the needs of visually impaired people. Informs persons with low vision of available services. Has support groups and chapters throughout the United States. Publishes *Vision Access.*

Council of Families with Visual Impairment
c/o American Council of the Blind
1155 15th Street, N.W., Suite 720
Washington, DC 20005
(202) 393-3666; (202) 467-5081
Serves as a support group of parents of blind and visually impaired children.

Council of Rehabilitation Specialists
c/o American Council of the Blind
1155 15th Street, N.W., Suite 720
Washington, DC 20005
(202) 467-5081; (800) 424-8666
Serves as an organization of professionals in rehabilitation and social services. Promotes the establishment of professional and academic standards and adequate rehabilitation services for all blind and visually impaired persons.

The Foundation Fighting Blindness
Executive Plaza 1, Suite 800
11350 McCormick Road
Hunt Valley, MD 21031-1014
(410) 785-1414; (410) 785-9687 (TTY/TDD);
(800) 683-5555
FAX: (410) 771-9470
Provides public education, information and referral, workshops and research through its main office and 60 affiliates. Raises funds for research into the cause, prevention, and treatment of retinitis pigmentosa. Publishes *Fighting Blindness News.*

Hadley School for the Blind
700 Elm Street
Winnetka, IL 60093-0299
(708) 446-8111 (voice/TTY/TDD)
FAX: (708) 446-8153
Provides tuition-free home studies in academic subjects as well as vocational and technical areas, personal enrichment, parent/child issues, compensatory rehabilitation education, and Bible study. Rehabilitation courses include topics such as braille, abacus, and independent living without sight and hearing for adults who are deaf-blind.

HEATH Resource Center
American Council on Education
One Dupont Circle, Suite 800
Washington, DC 20046-1193
(202) 939-9320 (voice/TTY/TDD); (800) 544-3284 (voice/TTY/TDD)
FAX: (202) 833-4760
Operates a national clearinghouse on postsecondary education for individuals with disabilities. Collects and disseminates information about educational services, policies, adaptations, and opportunities at U.S. colleges and universities, training schools, independent living centers and other post–high school training options. Publishes materials on related topics and a newsletter, *Information from HEATH.*

Helen Keller National Center for Deaf-Blind Youths and Adults
111 Middle Neck Road
Sands Point, NY 11050-1299
(516) 944-8900 (voice/TTY/TDD); (516) 944-8637 (TTY/TDD)
FAX: (516) 944-7302
Provides diagnostic evaluations, comprehensive vocational and personal adjustment training, and job preparation and placement for people from every state and territory who are deaf-blind through its national center and 10 regional offices. Provides technical assistance and training to those who work with deaf-blind people. Publishes *The Nat-Cent News.*

Mid-America Conference of Rehabilitation Teachers
c/o Alice Raftary
1846 Nightingale

Dearborn, MI 48128
As an independent organization of professional rehabilitation teachers and affiliates, holds an annual summer conference, awards scholarships for students in unversity rehabilitation teaching programs, and publishes a newsletter.

National Association for Parents of the Visually Impaired
P.O. Box 317
Watertown, MA 02272-0317
(800) 562-6265
FAX: (617) 972-7444
Provides support to parents and families of children and youth who have visual impairments. Operates a national clearinghouse for information, education, and referral. Publishes a newsletter, *Awareness.*

National Association for Visually Handicapped
22 West 21st Street
New York, NY 10010
(212) 889-3141
FAX: (212) 727-2931
Acts as an information clearinghouse and referral center regarding resources available to persons who are visually impaired.

National Association of Radio Reading Services
2100 Wharton Street, Suite 140
Pittsburgh, PA 15203
(412) 488-3944
FAX: (412) 488-3953
Provides information on and promotes radio reading services. Has closed-circuit radio broadcasts of daily newspapers plus other materials. Maintains circulating library of books and programs on tape. Publishes *Hearsay Newsletter* and *Directory of Radio Reading Services.*

National Braille Association
3 Townline Circle
Rochester, NY 14623-2513
(716) 427-8260
FAX: (716) 427-0263
Assists transcribers and narrators in the development and improvement of skills and techniques required for the production of reading materials for individuals who are print handicapped. Provides braille textbooks, music, career, and technical materials at below cost to blind students and professionals and helps meet other braille needs. Provides continuing education to groups and individuals who prepare reading materials for print handicapped individuals through seminars, workshops, consultation, and instruction manuals. Publishes *Tape Recording Manual, Tape Recording Lessons, Guidelines for Administration of Groups Producing Reading Materials for the Visually Handicapped,* and *NBA Bulletin*; provides reprints and workshops pertaining to all advanced braille codes, tactile graphics, and computer-assisted transcription.

National Clearing House of Rehabilitation Training Materials
Oklahoma State University
816 West 6th Avenue
Stillwater, OK 74078-4080
(405) 624-7650; (800) 223-5219
FAX: (405) 624-0695
Provides information on recent publications, videotapes, and other rehabilitation training materials. Publishes a quarterly newsletter, *NCHRTM Memo.*

National Federation of the Blind
1800 Johnson Street
Baltimore, MD 21230
(410) 659-9314
FAX: (410) 685-5653
Strives to improve social and economic conditions of people who are blind, evaluates and assists in establishing programs, and provides public education and scholarships. Publishes the *Braille Monitor* and *Future Reflections.* The Diabetics Division, a support and information network, publishes a quarterly newsletter, *Voice of the Diabetic.*

National Rehabilitation Association
633 South Washington Street
Alexandria, VA 22314

(703) 836-0850; (703) 836-0849 (TTY/TDD)
FAX: (703) 836-0848
Serves as a membership organization for professionals in the field of rehabilitation and as an advocate for the rights of persons with disabilities. Publishes the *Journal of Rehabilitation* and *Contemporary Rehab.*

National Rehabilitation Counseling Association
8807 Sudley Road, Suite 102
Manassas, VA 2210-4719
(703) 361-2077; (703) 361-1596 (TTY/TDD)
Serves as a professional membership organization representing rehabilitation counselors.

Prevent Blindness America
500 East Remington Road
Schaumburg, IL 60173
(708) 843-2020; (800) 221-3004
FAX: (708) 843-8458
Conducts, through a network of state affiliates, a program of public and professional education, research, and industrial and community services to prevent blindness. Services include screening, vision testing, and dissemination of information on low-vision devices and clinics.

Resources for Rehabilitation
33 Bedford Street, Suite 19A
Lexington, MA 02173
(617) 862-6455
FAX: (617) 861-7517
Provides training and information to professionals and the public about the needs of individuals with disabilities and the resources available to meet those needs. Publications include the Living with Low Vision Series and large-print publications.

Trace Research and Development Center
University of Wisconsin-Madison
S-151 Waisman Center
1500 Highland Avenue
Madison, WI 53705
(608) 262-6966; (608) 263-5408 (TTY/TDD)
FAX: (608) 262-8848
E-mail: info@trace.wisc.edu
Works to advance the ability of people with disabilities to achieve their life objectives through the use of communication, computer, and information technologies. Addresses the communication needs of people who have severe disabilities. Publishes the *Cooperative Electronic Library on Disability* (disseminated on CD-ROM as *Co-Net*) and the *Trace Resource Book for Assistive Technologies for Communication, Control, and Computer Access.*

Vision Foundation
818 Mt. Auburn St.
Watertown, MA 02172
(617) 926-4232; (617) 926-0290 (TTY/TDD); 800-852-3029 (Massachusetts only)
FAX: (617)926-1412
Provides information and publications in adapted formats for adults coping with sight loss and runs an AIDS project. For Massachusetts residents, provides free self-help services, including information and referral, peer-support groups, home survival skills for seniors who are not legally blind, and buddy telephone service.

Canadian National Organizations

Braille Authority of North America
See U.S. National Organizations listings

Canadian Braille Authority
Atlantic Provinces Special Education Authority
P.O. Box 578
Halifax, NS B3J 2S9, Canada
(902) 424-7765
FAX: (902) 424-5819
Promotes the use of braille in Canada and encourages research in the development of braille technology. Establishes, adopts, and monitors standards for the production and teaching of English and French braille.

Canadian Council of the Blind
396 Cooper Street, Suite 405
Ottawa, ON K2P 2H7, Canada
(613) 567-0311
FAX: (613) 567-2728

Provides social, recreational, and blindness prevention programs and advocacy on behalf of blind and visually impaired persons.

Canadian National Institute for the Blind
1931 Bayview Avenue
Toronto, ON, M4G 3E8, Canada
(416) 480-7580
FAX: (416) 480-7677
Provides services to people who are blind or visually impaired through a network of divisional offices throughout Canada.

Institut Nazareth et Louis-Braille
1111 St. Charles West
Longueuil, Quebec J4K 5G4, Canada
(514) 463-1710
FAX: (514) 463-0243
Provides rehabilitation and serves as a teaching center for visually impaired persons.

Library for the Blind
Canadian National Institute for the Blind
1929 Bayview Avenue
Toronto, ON M4G 3E8, Canada
(416) 480-7520
FAX: (416) 480-7700
Works to provide access to information, culture, education, and lifelong learning for blind and visually impaired Canadians. Transcribes textbooks and other books into alternative formats. Operates an audiotape and braille lending library. Publishes a catalog and *Off the Shelf* newsletter.

Regroupement des Aveugles et Amblyopes du Quebec
3740 Berri Street, 2nd floor
Montreal, PQ H2L 4G9, Canada
(514) 849-2018
FAX: (514) 987-9956
Works for the social integration of blind and visually impaired people by representing the interests of people with visual impairments in all fields of life. Fully administered and directed by blind and visually impaired persons. Publishes a French-language newsletter, *INFO-RAAQ,* in braille and large-print and on cassette and disk.

VIEWS for the Visually Impaired
3033 Palston Road
Station 205
Mississauga, ON L4Y 2Z7, Canada
(416) 277-4061
Strives to ensure that children who are visually impaired have the opportunity to reach their full potential and that their families receive the information, resources, and support they need.

SOURCES OF PRODUCTS AND SERVICES

Mail Order, Catalogs, and Distributors

Includes organizations and companies that carry a wide variety of products, including independent living, health care, and recreation products; low vision devices; and communication aids. Products can usually be ordered by catalog, which can be obtained from the individual companies listed.

American Printing House for the Blind
1839 Frankfort Avenue
P.O. Box 6085
Louisville, KY 40206-0085
(502) 895-2405; (800) 223-1839
FAX: (502) 895-1509

Ann Morris Enterprises
890 Fams Court
East Meadow, NY 11554
(516) 292-9232

Exceptional Teaching Aids
20102 Woodbine Avenue
Castro Valley, CA 94546
(415) 582-4859; (800) 549-6999

Guild for the Blind
180 North Michigan, Suite 170
Chicago, IL 60601-7643
(312) 236-8569
FAX: (312) 236-8128

Independent Living Aids
27 East Mall
Plainview, NY 11803
(516) 752-8080; (800) 537-2118
FAX: (516) 752-3135

Lighthouse Low Vision Products
36-02 Northern Boulevard
Long Island City, NY 11101
(800) 829-0500; (800) 334-5497
FAX: (718) 786-5620

LS&S Group
P.O. Box 673
Northbrook, IL 60065
(708) 498-9777; (800) 468-4789

Maxi-Aids
42 Executive Boulevard
P.O. Box 3290
Farmingdale, NY 11735
(516) 752-0521; (800) 522-6294

Microcomputer Science Centre
5220 Bradco Boulevard
Mississauga, ON L4W 1G7, Canada
(416) 629-1654
FAX: (416) 629-2321

Science Products
P.O. Box 888
Southeastern, PA 19399
(800) 888-7400; (800) 222-2148
FAX: (215) 296-0488

TFI Engineering
529 Main Street
Boston, MA 02129
(617) 242-7007; (800) 331-8255
FAX: (617) 242-2007

Communications

Audiodescription Services

Includes both training and production services producing audiodescriptions of videotapes, films, plays, television broadcasts, and exhibits.

Audio Description, Metropolitan Washington Ear
35 University Boulevard East
Silver Spring, MD 20901
(301) 681-6636

Descriptive Video Service, WGBH-TV
125 Western Avenue
Boston, MA 02134
(617) 492-2777; (800) 333-1203
E-mail: DVS@wgbh.org

Braille and Large-Print Producers and Publishers

Includes producers of books in braille, print, and large print.

American Bible Society
1865 Broadway
New York, NY 10023
(212) 581-7400

American Foundation for the Blind
11 Penn Plaza, Suite 300
New York, NY 10001
(212) 502-7600; (212) 502-7662 (TTY/TDD); (800) AFB-LINE
FAX: (212) 502-7777
E-mail: afbinfo@afb.org

American Printing House for the Blind
1839 Frankfort Avenue
P.O. Box 6085
Louisville, KY 40206-0085
(502) 895-2405; (800) 223-1839
FAX: (502) 895-1509

Associated Services for the Blind
919 Walnut Street
Philadelphia, PA 19107
(215) 627-0600
FAX: (215) 922-0692

Beach Cities Braille Guild
P.O. Box 712
Huntington Beach, CA 92648

Bible Alliance
P.O. Box 1549
Bradenton, FL 33506
(941) 748-3031

Blindskills
P.O. Box 5181
Salem, OR 97304
(503) 581-4224

Braille International
3142 S.E. Jay Street
Stuart, FL 34997
(407) 286-8366; (800) 336-3142

Canadian National Institute for the Blind
1929 Bayview Avenue
Toronto, Ontario, M4G 3E8, Canada
(416) 480-7417 (voice/TTY/TDD)
FAX: (416) 480-7700

Charles Crane Memorial Library
University of British Columbia
1874 East Mall
Vancouver, BC V6T 1Z1, Canada
(604) 822-6111
FAX: (604) 822-6113

Chivers North America
1 Lafayette Road
P.O. Box 1450
Hampton, NH 03842-0015
(508) 398-6566; (800) 621-0182
FAX: (603) 929-3890

G. K. Hall
70 Lincoln Street
Boston, MA 02111
(617) 423-3990; (800) 343-2806

Grant Wood Area Education Agency
4401 Sixth Street, S.W.
Cedar Rapids, IA 52404
(319) 300-6714

Grey Castle Press
Pocket Knife Square
Lakeville, CT 06039
(203) 435-0868
FAX: (203) 435-0867

HarperCollins
10 East 53rd Street
New York, NY 10022
(212) 207-7000

Herald House
Drawer 1770
Independence, MO 64055
(816) 252-5010

Horizons for the Blind
16A Meadowdale Center
Carpentersville, IL 60110
(708) 836-1400; (800) 318-2000
FAX: (708) 836-1443

I Can See Books
P.O. Box 601
Nanaimo, BC V9R 5L9, Canada
(604) 753-3096

Institut Nazareth et Louis-Braille
1111 St. Charles West
Longueuil, Quebec J4K 5G4, Canada
(514) 463-1710
FAX: (514) 463-0243

Isis Large Print Books, Transaction Publishers
Rutgers—The State University of New Jersey
New Brunswick, NJ 08903
(908) 932-2280
FAX: (908) 932-3138

Jewish Braille Institute of America
110 East 13th Street
New York, NY 10016
(212) 889-2525

Lehigh Valley Braille Guild
614 North 13th Street
Allentown, PA 18102
(215) 264-2141

Mary Lou Archer Communications Center
2200 University Avenue West, #240
St. Paul, MN 55114-1840

Matilda Ziegler Magazine for the Blind
80 Eighth Avenue, Room 1304
New York, NY 10011
(212) 242-0263

Multiple Services Media Technology
11 West Barham Avenue
Santa Rosa, CA 95407

Napier Publications
2323 7th Avenue, #B
Greeley, CO 80631
(970) 352-6946

National Association for Visually Handicapped
22 West 21st Street
New York, NY 10010
(212) 889-3141

National Braille Association
3 Townline Circle
Rochester, NY 14623-2513
(716) 427-8260
FAX: (716) 427-0263

National Braille Press
88 St. Stephen Street
Boston, MA 02115
(617) 266-6160
FAX: (617) 427-0456

National Federation of the Blind
1800 Johnson Street
Baltimore, MD 21230
(410) 659-9314
FAX: (410) 685-5653

Northern Nevada Braille Transcribers
Large-Cell Braille Book Lending Library
1015 Oxford Avenue
Sparks, NV 89431-3037
(702) 358-2456

Random House Large Print
201 East 50th Street
New York, NY 10022
(212) 572-2600; (800) 726-0600
FAX: (212) 872-8026

Royal National Institute for the Blind
224 Great Portland Street
London, England W1N 6AA

Seedlings: Braille Books for Blind Children
P.O. Box 2395
Livonia, MI 48151-0395
(313) 427-8552; (800) 777-8552

Thorndike Press
P.O. Box 159
Thorndike, ME 04986
(207) 948-2962
FAX: (207) 948-2863

Ulverscroft Large Print Books
279 Boston Street
Guilford, CT 06437
(203) 453-2080; (800) 955-9659
FAX: (203) 458-9841

Xavier Society for the Blind
National Catholic Lending Library
for the Visually Handicapped
154 East 23rd Street
New York, NY 10010
(212) 473-7800

Braille and Other Tactile Materials

Includes such products as slates and styli, braille typewriters, braille computer paper, and other braille accessories and tactile materials and kits.

Adhoc Reading Systems
28 Brunswick Woods Drive
East Brunswick, NJ 08816
(201) 254-7300
FAX: (201) 254-7310

American Printing House for the Blind
1839 Frankfort Avenue
Louisville, KY 40206
(502) 895-2405; (800) 223-1839
FAX: (502) 895-1509

American Thermoform Corporation
2311 Travers Avenue
City of Commerce, CA 90040
(213) 723-9021

Ann Morris
890 Fams Court
East Meadow, NY 11554
(516) 292-9232

Community Advocates
P.O. Box 83304
Lincoln, NE 68501
(402) 435-7423 (voice/TTY/TDD/FAX)

Fishburne Enterprises
43550 Cactus Valley Road
Hemet, CA 92543
(909) 765-9276

Guild for the Blind
180 North Michigan, Suite 170
Chicago, IL 60601-7643
(312) 236-8569
FAX: (312) 236-8128

Horizons for the Blind
16A Meadowdale Center
Carpentersville, IL 60110
(708) 836-1400; (800) 318-2000
FAX: (708) 836-1443

Howe Press of Perkins School for the Blind
175 Beacon Street
Watertown, MA 02172
(617) 924-3490

Independent Living Aids
27 East Mall
Plainview, NY 11803
(516) 752-8080; (800) 537-2118
FAX: (516) 752-3135

Inegra Products
10728 18th Street
Dawson Creek, BC V1G 4E2, Canada
(604) 782-3380

Lighthouse Low Vision Products
36-02 Northern Boulevard
Long Island City, NY 11101
(800) 829-0500; (800) 334-5497
FAX: (718) 786-5620

LS&S Group
P.O. Box 673
Northbrook, IL 60065
(708) 498-9777; (800) 468-4789

Maxi-Aids
42 Executive Boulevard
P.O. Box 3290
Farmingdale, NY 11735
(516) 752-0521; (800) 522-6294

Microcomputer Science Centre
5220 Bradco Boulevard
Mississauga, ON L4W 1G7, Canada
(416) 629-1654
FAX: (416) 629-2321

National Braille Association
3 Townline Circle
Rochester, NY 14623-2513
(716) 427-8260
FAX: (716) 427-0263

Braille Transcription Services

Includes organizations that take print material and render it into braille on either a voluntary or fee-for-service basis. Some services may also produce large-print or cassette tapes.

Associated Services for the Blind
919 Walnut Street
Philadelphia, PA 19107
(215) 627-0600

Braille, Inc.
184 Seapit Road
P.O. Box 457
East Falmouth, MA 02536-0457
(508) 540-0800
FAX: (508) 548-6116

Braille Institute
741 North Vermont Avenue
Los Angeles, CA 90029-3594
(213) 663-1111

Contra Costa Braille Transcribers
514 Freya Way
Pleasant Hill, CA 94523
(510) 682-4734

Library for the Blind
Canadian National Institute for the Blind
1929 Bayview Avenue
Toronto, ON M4G 3E8, Canada
(416) 480-7520
FAX: (416) 480-7700

National Braille Association
3 Townline Circle
Rochester, NY 14623-2513
(716) 427-8260
FAX: (716) 427-0263

National Braille Press
88 St. Stephen Street
Boston, MA 02115
(617) 266-6160
FAX: (617) 427-0456

Quik-Scrybe
14144 Burbank Boulevard, #4
Van Nuys, CA 91401
(818) 989-2137
FAX: (818) 989-5602

Region IV ESC Computer Braille Center
7145 West Tidwell
Houston, TX 77092-2096
(713) 744-8145

South Dakota Industries for the Blind
Interpoint Braille Printing Service
800 West Avenue North
Sioux Falls, SD 57104
(605) 367-5266; (800) 658-5441

Sun Sounds
3124 East Roosevelt
Phoenix, AZ 85008
(602) 231-0500
FAX: (602) 220-9335

TFB Publications
238 75th Street
North Bergen, NJ 07047
(201) 662-0956

Visual Aid Volunteers
617 State Street
Garland, TX 75040
(214) 272-1615
FAX: (214) 276-2839

Volunteer Braille Services
3730 Toledo Avenue, North
Robbinsdale, MN 55422
(612) 521-0372

Communications Aids and Devices

Includes such products as handwriting guides, tape recorders, telephones, and calculators.

American Printing House for the Blind
1839 Frankfort Avenue
Louisville, KY 40206
(502) 895-2405; (800) 223-1839
FAX: (502) 895-1509

Ann Morris
890 Fams Court
East Meadow, NY 11554
(516) 292-9232

Edison Press
6 North River Road
Des Plaines, IL 60016

(708) 298-0740
FAX: (708) 298-9507

Exceptional Teaching Aids
20102 Woodbine Avenue
Castro Valley, CA 94546
(415) 582-4859; (800) 549-6999

Guild for the Blind
180 North Michigan, Suite 170
Chicago, IL 60601-7643
(312) 236-8569
FAX: (312) 236-8128

Howe Press of Perkins School for the Blind
175 Beacon Street
Watertown, MA 02172
(617) 924-3490

Independent Living Aids
27 East Mall
Plainview, NY 11803
(516) 752-8080; (800) 537-2118
FAX: (516) 752-3135

Lighthouse Low Vision Products
36-02 Northern Boulevard
Long Island City, NY 11101
(800) 829-0500; (800) 334-5497
FAX: (718) 786-5620

LS&S Group
P.O. Box 673
Northbrook, IL 60065
(708) 498-9777; (800) 468-4789

Maxi-Aids
42 Executive Boulevard
P.O. Box 3290
Farmingdale, NY 11735
(516) 752-0521; (800) 522-6294

Science Products
P.O. Box 888
Southeastern, PA 19399
(800) 888-7400; (800) 222-2148
FAX: (215) 296-0488

Sense-Sations
Associated Services for the Blind
919 Walnut Street
Philadelphia, PA 19107
(215) 627-0600
FAX: (215) 922-0692

TFI Engineering
529 Main Street
Boston, MA 02129
(617) 242-7007; (800) 331-8255
FAX: (617) 242-2007

Computer Hardware

Includes adaptive equipment such as laptop computers, braille displays, braille printers, optical character recognition systems (scanners), and speech synthesizers.

Acrontech
2318 Danforth Avenue
Toronto, ON M4C 1K7, Canada
(416) 467-6800
FAX: (416) 467-1994

Adhoc Reading Systems
28 Brunswick Woods Drive
East Brunswick, NJ 08816
(201) 254-7300
FAX: (201) 254-7310

AICOM Corporation
1590 Oakland Road, Suite B112
San Jose, CA 95131
(408) 453-8251
FAX: (408) 453-8255

American Printing House for the Blind
1839 Frankfort Avenue
Louisville, KY 40206
(502) 895-2405; (800) 223-1839
FAX: (502) 895-1509

American Thermoform Corporation
2311 Travers Avenue
City of Commerce, CA 90040
(213) 723-9021

Arkenstone
1390 Borregas Avenue
Sunnyvale, CA 94089
(408) 752-2200; (800) 444-4443
FAX: (408) 745-6739
http:///wwwarkenstone.org

Artic Technologies
55 Park Street, Suite 2
Troy, MI 48083-2753
(810) 588-7370
FAX: (810) 588-2650
BBS: (810) 588-1424

Automated Functions
6424 North 28th Street
Arlington, VA 22207
(703) 536-7742
FAX: (703) 536-7920

Betacom Group
Montreal Betacom
723 Halpern Road
Dorval, PQ H9P 1G5, Canada
(514) 636-9267
FAX: (514) 636-9015

Betacom Group
Toronto Betacom
1515 Matheson Boulevard, Unit B5
Mississauga, ON L4W 2P5, Canada
(416) 629-1811
FAX: (416) 629-0328

Computer Conversations
6297 Worthington Road, S.W.
Alexandria, OH 43001
(614) 924-2885

Designing Aids for Disabled Adults
248 Concord Avenue, Unit 2
Toronto, ON M6H 2P4, Canada
(416) 530-0038
FAX: (416) 530-4917

Digital Equipment Corporation
20 Forbes Road
Northboro, MA 01532
(800) 344-4825
FAX: (800) 676-7517

Echo Speech Corporation
6460 Via Real
Carpinteria, CA 93013
(805) 684-4593
FAX: (805) 684-6628

E.V.A.S.
16 David Avenue
P.O. Box 371
Westerly, RI 02891
(401) 596-3155; (800) 872-3827

Frontier Computing
250 Davisville Avenue, Suite 205
Toronto, ON M4S 1H2, Canada
(416) 489-6690
FAX: (416) 489-6693

HumanWare
6245 King Road
Loomis, CA 95650
(916) 652-7253; (800) 722-3393
FAX: (916) 652-7296

Integrated Assistive Technologies
1257 Michigan Drive
Coquitlam, BC V3B 6T7, Canada
(604) 464-8245

LS&S
P.O. Box 673
Northbrook, IL 60065
(708) 498-9777; (800) 468-4789

Microcomputer Science Centre
5220 Bradco Boulevard
Mississauga, ON L4W 1G7, Canada
(416) 629-1654
FAX: (416) 629-2321

Octopus Audio Visual
Rural Route #1
Wilno, ON K0J 2N0, Canada

(613) 756-3938
FAX: (613) 756-2560

Optelec USA
6 Lyberty Way
Westford, MA 01886
(508) 392-0707; (800) 828-1056
FAX: (508) 692-6073

Schamex Research
19443 Superior Street
Northridge, CA 91324
(818) 772-6644
FAX: (818) 993-2946

Science Products
P.O. Box 888
Southeastern, PA 19399
(800) 888-7400; (800) 222-2148
FAX: (215) 296-0488

Sighted Electronics
464 Tappan Road
Northvale, NJ 07647
(800) 666-4883
FAX: (201) 767-0612

Syntha-Voice Computers
800 Queenstone Road, Suite 304
Stony Creek, ON L8G 1A7, Canada
(905) 662-0565; (800) 263-4540
FAX: (905) 662-0568
BBS: (905) 662-0569

Tash
70 Gibson Drive, Unit 12
Markham, ON L3R 4C2, Canada
(416) 475-2212

TeleSensory Corporation
455 North Bernardo
P.O. Box 7455
Mountain View, CA 94039-7455
(415) 960-0920; (800) 227-8418; (800) 345-2256
FAX: (415) 969-9064
BBS: (415) 960-0307
http://www.telesensory.com/indext.html

Visuaide 2000
1111Rue Street
Longueuil, PQ J4K 5G4, Canada
(514) 463-1717
FAX: (514) 463-0243

Xerox Imaging Systems, Adaptive Technology Products
9 Centennial Drive
Peabody, MA 01960
(800) 248-6550, Ext. 1
FAX: (508) 977-2148

Computer Software

Includes adaptive software such as large-print and synthetic-speech programs, braille translation software, magnification systems, and educational software and computer tutorial programs.

Adhoc Reading Systems
28 Brunswick Woods Drive
East Brunswick, NJ 08816
(201) 254-7300
FAX: (201) 254-7310

AI Squared
P.O. Box 669
Manchester Center
VT 05225-0669
(802) 362-3612
FAX: (802) 362-1670
E-mail: zoomtext@aisquared.com

American Printing House for the Blind
1839 Frankfort Avenue
Louisville, KY 40206
(502) 895-2405; (800) 223-1839
FAX: (502) 895-1509

Arkenstone
1390 Borregas Avenue
Sunnyvale, CA 94089
(408) 752-2200; (800) 444-4443
FAX: (408) 745-6739
http: www.arkenstone.org

Artic Technologies
55 Park Street, Suite 2
Troy, MI 48083-2753
(810) 588-7370
FAX: (810) 588-2650
BBS: (810) 588-1424

Berkeley Systems
2095 Rose Street
Berkeley, CA 94709
(510) 549-2300
FAX: (510) 849-9426
http://access.berksys.com

Betacom Group
Montreal Betacom
723 Halpern Road
Dorval, PQ H9P 1G5, Canada
(514) 636-9267
FAX: (514) 636-9015

Betacom Group
Toronto Betacom
1515 Matheson Boulevard, Unit B5
Mississauga, ON L4W 2P5, Canada
(416) 629-1811
FAX: (416) 629-0328

BioLink Computer Research and Development
4770 Glenwood Avenue
North Vancouver, BC V7R 4G8, Canada
(604) 984-4099

Blazie Engineering
105 East Jarrettsville Road
Forest Hill, MD 21050
(410) 893-9333
FAX: (410) 836-5040
http://blazie.com

BRL (Braille Research Literacy)
(formerly ARTS Computer Products)
1245 Hancock Street, Suite 4
Quincy, MA 02169
(617) 472-5848
FAX: (617) 472-6003
E-mail: pduran@world.std.com

Computer Conversations
6297 Worthington Road, SW
Alexandria, OH 43001
(614) 924-2885

Digital Equipment Corporation
20 Forbes Road
Northboro, MA 01532
(800) 344-4825
FAX: (800) 676-7517

Disability Accommodation Services
Sign It Yourself
1224 Alderly Road
Indianapolis, IN 46260

Duxbury Systems
435 King Street
P.O. Box 1504
Littleton, MA 01460
(508) 486-9766
FAX: (508) 486-9712

Frontier Computing
250 Davisville Avenue, Suite 205
Toronto, ON M4S 1H2, Canada
(416) 489-6690
FAX: (416) 489-6693

GW Micro
310 Racquet Drive
Ft. Wayne, IN 46825
(219) 483-3625
FAX: (219) 484-2510
listserv@gwmicro.com

Henter-Joyce
2100 62nd Avenue North
St. Petersburgh, FL 33702
(813) 528-8900; (800) 336-5658
FAX: (813) 528-8901
BBS: (813) 528-8903
http://www.hj.com

Hexagon Products
P.O. Box 1295
Park Ridge, IL 60068

(708) 692-3355
E-mail: 76064.1776@compuserv.com
http://ourworld.compuserve.com

HumanWare
6245 King Road
Loomis, CA 95650
(916) 652-7253; (800) 722-3393
FAX: (916) 652-7296

IBM Special Needs Systems
P.O. Box 1328
Boca Raton, FL 33429-1328
(800) 426-4832

Interface Systems International
P.O. Box 20415
Portland, OR 97220
(503) 665-0965

Kansys
1016 Ohio Street
Lawrence, KS 66044
(800) 279-4880
FAX: (913) 843-0351

LS&S
P.O. Box 673
Northbrook, IL 60065
(708) 498-9777; (800) 468-4789

Lyon Computer Discourse
1009 Kinloch Lane
North Vancouver, BC V7G 1V8, Canada
(604) 929-8886
FAX: (604) 929-8858

Mentor O&O
3000 Longwater Drive
Norwell, MA 02061
(800) 992-7557

Microcomputer Science Centre
5220 Bradco Boulevard
Mississauga, ON L4W 1G7, Canada
(416) 629-1654
FAX: (416) 629-2321

Microsystems Software
600 Worcester Road
Framingham, MA 01701-5342
(508) 879-9000; (800) 828-2600
FAX: (508) 626-8515
http://www.microsys.com

MicroTalk Software
917 Clear Creek Drive
Texarkana, TX 75503
(903) 832-3471
FAX: (903) 832-3517
BBS: (903) 832-3722

Omnichron
1438 Oxford Avenue
Berkeley, CA 94709
(510) 540-6455

OMS Development Systems
1921 Highland Avenue
Wilmette, IL 60091
(708) 251-5787

Optelec USA
6 Lyberty Way
Westford, MA 01886
(508) 392-0707; (800) 828-1056
FAX: (508) 692-6073

Raised Dot Computing
408 South Baldwin Street
Madison, WI 53703
(800) 347-9594
http://www.well.com/www/dnavy

RC Systems
1609 England Avenue
Everett, WA 98203
(206) 355-3800

SkiSoft
1644 Massachusetts Avenue, Suite 79
Lexington, MA 02173
(617) 863-1876
E-mail: info@skisoft.com
http://www.skisoft.com

Syntha-Voice Computers
800 Queenstone Road, Suite 304
Stony Creek, ON L8G 1A7, Canada
(905) 662-0565; (800) 263-4540
FAX: (905) 662-0568
BBS: (905) 662-0569

TeleSensory Corporation
455 North Bernardo
P.O. Box 7455
Mountain View, CA 94039-7455
(415) 960-0920; (800) 227-8418; (800) 345-2256
FAX: (415) 969-9064
BBS: (415) 960-0307
http://www.telesensory.com/indext.html

T-Maker
Handwriting Fonts Software
P.O. Box 2067
Secaucus, NJ 07096
(800) 955-1750

Low Vision Devices and Products

Includes such products as magnifiers, loupes, lamps, and closed-circuit televisions; encompasses optical and nonoptical devices, both electronic and nonelectronic.

Acrontech
2318 Danforth Avenue
Toronto, ON M4C 1K7, Canada
(416) 467-6800
FAX: (416) 467-1994

Acrontech International
5500 Main Street
Williamsville, NY 14221
(716) 854-3814
FAX: (716) 854-4014

American Printing House for the Blind
1839 Frankfort Avenue
Louisville, KY 40206
(502) 895-2405; (800) 223-1839
FAX: (502) 895-1509

DAAS Consulting
Vision Simulator Kits
P.O. Box 93545
Nelson Park Post Office
Vancouver, BC V6E 4L7, Canada
(604) 669-8529
E-mail: daas@mindlink.bc.ca

Exceptional Teaching Aids
20102 Woodbine Avenue
Castro Valley, CA 94546
(415) 582-4859

Gracefully Yours
12527 Olmerton Road
Largo, FL 34644
(800) 331-2211

Guild for the Blind
180 North Michigan, Suite 170
Chicago, IL 60601-7643
(312) 236-8569
FAX: (312) 236-8128

HumanWare
6245 King Road
Loomis, CA 95650
(916) 652-7253; (800) 722-3393
FAX: (916) 652-7296

Independent Living Aids
27 East Mall
Plainview, NY 11803
(516) 752-8080; (800) 537-2118
FAX: (516) 752-3135

Innoventions
5921 South Middlefield Road, Suite 102
Littleton, CO 80123-2877
(303) 797-6554; (800) 854-6554
FAX: (303) 727-4940

Lighthouse Low Vision Products
36-02 Northern Boulevard
Long Island City, NY 11101
(800) 829-0500; (800) 334-5497
FAX: (718) 786-5620

LS&S Group
P.O. Box 673
Northbrook, IL 60065
(708) 498-9777; (800) 468-4789

Magnisight
P.O. Box 2653
Colorado Springs, CO 80901
(800) 753-4767

Maxi-Aids
42 Executive Boulevard
P.O. Box 3290
Farmingdale, NY 11735
(516) 752-0521; (800) 522-6294

Microcomputer Science Centre
5220 Bradco Boulevard
Mississauga, ON L4W 1G7, Canada
(416) 629-1654
FAX: (416) 629-2321

Octopus Audio Visual
Rural Route #1
Wilno, ON K0J 2N0, Canada
(613) 756-3938
FAX: (613) 756-2560

Optelec USA
6 Lyberty Way
Westford, MA 01886
(508) 392-0707; (800) 828-1056
FAX: (508) 692-6073

Seeing Technologies
7074 Brooklyn Boulevard
Minneapolis, MN 55429
(612) 560-8080; (800) 462-3738
FAX: (612) 560-0663

Sense-Sations
Associated Services for the Blind
919 Walnut Street
Philadelphia, PA 19107
(215) 627-0600
FAX: (215) 922-0692

TeleSensory Corporation
455 North Bernardo
P.O. Box 7455
Mountain View, CA 94039-7455
(415) 960-0920; (800) 227-8418; (800) 345-2256
FAX: (415) 969-9064
BBS: (415) 960-0307
http://www.telesensory.com/indext.html

Radio Reading Services

Includes services that read on the air information that is difficult for visually impaired persons to obtain, such as newspaper articles; commentary; advertisements; best-sellers; consumer information; and discussion of issues of interest. They are typically broadcast on unused radio frequencies and require special receivers (often distributed free of charge), although some are distributed through local cable television companies as well.

In Touch Networks
15 West 65th Street
New York, NY 10023
(212) 769-6270
FAX: (212) 769-6266

National Association of Radio Reading Services
2100 Wharton Street, Suite 140
Pittsburgh, PA 15203
(412) 488-3944
FAX: (412) 488-3953

VoicePrint
The National Broadcast Reading Service
P.O. Box 1728, Station R
Toronto, ON M4G 4A3, Canada
(416) 489-5430
FAX: (416) 489-5430

Recorded and Computerized Media Producers

Includes organizations that produce talking books or other recorded material on cassette or transcribe printed material on computer disks.

American Foundation for the Blind
11 Penn Plaza, Suite 300
New York, NY 10001
(212) 502-7600; (212) 502-7662 (TTY/TDD); (800) AFB-LINE
FAX: (212) 502-7777
E-mail: afbinfo@afb.org

American Printing House for the Blind
1839 Frankfort Avenue
Louisville, KY 40206
(502) 895-2405; (800) 223-1839
FAX: (502) 895-1509

Braille International
3142 Jay Street
Stuart, FL 34997
(407) 286-8366; (800) 336-3142
FAX: (407) 286-8909

Chivers North America
1 Lafayette Road
P.O. Box 1450
Hampton, NH 03842-0015
(508) 398-6566; (800) 621-0182
FAX: (603) 929-3890

Choice Magazine Listening
Dept. 12
P.O. Box 10
Port Washington, NY 11050
(516) 883-8280
FAX: (516) 944-6849

G. K. Hall
70 Lincoln Street
Boston, MA 02111
(617) 423-3990; (800) 343-2806

Guild for the Blind
180 North Michigan, Suite 170
Chicago, IL 60601-7643
(312) 236-8569
FAX: (312) 236-8128

Horizons for the Blind
16A Meadowdale Center
Carpentersville, IL 60110
(708) 836-1400; (800) 318-2000
FAX: (708) 836-1443

Library for the Blind
Canadian National Institute for the Blind
1929 Bayview Avenue
Toronto, ON M4G 3E8
Canada
(416) 480-7520
FAX: (416) 480-7700

Matilda Ziegler Magazine for the Blind
80 Eighth Avenue, Room 1304
New York, NY 10011
(212) 242-0263

National Braille Association
3 Townline Circle
Rochester, NY 14623-2513
(716) 427-8260
FAX: (716) 427-0263

National Braille Press
88 St. Stephen Street
Boston, MA 02115
(617) 266-6160
FAX: (617) 427-0456

National Library Service for the Blind and Physically Handicapped
Library of Congress
1291 Taylor Street, NW
Washington, DC 20542
(202) 707-5100; (800) 424-8567
FAX: (202) 707-0712

PAL Reading Services
252 Bloor Street West
Suite 12-105
Toronto, ON M5S 1V6, Canada
(416) 960-1177

People Helping People
151 Colborne Street
Brantford, ON N3T 2G7, Canada
(519) 753-1362

The Reader Project
2631 Garfield Street, N.W.
Washington, DC 20008
(202) 667-7323
FAX: (202) 667-0559

Recording for the Blind and Dyslexic
20 Roszel Road
Princeton, NJ 08540
(609) 452-0606; (800) 221-4792
FAX: (609) 987-8116

Taping for the Blind
3935 Essex Lane
Houston, TX 77027
(713) 622-2767
FAX: (713) 622-2772

Activities of Daily Living

Dog Guide Training Programs

Guide Dog Foundation for the Blind
371 East Jericho Turnpike
Smithtown, NY 11787
(800) 548-4337

Guide Dogs for the Blind
P.O. Box 1200
San Rafael, CA 94915
(415) 479-4000

Guiding Eyes for the Blind
611 Granite Springs Road
Yorktown Heights, NY 10598
(914) 245-4024

Leader Dogs for the Blind
1039 Rochester Road
Rochester, MI 48063
(313) 651-9011

Seeing Eye
P.O. Box 375
Morristown, NJ 07906
(210) 539-4425

Household, Personal, and Independent Living Products

Includes such products as kitchen utensils; measuring devices; mobility aids; personal management items; talking clocks and scales; braille watches; money identifiers; and games and toys.

Ambutech Mobility Products
34 DeBaets Street
Winnipeg, Manitoba R2J 3S9, Canada
(204) 663-3340; (800) 561-3340
FAX: (204) 663-9345; (800) 267-5059

American Printing House for the Blind
1839 Frankfort Avenue
Louisville, KY 40206
(502) 895-2405; (800) 223-1839
FAX: (502) 895-1509

Ann Morris
890 Fams Court
East Meadow, NY 11554
(516) 292-9232

Exceptional Teaching Aids
20102 Woodbine Avenue
Castro Valley, CA 94546
(415) 582-4859

Guild for the Blind
180 North Michigan, Suite 170
Chicago, IL 60601-7643
(312) 236-8569
FAX: (312) 236-8128

Independent Living Aids
27 East Mall
Plainview, NY 11803
(516) 752-8080; (800) 537-2118
FAX: (516) 752-3135

Jim Jackson & Company
Reproductive Anatomy Models
33 Richdale Avenue
Cambridge, MA 02140
(617) 864-9063

Lighthouse Low Vision Products
36-02 Northern Boulevard
Long Island City, NY 11101
(800) 829-0500; (800) 334-5497
FAX: (718) 786-5620

LS&S Group
P.O. Box 673
Northbrook, IL 60065
(800) 468-4789; (708) 498-9777

Maxi-Aids
42 Executive Boulevard
P.O. Box 3290
Farmingdale, NY 11735
(516) 752-0521; (800) 522-6294

Pacific International Group
Activated Ceramic Laundry Discs
1844 North El Camino Real
San Clemente, CA 92672

Sense-Sations
Associated Services for the Blind
919 Walnut Street
Philadelphia, PA 19107
(215) 627-0600
FAX: (215) 922-0692

Labeling

Includes manufacturers and distributors of products that assist in labeling clothes, food, appliances, and other items for people who are blind or visually impaired.

American Thermoform Corporation
2311 Travers Avenue
City of Commerce, CA 90040
(213) 723-9021

Ann Morris
890 Fams Court
East Meadow, NY 11554
(516) 292-9232

Community Advocates
P.O. Box 83304
Lincoln, NE 68501
(402) 435-7423 (voice/TTY/TDD/FAX)

Exceptional Teaching Aids
20102 Woodbine Avenue
Castro Valley, CA 94546
(415) 582-4859

Fishburne Enterprises
43550 Cactus Valley Road
Hemet, CA 92543
(909) 765-9276

Gladys Loeb Foundation
2002 Forest Hill Drive
Silver Spring, MD 20903
(301) 434-7748

Howe Press of Perkins School for the Blind
175 Beacon Street
Watertown, MA 02172-9982
(617) 924-3490

Independent Living Aids
27 East Mall
Plainview, NY 11803
(516) 752-8080; (800) 537-2118
FAX: (516) 752-3135

Lighthouse Low Vision Products
36-02 Northern Boulevard
Long Island City, NY 11101
(800) 829-0500; (800) 334-5497
FAX: (718) 786-5620

LS&S Group
P.O. Box 673
Northbrook, IL 60065
(708) 498-9777; (800) 468-4789

Maxi-Aids
42 Executive Boulevard
P.O. Box 3290
Farmingdale, NY 11735
(516) 752-0521; (800) 522-6294

Science Products
P.O. Box 888
Southeastern, PA 19399
(800) 888-7400; (800) 222-2148
FAX: (215) 296-0488

W. R. Stewart
Aluminum Clothing Labels
477 Homestead
Union, NJ 07083

Medical Products

Includes distributors of adapted health care products such as blood glucose monitoring systems, talking or bold display thermometers, and pill dispensers and reminders.

Ann Morris Enterprises
890 Fams Court
East Meadow, NY 11554
(516) 292-9232

Fondation Centre Louis-Hebert
525 Boulevard Hamel Est, Aile J
Quebec City, PQ G1M 2S8, Canada
(418) 529-6991

Lighthouse Low Vision Products
36-02 Northern Boulevard
Long Island City, NY 11101
(800) 829-0500; (800) 334-5497
FAX: (718) 786-5620

LS&S Group
P.O. Box 673
Northbrook, IL 60065
(708) 498-9777; (800) 468-4789

Maxi-Aids
42 Executive Boulevard
P.O. Box 3290
Farmingdale, NY 11735
(800) 522-6294; (516) 752-0521

Meditec
9485 East Orchard Drive
Englewood, CO 80110
(303) 758-6978

Science Products
P.O. Box 888
Southeastern, PA 19399
(800) 888-7400; (800) 222-2148
FAX: (215) 296-0488

Recreation, Sports, and Leisure

Includes organizations that advocate for, arrange, and facilitate sports and recreational activities for people who are blind or visually impaired.

American Blind Bowlers Association
3500 Terry Drive
Norfolk, VA 23518
(804) 857-7267

Blind Outdoor Leisure Development (BOLD)
533 East Main Street
Aspen, CO 81611
(303) 925-8922

Canadian Blind Sports Association
1600 James Naismith Drive
Gloucester, Ontario, K1B 5N4, Canada
(613) 748-5609
FAX: (613) 748-5731

Find a Travel Agency
Society for the Advancement of Travel for the Handicapped
26 Court Street
Brooklyn, NY 11242
(718) 858-5483

National Beep Baseball Association
9623 Spencer Highway
La Porte, TX 77571
(713) 470-9574

Ski for Light
1455 West Lake Street
Minneapolis, MN 55408
(612) 827-3232

Ski for Light (Canada)
2520 Glenview Avenue
Kamloops, BC V2B 4L4
(604) 376-6504

United States Association for Blind Athletes
33 North Institute Street
Colorado Springs, CO 80903
(719) 630-0422
FAX: (719) 578-4654

Wilderness Inquiry II
313 Fifth Street, SE, Suite 327A
Minneapolis, MN 55414
(612) 379-3858

Signage

Includes companies that produce building, room, and elevator signs in adapted media.

Advance Corporation
327 East York Avenue
St. Paul, MN 55101
(612) 771-9297; (800) 328-9451

Lighthouse Low Vision Products
36-02 Northern Boulevard
Long Island City, NY 11101
(800) 829-0500; (800) 334-5497
FAX: (718) 786-5620

Wurtec Braille/Tactile Products
1326 Expressway Drive North
Toledo, OH
(800) 837-1066

On-Line Resources

These listings include Internet addresses for sources of electronic information. E-mail addresses for organizations listed elsewhere in this section are included with the main organizational listing and web-site addresses for vendors are included with their listings.

AbleData
gopher://valdor.cc.buffalo.edu:70/11/.naric/.able data

Accessible Web
General Services Administration
http://www.gsa.gov/coca/wwwcode.html

Adaptive/assistive Technology Information
http://www.lib.uwaterloo.ca/discipline/disability_issues/adaptive.html

Alex: A Catalogue of Electronic Texts on the Internet
Oxford University
gopher://gopher.rsl.ox.ac.uk:70/11/lib-corn/hunter

American Council of the Blind
http://www.acb.org

American Foundation for the Blind
http://www.afb.org/afb
gopher.afb.org 5005

Apple Disability Access
http://www.apple.com/disability.welcome.html

BLINDFAM
listserv@sjuvm.stjohns.edu

blind-I
Computer Use by and for the Blind
listserv@uafsysb.uark.edu

Canadian National Institute for the Blind
http://www.cnib.ca

Center for Assistive Technology
University of Buffalo
http://cosmos.ot.buffalo.edu/aztech/html

DSSHE-L
Disabled Student Services in Higher Education
listserv@ubvm.cc.buffalo.edu

EASI
Equal Access to Software and Information Project
http://www.rit.edu.-easi/easiem/html
listserv.@nas.rit.edu

guispeak
Access to GUI via Speech
listserve@vm1.nodak.edu

IBM Special Needs Solutions
http: //www.austin.ibm.com/pspinfo/snshome.html

Internet Book Information Center
University of North Carolina at Chapel Hill
http://sunsite.unc.edu/ibic/IBIC-homepage.html

MedWeb
http://www.cc.emory.edu.whscl/medweb.disabled.html

MOSAIC
National Center for Supercomputing Applications
University of Illinois
http://bucky.aa.uic.edu/#george

National Clearing House of Rehabilitation Training Materials
http://www.nchrtm.okstate.edu

National Federation of the Blind
http://www.nfb.org

National Library Service for the Blind and Physically Handicapped
http://lcweb.loc.gov/nls

National Rehabilitation Information Center
http://www.cais.net/naric//home.html

NIDR
National Institute on Disability and Rehabilitation
http://www.ed.gov

O&M Project
http://ccwf.cc.utexas.edu/-jshouman/OandM

Orientation & Mobility Listserve
oandm@msu.edu

RT-L
Rehabilitation Teaching on-line dialogue
RT-L@umbsky.cc.umb.edu

Toronto Adaptive Technology Centre
http://www.utirc.utoronto.ca/AdTech/welcome.html

Trace Center
http://trace.wisc.edu

Windows Access
http://ucunix.edu/-hamilt/wintip31.html

WWW NewsLink, online newspaper
http://www.newslink.org/newslink/ (graphics)
http://www.newslink.org/newslink/nongraphical.html (no graphics)

REHABILITATION TEACHER TRAINING PROGRAMS

Dominican College
10 Western Highway
Orangeburg, NY 10962
(914) 359-7800
FAX: (914) 359-2313

Florida State University
Visual Impairments B-172
College of Education
Tallahassee, FL 32306
(904) 644-4880

Hunter College of the City University of New York
Department of Special Education
695 Park Avenue

New York, NY 10021
(212) 772-4701
FAX: (212) 772-4491

Mohawk College of Applied Arts and Technology
Brantford Campus
411 Elgin Street
Brantford, ON N3T 5V2, Canada
(519) 759-7200
FAX: (519) 758-6043

Northern Illinois University
Department of Learning, Development, and Special Education
Dekalb, IL 60115
(815) 753-0657

Pennsylvania College of Optometry
1200 West Godfrey Avenue
Philadelphia, PA 19141
(215) 276-6293

San Francisco State University
Department of Special Education
1600 Holloway
San Francisco, CA 94132
(415) 338-1080

University of Arkansas at Little Rock
Department of Rehabilitation
2801 S. University
Little Rock, AR 72204
(501) 569-3169

University of Massachusetts at Boston
Graduate College of Education
Harbor Campus
Boston, MA 02125-3393
(617) 972-7434

Western Michigan University
Department of Blind Rehabilitation
Kalamazoo, MI 49008
(616) 387-3455
FAX: (616) 387 3567

INDEX

ABOUT THE AUTHORS

Paul E. Ponchillia, Ph.D., is a Professor of Blind Rehabilitation at Western Michigan University in Kalamazoo and a Certified Rehabilitation Teacher. A former plant nematologist, he holds a doctorate in plant pathology. After losing his vision in a hunting accident, he obtained a master's degree in blind rehabilitation. Dr. Ponchillia is the author and co-author of numerous articles, research studies, and presentations on various aspects of blind rehabilitation. He has been a board member of several national and state organizations, including the Association for Education and Rehabilitation of the Blind and Visually Impaired (AER), the Michigan Foundation for the Blind, the Michigan Blind Athletic Association, and the United States Association of Blind Athletes, and is a past chair of the Certification Committee of AER Division 11. Dr. Ponchillia is also an award-winning wood sculptor.

Susan V. Ponchillia, Ed.D. is an Associate Professor of Blind Rehabilitation at Western Michigan University in Kalamazoo and a Certified Rehabilitation Teacher. Previously she worked in private agencies as an itinerant rehabilitation teacher of children and adults. She has written and co-written many articles and presentations on rehabilitation teaching and visual impairment, with special interest in the areas of visual impairment and diabetes, children, native peoples, and sports.

Paul and Susan are co-authors of *A Course in Adapting Local Sports and Recreational Activities for Visually Impaired Persons.* They shared the 1990 Bruce McKenzie Award for Outstanding Service and Contributions to Rehabilitation Teaching from Division 11 of AER.

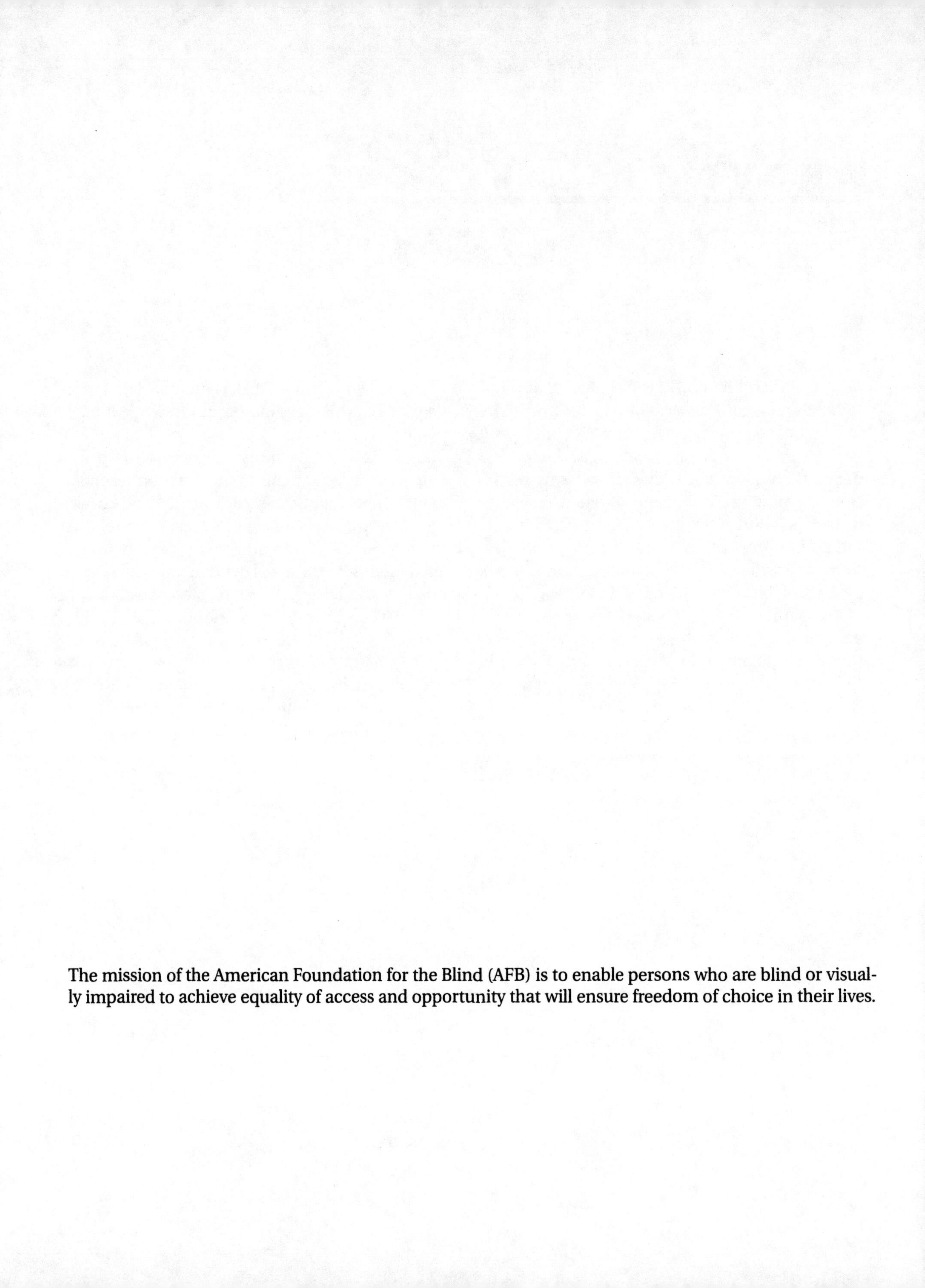

The mission of the American Foundation for the Blind (AFB) is to enable persons who are blind or visually impaired to achieve equality of access and opportunity that will ensure freedom of choice in their lives.

2006